ORIENTATION IN
RELIGIOUS EDUCATION

PHILIP   HENRY   LOTZ,   Editor

Orientation in
RELIGIOUS
EDUCATION

ABINGDON PRESS
New York   •   *Nashville*

ORIENTATION IN RELIGIOUS EDUCATION

Copyright MCML by Pierce and Smith

Library of Congress Catalog Card Number: 50-7274

D

SET UP, PRINTED, AND BOUND BY THE
PARTHENON PRESS, AT NASHVILLE,
TENNESSEE, UNITED STATES OF AMERICA

Introduction

RELIGIOUS EDUCATION is increasingly achieving the central place that it deserves in the life and work of the Church. When the history of religious education of the twentieth century is written, it will record the fact that the first half of the century was a period of tremendous growth and expansion. This book is a witness to the many and important areas that concern modern religious education. The inclusion of chapters on visual education, radio, and television indicates the desire of leaders to incorporate any instrument or agency that promises to be usable and useful to the cause. At the turn of the century a college department of religious education was practically unknown. Today a church college or seminary is not considered standard unless it offers courses in religious education.

Studies in Religious Education, the predecessor of this volume, was published in 1931. It was widely used in colleges, universities, and seminaries by the professional worker and the general reader. A number of the contributors to *Studies in Religious Education* have passed into the great beyond; others have retired from the active field of labor. Repeated requests have come to revise the earlier work or to provide an entirely new volume. The latter was decided upon, and only three persons have contributed chapters to both volumes.

The plan followed was to select specialists in their field for each chapter. No one person could possibly be a specialist in all these fields. Many of these persons have given years of study to their particular fields, and many of them have definite responsibilities for programs in these fields.

Time and experience have justified the use of multiple authorship. Variety of approach and viewpoint offers the reader and student the opportunity to become acquainted with a large number of the present leaders in the field of religious education and their respective attitudes. This variety also offers the teacher an opportunity to evaluate the various viewpoints and contributions of the writers. However, it will be helpful if the reader keeps in mind the fact that perhaps several chapters represent the author's particular convictions rather than a comprehensive review of the fields treated. It is perfectly proper for the author to express these convictions here. It should also be remembered that these chapters are greatly condensed. Many could be expanded into several times their present length—some even into entire volumes. Here in brief compass will be found each author's study and viewpoint.

It is hoped that this book will have a variety of uses. It was planned for the following persons: the college, university, and seminary student; the professional worker, such as the director, teacher, field worker, editor, and so on; the pastor and leaders in the local church; and the general reader who desires to keep abreast of the developments in the field of religious education. It might be used for the work of a semester, a quarter, or even a year's course of study. With the aid of the bibliographies it could be expanded according to desire and convenience. Certain sections or chapters might be selected for advanced work, such as seminars. It may be used either as a text or source book.

Deep appreciation is expressed to Dr. Nevin C. Harner, Lancaster Theological Seminary, and Dr. Ross Snyder, Chicago Theological Seminary, for their assistance as readers of the chapters. Their discriminating judgment and many helpful suggestions were invaluable. They also made many constructive suggestions on the organization of the book as well as the selection of the contributors. I am also deeply indebted to Dr. Roy G. Ross, of the International Council of Religious Education, who made it possible for me to have a most helpful conference with his entire staff.

Orientation in Religious Education is sent forth with a prayer in the heart, a paean of praise on the lips, and a deep sense of gratitude that this task has been completed. It is sincerely hoped that it will render a real service to the cause that is dear to all our hearts—the cause of religious education.

PHILIP HENRY LOTZ

Contents

I. The Cultural and Religious Setting of Religious Education

1. A Historical Study of the Religious Education Movement . . . 13
   Lewis J. Sherrill
2. Basic Christian Convictions 26
   John C. Bennett
3. Basic Psychological Concepts 37
   Ernest M. Ligon
4. Trends in Educational Philosophy 48
   Frank M. McKibben
5. Basic Causes of Progress and Decay in Civilization 61
   James Luther Adams
6. Educational Evangelism 75
   Harry H. Kalas
7. The Aim and Scope of Religious Education 87
   Luther A. Weigle

II. Materials and Methods of Religious Education

8. Curriculum Patterns for the Church School 101
   C. A. Bowen
9. The Use of Our Religious Heritage 114
   Frank G. Lankard
10. Worship in Religious Education 126
    Marie Cole Powell
11. The Creative Arts in Religious Education 137
    Amy Goodhue Loomis
12. Audio-Visual Method and Content 150
    Paul H. Vieth
13. Radio and Television in Religious Education 164
    Everett C. Parker
14. Play and Recreation 171
    Bob Tully
15. Individual and Group Counseling 183
    Harrison S. Elliott
16. Newer Techniques in Teaching 197
    Mildred Eakin

17. Building for Religious Education 207
      John R. Scotford

III. AGENCIES AND ORGANIZATIONS FOR RELIGIOUS EDUCATION

18. The Total Church as an Agency of Religious Education 221
      Donald M. Maynard
      The Total Program for Children 229
      Alice L. Goddard
19. The Home and Parent Education 236
      Wesner Fallaw
20. The Sunday Church School 248
      Harry Thomas Stock
21. The Vacation Church School 260
      Ruth Elizabeth Murphy
22. The Weekday Church School 274
      Erwin L. Shaver
23. The Youth Fellowship 287
      Oliver deWolf Cummings
24. The Christian Education of Adults 300
      Harry C. Munro
25. Agencies of Recreation and Group Services 312
      Paul M. Limbert
26. The Community as a Unit of Religious Education 325
      Helen Marie Edick
27. Camps and Summer Conferences 338
      Elizabeth Brown
28. Religious Education in Church Colleges and Theological Schools . 352
      Edward R. Bartlett
29. Religious Education in Tax-Supported Colleges and Universities . 365
      Edward W. Blakeman

IV. DIRECTING RELIGIOUS EDUCATION

30. The Educational Ministry of the Church 381
      Nevin C. Harner
31. The Education of Lay and Professional Religious Education Leaders 392
      Herman J. Sweet
32. Experimentation and Research 404
      Ross Snyder

V. Agencies for Co-operation in Religious Education

33. City and State Councils of Churches and Religious Education . . 419
John W. Harms
34. The International Council of Religious Education 431
Roy G. Ross
35. The Religious Education Association 445
Orville L. Davis
36. The United Christian Youth Movement 456
Isaac K. Beckes
37. The World Council of Christian Education 469
Forrest L. Knapp

VI. Wider Perspective of Religious Education

38. The Relation of Church and State 479
Ray Gibbons
39. The Relation of Religion and Public Education 491
J. Paul Williams
40. Jewish Education in America 501
Israel S. Chipkin
41. Roman Catholic Religious Education 519
Edward J. Heffron
42. The Development of Religious Education in Other Countries . . 533
Erich F. Voehringer
43. Protestantism's Strategy for Religious Education 549
Arlo Ayres Brown

Appendix

A Selected Bibliography of Religious Education 567
Leonard A. Stidley
Directory 584
Lemuel Petersen

Biographical Index 595

Index 611

PART I

The Cultural and Religious Setting of Religious Education

Chapter 1

A HISTORICAL STUDY OF
THE RELIGIOUS EDUCATION MOVEMENT

LEWIS J. SHERRILL

WHEREVER THERE is a living religion, there is religious education. As the moral code, the cult practices, and the beliefs of a given religion make their impact on the people of a given generation, and especially as religion awakens the dynamics of living, there religious education is going on. The forms which religious education takes are as varied as the forms which religion itself takes. But by its own inner compulsions a religion finds a way, or a form, or a type of "school," through which it can teach its code, its cult, and its creed. The "religious education movement," then, may be defined as the tendency of a religion to seek for, find, and use ways of teaching which are congenial to the particular religion in question, and which are suited to the general cultural conditions existing in a given time.

We are here concerned, not with religion in general, but with Christianity and its parent religion of Judaism. Within that Jewish-Christian stream the religious education movement is to be found, in one form or another, from the earliest days which our records describe to the present.

JUDAISM

Before the destruction of Jerusalem in 586 B.C. the Hebrews are depicted in the Bible as being at first a seminomadic, then an agricultural, people, who passed under a monarchy and eventually divided into a Northern and a Southern kingdom. In this long, formative period there were no formal schools, and yet this people carried on an effective education in which religion was intertwined with the other affairs of daily life.

The family was the center of this education. The first teachers of a child were his parents. The religious teaching had to do with the code of conduct, the religious rites, and the beliefs concerning God. Much of the teaching was done by means of ritual acts performed in the household, acts which provoked a child's curiosity, caused him to ask questions, and put upon the parents the necessity of answering the questions thus called forth. In this early period we evidently have the beginnings of the household

13

education, by means of symbolic ritual acts, which becomes so remarkable a feature of Judaism in all later times.

But in this early period there was the teaching of adults as well as children. The teachers were such persons as the priests, the prophets, the sages, the poets, and, in later days, the scribes, who became the custodians and official teachers of the Torah, or Law of God. Competing interpretations of the nature of God and the duty of man forced conflict in the mind of the adults as to the meanings in the religion and thus stimulated the development of the religion and the growth of individuals.

After the destruction of Jerusalem and the Exile, Judaism added to family education two other institutions having high significance in the education of an undying people in an undying religion. One of these was the synagogue, so familiar in the New Testament. The synagogue service was essentially a teaching service, containing prayers, the reading of Scripture, and the interpretation in the vernacular of a brief passage. The Christian service of worship carried forward this ancient custom of the weekly assembly of the congregation to hear the Word of God read and interpreted. This practice constituted a sort of continuing core of religious education, persisting in both Judaism and Christianity until this day.

The other institution was a system of schools. The first of these was the elementary school, or Beth Hassepher (House of the Book). Originating at an unknown date between 75 B.C. and A.D. 64, it received boys at about the age of six and taught them to read and memorize the Hebrew Scriptures. A school was supposed to be attached to every synagogue, and we have here perhaps the earliest instance of universal elementary education, at least for boys. It is possible that Jesus may have attended such a school.

Then there was a secondary school, the Beth Hamidrash (House of Study), where the interpretations of the Law were studied and memorized. These interpretations were meant to touch every aspect of daily life. They were transmitted orally, but with great precision, until reduced to writing about A.D. 190. The secondary schools probably originated earlier than the elementary schools, and it is believed by some scholars that Jesus attended a school of this character during the "silent years," thus gaining that minute acquaintance with the interpretations of the Law, or the "traditions of the elders," which make up so large a part of the background of his own teaching.

And the Jews had a remarkable third type of school known as "the academy," some of these existing in Palestine and others in Babylonia. An academy combined functions which are familiar to us under such terms as research institute, university, theological school, and supreme court.

Thus the parent religion from which Christianity sprang already had, and still maintains, a long tradition heavily weighted with respect for learning and the determination to carry forward the teaching of religion generation after generation in family, synagogue, and school.

EARLY CHRISTIANITY

In Christianity, as in Judaism, there is an inner compulsion to teach, a compulsion growing out of the nature of Christianity itself. This is strikingly expressed, for example, in the Great Commission: "All authority hath been given unto me. . . . Go . . . , make disciples [learners, apprentices] . . . , baptizing them . . . , teaching them to observe all things whatsover I commanded you: and lo, I am with you." (Matt. 28:18-20, A.S.V.)

Jesus himself was a teacher. That term, of course, does not fully describe him. For we in Christianity look to him as truly Son of man and truly Son of God, as Saviour, and as Lord of life. But that he took up the role of teacher and was commonly addressed as "Teacher" [Master] cannot be gainsaid after even a casual reading of the Gospels. Further, the *content* of his teaching is commonly regarded by Christians as being the norm for all Christian teaching, while some hold that his *method* of teaching should constitute the norm by which all our methods in Christian education are judged.

Before the books of our New Testament were written and collected into a "canon," the early Church was carrying on Christian education. It is possible to identify at least six types of content in this early Christian education, and these again illustrate the inner compulsion in Christianity to teach. These are: (1) the Christian reinterpretation of the Hebrew Scriptures; (2) the gospel of the suffering, death, and resurrection of Jesus Christ, for the gospel not only was proclaimed by preaching but was taught by what we should now call the discussion method; (3) the meaning of the Christian confession of faith, the earliest confession being "Jesus is Lord"; (4) the life and sayings of Jesus; (5) moral instruction concerning the way of life with its virtues and the way of death with its vices; and (6) instruction concerning the sacraments of baptism and the Lord's Supper.

Two institutions played a major role in Christian education in the early Church. One of these was the service of worship. Although this service grew both in richness and in length during the early centuries, it continued to have two clearly differentiated parts.

The first part was known as the *missa catechumenorum,* or the mass of the catechumens, which was a teaching service, patterned basically on the older synagogue service of the Jews. To this part of the service were admitted the catechumens, or persons receiving instruction prior to baptism. To them the Scripture was read and interpreted by the homily or sermon.

In this stage of their preparation the catechumens were known as "hearers." At the end of this part of the service the catechumens were dismissed, and the faithful remained for the second part of the service, known as the *missa fidelium,* or mass of the faithful. This part of the service was sacramental in character, culminating in the celebration of the Eucharist.

The second institution was the catechumenate, which flourished in the Church for some three centuries, say from A.D. 150 to 450. At a time when adult converts from paganism were coming into the Church in great numbers, the catechumenate may be said to represent adult Christian education with a threefold purpose: to provide a period of moral probation during which the candidate's sincerity could be tested; to give instruction in the Bible and the doctrines of the Church; and to admit the candidate into a limited but genuine Christian fellowship while he was preparing for baptism. As already indicated, part of the instruction was given during the worship service, but often there was careful instruction at other times also, individually or in groups. One was expected to remain a catechumen for two or three years.

Materials and methods used in the catechumenate varied greatly, but the plan as Origen knew it in about A.D. 248 may be illustrated by the following six steps: (1) A preliminary inquiry as to the candidate's occupation and moral character—many occupations were forbidden to a Christian. (2) Private instruction as needed by the candidate. (3) Admittance to the worship service as a "hearer." (4) Instruction outside the worship service in classes. (5) Further inquiry into the candidate's moral life. (6) Intensive instruction prior to baptism.

MEDIEVAL CHRISTIANITY

Consider first the situation of lay people in medieval times. After the disappearance of the catechumenate about A.D. 450 there was virtually no direct instruction of the laity during worship until the thirteenth century. Then confession was made obligatory at least once a year, and some priests began to instruct their people concerning the moral code, using catechisms as means of explaining the Ten Commandments, the Seven Deadly Sins, and the Seven Cardinal Virtues. But throughout the Middle Ages the laity received continuous informal education, through such means as observing and participating in worship; by learning some parts of the service, such as the Creed, the Lord's Prayer, the Ave Maria; by receiving the sacraments which were understood to convey the grace of God to the needy soul; and by watching religious dramas which began to be performed about the tenth century, portraying such biblical themes as the nativity and the suffering of Christ. And there was a sort of floating popular theology—a mingling of doctrine and superstition—passed along much as folklore is, and powerful in its hold upon the people. All these are note-worthy as forms of popular Christian education during the centuries when the Church was rising to unprecedented power, but when formal Christian education of the laity was almost nonexistent.

For those who embraced the religious life there were formal schools. For present purposes, three types of schools are the most significant—the monastic schools, the cathedral schools, and the universities. The monastic schools, established within monasteries, were designed to help novices prepare for the monastic life, while the cathedral schools served the purpose of preparing priests for a diocese. The core of the curriculum was the seven liberal arts—grammar, rhetoric, and dialectic making up the trivium; and arithmetic, music, geometry, and astronomy comprising the quadrivium. To these were often added a little theology, canon law, and medicine. It is often said that these church schools "kept the lamp of learning alight through the Dark Ages," and this is true. But it is to be kept in mind that the essential purpose was preparation for religious vocations rather than what we commonly call "learning."

Toward the end of the twelfth century universities began to be established in Europe, becoming centers for the advanced study of the liberal arts, medicine, canon law, and theology. Students thronged the universities in great numbers. Not all clerics were university men, but many were; and thenceforth higher learning became part of the great tradition in Christian education.

Modern Christianity

During the movements known as the Renaissance and the Reformation, from about A.D. 1400 to 1600, Europe was the scene of a vast ferment which penetrated into every phase of life. This ferment broke the power of the Catholic, or universal, Church. It sped the growth of nationalism in politics. It encouraged the use of reason and scientific method instead of authority as a way of arriving at knowledge. It fed the development of individualism in philosophy, religion, and morals. And it resulted in the appearance of numerous churches, or denominations, within Christianity.

Both movements left an indelible mark on education in general, and on Christian education in particular. The Renaissance exalted the individual, quickened an educational interest in *this* world as well as the next world, and revised the study of the ancient classics of Greece and Rome. Studies with such points of emphasis as these, under the general name of "humanism," stimulated the growth of new types of schools for the young and laid the foundation for the humanistic tradition in Christian education—the tradition, that is, that Christian education is properly concerned with the "humanities," human life present and past, as well as with revelation.

The Reformation, being a more distinctively religious awakening and revolt, laid down two principles having far-reaching consequences in education: The first was the authority of the Bible, as replacing the authority of the Church, in faith and morals. The second was "justification by faith," which meant that the individual is accepted by God, not in virtue of sacraments which a priest performs, but solely on the ground of the individual's personal faith in Jesus Christ as his redeemer and Lord. The first principle required that all persons should know the Bible, for thus would God confront them in present life. The second required that the individual should be approached through his reason as an avenue to understanding the Word of God, and through his feelings as a channel of response.

These two principles, taken together, inevitably demanded universal Christian education. To this end Protestants set themselves; and although the goal has never been reached, it has never been lost to sight. An approach to its realization was made along five general lines in early Protestantism:

The first was the translation of the Bible into the vernacular and its widest possible dissemination. Wherever Protestantism appears, it tends to follow the pattern of translating the Bible into the language of the people, reading the Bible in the vernacular during worship service, putting the Bible into the hands of the people, and encouraging them to read it.

A second was preaching, with biblical content as the core of the message. Early Protestantism was characterized by a revival of biblical and doctrinal preaching, and preaching has been an instrument in one after another of the great religious revivals since. Those who minimize the significance of preaching, or declare for a moratorium on it, have but slightly grasped the genius of Protestantism and Protestant Christian education.

A third was the teaching of Christianity in the family, especially by means of the Bible and systematic formulations of doctrine. The most characteristic document for this purpose was Luther's *Small Catechism*, early distributed in the form of a wall chart to be used by heads of families in instructing members of their households. The tradition of family teaching is especially strong among the Dutch and the Scotch.

A fourth was the establishment of Christian schools for all the youth of the community. The impulse toward universal Christian education is especially notable in Lutheranism and Calvinism. Luther, for example, in 1524 wrote his famous "Letter to Mayors and Aldermen of All the Cities of Germany in Behalf of Christian Schools," urging the establishment of schools for both boys and girls in every city. He advocated a threefold system comprising: vernacular primary schools for boys and girls; Latin secondary schools, important in preparing a trained clergy; and universities. His policies were partly put into effect in Northern Germany by Bugenhagen, who was especially interested in the vernacular primary schools, and in

Southern Germany by Melanchthon, who was especially interested in the humanistic tradition and in the Latin secondary schools.

Calvin in 1538 proposed a plan for the schools of Geneva to consist of elementary education in the vernacular for all. He held that the liberal arts and "good training" were essential to a knowledge of the Word of God. Secondary schools, called "colleges," developed according to his pattern, combined humanistic and religious training, and attained great influence. John Knox, under the impulse of Calvin, took the same principles to Scotland, where the *Book of Discipline* of 1560 proposed a schoolmaster for every town and would have the minister teach the school in smaller places where a master could not be employed. Comparable developments might be traced in the Netherlands. These two great branches of Protestantism—Lutheranism and Calvinism—brought the impulse to universal Christian education with them to America and wrote it deeply into our history.

A fifth approach to the goal of universal Christian education lies in the Protestant view that all education is, or should be, a unity. This, of course, is not a peculiarly Protestant view; but in all the typical Protestant schools just mentioned it was taken for granted. The humanistic and the religious contents were blended together into one curriculum.

American Protestant Christianity

We may regard the history of American Protestant education as falling into four periods:

1. The first American period—the colonial period of American history—extends from the earliest settlements by Protestants to the Federal Convention, about from 1620 to 1787. The principles of the Reformation and the resulting approaches to education were brought by Protestants to America and shaped the Christian education of this period along lines essentially the same as those prevailing then in Protestant Europe, except under pioneer conditions.

The Bible was commonly reckoned the supreme authority in faith and morals, the attempt being made to establish a code of civil law based on biblical moral codes. The sermon was the chief means of popular Christian education. To cite but one example of its importance, Alice M. Baldwin studied the election-day sermons of New England clergymen and found these sermons exerting great influence on political developments during a hundred years prior to the American Revolution.[1] As for religious teaching in the family, the classic document is Judge Samuel Sewall's *Diary*, which records, among other things, his conversations with his daughter, Betty,

---

[1] *New England Clergy and the American Revolution* (Durham: Duke University Press, 1928).

thus giving us a picture of parental education by a conscientious Puritan toward the end of the seventeenth century in New England.

In formal education the period was marked by a union of general and religious education within one and the same school. In elementary and secondary education the typical school of the Southern colonies was the private school, largely under parental control. In the middle colonies it was the parochial school, under church control; while in New England it was the common school, under community control. The typical college of the period was Harvard. In all these religion was an integral part of the curriculum.

2. The second American period, from 1787 to about 1847, was marked by the secularization, first of life in general, and then of education. In its outward aspects secularization meant the withdrawal of religious materials from the school curriculum, the withdrawal of tax support from private and church schools, and the elimination of religious controls over the public schools.

The causes underlying this gradual secularization had long been gathering force and included such factors as the spread of a secular and rationalistic view of life, the fragmenting of American Christianity into powerful sectarian movements which drove wedges into community solidarity and prevented Christians from making a united impact upon community or state, and the conflicts between religious sects as to the religious materials which might be taught in the schools. The last point is especially significant. In general terms it can be said that religious people forced secularization upon the schools by their controversies over the teaching of religion, particularly the Bible, in tax-supported schools. Controversies of this kind were especially bitter about 1840 in connection with the schools of Massachusetts and New York City, and about 1869 in connection with those of Cincinnati. In Massachusetts the strife was chiefly between conservative and liberal interpreters of Protestantism, while in New York City and Cincinnati it was largely a conflict between Protestants and Catholics.

These religious controversies over the teaching of religion in public schools left a remarkable imprint on American public opinion. Between 1844 and 1912 thirty-eight states wrote into their constitutions provisions forbidding the division or the diversion of public funds to private or parochial schools.

Thus the teaching of religion was increasingly left to the churches to handle as they might choose. And it was precisely at this turn in affairs that the Sunday school came into the American scene. The origin of the modern Sunday school is commonly attributed to Robert Raikes, a printer living in Gloucester, England. In 1780, moved by the plight of underprivileged children in his city, he began gathering them on Sundays, first in his own home, for instruction by paid teachers.

The pattern of Sunday teaching of the young by laymen quickly came to the United States. A Sunday school appeared in this country at least as early as 1785; and by 1790 the Methodist Conference of Charleston, South Carolina, was sanctioning schools of this kind. By 1816 city unions began to be established in larger centers to promote Sunday schools. In 1824 the American Sunday School Union began its long career, serving as a nondenominational missionary agency, establishing Sunday schools in neglected and pioneer areas. Denominations began to approve and push the policy of establishing and strengthening Sunday schools.

By the end of this period Sunday schools had become a recognized and familiar agency for religious education in the United States. The small Sunday school in America served a function not yet fully appreciated as the forerunner of an organized church in pioneer territory, or as a substitute for a church where the latter could not be organized, as an evangelizing agency, and as the scene of nondenominational Christian work by lay people at the very time when denominationalism was growing rampant in America.

3. The third American period may be regarded as extending from about 1847 to 1889, when the first World Sunday School Convention was held, and was characterized by the spread of the Sunday-school movement.

As just shown, by the late 1840's the American churches, facing the problem of finding a type of school suited to the purposes of religious education, were turning toward the Sunday school as a way of meeting this need. But there were many misgivings concerning the suitability of the Sunday school, and two efforts were made to turn that tide in some other direction.

One of these is represented by Horace Bushnell, who in 1847 published his famous *Christian Nurture* in brief form and then expanded his thought into a book with the same title in 1861. In this work he pleaded for a conception and a practice of Christianity which would make the family the chief agency for evangelism and religious education. But although the book aroused great interest it did not lead the churches to adopt a consciously family-centered type of education.

The second was the attempt made by the Presbyterians to establish a complete system of church-controlled schools at the elementary, secondary, collegiate, and seminary levels. One part of this general plan was the venture of the Presbyterians into the promotion of parochial schools. Other non-Catholic denominations also have established parochial schools in the United States since colonial days, but here let us take the Presbyterian experiment as especially illuminating because of its timing and the fate which overtook it. In 1846, and more strongly in 1847, the General Assembly approved the policy of parochial schools, with the goal of establishing such a school in every congregation. Some 260 Presbyterian parochial schools were actually set up—day schools combining general and religious subjects in one curriculum. But the system soon proved a failure and was abandoned in 1870.

The significance of these events is that Protestants, in one way or another, were ruling out three major types of schools for religious education—namely, the public school, the family, and the parochial school. Each of these possibilities was later to be re-examined, but for the time being energies were turned to the development and spread of Sunday schools.

Only three aspects of the spread of Sunday schools in this period can be noted here. One was the effort to train lay teachers. Inspired by the example of normal schools for public-school teachers, certain laymen pioneered in developing Sunday-school institutes for what we now call leadership education.

A second was the Sunday-school association and convention. Largely lay projects and nondenominational in character, they represent the organization of Sunday-school interests by areas, such as county, state, nation, and finally the world. National conventions were held at frequent intervals from 1832 to 1872. Beginning in 1875 they were held at three-year intervals and were called international conventions. As stated, the first world convention was held in 1889. These associations and conventions came to serve what might be called an interdenominational legislative function in religious education, in that they advocated policies which the denominations might adopt or reject, but which they could not ignore.

A third aspect was the development in curriculum. The long period from the rise of Sunday schools until about 1860 represents the search for types of curriculum suited to Sunday-school use. In 1872 the uniform-lesson system was adopted by the national convention. Opposed at first by denominational boards, it quickly won general favor, and, with frequent modifications, the system has continued in use until the present time. Warmly defended by some, as warmly assailed by others, it has provided the principal basis of Bible study for a significant portion of the people for some three quarters of a century.

Another general feature of this period was the rise of significant youth movements, more or less apart from the Sunday school, and commonly known as young people's societies. The classic example is Christian Endeavor, started in 1881 by Francis Clark in the Williston Congregational Church of Portland, Maine. The rapid spread of this nondenominational society and its appeal to youth were phenomenal and stimulated similar efforts along denominational lines, such as the Oxford League and the Epworth League of the Methodists and the Baptist Young People's Union.

4. The fourth American period, extending from about 1889 to the present, when it can be seen in perspective, will probably appear as a time of re-orientation and experimentation.

Three great series of events have made reorientation and experimentation imperative. One is on a national scale. The United States was becoming a world power, and state education was expanding to unprecedented lengths; yet state education was on an increasingly secularistic basis. The churches began to feel it necessary to parallel the developments in general education with correspondingly strong ones in religious education, and yet they found themselves with little more than the Sunday school as a basis of operations.

The second is on an international scale. After decades of belief in the possibilities of unlimited progress we were drawn into two world wars and now face the grim threat of a third. The need for a Christian philosophy of life and a Christian way of life never has been more urgent; and it has begun to be realized anew that education with such ends in view must be conducted by the churches or it will go undone. An atomic age requires a cosmically oriented education; and this the nationalistic, secularistic state cannot give.

The third, also on an international scale, is the development of psychology and pedagogy. As the profoundly disturbing events of our generation have swept over him, man has become almost obsessed by the desire to understand the demonic forces within himself and at the same time has been dreaming his dreams of a Utopia built upon a system of universal, democratic education, which will turn all the energies of the young to peaceful and constructive ends.

Accordingly there has been a growing recognition that we must have an adequate philosophy of Christian education, an adequate curriculum, a type of school suited to the job, and a staff of teachers and other professional workers competent to teach Christianity under present-day conditions. This is a job of staggering proportions when seen in its fullness; and much that has happened during the period can be understood as attempts to reorient toward, or experiment with, one or more of these three great problems.

The professionalization of religious education—a marked feature of the present century—represents the emergence of a self-conscious professional group devoting themselves to work upon these three, and other related, problems of religious education in a secular state. Only a few aspects of this professional movement can be noted here.

Some of these are best seen through their organizational expression. The Religious Education Association, formed in 1903, has stimulated a more scholarly use of the Bible in religious education, has pioneered in the scientific approach to problems in religious education, and has served as a liaison between the modern form of the religious education movement and other closely related fields.

The International Council of Religious Education, formed in 1922 by a merger of the older International Sunday School Association and the Sunday School Council of Evangelical Denominations, has carried forward the older type of lay interest and activity so characteristic of the Sunday-school movement, but now also co-ordinates both denominational and professional effort, and is perhaps the most influential single agency in the United States in the field of religious education.

The World Council of Christian Education, until recently the World Sunday School Association, is especially concerned with religious education in other lands and serves as a liaison between the nationals of many lands.

Professionalization is reflected also on the academic side. Many American universities have established departments of religious education and offer advanced work in this field. The subject ordinarily is present in the curriculum of American theological schools. Training schools have been established by many of the major denominations, one of their principal purposes being to prepare persons for positions in religious education. Research in religious education has now advanced far enough to give us a considerable and growing body of data obtained by using scientific methods in studying some of the problems encountered.

Professionalization is reflected further in the fact that religious education is now a recognized area for the investment of life in a church vocation. Open to both women and men, it now enlists a substantial number of persons in such positions as directors of religious education in local churches; denominational and interdenominational workers with children, with youth, with adults; teachers of religious education in colleges or universities, training schools, or seminaries.

Experimentation with new types of schools suited to the American scene is, as indicated, a feature of this period. We meet new types of schools on every hand. There are, for example, weekday schools of religious education, with numerous variations. The initial impulse is attributed to a paper read by Dr. George U. Wenner in 1905; courses in religion for high-school credit were introduced in certain situations by 1910; and the Gary, Indiana, experiment, begun in 1914, attracted wide attention. By 1930 weekday schools were being carried on in 861 towns or cities. These schools represent a form of co-operation between church and state which seemed to many our most promising avenue of expansion; yet the still-growing secularization policy of the state renders their future uncertain. There are daily vacation church schools, again with numerous varieties. These schools, dating in their modern form from about 1901, owe much to the vision and energy of Dr. Robert G. Boville. There are the graded church and the junior church. There are extended sessions of Sunday school on Sunday morning and numerous denominational variations of the young people's society. There are church nurseries and church kindergartens, and the question of parochial schools continues to be canvassed by Protestants.

Experimentation in curriculum and the more basic reorientation in philosophy will be treated in the following chapters and need not be further discussed here.

SUGGESTIONS FOR FURTHER STUDY

1. What is meant by the statement, "By reason of its own nature, Christianity has an inward compulsion to teach"? Illustrate the point from the Bible, or from Christian thought, or from Christian history.

2. Compare Jewish and early Christian practices in education.

3. From data on Judaism and early Christianity discuss and illustrate the statement, "Teaching is an act of worship."

4. Suppose that you confront an illiterate population and are responsible for teaching Christianity. What suggestions for procedure might you get from early Protestant history? What from medieval Christianity?

5. Certain Protestant "approaches" to the goal of universal Christian education are mentioned in this chapter. Take them up one at a time, and consider whether they are valid today.

6. Discuss and illustrate "the search for a type of school" in America.

7. Consider reasons for and against the following proposition: "Because of the inner nature of Protestantism, and because of the secularization of public education in the United States, Protestants should establish parochial schools."

8. Let one person prepare a eulogistic statement concerning the American Sunday school, praising the consecration that has been expressed through it, the service it has rendered in American life, and so forth. Let another person prepare a highly critical statement regarding the American Sunday school, pointing out its limitations. When the two have been presented, let the group contribute to the answers to two questions: (*a*) What values in the Sunday school do we wish to conserve and enlarge for ourselves as a result of our study? (*b*) What common defects in the Sunday school do we wish to find ways of remedying?

BIBLIOGRAPHY

Benson, C. H. *A Popular History of Christian Education.* Chicago: The Moody Press, 1943.

Brown, Arlo A. *A History of Religious Education in Recent Times.* New York: The Methodist Book Concern, 1923.

Bushnell, Horace. *Christian Nurture.* (Preferably, centennial edition.) New Haven: Yale University Press, 1947.

Cubberley, E. P. *The History of Education.* Boston: Houghton Mifflin Co., 1920. Chaps. X-XV.

———. *Public Education in the United States.* Boston: Houghton Mifflin Co., 1919. Chap. 6.

Culver, R. B. *Horace Mann and Religion in the Massachusetts Public Schools.* New Haven: Yale University Press, 1929.

Drazin, N. *History of Jewish Education from 515 B.C.E. to 220 C.E.* Baltimore: Johns Hopkins Press, 1943.

Erb, F. O. *The Development of the Young People's Movement.* Chicago: University of Chicago Press, 1917.

Lankard, F. G. *A History of the American Sunday School Curriculum.* New York: The Abingdon Press, 1927.

Sherrill, L. J. *The Rise of Christian Education.* New York: The Macmillan Co., 1944.

Chapter 2

BASIC CHRISTIAN CONVICTIONS

JOHN C. BENNETT

CHRISTIANITY IS A historical religion. This means that at its center is a series of events which culminate in Jesus Christ's life, death, and victory over death. Jesus Christ cannot be understood except against the background of the history of Israel that is recorded in the Old Testament. The preparation for his coming in that earlier history is essential also for our understanding of the way in which God deals with men and nations. As a result of what Christ was and what he did, the new community that we call the Christian Church was established, and participation in this historical community is an essential part of the Christian life.

This recognition that Christianity is a continuing historical movement that exists in virtue of something that happened in history means that Christian education must be related to what is *given*—to what in theological language is called "the revelation of God in Christ." Christianity is not what a group of contemporary Christians want to make it as a result of their own experience. It is the response within contemporary experience to what is given in the historical revelation. Christianity is not to be understood as a confirmation of what all good men know as a result of common experience. It is a new factor, an unexpected and a revolutionary factor that can transform experience.

This concept of the historical nature of Christianity raises many of the most acute problems and controversies in the field of education. There are various authoritarian ways of understanding the given elements in Christianity which naturally arouse the fears of the modern educator. Both Catholicism and Protestant orthodoxy confront the Christian with an external authority. The authoritarian Church, with its system of doctrine, and the Bible as an infallible book which is also often made to serve a rigid system of doctrine, should be rejected. What is given is not a system of doctrine; it is not a book; it is not a creed; it is not a teaching Church that claims authority to which the Christians must give uncritical assent. What is given is the Person who lived and died and conquered death, the preparation for his coming, the community of the Spirit that arose from the response of the first Christians to him. Our response to all of this that happened is itself a part of our contemporary experience. Moreover, it is *our* response, the response of whole persons, and not primarily a matter of intellectual belief.

26

This was illustrated by a leading Swedish Christian. He compared Christianity to what happened when the news came to Sweden and other parts of Scandinavia that Norway had been liberated from the Nazis. This news was about an event that had enormous significance for anyone living in Scandinavia. It was an event that changed the face of the world for them. News of this event was brought to the people by messengers of various kinds, by radio, and by newspapers. These messengers and these newspapers were not the event, but they pointed to it. The explanations given by commentators of why the Germans evacuated Norway when they did were not what gave the people a sense of deliverance. We may say that the newspapers in this illustration correspond to the Bible, which is the report of the central Christian events. Also we may say that the sense of deliverance—the changed face of the world that came to the people who first heard about the evacuation of Norway—is analogous to the sense of deliverance and the changed face of the world that Christians often receive as the result of their encounter with the central Christian events. Christians may continually recover this same fresh sense of deliverance; and each time it is a part of contemporary experience, though it always involves a relationship to what happened in the first century.

The explanation of the meaning of what happened should not be crystallized in intellectual formulas to be accepted uncritically. What is important is that each person be brought into the Christian movement, where he can see for himself what has happened and receive guidance from the response of others, both past and present, as he seeks to understand the meaning of the central Christian events for him. It is the characteristic Christian view that in this encounter with Jesus Christ one finds God, for God has acted in Christ to reveal himself supremely and to lift and redeem the life of men. By "Jesus Christ" is meant his life and personality and teaching together with his death and the event that we know as the Resurrection, which is the sign of Christ's victory over death. But this revelation and this act of redemption which in one sense took place so long ago become real to each person in ways that are always new and relevant to his condition now.

These doctrines concerning the revealing and redeeming acts of God in Christ are sometimes presented in an exclusive way that denies the existence of any other means of knowing God, but that is an error that limits the activity of God arbitrarily in the interests of a human theory. The most that can be said is that for the Christian what he knows of God through Christ is the norm by which the validity of all other claims to knowledge of God should be tested.

After this brief statement of the nature of Christianity as a historical religion and of the given elements that are recognized by Christians as the source of revelation, let us deal briefly with the central Christian beliefs that grow out of response to God's revelation of himself in Christ. It will be readily understood that in the Christian Church there is no unanimity about the formulation of these beliefs. The most that any individual Christian can do is to say what he believes as a member of the Christian community after he has attempted to understand what other Christians have said. These beliefs, which must be discussed so briefly, one after another, belong together as an organic whole.

God

God is known to men through his works as creator and redeemer. He is the Lord who as righteousness and power is above all the ideals and the powers of the world. He is, not the absolute of the philosophers, but the God who is living and active, who in his love is always seeking to save those who are lost in indifference or rebellion. The personal words borrowed from human experience—such words as will, purpose, wrath, love, and mercy—are the most meaningful that we can use as we seek to describe the nature and activity of God, but these words must always be used symbolically with full recognition of the difference between God and all finite persons. God is not identical with the world of our experience, but the world depends for its existence upon him. God is not the direct cause of every event that takes place, for he has created finite beings who have the freedom to resist his will. So while the possibility of evil is willed by God as a necessary condition of freedom, the actual evils which men bring upon themselves may not be willed by God, though God can use them for his purpose, and men who live in the midst of them can be redeemed so that for them all things do work together for good.

Perhaps the most startling statement in the New Testament is Paul's declaration: "But God shows his love for us in that while we were yet sinners Christ died for us" (R.S.V.). This view of God as one who does not dwell in lofty detachment from his creation, but who takes the initiative to visit and redeem his people, and who shares the suffering which is the consequence of their sin—this is the new factor which Christianity brings to our experience. It would be a surprise to anyone who has not become so familiar with the words and symbols that they have lost much of their meaning to see how Christian faith finds God present in a stable and on a cross—the instrument that was used to execute common criminals. It is essential to see beyond the conventional theological formulas which express all of these doctrines about God's work through Christ to the truly unconventional meaning that they carry concerning the nature and activity of God. The high and holy One who is the creator of the ends of the earth is with man, and he is with man at the point of man's greatest need.

The doctrine of the Trinity has enabled Christians to do justice to the conviction that the same God is both creator and redeemer.

MAN

Christian teaching about man always has two sides. One is the positive side that stresses the creation of man in the divine image, his responsibility as a person, his extraordinary potentialities of mind and spirit, his endless hunger for the true goals of life—hunger that can be disguised or can be apparently satisfied for a time by false gods which in the end lead to a sense of emptiness or to acute sickness in an individual soul or in a culture. The other side of the Christian view of man is the recognition of his tendency to see his life and all life in self-centered terms. The self-deceptions of pride, and the desire for power over others, and the innumerable ways in which men seek first to promote narrow interests that are closest to them are the forms that sin takes. Christian teaching about sin also stresses the ways in which the very capacities which are marks of the divine image in man may become perverted. It is this fact that makes human sin so much more destructive than the evil done by animals. Intelligence, imagination, and love when they are misdirected increase the scope and power of human sin.

This dual conception of man needs to be stressed constantly. It means in practice that Christians should be prepared for both the best and the worst. They should never be cynics or sentimentalists. There is always hope for the growth of the individual and for the solution of social problems. But in both personal and social life there are no simple cures. In both there is need for continuous repentance, for radical self-criticism in the light of our awareness of the ease with which we deceive ourselves.

This conception of man points to the need of something more than growth without conversion and something more than one conversion. The new forms of self-centeredness together with self-deception that appear on the higher levels of personal growth and in the lives of converted Christians need the attention both of those who stress growth and of those who stress conversion.

CHRIST

The central importance of faith in the incarnation for the Christian conception of God has already been emphasized. To affirm that God identified himself with man uniquely at a particular point in history is both the most distinctive and the most difficult of all Christian affirmations. Christian teaching about Christ has two great centers: the doctrine of the *incarnation* and the doctrine of the *atonement*. These two doctrines are interdependent, but there is a tendency for Christians to put their emphasis on one or the other. Those who emphasize the incarnation and neglect the atonement see only the fact that God has identified himself with man and are led by that to give a false sanctity to human activities, especially within the sphere of the Church. In the light of the atonement one can see that though God identified himself with man in Christ, man rejected him, and that the relation between God and man is one of persistent estrangement overcome by God's forgiving love shown forth on the cross.

The Church in its historic teaching has affirmed both the true humanity and the true divinity of Christ. Theories that have been developed to explain these affirmations have usually been defective in that they have failed to do justice either to Christ's humanity or to his divinity. Most often the traditional theories have undercut belief in his real humanity. This is one of the open problems of Christian thought that calls for continual fresh thinking.

The Church in its historic teaching has affirmed that Christ died for our sins, "that God was in Christ, reconciling the world unto himself." This underlies the various theories of the atonement, but there is no one theory which can be regarded as fully satisfactory. Two main emphases need to be guarded in any theory that may be developed. One is the emphasis upon the fact of deliverance by Christ, through his death and his victory over death, from many forms of bondage to evil in the world. The other is the realization that while God is a God of grace, mercy, and forgiveness, the sin that divides men from God cannot be overcome except by God's own act through which he shares the consequences of sin. The atonement in this context is a sign that forgiveness is not based upon moral indifference, but based upon love that is righteous and that fully faces the gravity of the evil in human life that must be overcome.

The historical life, teaching, and personality of Jesus are emphasized by some Christians without much reference to the convictions about what God has done in him; and by other Christians they are neglected entirely, and all of the emphasis is placed upon the death and the resurrection of Christ. Both of these one-sided approaches to Christ are wrong. It is of the utmost significance that the Christ who died on the cross and became victorious over death was the man about whose life, and teaching, and personality we read in the first three Gospels. It is also of the utmost significance that Christ was not an isolated "good man" who because of his moral perfections leaves us with a sense of his distance from us. If God was active in Christ for us, that distance between Christ and us can be overcome in the sense that by means of him God can get through to us.

SALVATION

Christian salvation presupposes the recognition that men are in need of radical change, that the true way of life is for us to be transformed so that

God—and nothing less—is the center of our world. It is true of all the great Christian traditions—though they differ in emphasis—that man cannot be transformed by his own efforts. He depends for his salvation on the grace of God. This does not mean that man is a helpless puppet before God, for he must himself be responsive to God. There is a problem here that has been a source of controversy throughout Christian history. It is best to recognize that no theory of how man's contribution to salvation is related to God's contribution is generally accepted among Christians, but that we are dealing with realities that were well stated by Paul when he wrote: "Work out your own salvation with fear and trembling; for God is at work in you, both to will and to work for his good pleasure." (R.S.V.) Gratitude before God, humility before God in relation to all the good that we experience in life, and a strong sense of the divine imperative to achieve the good—these should always go together.

The teaching about salvation is expressed in several technical theological words which should come to have meaning again because men still do recognize the significance of the realities to which they point. It sometimes seems that people will tolerate a special vocabulary in every field from sports to atomic science but reject it in religion. The *grace of God* primarily refers to the forgiving love of God that accepts man as he is without his having to earn such acceptance. What is needed on man's part is *faith*, which is primarily openness to God's grace. A secondary meaning of grace is the power for new living that men receive when they are open toward God, but this meaning of grace is very much the same as the meaning of the *Spirit of God*. *Justification* is the word that has been very much used in Protestantism to denote the fact that a sinful man is accepted by God and forgiven. *Sanctification* means actual moral and spiritual growth—growth in character and growth in religious faith and devotion. There can be much argument about the relation between the two aspects of the Christian life to which justification and sanctification refer. Many of our controversies arise when one or the other of them has been neglected. Today there is a strong tendency to return to the earlier Protestant stress on justification, because men in our time have become so much aware of the sin and anxiety in personal life and the massiveness of evil in the world. The forgiveness of God alone can overcome the deepest anxieties of the human soul, and to know that one is forgiven can be a cleansing experience that precedes all moral advance. Awareness of God's forgiveness, combined with full understanding of the dark consequences of human sin, has actually been brought home to men by the Cross of Christ.

There is great need of careful thinking about the problems of moral and spiritual growth. The fact that new forms of sin do appear among those who according to all usual standards are highly developed Christians should be a constant warning. But it should not cause us to fail to recognize the real possibilities of growth in love and loyalty and integrity. The best protection is to realize that no such growth is sound unless it is also growth in humility.

THE CHURCH

The discussion of salvation must never be individualistic, for the isolated Christian is a contradiction in terms. The result of Christ's work was the establishment of a community, the Christian Church, and this community is the bearer of the influences which make possible growth in the Christian life. The Christian community is the new environment to which the Christian becomes related, an environment that should be different from the world. It is not primarily an institution. Rather it uses institutions. It might be better to say that the Church is a people. It is within the Church that Christians worship, and it is within the Church that they are able to learn about the meaning of the Christian gospel. It is within the Church that they find those who share a common faith and purpose which should guide Christian action in the world. The great temptation of the Church is for it to forget that it is a human community. The danger of Catholicism is that it tends to make the institutions of the Church sacred and the teaching of its representatives so authoritative that criticism is discouraged. But the Church should always be under the criticism of Christ; and Christ, because he is known to the Christian, not only through the contemporary priests, preachers, or leaders in the Church, but also through the Bible, cannot be kept under the control of the Church. An open Bible and a community of Christians in which laymen as well as ministers are free to criticize the institutions and actions of the Church—these are among the essential marks of Protestantism. The Christian Church is not limited to any of the denominations. There is what we may call a universal Church within all of the churches. This universal Church has as its instruments the ecumenical movements, of which the World Council of Churches is the best known.

CHRISTIAN ETHICS

Central in Christian ethics is the commandment of love for the neighbor, and it has become clear both through the teachings of Jesus and through the development of Christian thought and experience in the New Testament that the neighbor is every man. This is the meaning of the story of the good Samaritan. Love in this context is not primarily an emotion, and it is to be distinguished from the kind of love that takes the form of affection in personal relations. Love is primarily caring for the neighbor. It is respect for the dignity of the neighbor as a child of God, and it is concern for the welfare of the neighbor. In all relationships love in this sense is the supreme Christian standard. In the life of the family the natural affection that binds together the members of the family needs to be both strengthened and corrected by Christian love—this respect for the dignity of the other persons and this caring for their real welfare. Not only is Christian love this caring for the real welfare of all neighbors, it also involves what we might call "unlimited liability." There are no sacrifices that are too great to be demanded by love. Though this demand of love is not heard very loudly in our conventional existence, from time to time, when issues become entirely clear and responsibilities are obvious, Christians do heed this demand, and they often suffer because they are loyal to Christ and because they love their suffering neighbors.

Love should control the purpose and attitudes of Christians in society at large. The standard that is more directly relevant to social institutions is *justice*. Justice is the standard that should govern us wherever human rights are involved, whether it is the right of the child to an education, or the right of a criminal to a fair trial, or the right of a nation to be free from oppression. But justice as a principle always needs to be under the criticism of *equality*. The Christian should know that whenever he supports policies and institutions which give to him and to his group special privileges, he is probably being led to do this because of the pressure of his own interests upon his judgment. Absolute equality in the conditions of life is seldom possible, but the burden of proof should always be on any forms of inequality. In the context of Christian ethics and Christian faith there is always a place for a kind of reversal of the inequalities of the world; and in the sight of God it is the lost sheep, the prodigal son, the publican and the sinner who rank above respectable ones who count themselves righteous. Jesus' parable of the Pharisee and the publican should forever disturb all who have come to trust in their own moral correctness and respectability.

The Christian Social Imperative

One of the most characteristic emphases in the modern Church is the emphasis upon the responsibility of the Christian and the Church for the whole life of society, for the policies of institutions, for the behavior of nations, for the relations of all of the large-scale social groups. It is clear that the individual soul cannot be detached from the body or from the environment, and that even though a mature person can rise above many environmental handicaps, the usual effect of an unfavorable environment upon persons is to distort the soul itself. So it is essential for Christians to seek to overcome the causes of war, of poverty, of racial discrimination, and of all the other evils which distort or destroy persons. Also, the very nature of the vocation of the Christian as a citizen and as a participant in economic life renders it impossible for him to escape responsibility for social decisions which make for justice or injustice, peace or war.

Not only is God, for the Christian, the Lord of the person in his inner life or in his personal relations with others; he is also Lord of the nations and of all the forces and movements that make history. Christianity must always seem negative and critical from the point of view of those who are at home in any social system, whether they live in America or in Russia. It is of special importance that in societies which have a strongly Christian background the Christian Church avoid the tendency to assume that the institutions that have grown up in that society have a special divine sanction. In some respects they may deserve approval, but there is no society that does not need radical criticism. Each one develops its own complacencies and blind spots, and it has always been a part of the divine strategy in human history to shake complacent societies by forcing them to face strong opposition and competition from without. This is part of the meaning of communism in relation to our American society. It shakes our society at the very point where it is weakest by promising what our society has never taken with full seriousness—economic justice and racial equality. Whether or not it can fulfill these promises is not the important point. What is important is that it will force our society to take seriously both the issue of economic justice and the issue of racial equality.

THE KINGDOM OF GOD

Christian thinking about the kingdom of God has always oscillated between emphasis upon the present and upon the future. This is true of the New Testament teaching about the kingdom as well as about subsequent teaching in the Church. There is one sense in which the kingdom of God is obviously past, present, and future, and that is when it is thought of as equivalent to the reign of God in the world. In this sense God's kingship is seen in judgment as in redemption. God would not be God unless he was King in this sense. But the kingdom of God is also thought of as present when we see beginnings of it or intimations of it in the results of Christ's work in history. In the New Testament there is great emphasis upon the faith that already there were manifestations of the kingdom in the life of the early Christian Church. This same emphasis upon the kingdom in the life of the Church has often been presented uncritically by Catholicism. It is the Catholic temptation to confuse the Church with the kingdom. It would be sounder for us to say that the Church is the sphere within which the manifestations of the kingdom have been concentrated, but that there is much in the Church which is a denial of the kingdom, and that there are manifestations of the kingdom outside the Church.

However much Christians may emphasize the kingdom as a present reality, they cannot limit it to the present or to our historical existence. The kingdom of God is the conception that points to God's ultimate triumph, a triumph for which all the manifestations of it in history are anticipations, but a triumph which extends beyond them. It is one of the clearest and most universal of all Christian convictions that we are pilgrims on this earth, and that God's kingdom is an eternal kingdom. Many Christian concepts and symbols are involved in this idea of the ultimate fulfillment that does not depend upon the conditions of our life on earth. This faith is the faith that the death of the individual person does not defeat God's purpose for him. It is the faith that neither cosmic changes nor atomic destruction can threaten God's kingdom.

How is the kingdom of God related to the social causes that men have often identified with it? It is important to realize that the kingdom both transcends and corrects every social system for which men may work. It is not identical with a new social order. But those who strive for a better order in history, for justice and fraternity among men, are serving the kingdom.

The Christian religion meets the needs of men when they face life's depths. It has much to say about sin and death, suffering and despair. Those who know what it is to be not far from despair can often understand best some of its teachings. It is this fact about Christianity which makes it natural that many who accept its ethics, and who respond to the more joyful elements in the Christian message, do not see the meaning of grace or forgiveness or of God's sharing our human lot. It is one of the most difficult problems of the educator that he must deal, not only with many age groups, but with differences of experience which can be found among adults. It should not be forgotten that our generation has seen the face of evil in startling forms, and that it is haunted by feelings of insecurity that are often not far from despair, even when these feelings are disguised. It is of the utmost importance that the whole Christian gospel as it can be grasped on the heights and in the depths of life be made available as people are prepared by experience to understand it, and that at every age children and adults alike should receive the true impression that there is more in Christianity than they have yet grasped.

SUGGESTIONS FOR FURTHER STUDY

1. What is the *given* element in Christianity?

2. How can Christian education do justice to this *given* element without the kind of indoctrination that lacks reality for the person?

3. In what way should we regard the Bible as the source of religious authority?

4. What is meant by the following concepts: God as creator, the love of God, the personality of God?

5. How do you understand the idea of the image of God in man?

6. What is the meaning of sin? Is it desirable to make use of the concept of sin in Christian education?

7. What do you think of the place of growth or conversion in the Christian life?

8. Discuss the meaning of Christ as divine. As redeemer. How do you think of the relation between the divinity and humanity of Christ? What is the significance of the idea of atonement?

9. Discuss the *underlined* words in the section on "Salvation." Is there any one of them to which you can attach no meaning?

10. Discuss the relation between the human weakness and sin in the actual churches and the claims made for the Church.

11. What are the differences between love and justice? How are they related to each other?

12. Do you agree that "the burden of proof should always be on any forms of inequality"?

13. Why does the Church have responsibility for social institutions? How far does your church recognize this responsibility?

14. Discuss the ways in which the kingdom of God is used in this chapter. Which ways do you find most meaningful?

BIBLIOGRAPHY

The Hazen Books on Religion (New York: Association Press), written primarily for young people, provide reading on several of the subjects discussed in this chapter. The following are especially relevant:

Calhoun, Robert L. *What Is Man?* (1939).

Horton, Walter. *God* (1937).

Lyman, Mary Ely. *Jesus* (1937).

Van Dusen, Henry P. *Reality and Religion* (1940).

Vlastos, Gregory. *Christian Faith and Democracy* (1939).

Five books which are intended for the lay reader are also recommended:

Easton, W. Burnet, Jr. *The Faith of a Protestant*. New York: The Macmillan Co., 1946.

Fitch, Robert E. *Preface to Ethical Living*. New York: Association Press, 1947.

Harkness, Georgia. *Understanding the Christian Faith*. New York and Nashville: Abingdon-Cokesbury Press, 1947.

Knox, John. *The Man Christ Jesus*. Chicago: Willett, Clark & Co., 1941.

Wicks, Robert Russell. *What Is a Man?* New York: Charles Scribner's Sons, 1947.

The following books are recommended for the more advanced reader:

Bennett, John C. *Christian Realism*. New York: Charles Scribner's Sons, 1941. This book will give some explanation of many of the ideas that are presented so briefly in this chapter.

Dodd, C. H. *The Bible Today*. New York: The Macmillan Co., 1947. A brief statement of the significance of the Bible by one of the leading biblical scholars.

Knox, John. *On the Meaning of Christ*. New York: Charles Scribner's Sons, 1947. One of the most helpful fresh discussions of the doctrines concerning Christ.

Temple, William. *Christianity and Social Order*. New York: Penguin Books, 1942. One of the best brief statements of the social implications of Christianity by the late Archbishop of Canterbury.

Van Dusen, Henry P., ed. *The Christian Answer*. New York: Charles Scribner's Sons, 1945. Especially the chapter on "Central Christian Affirmations," by George Thomas.

Whale, John S. *Christian Doctrine*. New York: The Macmillan Co., 1941. This book may seem rather difficult at first, but it is clear and brief.

Chapter 3

BASIC PSYCHOLOGICAL CONCEPTS

ERNEST M. LIGON

No RELIGIOUS EDUCATOR should dare attempt his task without adequate tools. Psychology is the chief and most effective tool for any kind of educational venture. Educators have no choice as to whether or not they use psychology. Their only choice is in what kind of psychology they use. They can use tradition, common sense, personal opinion, the latest fad, or the results of scientific research. But however they deal with human nature is their psychology. An educator trained in the techniques and skills of modern psychology has a great advantage over his colleagues who are untrained in them. The advances in this science during the last generation are as great as those of modern medicine over the techniques of the witch doctor.

Acquiring these skills and keeping abreast of the rapid progress in this field is an overwhelming task. This brief chapter can do little more than list some of the most important of these skills and suggest for religious educators methods of gaining some facility in their use.

The student will hear much about "schools" of psychology. Associationism, Gestalt psychology, group dynamics, depth psychology, Freudianism, and topological psychology are terms now used as common parlance among psychologists. To the nonprofessional this may sound as if one had to "join" one or another of them and to resist with vehemence all of the others. Actually, texts in general psychology contain much the same things, and representatives of any of these schools would teach them. Schools grow up around hypotheses set forth in the areas of differences. These in turn have to do with those phases of personality for which as yet we have insufficient evidence. Ernest Hilgard expresses it after discussing more than a dozen different theories of learning: "Because [we . . . have] been concerned with these more theoretical problems, the areas of disagreement have been emphasized above the areas of agreement. Many plain facts about learning, important in practice, have nothing of controversy in them." [1]

It will be attempted here to set forth a fairly conservative point of view from which the student may later explore as much as he wishes into the schools. Trying to learn all points of view at one time can lead only to

[1] P. 359.

confusion except to the professional psychologist, for whom this chapter is obviously not written. Gardner Murphy's *Personality* is an excellent but difficult text in which to see how one psychologist goes about investigating the known phenomena of personality.

This section on schools of psychology should not be concluded without giving the lay student of this field two orienting principles by which to use and evaluate his progress. It is difficult for professional psychologists not to lose their sense of balance concerning the schools, as well as for the layman in the field.

In the first place, the ablest leaders of these schools conceive of their hypotheses, not as being final, but rather as being promising hypotheses which need experimental exploration. The educator therefore ought to be intelligently eclectic about them. Each school has some principles which are of great value. The Gestalt hypothesis of field structure is certainly highly significant in understanding many sudden personality changes, such as conversion, falling in love, and mob phenomena. Similar illustrations could be drawn from each of them.

An even more important principle is that of studying and using actual experimental findings. Psychologists, like other scientists, do extensive experimental investigations and then endeavor to interpret the significance of the results. The findings are the basic things. The interpretations are likely to change. Thus the book by Barker, Kounin, and Wright is a series of actual investigations. The religious educator will find each of these studies of great value, quite apart from the theoretical interpretations given them by their authors. For example, the study reported by Barker, Dembo, and Lewin in Chapter XXVI of that book will certainly not be interpreted in the same way by everyone, but everyone will see the practical importance of the research itself for educational procedure. Most religious educators will not be able to keep up with the extensive experimental literature of psychology,[2] but they can read such books as the above one and become acquainted with the more important of them.

METHODS OF MEASUREMENT

Science progresses in proportion to the accuracy of its measurements. This can be said just as truly of education in general or of religious education in particular. One needs only review the work of the Character Education Inquiry—Hartshorne and May books—to recognize how important measurement is in any reliable evaluation of methods in terms of their effectiveness in reaching their objectives. Religious educators always ought to make sure they have three things—a clear understanding of what their objectives are,

[2] See my column "Significant Evidence," in *Religious Education,* designed to perform this service for religious educators.

criteria by which to determine whether and to what extent they have been reached, and scientifically constructed scales for measuring this progress. A book like that of Percival Symonds is essential to the training of every well-equipped student in this field. Some knowledge of elementary statistical techniques is necessary for clear thinking in any field involving subjective concepts. Courage and magnanimity can be measured almost as accurately as height and weight, but far greater skill is required to do so. Few problems are more fascinating than forging a precision tool for measuring such a seemingly elusive thing as a trait of character, and none pays bigger dividends. Armed with such tools, educators can progress many times more rapidly than by the blind efforts necessary without them.

THE PROBLEM OF TEACHING AND LEARNING

One of the obvious truisms which is so seldom used in practice is that if learning is to take place, the laws of learning must be obeyed. There is probably no field of educational endeavor which violates the known laws of learning so shamelessly and flagrantly as does religious education. Our curricular materials and methods are, in general, written and administered as if their religious nature exempted them from all the learning principles used in secular education. If any considerable learning did take place, a new group of data would be available for proof of miracles occurring outside the known laws of the universe.

Students of religious education therefore ought to learn the principles of educational psychology, recognizing that religious education is not exempted from them. They ought to have some insight into theories of learning. Hilgard is the best source—though fairly technical—in the field. Furthermore, they ought to see how research projects for evaluating educational methods are set up and carried out. Vernon Jones in his study of character education in the public schools made as great a contribution to methods of research as in the findings of the study as such.

The problems of learning and teaching are numerous and will require extensive study for even a minimum of skill in them. Leonard Carmichael and Barker, Kounin, and Wright are source books in developmental psychology which devote many chapters to various aspects of learning. But although there are many theories of learning, practical methods of teaching and learning are not widely different.

The adaptation procedure as used in the Union College Character Research Project [3] was developed as a result of years of research on effective teaching in the field of character education. This procedure demonstrates how exacting the teaching process is, not only in terms of hard work, but

[3] See my book *A Greater Generation*, chaps. xiv, xvii.

in terms of techniques and skills. It involves five steps essential in the learning process—essential because it was discovered that character education did not take place unless all five were carried out: (1) The child must be *exposed* to the material to be learned. (2) Review or *repetition* is necessary. (3) *Understanding* is a prerequisite for any intelligent use of the material. (4) Especially in such fields as character education, the child must become *convinced* of its value before he will make it a part of his personality. (5) He will have to *apply* it to every relevant part of his daily behavior to have it effective in his life experience. Students in religious education who do not wish to spend their lives in sterile futility must understand the intricacies of the learning process and plan their educational ventures in light of them.

The Nature of Personality Traits

It goes without saying that all educational programs must have objectives toward which they are working. It is not so commonly realized that the nature of human personality sets definite limitations and indicates definite directions for the selection of these objectives. Until the epoch-making researches of the Character Education Inquiry it was common procedure for any educational group to set forth whatever traits it considered desirable and to build a curriculum designed to teach them. When the Inquiry demonstrated the invalidity of considering such time-honored traits as honesty, service, and self-control as trait entities, the naïve era of trait manufacturing came to an end.

To suppose, however, that the specificity theory—which assumes that there are no generalized traits, only specific habits—is the only alternative has led to abuses of almost equal proportions in the other extreme. Catherine Cox and her associates clearly demonstrated that men of eminence did possess clearly identifiable characteristics. Gordon Allport showed many evidences of consistency in behavior and the possibility of generalized traits.

The choice of trait goals, however, is a problem of research discovery, not of armchair opinion. Religious educators ought to become thoroughly familiar with the growth of trait theory in psychology. In my books I have attempted to set forth under the title "The Christian Hypothesis" a trait theory based on the Christian philosophy and the findings of personality psychology. Its attitude list formed the basis for an extensive research for more valid trait concepts. This had to be done in such a fashion that the practical educational training of children would be valid and wholesome, whatever theoretical concepts might grow out of it in the future.

A preview of the type of trait theory to be expected as a result of modern research is found in Raymond Cattell's work. Using such modern statistical techniques as factor analysis, he starts with several hundred trait names and by a series of steps arrives at twelve "source traits" such as cyclothymiaschizothymia and surgent cyclothymia-paranoia. It is highly probable that all of our common-sense trait names will be found not to be simple traits at all. The basic personality trait names will be as foreign to our daily conversation as the names of the chemical elements are in our daily descriptions of our common foods. The fact remains that the religious educator who does not keep abreast of this development will be as helpless as a person who attempts to solve chemical problems without a knowledge of the periodic table.

A personality trait has no meaning apart from the individual of whom it is characteristic. Another section of this chapter will start with this same statement. There the emphasis is on individual differences. Here the emphasis is on the nature of traits. It was customary in former days to teach traits as if they were things in themselves which could be instilled in children like a hypodermic needle. Modern psychologists would probably all agree now—whatever our concept of traits—that each is simply a characteristic of the total personality of the individual. It cannot be either understood or modified except as one deals with that total personality. For example, educators will not teach purposiveness successfully by simply extolling its virtues and describing some great men who had it. Purposiveness for each child is a separate and distinct thing from every other child. It involves his native endowment, his training, the social culture in which he lives, the basic drives which motivate him, and all of the evaluative attitudes he has already formed. A careful examination, for example, of the study made by Lippitt and White and reported in chapter 28 of Barker, Kounin, and Wright on "social climates" is only partially understood in comparing autocratic, democratic, and laissez-faire climates. Individual differences are constantly creeping into the picture. Boys who had autocracy in their past experiences behaved differently from those who had not. The important thing to remember is that traits apart from the individuals of whom they are characteristic are as meaningless as the grin of the Cheshire cat without the cat. A personality trait, then, is an abstraction and has meaning only as one studies the total personality.

The Problem of Motivation

The great problem of psychology is the problem of motivation. A concept of motivation as far-reaching as Newton's laws of motion or Darwin's theory of evolution is still to be discovered. Its discovery is brought nearer every day by the increasing mass of experimental evidence concerning human motivation. Why do we behave like human beings? What are the biological and psychological drives which bring about our behavior? How are desirable motives taught and learned? Religious education would be sterile indeed if it took no account of the basic motivational nature of man himself. This in turn requires some fundamental knowledge of general psychology. Ruch is an excellent text for students wishing the most practical possible approach to the general field. Many of his chapters deal with such topics as motives, physiological drives, and the like.

Many efforts have been made to construct practical diagrams of behavior. Watson, Woodworth, and Lewin are among those who have used such schematic diagrams of human behavior. In *Their Future Is Now* and elsewhere I used the following diagram:

$$S - PS - T - R$$
$$| \quad / \text{Att}$$
$$Om$$
$$| \quad \backslash Sk$$
$$| \quad /$$
$$Oi$$

In this diagram S (situation) is the external world in which the individual adjusts. PS (perceptual situation) is his interpretation of that situation. This is quite as much a function of the individual—O (organism)—as of the situation itself. His inherited characteristics—Oi (inherited organism)—set definite limits on his ability to sense and comprehend the world correctly. His learned characteristics—Om (modified organism)—consisting of his Sk (skills) and Att (attitudes), exert the greatest influences upon his behavior. His attitudes constitute his real philosophy of life. All character education is effective to the extent that it formulates or modifies attitudes. Any immediate action is brought about by T (tensions). The primary tensions are the appetites, the drive for achievement, and the social drives. They are augmented by the feelings and emotions—the secondary tensions. All behavior—R (response)—is for the purpose of satisfying these tensions singly or in groups. The strength of these tensions differs from individual to individual, and his attitudes are developed as he finds ways of satisfying his basic needs or tensions.

It is not likely that the student will feel that the preceding paragraph is an adequate description of human motivations. And so it is not. This diagram is the basis of an advanced semester course in college. It is set forth here to demonstrate to the student how complex the problem is, and how much study is in prospect before he can grasp it.

One factor in this diagram needs to be examined with a little more care. It is the perceptual situation (PS). A very common error in people's thinking about human behavior is in considering the S as if it were an adequate determiner of behavior. Parents show this error in a question like this one: "How can two children brought up in the same family behave so differently?" The answer is that two children are brought up in the same family only in terms of the S, and not entirely so even there; but in the PS the two children may have families as different as humanly possible. If one child looks upon his parents as saints, that is how he adjusts to them and because of them. If the other thinks of them as unjust, tyrannical taskmasters, that is what they are as far as his adjustment is concerned.

Psychologists are not always immune to this error. A great deal that is being written in the literature today about frustration deals with it as if it were an *S*. It seems far more likely that frustration in the sense of being a disturbing personality factor is a *PS*. Blocking one's desires and purposes in the external world may prove to be a frustration for one individual and a challenge to another. Failure to some people certainly produces all the characteristics of frustration. They show fear for it and engage in many varieties of behavior to avoid it. However, let us instill in the child the attitude that failure is the forerunner to high achievement, that objectives which can be reached on the first trial are not worth doing, that great men have regularly failed many times before they achieved success. Then the child may see failure as highly desirable, a thrilling form of challenge. It is clear that even this idea can be carried to the extreme. One must take the child's aptitudes into consideration and probably many other things. The point is, the sociological ideal is not valid if it considers only *S*. The important environment of the individual is not *S* but *PS*, in which *S* plays only a single role—and usually not even the most important one.

The psychological problems of religious education are almost always problems either of educational psychology or of social psychology. The religious educator cannot hope to master these two extensive fields of investigation. However, he ought to keep abreast of their findings and their methodology. Murphy, Murphy, and Newcomb, for example, will open up vistas of research of which he probably is totally unaware.

The Development of Personality

Developing any kind of personality traits or teaching any kind of material is a function partly of nature and partly of nurture. The latter is futile when out of step with the former. As the infant progresses toward maturity, at each age level the extent of his maturity sets the limits both in the amount and the nature of the education he is capable of acquiring. The nursery or kindergarten child may enjoy the rhythm of "Jesus Loves Me." He most certainly cannot understand its concepts. The first ten years of the Union College Character Research Project were in large part spent in determining what could be taught and when.[4] There are few ways in which religious educators can make themselves more absurd and their educational efforts more futile than by failing to submit their methods and materials to age-level calibration.

---

[4] See Ligon, *A Greater Generation* and *Their Future Is Now*.

An interesting problem which shows the significance of this developmental calibration is the age-old one of discipline. Which is better, strict discipline, or letting the child work out things for himself, or democratic procedures? This problem has many aspects. Here let us deal only with the matter of developmental calibration. It sounds very noble to speak of democratic methods being used in the home and school, in which children as well as parents and teachers have a voice. And so it is. But how much voice shall they have? If the father is a doctor and sickness comes in the home, should diagnosis and treatment be determined by simple majority vote, or should the father probably have the determining vote? In a problem such as making some new business investment or buying a new home, is the opinion of the five-year-old to be weighed as heavily as that of his parents? Of course not. Clearly, then, the child can be given a voice in his own or the family's decisions as rapidly as—but only as rapidly as—he has wisdom and stability to use this privilege wisely. The characteristic emotional instability of the high-school boy or girl makes it highly desirable that he have stabilizing controls from his elders. One shudders to think what would happen to a college if it were run by the student body.

This is not all there is to be said about discipline. There are many answers which we do not know as yet. Religious educators will need to follow with care the work of psychologists—including the nonfrustration enthusiasts—and to be constantly revising their thinking about it. Of one thing they can be sure, however—developmental calibration will always be a factor to be considered.

Florence Goodenough has furnished an excellent text from which to learn the basic characteristics of growth. This foundation, however, is not sufficient for those who expect to do curriculum construction or effective direction of educational program. Such extensive sources as Barker, Kounin, and Wright and Carmichael will need to be studied thoroughly before one can profess any real competence in the field.

When the more extensive curriculum projects, such as those of the various denominational publishing houses, are undertaken, a thoroughly trained psychologist should test every aspect of them for age-level calibration. Furthermore, each writer needs an exhaustive description of the characteristics of the age level for which the materials are designed.

For example, in the Character Research Project at Union College, curricular writers are provided with extensive summaries of all the findings in the field of child development with respect to the age level. The chart in *Their Future Is Now* shows in its three left-hand columns such a summary of the physical, mental, emotional, and social stages of development. All other studies are examined for added information. The growth of vocabulary, capacity for rote memory, development of concepts, and characteristic interests and skills are all necessary information. The results of parent-interview outlines of interests and abilities, the data from attitude scales, and parent and teacher reports are added to this basic information. The final step in this procedure is in testing these materials by actual use. The ablest and best-trained psychologist would make errors if he omitted this testing process. No competent psychologist would even consider putting his materials into permanent form without trying them out in actual test situations. These curricular materials, then, are revised each time they are used, on the basis of the actual experience of parents and teachers with them, which of course implies better age-level calibration.

When the depression of 1929 produced its consequent economies among churches, directors of religious education were usually the first "luxuries" to be cut from the budget. The fact is that they could hardly have made themselves otherwise because of our lack of knowledge in the field of child development. Developmental psychology as represented by Arnold Gesell and the child-development research laboratories had just been born. If our present corps of directors keep abreast of this rapidly growing mass of data in developmental psychology, they can do such effective jobs that never again can they be thought of as "luxuries." Failing in this basic training, they most certainly will be.

INDIVIDUAL DIFFERENCES

A character trait has no meaning apart from the individual of whom it is characteristic. One can no more solve the problem of the personal equation without knowing the factors in that equation than he can solve the problem of a mathematics equation without knowing its factors. This means that an adequate knowledge and use of individual differences is a prerequisite for effective education of any sort. The religious educator ought to inform himself fully concerning the nature, extent, and measurement of individual differences. James Mursell's is one of the latest texts designed as an introduction to this field.

A great deal has been said and written about child-centered education. The fact is that most of it is thoroughly content-centered, with little more than a polite gesture of recognition of individual differences. There are, perhaps, two ways in which curricular materials can be made child-centered. The more common one is to determine the content first and then to adapt it to individual differences. The second is to start with an objective, to study successively a number of individual children, to select materials and methods suitable for each child, and then to organize the individual materials into an integrated lesson plan or curricular unit.

The first of the two is far less laborious and more logical in content organization. It is questionable as to whether it can ever be very effective. The latter is time consuming and difficult indeed. Its content organization is correspondingly difficult to achieve. In terms of permanent effectiveness it seems to outdo the other approach a hundredfold.

The extent of individual differences is very wide as becomes obvious from a careful study of Mursell; Barker, Kounin, and Wright; Carmichael; and *Their Future Is Now.* The last of these is listed here because it relates the problem specifically to religious education. The existence of an enormous variety of individual differences, however, does not mean that standardized curriculums are impossible. These individual differences follow very definite and predictable laws. Individuals differ widely, but groups are astonishingly alike. If one aims at the "average child," none will be dealt with adequately, for there is no such thing as an average child. He may be average in some respects but certainly never in all. Only those curriculums which are written with a full recognition of individual differences and revised in light of repeated group experimentation can hope to be effective, no matter what educational objectives are being sought.

SUGGESTIONS FOR FURTHER STUDY

The principles set forth in this chapter can best be learned by a project of curriculum construction. How far the project can be carried will depend on the time and resource limitations of the individual student. The following suggestions are put in order of increasing difficulty so that they can be carried out as far as desired. All of them are necessary for effective curriculum construction.

1. Select an educational objective. It may be teaching a Bible story, a religious principle, a character trait, or a step in a progressive course of some kind. Make sure that the objective is stated fully in terms of who is to be taught what, and what ought to be achieved in the process.

2. Prepare some sort of scale—examination, attitude scale, or behavior situation—by which to evaluate the pupils to be taught in terms of the objective before the unit is taught and again at the end to measure progress. (A control group will have to be used in an actual experiment.)

3. Try to make an age-level calibration of your material by submitting it to several age groups and examining carefully their comprehension of its concepts. Select the age level which it best fits.

4. Select a tentative class for experimentation. Choose not more than five boys and five girls of the age level determined in Step 3. Talk with each child individually, having previously learned everything about him that you can. Try to teach him the lesson involved in your objective. That is, by trial and error try to determine what methods and materials have to be used to achieve the objective with the child being taught. Study his aptitudes, interests, and motives until you are able to achieve your objective. This will require several hours for each child. Use tests or test results if you are competent in their use and interpretation. Do not assume that you are. Find out from a professional psychometrist.

5. Build a lesson from these individual materials. Integrate them into a unit as a dramatist might weave the details of his plot into a play.

6. Choose another class (with control group, equated for intelligence, education, age, socio-economic status). Give the evaluative scale prepared in Step 2

to both groups. Use the curricular materials prepared with one group and measure the effectiveness or ineffectiveness of your efforts.

BIBLIOGRAPHY

Allport, Gordon W. *Personality*. New York: Henry Holt & Company, 1937.

Barker, Roger G.; Kounin, Jacob S.; and Wright, Herbert F. *Child Behavior and Development*. New York: McGraw-Hill Book Company, 1943.

Carmichael, Leonard, ed. *Manual of Child Psychology*. New York: John Wiley and Sons, 1946.

Cattell, Raymond B. *Description and Measurement of Personality*. Yonkers-on-Hudson: World Book Company, 1946.

Cox, Catherine Morris. *The Early Mental Traits of Three Hundred Geniuses*. (Vol. II of "Genetic Studies of Genius," ed. Lewis M. Terman.) Stanford University: Stanford University Press, 1926.

Goodenough, Florence L. *Developmental Psychology*. New York: D. Appleton-Century Company, 1945.

Hartshorne, Hugh, and May, M. A. *Studies in Deceit* (Book I, *General Methods and Results;* Book II, *Statistical Methods and Results*). New York: The Macmillan Company, 1928.

———. *Studies in Service and Self-Control*. New York: The Macmillan Company, 1929.

Hartshorne, Hugh; May, M. A.; and Shuttleworth, F. K. *Studies in the Organization of Character*. New York: The Macmillan Company, 1930.

Hilgard, Ernest R. *Theories of Learning*. New York: Appleton-Century-Crofts, Inc., 1948.

Jones, Vernon. *Character and Citizenship Training in the Public School*. Chicago: University of Chicago Press, 1936.

Ligon, Ernest M. *A Greater Generation*. New York: The Macmillan Company, 1948.

———. *The Psychology of Christian Personality*. New York: The Macmillan Company, 1935.

———. *Their Future Is Now*. New York: The Macmillan Company, 1939.

Murphy, Gardner. *Personality*. New York: Harper & Brothers, 1947.

Murphy, Gardner; Murphy, Lois B.; and Newcomb, Theodore M. *Experimental Social Psychology*. New York: Harper & Brothers, 1937.

Mursell, James L. *Psychological Testing*. New York: Longmans, Green & Company, 1947.

Ruch, F. L. *Psychology and Life*, Chicago: Scott, Foresman & Company, 1948.

Symonds, Percival M. *Diagnosing Personality and Conduct*. New York: D. Appleton-Century Company, 1931.

Chapter 4

TRENDS IN EDUCATIONAL PHILOSOPHY

FRANK M. McKIBBEN

EDUCATION OF ANY TYPE needs a supporting and guiding philosophy. It is the function of philosophy to focus attention upon the totality of experience. It attempts to bring into unity and consistency the various elements involved in a comprehensive, all-inclusive view of life. The more particular role of educational philosophy is to see education steadily and to see it whole. It must critically examine all the assumptions upon which educational theory, science, and practice rest. It should give direction to the total enterprise and therefore will help determine the ends sought through education. This inevitably involves education in a theory of value, which cannot be developed without reference to morals, ethics, and religion. A philosophy must express some point of view on ethics and religion. A philosophy of education will be concerned with the metaphysical foundations upon which its procedures will be based, for professional thinking in education will be without adequate foundations unless it rests upon well-considered conceptions of the way things really are in this world. It will inquire into the nature of ultimate reality.

This philosophy must develop some theory of knowledge—how one comes to know and how he knows that he knows. Here arises the fundamental question regarding the nature of truth and the authority of the knowledge that enters into the educative process. An educational philosophy is also concerned with the psychology of learning, with the various factors that determine the physical, emotional, and mental responses of the learner to the procedures of education. The view held of the nature of the mind and its relation to the body will determine many of the educational practices to be engaged in. Education will be carried forward upon the basis of some interpretation of the origin and nature of the human organism, the raw material with which the educator deals.

Education is likewise interrelated with the social process. It does not occur in a vacuum. Whatever else education is, it is the continuous interaction of the individual with his environment. Therefore the nature of the social order in which it is carried on—whether it be a democratic, a fascist, or any other type of state—will have profound implications for the purposes and methods of education. This concern extends also to the economic ideals and practices of the social order as they influence the nature and

48

method of inducting the young into its culture. This social order has a dynamic quality and is subject to constant change. The nature, direction, and rapidity of social progress is inevitably determined, in part at least, by education. Education must have a theory of social progress.

These then are some of the major philosophical considerations that are ultimately brought to bear upon the educative process. The details of this process at every point hinge upon the answers given to the questions arising with respect to the major considerations mentioned above. Any trends to be discerned in educational philosophy will be found in relation to these major issues.

Dominant Philosophies of Education

Before we can intelligently discuss trends, we must have some notion of prevailing philosophies of education. Various classifications of identifiable schools of philosophical thought may be made, although many would hold that educational thought is so unsettled as to make "schools of thought" unidentifiable. Doubtless the simplest and most serviceable analysis for this brief review is that made by John Brubacher.[1] He identifies two main streams of philosophical thought. These are (1) progressivism and (2) traditionalism or essentialism. In the progressive school two major emphases are identified: the pragmatic and the naturalistic; and the traditionalist view of education is characterized by idealism and realism. A mere sketch of the most characteristic features of these points of view will be given here, since it is assumed that the serious student of the problem will seek fuller interpretations in more substantial treatments of the philosophy of education.

The distinguishing characteristics of the progressive school of thought are briefly the following: the emphasis upon pupil freedom; the cultivation of initiative, self-reliance, and independent thinking; the recognition of individuality in capacity and aptitude; the utilization of pupil interests and needs as the organizing principle of curriculum making and the dominant type of motivation of study and achievement; the recognition of membership in the group—society—as a most essential and effective means of developing the total personality of the individual. A cardinal principle of this point of view is the recognition of change. "Progress means change." But "progress" is a value word. "From the pragmatic point of view values are instrumental. They implement a person to gain ends. Progress occurs if these ends are achieved." But, one may ask, are the ends worthy or good? The progressive sets up no fixed aims or values in advance. No matter how well authenticated by the past, educational aims are not to be projected

---

[1] *Modern Philosophies of Education*, chap. xiv.

indefinitely into the future. Hence, knowledge takes on instrumental meaning. The pragmatist holds that knowledge is something which is wrought out in action. Information is transformed into knowledge when it is judged to be pertinent to the solutions of a particular problem, and that judgment is tested out in experience.

Closely related to the pragmatic, instrumental philosophy as a form of progressive education is the naturalistic school of thought. Sharing much that has been described above,

it denies that educational philosophy in its inclusive sweep need take into account concepts of the supernatural. If there is anything hidden from man in his search for the solution of educational problems, it must lie hidden in the system of nature of which he himself is a part. . . . Ultimate reality is materialistic or at least energistic. . . . [This] educational philosophy . . . omits the eternal, the timeless, from the space-time frame of reference. . . . If religion enters this philosophy of education, it is only as a deified nature. God is immanent in nature, and nature is His temple of worship.[2]

To religious naturalism this interpretation is not adequate. Naturalism needs supplementation by the superior insight of revelation and grace. Back of any grand design found in nature is a God guiding and directing it. For such problems as nature reveals, God supplies the clues in the cosmos for their solution.

Over against this philosophy of progressivism, with its pragmatic and naturalistic wings, stands that of essentialism or traditionalism. The essentialist believes that there are some points of the educational compass that are relatively fixed, and he firmly and resolutely insists that the child experience these essentials of education. He believes that they should constitute a considerable part of the curriculum. Individual freedom is recognized, but freedom is won as a well-deserved reward by the youth who has learned to discipline himself through a mastery of the social experience of the ages.

Experience refined and generalized in the mill of preceding generations must have an authority which surpasses that of any individual child and his epoch. The more confidence one has in this authority, the more authoritarian is the structure of society likely to be. . . . Essential values in education are ultimately sanctioned and consecrated by religion. . . . Its concern is with an unassailable authority, an authority which is above and beyond nature, the supernatural. Its main inspiration is a divine being, God, the author of all values, educational and otherwise.[3]

The idealistic wing holds that certain ideas that determine the frame of a world in which the child lives are final and fixed. This means that they

[2] *Ibid.*, pp. 332, 335.
[3] *Ibid.*, p. 420.

must furnish the core of his education. Truth and goodness are absolutes and set the models to which the child's learning should conform. Learning thus becomes a realization, not a creation.

Realism stresses the fact that objects have a reality independent of ideas about them. "Reality simply is; truth is what reality is reported to be." One finds the tests of truth, therefore, in its correspondence to reality. There are scientific realists and scholastic realists, but the latter play the larger role in education. Scholastic realism is the underlying philosophy of the Catholic church, stemming from the medieval scholastic Thomas Aquinas. It is fundamentally dualistic, holding that certain verities exist independent of our ideas about them, and that God himself is changeless and eternal. Certain objectives may be held unwaveringly; prescribed curriculums are justified; and educational values take on an immutable character.

It must be admitted that these schools of thought are greatly intertwined, and even the terms used to designate them may defy successful definition for any considerable body of educators.

Trends

Trends in educational philosophy need not be taken seriously until they begin to affect practice. Some will hold that the only way to discover any philosophy or trend in philosophy is to review and evaluate practice. The following are among those trends discernible in dominant conceptions and practices in education today: the more broadly-conceived aims of education; the growing concern for the total personality of the student; the identification of the school life with the environing society, and the incorporation of more of contemporary life in the curriculum; the fuller utilization of the democratic, creative method in teaching and learning, with greater freedom for the pupil; the serious evaluation of the direction in which the social order is moving; and the disposition to state the ends of education in spiritual or religious terms. It must be recognized that trends develop slowly in both formulation and expression in practice, and that certain of them are often counteracted by trends in the very opposite direction. The trends mentioned above group themselves about the two schools of educational thought just considered—the progressive and the traditional. It is therefore highly important that these major schools of thought be identified—not that we should be particularly concerned with names or labels—because most of the current problems in educational philosophy relate to conflicting viewpoints represented by their respective proponents. Both philosophies hold important points in common, and both have right and left wings within their group. But each school of thought has its own point of view on many of the basic issues listed earlier as those upon which a philosophy of education is formed. The weight of

practice stemming from the past is overwhelmingly on the more conservative or traditional side. Therefore, most of the trends discussed here are
those which *challenge past practice* and seem to move in a different direction.
It seems also that these trends, among those that might have been discussed,
are of greatest concern to religious education.

OBJECTIVES: INCLUSIVE AND DYNAMIC

The ends sought through the educative process are central in any philosophy of education. Various possibilities confront the educator. He may
conceive the purpose of education in terms of transmitting the end products
of the past experience of the race as systematized knowledge. Or he may
regard the objective of education to be molding the immature into the
patterns of contemporary thought and behavior. This will constitute
largely adjustment to, and participation in, the status quo. Or he may regard
the objective to be that of guiding the interaction of the young with their
environment, with special concern that they view it intelligently and critically and seek to bring about improvement. There can be no question that
educational practice continues to move in the direction of the last of these
three alternatives.

This trend manifests itself in several ways. It means that education is
increasingly concerned with *living* persons, as individuals and in association
with other individuals and institutions. It is shown in the tendency to recognize the wholeness and unity of living—in a concern for the total personality.
The total child, in the home, the school, the community, and the world,
represents the scope of modern education. It is revealed in innumerable
statements of objectives of representative bodies of educators, prominent
among which are *Character Education,*[4] and Brubacher's *The Public Schools
and Spiritual Values*, the Seventh Year Book of the John Dewey Society.
These objectives embrace that comprehensiveness that is life itself. Education is concerned with all aspects of growth, and no area of human knowledge and activities lies outside its interest.

ADJUSTMENT OF EDUCATION TO THE INDIVIDUAL

This trend is further manifested in the growing recognition of individual
capacities, needs, and problems. This concern is not expressed alone or
primarily in terms of the problem child, but rather it is directed toward
making education more meaningful to all individuals. The more traditional
concept of education has been that of adapting the individual to the curriculum and the school. The newer approach is to adjust the curriculum

[4] Tenth Year Book (Washington, D. C.: Department of Superintendence, N.E.A. 1932).

and the school to the individual, letting his capacities, interests, needs, and problems determine a large part of the program planned for him. This trend does not have to do with the more formal aspects of learning only, but it involves the total situation—the response of the student to his fellows, his teachers, the total school, and the larger world about him. One striking manifestation of this tendency is the rapid and extensive development of guidance and counseling as a normal and indispensable part of the school program. In spite of increasing enrollment and the greatly enriched school program this trend to get away from undifferentiated, uniform, "assembly-line" education is most pronounced.

However, this rather exclusively child-centered concept of education is being challenged and supplanted by a community-centered approach. The child is not an individual apart from the stream of humanity about him; he is part of a company of people—old, middle-aged, and young—whose interests, problems, achievements, and values are bound together in the "bundle of life." Such interpretations of education for tomorrow as are found in *Learning the Ways of Democracy* and *Education for All American Youth* are vitally concerned for the fully rounded development of all individuals, but are concerned also that such development take place in, and take account of, the enrichment and growth of the community of which they are a part. Thus we have a definite trend from the child-centered school to community-centered education, in line with basic concepts of the purpose and nature of education as held by the more liberal progressive educators.

Furthermore, in this trend is noticeable a much greater disposition now than formerly to place a high value on racial experience in whatever form it has been preserved. There is greater recognition of the limitations of the child's experience in comparison with that of the race. The neglect of the racial experience characteristic of the child-centered movement is being corrected. This trend is finding expression throughout education from the kindergarten to graduate schools. On the college level it is expressed in the growing effort to provide general courses of shared experience covering a wide spread of human knowledge and experience, upon the basis of which specialization takes place in the last two years and graduate work. And through it all there is great concern as to the quality of educational experience being provided and the kind of person being developed.

EDUCATION IS LIFE

Changes taking place in the curriculum seem to be moving in the direction of including more of the personal interests and problems of the pupils and embracing more of contemporary life in the classroom. Education, it is held, is life—life in the here and now. In contrast to the conception of education as preparation for life in the future, it is believed that the best possible preparation for tomorrow is to be found in meeting most effectively the demands of living fruitfully today. Therefore, anything common to the everyday life of pupils is legitimate subject matter for the school. All the major interests of life are to be caught up in the curriculum and in the increasing spread of attractive and developmental extracurricular activities. "[Interest] is, after all, the core of educational value theory. It is both a guide to the selection of curriculum materials and the single best dynamic by which to motivate them." [5] This means also that the walls between the formal subjects are disappearing and the unity of subjects is being emphasized. Probably no finding in educational psychology has secured more universal support today than the principle that we learn as we live, and that information, knowledge, skills, habits, attitudes, appreciations, beliefs, and ideals are acquired in one and the same process.

Coincident with these changes in the curriculum is the definite attempt to make the teaching-learning process more democratic in method, with the pupils sharing more fully in determining the emphases, if not the content, of the curriculum and finding their motivation for work in the opportunity to direct their own learning activities and in their sense of the real worth inhering in the things that constitute the school program. They are increasingly encouraged to be more creative, to assume more initiative and responsibility, to make original contributions to the process, to sit in critical evaluation of their own achievements, and to help manage school life through student government.[6] The quality of life in the classroom, in the relations of pupil to pupil, and pupil to teacher and to the larger school community, is a matter of primary concern. Pupils are living meaningfully in a democracy—the smaller democracy of the school—which, it is held, constitutes the best possible training for effective participation in the democracy outside the school.

With the development of the progressive education movement during the early part of this century the traditional notion of education as imparting facts and indoctrinating with ideas was sharply challenged. The educative process came to be conceived as active rather than passive, as centering in the learner's felt needs and purposes, and as depending for its effectiveness on his own confirmatory response to what was presented to him, and its purposeful incorporation in his life. . . . It has been vigorously attacked on the score of its alleged inadequacy in social discipline and in equipping the young with the knowledge and skills which the community has a right to expect in the product of its schools.[7]

[5] Brubacher, *op. cit.*, p. 308.
[6] See *Learning the Ways of Democracy*.
[7] *The Relation of Religion to Public Education*, p. 12.

Yet the products of such education have consistently made good in college and graduate work. Throughout this discussion of trends it will be noted that both trends and countertrends are taken into account.

CONCERN FOR SOCIAL PROGRESS

All attempts to relate the individual more directly to the social setting in which his education is occurring, and efforts to embrace in the curriculum the common activities of his everyday living, mean that education is concerned with the direction of social progress. At least it strives to develop ever greater intelligence about, and a more evaluative attitude toward, social issues and problems. Students are encouraged to study the social structure, to observe keenly the wide sweep of current events, and to develop a forward-looking, constructive approach to democratic living. Efforts are being made to acquaint them realistically with the operation of affairs in their community and to develop them as world citizens. The present dynamic social situation will increasingly challenge educators to deal with it critically and constructively throughout the school program. To what extent schoolmen themselves will assume the role of statesmen and attempt leadership in pointing the direction of social progress is an open question. The writings of such men as John Dewey, George Counts, J. L. Childs, and others would seem to place a heavy and inescapable responsibility in this connection upon all educators. Attempts to assume such leadership are resulting at once in both strong commendation and sharp criticism from various elements in our democracy. Many educational theorists and practical schoolmen have been the subjects of close scrutiny and frequently of vigorous criticism for positions they have taken on social issues in their writings and teachings.

Socially minded educators have defended the introduction of controversial social and economic questions at the appropriate age level on the ground that the students need to know what the issues are, to be guided in their analysis of them in the light of the American tradition, and to have a sympathetic understanding of all honest proposals for their solution.[8]

While it may be admitted that few schoolmen are at present assuming vigorous and outstanding leadership in attacking major social problems, it may be said that the great majority of rank-and-file schoolteachers and administrators are committed to fundamental equalitarianism and other democratic ideals, and are quietly and effectively developing these essential principles in American democracy in the experience of millions of American youth in their day-by-day work in the public school. There is probably

[8] *Ibid.,* p. 16.

no single body of people in society today more uniformly committed to, and actively working toward, the realization of values inherent in the democratic way of life than public-school people. This is the outcome of a philosophy of education that has increasingly acknowledged the responsibility of the public schools of a democracy to incorporate such practical training in its program.

THE ROLE OF RESEARCH

There is every evidence of the increasing reliance of public education upon research of all kinds for the determination of its procedures in the classroom. The practitioner is leaning more heavily upon the research expert than upon the normal-school theorizer or armchair philosopher for guidance in the direction and improvement of practice. In normal schools and teachers' colleges, and particularly in graduate schools of education, research departments are assuming ever greater significance. Most large school systems have their own research staff. Painstaking studies of all aspects of education, experimentation, and laboratory and seminar activities are producing scientific data for the revision and improvement of educational procedure. A real science of education has emerged in the last quarter-century. All kindred sciences—anthropology, sociology, psychology, statistics, and testing procedures—are being drawn upon for whatever light they may throw upon the practice of education. This reliance upon the scientific attitude and method in education serves at once to free educational procedure from the binding grip of tradition and custom and also to furnish it with the tools by which it may test its own activities and discover better ways of directing growth.

SPIRITUAL VALUES IN EDUCATION

Closely related to the tendency to broaden the objectives of education is the disposition to state these objectives in idealistic and near-religious terms. The marked emphasis upon character outcomes of the past several decades has left a strong impression upon the confessed objectives of education. The stress upon guidance and counseling mentioned earlier likewise grows out of a concern for the development of well-rounded personality and for assisting the individual to realize all his potentialities. The goals of education have been conceived as spiritual values and stated in the following terms: "Moral insight; integrity of thought and act; equal regard for human personality wherever found; faith in the free play of intelligence both to guide study and direct action; and finally, those further values of refined thought and feeling requisite to bring life to its finest quality." [9]

[9] Brubacher, *The Public Schools and Spiritual Values.*

These spiritual values, which are the confessed objectives of education, are most commendable. Any educator, parent, or citizen would give hearty approval of them as the goals of education. Anyone interested in the more adequate religious education of children cannot help sensing the identity of these objectives with much that church leaders are primarily concerned for.

A crucial problem arises, however, over the relation of these spiritual values to religion. The metaphysics of the traditional or conservative point of view includes for many a strong commitment to a theistic conception of the universe. This position holds that these values, which education most deserving of support seeks to realize, have not emerged accidentally or merely as by-products—however worthy—of the social process. It holds that they correspond to something eternal, that they are grounded in the moral structure of the universe, that their roots are laid deep in the religious strivings of mankind. Since, it is held, these values arise out of, not apart from, the religious thought and experience of men, they must have religious reference and sanction. Therefore a theological framework—however simple— is essential to their best understanding and their finest expression in life and conduct. It is felt that this is also the position of a considerable proportion of the rank-and-file schoolmen throughout the country, as well as of most religious leaders.

Conflicting Metaphysics

Thus it is that educators—both inside and outside the Church—who hold to a theistic interpretation of the universe will join most heartily with educators of all schools of thought who subscribe to "spiritual values" as goals of education but will insist that for their proper understanding and full realization they will require religious interpretation and support. Here we find a significant parting of the way in educational thought. This radical difference is seen, in the comparison, not only of representative statements of religious bodies with those of many educational agencies, but also of such writings as *The Relation of Religion to Public Education*—produced under the auspices of the American Council of Education—on the one hand, and *The Public Schools and Spiritual Values* already referred to. The Commission of the American Council of Education says:

But to assume that spiritual values embody the full, valid content of religion is quite another matter. The words "spiritual" and "moral" denote the value-structure of life. Religion seeks personal identification with some ultimate source of values. It involves faith in the permanent validity and durability of these values. Religion has always supplied moral sanctions for men's actions. No person is fully educated who has not gained a knowledge of the faiths men live by. And unless the schools are content to leave one of the major areas of life unexplored, the specifically religious beliefs and aspirations of human beings must have attention.[10]

Brubacher and his associates, on the other hand,

propose to maintain both the logical possibility and practical potential adequacy of the public schools to teach such spiritual values as those named above, and this on the basis of human reason and experience and without necessary recourse to religious authority.[11]

The instrumentalist or experimentalist approach contends that such spiritual values are relative. The origin of such values is to be found, not in an order "eternal in the heavens," but in the slowly evolving experience of the human race, where the values have been found to be, not necessarily the *Good*, but the highest good yet experienced.

This empirical orientation holds that the advance of knowledge in the biological and social sciences requires that we reject the traditional dualisms of man and nature, of mind and body, of spirit and flesh, of mechanism and purpose, of practice and theory, of utility and art, and of morals and the affairs of ordinary experience. In sum, this conception holds that morals and values do not constitute a realm apart, that they are properties of a transcendental realm to be known by revelation or mystical intuition, but rather that they are in the nature of group judgments about affairs of human history, social institutions, and evolving modes of life and thought.[12]

These values are not ultimates—no one knows what future experience may bring forth. A dynamic, emerging environment will demand new responses and learnings. The primary source of values, they claim, is successful adaptation. If effective adaptation to this dynamic environment suggests other and higher values, education should seek these as goals.

What we observe, then, in noting this strong trend is the disposition in various educational circles to adopt broadly conceived, elevated objectives, with both traditionalists and progressives supporting them, each relying upon his own metaphysics for interpretation and support. What support they have in common is not clear. The John Dewey Society says, "In the matter of teaching, we believe specifically that there is a large area of ground common for both public school teachers and religious teachers to the end that they should have common concern for the spiritual values herein upheld and can likewise find a common support for these values." [13] On the other hand, Boyd Bode writes: "It could be that the alliance with

---

[10] *The Relation of Religion to Public Education*, p. 19.
[11] *The Public Schools and Spiritual Values*, p. 3.
[12] *Ibid.*
[13] *Ibid.*, p. 9.

theology, which was a source of strength to democracy in the past, is now become a hindrance to it. It could be that the non-theological conception of moral values comes closer to the deeper meaning of the Gospels than the traditional interpretation." [14] There can be no doubt that there is a strong and vigorous group of education leaders who share the position just stated, made articulate for them by such writers as Dewey, Bode, Brubacher, Childs, and others. The future of the relation of religion to the education our society provides for its young and the nature of the sanctions of its goals will be determined by the manner in which this issue is resolved in practical school programs.

SUGGESTIONS FOR FURTHER STUDY

1. What issues or problems should a philosophy of Christian education treat? How do these issues relate to those listed in this chapter?

2. Develop in greater detail positions (1) held in common, and (2) those representing differences, in the two major schools of philosophical thought discussed in this chapter. Distinguish if possible other systematic philosophies of education.

3. Discuss and interpret such terms as "traditional, creative, democratic, dynamic, experience-centered, value," in relation to an over-all theory of the educative process.

4. Interpret "method" in education. Indicate how it is influenced by basic philosophic concepts of education.

5. Outline your own position with respect to the nature of the authority to be used in education. What constitutes such authority, and how may it be used effectively in teaching?

6. To what extent and how should educators deal with "live social issues" in the curriculum of the schools?

7. Give your own interpretation of "spiritual values" as goals of education. In what ways do they represent what educators seek through Christian education?

BIBLIOGRAPHY

Bode, Boyd. *Fundamentals of Education.* New York: The Macmillan Company, 1939.

Brubacher, J. *Modern Philosophies of Education.* New York: McGraw-Hill Book Company, 1939.

Brubacher, J., ed. *The Public Schools and Spiritual Values.* New York: Harper & Brothers, 1944.

Chave, E. J. *A Functional Approach to Religious Education.* Chicago: University of Chicago Press, 1947.

Childs, J. L. *Education and the Philosophy of Experimentation.* New York: D. Appleton-Century, Inc., 1931.

Dewey, John. *Democracy and Education.* New York: The Macmillan Company, 1916.

Education for All American Youth. Washington, D. C.: National Education Association of the United States, 1944.

[14] "Religion and the Public Schools," *School and Society*, March 27, 1948, p. 228.

Horne, Herman. *The Democratic Philosophy of Education.* New York: The Macmillan Company, 1935.

Learning the Ways of Democracy. Washington D. C.: National Education Association of the United States, 1940.

Marque, P. J. *The Philosophy of Christian Education.* New York: Prentice-Hall, Inc., 1939.

Relation of Religion to Public Education, The. Washington, D. C.: American Council on Education Series. Vol. XI, April, 1947.

Washburne, C. W. *A Living Philosophy of Education.* New York: John Day Company, 1940.

Chapter 5

BASIC CAUSES OF PROGRESS AND DECAY IN CIVILIZATION

JAMES LUTHER ADAMS

"When i mention religion, I mean the Christian religion; and not only the Christian religion, but the Protestant religion; and not only the Protestant religion, but the church of England." So says the clergyman in Fielding's novel *Tom Jones*. If his words reflect a certain provincialism, they also exhibit some precision of definition.

In the present essay I shall attempt at the outset to define the concept of "civilization" precisely, but we shall proceed in the direction of a sort of provincialism, for principal attention will be devoted to our Western industrial, democratic civilization and to the progress and decay in that kind of society.

The Meaning of "Civilization"

In its generic meaning the term "civilization" denotes an order of society distinguished from primitive society. The latter is a "small, isolated, non-literate, and homogeneous society, with a strong sense of group solidarity"; behavior is "traditional, spontaneous, uncritical, and personal"; apart from differences in age and sex there is little division of labor; the motive of commercial gain is absent, for the members are bound decisively by kinship and religious ties. This is the sacred, folk society. It has a culture—a system of acquired patterns of behavior—even though it is not civilized.

Literally the term "civilization" implies that groups are organized on a civil basis rather than on the basis of kinship; it suggests the city—or fixed habitations. Accordingly, it denotes a vast, complicated, literate, heterogeneous society, hospitable to influences from other societies and to criticism from within. It also includes diverse and conflicting loyalties, leisure for invention, elaborate division of labor, formulated and modifiable law, and the choice of group policy through an at least partially rational consideration of alternative solutions as they arise. Sanctions other than those which are traditional and explicitly sacred may operate.

Somewhat different connotations are suggested by the term "civility." The word stems, of course, from the same root as civilization, and it is the opposite of barbarism. Here urbanity, poise, moderation, courtesy, the

61

disciplined use of leisure, cultivation in the arts, the ideal of the gentleman, are implied. Like "civilization," the word "urbanity" connotes the urban milieu. In Western civilization, the disciplines of civility have been sponsored and transmitted mainly by what is called "humanism"; they have been largely associated with the sophistication of the city and the university.

Within a given civilization, and also within a religious tradition, basic differences of evaluation may appear with respect to civilization and civility, and therefore also with respect to the nature of progress and decay. Widely different evaluations of religion may also appear. Some people view religion as the enemy of civilization; others think of it as the mother of civilization and culture; still others think of civilization and especially of civility as the enemy of true religion. Because of its tendency to preen itself on man's sophistication and on his cultural achievements, urbanity, Spengler asserted, long ago "killed Christianity." In contrast, Gibbon attributed the fall of Rome to the rise of barbarism and religion. Kierkegaard, on quite different presuppositions from Spengler's, insisted that there is a world of difference between the roots and fruits of Christianity and the roots and fruits of urbanity. For Kierkegaard urbane poise freezes the knees of the "man of the world": being completely self-sufficient, he is not capable of genuine religious humility—he aims to be his own redeemer. With still different presuppositions John Henry Newman contrasted the ideal of the gentleman with the ideal of the Christian, sardonically defining the gentleman as one who refuses to cause pain. Harold Laski believes that progress in civilization is possible only with the elimination of religion. In contrast to certain of these views we find Hegel asserting that religion is the womb of culture; Arnold Toynbee believes civilization is the womb of religion, and indeed religion is the only enduring product of civilizations in their rise and fall; and Edmund Burke held that civilization is the result of two things—the spirit of the gentleman and the spirit of religion.

Within any general conception of civilization we see that room exists for a great plasticity in the expenditure of man's biological and social inheritance. A multitude of different familial, political, economic, religious, and nonreligious patterns appear, even within the same civilization. To a traditional Chinese, the typical American urban family has surrendered the chief civilizational values of the family. The contrasts between the religions are no less marked. It has been said, for example, that the Christian idea of heaven is the Buddhist idea of hell. Analogous contrasts may be observed also between different types of Christianity. Such contrasts imply markedly different conceptions of history and its meaning. Any completely other-worldly religion will entertain no conception of progress in history; progress, if any, will come only through escape from history. But, without stressing world-denying asceticism, many religions and civilizations have possessed no conception of progress, even though they have reached a high stage of development.

THE IDEA OF PROGRESS

The doctrine of progress was a late arrival in Western civilization, Ancient civilizations—apart from a few rare individuals—held that the "Ages of the World" succeed each other on a descending line. Among the Greeks, for example, civilization was believed to be in process of gradual deterioration from a Golden Age; and the end would issue in a new beginning of the cycle of genesis and decay. "Time is the enemy." Plato equates change with decay; the perfect is static. In ancient Jewish tradition one finds the myth of paradise and the doctrine of the four successive world kingdoms; in the last of these kingdoms the world was to come to an end. In the prophetic philosophy of history, modified by primitive Christianity, a Golden Age was projected into the future also—an age to be brought in by divine decree. This view did not imply the idea of progress in the modern sense. Jesus believed the new age was coming with great suddenness. Moreover, he did not believe that man was to usher in the new kingdom, which was already breaking in; rather man was to *prepare* for it by repentance. In the course of time the eschatological hopes of early Christianity were displaced by a new static view of history. Expectations of a new heaven and a new earth were harbored mainly by small groups resisting the conservative, established Church. The doctrine of the four kingdoms reappeared in the dominant outlook. But as early as the twelfth century emerging eschatological movements predicted an imminent, providential, new age. In general, however, the medieval thinker would have recognized no progress since fifth-century Athens, with one important qualification—the divine revelation in the events and the truth of the Bible, which gave rise to the Church, the mediator of salvation in the present last age of the world.

In the Renaissance and the Reformation the humanists and the left-wing sects of Protestantism in varying ways proclaimed a new age. Gradually the "periodization" was accepted which is now taken for granted by the typical modern man—the division of history into three periods: Antiquity, the Middle Ages, and the Modern Era. Time is no longer the enemy, for history is believed to be the arena of progress. The forward-driving impulse of Jewish and Christian dynamic conceptions of history was implicit in the movements for renewal and reform—movements looking toward the liberation of man from ecclesiastical and political tyranny, movements that made headway, not without dust and heat. But other new elements also appeared. For example, the notion that in literature and art the modern age exhibits superiority beyond earlier ages; the notion that social progress is possible by means of man's newly discovered knowledge and by means of the freedom of self-determination and world-transformation; and also the idea that if men would but break the shackles of superstition, they could, with or without divine aid, create a new kingdom of man, especially through the use of inductive science and technology. The seventeenth century became the age of scientific genius and also of a vigorous struggle for religious and political freedom; the eighteenth-century Enlightenment looked forward to a pedagogical era when men would cut completely the apron strings of childish docility to tradition and achieve autonomous maturity. Some thinkers adopted the belief in the perfectibility of man.

Early in the nineteenth century a change of emphasis appeared. For example, the biologist Lamarck asserted that nature is compelled, by a law the Supreme Being has imposed, to proceed by the constant fresh creation of simple forms which develop by gradual steps toward the highest level of intelligence and organization, partly through their own inherent tendency to perfection, partly through the force of external circumstances. With the later appearance of the Darwinian theory of evolution, the idea of progress seemed to receive full scientific sanction. The earlier belief in the evolving goodness of man, and in a pre-established harmony that was to make public benefit out of the pursuit of individual interest, was appealed to in order to mitigate the seemingly callous operation of the law of the survival of the fittest. The transition from classical Manchester economics to social Darwinism was easy, for both philosophies of progress served to vindicate the triumph of the strong. Meanwhile, a new industrial technology and a world-encompassing imperialism had given rise to a new class—the middle class—and to enormous material progress. By virtue or by election the new class believed itself to be on an escalator. The phenomenal extension of education and the increase in medical and other scientific advances helped to engender the expectation of a far-off divine event of fairly complete fulfillment. Progress had taken over the functions of a beneficent providence.

Beginning and continuing for a long time only among a few, the doctrine of progress had become by the end of the nineteenth century "the animating and controlling idea of Western civilization." In the main the ground of hope was found in the increase and power of knowledge and in a new faith in man and the historical process.

CRITICISMS OF THE IDEA OF PROGRESS

The criticisms that have been directed against the doctrine are legion. The most convincing one for those who have eyes to see is, of course, "the logic of events"—the turmoil, the confusion, the chaos, in civilization which have culminated in two world wars in a single generation. If the turmoil has not destroyed civilization, this is not because any sphere of life has escaped the confusion. At the level of the embracing industrial structure periodic "boom and bust" seems to be the order of progression. At the level of political organization humanity has been thrown into "one world" before it is civilized enough to be ready for it.

In the twentieth century many people—especially the victims of the catastrophes—have recognized that historical change is different from what it was conceived to be by earlier exponents of the doctrine of progress. It is not, as Lamarck seems to have believed, an inherent tendency to perfection. Nor is it, as Hegel speculated, a progressive, rational interpenetration and gathering up of the best in opposite tendencies leading to ever richer and higher synthesis—the unfolding of God in history. Tragedy is not, as Hegel supposed, merely the conflict between incompatible good things.

Progress in any sphere of social life produces new problems which the original impulse may be inadequate to cope with. If the maladjustment is a major one, the gradual progress that was expected turns out to be sudden catastrophe. There are structures of disintegration as well as of integration, and they can work like a thief in the night. Shattering crisis can be the outcome of what seemed to be gradual progress.

The gradualistic and simply optimistic doctrine of progress was bound up with a grossly inadequate conception of human nature. The myth of the Fall and the doctrine of total depravity were no longer tenable; they formed the core of an inadequate doctrine of man. But now sin was viewed in a new light; it was interpreted as a residue from the jungle—a residue to be eliminated by new knowledge or by reforming the institutions. Thus the new possibilities of perversion that come with new human powers were overlooked, as also was the human propensity to appeal to high-sounding moral maxims in order to rationalize self-interest. The consequence was a sentimental interpretation of human nature, an interpretation that placed heavy reliance upon man's spontaneous, natural sympathy for others. One is reminded here of the popular plays of the eighteenth century in which "men of feeling" wept with ecstasy on observing that "man is so good." This sentimental reliance upon man's "natural" propensity to benevolence was coupled with a Baconian dependence upon knowledge as power. But progress in knowledge does not necessarily carry with it moral progress and social responsibility, and feeling has its own cunning. This should be clear if we consider the fact that nationalism, racism, and imperialism have produced more martyrs than has any religion in history. All our inventions are as potent for evil as for good. Improved means with unimproved ends, as Thoreau suggested, make a possible blessing into a blight. Technical means may be transmitted, but moral progress requires the acquisition of habit and discipline anew by each individual as a social being living in a changing world.

"Progress" has ever been self-defeating where men have assumed that because an idea or a practice is new it is therefore superior. This notion that older times and ways are a "back number" is almost a dogma in wide circles of the "educated" classes. It has produced in some quarters a fanatical provincialism in time—ideas or standards are judged by the recency of their flourishing.

A sort of provincialism in space has also appeared. The middle classes in their growth have extended the benefits of civilization, but those who have profited most from the progress have identified *their* success with progress. Here standards or policies are judged by their compatibility with middle-class comfort and convention. The consequence—also in middle-class Protestantism—is an insensitivity to the general welfare and to the brutalities and injustices created by bourgeois culture.

A secularistic provincialism has bolstered the provincialisms of time and space. From believing that progress is a law of being, many have adopted a matter-of-fact attitude of self-sufficiency. They overlook the contribution of "our neighbor the universe"; they neglect to observe that the source of being and meaning is not something man-made, but rather is a creative, sustaining, transforming power tnat man can neither manipulate nor escape. Besides, however important knowledge is, the power that is the ground of human fulfillment cannot be fully known merely through the increase of knowledge, for it demands commitment of the whole man as he opens himself to its working. Without this commitment he becomes a dupe of presumption, a believer in self-salvation who ends by seeking sanctions to support only his own interests—the pleasure principle separates him from the reality principle. In short, he gives his loyalty to only a section of reality and inflates that into a false god, a projection of himself.

But an inadequate idea of progress and of the ground for fulfillment is not a sound reason for rejecting every conception of progress. To assert that man in his striving for freedom, or in his achievement of knowledge concerning the world and himself, has exhibited only futility is to accept a simpleton's idea of progress in reverse. The extreme revulsion to every idea of progress deserves the comment, "Nothing is so much like a swelling as a hole."

Justification for belief in progress as a fact or a possibility depends, of course, upon the standard chosen for measuring it and upon the limits one places upon the expectation of human perfectibility. It depends also upon the time schedule by which progress is measured. Obviously there was a time when none of the values of civilization nor any other values of spiritual life were known. The longer perspectives of terrestrial and cosmic history, past and future, lie beyond the scope of the present chapter, as does also the question regarding the ultimate victory of the good. But even within the context of the shorter perspectives there has been a great deal of confusion concerning the meaning of progress. Much of this confusion has been the result of the failure to distinguish between the areas in which progress can occur and those in which it cannot. There can be progress, or cumulative achievement, in technology, in social or political organization, and in the spread of humanizing sentiments affecting the ethos of a culture. But the concept "progress" is relevant in only a very limited way for a consideration of cultural creations (*e.g.*, art) or of moral decision, where meaning appears not only in cumulative insight and achievement but also, and especially, in inexplicable, unrepeated individuality and novelty. In none of these areas is there ever for long a unilinear progression. The new situation demands new creation. We can never have a guarantee that accumulated achievements may be kept intact. As we have already observed, history is full of tragic as well as creative possibilities. Of history it must be said, "He hath founded it upon the seas, and established it upon the floods."

In the Modern Era in the West certain advances must be recognized, not only as impressive, but even as characteristic. The idea of progress began by introducing a critical attitude toward the status quo; it stimulated men to envisage new possibilities of human endeavor. With its concomitant ideas it helped men to judge more detachedly and more rationally the whole character and development of civilization and even of sacred literature and tradition. It produced an efficiency hitherto undreamed of—an efficiency that has raised the standard of living for uncounted millions. It promoted the dynamic attitude towards history which was the matrix for the development of democratic ideals and institutions. It released the energies of men to struggle for liberation from tyranny, from ignorance, from intolerance and persecution. The advances of medical science in relieving suffering and in prolonging life have been enormous. The development of the scientific attitude has created an immeasurable possibility for religion as well as for civilization. But none of these triumphs carries with it more than a new possibility—a possibility of progress or regress, of fulfillment or perversion.

We must therefore pursue still further our discussion of the questions: What are the proper criteria of progress in civilization? And what are the causes of this kind of progress?

A PROTESTANT ATTITUDE TOWARD CIVILIZATION, PROGRESS, AND DECAY

The Protestant does not place his confidence in civilization or in progress; nor does he place it in Protestantism. He places his confidence in the creative, judging, commanding, forgiving, transforming power manifest especially in Jesus Christ. This sovereign power is the Lord of history; it is active wherever truth and beauty, love and justice, are being sought or served; and it is working—in "wrath"—wherever these manifestations of the divine abundance are frustrated or perverted. To this inescapable, commanding power the Protestant is called to respond in trusting obedience and in continual repentance and renewal. This response involves personal responsibility for belief and action. As Luther was wont to say, "Everyone must do his own believing as he must do his own dying." But belief, like action, is social as well as personal.

The Protestant principle of the universal priesthood of believers expresses both the personal and the social dimension of response to the Divine. It demands personal responsibility for belief and also co-operative effort for the explication of belief. Implying as it does the radically lay character of religious fellowship, it presents to all men the vocation, the call, to manifest the freedom of the Christian man through love for God and love for man. Therefore it demands personal and social responsibility for the promotion, not the ecclesiastical control, of a free society that can give expression to the divine fecundity in forms of beauty, truth, and justice. This free society requires material as well as spiritual resources; salvation is for the whole man—body, soul, and spirit—and it is for man in society as well as for man in solitude. One of the reasons the society must be free is, as Milton observed, that no man or group of men is good enough to be entrusted with another's destiny. The sinfulness of man may be checked only where there is liberty of prophesying. On the other hand, the moment freedom cannot be perverted, it will no longer be freedom—and life will have lost its meaning.

The achievement of freedom is a social achievement. Every personal problem is also a social problem, and every social problem is also a personal problem. All the areas of life must be maintained in freedom—art, science, politics, education, industry, and Church; that is, they must be free from merely external, coercive domination, and yet also under the great Taskmaster's eye. Thus not only are free speech and free assembly a privilege; they are a duty if the spirit is to blow whither it listeth, and if strength of spirit and mutual enrichment are to result. The goal is not uniformity but rather *e pluribus unum*. Only in this sort of society can tyranny be prevented, and only in this kind of society can there be progress in problem solving.

The Left Wing of the Reformation, from which many American denominations derive historically, gave these principles an application decisive for modern democracy by promoting the idea that every believer must understand his faith—Protestant explicit faith in contrast to medieval or secular implicit faith—the dependence upon consensus rather than upon coercion, the separation of church and state, the autonomy of local groupings, and the rule of the majority under a growing conception of law and justice—that is, under the headship of Christ. After having been applied to Church life in the seventeenth century, these democratic ideas were in the eighteenth and nineteenth centuries applied in the realm of government, and in the twentieth century we see the struggle to apply them to the sphere of labor and industry. The Left Wing of the Reformation and its descendants have undertaken a centuries-long struggle against domination, insisting that: "If we are responsible to God for our way of living, then our leaders must be responsible to us." The course and goal of the modern pilgrim's progress has been: from compulsion to discussion and consensus.

A further word must be said here concerning humanism and its relation to the Protestant outlook. Humanism has encouraged tolerance—along with the pursuit of civility, the promotion of art and science, and the maintenance of unprovincial perspectives—though it has, like middle-class Protestantism, shown a meager concern that the abundance of life shall be in widest commonalty spread. In a Protestant figure like Milton or Schweitzer we see a fusing of the impulses of both the Left Wing of the Reformation and humanism—impulses that were expressed in personal piety, social and political responsibility, and artistic creation. There is no necessary conflict in principle between Protestantism and civility. Each has something important to offer the other, though both may become idolatrous. Thus both, even when they are working together, must stand under an inspiration and judgment higher than either of them. Neither of them is worthy of ultimate trust: in their actuality they will always exhibit the sinfulness as well as the meaningful possibilities that inhabit the heart of man.

The principles which have here been adumbrated may serve as the criteria of progress as understood by the radical Protestant. And withal they indicate a critical as well as a positive attitude toward civilization and civility, and a sharply negative attitude toward the doctrine of the perfectibility of man.

Some Causes of Decay

We have seen that one cause of decay has been certain false doctrines of progress. But the causes must be sought in many quarters and at many levels. One can find them in idolatrous devotion to class, to nation, and to race; in exploitation which blights both the exploiter and the exploited; in the lag of social skills behind technical skills; in the insecurity and anxiety incident upon periodic inflation and depression; in the average man's sense of his own impotence and insignificance; in his sense of emptiness and loneliness; in the phenomenal changes in the structure and role of the family; in the frustrations and neuroses of prolonged adolescence; in the loss of overarching loyalties that create participation in wider and wider community.

These factors are all interrelated, but one cause that lies beneath all decay in modern civilization is the mentality and character of what is called the "mass man." In view of the fact that religious education can and does play a major role in confronting this cause of decay, let us here concentrate attention upon it.

John Stuart Mill, in his essay on "Civilization," asserts that "there is no more accurate test of the progress of civilization than the progress of the power of co-operation." This co-operation, he says, is possible only through the diffusion of property and intelligence. But our civilization by its very nature militates in certain ways against the achievement of this kind of co-operation; it brings about a relaxation of individual energy and tends to concentrate it "within the narrow sphere of the individual's money-getting pursuits." It enables those who enjoy the benefits of civilization to keep the pain of others more and more out of sight. Because of the influence of anonymous ruling "opinion" our civilization makes many men submissive and thus represses the active qualities of heroism. It weakens the influence of superior minds and gives rise to the easy success of mediocrity, unformed taste, and charlatanry; and it makes difficult the shaping of sensitive and intelligent public opinion and policy. Here we see a tragic aspect of civilization itself; it makes possible the values noted in our definition of civilization, and at the same time by nature it provides obstacles to their realization.

The impulses of both humanism and radical Protestantism are also frustrated by this "society" of the mass man. A sort of authoritarianism—a disintegrating, nihilistic authoritarianism—supervenes. The "idea industries," under highly centralized control, belch forth a steady stream of images, headlines, catchwords, novelties, mass appeals, and agitations. Social policy is largely determined by special-interest pressure groups; the concerns promoted by these groups and by centralized powers of property and communications invade the schools, the legislative assemblies, and the churches. Only segments of human personality are brought into play, and men use each other as objects; they treat both nature and other men merely as means, or "things," rather than as ends, or realities possessing intrinsic qualities, or objects of love. Thus men are brought under the domination of the goddess Success. "Any voice not pitched in an exaggerated key," says Mill, "is lost in the hubbub. Success, in so crowded a field, depends not upon what a person is, but upon what he seems: mere marketable qualities become the object instead of substantial ones." In so far as the contemporary man has lost his attachment to a cultural and cultic community that gives him an unconscious as well as a conscious sense of belongingness, discipline, and direction, he is adrift—he is a mass man. Either he has no civilization world view, or he has none that is able to produce spiritual integrity and wholeness in the contemporary situation. He is merely the object and victim of forces that push him around and that push him down. It is little wonder that in times of crisis he reveals his loss of commitment to universal values by resorting to a worship of blood and soil and to the suppressions and brutalities it demands. This is the ever-present possibility of civilization—rebarbarization. "Civilized" co-operation can be co-operation in the dehumanization of man. When it resorts to force in war for the annihilation of man, it risks the collapse of civilization.

SOME CAUSES OF PROGRESS

The test of the progress of civilization is the progress of co-operation—in the diffusion of intelligence and in the diffusion of commitment to the religious, aesthetic, and ethical principles and practices that maintain dynamic democracy. The crucial test of loyalty to these principles is the period of change or challenge when the decision has to be made whether coercion or discussion will be the method adopted. The economic crisis in our highly centralized—and increasingly militarized—American society is largely the consequence of the feebleness of application of these principles for the achievement of freedom and of a security compatible with it; it is a judgment especially upon the Protestant churches that have provided a spuriously "religious" embellishment for the very causes of the crisis.

Elton Mayo of Harvard, who had much to do with the revealing Hawthorne experiments in industrial psychology at the General Electric Company in Chicago, has succinctly indicated the demands of progress:

Every social group, at whatever level of culture, must face and clearly state two perpetual and recurrent problems of administration. It must secure for its individual and group membership:

(1) The satisfaction of material and economic needs.

(2) The maintenance of spontaneous cooperation throughout the organization.[1]

Two things stand out here as basic demands. First, the progressive society moves toward the possibility of meeting the material needs of all its members; it is not content so long as anyone is "left out." This idea that none should be left out was central in Jesus' hope for the Kingdom; although he did not concern himself directly with material needs, he addressed himself primarily to the "little ones" of the human family, and to the oppressed. Second, spontaneous co-operation is the method: ideally, compulsion should be reduced to a minimum. This means that equal opportunity for work, for significant leisure, and for participation in the making of social decisions is required.

[1] Elton Mayo, *The Social Problems of an Industrial Civilization* (Boston: Graduate School of Business Administration, Harvard University, 1945), p. 9. In this book and in his other publications, Dr. Mayo sets forth certain principles and policies that have striking relevance for the work of the religious educator, as does much of the recent literature on group-dynamics research.

In stressing these particular demands one should reject what may be heard in certain Protestant circles—namely, the moralistic notion that the sole cause of progress is individual character and integrity. This conception of social causation tends to overlook the fact that personality develops and expresses itself only in a social matrix; it overlooks also the fact that human responsibility includes responsibility for the character and institutions of society as well as for the "private virtues."

The major causes of progress implicit in the principles of radical Protestantism and humanism may now be summarized. These causes are the conditions necessary to produce both the satisfaction of material needs and spontaneity of co-operation. They must operate if the hazards of a mass-society, the hazards of civilization, are to be overcome. They must operate if the Protestant is to fulfill his vocation of entering into the struggle of justice against injustice, of love against hate, of beauty against ugliness, in order to receive the salvation in time and community which is offered by the Lord of history.

1. Participation in groups that develop an explicit faith—in contrast to the implicit faith of the medieval and also of the present-day mass culture—a faith which (a) relates the transient to the enduring, recreative powers; (b) elicits commitment to a Protestant conception of vocation, in family, work, and community, of striving for truth and beauty, love and justice; (c) is the shared possession of persons living in primary relations to each other and of persons sensitive to the divine sources of judgment and fulfillment and responsible in personal and social ways for belief and action. For the achievement of a universal faith, these groups must include various classes and races of people. We learn only from those we love.

2. An education that keeps alive a vision of greatness by "lifting up" the formative figures, the literature, art, and science, and the decisive events of the religious and cultural tradition—figures and events whose analogues appear in contemporary human enterprises. In our new "one world" the figures and events presented should include those of other religions and civilizations.

3. A cultus that gives gracious, symbolically powerful expression to these values and traditions, figures and responsibilities, that gives a sense of belongingness and direction to the members of the group, and that relates the individual in unconscious as well as in conscious ways to the divine powers of abundance.

4. The application of religious, ethical, and aesthetic principles to immediate personal, social, and institutional changing situations, lacking which the cultus and the education, as well as the ultimate religious powers, are frustrated and rendered stultifying.

5. Individual and group participation in those organizations that on the

basis of rational consensus and on behalf of the general welfare shape social policy and bring about effective social change and creativeness in home and school, in government and industry, in the arts and sciences, and in the religious fellowship itself. From this participation alone can come the meeting of the material needs and the creation of spontaneity in response to the sovereign, righteous Lord of history and in the application—and vindication—of the Protestant principle of the universal priesthood of believers.

All of the efforts listed here will always require the leadership or the stimulus of the small, devoted cell group—a perennial cause of progress.

These are certainly among the causes that create a growing fellowship of memory and hope, the kind of society that can withstand the ravages of civilization and the slings and arrows of personal and social fortune, a fellowship that can be at the same time civilized and progressive.

The wide dimensions of progress demanded if the present civilization is to survive in an atomic age have not been made wholly explicit here. The dire necessity of our changing certain fundamental social and economic structures has been stressed—concern with this problem belongs inextricably to the Protestant vocation and involves the prophethood as well as the priesthood of all believers.[2] For the Protestant, the exercise of the liberty of prophesying—interpreting the signs of the time—is inextricably bound up with the practice of the priesthood of all believers.

The moral and spiritual forces and procedures that can make a frontal attack on these immense, complicated problems have been pointed to. They begin where *we* are—in the small, intimate fellowship—and they reach out from there through the participation of individuals invigorated by personal faith and by a vocation of social responsibility. A society is renewed when its humblest element acquires a value and a function. This sort of faith recognizes that men cannot reap where they have not sown. It calls for strong men and women and then makes them stronger in the power that groweth not old, in the power that is a gift to them who will humbly and boldly open the door.

SUGGESTIONS FOR FURTHER STUDY

1. Read the brief first two chapters in T. R. Glover, *The Influence of Christ in the Ancient World.*[3] Note the causes listed by the author for the decay of ancient society. Then read Chapter IV—"Character"—and note the causes of progress which the author ascribes to the influence of Christ. Compare with these the causes of progress and decay listed on pages 69-73. Would it be correct to say that in Glover's opinion the causes of decay in ancient society were epitomized in the mass man of that period? Would it be correct to say that the causes of progress in the early Christian period were the elements of the Christian char-

[2] See my article "The Prophethood of All Believers," *Christian Register*, March, 1947.
[3] Cambridge: Cambridge University Press, 1932.

acter which served to convert this mass man into a person of responsibility, free initiative, and affirmative hope for the future?

2. Read the chapter entitled "Primary and Secondary Groups" in Paul H. Landis, *Social Policies in the Making*.[4] Using the criteria of progress and decay set forth on pages 69-73, note the elements of progress and decay which are characteristic of primary groups; then note the elements of progress and decay characteristic of secondary groups. Note the irrelevance, if not the evil influence, of the Church cited in the Landis chapter. How can religious education help to overcome the forms of decay you have noted? If you cannot secure the volume by Landis, use some other sociology textbook that deals with the role of primary and secondary groups in contemporary American society.

3. By means of direct questioning or a questionnaire determine the number of organizations supported—through money and active, personal participation—by five or ten typical members of your local church. How many of these organizations aim directly to help shape public social policy? How many of them serve merely special class or vocational interests? How many are clearly concerned for the general welfare, regardless of race, class, or vocational divisions? Evaluate your findings in the light of Items 4 and 5 in the list of "Causes of Progress" on page 72. On the basis of your findings how would you characterize the conception of Christian vocation practiced by these members of your local church?

4. Read Chapter IX, "The Social Test of Religion," in Walter Rauschenbusch, *The Social Principles of Jesus*.[5] Then list the causes of progress and decay attributed by Rauschenbusch to religion. Which of these causes of progress and decay do you detect in the program of religious education promoted by your own local church?

BIBLIOGRAPHY

Barker, Ernest. *Traditions of Civility*. Cambridge: Cambridge University Press, 1948.

Brunner, Emil. *Christianity and Civilization*. New York: Charles Scribner's Sons, 1948.

Bury, J. B. *The Idea of Progress*. New York: The Macmillan Co., 1920.

Mannheim, Karl. *Diagnosis of Our Time*. New York: Oxford University Press, 1944.

Minear, Paul. *Eyes of Faith*. Philadelphia: Westminster Press, 1948.

Niebuhr, Reinhold. *Faith and History*. New York: Charles Scribner's Sons, 1949.

Oldham, J. H., ed. *The Kingdom of God and History* (Oxford Conference volume). Chicago: Willett, Clark & Co., 1938.

Schweitzer, Albert. *Decay and Restoration of Civilization*. New York: The Macmillan Co., 1924.

Tillich, Paul. *The Protestant Era*. Chicago: University of Chicago Press, 1948.

Toynbee, Arnold J. *The Study of History*. New York: Oxford University Press, 1947.

Troeltsch, Ernst. *Protestantism and Progress*. New York: G. P. Putnam's Sons, 1912.

Whitehead, Alfred North. *Adventures of Ideas*. New York: The Macmillan Co., 1933.

Wieman, Henry Nelson. *The Directive in History*. Boston: Beacon Press; and Glencoe, Ill.: Free Press, 1949.

[4] Boston: D. C. Heath & Co., 1947. Pp. 62-76.

[5] New York: Association Press, 1916.

Chapter 6

EDUCATIONAL EVANGELISM

H. H. KALAS

THERE ARE, IN THE CHURCH, two arms for outreach—two plans for bringing people into relationship with God. They are evangelism and Christian education. It is wrong to say that the distinction between these two arms of outreach did not exist in the New Testament. The Apostle to the Gentiles must have had some precedent in the practice of the first-century church for saying,

His gifts were that some should be apostles, some prophets, some evangelists, some pastors and teachers, for the equipment of the saints, for the work of ministry, for building up the body of Christ, until we all attain to the unity of the faith and of the knowledge of the Son of God, to mature manhood, to the measure of the stature of the fullness of Christ. (Eph. 4:11-13, R.S.V.)

Distinctions as to function need not always be contradictory. They can be complementary. A mere blending of two functions in the Christian enterprise is not always desirable, but in the case of religious education and evangelism the blending seems necessary. This is not to imply that educational evangelism as later described in this chapter will supplant other elements in religious education and other methods of evangelism. It is important to assert that educational evangelism will provide a dominant objective for religious education and will have an effect on all other forms of evangelism. Therefore this chapter begins by a consideration of an exchange of criticisms between the educator and the evangelist. By criticisms, of course, denunciation is not meant. Rather it is sympathetic and objective analysis, with a view to more effective human redemption. The motive for mutual criticism is, not jealousy *against* another type of enterprise, but jealousy *for* God's will and human peace. For that reason, each criticism has a statement of a constructive alternative added. It is assumed that the object of each criticism is remediable.

THE EDUCATOR'S CRITICISM OF THE EVANGELIST

1. The educator criticizes the evangelist when the latter emphasizes the momentary phenomenon of conversion, or the moment of decision,

without adequate regard for the many life processes which alone can give it significance. "The error in evangelism is not in having a simple aim, but in assuming that the attainment of the simple aim is the end of the process." [1] The educator, unless he is an extremist, duly appreciates the importance of great crises and high moments in human decision. He believes, however, that these crises and high moments can have little significance if induced without regard to antecedent experiences, immediate assimilation into group church life, knowledge of the nature of God and man, and appreciation of the many symbols and resources of religion.

2. Many educators believe that evangelism is too frequently identified only with response to verbal appeal. The educator agrees that the evangelistic appeal must be made to the will in terms of a surrender to the purposes of God. He however holds that surrender is most significant when it involves an intelligent turn of life, based on cumulative emotional experiences and rational insights. The educator believes that God deigns to change a life through processes which are consistent with man's nature. Through the patient processes of education the evangelized person learns how to make of the Christian life a vocation touching every experience and need. God is as much at work in such a functional process as he is in the most fantastic miracle.

3. Visitation evangelists in their emphasis upon techniques frequently seem to reduce methods of evangelism to the devices of salesmanship. We would not go so far as one educator who says, "Most evangelistic efforts could be likened to the action of forest rangers who, finding a man lost in the woods, would turn him around in the direction of civilization, and then would go off looking for other lost souls, trusting that the bewildered fellow could find his own way back home." [2] To be sure, the writers of books on visitation evangelism presuppose that before and after visitation evangelism has done its work, someone will have done the more difficult and continuous task of giving realism and content to the decision. The cure for a wrong use of visitation evangelism, especially among laymen, is to get beyond mere vague assumption and definitely to relate the visitation evangelism program to some assimilative process.

4. Educators sometimes accuse evangelists of being more interested in quantitatively measured results than in the less measurable qualitative results. Educators who are committed to the patient processes of growth see in emphasis upon numbers a temptation to attach superficial motives, such as the enhancement of an institution, rather than a deep motive based upon concern for persons. When the interest in numbers is based upon

[1] J. Paul Williams, "Evangelism and the Social Pattern," *Religious Education*, May-June, 1948, p. 167.
[2] *Ibid.*, p. 166.

an honest concern for persons, the concern is even then often defeated because of the absence of disciplined effort to "feed the flock." Every increase in numbers by the evangelist increases, by a geometric ratio, the necessity of a continuous stimulation, assimilation, and teaching of every person reached.

5. Lack of regard for known psychological laws involving growth, readiness, and individual difference is another common accusation by the educator as he regards evangelism. Perhaps the most dramatic illustration of this is the educational criticism of such evangelistic groups as Child Evangelism Fellowship, Inc. The accusation is that this group tends to impose upon children religious concepts and practices which are not adapted to their age. It does not assimilate them normally into the Church. The Church can give them the undergirding of its eternal existence and the environment for the continued growth and endeavor. Edna Acheson rightly says that "there is no one great pattern of lostness for which one wholesale panacea of salvation can be found. There are individual differences in integration." [3]

6. The Christian educator frequently takes issue with the evangelist because he relies in his terminology upon terms which are admittedly deep in their historic and theological content, but which become superficial when the person evangelized uses them largely like a patent medicine. Orthodox terminology, says the educator, often becomes the equivalent of magic. This problem will be touched upon again later. Suffice it to say here that the solution is probably at some meeting point between the educative and evangelistic processes which gives relevant meaning to the orthodox terms and a translation of these terms into the idiom of the people.

7. Use of extravagant terminology in the gospel songs which have been associated with evangelism as it is commonly known is a symbol of a lack of realism which educators often sense in the evangelistic appeal. It is educationally unsound to ask people to sing songs about "carrying crosses," "dying with Jesus," "surrendering all," unless these extravagant expressions are closely attached to some honest realism. Incidentally, it should be said that no language is too superlative when used in the objective worship of God; but the hymnody of evangelism is frequently subjective, centering on man's needs and impulses rather than on God and his purposes. The more moderate educator will not go so far as to say that courageous commitment is out of order. He legitimately calls attention to the burden which extravagant religious expression places upon agencies in the church whose function it is to help men to live out their commitments.

[3] "The Educative Process in Evangelism," *Religious Education*, May-June, 1948, p. 160.

The Evangelist's Criticism of Religious Education

1. The evangelist accuses the religious educator of inadequate conceptions of "pillars of faith." Men are not likely to be brought to the fullness of Christian faith and life if their teachers have inadequate conceptions of God, the nature of man, the lordship and saviourhood of Jesus Christ over and above his obvious human appeals, the reality and penetrating power of the Holy Spirit, and the Church as a mystic fellowship and reality. The evangelist considers the fundamental revelations of God as contained in the Bible and as revealed in Christ to be both comprehensible and necessary of comprehension. The kind of evangelist who will commit himself to a program of educational evangelism will certainly not insist upon the enforcement of abstract theological realities until readiness has been created for them on the part of the learner. He knows that these great realities are, not so much comprehended, as emotionally accepted when need for them arises. But he says, with Edward Paisley, "Evangelism is an educational process based upon what we know of a gracious God." [4]

2. The evangelist accuses the religious educator of a romantic faith in the educational process, which is as superficial as are any of the inadequate evangelistic expedients of which the evangelist is accused. He insists that educative processes and devices are but the channels through which the divine power and will may flow. Religious education, to the evangelist, if it is to be called Christian, must be theistic in its emphasis and in its reliances.

3. The educator is accused of inadequately recognizing the significance of great moments and crisis decisions. From the psychological point of view it is not realistic to assume that the growth of an individual can be plotted in one continuous upward curve. There are deep recesses and there are high pinnacles. These are coexistent with the physical and psychological development of a person. Some of them are circumstantial in character. In educational evangelism the normal points of crisis in human development are given eternal accent.

Man is by nature a sinner, says the evangelist, and one of the first steps in his redemption is his recognition of his own sin and the adequacy of God's redemption for that sin. Moments of crisis or high points of decision even without the fact of God and sin would be great, but they take on eternal significance when considered in the light of the above theological realities. The evangelist wants the educator to point at least some of the educational processes to inevitable crisis moments of life. It is more than a matter of "decision" on the part of the individual. It is also a matter of "consent" to the redemptive reality and process about which he has

[4] "Educational Processes Involved in Evangelism," *Religious Education*, May-June, 1948, p. 179.

learned in Christian education, and to which he now commits himself unreservedly.

4. Because of the above and other considerations evangelists have frequently accused educators of lacking the sense of urgency which comes to anyone who feels that without God men are lost. This urgency, says the evangelist, need not rob the teacher of poise, nor need it make him so tense that he does not live life normally. Evangelists of the better type will also say that this sense of urgency need not cause the teacher and the evangelist to take expedients and short cuts. Evangelists of the better type will look to the teacher to keep intact principles of thoroughness and of patience, even while feeling under a divine urgency.

5. The evangelist has sometimes accused the religious educator of becoming so absorbed in immediate projects that he loses a sense of their ultimate meanings. He has a suspicion that an overemphasis upon procedural considerations tends in that direction. It is possible, for instance, for a teacher to become so absorbed in such things as "learning a song" or "building a worship center" that the teacher does not have either the time or the inclination to drive through to ultimate meanings. This, says the evangelist, is the weakness of the project principle in religious education.

Synthesis and Interaction

1. Educational evangelism assumes that there is a correlative relationship between the process of redemption and the laws of growth. The God who redeems the sinner created man. "He knoweth our frame." It is inconceivable that the plan for human redemption should be inconsistent with man's physical and psychological make-up. In the fact of the incarnation of Jesus Christ there is the greatest possible evidence that we can find true synthesis between an educational approach which is concerned with the normal laws of human development and an evangelistic approach which is concerned with the divine activity in human regeneration.

2. Life does not always move smoothly and uneventfully. There are in most lives crisis moments of decision. They are no less important than the average human experience—and no more important. They are simply essential. Evangelism is particularly concerned with crisis moments of decision from which new life emerges. It is concerned with the surrender of the individual to the divine act in those times of crisis. Christian education, which is interested in all of life, certainly should build toward those crises. In addition, it is the responsibility of Christian education to see that the divine power is poured into the normal experiences of life, and that human consent is given to God's purposes and power in these normal experiences.

Christian educators believe that evangelism need not be limited in its definitions to crisis moments. If this interfusion ever takes place, every Christian educator will become an evangelist.

3. "Things learned" and "things felt" should become more or less identical if evangelism and Christian education are to complete their work. Intellectual comprehension and emotional consent must be interfused. I have already said that some of the great doctrines must be emotionally appreciated before they can be intellectually defined. Someone has said that the great doctrines must be sung. Evangelism is interested in having them sung. Both evangelism and Christian education are interested in having them lived. Only then comes understanding. "If any man wills to do his will, he shall know whether the teaching is from God."

4. Both evangelists and Christian educators are aware of the fact that "divine-human encounter" resulting in conversion is not the last crisis for decision. Deep experience prepares one for subsequent experiences. The psychological law of a chain of experiences has long been recognized. Evangelists and Christian educators share the conviction that intelligent people can seek, by their own will and self-determination, an enrichment of this chain of experience which does not come to one who is not a "seeker." The idea of a "seeker" is as much an educational concept as it is an evangelistic concept.

SOME IMPERATIVE REALITIES

1. God loves man. This is a basic fact. Its elementary realities can be grasped by the child upon his first experiences of parental love. Its ultimate realities are never completely comprehended. God's love is a lavish love. To comprehend this fact is to appreciate the fullnesses of the universe, the abundances of providence with which all of us are blessed. God's love is so desperate as to be vicarious. To comprehend this is to understand the full meanings of the New Testament and the Christ who stands at its center. God's love is purposeful. To comprehend that is to be possessed with the conviction that the ultimate end of every man's life is to discover the specific purposes of his Creator for that life. God's love is indispensable. It is impossible to live in the intimacies of a home without love, so it is impossible for man to be comfortable or secure in the universe without living in that universe as though he is a child of the Heavenly Father.

2. Man by himself cannot respond to God's love, even though he wishes to do so. This arbitrary theological dogma has had renewed emphasis in recent years. It challenges romantic belief in the inevitability of human progress. It declares that human redemption awaits the divine initiative and that the teacher and evangelist are but the heralds of a potential impact of the divine Spirit.

On the other hand, it says too much if left unmodified. It negates the possibility of the improvability of human nature. No child needs to re-capitulate all of the moral stupidities of the man. His status between the alternative possibilities of sainthood or moral ruin is partly determined by the impacts which have been made upon him in his environment. He is endowed with capacities to make right choices at each stage of his growth, and his moral descent is not inevitable. He is as ready to respond to the upward pull of Christian teaching as he is to respond to the impacts of an immoral society. His guided inclination toward God can be so stimulated that his "acceptance of Christ as saviour" can hardly be distinguishable in terms of any single moment. When one day he is formally accepted into the Church "on confession of faith," he but summarizes in that confes-sion a long sequence of responses to the divine Spirit. Evangelism goes on whenever a teacher helps children to make the deepest responses and the highest decisions of which they are capable. God is at work in this guided experience. The actual act of turning toward God needs both the moving power of God's spirit and the guided human impulse.

3. It is not enough to absorb information about life and to pass through controlled experiences. The child must be given a frame of reference and experience so that he can interpret his day-by-day experiences in the light of Christian faith. That is a true blending of evangelism and Christian education. Granting that there is a "given" in the universe, the Bible is eloquent with the idea that it was not "given" all at once. The fact of "progressive revelation" is a precedent for the idea of educational evange-lism—that the great realities and experiences which can come to man must be absorbed gradually. This interaction between a predetermined frame of belief and one that is achieved gradually brings us to a well-known point of controversy among religious educators. There are extreme de-fenders of a philosophy of democracy in education who would say that any emphasis upon educational evangelism plays into the hands of "author-itarians." In part they are right. Evangelism does assume certain realities which are "given." The Christian fellowship is centripetal. Its center is a God who is at once a person and an indispensable, universal reality. Theism and evangelism are historically interrelated. But the fact of fundamental reality does not cancel out "the variety of Religious Experience."

4. As a rational being, man must be appealed to on the basis of intelli-gence. At the same time, human passions are not amenable to reason. This is not to say that the appeal to intelligence is apropos to one and not to another. It is better to say that every person is at some time in his life susceptible to reason, and at other times he must be approached on an emotional basis. The appeal to intelligence is much easier to standardize than is the appeal to emotions. Both are the concerns of educational evangelists.

5. One cannot complete a statement in imperative realities without asserting the truism that the goal of educational evangelism is the good life. By this is meant both a satisfied life and a satisfactory life. The person evangelized has a right to expect "peace of mind" and the satisfaction of a purposive life. He also has the right to expect practical resources which will help him to meet the moral demands of the universe.

6. It is possible and necessary in educational evangelism to clearly define the function of the teacher in the evangelistic process at each level of age and circumstance. Then evangelism becomes more than a technique or method. It becomes a process of guiding people *into* and *beyond* the time—usually in early adolescence—when he makes public confession of his faith and declaration of his willingness to assume a responsible relationship to the Church. At the ages of two and three, for instance, the child may be made conscious of God by identifying the fact of God with all that gives him pleasure or security. At this age he may be conditioned to the "habit of belief." There is no reason why at four and five the child should not be given first impressions of Jesus through carefully chosen stories about him. At the ages of six to eight, first impressions of an admirable life can take a form of allegiance. Simple moral distinctions can be developed, and the child can be guided to a consistent dependence upon a Power beyond himself to assist his desire to live the good life. During late childhood the growing person is guided—more by example than by precept—to make life's choices, of which the greatest is personal commitment to Christ as saviour. Anticipation is created for the time when the child is formally received into the fuller fellowship of the Church.

In early adolescence the person is fully oriented to the church—its teachings and its requirements—and is carefully guided to an emotional "surrender" to God as the ruler of life.

This sketchy overview of the role of the teacher in evangelism needs the following additional summary.

1. The teacher cultivates the seeds of trust which seem to be innately planted within the human being.

2. The teacher becomes a living example of the Christian way. Response to God and loyalty to Christ and the Church are better exemplified than verbalized. That is why home religion is essential to educational evangelism.

3. The teacher guides the growing person into the experience of prayer. It is my conviction that it is the major function of the Church to teach men to pray. This is a process which goes on through life. Without a prayer life which is as normal as any other human function, educational evangelism is impossible. If religious education could guide people at every age and circumstance into prayer, the evangelistic task would be done.

A PRACTICAL PROGRAM

Recently most denominations in Protestantism have recognized the need for a clear synthesis between evangelism and education in some practical program. To be sure, liturgical, confessional, and sacramental churches have always emphasized the importance of the teaching process in preparation for churchmanship and the Christian life. It has been done through parochial instruction, indoctrination, orientation to the sacraments and to the worship of the cultus, as well as through many other forms of special preparation for great moments of initiation and induction. Sometimes to the more liturgical churches the emphasis upon the integration between evangelism and Christian education sounds strange. They are, however, proving to be very much interested both for what they can contribute and for what they can receive.

In America the Sunday-school movement, which symbolized religious education in the more evangelical churches, and the revival movement, which became the expression for evangelism of the more evangelical churches, became closely identified. The great evangelists and the great Sunday-school leaders were friends and colleagues. Sunday-school conventions were tense with evangelistic fervor. It is safe to say that the Sunday school was more evangelistic than it was educational. Education was, at best, secondary, contributive, and partial, striving chiefly to bring the Bible to bear upon individual life.

America has been known for its pendulum swings. The Christian-nurture concept of Horace Bushnell and of those who followed him led Christian educators to a much more thorough consideration of measures by which a child would never know himself to be other than a child of God. The effects of the educational disciplines of Horace Bushnell are beyond all comprehension, and they are all to the good.

That Christian education should take on the character of each new development in American public education was inevitable. That it should, by that token, have become frequently differentiated from the evangelistic function was also inevitable. It is my conviction that this differentiation is not to be deplored. A cycle in the history of Christian education which rather closely identifies it in method and principle with the philosophy of general education in America will, it is hoped, not be abandoned when we achieve the integration between education and evangelism which is the burden of this chapter. Be that as it may, it is more important for Christian education in the American Church to achieve its basic purpose than it is for it to educationally emulate current American practice.

After the last World War a number of the more evangelical denominations attempted to develop new integrations between Christian education and evangelism. Particularly did it seem necessary to project programs for the stimulation of church-school teachers in their evangelistic tasks. A thorough review of developments in several of our denominations along this line needs to be written. Suffice it here to say that the result of some of these denominational experiences was the Mission to Teachers, which in 1944 was projected by the International Council of Religious Education. This mission had as its slogan, "Every Teacher an Evangelist." A nation-wide series of studies and mass meetings was designed to bring a new consciousness on the part of all church-school teachers of their relationship to the redemptive process, and also to clearly define the specific function in the redemptive process of the church-school teacher at each age level. It soon became evident that a program was needed which would relate itself much more adaptively and comprehensively to local communities and to the churches within those communities. The result was the National Christian Teaching Mission.

The fact that this mission and its immediate predecessor, the Mission to Teachers, is under the joint sponsorship of the Department of Evangelism of the Federal Council of Churches of Christ in America and the International Council of Religious Education is in itself symbolic of an integration between education and evangelism. The joint committee under which it operates consists in equal part of persons whose professional leadership and interest lie in the direction of evangelism and religious education. The national director and his assistant are chosen for their training and competence both in religious education and in the general evangelistic program of the Church. The forty-two denominational directors who serve as associate directors in Christian Teaching Missions over America are now chosen for their competence in both fields.

The mission has been conducted in fifty-four communities already. After the United Evangelistic Advance, between October 1, 1949, and January 1, 1951, missions will have been projected in seventy-five more communities. In the communities in which it has been held the mission has drawn together churches of widely variant religious emphasis, both as to theology, polity, and emphasis upon religious education and evangelism. This bringing together of many temperaments and of many types of churches is possible because the mission imposes a pattern of uniformity upon no local church. It insists upon complete adaptation of its integration between evangelism and Christian education on the part of every local church.

Each church invites a guest leader who comes in during the week of the more formal part of the mission. The guest leaders and the host pastors of the churches make up a seminar which meets approximately sixteen hours during an intensive week, under the direction of a national director or more than one director if the size of the city makes that necessary.

It is the function of the seminar to project a fourfold program in every local church:

1. Through the guest leader and the pastor the seminar projects into every local church a self-study entitled "Your Evangelistic Potential." It is not the purpose of this study to test the total educational or evangelistic program of the church. Rather its purpose is to discover on an evaluative basis the present concern for persons by the organized life of the church, and its capacity for outreach. To this self-study is brought a committee from each of the organized groups of the church. This includes the study groups, the fellowship groups, and the service groups. The entire mission rests upon the assumption that the evangelistic task of the church will be done, not by the setting up of new machinery, but rather in the using of the existent organized life of the church in ways which are normal to the groups of the church, with special emphasis upon the assimilative and educational functions of those groups. The self-study has educational and evangelistic significance because it highlights concern for persons above considerations which are institutional or academic.

2. A community-wide census is made to discover the people who are not related to the church.

3. The seminar directs the guest leaders to project a program known as "fellowship cultivation" in each local church. The organized groups who made the self-study are asked, by this device, to take their share in the assimilative process of evangelism, which is achieved through fellowship in normal groups. The purpose of fellowship cultivation is to surround every man, woman, and child on the responsibility list of each local church with the warmth of Christian fellowship in a group which might normally appeal to his or her age and interest.

4. The fourth phase of the program, now known as "program enlargement," more specifically deals with educational evangelism. As national norms develop, it will be through this phase of the program that a clear definition is given as to the function of teachers at every age and interest level in the total redemptive process. Meantime, local church groups are organized to discuss this matter and in other ways to stimulate local church-school teachers to a full realization of the evangelistic aspect of their task.

Program enlargement also endeavors to focus upon the points in the educational program of that local church in which the task of outreach seems to be least effectively accomplished. Sometimes this involves the organization of new agencies or new groups. Sometimes it involves the reorganization of the existent ones so that they may better meet the demands made incumbent upon them by the self-study.

This phase also involves a clear plan by which people, as they are assimilated into the group life of the church, are brought into contact with its more intensive educational programs through a clearly defined process.

SUGGESTIONS FOR FURTHER STUDY

The International Council of Religious Education has a Committee on Educational Evangelism. On February 5, 1949, this Committee met to consider matters pertaining to educational evangelism which do not normally fall within the pattern of the National Christian Teaching Mission. Matters which are listed below, and many others which will later emerge, will require a great deal of discussion, experimentation, and research. The matters on the agenda of this meeting are listed here because they may serve as a basis for discussion in groups or for thoughtful consideration by individual readers:

1. Creating integration between pastors' classes in religion such as catechetic classes, confirmation classes, and so on, and the Sunday church school.
2. Evangelism to and through homes.
3. The theological orientation of the Sunday-church-school teachers.
4. The Christian education task in blighted urban areas.
5. The Christian education of children in temporary housing areas.
6. The enlistment of lay church participation—an evangelistic task.
7. Audio-visual aids to educational evangelism.

BIBLIOGRAPHY

Bryan, Dawson C. *A Handbook of Evangelism for Laymen.* New York and Nashville: Abingdon-Cokesbury Press, 1948.

Ferré, Nels. *Pillars of Faith.* New York: Harper & Brothers, 1948.

Mott, John R. *The Larger Evangelism.* New York and Nashville: Abingdon-Cokesbury Press, 1944.

Munro, Harry C. *Fellowship Evangelism.* Chicago: National Christian Teaching Mission, 1947.

Ownbey, Richard L. *Evangelism in Christian Education.* New York and Nashville: Abingdon-Cokesbury Press, 1941.

Religious Education, May-June, 1948.

Richardson, Norman E. *What Is Educational Evangelism?* Study Unit No. 2. Chicago: McCormick Extension Service.

Toward the Conversion of England (Report of a Commission on Evangelism). Toronto: J. M. Dent & Sons, 1946.

Trimble, Henry Burton. *To Every Creature.* New York and Nashville: Abingdon-Cokesbury Press, 1939.

Chapter 7

THE AIM AND SCOPE
OF RELIGIOUS EDUCATION

LUTHER A. WEIGLE

WHEN JESUS WAS ASKED what commandment was first of all, he replied in terms familiar to his hearers, quoting from the books of Deuteronomy and Leviticus. But as usual his answer contained something new. He gave to the word "neighbor" a new depth and range of meaning; and he added to the commandment to love God a new phrase "with all thy mind." He explicitly associated intelligence with religious faith. "Thou shalt love the Lord thy God with all thy . . . mind."

In Jesus' answer is implied that intimate relationship between democracy, education, and religion which is characteristic of the Christian faith. Democracy is respect for persons; education is devotion to truth; religion is faith in God. These three belong together. They are interdependent and organically related. Each finds its full realization only in association with the other two.

This does not mean that the vital union of democracy, education, and religion is exclusively Christian, for it has its roots in the Hebrew heritage which is common to Jews and Christians. Neither does it mean that it has been understood and maintained throughout Christian history, for what we call "Christendom" has fallen short of it many times and our own time is in this respect notorious. Again, this does not mean that true religion is tied to political democracy; for democracy is more than a form of government. It is an ethical principle which is not dependent upon any one type of political structure. It may be realized in a monarchy and may fail in a republic.

This does mean that there is an intrinsic relation between faith in the God whom Jesus Christ revealed, and that respect for persons which is the central principle of democracy, and that obedience to truth which is essential to education. Only as this relation is strong, and clear, and consistent is faith rational, liberty secure, and knowledge safe.

Jesus did not present a code of laws, either for his time or for ours. He revealed God to men and sought to bring them into right relation with him. Of commandments, in the proper sense of the term, he affirmed only two: "Thou shalt love the Lord thy God," and, "Thou shalt love thy neighbor as thyself." The rest of his ethical teaching follows by way of application or counsel from these. Just what in specific detail are the decisions to be made and the paths of action to be followed by those who in the successive generations seek first the kingdom of God and his righteousness is left to their mind and conscience to learn through experience in the light of his Spirit. He did not deprive his followers of their freedom and responsibility, under guidance of the Holy Spirit, to discern what is the will of God in the changing tides of circumstance and the onward march of events. The ideas of learning, investigation, discovery, and education are intrinsically related to the Christian faith.

The totalitarian governments of our time have set their might against the religious faith, democratic freedom, and education in truth and for truth which are basic to Christianity. We of the democratic countries can meet their challenge only by a more complete achievement and maintenance of that vital union of religion and education with democracy which is our ideal as Christians. But we are at present far from doing this. These three great interests of the human soul have pulled apart, and the result is that democracy is gravely threatened from within. The fault lies, not with any one of the three, but with all. Each has tended to go its own way.

When Religion Is at Fault

Religion is at fault when it fails to respect human personality and sets itself in opposition to the human mind. It may do this in various ways: by asserting that arbitrariness marks God's sovereignty and by overemphasizing his "otherness" to man; by making miracle supreme, to the relative neglect of those laws of nature which are God's accustomed ways; by conceiving the grace of God as a mechanical and overpowering denial of human freedom rather than as a personal relation which affirms it; by regarding conversion as invariably emotional and episodic and by confusing evangelism with revivalism; by too sharply sundering revelation and reason, faith and knowledge; by regarding the kingdom of God as otherworldly only and by failing to pray and to labor that his kingdom may come and his will be done on earth; by acquiescing in political and social and economic injustice; by making of itself an escape or an opiate; by undue emphasis upon theological doctrines which are secondary and inferential; by jealous and divisive insistence upon some cherished feature of ecclesiastical polity.

When Democracy Is at Fault

Democracy is at fault when it tends to rely upon propaganda rather than upon education, and when it tries to do without God. When Thomas

Hooker, the first great exponent of political democracy in this country, asserted that "the foundation of authority is laid in the free consent of the people," and that "the choice of public magistrates belongs unto the people by God's own allowance," he added—what we are in danger of forgetting—that the right of suffrage which belongs to the people ought not to be "exercised according to their humors, but according to the blessed will and law of God." If democracy has no foundation and frame of reference in standards of right, and truth, and duty, such as faith conceives to be the will and law of God, it becomes a mere conflict of desires where the majority rules by might or the minority rules by cunning, and freedom is mocked by social and economic injustice. The end of that road, as Plato told us long ago, is dictatorship.

Professor M. L. Jacks, of Oxford University, has put the present situation vividly in his recent book on *God in Education:*

Democracy is in danger because it is abandoning the spiritual basis of its own welfare. The liberty which it professes is liberty without an end, and therefore no true liberty; the individual whom it spoils is an individual without a purpose, and therefore no true individual. In these days of panic and power politics, the democratic state needs discipline and authority no less than the totalitarian: only so can it compete with its enemies on equal terms. But the democratic authority must by definition come from within and cannot be imposed from without, and the discipline must be the self-discipline of a man who believes in himself because he believes in God and sees a meaning and a purpose in his existence.[1]

WHEN EDUCATION IS AT FAULT

Education is at fault when it ignores God and drifts into secularism. We have gone too far in that direction.

The bitter struggle between totalitarianism and democracy in our time has thrown into sharp contrast the distinction between reliance upon psychological conditioning and respect for objective truth. And this has been leading to a new realization of the importance of subject matter—the content of teaching. The dogma "not what to teach, but how to teach" is now seen to be misleading because the truth of what it affirms is spoiled by the falsity of its negation. Both *what* and *how* are essential to education. Psychology is an indispensable aid, but only an aid. Psychology cannot determine the ends or final values of life, or spin out of itself the web of knowledge. It cannot take the place of history, or literature, or the physical sciences, or ethics, or philosophy, or theology, or the Word of God. The experimental method is fruitful, not when it is used without presupposition or content, but when it is applied to new material in the

[1] London: Rich & Cowan, Ltd., 1939. Pp. 41-42.

full light of what we already know and believe. Genuinely creative teaching takes place, not in the absence of transmission of a heritage, but where transmission is so adequate that it serves as a base for further action and inquiry.

A new sense of community is inevitable in these tragic days. It links us horizontally—across the world—for none can help feeling how closely bound in common fate are all the races and nations of mankind. It joins us vertically—across the generations—for there is a new community of old and young in interests, in dangers, in sacrifices, and in service, which makes obsolete and worse than useless many of our old neat schemes of classification and partition. Young and old are being educated together by the impact of life. The community itself is educating the young as truly as do the schools. The better education of adults is now seen to be of vital importance to the education of the young. More things can be done and learned by old and young together than we formerly thought. Stanley Hall's idea that children should be taught what their elders do not believe, in the interest of their recapitulation of race experience, has disappeared; and with it should go into oblivion the new opinion that children are incapable of learning anything articulate about God. We must share with our children, honestly, freely, intelligently, what we ourselves know and believe in matters of religious faith and moral principle as well as of loyalty to our country.

In the first heyday of the movement lately known as progressive education it was held that at all points where decision may be involved and attitudes are being formed, the teacher must not intrude and the school must be neutral. For the teacher or even the parent to share his faith with the children and to hope to win them to a like faith was regarded as an unwarranted imposition, a sin against the child's individuality. This extreme view is now being given up. It has been sharply criticized by John Dewey and George Counts and J. H. Newlon, among others. Newlon strongly opposes what he calls "the myth of neutrality" in education and holds that education should be consciously planned to win American youth to "an informed loyalty to a democracy as a way, the best way of life." He goes on to say:

Education that does not dispose to action is not education. To win youth thus to democracy is to assure the preservation of the "essential values" of our culture, such as freedom of inquiry, speech, and press, religious freedom, freedom of teaching, and government by the people. A century ago democracy was truly evangelical. Has it lost its vitality? Will it be able to withstand the onslaughts of authoritarianism in the twentieth century if it has not the will to make converts to its values?[2]

[2] *Education for Democracy in Our Time* (New York: McGraw-Hill Book Company, 1939), p. 214.

THE SECULARIZATION OF EDUCATION IN AMERICA

For more than two centuries the schools of America gave ample place to religious faith, but about one hundred years ago a process of secularization began which has now led to the almost complete exclusion of religion from public education. In the nineteenth century this process was incidental rather than purposed. It was due chiefly to our religious sectarianism and to the fact that we held our diverse religious beliefs and practices in so jealous and divisive a fashion. Adherents of all faiths in America were more concerned that the public schools should not contain any element to which they could object than they were to conserve in these schools the great principles of morals and religion upon which they agree.

In the twentieth century another powerful factor was added, which bore more purposefully and directly upon the exclusion of religion from education. This was the popular vogue of pragmatism, instrumentalism, and experimentalism—to use the successive names which the movement bore— and there was the tremendous influence of this pragmatic point of view in education, together with the fact that in the thought of its greatest protagonist, John Dewey, this point of view was associated with opposition to Judeo-Christian theism.

Professor Hocking has so well stated the danger in the present situation that his striking sentences merit quoting. He was answering the objection which Bertrand Russell voiced against "immersing defenseless children" in the atmosphere of the older generation's faiths—political and religious.

The greatest danger of politically guided education, particularly in democracies which feel themselves obliged in their educational enterprises to cancel out against one another the divergent opinions of various parties, is that the best places will be left blank, because it is on the most vital matters that men most differ. . . . Children have rights which education is bound to respect. The first of these rights is not that they be left to choose their way of life, i.e., to make bricks without either straw or clay. Their first right is that they be offered something positive, the best the group has so far found. Against errors and interested propaganda the growing will has natural protection; it has no protection against starvation.[3]

The ignoring of religion by the public schools inevitably conveys to children a negative suggestion. It is natural for them to conclude that religion is negligible, or unimportant, or irrelevant to the real business of life.

The danger is greater today than ever before just because the public schools are greater today than ever before. The public schools of today have the dimensions of life itself. They undertake to afford to children an

[3] *Human Nature and Its Remaking.* (New Haven: Yale University Press, 1918), pp. 233-34.

environment simpler, purer, wider, better balanced, and more rightly pro-
portioned—to repeat some phrases of John Dewey's—than the environment
in which they chance to be born. They provide for the education of
children in practically every other human interest—*except religion*. The
omission and ignoring of religion by such schools conveys a powerful con-
demnatory suggestion.

THE PERIL OF WEAKENING DEMOCRACY

If this were all, it could be withstood. Parents and churches would find
it harder to share their faith with their children than they would if the
public school were pulling with them rather than against them; but they
would still succeed, as they have been succeeding for a good many years.
The issue is far wider and deeper than the question of the child's positive
or negative attitude toward his parents' faith. The peril is that of the dis-
tortion of education itself and the consequent weakening of democracy.
When it omits faith in God from its teaching, the school gives a distorted
and untrue view of history, and of literature, and of human society. It puts
itself in the anomalous position of attempting to perpetuate and advance
a culture without informing our children concerning the faith that inspired
and sustained that culture. It seeks to pass on to children the great heritage
of our founding fathers but despoils it by eliminating all reference to what
they deemed to be their highest motives. Its hope is that the children will
in maturity do what is just and right; but it carefully refrains from letting
them know what our fathers regarded as just and right, and why they
did so. It undertakes to launch the children upon citizenship in a democracy
without equipping them with those inward controls of conscience and faith
which are necessary if democracy is to be anything other than a welter of
conflicting wills. The public school is not fulfilling its primary purpose of
education for citizenship in American democracy if it maintains a policy of
silence with respect to faith in God.

There is a little book that was published for use in the public schools of
one of our New England cities which recently celebrated its tercentenary.
It is a city that was founded in Puritan religious faith, and that has had a
notable history. Not only were events of high significance omitted from
the account, but the only reason stated for what the founding fathers did
was that they did not like the laws of England. Again and again, as reference
is made to major crises in the life of the city and the nation, this same
statement is the only reason given—"they did not like" something or other.
How can a child know that great moral and political issues were at stake?
How indeed can he know that there are any such moral issues if men are
always moved simply by what they like or do not like? The trouble with
the book—which was written by the city supervisor of social studies—is

not so much that it is false as that it lacks depth and perspective. It is superficial; the story it tells is thin and flat.

AMERICA'S COMMON RELIGIOUS FAITH

Underlying all her differences America has a common religious faith: common, not in the sense that everybody shares it, for there are some among us who deny or ignore God, but in the sense that it is common to the three great religious groups—Protestant, Catholic, and Jewish—to which the great majority of American citizens profess to belong. These citizens—Protestant, Catholic, and Jew—worship the one God, Creator of all things and Father of men. They believe that his will has been revealed in the life and literature of the Hebrew people, as this is recorded in the Bible, and that it is discernible in nature about us and in conscience within. They acknowledge the principles of human duty set forth in the Ten Commandments, in the teachings of the Hebrew prophets, in the Golden Rule, and in the law of love to God and to fellow men. They sing hymns and psalms that transcend differences of creed. They can all unite in the Lord's Prayer: "Our Father who art in heaven. . . . Thy kingdom come. Thy will be done."

The religious faith of America has inspired our history as a people and is embodied in our most characteristic institutions. It is avowed in the Declaration of Independence and in the constitutions of forty-two out of the forty-eight states. It is expressed in various public acts and customs of the federal, state, and municipal governments—the annual proclamation and observance of a day of Thanksgiving to God, the setting aside of Sundays and certain religious festivals as legal holidays, the opening of the sessions of legislative assemblies with prayer, the form of oath used in courts of law and in the inauguration of public officials, the appointment of chaplains for the Army and Navy, and so forth.

There is nothing in the status of the public school as an institution of the state, therefore, to render it godless. There is nothing in the principle of religious freedom or the separation of Church and state to hinder the school's acknowledgment of the power and goodness of God. The common religious faith of the American people, as distinguished from the sectarian forms in which it is organized, may rightfully be assumed and may find appropriate expression in the life and work of the public schools.

In most states the public schools may continue the well-established custom of reading a brief selection from the Bible and engaging in the Lord's Prayer; and by the careful selection of biblical materials, this practice may be made of more educational value than it often is. The public schools may and should refer to religion, as occasion arises, naturally and wholesomely, without dogmatism, without bias, and without affectation or strain. In all of their teaching they should manifest reverence for God and respect for religious beliefs. Teachers should understand that the principle of religious freedom is designed to protect rather than to destroy religious faith, and that this principle gives them no right either tacitly to suggest or actually to teach secularism or irreligion. The public schools should aim at the development of a citizenship which is founded upon character; and they may, in their efforts to educate for character, give due place to religious motives. They can teach that morality is more than custom, public opinion, or legal enactment; they can point to its grounding in the structure of the universe and in the nature of God. In the teaching of history, literature, and the social sciences they can afford to religious faith its normal and proper place.

THE AIM AND SCOPE OF RELIGIOUS EDUCATION

How, then, shall we describe the aim and scope of religious education? It must be in terms no less inclusive than those in which we seek to describe the aim and scope of democracy and of education. "I came," said Jesus, "that they may have life, and may have it abundantly." Religion is no mere compartment of life; it is not a narrow special interest; it must not be—as one writer has put it—a set of scruples impeding our faculties. All that is best in democracy and in education is enhanced and made more vital by the faith in God which Jesus opened to mankind. Nothing less than the whole range of life and education is to be conceived and fulfilled in the spirit of religious faith.

A statement of the aim and scope of Christian religious education which is compact and comprehensive was drawn up by the Chinese delegates to the Jerusalem meeting of the International Missionary Council and by them presented to that body. It reads:

Religious education in the Christian sense includes all efforts and processes which help to bring children and adults into a vital and saving experience of God revealed in Christ; to quicken the sense of God as a living reality, so that communion with Him in prayer and worship becomes a natural habit and principle of life; to enable them to interpret the meaning of their growing experience of life in the light of ultimate values; to establish attitudes and habits of Christlike living in common life and in all human relations; and to enlarge and deepen the understanding of the historic facts on which Christianity rests and of the rich content of Christian experience, belief, and doctrine.[4]

CHRISTIAN EDUCATION IN THE FAMILY

The fulfillment of these aims depends more directly upon the family and upon the church than upon the school, the community, and the state.

[4] Weigle and Oldham, *Religious Education* (New York: International Missionary Council, 1928), II, 4.

The major principle underlying the Christian education of children is that of their fellowship with older folk in primary social groups which are genuinely Christian in spirit and life. Of these groups by far the most important is the family. Horace Bushnell found in what he called the organic unity of the family the natural basis for his principle of Christian nurture: "That the child is to grow up a Christian, and never know himself as being otherwise."

The influences of family life are of especial importance in their bearing upon the growing character of the child. Here is a little group of old and young, mature and immature, living together in mutual affection, placing personal values first, constrained by the manifold contacts of their common life each to have regard for the things of the other, always giving and receiving service, with opportunities for helpfulness, unselfishness, and even self-sacrifice so constant as to make these a matter of course—what finer soil for the virtues, what better training ground for character, could there be? We may well doubt whether this moral function of the family could ever be fulfilled by any other institution. Schools may take over the larger part of the education of children; and the state may exercise supervision and control in many matters that, under simpler conditions of life, were left to the parent. The life of the school and the service of the state moreover can do much to bring out the sturdier virtues and to train the character of the young. But these must deal with children in large groups and in relatively cold and impersonal ways. They can never beget and train the inner emotional springs of the moral life as the family does in its atmosphere of personal affection, love, and loyalty.

There is an essential relation, moreover, between Christianity and the institution of the family. The Christian religion universalizes the relations of family life. Jesus' teachings concerning God as well as concerning human duty are based upon these relations. God, he tells us, is our Father, and we are all brethren. Our understanding of these teachings depends upon the quality of our own family life. It is the privilege and responsibility of the parent to interpret God to his children in terms of his own character, and so to direct the spirit of his family that it may fitly serve as the type for all good social living.

THE EDUCATIONAL WORK OF THE CHURCH

In a general but vital and fundamental sense the whole life and work of the Christian Church is to be conceived in educational terms. The primary interest of the Church is in persons; its concern is for the enrichment of their experience, the development of their character, and the quality of their service as free, responsible, co-operative members of the human race. In the power of the Spirit of God, the Church undertakes the regeneration of society through the regeneration and Christian education of individuals.

In a more direct and immediate sense the educational work of the Christian Church includes at least these major aspects:

1. The fostering of growth in grace as the individual's powers mature and his experience deepens and widens. This includes both the Christian nurture and education of children and provision for the religious growth and development of young people and adults.

2. The lifting of the Christian life above the level of habit and custom to the level of intelligence. This includes the intelligent understanding of the Church's own convictions as these are grounded in the life and teachings of Jesus, the discovery of new truth and the discernment of the witness of the Spirit in the life of today, the application of Christian principles to the ever-new problems of changing civilization, the training of Church members to render intelligent and effective service in the various fields of their opportunity, and the creation and maintenance among folk generally of a sound, true, and effective public opinion.

3. The fitting of young people, through institutions of higher education, for service in places of initiative, responsibility, and leadership.

CO-OPERATION IN RELIGIOUS EDUCATION

There is need of more effective co-operation between the churches, as well as between churches and families and schools. Without infringement of the principle of religious freedom, and without disregard for sincere differences of belief, the churches may engage in three contexts of co-operation:

1. Each church remains free, of course, to teach the full range of doctrines and duties which are included in its heritage and present belief, and to provide materials and counsel for such teaching in the families associated with it. But the spirit of co-operation—as well as the spirit of Christ—requires that such teaching be positive and without invidious comparison with the supposed defects and errors of other churches. If the distinctive doctrines of a church cannot be set forth positively in terms of the basic revelation of God through Christ, they are probably not worth setting forth.

2. We must extend as widely as possible the range of doctrines and duties which we hold in common, and which serve as a basis for united action and teaching. We are making progress in this respect through such conferences as those held within the last twenty years at Stockholm, Lausanne, Jerusalem, Oxford, Edinburgh and Madras, through the plans of the World Council of Churches, organized at Amsterdam in 1948, and through the work of the Federal Council of Churches and the International Council of Religious Education. But we must move more rapidly. And we must all

recognize that the need for common action and teaching is so urgent that no group will hold back because its own distinctive formulation of some point is not generally accepted.

3. We must do all that we can to reach an understanding with our Roman Catholic and Jewish brethren that will permit the inclusion in community provisions for education of the faith in God which we share with them and they with us.

These three contexts of co-operation are all valid. They are not competitive but complementary. They mutually reinforce one another. It is a mistake to suppose that the inclusion of theistic faith in the life and teaching of the public schools would hinder or replace the teaching of the churches, or that strengthening the common program of the churches would weaken interest in the program of the denomination. The effect would be quite the opposite. More adequate teaching, more effective co-operation, in all three contexts, would strengthen both education and religion, and would more amply undergird democracy with faith in God.

SUGGESTIONS FOR FURTHER STUDY

All of the books in the following Bibliography are well worth careful reading and study. The following topics may be suggestive:

1. The place of religious faith in the development of American democracy: Gabriel, Perry.
2. Education and faith in God: Jacks, Murry, Powell.
3. The psychological and ethical bases of education: Hocking.
4. The inadequacy of conditioning as a substitute for education: Lewis.
5. Christian nurture in the family and the church: Bushnell, Vieth.
6. Religious faith and moral training in the public schools: Newlon, Rugh.
7. A world-wide philosophy of Christian religious education: Weigle and Oldham.

BIBLIOGRAPHY

Bushnell, Horace. *Christian Nurture* [1847]. Rev. ed. New Haven: Yale University Press, 1948.

Gabriel, Ralph H. *The Course of American Democratic Thought*. New York: Ronald Press, 1940.

Hocking, William E. *Human Nature and Its Remaking*. New Haven: Yale University Press, 1918.

Jacks, M. L. *God in Education*. London: Rich and Cowan, 1939.

Lewis, C. S. *The Abolition of Man*. New York: The Macmillan Co., 1947.

Murry, Middleton. *The Price of Leadership*. London: Student Christian Movement Press, 1939.

Perry, Ralph B. *Puritanism and Democracy*. New York: Vanguard Press, 1944.

Powell, Wilfred E. *Education for Life with God*. New York: The Abingdon Press, 1934.

Rugh, C. E., ed. *Moral Training in the Public Schools.* Boston: Ginn and Company, 1907. Chap. II, pp. 53-88.

Vieth, Paul H. *Objectives in Religious Education.* New York: Harper & Brothers, 1930.

Weigle, L. A., and Oldham, J. H. *Religious Education* (Vol. II of the Reports of the Jerusalem Meeting of the International Missionary Council). New York: International Missionary Council, 1928.

PART II

Materials and Methods
of Religious Education

Chapter 8

CURRICULUM PATTERNS FOR THE CHURCH SCHOOL

C. A. BOWEN

THE USE OF THE WORD "patterns" does not imply that curriculum is looked upon as something to be "cut out" just as you design an item of wearing apparel. "Patterns" is interpreted to mean a way in which the curriculum is planned, also how it is used. When we observe how the curriculum has been constructed and used, we discover the various patterns of curriculum used in our church schools.

Curriculum itself is something which all but evades definition. In the more rarefied sense of the term it is whatever teacher and learner use to aid learning. This leaves us nowhere, of course, when we think of patterns of curriculum. It is necessary in this statement arbitrarily to restrict our thinking to the idea of curriculum as something formulated, or capable of formulation, in writing. Now for the patterns.

PREPARATION, SELECTION, AND USE

One group of patterns will be discovered when we inquire into how curriculum is prepared, how it is selected, and how it is used.

In this connection let us think of curriculum committees, libraries of books dealing with education and the use of materials in learning, the Bible as the basis of our teaching, various resource materials, editors, publishers, leadership schools, and the teaching force in the local church. An examination on this basis reveals within this general classification certain very interesting patterns of curriculum.

Let us begin with what has been called the *main-line materials*. These are usually prepared by a denomination and used as directed in the local school. It does not follow necessarily that the construction of such a pattern of curriculum is undemocratic. The builders of the courses at the denominational headquarters may work in close co-operation with persons in selected homes and church schools. They may keep in close touch with the grass roots. The teaching forces in the local schools may be entirely satisfied in thus delegating a difficult and technical responsibility to the persons to whom it has been assigned by the church.

Next, there are what might be called *main-line materials with variations*. Here the local school uses the denominational curriculum for the most part. However, interests emerge which can be met only by securing additional materials elsewhere. Often the educational leaders of the denomination give guidance as to where such other approved materials may be located. Sometimes the tendency to vary from the strict denominational pattern is locally initiated.

Then there is the *local-church curriculum* chosen from various sources as the school projects its plans. Here leaders use whatever they think will serve their purpose. They find these materials wherever they can be located. Often these leaders work in co-operation with the board of education of the denomination. Often they plan apart from any denominational guidance. There are values in centering the curriculum more definitely in the needs and interests of the local situation. Such procedure also faces the dangers of spottiness, imbalance, and aloofness from the life of the denomination and the ecumenical church. The assumption of responsibility for locating needs and building a curriculum upon correct principles calls for wise and well-trained local leadership.

The local leaders may draw their materials from various sources, with little evidence of planning. This might be called the casual or unplanned curriculum. Here the dangers just outlined are accentuated. It is easy for certain strong-minded persons who know how to secure favorable action on their proposals to dominate the operations of the curriculum in the local church. The results will follow the vagaries of the individuals in charge. A plan worked out in co-operation with well-qualified curriculum builders is necessary no matter where the materials are obtained.

There are schools in which the teaching materials are largely created on the spot. This is sometimes called *free curriculum*. The assumption followed is that only the teachers and learners in this particular situation are in a position to locate and supply the educational and religious needs found there. Only in this way can the curriculum be alive. Only thus can teaching be creative. Both the truth and the exacting demands of procedure based on these assumptions are easy to see. Only thus can the process of curriculum construction be democratic. Of course there are risks. Besides, this type of curriculum is a daring challenge to educational leadership in the local church.

The reader may easily be able to think of illustrations of each of the patterns—classified on the basis of preparation, selection, and use—just enumerated. Sometimes the polity of the church binds local congregations together closely. In other cases the structure of the denomination allows each congregation to serve as its own educational guide and director. In addition to the structure of church organization differences might be pointed to in the educational organization of the denominations. Where this organization is strong and aggressive, the materials will tend to become main-line. Where the organization is weak and passive, the opposite will be true. A denomination with a rigid theological position will tend to regularize the local congregation as to the doctrines taught in the curriculum. A denomination in which flow diverse doctrinal currents will be apt to have local schools with varied patterns of curriculum. Some situations provide aggressive and able leaders who insist on developing the curriculum apart from denominational or interdenominational advice. It should be said that the present confusion in educational and religious thinking tends to provide conditions where varied patterns will appear.

GRADING

Let us look at another basis of differentiation. This time curriculum will be classified in terms of the way the principle of grading is applied. This provides several interesting patterns also.

There are the *broadly graded lessons*. These materials make it possible for very small schools with limited resources and leadership to provide materials suited to some extent to the needs of pupils of various ages. The younger children can have their graded materials—also the older children, the youth, and the adults. Broadly graded lessons furnish an answer to the problem of meeting the needs of schools which have felt that they must use uniform lessons.

There are also the *cycle-graded lessons*. Some denominations term materials of this type "group-graded" or "departmentally graded" lessons. This curriculum is built around the plan of organization capable of use in the majority of church schools. The materials are graded by departments through the youth division. There is a two-year course for beginners, and there are three-year courses for primaries, juniors, intermediates, seniors, and older youth. There is no gradation within each department. The advance to more difficult materials comes when the pupil passes from the beginner's department to the primary department, from the primary department to the junior department, and so on. When a school uses cycle-graded lessons in the children's and youth divisions, it tends to "grade" its materials for adults also. When its adult classes use uniform lessons or elective courses, it is easy to fit them to the needs of older pupils and therefore to make them "graded." When this is true, the entire curriculum for that school is graded, though not according to a single pattern.

There are also the *closely-graded courses*. In this instance the school provides a course for its kindergarten or beginner's department two years in length on a single level of difficulty. Beginning with the primary department, the curriculum is graded by years. For example Course One, for a six-year-old child, corresponds with the materials in the first grade in the public school.

Course Two, for the seven-year-old, corresponds with those in the second grade; and so on through Course Nine. Some denominations have provided closely graded courses for pupils fifteen to seventeen years of age. Others provide cycle-graded or elective courses for this age group. Some experimentation has been carried on in shifting the boundaries of the primary and junior departments by assigning two years to a department. This does not affect the year-by-year grading of the curriculum for these children, however. The closely graded pattern is not practicable for use above the senior department. The school with closely graded curriculum through the seventeenth year usually provides electives, uniform lessons, or some specialized form of materials for its older age groups. It is easy to see the advantages of drawing a fine bead on the stages of growth of the pupil. However, the learning ability of the pupil does not always correspond to his calendar age. This would not make a great deal of difference in the use of cycle-graded curriculum. It would create a problem where the materials are closely graded. In places where the closely graded curriculum is used, the operations of the school become intricate. The demands for equipment and leadership personnel multiply rapidly.

There is also what we have already referred to as *free curriculum*. The courses might also be described as "loosely graded." They do not presuppose any framework which might be worked out by some outside agency responsible for curriculum construction. The structure of the curriculum would vary with different periods of the year. At times the school might appear to be graded rather completely. At other times the evidence of grading as we understand the term would be hard to discover. Those who advocate free curriculum insist that it alone provides for vital learning. They also point out that they are working at the frontier and must move away from the accepted patterns and experiments to discover new truths about curriculum. Certainly this is a function which should be performed by schools which prefer to operate as curriculum laboratories. Both the advantages of free curriculum and the difficulties involved in administering it are many. They are too evident to call for description.

Some of the denominations are working out what we might call a *unified curriculum*. The curriculum committee of the denomination decides upon an emphasis for a year—or a quarter. The courses for the various grades are in the area of that emphasis. Real skill has been developed in making it possible for children, youth, and adults to carry on their learning activities in the same general field of study. It is claimed that this type of curriculum organization will unify the life of the church. It will bring the family closer together in its relation to the church school. It will make it easier to plan worship and activities. In the unified curriculum we have a natural reaction to the extreme practices of grading which have come into vogue in some places. It is also an effort to deal with what has become an apparently confused curriculum situation in some church schools. We hear many voices. Many plans are suggested. Curriculum courses are many. Certain denominations take the situation in hand and work to bring order out of chaos. These denominations claim that what we call the unified curriculum is especially practical for use in the smaller schools—also that it does not provide the administrative difficulties of the broadly graded materials already referred to.

While it is contrary to the principle of grading, we should mention one of the most popular patterns of all—the *uniform lessons*. In these lessons a passage of Scripture is the organizing center of the curriculum. At one extreme we find groups which tend toward a rigid system of teaching the passage selected to pupils old and young. The effort is made to adapt the materials to the various age groups. The adaptation for use by children involves efforts to simplify words and to explain difficult theological concepts. At the other extreme we find groups which use material prepared to meet the needs of the younger pupils. The "babes in Christ" have a "semiliquid food" with considerable amounts of finely ground theological "meat." The more mature "saints" have a liquid diet with the meat in larger portions. Of course, the "babe in Christ" should have "milk" and the full-grown Christians "meat"; but in denominations less rigid in their teaching procedures, uniform lessons are used which are built around a core of several loosely related passages of Scripture grouped into a single area of emphasis. The simpler narrative passages are developed for the children. The other passages are used with various age groups. It might be suggested that this is a strained usage of what might be called uniform materials. It is certainly far from the usual meaning of the term.

The history of the struggle to provide graded curriculum for the church school is well known. It has been going on for nearly half a century. About the year 1930 it seemed as if graded materials would get into use in all of the larger denominations, thereby supplanting uniform lessons. Then the tide seemed to turn against the graded materials. Even the International Council of Religious Education ceased to "hold the line" and began to approve uniform-lesson outlines for all ages except the younger children. At present the uniform materials are more widely used than any other type in the Protestant churches of America. A few denominations have eliminated all uniform materials for children and youth, making the uniform lessons definitely adult-centered when used. This movement has affected favorably the circulation of their lesson periodicals.

The reader may be able to identify church schools in which the curriculum has followed some of the patterns of grading—or nongrading—which have been mentioned. The educational point of view of the denomination, its theological outlook, the strength and aggressiveness of its educational leadership, and the skill, point of view, conservatism, or vitality of the local church leadership might well explain whatever situation is discovered.

CONTENT

Let us look at still another basis of differentiation. In this instance the patterns of curriculum will be classified in terms of the place which is given to content. There is considerable variety in the way content is chosen, placed, and used.

Some materials are *content-centered*. Passages from the Bible are chosen to be transmitted to the pupil with whatever understanding and appreciation is possible. Other materials are selected or prepared by the authorities within a denomination, to be accepted likewise by the pupils and teachers who use them. The determining assumption is that the intrinsic worth of certain formulated truth is far more important than any other element in religious learning. The repeating of precious phrases or the mental acceptance of glorious ideas will work complete transformation in life and conduct. The learner is the subject of this process. The more passive he is, the more successful the teaching. The teacher is likewise the servant of the material. He is not to disturb the conclusions already stated by interposing his own personal interpretations. Content-centered materials are not easy to use in vital teaching; they are easy to use in mechanical fashion. It is simply a problem of moving a certain pile of information from the pages of the book into the memory of the learner. The problem is almost one of logistics.

Within this pattern we may also discover curriculum that is only *partly content-centered*. In this case we have solid materials prepared so as to be transmitted. The logistic aspect is not so evident. The content is adapted to some degree to the learner's capacities. Some account is taken of his needs. However, when such a compromise is carried out, it must be kept clearly in mind that in such curriculum the emphasis is really upon content after all. Some tribute is paid to the pupil and his needs. Some thought is given to effective ways of teaching; but, after all, the content itself is most important. The learner and the learning process are secondary. Such curriculum lends itself to mechanical use. It is not easy to use in vital teaching.

Curriculum is *basically life-centered* when the nature of the pupil, the laws of learning, and the spirit and teaching of Christianity affect strongly the way materials are prepared, selected, and used. Content is considered important—the Bible is the essential source of materials. But a new interpretation is given to content. It is seen as vital religious experience which has come to us in certain formulations—the pupil sees behind the form as he locates the basic spiritual meaning. This places the emphasis in curriculum building upon the sharing and enrichment of experience. The pupil reads and studies the Bible just as he gets acquainted with a person who becomes an intimate friend. As a result he becomes ever more alive to the message of God which it contains. The same process goes on as other types of content are used. Religion itself is primary. The believer who is learning is also primary. Content is chosen with its value for vital use in mind. The preparation of other materials is guided by the same principle. The teacher uses these basically life-centered materials vitally—that is, in the way they were intended to be used. The worker who tries to use such materials mechanically finds that it is difficult. He is disappointed.

Finally there is curriculum which professes to be *completely life-centered*. The difference between this and the pattern just mentioned is found in the words "completely" and "basically." The so-called "completely life-centered curriculum" emphasizes the learning experience at the expense of content. The implication is that the use of content prevents vital learning from taking place—that is, unless the use is made contingent upon the relevance of the content to the experience. This pattern says that the Bible and other religious content have no intrinsic value for Christian learning. Their value is entirely contingent upon whether they can be used on a particular occasion to aid the process of learning. It is easy to see that this is an extreme position. When the reaction against the blind and mechanical methods of a given body of teachers reached its farthest point some years ago, there was considerable interest in all but doing away with the use of content in religious teaching. The free self-activity of the learner was all-important. The material to be used must tremble as a suppliant before him. His teacher must "empty himself," also, taking "the form of a servant." Nothing must interfere with the complete sovereignty of "His Majesty, the Pupil." This reaction has reached its limit, and the position of our current thinking has moved nearer toward the center. Yet this pattern of curriculum had to be listed and described, at least in brief fashion.

AGENCIES

A final basis of differentiation awaits our consideration. In this instance we classify the patterns of curriculum according to the agencies in which they are used. There are real differences in curriculums as used in various agencies of religious teaching.

The curriculum used in the *weekday school of religion* is probably the most highly developed type. These courses operate alongside the materials which make up the curriculum of the public school. Teachers in the weekday church schools are apt to be well versed in the general principles of teaching. Units of study will be longer and more thoroughly developed. Periods of teaching will be protected against interruption. Equipment, supervision, and the other educative factors taken for granted in a good public school will operate here. The close relation with the life of the public school, the opportunities for visual education, access to libraries, the drive of the school situation—all these may contribute to making the curriculum of the weekday school of religion far more adequate and effective than that used in other agencies.

Recently the *church camping movement* has gained momentum. Immediately the curriculum architects were called upon to develop proper materials. There was the usual research and experimentation. It was discovered that a new pattern of curriculum must be developed. Curriculum for a camp must be differentiated from that of a vacation school. It must be centered in the intensive and close fellowship provided over a brief period by the camp situation. Within definite limitations camp curriculum must be free curriculum. It must be created, in large part, out of the search for God, and the discovery of God in nature, and the experience of living as a Christian fellowship. It is surprising to find how much Christian learning can take place when curriculum of this type is properly used.

The curriculum used in the *vacation church school* also has its peculiar pattern. It is constructed for use in an intensive teaching operation. For five successive days in the week during several weeks the school goes on. The time of year makes it possible to bring in actual experiences of nature with the proper religious interpretations. It is possible to carry through completion projects calling for serious planning and determined execution. The use of play and drama in teaching has a favored chance. The length of time devoted each day to the program adds drive and zest to learning. Further momentum comes out of the daily sessions. The school gets a strong hold on the pupils. Besides, close association with the church building and continuous fellowship with children and adults in the circle of church life accomplish much in Christian learning. The curriculum of the vacation church school must take account of all these elements in the situation. We have already noted how it must be differentiated from the curriculum for the church camp. It must be different from that of the Sunday church school. Its pattern must be distinctive.

In the *Sunday-morning church school* we find a rather unpromising situation in which to use an extensive and thoroughly formalized curriculum. Some of the best-laid plans come to grief when materials so developed are used in this agency of Christian education. Perhaps the strongest element in the church-school session held on Sunday morning is Christian fellowship. Folks enjoy meeting each other at church. They worship together. They allow various interests to invade the regular period set apart for teaching. Why not? Everybody is having a good time. The workers gladly give the odds and ends of their time, strength, and ability to make the school go. Yet, try as it may, it is difficult for the local board of education to carry out fully the serious plans for effective teaching through this agency.

Some have pointed to this session of the church school as an effective opportunity for educational evangelism. Others are reluctant to admit that any one agency is more valuable for evangelism than another. Certainly the spontaneity and casualness of operation which we are apt to find on Sunday morning in the church school affects the curriculum. Some weary and frustrated educators have suggested giving up the church school as held on Sunday morning. To do so would be to make a serious mistake. What must be done is to use care in setting the desired outcomes for this agency. Let us give up the expectation that always there will be extensive and thorough learning in the Sunday-morning sessions such as might take place in other agencies. Let us look to these sessions as the time when the whole idea of Christian learning is popularized. It is well to gather in crowds. Expose these people to a little teaching anyway. Introduce them to the disciplines of Christian learning. Then guide them into the more intensive and effective groups or agencies where more adequate Christian teaching can take place. This does imply that little effort should be made to carry forward a thoroughly implemented program of Christian education at this time. Rather more emphasis will be given to the more spontaneous elements of the program. On Sunday morning let us go as far as we can in our teaching.

Of course all this affects the preparation of materials for the Sunday-morning session. They should be planned and constructed with the idea in mind that the church school on Sunday morning is a distinctive agency in which the curriculum must not exact too much of pupil and teacher. The materials must be pliable. They must be provocative. They must provide stimulus to real effort in learning. They must provide resources for those who desire to give themselves to this discipline. This is not a close description of a pattern of curriculum. Rather it explains in part the frequent failure of the church school of this type to use the materials provided for it. Our sympathy is with the workers and pupils in this situation. We have already noted the need for curriculum of a distinctive pattern for the Sunday school.

Some mention should be made of the pattern of curriculum now being used in the *youth and adult fellowship meetings*. It stands in contrast with those youth materials used on Sunday morning, which are dominated by the teacher. The fellowship curriculum is learner dominated. The initiative is in his hands. He plans. He carries out. The teacher is really an adviser or counselor. Such a curriculum is apt to be spontaneous. It is often contemporary. Discussion is free and often leads to action. It is hard to predict what a session will bring forth. For this reason the materials prepared for such use must be stimulating. They must furnish principles of guidance and desired outcomes to be sought. They must provide adequate resources.

It is difficult to place in a separate pattern of curriculum the use of projected visualized materials, which have been coming into more widespread use of late. At the same time, some mention should be made of this development.

At first glance the use of *audio-visual material* gave promise of great usefulness. It was different. The appeal of this new instrument was strong. For a time it seemed possible for the screen and projector to displace the printed text and the nonprojected visual materials. One enthusiast outlined a plan to devote an entire period of the Sunday church school to the showing of a single motion picture. On the following Sunday stills of important scenes taken from the picture were to be shown with some verbal explanation. On a third Sunday discussion would follow. The entire school would thus be given a complete curriculum. Then the process would start again with a new picture on the fourth Sunday.

As church-school workers gained more experience with audio-visual materials, it was possible to develop certain units which were visualized to a considerable extent. Other units were found to be capable of enrichment through the use of materials of this type. It was also discovered that it is possible to make significant educational use of this medium, even though the temptation to use it for entertainment is always present. Recent progress in this field gives promise of a far deeper integration of audio-visual materials into the curriculum of the church school.

Summary and Conclusions

Patterns of curriculum for the church school classified under four groupings have been pointed out. We have observed how the selection, preparation, and use of materials bring certain patterns of curriculum to light; how the application of the principle of grading brings to light other patterns; how the place given to content and the way in which content is used provide still other patterns. Finally, the agencies for which materials are prepared reveal still other patterns of curriculum. The examination of these various forms in which the materials are appearing should impress us with the wide differentiation which has come to the curriculum during the years in which the church school has flourished.

Are we in a twentieth-century "Babel Period"? We recall the confused period coming at the middle of the last century. Has the same chaos in curriculum descended upon us again? The uniform lessons came out of a revolt against such a time of confusion nearly a century ago. Then came a reaction against the deadly uniformity of our Sunday-school lessons. Most of what has been discussed in this chapter might be described as various reactions to the principle of uniformity. Leaders have tended to be somewhat hysterical as they have tried to establish the vital principle of curriculum construction. During the last few decades some of them have trailed after the various fads of the general educators. One of our saner leaders in the Church pointed out with some bitterness that the "Ziegfield Follies" of each year must be matched by the novel educational philosophies of the same period. Out of it all have come our present difficulties. The church school finds itself beset with numerous widely differing patterns of curriculum. All of us should be disturbed. This includes both the workers in the local school and those who provide the materials. Church schools are better. Teachers are better trained. Programs are more effective. The materials are nearer to the needs of the learner and teacher. Still the present confusion presses upon us. Are we sufficient for the demands now being made upon us?

First, let us admit that we are all the richer because of the varieties of materials which have been developed. It is possible to select among several types of curriculum. The Christian faces a new world, no matter where he turns. Those responsible for guiding Christian learning must make many approaches to the problem of providing the materials needed. Let us admit also that we cannot return to the past. That would be to take flight from our problem. We will refuse to do this. We must face firmly the difficulties which now frown upon us—no matter the degree of their fury. The only passage is straight through our problem. We must find the solution as we move forward.

Are we sufficient for the demands now facing us as builders and users of curriculum? Yes; if we turn our attention to the central emphasis of Christian teaching and construct a rich and varied curriculum around it. All the elements of teaching are not of equal importance. Christian teaching finds its center in faith in God as revealed in Jesus Christ. Faith is viewed as the core of Christian teaching and it must be guided to expression. It must be nurtured till it controls life. Such guidance and nurture is Christian teaching, which affirms that faith does not reach its highest form apart from the help of teacher, school, home, and curriculum. Christian teaching drives faith to deal with every facet of life. Christian teaching helps the learner to find the very motive for living in the purpose of God. It helps the learner to discover that purpose for himself and for all of life. When Christian faith is central to teaching, unity is found amidst diversity. The curriculum is unified at the very time when it is rich and diversified. The curriculum has a central core and drive while it draws upon every significant experience which comes to the learner.

This is a far cry from uniform lessons. The integrated curriculum will be graded and will be relevant to the needs of the person and the situation which he faces. It will take many forms. It will be as much in motion as life itself. At the same time, it will be as unified as life itself.

An individual is integrated when he is normal. One phase of our curriculum might also be integrated about the experiences of the learner in terms of his relation to God. Someone has pointed out that "the curriculum is ninety per cent teacher." Here, then, we have another point of integration. The depth and degree of the teacher's Christian faith will relate his teaching to the central objective of the curriculum—faith in God as revealed by Jesus Christ. Teachers can be trained to be persons of faith in the vital sense which educators understand. Those teachers in the home can be trained to the same end. The result will be a curriculum vitally related to the great purpose of Christian education.

The importance of parent and church-school teacher may have been overstressed. Maybe the Christian fellowship provided by the Church is more effective than any person or agency impinging upon the learner. If so, here again we may have a point of integration. The depth and degree of the Christian faith of the Christian fellowship will tend to bring the curriculum close to the central objective of teaching. A unifying force will operate to bind divergent and widely separated elements into a common center.

We need not worry about the various patterns of curriculum. These have flowered partly out of confusion. They have also come about because of the vigor and daring of those engaged in the processes of Christian learning. They may reach a danger point if we cannot find some central principle of unity. Several possibilities have been mentioned—those presented by the individual learner himself, by the teachers in home and church school, and by the Christian fellowship. Somewhere the construction of curriculum materials will go on. Architects and planners will continue at their tasks. They will contribute significantly to the making of an integrated curriculum of Christian education so long as they remember that they are working in the area of learning, handling the materials of the human spirit, accepting the control of the laws of personal growth, and sensing dependence upon the great Master of the task of curriculum construction and use.

SUGGESTIONS FOR FURTHER STUDY

1. Study the curriculum used in some local church school. Classify and evaluate it in terms of the categories used in this chapter.

2. Secure from your denominational headquarters information concerning the lesson and program materials produced for its church schools. Check the materials used in your own church school with those provided by the denomination.

3. Study the materials used in your church school during the current church-school year. Discover its plan of organization. Evaluate its effectiveness. Prepare a report to be discussed at a meeting of the workers' council.

4. At the beginning of the church-school year prepare a series of suggestions to your workers' council proposing curriculum materials for use during the next twelve months.

BIBLIOGRAPHY

Bowen, C. A. *Literature and the Christian Life* (Rev.). New York and Nashville: Abingdon Press, 1947.

Bower, W. C., and Hayward, P. R. *Protestantism Faces Its Educational Task Together*. Appleton, Wis.: C. C. Nelson Co., 1949. Chap. 4.

Christian Education Today. Chicago: International Council of Religious Education, 1940.

Curriculum Guide for the Local Church. Chicago: International Council of Religious Education, 1945.

Smither, Ethel L. *The Use of the Bible with Children*. New York: The Abingdon Press, 1937.

Study of Christian Education. Chicago: International Council of Religious Education, 1947. Chap. 4, "The Curriculum of Christian Education."

Chapter 9

THE USE OF OUR RELIGIOUS HERITAGE

FRANK GLENN LANKARD

IN ANY CONSIDERATION of the materials and methods of religious education one needs to give a large place to the Bible, to religious biography, and to the classics.

THE BIBLE

There have been periods when the Bible was the sole source of the religious curriculum. During the years 1790-1815, instruction in the Sunday school centered in the catechism; but because of the English Evangelical Movement of the eighteentth century and the great revivals of religion in America—movements which drew their inspiration from the Scriptures— interest had shifted rapidly by the second decade of the nineteenth century from the catechism to the Bible.

Even though the Bible assumed first place in the religious curriculum, this must be described as the period of unorganized Bible study. There were two reasons for this: First, the Bible is an ungraded book for various age groups; and, second, the common method of learning in that period was that of memorization. Hence the children memorized large portions of the Scriptures to be recited each Sunday with little or no supervision. Motivation was supplied by various prizes and rewards. Some children indulged in almost unbelievable marathons of memorization. The results were that the memory was exercised, but reason and judgment suffered. Memorization of biblical material became an end in itself, and the application of biblical truths to character and conduct received scant attention. This type of study, as might be expected, fell of its own weight, the prizes and rewards notwithstanding.

Soon a system of prepared material appeared, known as the selected-lesson system. A selected-lesson plan could be prepared by an individual or by an organization for purposes of instruction. At any rate, it was in contrast to the haphazard, meaningless selection of verses by the pupils themselves. The new plan might center in the life of Christ, or it might be a study of the prophets or of the journeys of Paul. The selections, however, were wholly Bible centered and gave little or no attention to the needs or problems of the pupils. They proved difficult for younger pupils, and by 1830 the plan fell into disrepute.

A period of great confusion in the religious curriculum followed, which lasted for approximately forty years. The several denominations had taken on a more definite Sunday-school consciousness, and their publishing houses were attempting to meet the needs of the pupils. Private publishing houses also sprang up which competed with denominational houses by printing their own systems. The net result was confusion and competition. It has been aptly described as the "Babel Period" in Sunday-school materials. But it must be noted that in every instance the lesson materials were taken from the Bible.

By the third quarter of the nineteenth century a number of forces combined to influence the religious curriculum. The public schools, for example, were making valiant attempts to bring their materials within the comprehension of the pupils. Alert Sunday-school teachers were looking for a way out of the confusion in Sunday-school materials. The Sunday-school Institute Movement was more and more centering attention on the needs of the children. The net result was a strong reaction against competition and confusion and a desire for closer unity and co-operation. The answer came in what is known as uniform lessons, a type of lesson in which the same Bible text was used for all ages on a given Sunday. The pedagogical error was that the same Bible text was used for all ages, but the several denominations sought to offset this defect by preparing helps and teaching techniques for the various age levels. We need to bear in mind, however, that the lessons were wholly from the Bible, which was regarded as the treasure house of religious experience. The uniform lessons reached their zenith about 1910, when the closely graded lessons came to occupy a prominent place in the Sunday-school curriculum.[1]

By 1910 there was a feeling that Christians might well go beyond the Bible for teaching materials, but the Bible was by no means discarded. A study of the closely graded lessons reveals that 52.7 per cent of the material was biblical, 31.1 per cent quasi-biblical, and 16.2 per cent drawn from history, biography, nature, and literature. There was a shift in emphasis, however. The Bible was not to be used for its own sake, primarily, but to meet the needs and problems of the age level where it was used.

In present-day curriculums the emphasis has shifted largely from the subject matter to the pupil. Only that material is chosen which is calculated to enrich the pupil's experience and give it Christian quality. Among all types of subject matter, however, the Bible is regarded as pre-eminent. The pupil is at the center, and that biblical material is chosen which is thought to assist the pupil in his growing experience. The newest curric-

[1] See also Chapter 8, "Curriculum Patterns for the Church School."

ulums appearing are making even larger and more definite use of the Bible. The lessons draw upon the Scriptures, biography, travel, nature stories, hero stories, and any other type of material that will enrich the pupil's experience, but the Bible is at the very heart of the curriculum.

Why does the Bible have this commanding place in the thinking of Christian people? It grows out of the fact that it is our religious classic par excellence. It contains the life and teachings of Jesus of Nazareth, who gave birth to the Christian religion. All of our Christian virtues and standards are either implicit or explicit in the teachings of Jesus. The Bible contains the record of the founding and growth of Christianity from the death and resurrection of Jesus to the culmination in the organization of churches in all the vital centers of the Roman Empire. It contains the missionary efforts and thought of Paul, of whom John Lord says: "After Jesus, St. Paul is the most colossal figure of the ages." It contains the history and religious literature of the Hebrew people, out of which Christianity came. It contains the Word of God to man. It is the historical record of God's self-revelation. Thus the Bible is more than a source of good morals; it contains a total religious view about life. The Old and New Testaments together constitute the source of our religious heritage.

The Scriptures constitute a dominant stream of influence in our Western culture, and without a knowledge of the Bible one will be forever ignorant of his cultural heritage. One cannot read English literature intelligently, all the way from Chaucer to Browning, without a knowledge of the Scriptures. Shakespeare leans heavily upon the Bible, and in Browning's *The Ring and the Book* alone there are over six hundred allusions to the Scriptures. The Bible not only has inspired, but to a large degree has set, the standard of excellence in much of our literature. The translation of the Bible into German, for example, fixed the standard form and idiom of the German language and literature from Martin Luther until the present. In no other field of literary effort, perhaps, have the Scriptures been more often drawn upon for illustration than in public address. The orations of Edmund Burke, Abraham Lincoln, John Bright, and William Lloyd Garrison bear witness to this fact. One might well ask, Why should our young people be introduced to the orations of Burke and Webster and be ignorant of the great and noble themes of Isaiah?

The greatest art of the Western world is based largely upon biblical themes. The art of the Renaissance Period has never been excelled, and it is steeped in biblical lore. Some years ago the director of the Art Institute in Chicago said that certain pictures were always included in the great art anthologies of the world. Of the ten which he named, nine were inspired by the Bible.

The great music of the Western world issued from the wellsprings of the Old and New Testaments. *Creation*, by Haydn; *Elijah and St. Paul*, by

Mendelssohn; *The Messiah* and seventeen other oratorios, by Handel; *The Apostles* and *The Kingdom*, by Sir Edward Elgar; *St. Cecilia and St. Peter*, by Sir Julius Benedict; the oratorio *The Woman of Samaria*, by Sir William Bennett; the oratorios *The Prodigal Son* and *The Light of the World*, by Sir Arthur Sullivan; the chorales and hymns of Bach, Charles Wesley, and Isaac Watts; the *Hora Novissima*, by Horatio Parker; and the powerful and dramatic oratorio *Job* by Frederick S. Converse—strip these from our culture, and we should begin to realize the seriousness of our loss.

The Scriptures have exerted their influence also on the development of the drama. The miracle, mystery, and morality plays of the Middle Ages, for example, were wholly moral and religious.

The great architecture of our Western culture is to be found in the chapels and cathedrals of the Christian Church. We think at once of St. Peter's in Rome, the Milan Cathedral, Notre Dame of Paris, the cathedrals of Amiens, Rouen and Chartres, the Cologne Cathedral in Germany, the Salisbury and Lincoln cathedrals in England, and St. John the Divine in New York City, to name but a few. In the cathedrals of Europe and America also are to be found many of the great paintings of the world. On a wall in the refectory of Santa Maria in Milan, Leonardo da Vinci painted "The Last Supper," and Raphael's "Sistine Madonna" adorns the Sistine Chapel in Rome. Fifteenth-century art came to its climax in the Sistine Chapel frescoes of Michelangelo, among which are "Creation of Adam" and "Jeremiah." The painting "Ascension of Our Lord," by the American painter John La Farge, occupies the central panel in the Church of the Ascension in New York City. And to describe the reproduction of biblical scenes and characters in the stained glass of the cathedrals of Europe and America would take a volume.

There can be no doubt that the Bible has been the most potent influence in the great art, literature, music, and architecture of the Western world. The skillful teacher will seek out the art materials best adapted to his pupils and will introduce the great religious music to them in worship, in periods of appreciation, and, best of all, by actual participation in religious oratorios and cantatas.

But most important of all, perhaps, when put to work in human living, the Bible is the most vital book in existence in meeting the needs of bewildered men and women today. Where is the man who at some time has not said, "Does the universe care whether or not I make a go of it?" The Bible declares with certainty that the universe is not a runaway train with the engineer dead at the throttle but is guided by a Great Intelligence interested in the men and women whom he has created. People are on the planet, not to kill and destroy one another, but to live together in a spirit of co-operation and good will. The ways by which men get on together are more than mere mores; they are a part of the very structure of the universe itself. The Bible says, in effect, that men and women can master life and overcome their difficulties through the help of God. Human history is not a blind alley but a march, with God leading the column of progress. The present may be dark and disappointing; but the future is assured if men live their lives in the spirit of God, who guarantees by his own character that his purposes will not fail, and that his children consequently will yet have the abundant life.

The Bible, it is true, is not graded to the several age levels. This fact has its advantages and disadvantages. If the book had been handed down in graded form, it would be lacking in flexibility, and its rigidity would be unfortunate for pupils more advanced or retarded from the norm, as the case might be. As it is, the teacher and the lesson writers are free to utilize the Bible according to the comprehension of the pupils in a given area or on a certain cultural level.

Little children need a sense of care and protection. There is much in the Gospels to indicate the care of the Heavenly Father for his children, such as the sending of the rain and the sunshine, and the care of the birds of heaven and the lilies of the field (Matt. 6). Children love nature, and the Bible is filled with the wonders of nature. They might not be able to grasp the Hebrew concept of nature as the brother of man, so to speak, but they can understand the placing of the rainbow in the sky as a sign of God's thoughtfulness and protection. The twenty-third psalm is a succession of pictures setting forth the loving care and protection of God and can be applied to all ages.

Juniors are captivated by stories that contain qualities of heroism and courage. They need to learn to be truthful, dependable, helpful, and appreciative. In the eighteenth chapter of Second Chronicles there is a story of the prophet Micaiah, who declared he would tell the truth no matter what the consequences. Gideon and his three hundred men are a symbol of courage and faithfulness. There is magnificent courage in the words of Caleb and Joshua as they challenged the fainthearted spies and called for an immediate advance into the Promised Land (Num. 12:17–14:10). What junior would not thrill to the courage of Commander Joshua as he takes his place at the head of the people and says: "Choose you this day whom ye will serve; . . . but as for me and my house, we will serve the Lord" (Josh. 24:15)? It would not be hard to teach appreciation from an incident in the life of David: When David realized that three men had risked their lives to satisfy his desire for a drink of water from the ancestral well at Bethlehem, he was so appreciative of their courage and devotion that he denied himself and poured out the water as an offering to Jehovah (II Sam. 23:13-17). There is a lesson on the spirit of dependability and helpfulness in the story of Joseph, who journeyed to Dothan to carry provisions to his brothers, who were not worthy of him (Gen. 27:12-17).

Life in the adolescent years becomes more complex. Conscience becomes more keen, and standards of right and wrong emerge with a new sharpness. There is also the quickening of the social consciousness. Racial discrimination is detestable, as the adolescent thinks of a man as a man "for a' that, and a' that." And the adolescent is peculiarly susceptible to the appeal of great and noble causes. What adolescent, in the hands of a skillful teacher, can possibly miss the appeal that Jesus makes as he is captured by a great cause which he calls the kingdom of God, for which he lives and finally dies? The adolescent mind is hospitable to the idea of equality of opportunity so implicit in the Sermon on the Mount, which furthermore presents a program of action big enough to command of these young people their best and their all. The adolescent's standard of right and wrong will be quickened by a study of those scriptural characters who refused to sell out for a price. Elisha, for example, could have made a handsome profit out of the cure that came to Naaman the Syrian had he been willing to yield to a spirit of avarice (II Kings 5:14-27). A beautiful and high loyalty is to be found in the character of Ruth. The love of Jonathan for David is a classic of devotion and understanding (I Sam. 19:1-7). An astonishing spirit of magnanimity characterizes Ornan as he sells his threshing floor to David (I Chron. 21:15-30). The awakened social consciousness of the adolescent will be stirred by a study of the book of Amos. All of the eighth-century prophets, in fact, take their stand on the side of social justice. The adolescent will read with approval the story of Philip as he goes up into the Ethiopian's chariot and shares with him the mysteries of the kingdom of God (Acts 8:27-35).

The development of a life philosophy is the business especially of the adolescent years and early adulthood. The Scriptures teem with helpful materials. If life is worth the living, there must be a feeling that it has real significance. The Bible has as its thesis from beginning to end that this is God's world because he made it and he placed his children here to live a good life. The good life is possible only as we tie in with some great cause that has cosmic significance. The prophets of the Old Testament and the Prophet of Nazareth in the New had given themselves to a cause which demanded their all. In the building of a life philosophy we need a sense of responsibility for others. Paul experiences it in the description of meat offered to idols (I Cor. 8:13). To live the good life we need to live above fear. Let him who is afraid refer again and again to the quality of courage in the lives of Joshua and Caleb as they rallied a discouraged people to the Lord of hosts (Num. 14:8-9). Continents may change and political systems have their day, but if we make a go of life we need to lay hold on the great stabilities which abide. We need to believe with Paul: "But now abideth faith, hope, love, these three; and the greatest of these is love" (I Cor. 13:13, A.S.V.). And, "finally, brethren, whatsoever things are true, whatsoever things are honest, whatsoever things are just, whatsoever things are pure, whatsoever things are lovely, whatsoever things are of good report; if there be any virtue, and if there be any praise, think on these things" (Phil. 4:8.). Paul would fashion our life philosophy out of the great stabilities of life.

Only a few illustrations have been listed out of a countless number to show the relevancy of the Bible as a rich source of zestful and successful living. The intelligent teacher will grade his own Bible to the particular age level which he serves.

How shall we use the Bible in our teaching? Shall we approach it as a book set apart, sacrosanct, to be studied differently from any other book? We shall do well to use the historical method with which our pupils are familiar. They know the historical method as the fearless and careful study of a literature or a book to ascertain who wrote it, why it was written, to whom it was written, and what its message is. We get the best results when we apply the historical method to the Bible.

When we teach the Scriptures, let us assume that we live in a well-ordered world. It is true that there are miracles in the Bible. There are also miracles in our world. Miracles are things which are wonderful rather than things which have no explanation. Because the people of Bible times thought insanity to be the result of evil spirits, that did not make it so in fact. It is much better to tell our children that we live in a law-abiding world even though the Bible people did not always grasp this concept. For example, it was because Walter Rauschenbusch—an early American leader of the Christian social emphasis—approached the Scriptures as though we live in a law-abiding world that his children did not have a lot of things about the Bible to unlearn when they went to college.

We can afford to run the risk that our pupils may for a time think of the Bible as being just like any other book. The skillful teacher will let her pupils see that the plays of Shakespeare, by their own intrinsic worth, are greater than any other plays in the English language. The skillful teacher of art will lead his pupils to realize that the art of the Renaissance has been unequaled in our Western culture. The skillful geographer will help his pupils to understand that mountains are not the same, and that no mountain reaches the height, and in some respects the grandeur, of the Himalayan range. In the same way the skillful Bible teacher will study the Bible with his pupils as they do any other book; but acquaintance, time, and experience will bear home the truth that in the field of religious experience the Bible stands without a peer. Like Mount Everest of the Himalayas, it towers over all the others because of its intrinsic beauty, power, and majesty.

It must be apparent, therefore, that it is imperative that teachers of the Bible be so familiar with the content of the Scriptures—both Old and New—

that they can call to mind the character, illustration, or story that is most apt to challenge, stimulate, and motivate the pupil when the iron is hot.

RELIGIOUS BIOGRAPHY

Biography makes a strong appeal to youth. Fortunately for our purposes, we have a vast lore of religious biographical material.

When Jesus reawakened the consciousness of his disciples they began their penetration into the Roman Empire, in spite of the sword, fire, and wild beasts, to make converts to the Christian faith. Their deeds live after them. The intrepid spirits who carried the good news to the Teutons of the Black Forest, to the Hibernians of the Island Kingdom, and to the Vikings of Scandinavia, left their records in legend, story, and history. Missionaries have braved high mountains, dangerous jungles, and cholera-infested areas of the earth to bring the gospel to less fortunate people. Their heroism and Christian devotion stiffen our courage. Ministers of the gospel followed the restless pioneer as he journeyed farther and farther to new lands and richer opportunities, and their life stories are interwoven with the saga of the advancing frontier. Others have gone to the poor and ignorant of great cities and have gathered the children from the streets for religious instruction and the young people and their parents into settlement houses; they have labored indefatigably for playgrounds, better housing, and recreational facilities. They all join hands across the years and from many lands, and their efforts combine to make a story to tell to the nations.

This treasury of biography, like the Bible, is not graded to the several age levels. Biography, however, has a kind of universal appeal, and each age level has a way of appropriating that which appeals most to it. This is no argument, however, for any lessening in our efforts for the most meticulous selection wherever possible. The skillful teacher will select out of the several life stories the traits of character, the qualities of mind and heart, the scenes and incidents, which will most enrich and motivate the lives of the pupils of each age group.

SUGGESTIONS FOR FURTHER STUDY

1. Select an age group, such as primary or junior, and choose from Genesis, First and Second Samuel, and the Gospel of Mark the biblical stories and incidents best suited to their needs.

2. Study Shakespeare's *Richard II* or *Hamlet*, and note his allusions to the Bible.

3. Select the public addresses of Edmund Burke, James A. Garfield, John Hay, Theodore Roosevelt, or Abraham Lincoln and note the references to the Bible.

4. Study the Negro spirituals with reference to their themes and sources.

5. What picture materials are available and useful for teaching purposes? Be selective and specific.

6. Select an age group and choose a character from biography, noting qualities or incidents best suited for purposes of teaching.

7. Select one or more of the religious classics and suggest how it may be used to meet the needs of a particular age group.

BIBLIOGRAPHY

BIOGRAPHY

For the use of the teacher some sources of material are recommended here. The list is by no means complete. Many of the books suggested doubtless are out of print and are available only in libraries. It is quite possible that many good collections have escaped attention altogether. One-volume biographies of individual men and women are so numerous that, for the most part, no attempt has been made to include them, but this has been kept to collections of biographical material only.

Adams, John Coleman. *Christian Types of Heroism*. Boston: Universalist Publishing House, 1891. A study of heroic spirits—martyrs, hermits, monks, reformers, missionaries, philanthropists, and statesmen.

Axling, William. *Kagawa*. New York: Harper & Brothers, 1932. A moving story that reveals the mind and heart of this great Oriental Christian.

Banks, Louis A. *Heroic Personalities*. New York: Eaton & Mains, 1898. Men and women who had, or who developed, "what it takes" to emerge successful and of great service in their fields of endeavor. Suitable for juniors and early adolescents.

Begbie, Harold. *Painted Windows*. New York: G. P. Putnam's Sons, 1922. Studies of some of the greatest religious personalities who have reflected the power of Jesus in human lives.

Carpenter, William B. *The Prophets of Christendom*. London: Hodder & Stoughton, 1884. A study of the lives, teachings, trials, and persecutions of such men as Augustine, Jerome, Martin Luther, and Jeremy Taylor.

Cheney, Sheldon. *Men Who Have Walked with God*. New York: Alfred A. Knopf, 1945. A study of mysticism through the centuries as found in the biographies of representative seers and saints.

"Creative Personalities Series." P. Henry Lotz, ed., Vols. I, II, III, V, VI. Mabel H. Erdman, ed., Vol. IV. New York: Association Press.

Answering Distant Calls. Vol. IV, 1942. A study of some of the persons whose courage, fortitude, and devotion carried the Christian faith to the far-flung areas of the world.

Distinguished American Jews. Vol. VI, 1945. A portrayal of some American Jews prominent in medicine, statecraft, music, writing, and so forth.

Founders of Christian Movements. Vol. III, 1941. A study of fifteen men who, through their convictions, have founded Christian movements which shape our lives and thought today.

Rising Above Color. Vol. V, 1943. A study of thirteen prominent Negroes and their notable achievements.

Vocations and Professions. Vol. I, 1940. A study of such men of achievement as Luther Burbank, Charles and William Mayo, Jacob Riis, David Livingstone, and Thomas A. Edison.

Women Leaders. Vol. II, 1940. Stories of women of contemporary and recent times whose lives have changed human history.

Hagedorn, Hermann. *Prophet in the Wilderness.* New York: The Macmillan Company, 1947. A story of Albert Schweitzer's richly varied and exciting life.

Howard, Harry C. *Princes of the Christian Pulpit and Pastorate.* 2 vols. Nashville: The Cokesbury Press, 1927. The "princes" studied range all the way from those of the twelfth century to preachers of the more immediate past.

Jeffs, Ernest H. *Princes of the Modern Pulpit in England.* Nashville: The Cokesbury Press, 1931. A study of twenty of the most influential British preachers of the present and the immediate past.

Jones, E. Stanley. *Mahatma Gandhi.* New York and Nashville: Abingdon-Cokesbury Press, 1948. An interpretation of a great Indian by a man who believed in him and loved him in spite of fundamental differences.

Kavanagh, Julia. *Women of Christianity.* New York: D. Appleton Century and Company, 1852. An encyclopedic study of women around the world who were essentially simple and true.

Kepler, Thomas S. "The Centuries Speak to the Hours," *Christian Advocate,* Nov., 1948-Feb., 1949. A study of significant characters throughout the span of history who have influenced our thinking and living.

Mead, Frank S. *The March of Eleven Men.* New York. The Bobbs-Merrill Company, 1932. A story of the spread of Christianity in the Greco-Roman world by the Disciples of Jesus. This book is partly historical and partly biographical.

Mudge, James. *The Saintly Calling.* Cincinnati: Jennings & Graham. New York: Eaton & Mains, 1905. A study of a number of men whose inspiration may guide us to the deeper things of life and God.

Nigg, Walter. *Great Saints.* Hinsdale, Illinois: Henry Regnery Co., 1948. A study of the innermost motives of nine great saints.

Peabody, Francis G. *Reminiscences of Present-Day Saints.* New York: Houghton Mifflin Company, 1927. Teachers, preachers, men of affairs, and others known to the author.

Powell, Lyman P. *Heavenly Heretics.* New York: G. P. Putnam's Sons, 1909. A study of five representative preachers who have profoundly influenced the religious life of their contemporaries.

Wallace, Dillon. *The Story of Grenfell of the Labrador.* New York: Fleming H. Revell, 1922. Some of the marvelous achievements of Grenfell as witnessed by the author himself.

RELIGIOUS CLASSICS

Any movement which is as well established and virile as the Christian religion can be expected to produce its classics. What is a classic? The answer, of course, depends upon whether the book endures or not. In other words, a classic must meet the test of time. Probably no two people would choose identical lists, but the following books deserve to be considered as classics. The books selected in some instances cannot be said to have been inspired by the Christian religion, but the qualities of mind and heart and the lessons drawn or suggested are distinctly Christian.

The great religious classics are not particularly valuable as teaching material for children. They have their greatest value for adolescents, young people, and adults.

Boethius. *The Consolations of Philosophy*. Boethius, a faithful subject of King Theodoric, is placed in prison and finally is put to death. In his contemplation of the question "Why does a good man suffer?" Boethius finds consolation in philosophy and eventually arrives at a satisfactory belief in the existence of Providence.

Browning, Robert. *The Ring and the Book*. One of the greatest poems in the English language. Browning here grapples with the complex elements in human nature. A powerful testimony to the ultimate triumph of the good.

Bunyan, John. *The Pilgrim's Progress*. This remarkable story is a delineation of the Christian's course with its difficulties, temptations, perils, conflicts, and consolations. Lessons for all age groups may be drawn from this book.

Confessions of St. Augustine. An autobiographical account of the temptations and struggles of a titanic soul finally redeemed by the grace of God.

Dante, Alighieri. *The Divine Comedy*. The autobiographical description of the redeeming power and influence of love as an instrument of divine grace.

Dostoevsky, Feodor. *Crime and Punishment*. That "crime does not pay," even though not detected, is one of the lessons of this powerful psychological study, but a greater one is the regenerating influence of deep human love.

Eliot, George. *Adam Bede*. A profoundly religious study of the heroism in common men and women and the strength and beauty of noble character wherever it is found.

Herman, Nicolas (Brother Lawrence). *The Practice of the Presence of God*. The ecstatic experiences of the divine Presence which Brother Lawrence had as he toiled in his kitchen for forty years. Valuable lessons for contemporary living.

Kempis, Thomas à. *Imitation of Christ*. Meditations of rare charm that draw us to Christ as our great leader and Lord.

Law, William. *A Serious Call*. This book had a profound influence on the Evangelical Revival of the eighteenth century and was one of the books which deeply influenced John Wesley while a student in Oxford University, giving him a deepened purpose and a new seriousness in life.

Luccock, Halford, and Brentano, Frances, eds. *The Questing Spirit*. New York: Coward-McCann, Inc., 1947. A volume of encyclopedic proportions containing the earnest outpouring of the yearnings and deepest thoughts of men and women around the world. A rich mine of thoughtful and devotional literature.

Luther, Martin. *On Christian Living*. A bold declaration of Christian faith, containing the whole of Christian living in brief form, with faith as the keystone of the arch.

Milton, John. *Paradise Lost*. In this great epic we have profound delineations of character as well as great poetry. It describes the causes and consequences of the Fall of man.

Rauschenbusch, Walter. *Prayers of the Social Awakening*. Boston: Pilgrim Press, 1925. Devout prayers, breathing a deep social passion.

Tolstoy, Lyof. *Resurrection*. A moving story of a wealthy Russian who, through his efforts to win and marry an exiled girl whom he has wronged, finds the higher life for himself and a new and constructive outlook on society.

Woolman, John. *Journal*. The experiences of a devout man, down to earth, sincere, contemporary, and American.

Truly, our religious heritage is like a fountain from which issue the living waters for the healing of the nations, giving inspiration and power to countless men and women everywhere who bear the heat and burden of the present hour.

FOR FURTHER READING

Bower, William Clayton. *The Living Bible*. New York: Harper & Brothers, 1936.

Coutts, John W. *How to Use the Bible*. Nashville: Cokesbury Press, 1936.

Crook, Margaret B., ed. *The Bible and Its Literary Associations*. New York: The Abingdon Press, 1937.

Culler, Arthur J. *Creative Religious Literature*. New York: The Macmillan Company, 1930.

Fosdick, Harry Emerson. *The Modern Use of the Bible*. New York: The Macmillan Company, 1924.

Gardner, Helen. *Art Through the Ages*. New York: Harcourt, Brace & Company, 1926.

Lankard, Frank Glenn. *The Bible Speaks to Our Generation*. New York: Oxford University Press, 1941.

McNeill, John T. *Books of Faith and Power*. New York: Harper & Brothers, 1947.

Martin, Hugh. *Great Christian Books*. Philadelphia: Westminster Press, 1946.

Smither, Ethel L. *The Use of the Bible with Children*. New York: The Abingdon Press, 1937.

Chapter 10

WORSHIP IN RELIGIOUS EDUCATION

MARIE COLE POWELL

FROM WHATEVER STANDPOINT we view it, worship is one of the most important aspects of religious education. In Evelyn Underhill's words, "Worship is the response of man to the Eternal." Whether we think of God as being a cosmic force, that Power in the universe other than and greater than ourselves, whether God is to us an "integrating process," [1] the sum total of all that is good, or whether we think of him as having a more distinctly personal character, the need to feel ourselves one with him is a fundamental need of the human spirit.

When the religious educator begins to think in terms of a program of worship for any group, he knows that in that group he will have some who do not recognize that they have this need; some, perhaps, have never experienced satisfaction through worship and therefore do not know what they are missing of fullness of life; others think of religion as a way of living or a way of thinking, but only dimly, if at all, apprehend its other aspect—a way of fellowship with God.

It is one of the chief functions of any program of religious education to help old and young to recognize their need for the experience of worship, to discover satisfaction through participation in this experience, and to grow in the ability to worship on higher and higher levels of communion with God.

THE PURPOSES OF WORSHIP

Although the purposes of worship have been stated by a number of writers, let us think for a moment of some of the most important functions of worship in the life of an individual or a group. It is the function of worship, first of all, to make God seem real and near, a living Power with whom the worshiper may have a continuing fellowship. Edwin Goldsworthy entitles one chapter in his book[2] "At Home with God." It is this feeling of at-homeness with God which any program of worship seeks to cultivate.

It is the purpose of worship, furthermore, to provide an opportunity for

[1] Henry N. Wieman, *Methods of Private Religious Living* (New York: The Macmillan Co., 1929), pp. 46-47.

[2] *Plain Thoughts on Worship.*

126

the sense of God's presence in all of life to grow and develop, and to provide opportunities for the worshiper to express this growing feeling of fellowship when alone and with groups of other worshipers.

It is the function of worship to stir feelings of wonder, appreciation, and gratitude in the presence of a spiritual universe, and to give significance to all of life.

But worship should also challenge and inspire; it should provide insights into the nature of religious living and release spiritual energies to enable the worshiper to meet the ethical demands of everyday life. These challenges should, through worship, extend his social sympathies until as a child of God he thinks and feels in terms of the "kingdom of God."

Whether all of these functions are primary ones in worship, or whether its one supreme objective is awareness of God and all these other outcomes are the results of this awareness, has been discussed by writers of differing schools of thought. But the religious educator can test the reality of the worship experiences through which he guides groups of worshipers by the presence of at least some of these outcomes.

While we are considering the purposes of worship, we should caution ourselves about the temptation to exploit the experience of worship for other ends. It is very easy to fall into the habit of utilizing a service of worship to give information. With children it may be necessary to supply a needed bit of information which will make their worship more vital, but the primary purpose of a service of worship is not to instruct the group about missionary work in China or refugee orphans in Europe. The line between the legitimate use in worship of informational material which will expand horizons of thought and feeling, and which will stir the desire to worship God, and the use of information for its own sake is a very thin one. The sensitive leader will know whether the service has brought the child nearer to God.

There is a thin line of distinction, too, between the use of memorized passages of Scripture to express feelings of worship which are genuine and the exploitation of the service for the purpose of providing drill and practice in memorization.

Even in the field of ethical values it is easy for a leader of worship to utilize the service for the purpose of pointing out a wrong done or to reform Christian character. Worship that is vital will often make us aware that we are children of God and can live like God; it can reveal an ideal of ethical living against which our own failure stands out and thus can arouse in us true repentance. It is one thing to meet the everyday needs of boys and girls through worship; it is quite another to use a service of worship to preach at them or to bring home a sense of guilt for wrongdoing.

The Leader and the Program of Worship

If worship is to be an increasingly vital experience, the religious educator must be aware of certain fundamental needs of boys and girls, young people and adults. He must know something of the present-day trends in worship and the guidance of worship. And he must think of the worship program in the church as a total program. Let us see what each of these phases of worship guidance might include.

The leader of worship is primarily concerned that the worshipers shall be present at a service not in body only, that they shall not merely go through the forms of worship, but that the experience shall be so real and vital to them that they will leave the service with some changed attitudes and desires, to walk in "newness of life." To secure such reality, what are some of the fundamental needs which the religious educator should try to meet?

First of all, there is the need that the experience of worship shall begin at an early age. Even though some writers maintain that the act of worship is an adult experience, they would not deny that early influences are important. Other writers caution us not to urge a little child to "say prayers" before he has experienced those things for which his prayer words are symbols. It would be well for all parents and teachers of young children to ponder this thought and to study its possible significance in building worship attitudes.

Whether we would postpone the use of the word "God" until such time as the child has built up experiences that will give it meaning, or whether we feel that somehow or other the name of God should be associated with his growing experiences all along the way, the fact remains that the promise of fullness of life can and should be made to children as well as to adults. The fulfillment of this promise involves providing the little child with experiences such as wonder at the beauty and law of the universe in which he lives, knowing that he is loved and that he too can love others, seeing goodness at work in the people around him, working creatively to make his world of home and neighborhood a happy place for all to live in. It is from experiences like these that an understanding of God comes, and in such experiences are the springs of worship.

Some religious educators feel that such experiences as the above are the only meaningful ones for the preschool child.[3] Others say that since the little child shares with his father and mother and older brothers and sisters many experiences—even those of play—which he does not yet fully understand, so he should not be denied the richness of sharing in family worship and of offering his prayers, just as Jimmy or Mary do. These educators

[3] Manwell and Fahs, *Consider the Children.* Verna Hills, "Introduction" to *Martin and Judy* (ed. Sophia Fahs; Boston: Beacon Press, 1944-45), Vol. I.

feel that merely sharing the act of worship with the adults that he loves will establish in the child a receptivity for further worship experiences. There are some educators who feel that you cannot begin too early to let a child share with his family the experience of church worship. But all of these thinkers agree on the basic fundamental need of beginning with some type of worship experience when the child is little.

Another fundamental need is that the experience of worship shall at every age level be accompanied with a feeling of satisfaction and enjoyment. Enjoyment is an important factor in making worship vital. The laws of learning apply here as well as in other areas of habit formation.

The worshiper must feel relaxed and therefore open to suggestion. This is one reason why *beauty of environment* is desirable. It partly accounts for the fact that so many young people say that they have had their most stirring worship experiences at sunset meetings on a hillside or beside a lake. Children respond quickly to an environment in which flowers, autumn leaves, or beautiful pictures quicken the aesthetic feelings.

But beauty is not the only source of satisfaction. It is a satisfying experience in worship to *recall past experiences* which hold a cherished place in our memories and also to find that our present-day living is given a new meaning.

The worshiper feels a warm glow when the content of worship, the words of hymns, Scripture, and prose selections, are *easily comprehended.* Many services of worship are considered "dull" by young people and induce only inattention from children because the materials are either too difficult for their comprehension or too childish for their maturing needs.

The worshiper is also warmed if these materials *present challenges* or lead him on to goals he has not hitherto glimpsed so clearly. To interpret the past, to relate it to the present, and to endow the future with possibilities of creative living, and to do this in terms of the everyday experiences of a certain age group—this is to ensure happiness and satisfaction in the act of worship.

This suggests another need which the religious educator should plan to meet. Perhaps the greatest satisfaction a worshiper can have is the realization that a service of worship seems to be an *answer to his own spiritual needs.* Young people and adults are aware of many of their own needs; children seldom are, though their wants and problems are very real to them. But in either case the leader of worship must be sensitive to the personal longings, frustrations, or causes for thanksgiving which are most likely to be absorbing the attention of the worshiping group—as a group and as individuals.

This sensitivity to group and individual needs is greatly deepened by an understanding of the psychological laws of growth and the normal psychological reactions of the age group for which worship is being planned. A sound psychology of childhood, of youth, and of adulthood provides part of the groundwork for every leader of worship.

Readiness for worship helps to bring satisfaction also. How to secure such readiness is a vast subject in itself and involves the total program of religious education. Children and young people do not come from the absorbing activities of their homes, schools, and playgrounds to a service of worship able to make a quick transition from their active lives to communion with God. This requires preparation. The prelude of music inducing a quiet mood, the opening sentences or call to worship by the leader, revealing some common interest around which the service is to be built—these will help to bring about a certain readiness for worship.

If the curriculum of religious education is vitally interesting to the group, and if the worship experience is an inevitable consummation of the entire curriculum activity, then the transition from discussion and activity to worship is natural, and worship illuminates what the group has been doing and thinking. Let us imagine a group of junior-high-school students who have been studying about "Men and Women Who Knew Jesus." At each of their class sessions they have projected on the screen slides revealing these men and women as the artists have painted them. The students themselves have tried their hands at making some slides illustrating events in the lives of these early followers of Jesus. As a climax to all their study and activity they plan a service of worship on the theme "They Knew Jesus." To this service they invite other groups in the church school; they show the best of their slides; they read materials which they have written about each of the men and women who knew Jesus. Such a service of worship will be full of meaning for these young people because it has grown out of their own thinking and feeling and is closely related to their total curriculum experience.

With children, informal conversation in which they share as leaders guide them to a worshipful mood will often lead naturally into the worship experience. Children need plenty of opportunity to discover the meanings of hymns and scripture, to understand the implications of a picture or a story. This is one reason why the informal pattern of worship lends itself to vitality in worship by children.

Recent Trends in the Guidance of Worship

The religious educator should be familiar with the historical trends in worship and also with more recent trends. The historical background for an understanding of worship has been ably described in books upon that subject.[4] Let us consider briefly some recent developments.

[4] For instance, William D. Maxwell, *An Outline of Christian Worship* (New York: Oxford University Press, 1936).

Worship for Children. With growing understanding of the educational needs of children, religious educators have re-examined the historic worship patterns, trying to discover in what kinds of environments and in what situations children seem to worship most genuinely.

There has been a growing conviction that young children need an immediacy of expression of their worship feelings when these arise spontaneously, rather than being asked to postpone such expression until some set period of worship. So, many teachers of little children, when something in the child's experience seems to have brought God near, are ready to pause in the midst of a story or an activity for a moment of quiet or joyful communion with God. Many curriculum units for young children are so planned that worship may come at the beginning of the session, at the end, or in the middle. Older boys and girls, too, often respond with quickened worship feelings to such natural and spontaneous worship situations.

There is a trend among some leaders of worship for children never to plan for a definite period for the service of worship but to so guide the group's activities and discussions that there may arise naturally a felt need for worship. They believe that to gather a group together and to say "Let us worship" may result in making worship a mere form. They would prefer to have a Sunday-morning session without any worship if no felt need for it arises.

To this point of view others say, "It is a good thing to set aside certain times which we recognize as quiet times, times when we seek God in worship." Much is being written today urging adults to set aside definite periods every day for quiet thinking and personal devotions. Why not start with the boys and girls? In a period where every effort is made to stimulate the religious feelings, to motivate quiet thinking about the things that concern ourselves and God, and to create the assurance that God is with us and in us, one can be about as sure of a genuine worship response as if we relied only upon the sudden emergence of a felt need for this in the midst of other curriculum activities. It is seldom a case of "either-or" but rather of "both-and." Children and young people and adults need to experience the sudden turning to God with life's problems. They also need the quiet habitual practice of his presence when life as a whole is reviewed and revealed with new meanings.

There has been a growing trend, also, to follow a less formal pattern for worship with children than with adults. We must not mistake an informal worship service for an unplanned service. Children need the insights and illuminations which come through informal conversation, through the sharing of ideas with each other and with the leader, and through the consequent feeling of togetherness. Worship for children can include such informal elements and yet follow a basic form which lets the worshipers start with a quiet feeling of God's nearness; follow this by expressions of gratitude and praise in song and prayer; catch up new visions of goodness through story, scripture, and picture appreciation; and climax in a feeling of being a child of God and wanting to live as God's child. This, very simply stated, is the basic form or pattern for all worship. An informal, friendly atmosphere clothes the form with life.

Worship for Young People. The trends in worship for young people, and even for adults, in recent years reveal a greater fluidity of treatment. We may find an emphasis upon a return to some of the more historic patterns of corporate worship, but that return is likely to be characterized by a new adaptation to the needs of twentieth-century worshipers. In a Methodist church, for instance, John Wesley's order of worship may be revived, but with a few significant differences. The creed may be one chosen to meet the religious thinking of young people and adults living in today's world.

One of the very evident trends is toward finding ways of incorporating the young people into the adult fellowship of worship. This outcome may be sought for in various ways. One way is by enriching the worship in young people's groups so that they are prepared for participation in a more mature worship experience. In some churches the young people meet in church-school classes for study, discussion, and activity, but unite with the adult congregation in the Sunday-morning service of worship.

Another trend is that toward broadening the types of worship experiences for young people. From the rather haphazard "opening services" provided in church schools some years ago, the trend has swung to a dignified and formal worship service for all ages. This is a much-needed emphasis. But there are values also in the less formal type of worship. We should not limit the inspiration of informal worship moments to children only. It is undoubtedly true that people of all ages need for their spiritual nourishment both types of worship. Young people around a campfire or a group of parents before an open fireplace will find a certain reality in such informal worship gatherings with their intimate suggestions of a group solidarity. Such informal experiences ought to make them feel their need of the more formal Sunday-morning service.

While corporate worship is important, we find an accompanying trend to emphasize the need of every individual for moments of private worship. In youth magazines and at youth conferences, as well as in the curriculum materials for youth, suggestions are given for the enrichment of living through some pattern of personal devotions. Where once this need for a personal life of the spirit was left almost to chance, it is now definitely planned for as an integral aspect of the total program of worship.

Another plainly discernible trend is that of making all worship materials more meaningful and vital. Books of source materials in the field of worship have increased by the dozens in recent years, many of these prepared distinctly for young people's groups. Magazines have spent hours of research in discovering materials that are vitally related to the interests and the problems of modern youth. New hymnals have been edited and published with young people distinctly in mind.

There is noticeable the use of a great variety of worship materials. Not Bible selections alone, but great poetry and prose which can lift the human spirit on the wings of prayer and which have been written out of the needs and aspirations of more recent centuries. Lowell wrote:

> God is not dumb, that He should speak no more;
>
> . . . .
>
> Slowly the Bible of the race is writ,
>   And not on paper leaves nor leaves of stone;
> Each age, each kindred, adds a verse to it.[5]

A Lenten service takes on new significance when to the story of the centurion at the foot of the cross are added selections from John Masefield's *The Trial of Jesus*.[6]

When the Bible is used in worship there is a trend to discover ways in which to make it more meaningful. In adult services it is increasingly noticeable that the minister introduces the scripture reading by giving the setting for it, or by a few words of explanation in the printed order of service. In young people's services, also, there have been dramatic ways of presenting the biblical passages.

Both drama and the pictorial arts offer a rich opportunity for stimulating attitudes of worship and presenting the central theme of a service of worship. Many churches are continually adding to their art collection so that both children and young people can have access to reproductions of the best paintings on religious themes.

There is a trend toward experimentation with new forms and materials of worship. The use of choric speaking is only one illustration of this experimental trend. A college choir as well as a group of junior-high students enriched their services of worship by the choric recitation of some of the psalms and the sayings of Jesus. As an illustration of rather radical experimentation suggestions have been made for a service of worship in which voices here and there in the midst of the worshiping group cry out with prophetic utterance some of the social wrongs in modern society, while at intervals the worshipers sing together stanzas of the hymn "Once to Every

[5] From "God Is Not Dumb."
[6] New York: The Macmillan Co., 1925.

Man and Nation." These are only a few illustrations of the ways in which new materials and forms are being introduced into worship.

This last trend suggests broader movement toward greater creativity in the whole approach to worship. In the early days art belonged to the people and was their natural expression. The medieval cathedral became, through its carvings in wood and stone, its frescoes and its stained glass windows, the pictorial Bible of the people. There was a time in the history of religion when the people participated as actively in worship as did the priest. It is an encouraging sign that today the emphasis seems to be upon participation in the creative act of worship.

Young people meet in small groups to study the principles of worship and methods of planning and leading their own services. Young people's departments in the church have their worship committees or commissions which study the worship needs of their groups, search for appropriate materials to meet these needs, and attempt to develop the leadership of worship among their own group members.

The Environment of Worship

No discussion of worship should overlook the increasing interest in creating for each age group an environment in which genuine experiences of worship will be stimulated. Some churches have built small chapels for young people and even for children. Attempts have been made to discover in just what types of environment children worship best. Efforts are noted to provide not just one type of environment but a variety, so that in the change from a sunlit room with a homey atmosphere to the more formal churchlike setting, God may be felt to be near at all times.

Whether the church provides chapels especially built for worship, or whether the group of children or young people meet in a pleasant room, the worship center is planned as a focal point which suggests the presence of God to the worshiping group. This center may be an altar with a simple hanging behind it or a table on which a bowl of flowers is placed; a single beautiful picture may suggest the theme of worship, or for older groups a cross may symbolize the Christian faith. But whatever object of beauty the worship center holds, it suggests that

> Here is a quiet room!
> Pause for a little space.[7]

Planning the Program of Worship

A third concern for the religious educator is that the program of worship in any local church shall be an all-inclusive one—a whole program for

[7] Donald Cox, in *Youth at Worship.*

the whole church. The program of religious education can never be confined to children and young people only. Children who worship in the church school and return to worshipless families cannot bring to worship the same type of participation which comes from children who have enjoyed experiences of worship in the home.

One of the weakest points in religious education at present is the lack of sufficient guidance and appropriate materials for use in family worship. It is not easy to plan worship which will meet the needs of the businessman, the mother in the home, four-year-old Jimmy, Susan in grade five, Tom in high school, and perhaps Grandma. A curriculum of religious teaching and worship for the family is an alluring challenge to religious educators.[8]

What will a thorough program of religious education include by way of worship experiences and education for worship? First of all, there will be worship planned and led for age groups by leaders who understand the principles of worship building and guidance and the needs and abilities of each age division. This division into age groups means that worship can be planned to meet the specific interests of each age.

In the second place, the problem of guidance in worship will be thought of as being shared by department leaders and teachers; and teachers will be trained to discover the possibilities of guiding their classes into informal moments of worship. They will also discuss with the department leader and other teachers the purposes of worship and the special worship needs of the boys and girls in their classes.

In order that worship may be planned and guided so that it will bear the richest results in group and individual life, leaders of worship and teachers will be provided with opportunities to enroll in classes for the study and discussion of the principles and methods of worship.

Someone has remarked that this generation is hungry for great affirmations. People living today need to feel that the world of values is as real as the world opened to us by science. Boynton Merrill's story of the twelve-year-old boy whom he discovered sitting all alone in the church sanctuary early one Monday morning suggests what men, women, young people, and children ought to find through worship. The boy said to Dr. Merrill, "This is a beautiful church; it does something to you, doesn't it?"

"What does it do for you my boy?" asked Dr. Merrill. "I would like to know."

After a moment of silence the boy said, "Well, it makes you all quiet inside, and it makes you feel bigger than you are." In the days in which we are living there is great need that we shall feel "all quiet inside," and in how many overwhelming situations we need to "feel bigger than we are"!

Those who guide the programs of religious education, and especially

[8] See Fallaw, *The Modern Parent and the Teaching Church*, chap. viii.

those who are parents or teachers and leaders of worship, must themselves have entered into a fellowship with him in whom we live and move and have our being. On their own altars must the fires of worship first be kindled. Then will their program of worship be more than a plan, more than a set of objectives. The program will become a living way along which parents, teachers, and youth will walk together—a way of fellowship with the Eternal.

SUGGESTIONS FOR FURTHER STUDY

1. After further reading, expand the statement, "Worship is one of the most important aspects of religious education."

2. How do the laws governing the development of appreciation relate to worship?

3. Read carefully Coe and Hislop (see Bibliography). How do the points of view of these writers compare with the more traditional ideas about worship for the little child? What is your own point of view?

4. Choose at least three curriculum units in some recently published series and evaluate the suggestions for worship in these units.

5. Plan in detail a series of four services of worship for some age group in the church school. First describe the specific situation which is the background for the group, and then describe the group's specific problems and interests as you see them.

6. Plan a total program of worship for some specific church in which you are interested, including related units of study, any Sunday or weekday services, training for leaders of worship and for teachers.

BIBLIOGRAPHY

Chave, Ernest. *The Functional Approach to Religious Education.* Chicago: University of Chicago Press, 1947.

Coe, George A. *What Is Christian Education?* New York: Charles Scribner's Sons, 1929.

Fallaw, Wesner. *The Modern Parent and the Teaching Church.* New York: The Macmillan Company, 1946.

Goldsworthy, Edwin A. *Plain Thoughts on Worship.* Chicago: Willett, Clark & Company, 1936.

Hislop, D. H. *Our Heritage in Public Worship.* New York: Charles Scribner's Sons, 1935.

Lotz, Philip Henry, ed. *The Quest for God Through Worship.* St. Louis: Bethany Press, 1934.

Manwell, Elizabeth M., and Fahs, Sophia L. *Consider the Children.* Boston: Beacon Press, 1940.

Perkins, Jeannette. *Children's Worship in the Church School.* Harper & Brothers, 1939.

Powell, Marie C. *Boys and Girls at Worship.* New York: Harper & Brothers, 1943.

————. *Guiding the Experience of Worship.* New York and Nashville: Abingdon-Cokesbury Press, 1935.

Thoughts of God for Boys and Girls. The Connecticut Council of Churches. A quarterly booklet for worship in the home.

Vogt, Von Ogden. *Modern Worship.* New Haven: Yale University Press, 1927.

Chapter 11

THE CREATIVE ARTS IN RELIGIOUS EDUCATION

AMY GOODHUE LOOMIS

"I AM SIMPLY CALLING ATTENTION to the fact that fine art is the only teacher except torture," said Bernard Shaw. With this trenchant quotation, Herbert Read, the contemporary art critic, educator, and essayist, has chosen to introduce his book *Education Through Art*, which served to stimulate the thinking of teachers and art critics to the point of heated controversy verging on the violent. That Read selected such a provocative statement is appropriate to his subject, which contains in its title two very controversial words. For when "education" and "art" have been satisfactorily defined for all time, we may rightly become suspicious of their quality. But the statement is of interest to us as religious educators because it is suggestive of an entire change of attitude in recent years, which has marked not only the popular but particularly the professional, approach to and use of the fine arts in religious education. We are still in the midst of that change. And any comments made herein must be thought of as having merely temporary value.

As recently as 1931, when the volume of *Studies in Religious Education* was published, it was both necessary and proper for the writer of the section devoted to the arts in religion to spend a good deal of time "selling" the idea of their religious and educational importance. The intervening years have served to influence profoundly the curriculums of the church schools throughout the country, with the result that the church which does not make any effort to use music, art, or drama for the extension of its teaching program may be considered the exception. The wisdom of making appropriate use of *every* art form in the service of genuine religious education has been tested through the centuries and richly experienced in our twentieth century. But it is within the last fifteen or twenty years that the impact of a changed attitude toward the place of the fine arts in the curriculum of the church school has been most keenly felt. For instance, there has been a noticeable and fairly recent swing toward formal, carefully designed, reverent, and beautiful usage in worship. Junior choirs, youth choirs, speaking choirs, are becoming an accepted part of our worship experience, adding their fresh voices to the interpretation of scriptural and worthy musical

137

literature. And a form approaching ritual has crept into some of our most traditionally conservative denominational patterns.

That the tendency toward informal, conversational, deplorably "folksy" services of corporate worship has swung sharply toward borrowed or adapted liturgies, and that these borrowings and adaptations have not been uniformly successful, is, perhaps, beside the point. To impose meaningless litanies and elaborate written prayers with their accompanying ceremonial on a simple Protestant church service would seem injudicious to a degree. But it is a situation which has grown out of "hunger and thirst after righteousness" of beauty, and it is rapidly correcting itself as creative-art experience is improving the level of congregational taste.

This new interest has carried with it the obligation to train and equip the congregation with the means of appreciation of, and participation in, such revitalized experience. And in this very process of training, our pupils have helped us, as teachers, to discover whole new areas of religious education through creative-art experiences. The old egg and chicken dilemma confronts us; which came first, the psychic hunger of the congregation, too long deprived of legitimate nourishment, or the means of its religious and artistic satisfaction?

For it seems to be true that the more we deal with the methods of training necessary to the basic satisfactions of the human soul, the more frequently we discover new and challenging areas of exploration in religious education. Since last was written an inclusive volume of instruction for this highly specialized professional work, many leading colleges and universities have begun to use a whole new vocabulary of terms made popular by the grim needs of a postwar society. In somewhat frantic efforts to democratize a reluctant world, educators have fallen into the common use of such terms as "community," "fellowship," "group sensitivity," and "togetherness" with self-conscious insistence. But how graphic, how dramatic, the words are in their fresh import! How vividly they *symbolize* the desperate plight—and our Christian hope.

How it has all come about is too involved for further discussion here. But that the attitude has changed, and that the revival of religious art seems to be dawning, is cause for rejoicing and gratitude to those visionaries and honest craftsmen who have made the renewal possible.

It is the problem here to consider together and discover, if possible, *how* we may most effectively use the arts to deepen religious experience among our pupils and students.

MUSIC AS CREATIVE EXPERIENCE

"You feel that the fellow next to you is an important human being, and you like him, and you try desperately to understand how he feels about what he sings about, and pool your creative passions to make something bigger than either of you could make alone," said Robert Shaw. This selection was discovered on a page of the *Saturday Evening Post*, purchased from a pile of several dozen on the corner newsstand, a distinctly popular source! But it is a quotation that takes on real meaning when we note its author. For it is probably fair to consider Robert Shaw the outstanding example of social-religious art leadership in the year 1948.

This young American-born conductor of the Collegiate Chorale of New York has accomplished the almost incredible feat of gathering a group of music-loving people of many nations and races together every week to sing great music, to be prompt and regular in attendance, to work so hard that coats have to be removed, and to pay ten dollars a year for the privilege! And it is important to us that while Shaw has succeeded in unifying the basic interests of an interracial, international group in the chorale, while he has served the aims of social religion by developing other choral units in such therapeutic institutions as veterans' hospitals, while he has carried religion and music into industrial situations involving management and labor, he still has the wisdom and courage to say "*music* comes first." This insistence upon standard and ideal springs from a soundly religious motive. How often the young religious educator hears some such questionable piece of advice as, "You must begin where the people are." It is too often the experience of leaders that, having begun at the popular level, leadership is dragged down to that level. There is nothing in the lofty impulse of religion or great art to justify this approach. It is the prime obligation of leadership in the joint field of religion and art to assume that the people are ready for the best. History will justify this approach.

Nor is the discussion of this community project a digression. It is rather evidence that the entire problem of the use of music as a religious educational method is being explored far from the confines of the church-school classroom. Our entire concept of religion has been opened wide to such exploration, too, since our prewar theological clichés apparently could not keep us back from the brink of self-annihilation. People, hungry for emotional stability and moral security, are seeking the Good where they can find it nowadays. If their search does not always lead them to the church door, we had better consider our own failure rather than condemn their efforts to find satisfaction. That one of the very real satisfactions people have discovered is the joy of group participation in the making of music would seem to justify the earnest effort to include opportunities for such creative experience in religious educational programs. It is a wise board of religious education that moves in this direction.

But it should also be evident from the brief description of the successful enterprises above discussed—secular in method although we may consider them to be religious in impulse—that success has sprung largely from the quality of leadership. Where may we look for such leadership for religious groups in church situations? And what may we expect of such leaders?

It is a hopeful state of affairs that almost without exception our denominational boards have offered some sort of answer to these questions. Many seminaries and church schools now include adequate courses in church music in their curriculums. One has only to visit the nearest public library to be fairly overwhelmed by the rich opportunities for study which the rows of tempting catalogues of colleges and seminaries offer. In justice no specific schools can be recommended here. Too much depends upon the needs of the individual student. But the student who aspires to genuine educational leadership through the channels of religious music will never be content with a degree from a seminary—even a degree in his field of musical specialization. Too many avenues, exciting with promise, beckon to further research. His knowledge of methods and materials will require constant refreshment during the seasons and years of his service.

For this purpose several summer schools of choral leadership in the field of church music have been successfully established. One thinks of the summer schools of religious music at the Stambaugh Music Center, Northern Baptist Assembly, Green Lake, Wisconsin; the Institute for Church Choir Directors at Northwestern University School of Music; and the special institute held each summer at St. Olaf College, Northfield, Minnesota. And such standard institutions as the affiliated School of Sacred Music of Union Theological Seminary in New York City, and the Westminster Choir College at Princeton, New Jersey, offer full-term summer schools and credits toward degrees in this area of specialization.

POSSIBLE ACTIVITIES IN CHURCH MUSIC

In addition to the volunteer chorus choir which sings in the morning service of worship throughout the season in the average evangelical Protestant church, there are many weekday channels for musical activity offered to the imaginative board of religious education. Junior choir and teen-age choir groups, girls' choir and boys' choir—all demand highly specialized knowledge on the part of the conductor. Small instrumental ensembles, congregational hymn sings, interdenominational and interfaith hymn festivals and choir festivals, and joint programs of music and drama offer fascinating avenues of expansion.

Why should we assume, for instance, that congregational singing will arrive at a high degree of excellence and maintain its fine tradition unless specific training is given in the art of singing hymns? The old-fashioned singing school of the nineteenth-century village community moved in the right direction. Occasional weeknight hymn sings, including the discussion of the musical structure of well-loved hymns and their backgrounds, will flourish under competent leadership and promotion. And the experience will contribute richly to the resulting joy in worship.

In general, the above discussion of creative activity through religious music may be summed up by suggesting the following important points: (1) The attitude toward corporate participation in musical activity is basically religious in impulse. (2) Changing attitudes within the community have resulted in such extensive use of musical ensembles that the church must meet a lofty art and social standard in order successfully to satisfy the needs of its constituency. (3) Since art and religion seem to spring from common impulses, it is imperative that the director of music and the leader of any religious educational use of music be, first of all, an honest craftsman. The use of the quotation "*music* comes first" does not imperil the quality of religious leadership. Rather it reinforces and stimulates.

The Place of Creative Art Activity in Religious Education

The parables of Christ, of Lao-Tzu, of Tolstoy, or of any great moral teacher, are works of art, and are intended to operate (and this is the important point) on the perceptual and non-ratiocinative level of mental consciousness. . . .

It is the perception of rightness, and not the knowledge of it, which is possible to, and characteristic of, childhood.

The above words are again from the pen of Herbert Read and are quoted from his important volume *Education Through Art*. One of the greatest art educators of our contemporary society, Read might also be quoted for his pertinent comment in an interview in *Time* magazine: "The minds of men are controlled only by some form of moral discipline. . . . Discipline [is] the end, not the means of education."

The two quotations seem to suggest a slight difference in point of view. But in practice, any teacher would be quick to discover that this difference is one of age level. What is important to us in this discussion is the significance of that word "perceptual," and we will return to it after a brief digression.

The function of art in the service of religious education might well be the subject of an entire volume of essays. Its influence is hard to define. For instance, one seldom thinks of the decorations and design of a classroom as creative. But such art creates an atmosphere which usually becomes indelibly associated in the mind of youth with the words "church" and "religion." And since most church buildings are pretty bad architecturally and esthetically, those of us who can recall the days when the kindergarten and primary children were crowded into basement rooms breathe a sigh of relief at the space and clinical functionalism of more modern surroundings. To the degree that these surroundings are genuinely expressive of the purpose for which they are to be used, they are aptest to be beautiful. And just to the degree that they are adorned with the evidences of preconceived adult taste in ornament, they are dangerously apt to lose their meaning and functional beauty.

Too many church schools in our country are setting before the children each Sunday sentimentalized pictures of Jesus and the children—simply because of the story content of those pictures and their association with an accepted religious ideal—without any concern for the art quality of the work. And yet we have the word of such a distinguished authority as Herbert Read—backed, we may feel confident, by the best knowledge of contemporary psychology—that the child's experience is basically "perceptual," not "conceptual." What he sees is more important than what he knows. His understanding, we are to believe, will be colored by what he sees.

Therefore it has seemed wise to many contemporary educators to leave the wall space and screen areas of the classroom in the lower grades blank and ready for adornment by the children's own work or by their selected material. The sources of selection will need to be carefully determined by competent art authorities.

Murals painted on large sheets of coarse paper by a group of children— the subject matter drawn out of Bible stories or life experiences—may be appropriately used to cover large wall spaces. "Painted-glass" windows, similar to those in the church, may be made out of simple materials and hung above the worship center. But what is vitally important to the religious education of the child is that these murals or windows shall be the product of his *own* genuine art experience and creative effort.

ART AS ACTIVITY

The impulses of artistic and religious feeling are too closely entwined to attempt to separate them in this limited space. How important it is that the child be permitted to express himself esthetically within the limits of his capacity if he is to learn to express himself religiously! Freedom and self-discipline seem to be essentials of a good society. How can the child learn the sense of freedom and the need for self-discipline more effectively than through an art experience? In many church schools, following the relating of the story the children are supplied with large pieces of butcher paper and an adequate supply of water colors and crayons—with care taken that property and pinafores are protected. But beyond the mildest imposed controls the children should be left to interpret the story they have heard. Or they may prefer to paint episodes from life, with which they have been recently concerned. The Sunday *after* Christmas, the first Sunday *after* Easter, make excellent periods for discovering what the child has really learned during the preceding holiday season. Left to himself, with the simplest materials and a confidence that no adult is going to impose a grown-up idea of what is "pretty," the child will usually reveal a keen sense not only of what he has perceived but also of what he has learned.

To hurry that experience by insisting that pictures be finished at a given moment is to defeat much of its usefulness. The child can easily be led by a trained teacher to discover the need for discipline. He prefers design. He deliberately chooses form. A persistent failure to respond to the limits of his paper, with its fascinating spaces to be filled, suggests the need for psychiatric help. Far from imposing a preconceived notion of beauty is the teacher's obligation of guiding into beauty.

Activity Without Art

Many church schools and denominational publishing houses provide so-called "activity" materials. This busywork may serve to give a burdened teacher with a room full of active children a few moments respite, but its total impact upon the child is not very profound. There is nothing intrinsically wrong with making napkin rings, filling in printed outlines of Indian and Eskimo villages, or creating Palestinian houses out of pasteboard. But it is not necessarily a religious experience, and it is almost certainly not one of art. Creative art activity implies three basic processes: (1) perception or observation, (2) appreciation, and (3) the urge to individual interpretation. To guide from one into the other of these processes is part of the business of the religious educator who seeks to use art methods creatively.

One outstanding teacher uses an interesting method to secure response to the first two processes. Each Sunday during the period reserved for worship she brings out a carved box known as the "Treasure Chest." In it is some object—an autumn leaf, a cunningly wrought shell, a choice poem, a butterfly, a parable, a song, some lovely thing—to capture the entranced attention of the children. They crowd about her, striving to see, observing under her guidance and through her interpretation, appreciating the treasure for the morning. During a later period they are provided with adequate means of art expression, and frequently choose to reinterpret in their own way the knowledge of breathless wonder and the object of loveliness which they beheld. When this process under expert guidance reaches fulfillment, it is genuine art and, in my opinion, genuine religion.

The Place of Drama in Religious Education

When the artist succeeds in segregating a small part of his life struggle into the compass of one climax situation, we have a play or drama. If this drama comes alive before a participating group as audience, and gives that group motivation for action that sends it out to live effectively in spite of its human weakness, ... then the play is of religious consequence.

This quotation from Harold Ehrensperger's definitive work on religious drama *Conscience on Stage* has been used here for several reasons. It points up the basic conflicts to be found in all truly great drama. It emphasizes the test of heroic tragedy. And it has interest because it suggests a new standard for the selection of religious dramas for presentation, a standard more in harmony with our present needs and uses than were the early dramatic efforts of this century with their insistence upon biblical characters, crepe hair, and conformity to Edwardian theatrical conventions. Also, it calls educators' attention to the basic honesty of contemporary youth. Religion must enter into the very life of young people, must be part of their daily attitudes and actions, or it has no meaning for them. By the same token, we must revise our concepts of what religious drama is if we hope to interest youthful participants in it to the point that they will give up some of their precious free time for the study, memorizing, and rehearsal necessary to a complete dramatic experience.

The historic line of religious drama, from the earliest recorded times to the present day, has been relatively uninterrupted. Sometimes the trunk is so entangled with other branches of the sturdy vine of dramatic literature that it is almost indistinguishable. But it does maintain its own individuality. The need for beauty in expression, the satisfaction to be obtained from group participation in such expression, seems to be basic to the finest and most sensitive development of humanity.

Writing for the anniversary edition of *motive* magazine, R. H. Ward, the British playwright, said,

It is in fact unnecessary to make very profound examination of the nature of any considerable artist in order to discover that the impulse which drives him to write, paint, or compose music is the same impulse which leads some men to the practice of the greatest art of all, that of living a life in the imitation of Christ.[1]

Ward mentions the names of Shakespeare, Keats, Wordsworth, Michelangelo, El Greco, Bach, Beethoven, and Wagner in support of his theory, and says further,

There shines clearly through the works of all of them direct contact with the wells of the spirit, a certain sense of indwelling ministry, a certain perception of spiritual and natural laws, ... a steady reference ... to a single inward reality which is the basis of art and of religion.

While we may not hope that in our local church-school groups we shall develop the Michelangelo and Beethoven of the twentieth century, yet we

[1] "To Open the Doors of Perception," February, 1948.

have an obligation as religious educators to explore the environments from which these titans of the spirit have emerged. And religious drama would seem, by its very nature, to provide such an atmosphere.

The truth of this fact may be tested in terms of time. The Church of the eleventh century understood the principle involved. And while it would seem unwise to impose a medieval Catholic ceremonial tradition upon a present-day Protestant youth group, it would be equally unfortunate to deprive our youth of acquaintance with the great mystery, miracle, and morality plays of the eleventh through the fifteenth centuries. *Everyman*[2] remains the greatest example of Church drama.

The same impulses which drove the Church fathers of A.D. 1120 to experiment with *Quem Quaeritis?* [3] persuaded modern educators that perhaps through the drama we can most effectively uplift, instruct, and inspire to action our contemporary youth. It would seem obvious, therefore, that we too should explore our biblical heritage, the historical traditions of the particular denomination through which we function, and the society in which we live to discover new experiences of dramatic worship and fellowship. As religious people, we are all concerned about the following subjects: evangelism, missionary outreach, responsibility to the social order—including the dignity of labor, the obligation to use the franchise wisely, the privilege of sharing with the underprivileged, the inclusion of *all* mankind in the ecumenical society. May we not hope, therefore, that out of these concerns may be woven and developed new drama experiences? We will not always find so-called religious dramas written to our order. That is good. It means that we are thrown upon our own resources of Christian conviction and creative spontaneity to make our own expression.

METHODS OF USING RELIGIOUS DRAMA

In some denominational organizations, elaborate dramatic clubs have been developed. Where the youth body of a given church is accustomed to the complexities of organization, these clubs offer an effective outlet for dramatic activity. However, in smaller churches less highly organized it may be advisable to let the dramatic impulse of the congregation find its own expression through occasional seasonal dramas. In one case—that of a midwestern Baptist church—a drama department was developed with a full-time weekday and Sunday schedule. Among the groups included in such a department were a verse-speaking choir of women; a speaking choir of young girls; a teen-age drama guild for girls, which met in the middle of the week and studied some of the techniques of playing and production in order that

---

[2] See Phillips Osgood, ed., *Old Time Church Dramas Adapted*.
[3] *Ibid.*

its interpretations might have added dignity and merit; a builders' guild of teen-age boys, primarily concerned with the construction of scenery and lighting; a junior guild for children under ten years of age, meeting on Saturday morning primarily for training in the reading and memorizing of scriptural and related material and the developing of simple creative dramas; and a play-readers' guild, made up of adult men and women interested in discussing the religious implications of contemporary successful commercial drama. Because this department was unique and included many of the approved contemporary techniques of religious drama, it seems advisable to consider some specific aspects of its success here.

Speaking Choirs. The use of a speaking choir for occasional variation in the church service of worship has become an accepted and popular technique in many churches. However, its primary interest to educators lies in the long-term experience of the members of such a group. As has been mentioned in the discussion on music as creative activity, the *choir* experience is of inestimable value in developing a Christian society. This is equally true of the Speaking Choir. The Walter H. Baker Company publishes an excellent separate catalogue of speaking-choir materials, among them one particularly useful volume of instruction—*An Approach to Choral Speech*, by Mona Swann, which has proved extremely helpful to directors in this tempting field. The Division of Education of the Northern Baptist Convention also makes available a revised and complete list of scriptural materials and religious poetry suitable for speaking-choir use. It should be noted that a group of persons hastily assembled for an occasional appearance in a Chrismas or Easter drama, reading as a group from notebooks, is not the same thing as a real speaking choir. The latter is a group of persons with related interests, rehearsing not less than once a week consistently throughout the church year, and making a regular contribution to the church service through worship participation in an occasional drama or even in special recitals. These choirs lend themselves to effective use by children, youth, and adults. Leadership requires a love of poetry, some speech training, and an unlimited capacity for learning and absorbing new ideas.

Creative Drama. Winifred Ward's book *Play Making with Children* has at last given us a definitive and long-awaited volume covering the entire range of this fascinating use of drama. Miss Ward has concerned herself primarily with creative drama in the public school situation, but every word she writes is applicable to our religious dramatic problem. It is well for the director of religious education to remember that informal creative dramatization of subject matter or life experience depends for its success upon spontaneity, adequate time, and *absence* of audience. It is an activity primarily for the participants.

Hulda Niebuhr has also made rich contributions in her experiments with dramatizing Bible stories, and Mrs. Isabelle Kimball Whiting of Kings Chapel,

Boston, has developed several unusually successful *Dramatic Preludes and Services of Worship*[4] out of creative dramatic experiments.

It has sometimes been felt that the use of this particular technique with youth is doomed to failure because of the increasing self-consciousness of teen-agers. However, I have used it with considerable satisfaction in a mixed group of eighth- and ninth-grade boys and girls. In this situation a study was made of the boyhood of Paul. Considerable research was necessary, and imagination was brought to bear upon the problem. Eight little dramas were the result—all very brief and to the point, but sufficiently good that the members of the class asked to have them copied and bound for future reference. It is interesting to note that all of these dramas used material preceding Paul's vision on the road to Damascus. This is important, because it shows clearly how much creative imagination had been brought to bear upon the part of the story that is scarcely told.

In her extensive work with college-age youth in the Wesley Foundations, with which she has been associated, Mrs. Ruth Winfield Love [5] has drawn out some remarkably meaningful dramatic group writing. Young people, after several sessions of earnest discussion of any given contemporary youth problem, have recorded their conversation, selected a basic dramatic conflict, and *as a group* worked out a dramatic scene or service of worship. This activity requires patience, sincere concern that the young people shall unself-consciously express their opinions, willingness to wait, and a stanch discipline which prevents the leader from intruding her own suggestions. Mrs. Love's work has been remarkably free from any intrusion of an adult point of view. To watch the faces of the young people participating in her creative-drama groups, and to read the finished product of their pooled efforts, is to salute the sincerity of the director and the quality of thinking involved in the process.

Formal Dramatics. There is little opportunity for, or emphasis upon, the production of ready-made plays in the foregoing discussion. That is because the present concern is in harmony with present trends. The creation of dramatic experience in terms of religious values is far more exciting than the memorizing and producing of another author's words and situations. However, in the church which has had no exposure to dramatic methods it is certainly advisable to begin with published dramas. Three books which are absolutely essential in the library of the director of such activity are: *Conscience on Stage*, by Harold Ehrensperger; *Best Plays for the Church*, by Mildred Hahn; and *A Treasury of Religious Plays*,[6] by Thelma Sharman Brown. Several other useful volumes are listed in the Bibliography.

[4] Boston: Walter Baker Co., 1940.
[5] Presently associated with Scarritt and Peabody colleges, Nashville, Tennessee.
[6] New York: Association Press, 1947.

As to places and means of preparation for specialization in the field of religious drama, there can only be the reiteration of what was implied in the discussion of music as creative activity. The schools of religious education can serve us best by suggesting *how* we are to incorporate such specialized technique in the general pattern of religious education. The techniques themselves, however, can be best learned in colleges or technical schools offering extensive and detailed courses in playwriting, play production, play direction, acting, and so forth. Unique in the United States is the Interdenominational Religious Drama Workshop, co-operatively sponsored through the International Council of Religious Education and the Northern Baptist Assembly, on the Assembly Grounds at Green Lake, Wisconsin.

THE DANCE

The use of the dance as a further enlightening experience in religious education has been explored in only a few outstanding American Protestant churches. Yet the development of dance as a group-art form has been America's outstanding contribution to the arts of the twentieth century. And the early dance groups of the period immediately following World War I were developed in Switzerland as distinctly *religious* groups. Phoebe Guthrie of New York; Ruth St. Denis and Ted Shawn, exponents of the dance in its noblest form in the church chancel; the Department of Fine Arts of the Fountain Street Baptist Church in Grand Rapids, Michigan; and Mrs. Chester Fisk, the wife of the minister of the Congregational Church of Hanover, New Hampshire—all have made notable contributions in this direction. It is unfortunate that the dance per se has retained an aura of frontier-town saloons in the minds of many otherwise educated religious people. For the art itself, at its noblest, is fully worthy to be reinstated in its service to the Church. As a religiously expressive activity it is a superb vehicle for the transmission of thought, feeling, and exhortation.

SUGGESTIONS FOR FURTHER STUDY

1. In your local community what evidence is there of religious impulse and leadership in secular group activities? Visit and investigate the classes at the art gallery, the civic orchestra, civic choral groups, the little theater, college theater, and so forth.

2. This assignment is borrowed in full from the chapter by Edith L. Thomas on music, drama, and art in *Studies in Religious Education.* "In churches with which you are familiar how much money in equipment and staff is invested in music? Compare this with the minister's salary and the relative returns in religious education results."

3. Design a program of religious instruction through drama for an entire year in your local church, emphasizing the three general areas of liturgical drama, social drama, and creative drama.

4. Devote a year's research to the present state and possible improvement of the art environment, including architecture, furnishings, pictures, and materials for creative art activity, in your local church school.

5. Adapt a contemporary poem, or nonfiction, or fiction work of art for interpretation by a speaking choir, dividing it into appropriate narrative and lyric passages with soloists and choir voices.

BIBLIOGRAPHY

ART

Bailey, Albert E. *Christ and His Gospel in Recent Art*. New York: Charles Scribner's Sons, 1948.

Dewey, John. *Art as Experience*. New York: Minton, Balch & Co., 1934.

Lowenfeld, Viktor. *Creative and Mental Growth*. New York: Macmillan Co., 1947. Chapter on art education.

Read, Herbert. *Education Through Art*. London: Faber & Faber, 1944.

————. *The Grass Roots of Art* (Problems of Contemporary Art Series, No. 2). New York: Wittenborn & Co., 1947.

DRAMA

Bates, Esther. *The Church Play and Its Production*. Boston: Walter Baker Co., 1938.

Ehrensperger, Harold. *Conscience on Stage*. New York and Nashville: Abingdon-Cokesbury Press, 1947.

Hahn, Mildred B. *Best Plays for the Church*. Philadelphia: Christian Education Press, 1947.

Osgood, Phillips E. *Old Time Church Dramas Adapted*. New York: Harper & Brothers, 1927.

Swann, Mona. *An Approach to Choral Speech*. Boston: The Expression Company, 1934.

MUSIC

Dearmer, Percy, and Others. *Songs of Praise for Boys and Girls*. New York: Oxford University Press, 1929-30.

————. *Songs of Praise for Little Children*. New York: Oxford University Press, 1932.

Dickenson, Clarence, ed. *Choir Loft and Pulpit* (collection). New York: Novello Co.

The Gateway Collection. New York: G. Schirmer, Inc.

The Green Hill Junior Choir Book. New York: G. Schirmer, Inc.

Jaques-Dalcroze, Emile. *Rhythm, Music, and Education*. New York: G. P. Putnam's Sons, 1921.

Oxford Book of Carols. New York: Oxford University Press, 1928.

Prayers and Hymns for Junior Schools. New York: Oxford University Press, 1933.

Smith, Henry Augustine, ed. *New Hymnal for American Youth*. New York: Century Co., 1930.

Vaughn Williams, Ralph, and Shaw, M. F., eds. *Songs of Praise* (Prayers and Hymns for Use in Church Schools; Prayers and Hymns for the Little Child). New York: Oxford University Press, 1931.

Chapter 12

AUDIO-VISUAL METHOD AND CONTENT

PAUL H. VIETH

AUDIO-VISUAL METHODS AND MATERIALS are a means toward achieving effective teaching. Better religious teaching can be done through their use. Therefore no church can afford to overlook them. The term "teaching" is used broadly to include all efforts and processes through which the church and the home seek to achieve the objectives of religious education.

Active personal participation in life's activity under guidance is the most direct road to effective and permanent learning. At the other extreme is talking about life and the ideals under which life should be lived. The alert teacher is constantly aware of the need for producing teaching situations in which the attitudes of interest, effort, and experimentation which characterize life situations are reproduced in his class.

By no means all, nor even a major portion, of religious education can be provided in actual life situations. Hence the teacher is under the necessity of providing a learning experience which will have the greatest likelihood of carrying over into life experience. Audio-visual aids have meaning and value because of their capacity to help bridge the gap between teaching and life. Audio-visual aids include all those techniques and devices which are used to appeal to the eye or ear, or to the eye and ear simultaneously, so as to enhance learning. It is their function to provide concreteness and vividness for the learning experience. They have the capacity to make a multisensual appeal, to heighten interest and emotional tone, and thus to make an indelible impression. They can take the class from the here and now to the then and there—or, better, can bring the then and there into the here and now. They can vividly portray manners and customs of people in distant places and faraway times; they can give persons and groups life and character; they have the power of making ideals and ambitions vividly articulate and of motivating the pupil to desire to emulate and achieve.

ARE AUDIO-VISUAL AIDS EFFECTIVE?

There is no longer any doubt that audio-visual methods and materials are effective when properly selected and used with skill. Scientific research has established their value. An extensive review of research in the effectiveness of audio-visual aids is given in Chapter 4 of Elliott's *Film and Educa-*

tion. He concludes that these studies tend to indicate a rapid rate at which attitudes, insights, relationships, and concepts are developed through the use of such aids. So convincing are these results that teaching methods in certain subjects such as social studies are rapidly being changed because of this quality of films. Moreover such studies have shown that not only is immediate learning increased but retention over longer periods of time is enhanced. The greatest benefit from the use of audio-visual aids seems to accrue to the dull pupils in the school, who find it difficult to learn through the more abstract verbal types of communication.

Typical of studies of this kind is that made by Harry Arthur Wise in the high schools of southwest Missouri. His purpose was to determine the effectiveness in the teaching of American history of the use of the "Chronicles of America" photoplays. Through the standard procedure of using control and experimental groups, including 436 pupils, he discovered that students who had the benefit of motion pictures in their teaching learned above 20 per cent more history than those who were taught by the usual method. Greatest improvement was shown in the learning of causal relationships, such as social and economic ones. The use of the motion pictures aroused greater interest in American history, which resulted in more outside reading being done by those pupils who were taught by the audio-visual method.[1]

While most of these studies have been made in general education, we have every reason to suppose that audio-visual aids are just as effective in religious education. B. F. Jackson, Jr., investigated the value of using filmstrips and sound motion pictures in teaching Bible. Taking the life of Paul as his subject and Bible classes in relation to the public high schools in Fort Worth, Texas, as his setting, he established three comparable groups of students. One group was taught without the use of audio-visual aids; the second had the same course with the aid of the "Life of St. Paul" series of sound motion pictures of the Religious Film Society of Great Britain; the third had the same course with the aid of filmstrips made from selected frames of these motion pictures. He found that the filmstrip group learned 24.51 per cent more, and the motion picture group 38.52 per cent more, than the control group. Both experimental groups learned more of the entire life of Paul than the control group, but the gain was proportionately greater in those portions which were actually included in the film and slide material.[2]

These scientific studies are valuable in establishing conclusively what common observation affirms. Thousands of teachers have proved through

[1] *Motion Pictures as an Aid in Teaching American History* (New Haven: Yale University Press, 1939).

[2] *Film Strips and Sound Motion Pictures in Teaching High School Bible* (1948). An unpublished dissertation in the library of Yale University.

experience that teaching can be made more effective through the wise use of such aids. Student application, interest, and effort are notoriously poor in the usual type of religious teaching. If this handicap can be overcome by a use of audio-visual aids which is comparable with the best practice in the public and private day schools, it is conceivable that the advantage of the use of such methods and materials in religious education may be even greater than in general education.

The emphasis in research has shifted from the broad question of the value of audio-visual aids in teaching—that has been sufficiently established—to more specific questions of effective utilization. Typical of this type of research is that carried out by the Motion Picture Research Project, under the direction of Mark A. May at Yale University. A study was made to determine the effect on factual learning of the simple showing of a film; the showing of the same film with "motivation" through questions at the beginning of each of seven sections designed to make the pupils more alert to the material presented in each section; the showing of the same film with "participation" exercises introduced at the end of each of the seven sections requiring the pupils to answer questions on a work sheet; and the showing of the same film with both the motivation questions and the participation exercises included. Controlled experimentation revealed that these four ways of using the film yielded, respectively, 8.2 per cent, 10.5 per cent, 12.2 per cent and 14 per cent gains in learning. The significant gain in learning in the "participation" group was on those items covered by the participation questions, while on other items of information the gain in learning was about the same as that of pupils who had a simple showing of the film without participation procedure.[3] The implication which may be drawn from this study is that careful planning for the showing of a film and the use of the right educational techniques will greatly increase the results in pupil learning. The method of audio-visual education is as important as the material.

The increasingly effective use of audio-visual aids in the church awaits the results of many studies which should be undertaken to determine what types of aids are most effective for given purposes, and what methods of utilization will yield best results. In the meantime the movement must proceed on the growing body of experience already available. Imagination and ingenuity will enable the alert teacher to do the basic planning which will yield rewarding results even with unsatisfactory material and less than perfect conditions.

TYPES OF AUDIO-VISUAL AIDS

The resourceful teacher who has some imagination will find a wide range of materials and devices which serve the purpose as audio-visual

[3] From *Educational Screen*, XXVI: 4, 5.

aids. These include not simply motion pictures and other projected material, but also a rich resource of nonprojected aids.

Nonprojected Audio-visual Aids. The field trip is an educational technique which stands closest to life experience because it enables the pupil to see the actual situation, institution, object, or setting with which a unit of learning is dealing. Most communities provide many opportunities for field trips. Simple visits to the church sanctuary, nature hikes, visits to churches and synagogues of other faiths, visits to institutions which are expressing Christianity in action, visits to situations which illustrate the need for Christian service and action—all of these are fairly readily organized and carried out in most churches. They require basic planning if they are to achieve their educational objectives, but this constitutes a part of all good teaching.

In the classroom and department assembly there is opportunity for the use of various types of nonprojected visual aids. In fact, there are few teachers who are so devoid of imagination in teaching that they are not already making some use of such aids, although their practice may be haphazard and ineffective. Blackboard illustrations, maps, charts, and diagrams may be used to illuminate and illustrate what would otherwise be abstract teaching. Objects representing the art and culture of other peoples may be used to introduce pupils to the life and customs of these near-by or faraway neighbors.

Printed pictures are a time-honored aid in religious teaching. Their advantage over slides is that they can be used in any classroom and can be displayed for longer periods of time. Pupils may study them in detail and benefit from them, even when they are not in actual use as a part of class procedure. Printed pictures are of particular importance in religious education in the home.

Illustrated textbooks provide a combination of pictures and reading material in relation to each other. The effectiveness of such illustrations depends on the quality of the pictures and their relevance to the subject matter presented. Unrelated pictures may serve to lighten up what would otherwise be a solid page of print but serve no other useful purpose. Publishers of religious education materials are aware of the need for high-quality illustrations and attractive page format but have been prevented from achieving their ideal in textbooks because of the inability or unwillingness of churches to pay the higher costs involved. The local church which senses the value of visual aids can help to support much-needed improvement by buying and using the better-grade materials.

The action picture, so familiar in the comic supplements and comic magazines, has appealed to some as a technique through which religious materials and values may be effectively taught. There is reason to believe that the avid interest of children in such pictures springs not simply from the content but also from the method of presentation. If this judgment is correct, then much of what the church school seeks to teach might effectively be taught through this device. There are some handicaps to be overcome because of the extent to which the action pictures are being used to portray lurid and undesirable material, and because the pupil may find the portrayal of religious subject matter "tame" in comparison with his usual diet of comic magazines. Some ventures have been made in this field. Most of them have been inferior from an artistic standpoint and from the standpoint of the selection of subject matter. Even under these handicaps, however, there is evidence that action pictures may have value for the vivid portrayal of lessons in religion. It should not surprise us if, in the near future, enterprising publishers will recognize the huge potential market for such material in the religious field and provide them for church schools and homes. It is tragic that at this juncture the religious education forces should not be engaged in research on the possible use and value of action pictures in religious education, and in experimentation in the production of high-type publications, judged from both the artistic and content standpoints.

Phonograph records are becoming increasingly significant for presenting incidents, stories, and even lectures in an effective way. Music and drama are added to simple storytelling, and the effective use of characters has the capacity of carrying the listeners into the very setting which is being depicted. By means of the phonograph record the voices of important persons may be brought right into the home church.

Projected Visual Aids. Projection on a screen makes some of the aids already mentioned more available for class use, and it is a necessary device for bringing other aids into being. All still pictures are of the first type and motion pictures of the second.

By means of the opaque projector any pictures or other material of appropriate size may be projected on a screen so that a whole class may view them at one time. Illustrations from books and magazines, diagrams, drawings by pupils, photographs, and small objects may be brought to the screen by this device. Pictures may also be converted into transparencies either in black and white or natural color and may be projected by means of the stereopticon or slide projector. Slides may be in the form of individual transparencies, or printed in series on a strip of film, popularly known as filmslide or filmstrip. The phonograph record may be combined with the projection of pictures so as to provide continuous narration, sound effects, or musical background.

While projected transparencies are but still pictures shown on a screen, it is probably not entirely correct to say that only the element of projection has been added. When a continuous story is told, requiring pictures to be shown in rapid succession, accompanied by narration or music, something approaching the motion picture has been produced, which would never be quite the same if the pictures were presented as prints in rapid succession. The combination of filmstrip and phonograph record is one of the most promising of recent developments in audio-visual education, and one which will probably have extensive use in the future.

There are other elements which are added to the effectiveness of audio-visual aids through projection. The larger picture makes it easily possible for a whole class or audience to see the same picture at the same time. The teacher can be in a position in relation to the screen and the class which enables him to direct proper interpretation and discussion to the picture being shown. The single illuminated picture in an otherwise darkened room tends to focus attention and to remove distractions. The comparative comfort with respect to seating and eyestrain in which an entire class or audience may see a well-arranged projected program is conducive to heightened pleasure and enjoyment in the experience.

It should not be assumed that projected still pictures are always inferior to motion pictures. Each method of projection has its own purposes and values. For example, when slides are used, the program is always under the control of the teacher, who may interpret each picture as fully as he chooses. Also, the subjects in a set of slides may be rearranged to suit the teacher, or single slides may be selected for more intensive attention. On the other hand, the motion picture has certain values of its own. It adds the dramatic element of motion—which while it is an optical illusion is nevertheless very real. This makes it possible to transport persons in imagination to the actual time and place which is being depicted. To this the sound film adds dialogue or off-stage explanation, sets the mood through music and other sound, and thus constitutes a fusion of sight and sound which may be exceedingly effective for intellectual and emotional response.

The moving picture is a veritable magic carpet, and more. Presenting its subject in lifelike motion, it casts a spell of reality over its audience. It can enable them to travel in far places, take them into the distant past or an imagined future, cause them to run the scale of the human emotions, show the actions of life too small to be seen with the naked eye, and processes such as the growth of a plant which are too slow for the unaided eye to catch. It can present individual persons or whole peoples in such a way that they are admired or despised, loved or hated. It can take its audience behind the scenes and show people as they really are, what they do, what they think, what they love. It can give vicarious experiences which could never be had in the real world.[4]

Films may be used in religious education to present Bible stories or characters, Church history, missionary activities, or aspects of the broad scope of the work of the Church. They may be used to present problems for discussion. They may show social situations illustrating the need for

[4] Rogers and Vieth, *Visual Aids in the Church*, p. 56.

Christian action or social work. They may serve as vocational guidance, showing the need for Christian workers and the kind of work performed by different types of leaders. They may demonstrate how to perform certain duties or acts, such as leading a worship service or teaching a class. They may illustrate Christianity in action, so as to motivate conduct and to develop character. In fact, the possible use of films is almost endless.

Some films are made for a specific purpose and will serve that purpose only. Most of them are more general and may serve any one of several purposes, depending on the aim of the teacher and his ingenuity in working it out. Educational use of film should be distinguished from entertainment use. An educational film should be interesting but need not entertain. Comparison of educational with theatrical films is irrelevant. Until a church can get its pupils past the stage where they expect to be entertained whenever a film is shown, it has not entered on effective utilization. This affects such matters as whether a film should be shown two or more times for best learning value, whether it should be preceded or interrupted by motivation or participation questions and exercises, and whether it should be followed by testing or discussion. In this review no mention has been made of radio, television, or drama. While these media might rightly be classed as audio-visual aids, they have such important functions of their own that they deserve treatment under separate categories. (See Chapters 11 and 13.)

Audio-visual Aids and the Church

The present possibility of, and prospect for, better religious education through the use of audio-visual aids are promising. Will the Church take full advantage of its opportunities? Past performance in religious education in most churches gives little ground for optimism. Yet audio-visual aids may prove to be the open door through which new insights will be gained into what the Church might do, as well as new methods for doing it.

There are problems in church religious education which put those under a handicap who would use audio-visual aids. One of these is that of availability to the church of a sufficient quantity, quality, and variety of aids. This involves production, distribution, and facilities for acquainting prospective users with the nature and content of what is available.

We have come a long way since the day when religious education had to be satisfied with inferior material on the Bible or to make its own adaptations of material not planned for religious teaching. Those who pioneered through that stage, because they saw better days ahead, made a contribution to the improvements which have come to pass by encouraging production. Today there are offerings in all types of audio-visual aids which are acceptable and usable even though far from perfect. The advent of color film has given great impetus to the production of slides and filmstrips. The increasing use of recordings with or without slides or filmstrips has released many attractive programs. The service of such organizations as the Protestant Film Commission in production or encouraging production of high-quality audio-visual aids and the exacting work of J. Arthur Rank in Great Britain have speeded the production of quality materials. Denominational boards have added their quota of audio-visual productions with a purpose. Even if that purpose is promotional, it may yet yield usable materials for religious education, because promotional aims are not necessarily inconsistent with educational aims. Commercial producers such as Cathedral Films, Inc., are offering to the churches quantities of materials which are improving as increased use makes more money available to apply more exacting standards of production. Yet, in face of this improving situation a current writer can say, with some justice: "The film resources of the church today are a heterogeneous mass of unorganized and unrelated materials which were produced to some extent by the church, but principally by those having a financial rather than educational interest in films. Generally, existing films are of low quality on most counts." [5] To get better, more usable films, Hockman suggests, there must be closer cooperation between the producer and consumer, between those who plan religious education and those who provide the audio-visual materials for it. Only thus will it be possible to get aids which cover the core of curriculum instead of being on the periphery, which act as a pivot for educative situations instead of being mere adjuncts.

The problem of distribution is one of making audio-visual aids readily available to users in the church. No matter how abundant the supply, it will help the local user only to the extent that he can get what he wants when he needs it. This requires that source libraries be readily available to the consumer. The Religious Film Association is an agency of denominational publishers seeking to ease this problem. Through its service, churches may send their orders to their own denominational publishing houses and have delivery made from a few central distributing agencies. But the plan is cumbersome, and resources are still far removed from the ultimate consumer. Churches in a locality need to learn the value of having a film council through which they co-operate to lease or buy the more important materials and provide equipment for use of all the members. "Pick-up and carry" availability will greatly enhance use. Sometimes such a service may be rendered by a local business with which the churches co-operate.

Such local availability will also enhance effective use if provision is made for preview of materials. It is almost impossible to learn the exact

[5] W. S. Hockman, in Elliott, ed., *op. cit.*, p. 342.

nature and quality of an aid from a catalogue description. It is also difficult to make the necessary preparation for effective utilization if the aid is delivered from a distant distributor only a day or two before its scheduled use. A central community agency whose primary interest is education can provide a service which will go a long way toward solving these problems. Certain aids such as slides, filmstrips, recordings, prints, should be included in the church's own library of resources so as to be readily available to the workers.

Certain other developments are necessary before churches can make adequate and proper use of audio-visual aids:

1. Closer integration with curriculum. If audio-visual aids are to serve their purpose, they must have a central relation to the curriculum, rather than be lightly attached to what is already complete without them. Church-school curriculums are constructed, in the main, by denominational committees rather than by the local churches in which they are used. It is only the occasional curriculum unit which has audio-visual aids related to it at the point where the unit is originally constructed. One reason for this is that lesson-writers have not been trained in the use of audio-visual aids, but perhaps a more important reason is that few churches would be able to utilize such suggestions if they were made. Publishers of public school texts are considering co-ordinating films and other audio-visual aids with textbooks. It is time that publishers of religious education material gave thought to similar procedure.

There is opportunity also at the local church level to correlate audio-visual aids with curriculum, since printed curriculums are rarely used in their entirety, and most churches have phases of curriculum which are locally developed. Successful experiments have been carried out in selecting audio-visual materials as the core of a curriculum and relating reading material to them. This, however, requires a type of creative work for which leadership is not available in most churches.

2. Responsibility in the church. The church committee on Christian education may take the lead in sponsoring the use of audio-visual methods and materials, but it must be remembered that all phases of the church's program may benefit from such use, not just the work in the church school. A good plan is that of having a church committee on audio-visual aids, related to the committee on Christian education. Such a committee should serve the church in providing facilities, equipment, and a library of materials, be a clearing house for catalogues of rental libraries, care for equipment, provide technicians in the use and care of equipment, and train the workers of the church in the meaning and use of audio-visual aids.

3. The training of workers. Can church-school workers develop the competence needed for effective utilization of audio-visual aids? Unless this question can be answered in the affirmative, there is little to be gained

from introducing such materials into the curriculum. This requires a new type of teacher training.

Effective utilization requires such knowledge and skills as the following:

a) Acquaintance with the resources in equipment and materials. Teachers should know what is available in the local church library and how to secure rental material through use of catalogues of rental libraries, which the committee on audio-visual aids may provide. They should be familiar with the various types of equipment used in presenting audio-visual aids, though it is not necessary that every teacher be a projectionist if the church committee is prepared to supply technicians.

b) Ability to define an objective to which an audio-visual aid may be related and to select a suitable aid. The objective may come out of questions or discussion which arise in class, or it may come from the teacher's own conception of what the pupils most need. It must be specific enough so that the relation of the aid to the objective is clearly established.

c) Ability to prepare the room for proper use of audio-visual aids. This will require consideration of such matters as darkening the room, the best location of screen and projector, the seating of the pupils, the most effective use of electric equipment so as to provide efficient change from regular class procedure to projection and back again to class procedure.

d) Ability to prepare the class for the presentation of an audio-visual aid. If this use has grown out of previous discussion, the aid to be presented must be related to such discussion. In other cases it may be necessary to raise pertinent problems which are to be answered by the aid, to tell the class why the aid is being used, to ask that certain points be especially observed, or to use similar introductory procedures. Great skill is required in this step of procedure to give just enough introduction for the best use of the aid without destroying the interest of the pupils in that which is to follow.

e) Ability to present the aid effectively. This requires consideration of such matters as the timetable to allow adequate time for preparation, presentation, and follow-up. Church-school schedules make this difficult, because class periods or assembly periods are usually not long enough for the effective use of an aid in a single period. Producers have not helped with this problem by their tendency to make most aids over fifteen minutes in length. When follow-up must be delayed for a week, much of the impression of the aid will have been dissipated. The vacation church school offers better opportunities for the use of aids than the Sunday school. If pupils are to assist with projection, they must be rehearsed for the tasks they are to perform; and, in any case, care must be taken that the projection is done with the maximum smoothness and effectiveness possible under existing conditions.

f) Ability to follow through with questions or discussion to make sure that the purpose of the aid has been achieved. Sometimes the picture should be presented a second time for best effect. The type of follow-up depends on the purpose in using the aid. It may consist of test questions to check on knowledge acquired or class discussion to develop problems or points of view. This step is most important if aids are to have their best effect but is one which is frequently omitted or badly handled in church schools.

These steps in procedure apply primarily to the classroom use of audio-visual materials which are closely related to curriculum. The church field has produced many films which are of a more general nature. These will usually be used with larger groups and in settings other than the church school. Some of these carry their own impact and message without need for, or possibility of, setting them in a teaching pattern. These may be useful in religious education. Their use does, however, have a tendency to return the church school to an ungraded curriculum pattern; and the mere availability of such films should not lead workers to think that this is the solution to their need for audio-visual aids closely related to teaching. The effective use of such longer films presents a peculiar problem of utilization involving projection to larger groups, but it permits more specific application to smaller graded classes in discussion and follow-up. Public school practice will give little help in the solution of this problem.

The increasing quantity of audio-visual materials requires church workers to develop competence in evaluation so that selection may be carefully made. Opportunities need to be provided for previews which will enable a church committee to build up a file of evaluations. This is a service which a community council can render. One group has worked out the following evaluation schedule.[6]

AUDIO-VISUAL AID EVALUATION

Subject field: _____

Type of aid: Record___Slides___Filmstrip___FS or S and R___Movie: Si___So___

Title _____Length _____Cost: Rental _____Purchase _____

Where secured _____

Synopsis of Content:

Suitable for: Kg.____Pr.____Jr.____JHS____HS__ _YP__YA__Adult___

A. *Technical Quality* (E—Excellent, G—Good, F—Fair, P—Poor, VP—**Very Poor**)

1. Logical sequences of plot_____
2. Movement sufficient to hold interest_____
3. Definite beginning_____, climax_____, ending_____
4. Comprehensive titles_____
5. Variety in shots_____

[6] Based on Dale, *Audio-Visual Methods in Teaching*, p. 507.

6. Good acting_____
7. Good music_____
8. Good use of music_____

B. *Mechanical Quality*
   1. Are the color tones true to life?_____
   2. Good sound?_____
   3. Clear shots?_____
   4. No flickering?_____

C. *Content*
   1. Purpose: Is it definite?_____ Properly fulfilled?_____
   2. Suitable to age group in mind?_____
   3. Is it for purposes of instruction_____, inspiration_____, recreation_____, entertainment_____?
   4. Is it accurate regarding place, event, and time represented?_____
   5. Is it in accord with the goals of religious education?_____
      Comment:

Training in the use of audio-visual aids will assume some understanding of the meaning of teaching. In turn, such training may be a help to a better understanding of teaching techniques because of its specific and practical nature. Workers' conferences may be used for instruction in, and demonstration of, effective utilization. Classes in leadership schools and audio-visual workshops will be helpful. But the best type of training is that given through guidance of teachers in personal supervision as they undertake the several stages of good utilization. In the training of teachers audio-visual materials and methods should be used, such as the filmstrip with records *The Use of Visual Method in the Church* and the films *Using the Classroom Film* and *How to Teach with Films.*

4. Securing a budget. A program such as that outlined here cannot be carried out without a proper budget. It is best to have the budget of audio-visual aids included as an item in the general church budget. When this is not possible, the committee may use other methods of securing funds, such as the giving of an entertainment to which admission is charged or at which an offering is taken. The budget should provide for the addition of permanent equipment from year to year and for the rental of necessary materials to carry out each year's curriculum. Making a budget for a year implies that curriculum planning will also be done well in advance so that estimated expenditures can be based on specific request for needed equipment and materials.

Conclusion

Audio-visual aids offer a new tool for religious education. They do not change the nature and purpose of religious education, but they do revolutionize method. They are not self-teaching or a substitute for skillful work on the part of the teacher. In both material and method the field of audio-visual aids is in its beginning stages. Encouraging results have been achieved by some churches through careful selection and well-planned utilization. Most churches have much to learn, and such learning will not come without hard study and intelligent experimentation. The prospects for the future are bright; and if these prospects are realized, we may expect increasingly effective religious education through the use of this new tool which modern science has put into our hands.

SUGGESTIONS FOR FURTHER STUDY

1. What is the maximum length of a film or other audio-visual aid for effective use in a one-hour church-school session? How can provision be made for utilizing pictures which run one hour or longer?

2. Can younger children profit from the use of projected pictures? At what age can a child get meaningful impressions from a projected slide? A movie?

3. Is it practical to build an entire curriculum *around* audio-visual aids, rather than to let them *supplement* printed materials? If practical, would it be desirable?

4. In teaching a Bible narrative, such as the life of Paul, what is the relative effectiveness of slides or filmstrips and motion pictures? The relative cost and ease of utilization?

5. When Bible incidents, such as the story of the good Samaritan, are "built up" so as to make a twenty-minute movie story, do pupils get a confused and erroneous idea of what is actually in the Bible? How could this danger be avoided?

6. Will audio-visual aids tend to be a substitute for more rigorous mental application on the part of pupils?

7. Does your community have a film council? If so, what is it doing? If not, how might you proceed to organize one?

BIBLIOGRAPHY

ABC's of Visual Aids and Projectionists' Manual. M. O. Publishers, Box 406, State College, Pa.

Chandler, Anna Curtis, and Cypher, I. F. *Audio-visual Techniques for Enrichment of the Curriculum.* New York: Noble Co., 1948.

Dale, Edgar: *Audio-visual Methods in Teaching.* New York: Dryden Press, 1946.

Educational Screen. Magazine for audio-visual aids in education. 64 E. Lake Street, Chicago, Ill.

Elliott, Godfrey, ed. *Film and Education.* New York: Philosophical Library, 1948.

Film World (also *Church Film Quarterly*). Magazine of audio-visual aids. C. J. Ver Halen, Jr., Publishing Co., 6060 Sunset Boulevard, Los Angeles, Calif.

Hoban, Charles F., Jr. *Focus on Learning.* American Council on Education, 744 Jackson Place, Washington, D. C., 1942.

Hockman, William S. *Projected Visual Aids in the Church.* Boston: Pilgrim Press, 1947.

Master Guide to Religious Films. Selected Films Release Service, Whittier, Calif. Describes all types of religious audio-visual aids as advertised by the distributors. No attempt to evaluate items.

1000 and One—the Blue Book of Nontheatrical Films. The Educational Screen, 64 East Lake Street, Chicago, Ill.

Religious Film Association Catalogue. The Religious Film Association, 347 Madison Avenue, New York 17, N. Y., or nearest depository. Each item is well described and carefully evaluated.

Rogers, William L., and Vieth, Paul H. *Visual Aids in the Church.* Philadelphia: Christian Education Press, 1946.

Wittich, W. A., and Fowlkes, John G. *Audio-visual Paths to Learning.* New York: Harper & Brothers, 1946.

Chapter 13

RADIO AND TELEVISION IN RELIGIOUS EDUCATION

EVERETT C. PARKER

IN USING RADIO OR TELEVISION for religious education, remember that both are mediums of communication, not ends in themselves. The radio speaker and the television screen are as impersonal as the telegraph or the telephone. They will transmit any message fed into them. In and of themselves they have no power to influence, except that people tend to be unduly impressed by ideas and information received through radio and television because of the aura of magic and power surrounding radio communication.

Radio can supplement, but cannot replace, organized group activity under skilled leadership in the church school or the home. As yet there has been almost no experimentation with in-school listening in the field of religious education. It seems apparent that the success of radio listening in the public schools should point the way to development of similar educational religious programs, geared to the curriculum and broadcast at times when church schools can listen as a body. The teaching program, especially in the small church school, would be enriched far beyond the achievement possible to a single church. Weekday religious education classes also could benefit from directed listening to radio programs or recordings planned as part of their study program.

IMMEDIACY AND PERSONALIZED NATURE

The essence of the success of radio and television lies in the immediacy and speed of the two mediums, their ability to let the listener or viewer meet the performers face to face in an intimate "I-thou" relationship, and in the fact they exercise all these functions right in the listener's home. The clue for religious educators is apparent. The most important function of radio and television is to bring the Christian message right where we live. Via radio we can extend the program of Christian education beyond the walls of the church, bringing it on a friendly and informal basis into the home—which is exactly where every Christian educator wants it to be, but where it seldom gains entry by means of books, pamphlets, or informal home teaching.

We cannot overemphasize the need to get into the homes of America with educational radio programs of a religious nature. The 1949 edition of the *Yearbook of American Churches* lists only 77,000,000 church members of all faiths in the United States. And Samuel McCrea Cavert, in the Foreword, states that only 30 per cent of these nominal members attend church except at Easter. It seems apparent the only hope we have of reaching the overwhelming majority of Americans with a Christian message is to make contact with them outside the normal channels of church activity. Radio, which crosses freely all boundaries of thought and status, is the natural medium to use for reaching the mass of people. Indeed, it may provide the only opportunity we have for catching the ear of our secularized society with the gospel story.

If the Christian teaching is effective over the air—that is, if the subject matter is presented in terms listeners can understand, if the problems dealt with are pertinent to the listeners' experience and their personal problems, if the solutions offered help listeners think through their own situations and rise above their personal frustrations, and if all this is done in an entertaining manner—listeners may be led to identify themselves with the cause and the institution of the broadcaster. Christian teaching over the air should strive to give people the opportunity for personal identification with the kind of persons and the kind of group life through which they can discover both their real selves and a successful way of life under God's will. To be effective such an identification with Christian persons and group movements must be an emotional one. There must be a "warming of the heart" as well as a quickening of the mind.

DRAMA AND EMOTION

The educational program which wishes to reach the unchurched will therefore deal in terms of human drama—not necessarily in dramatic format—introducing a real person of the Christian faith, quickly establishing sympathy for him, and through this sympathy leading listeners into an inescapable identification with the struggles, the defeats, and the victories of that person. That is the kind of emotional absorption that makes people decide: "I want to follow this leader, because his experiences are common to my experience." Fortunately radio is admirably suited to this form of educational approach. Radio makes its basic appeal through emotion. Radio relies, not alone on words with their intellectual connotations, but on words placed in an ever-changing sequence of sound organization. Radio has three tools, and only three: words, music, and sound effects. The latter two have few intellectual connotations in arousing response from listeners, while the words themselves are highly colored emotionally by the inflection of the voice. (In television the emotional reaction to speakers and to sets must be considered.) This emotional quality of radio is an asset, not a handicap, where action is desired. *Emotion* and *motivation* look alike and belong to the same family. People act when emotions are aroused.

NEED FOR PERSONAL FOLLOW-UP

The educational program will be most effective when there is a personal follow-up to the individual listener. It is necessary to have some element in the program which will elicit listener response. Even if this response is critical of the program itself, it will provide the opportunity for a personal call. The most common method employed for prompting listener response is to offer a free premium to anyone who will write for it. In the transcribed children's series "All Aboard for Adventure," produced by the Protestant Radio Commission, a free booklet "telling all about the people and places visited on the program" is offered listeners. The booklet has a twofold purpose. First, it is a pamphlet text giving information additional to the broadcast. It becomes a part of the listener's library, thus widening the scope of the program series. (Radio educators demand that premiums offered on educational programs be useful teaching aids. It seems unfair, especially to children, to offer useless trinkets just to obtain mail response. The commercial programs do this because they are interested only in finding out how many persons are listening to their advertising message. On the other hand, educators should pause to remember that many children will write for "a compass you can wear on your wrist, just like a wrist watch" who would never bother to write for a book or even an album of pictures. The real question to determine what premium is justified is: What will you do with the names after you get them?) The second purpose of the booklet deals with what to do with the names. It is hoped that when a child writes for a booklet, the council of churches or other body sponsoring the broadcasts will send him his premium, then transmit his name to the church nearest his home. The church, in turn, is expected to call on the family to determine church-school status and to establish a church affiliation if none exists.

A further refinement, and one of major importance in the educational experience, is to organize formal or informal educational groups around the radio program. The radio program then becomes both an educational experience in its own right and the motivator of a further group experience. This system of radio-centered group education is now being tried by the churches in Glendive, Montana, and the ranch area surrounding that community. The churches of Glendive co-operate in presenting a weekly half hour on the local radio station, which covers an eighty-five-mile radius. The first fifteen minutes are devoted to the broadcast of an "All Aboard for Adventure" recording. The second half of the program is a meeting of "The Adventure Club." Children join the club merely by sending their name and address to the radio station. In return they receive a copy of the "All Aboard for Adventure" premium pamphlet and an "Adventure Club" badge. When five or more children have registered from a neighborhood, a field worker from Glendive visits them and organizes a local Adventure Club. Continuing leadership for the local club is provided by parents. The central club furnishes study materials and, through the radio program, suggests work projects, reports on local club activities, carries on direct teaching, and gives local club members the opportunity to broadcast.

The Glendive project is still too new for definitive analysis and evaluation. The club members are enthusiastic for the program, and the co-operating churches are satisfied with results so far. If the project succeeds in holding the interest of the children, Glendive may well have discovered an important method of educational evangelism.

Radio Production Workshops as an Educational Tool

Public-school teachers have found that a tremendous amount of learning can take place in the production of a radio program. This fact accounts for the recent rapid increase of school radio-production workshops, especially in high school. Whenever students—adults as well as children—know they will have a chance to say something significant over the air about the subject they are studying, they do a great deal of research and spend as much time as is necessary to clarify their views so they may be communicated to persons who have less understanding of the subject. In church schools, where little outside study can be expected, the use of radio production as a creative outlet can assure a prodigious amount of outside thinking and activity that would never take place otherwise. Even an imitation radio broadcast prepared for the church school or a department will excite the interest of students and lead to sustained creative work.

Young people and young adults are especially keen to participate in live radio programs sponsored by their churches. Already many churches can tap a reservoir of radio talent among young adults who have had experience in college or high-school radio workshops. They will accept eagerly the opportunity to make an important use of their creative talents in behalf of their church or a council of churches.

Production workshops can be organized in co-operation with a local radio station or with an educational institution that offers radio courses. But the church must provide competent leadership—leaders who know both radio and the proper content for religious educational programs.

Distinctive Educational Functions of Radio and Television

Either radio or television may be employed for the basic educational objectives of arousing interest, imparting information, gaining the allegiance and the active participation of members of the audience. But the educational effectiveness of specific material may be vastly different when transmission is by radio from what it would be if transmission were by television; and the advantage does not always lie with television. The superiority of a combination of sight and sound seems obvious in a teaching situation requiring definition, identification of objects—for example, What were houses like in Jesus' day?—explanations of how objects, or even of how ideas, function, or comparisons between objects or ideas. When a person is speaking, especially if he is someone the audience would like very much to meet, it is almost always better for him to be seen than to depend upon voice quality alone for effectiveness. (But women should beware of appearing on television without adequate make-up. The harsh lighting enhances lines and hollows.) Television, like other visual mediums, is an excellent means to use to impress upon minds the structure, the dimensions, the general appearance, the inner workings of something. Television is a tool for concretion; it shows things as they are, banishing vagueness in the comprehensive process.

When radio and television are viewed objectively, there seems to be little reason to doubt that the latter, provided program fare is improved, will largely banish radio listening in those areas where a television signal is receivable. No one would be blind who has the gift of sight. But the religious educator who wishes to spark creative thinking may well turn to lowly radio to accomplish his aims. One weakness of television—as of any pictorial medium—is that it may do too well the job of imparting a rigid structure to the mind. A thing or a person is seen, and no play is left in the mind for enlarging or modifying the visual concept. A generation of Americans equate Disraeli with George Arliss. Historical religious characters—the prophets, the Church fathers, Paul—are usually pictured as white-bearded, stern-looking creatures, indelibly impressed upon our minds today as forbidding persons, untouchable, aloof from the struggle of living. Such pictures are a current visualization of what a former generation thought these persons ought to be. They have no relevance for us, are only blocks to our understanding of the real characters of these leaders. How much better it is to introduce our young people to Paul by means of radio or recording! There is no preconception as a strong, virile voice says quietly: "I am Paul, a Jew, born in Tarsus, but brought up in Jerusalem at the feet of Gamaliel, instructed in the law of our fathers, and zealous for God. I was a Pharisee, and lived after the strictest sect of our religion. I verily thought with myself, that I ought to do many things against the name of Jesus. And this I did." [1] Here is **Paul** speaking for himself. The visual image created in the mind of the listener is one satisfying to him. Paul becomes a real, living person, because the listener has created him in a face-to-face situation in his imagination.

Whereas television is bound by the confines of the studio set and the screen, radio knows no boundaries of time or space. The mere turn of a phrase, a strain of music, sets the scene in radio. For radio's stage is the imagination, and the listener peoples it with those persons and things that best suit his fancy in understanding the story being told. Radio's stuff in trade is the awakening of the creative activity of the world of experience of each listener. There is free play of communication from the mind of the broadcaster to the mind of the listener, unencumbered by stereotyped visual symbols. This situation gives radio the greatest potentiality of any medium of communication for creative interaction between educator and auditor.

Both radio and television are part of the new and growing field of educational resources. The advantages and limitations of each medium will determine the format in which the educational message is cast. Whichever medium he uses, the religious educator will be concerned with connecting everyday living and religion. He will want to show "how Christianity works"; to present concrete situations in which the great Christian ideas are in action and can be understood as concepts that work. He will be sure to present his message through stories of Christians living, because Christianity can be understood only if we are exposed to it in personal form. Ideas take on meaning when they become clothed in life experiences. When people experience such meaning, they can be persuaded to intelligent, independent action.

SUGGESTIONS FOR FURTHER STUDY

1. Use of phonograph records, such as the *All Aboard for Adventure* recordings, in teaching junior and junior-high school children (see *Religious Radio*, pp. 221-33). Records can be purchased through denominational publishing houses.

2. The use of radio-production workshops to lead children and youth into productive effort based upon curriculum material (see *Religious Radio*, pp. 233-35).

3. A vocabulary research project, using a cross-section control group of adults, both church members and nonchurch people, in which the words, phrases, and ideas in current religious programs are studied to determine how well they are understood by listeners.

4. Utilization of current educational radio programs in religious education work.

5. Development of Christian education programs in radio and television for actual production over local radio stations.

[1] From *The Radio Edition of the Bible*, produced by the Protestant Radio Commission.

6. Leadership training for broadcasters in the field of Christian education.
7. Working with station management for the inclusion of Christian educational material in standard educational broadcasts.

BIBLIOGRAPHY

Barnouw, Erik. *Handbook of Radio Production.* Boston: Little, Brown & Co., 1949.

_____. *Handbook of Radio Writing.* Rev. ed. Boston: Little, Brown & Co., 1947.

Crews, Albert. *Professional Radio Writing.* Boston: Houghton Mifflin Co., 1946.

_____. *Radio Production Directing.* Boston: Houghton Mifflin Co., 1944.

Institute for Education by Radio, Ohio State University: *Proceedings of the Annual Meetings.* Columbus: Ohio State University, 1940-49.

Levenson, William B. *Teaching Through Radio.* New York: Rinehart and Co., 1945.

Parker, E. C.; Inman, Elinor; and Snyder, Ross. *Religious Radio.* New York: Harper & Brothers, 1948.

School Broadcast Conference. *Proceedings of the Annual Meetings.* Chicago: School Broadcast Conference, 1937 to date.

Wisconsin Research Project. *Radio in the Classroom.* Madison: University of Wisconsin Press, 1942.

Woefel, Norman, and Tyler, I. Keith. *Radio and the School.* New York; World Book Company. 1945.

Chapter 14

PLAY AND RECREATION

BOB TULLY

A FLAT TIRE HAD DELAYED our entrance into the neat white church. The alert superintendent met us and offered to take the boys down to their classes in the basement. We went into the children's and youth's department. At one side the primary children surrounded the sand table. The beginners were maneuvering pictures on a flannel-covered board. Dickie, our younger, entered into the fun of learning at once. The Junior Boys were planning an overnight hike. Bobby, our older boy, was sorry he was only a visitor, but he soon was sharing his ideas. In the adult class I was handed the Sunday bulletin and program:

Kingdom News:

The Ladies' Missionary Society is planning a church supper June 5th. Keep the date open.

The Young People will hold their monthly social at the home of Jim Wasser Wednesday night.

The Dorcas Class will sew at the home of Mrs. Nina Brown on Thursday. The meal will be a covered-dish dinner at 12:15. Husbands are invited to attend. Come in your work clothes.

Messrs. Ted Banks, Victor Reed, and John Saylor are the members of the Annual Church Picnic Committee. Date: July 4. Games, contests, variety program, and evening vespers are being planned.

Play and recreation are accepted activities on the part of churches for the development of fellowship. But they should be more than that; they have possibilities to achieve the greater ends of religious education. Play is a method—a way to achieve religious concepts so that man may live religiously.

Throughout the ages there have been varying influences that have molded the play and recreation of the Church as an organization and as individual members. The early Church was so interested in the immediate return of Jesus and the personal joys of his gospel that its members functioned normally in the fellowship and proclamation of that gospel. As the Church lived on, it had to become very conscious of the world

173

about it; and beginning about the second century it struggled to move out of the world, and two great movements came into being. Remnants of these fully developed Dark Ages points of view are still with us:

1. *Scholasticism.* The basic idea here was that the mind, thinking, discussing, lecturing, and so on, were the important things. The body, play, and recreation were neglected in the intriguing development of the mind. Scholasticism is still with us in many forms, centering in many schools of "higher" learning.

2. *Asceticism.* This conception did not just lead to the neglect of the physical, the joyful play experiences; it directly opposed fun, play, and recreation. Religion was not only serious business; it was a solemn ordeal. Joy, pleasure, happiness, play, recreation, were not signs of religious understanding and growth. Natural desires were to be subdued, not religiously directed.

Asceticism showed up in the United States during the time of the Puritans. It comes to light today in the religious educators who condemn play and recreational activity as foolish and worldly. These educators do not analyze the values of the material or activity itself. They do not see the opportunities of religious development through play and recreation.

Although present—and often troublesomely so—these two major attitudes are not extremely powerful. Most religious educators now accept play and recreation as valid materials to supplement the process of education. Play and recreation are accepted as something the church will have to get along with because all children play, and all adults probably need recreation. Therefore, to hold the interest of all there will have to be sand tables for the little ones, hikes under church leadership for the boys, parties for the youth, and a periodic picnic for all to maintain the church fellowship. But these are not seen as a method to achieve religious education's aim of teaching individuals to live religiously, to build a total personality pattern within a framework of religious concepts and ideals.

A Modern Religious Philosophy of Play and Recreation

Throughout the ages, from Aristotle to the present generation of psychologists and educators, there have been many ideas or theories of play. The modern point of view is often termed the "self-expression theory" and is founded on many outstanding physiological and psychological studies which, in brief, indicate: (1) Man is naturally active in body and mind. (2) He is organically constructed so that there are limits to his activity. (3) Within the limits of this organism man is affected by his degree of physical fitness. (4) There seem to be psychological inclinations—human desires—which would lead men to certain types of play activity.[1]

[1] See Mitchell and Mason, *Theory of Play*, chap. 3.

On this scientific point of view the religious educator should build scientifically to bring to pass, through play, his objectives of religious education.

It is wise to remember that play for the child is his life. It is his natural environment. Many educators are seeing, as Caroline Pratt saw years ago, that childhood's work is learning, and it is in his play that the child works at his job.[2] Play for the adult is usually his recreation. The adult strives to rebuild himself through pleasant, self-chosen activity. This recreation in most cases isn't as active as the play of childhood or youth. Youth stands at the period of transition—the period of movement from childhood into adulthood. Much of youth's play is its life—an all-consuming interest. Yet youth is learning also to make play recreational, to make it rebuild tired bodies and minds. Many religiously minded adults question and criticize during this transition period, rather than serve and aid in the transition so that the coming adult generation will have habits of creative, Christian recreation.

There are few in today's society that do not see the values in play for children, youth, and adults. Our modern society, geared to industrialized and assembly-line techniques, creates great needs that can be answered only through natural and creative play.

But more than this, play properly guided and motivated can bring to pass religious and moral concepts and values. It can be of extreme value in the development of character, since man's conduct is more dependent on his feelings than upon his thought. It is recognized that the worth of an activity for the building of character is determined by the opportunity it gives to develop attitudes and by the kinds or types of emotion it arouses. And play is the best type of activity to develop attitudes and to bring out emotions.

Therefore it is well for a play leader to know how character is built and to purposely use the following three methods:

1. *Imitation.* Man takes on the ways of others that he admires. Children imitate their play group, which, next to the home, is the most powerful group in influencing conduct. Hero worship is a common characteristic and is a force deeply affecting character. Play leaders should encourage proper imitation.

2. *Suggestion.* Many ideas and ideals are accepted without much critical analysis. They come by suggestion, are encountered at many turns of life in common, matter-of-fact experiences. Scientific studies indicate three important things that make suggestions work: (*a*) character or position of the person making it; (*b*) repetition, over and over again for a long enough time, of the positive suggestion; (*c*) intensity of suggestion. Spec-

[2] *I Learn from Children.*

tacular events and suggestions stick in memory. Play leaders need to constantly suggest proper attitudes and methods of conduct.

3. *Instruction.* Two types of instruction are usually under discussion—direct moral instruction and the indirect or incidental moral instruction. Both have a place, but the play leader will wisely use the latter method. This is the method of teaching moral concepts in all acts of the learner. Honesty is best taught in acts calling for honesty, truth in situations calling for truth, love in acts calling for love or hate, and so on. In the natural environment of play and recreation the play leader has many opportunities to give character instruction.[3]

There are many activities through which the play leader can instruct in character education, but only a few will be mentioned here:

a) Games, contests, sports, hobbies, and so on. Moral choices have to be made every instant in games and contests and hobbies. At the time of those choices is the time to be ready for instruction, so the play leader should have in mind the following specific steps: (1) Know the learnings that are desired and have a chance to be taught in the activity. (2) Praise—commend—the desirable response. (3) Condemn the undesirable response. (4) Point out the consequences of the act. Be fair and point out both the good and bad consequences. (5) Lift the eyes of the participant to the far-reaching consequences of the act. It is always wise in games and contests to enforce the rules at once and fairly. Show no partiality.

b) Storytelling and dramatics. The spoken word is an excellent method of influencing behavior.[4]

c) Personal counseling. Perhaps no other individual has as much opportunity for this type of instruction as the play leader. He has entrance into conversation because of the universality of play and the naturalness of the play fellowship.[5]

Other than in character education, play offers values in physical well-being, in mental development, in developing the democratic process. Play, well taught, will help overcome provincialism, bring about world-mindedness. Play, well guided, can help develop the attitude of service to mankind. The late World War taught us some of the techniques—paper and scrap drives, overseas recreational units, and so forth. The Church, with its missionary and service interest, could and is doing in peace what recreational-educational organizations attempted in the war. Children, youth, and adults in the spirit of play and recreation collect grease, make soap, can food, collect old clothes, raise heifers, sew, write letters, give programs—all in the interest of serving the world and their God.

[3] See Mitchell and Mason, *op. cit.*, chap. 12.
[4] See Chapter 11.
[5] See Chapter 15.

BUILDING THE TOTAL CHURCH RECREATION PROGRAM[6]

The foregoing philosophy can be placed in the local church through avenues of formalized teaching, as themes for sermons, in class or age-group discussions, in forums, and in other ways. But better still it should enter through a total church-recreation program—a program which functions in each of the component groups, departments, classes, fellowships, and the like. It should be an active recreational program which places the play and recreational life of the members in relationship to the ideals, concepts, and broader activities of the religious group and brings about religious living—the aim of religious education.

Organizationally there probably is no definite pattern that will meet the needs of each local congregation, so the following outline is only suggestive. Each item is discussed briefly to point up basic considerations.

1. *The church recreation committee or director.*[7] Many local churches are not ready for this recreational step, but others could take it if they had vision of the functions of such a person or committee. Some large congregations do have a full-time paid director of recreation. Others might use a qualified individual on a part-time voluntary basis. Many churches could have a church-wide committee. The following are some major functions of such a person or committee:

a) Co-ordinating the social functions of the church. An easy way to begin is with a central recreational calendar. It is too bad to find groups within the church in conflict because there is no one through whom they can clear dates and facilities.

b) Leading all-church social functions. Annual picnics, church nights, and other all-church social functions could be planned and guided.

c) Resource leader or group. The leaders of small groups often need helps in the areas of materials, facilities, and leadership.

d) Recreational librarian. Each church should have a collection of recreational source materials for the use of individuals who conduct social recreation infrequently.

e) Research. Knowledge of local needs, abilities, and interests could well be sought out. The entire community could be studied.

f) Training leaders. Each of the groups within the church should have trained leadership in it, trained by the church, and with a religious point of view.

2. *The small-group recreational leader or committee.*[8] In the vast majority of churches this is the heart of the present recreation program of the

---

[6] See Powell, *Recreation in Church and Community.*
[7] See Tully, *Social Recreation Primer.*
[8] See Tully, *op. cit.;* Harbin, *Fun Encyclopedia;* Rohrbough, *Handy* and *Handy II.*

church. This leader or committee is untrained but willing and in the light of providing social fellowship is doing a fair job. But there the job stops. Many individuals do not think of the religious educational values of play as outlined in the first part of this chapter. The following are steps that could be taken to point up the values:

a) The committee or leader could function for a longer period of time than one social or even a half-year. Thus there would be a chance to build a progressive program and time to study the purpose, problems, and methods of recreation.

b) The group might investigate the possibilities of participation in more than just parties or socials. There are other interesting elements in a recreation program.

c) The group could help their leaders financially so they could attend recreational institutes and conferences to obtain a broader point of view.

In the children's department the play leader is usually the teacher. Each teacher could well learn the methods of using play to teach religion. Here play is a method in the classroom as well as an activity for recess, relaxation, or the development of fellowship.

3. *Program elements.*[9] True, the crux of a good recreational program will be found in the leadership. One consecrated leader is more valuable than tons of material. But many potential leaders have not gone far because they have failed to comprehend the possibilities of good recreation. They confine their program to only a few elements and fail to expand it to meet the interests, desires, and needs of the total group.

The church's major recreational program has centered about socials, parties, and picnics, the major aim of which is to develop fellowship. This has been an excellent aim, but in this complex society the church must find additional recreational activities in which fellowship is not neglected, but other objectives are reached. Following are a few other suggested program elements.

a) Hobbies: Hobbies bring out creativeness; they can be centered in the home and are much more enjoyable when shared. To encourage hobbies the group can sponsor four types of activities: a hobby exhibit, a hobby night, a hobby workshop, and a hobby club.

b) Dramatics: Dramatics call for great variety of ability and interests—music; rhythm; handicraft for making stage sets; art for making costumes, posters, sets, tickets; acting. At the same time there are great social values in a cast working together. Dramatics are more fully discussed in Chapter 11, so here there will be mentioned four types of fun dramatics: (1) Suggested dramatics—acting out something suggested, such as a nursery rhyme or fairy

[9] Harbin, *Recreation for Youth;* Powell, *op. cit.;* Tully, *op. cit.*

story. (2) Spontaneous dramatics—acting out the ending to a partly told story or play by ad libbing the lines and actions. (3) Game dramatics—using games with the dramatic principle, such as charades, slogans, dumb crambo, and so on. (4) Stunt dramatics—asking small groups to prepare stunts which will be given before the whole group. The aim is fun and creativeness, not perfection. Yet there is no need for poor humor or lack of preparation. Sacred subjects should not be caricatured for a stunt.

c) Group play reading: A recreational activity, related to dramatics, wherein the values are in the script of the play.

d) Movies: Audio-visual method and content are discussed in Chapter 12, but it should be added that the recreational leader faces two special tasks: First is the giving of guidance in the area of movie evaluation. A modern sin is indiscriminate attendance at movies. Second is the using of good motion pictures—full-length features and shorts—in the recreational program of the group. There are good motion pictures that can be secured for recreational showing. Check with denominational and interdenominational sources.

e) Music: There are three important areas in the field of music that the religious-recreation educator can well study and plan to use. (1) Music appreciation may be increased by the following activities: music appreciation vespers, music appreciation clubs, radio clubs, church offertories, record library. (2) Music interpretation may be done by choral clubs, choirs, choruses, quartets, octets, trios, solos, bands, orchestras, composing, arranging, transposing, and conducting—all means of interpretation. The area of recreational song-leading is also challenging. (3) Musical games and folk dances have been increasing in popularity because they answer so many healthy and fundamental interests of people, giving opportunity for rhythmic expression without all the attendant evils of the social dance, developing cultural interests and helping to destroy race barriers, developing sociability and destroying social barriers. Because musical games are fun, many groups overuse them, neglecting other program elements.

f) Team games: With the growth of competitive sports we find many individuals skilled in team games who do not get to participate on highly skilled high-school, college, or professional teams. Having the skill, they wish to play, and the church can use that desire for valuable religious educational purposes. There are many problems encountered in sponsoring church-related teams and leagues, but they can be answered. The objectives of a sports program—to give pleasurable and healthful physical activity, to develop co-ordination and physical skill, to establish friendship within one's own and other groups, and especially to develop character through the teaching of sportsmanship—should be met through careful organization of the team and the leagues. The objective of winning must never overshadow the other objectives.

g) Hikes: Even in this air-minded, atomic-energy age, there has been an increasing interest in hiking as a recreational activity. Of course, one of the objectives of sponsoring hikes is to develop a pleasure and an interest in walking, but other objectives might be learning of nature and nature crafts, camping, woodcraft, outdoor cooking, and developing self-reliance and initiative in the out of doors.

h) Banquets: The major purpose of a banquet should be genuine fellowship and fun, but it may have other objectives also—to sell a project, to bestow honors, to hear an address. However, don't forget to plan for fun and fellowship.

i) Reading: The church can well launch a recreational reading program to improve and increase the reading habits of its people. To do so, the following can be sponsored: a church library, a book shelf or table, a reading club, book reviews, printed reviews, a book party, or a poetry club.

Planning Specific Social Activities[10]

Whenever a group meets, it moves. There is always group change, although sometimes unguided and aimless. Many recreational leaders have noted and identified the elements that make for good movement. So the recreational leader uses a definitely planned organization of these elements and weaves them together into what is termed a "social-activities pattern." Inexperienced leaders should find the following outline of these elements helpful in making plans for any type of social activity.

The following items call for general planning:

1. *Theme.* This is the subject or idea around which the whole is planned.

2. *Time.* Don't set it for before the majority can arrive; but once it is set, start on time.

3. *Place.* The location will greatly determine what activities can be entered into.

4. *Crowd.* It is never the "same old crowd." The relationships in numbers, attitudes, and interests of a group change from meeting to meeting. The size also determines what activities can be done.

The following items must be planned in detail if there is to be good group movement:

1. *Invitations.* Raise the joy of anticipation by making clever invitations.

2. *Decorations.* These, as well as the invitations, should fit the theme, be simple and inexpensive but neat and lovely.

3. *Refreshments.* It is not always necessary to serve refreshments to a group; but if they are used, they should be well planned so they fit into the program easily.

4. *Program.* Now comes the actual planning of the fellowship of the

[10] See Tully, *op. cit.*

group. After the invitations are out, the decorations are up, and the refreshments are prepared, the next task is the handling of the crowd, and the planning for this falls into five parts: (*a*) Activities for first comers: Something should be planned for those who arrive early; if not, everyone will soon be arriving late. (*b*) Mixer: This is a type of activity that the entire group can enter easily and quickly. It should unify the group. In groups that are unacquainted, mixers are often used to learn names. (*c*) Social activities: This is the body of the program and should include moments of active participation, a number of activities for the entire group, intermingled with moments of quiet participation, when interest is maintained, but the entire group need not actively participate. (*d*) Refreshments: At some time during the group fellowship the prepared refreshments should be served as a part of the total program, not just tacked on. (*e*) Climax: How to close a social gathering effectively has always been a major problem. Many leaders just let interest fizzle out after the refreshments are served. Some leaders suggest saving the best activity till the last. But for church people, interested in religious education, why not close with a short inspirational worship experience? Worship is the highest type of recreation known to man, and Christians should not fear to use it for its recreational value. There should be no fear of worship losing value or being degraded when it supplements the recreative values found in play and fellowship.

This climax of worship should be the lifting of the thoughts and emotions of the group members outside themselves to something bigger than the individual or the immediate group. It is the continuing of the already-built-up fellowship into an expanded fellowship. Therefore this worship should be more than a prayer tacked on to give religious sanction, or a lecture or talk stuck in. It must be a part of the total planning that fits the theme and must be woven in as an integral part of the program. Group worship implies group movement toward God. If the social program has built a group out of individuals, then the closing worship calls only for the moving of that group into an experience above the commonplace—an experience that lifts the group to a higher appreciation. If a talk, scripture, poem, song, or picture will do it, then it should be used. Climaxes should be planned well in advance, and the leader should work for group unity and group feeling before the climax in worship is approached.

5. *Clinic*. After each social experience the leader and his planning group could well conduct a clinic to examine the results. The social event should be analyzed as to movement, as to attitudes taken, as to mistakes made, also as to good points and qualities. On the analysis found in a good clinic experience the next social gathering can be planned and former errors corrected.

Areas, Facilities, and Finances

Several factors should determine the extent of recreational facilities that the church should provide: (1) The need of individuals and the community for play areas, both outdoors and indoors. (2) The leadership available that can get religious educational results. (3) The ability of the religious group to finance both the areas and the leadership.

Most churches, following the above criteria, would not build gymnasiums or stadiums; but many would provide, supervise, and finance social recreational rooms and small playgrounds. Under this setup the congregation could recreationally build homemade equipment and provide voluntary leadership to supervise areas and activities, cutting down on total financial expense.

Recreation should be financed just as any other activity in the church. Ideally it should have a place in the regular church budget and should be met as a part of the total church program. But there are other ways of financing the program: (1) Special group sponsorship, with men's group, mothers' club, and so on, standing behind the need of finance. (2) Special contributions by pledges received and recreational finance campaigns inaugurated. (3) Donations, collections, and admissions received at special recreational events. (4) Sales of arts-and-crafts materials, rummage, old records—or auction sales—can be conducted.

The Church and Questionable Recreational Practices[11]

There are three attitudes that the church can take toward questionable recreational practices its members participate in. (1) Ignore—go on as though unseen or unnoticed. At the same time the problems go unanswered and become greater. (2) Abhor—stand off and condemn, crying from the steeple top the evils, not recognizing individual needs nor trying to find positive answers. (3) Educate—provide a sound basis of intelligent self-judgment of an activity, and then provide outlets for wholesome desires if other well-organized and well-directed agencies do not provide the outlets.

Areas in need of study, research, and then creative action are commercial recreation, gambling including bingo games and quilt raffles, the present trend toward nudity in bathing apparel, comic books, motion pictures, horse racing, and the radio.

Training for Religious Recreational Leadership

There are two major attitudes toward play and recreation. Public recreationalists advocate the point of view that play in itself is its own end: "Play for play's sake." They avoid religious implications and discussions. The re-

[11] Rohrbough, *op. cit.*

ligious educator advocates that play is a method through which individuals not only can but should grow toward Christlikeness. They use recreation for a higher goal. This point of view has implications for the church as it plans the training of its recreational leaders.

First, the church must train them in the religious philosophy of play and recreation. Second, it should teach leaders the methods of religious recreational leadership. Their methods should be different because their objectives are different. But in the third area—the area of materials, the skills of recreation—the church recreationalist can secure help from many sources outside the church. These then can be applied, using the religious method to reach the church's goal of education.

It is the task of the church to see that its leaders are trained in how to eliminate the questionable and undesirable things that are "activity for activity's sake." To do that, the philosophy and point of view of the church must be well taught during the time that skills are learned. The aims and objectives of religious recreational leadership should be taught under church leadership; then skills can be picked up from many areas.

Following are fruitful areas for the training in philosophy and method along with skills: (1) National or regional denominationally sponsored recreational institutes. Example: Methodist Regional Recreational Institutes. (2) Interdenominational leadership-training classes or camps. Example: U. C. Y. M. Regional Planning Conferences. (3) Recreational Laboratories. Example: Ihduhapi Recreation Leaders Laboratory. (4) Denominational colleges, if their recreational departments have the religious point of view rather than the public recreational point of view.

Also there are excellent areas in which recreational skills of leadership can be learned, but there is little or no help in the development of the religious point of view and method: (1) National Recreation Association Training Institutes. Note the association's magazine, *Recreation*, for listings. (2) State universities and their extension program, including the Four-H leadership training. (3) National Recreational Conferences. Example: National Recreation Congress.

SUMMARY

Play and recreation are both material and method to the trained educator. The activities of play and recreation are materials used for fellowship, relaxation, and fun; but they are also methods—methods of reaching objectives of religious education. To handle the task of using recreation as a method, the objectives must be clearly in mind. The program content should contain many different elements, each one conducted well, following a social activities pattern that will lead to the desired results. Leaders need church-guided training, facilities should be adequate and finances in order.

SUGGESTIONS FOR FURTHER STUDY

1. Formulate your own "theory of play" and "philosophy of recreation" (Cabot, Mitchell and Mason, Neumeyer and Neumeyer).

2. Analyze some present trends in leisure and recreation, and list their implications for religious education (Mitchell and Mason, Nash, Neumeyer and Neumeyer).

3. Evaluate the recreation program of a local church as to objectives, program elements, leadership, facilities, finance (Powell, Tully).

4. Build a proposed recreational program for the church that you examined (Harbin, Powell, Tully).

5. Following the outline suggested under "Planning Specific Social Activities," build a complete social evening's fellowship for a group of twenty-five persons. Choose your own theme, place, time, and group (Tully).

BIBLIOGRAPHY

In keeping with the suggestions of the chapter, this brief biblography has been divided into three divisions—philosophy, method, and materials. Many works overlap, giving aids in each division, so they are listed under their major contribution.

PHILOSOPHY

Cabot, Richard C. *What Men Live By*. New York: Houghton Mifflin Co., 1914.

Mitchell, Elmer and Mason, Bernard. *Theory of Play*. New York: A. S. Barnes & Co., 1948.

Nash, J. B. *Spectatoritis*. New York: Sears, 1932.

Neumeyer, Martin H., and Neumeyer, Esther. *Leisure and Recreation*. New York: A. S. Barnes & Co., 1936.

Pratt, Caroline. *I Learn from Children*. New York: Simon & Schuster, 1948.

METHOD

Harbin, E. O. *Recreation for Youth*. Nashville: Methodist Publishing House, 1941.

Meyer, Harold D., and Brightbill, Charles K. *Community Recreation*. Boston: D. C. Heath and Co., 1948.

Powell, Warren T. *Recreation in Church and Community*. New York: Abingdon Press, 1938.

Tully, Bob. *Social Recreation Primer*. Elgin, Ill.: Brethren Publishing House, 1944.

MATERIALS

Harbin, E. O. *Fun Encyclopedia*. New York and Nashville: Abingdon-Cokesbury Press, 1940.

Mason, Bernard S., and Mitchell, Elmer D. *Social Games for Recreation*. New York: A. S. Barnes & Co., 1936.

Rohrbough, Lynn. *Handy* and *Handy II*. Delaware, Ohio: Cooperative Recreation Service.

Chapter 15

INDIVIDUAL AND GROUP COUNSELING

HARRISON SACKET ELLIOTT

Counseling is both an emphasis in the entire program of religious education and a special aspect of that program. As an emphasis in the entire program it represents an acceptance of the responsibility in and through religious
education to help individuals in meeting the everyday situations of life. As a
special aspect of the program it involves a recognition of the fact that each
individual's situation and problems are unique, and that he may need personal help on his own particular problems and decisions.

Individual and group counseling is based upon a distinctive possibility in
human beings. They do not have to be at the mercy of immediate circumstances and to meet life on a trial-and-error, trial-and-success, basis. They can
arrange for alternations from the traffic of life and can through memory and
imagination explore a situation apart from their immediate involvement in it
and in advance of action. Such periods of temporary withdrawal can also
be used to review and appraise the consequences of actions and attitudes and
to remake one's plans for future situations, thus having opportunity really
to benefit from experience. Human beings can carry on these types of exploration in alternation from life's activities alone, but they often find it
helpful to carry on this process in a group, the members of which are facing
similar situations and problems, or individually with a counselor in whom
they have confidence.

Basic Process in Counseling

Whatever the type of counseling, the basic process is the same. Indeed,
the procedure in counseling is not different from that in any aspect of the
program of religious education where the purpose is to help individuals or
groups find the answers to their problems. Further, the basic process in helping people with ordinary life problems is similar to that used for helping
individuals with personality and behavior difficulties.

The first step is coming to a real understanding of the problem or question under consideration. This involves describing and exploring the situation or situations in which it has arisen so that the environmental factors and
pressures are taken into account. It is necessary also to give free opportunity
for the individual facing the situation to express his feelings and attitudes

183

so that the problem as he sees and feels it may be considered and the emotional factors may be taken fully into account.

The second main step is to secure a clarification of the actual choices which the individual is facing, or of the alternative possibilities which he is willing to consider in answer to the problem. These need to be explored by the counselee as to what he feels will be the probable consequences of each if adopted. This will bring still further into the open his attitudes and feelings. Particularly important is it for the counselee to express *why* each alternative appeals to him or why he resists it. This will reveal his basic outlook on life and where the underlying conflicts are in arriving at a choice.

The third major step is coming to a choice or a decision. On an important problem this will not be arrived at easily. There will be discussion back and forth as between the alternative possibilities, and there will be real struggle on the part of the counselee over his personal attitudes and feelings and in relation to his basic outlook on life.

A fourth major step—which sometimes is omitted, to the harm of the counselee—is foreseeing the difficulties and making plans for carrying out the decision. If the choice represents a different way of action or a change in his basic attitudes, there will be difficulties in carrying it out. Sizing up these difficulties and working out ways and means will help to prevent defeat.

EMOTIONAL ATTITUDES AND PREDISPOSITIONS

The emotional factors are especially important in counseling. The actual facts about the situation are not as important as how the counselee feels about it. Every individual looks at a situation through the glasses of his past experience; and no two individuals wear the same glasses, since all have had different experiences. It is important, therefore, that the counselee be free to express his feelings so that the situation as he sees it shall be dealt with. For example, a boy comes to talk with a counselor about difficulties he is facing in relation to rules and regulations at school. They seem to him unfair and unreasonable. He feels like defying or side-stepping them. He hates the teacher who seeks to enforce them. What should he do? He has so much emotion about the matter that the counselor suspects he views the present situation through the emotionally tinged glasses of his experience with the exercise of authority. As the boy expresses himself, he reveals that he has an autocratic father and a home conducted with strict and seemingly unreasonable discipline. The boy has inwardly rebelled although outwardly conforming. Out of this experience he has developed attitudes toward discipline and authority which make him feel in advance that any restrictions upon him are unwarranted and unreasonable. Unless he gets these feelings out into the open and comes to see why he feels as he does about all exercise of authority, he will not be able to make a reliable decision as to what to do in the present situation, which may or may not represent an unwarranted restriction upon him; nor will he come to a more mature attitude toward authority.

Another example is that of a girl who is having difficulty in deciding whether to accept an important post of responsibility in a local church. As she expresses herself freely, it becomes evident that she has an extreme fear of failure and has come to look on situations where she must assume responsibility as dangerous. As she talks further, she comes to realize that the insecurity of her home and certain devastating disappointments she has had have so influenced her that she is looking at the situation as she feels it to be and not as it really is.

A third example is that of a young man who is baffled on a vocational decision. He has narrowed the alternatives to a choice between being a lawyer and being a minister. He seems to have the abilities which fit him equally well for either calling. His life purpose seems clear, and yet he cannot be sure as to what is God's will for his life. As he expresses his feelings about the two possible callings, he becomes aware that he is at the mercy of influences from his past experience which are confusing his present choice. His mother is a devout member of the church and dedicated him to the ministry before he was born. On the other hand, his father is a judge, comes of a long line of lawyers, and wants him to choose the law. The conflicting attitudes and desires of his parents have so influenced him that he brings confused and conflicting feelings to his vocational choice. Until he can get these feelings out into the open and deal with them, he will be torn between his conflicting loyalties to his parents. Often the individual is not aware of why he feels as he does. But he cannot meet the present situation positively until these unconscious motivations and compulsions are brought into consciousness and are dealt with.

Emotional Factors in a Counseling Situation

Not only are the emotional attitudes and predispositions which the individual brings to a counseling situation important, but there are emotional factors in the situation itself which must be given due recognition. Seward Hiltner gives an example of a conscience-stricken student who went to a minister to confer about cheating he had done in a crucial examination. He had cheated because he would fail the examination if he did not cheat; and he could not stand the threat to his security, recognition, and acceptance which seemed involved in his failure. When he explored what he should do, the same emotional factors were present and made it as difficult to decide what to do to set this right as it had been to resist cheating in the first place. If he made a clear breast of it to the dean, he might be dismissed from school;

and again there were the threats to his security, sense of worth, and his acceptance by others.[1]

These three emotional factors of security, recognition, and acceptance are present in varying degrees in every counseling situation. Security is perhaps the most basic. A situation with threats to the security of the individual greater than he feels he can negotiate warps decisions. This factor is particularly important in dealing with children who are so completely at the mercy of parents and other adults and of other environmental factors. Recognition, or a sense of achievement and worth, is also important. Too great a threat of failure in the situation may warp the decision, as will also too easy success. Acceptance by others and a sense of belonging are also basic. A threat of rejection by others may powerfully influence a decision. These environmental factors may develop basic anxiety in the individual and, as Karen Horney has pointed out in relation to neurotic individuals,[2] lead to either of three types of decision: making the choices and adopting the courses of action which lead one to be recognized and accepted by others without due reference to one's own convictions and beliefs; or aggressively fighting others in the interests of one's own security and achievement; or seeking in some way to get out of the situation and to avoid decision and action altogether. These emotional factors in the situation must be brought out into the open and dealt with in any group or individual counseling. Otherwise the problem will not really be solved, and unhealthy results may occur.

Conflicts in Life Purpose

The counseling process involves for the counselee underlying conflicts as he seeks an answer to his problems, or as he tries to come to a decision in a baffling situation. These underlying conflicts take various forms, depending upon the age and circumstances of the counselee; but they actually involve the counselee's controlling purpose in life—that to which he is supremely devoted. Frequently the issue for the counselee is between ego-centered goals on the one hand, in which his life will be centered on his own welfare, security, and achievement; and alter-centered purposes, on the other hand, where his concern will include the welfare of others and service to the common good. For children the issue between looking out for Number One or thinking about others arises in the more restricted areas of life in relationships in the home, in play and games, in schoolwork and school activities, in church or synagogue programs and projects. Adolescents often face the question in fundamental form in their relations with the opposite sex and in their goals for marriage, in their lifework choices, and in their

[1] *Pastoral Counseling*, pp. 22-23.
[2] *Our Inner Conflicts*.

decisions about their relations to church or synagogue. For adults the issue may arise in face-to-face relationships in home, church, and social affairs, or in the wider aspects of life in business or profession, in community life and organizations, and in racial, economic, and other relationships. For the ego-centered individual, who has been living his life in terms of himself, the crisis in the counseling process comes when he really has to face the issue between a self-centered life and his obligation to others than himself.

For some the underlying issue of life purpose is defined in terms of authority—whether they will insist on doing as they please, no matter what the effect upon others, or will recognize their obligation to accept various forms of control in the interests of the common good. For children and adolescents this form of the issue usually arises around their relationships with parents, teachers, club leaders, and others in positions of authority. It is often confused because of the unreasonable demands of autocratic parents or teachers. For the dependent, immature individual, who wants to be looked after and have someone else make his decisions and plans for him, the basic question as to his outlook on life is whether or not he will assume his share of the load and take responsibility proportionate to his age.

The religious counselor recognizes that these underlying issues as to controlling life purpose are basically religious and will need finally to be interpreted in religious terms. They involve living life for oneself versus seeking first and making one's supreme loyalty the furthering of the kingdom of God; doing as one pleases versus finding and following the will of God for one's life; expecting to be looked after in life versus doing one's part in making God's will operative in human life.

Issues of Basic Confidence

A second type of underlying issue is often involved: namely, the possibility of carrying out the decision, even if one makes it. To a greater or lesser degree, the counselee may have uncertainty, anxiety, and even fear because of his lack of faith in himself and trust in others. Has he the resources which will enable him to make good on his decision? If he changes his attitudes and manifests outgoing good will and concern in his relations with others, will he find that love really conquers suspicion and ill will in a competitive world? Can others, life itself, really be trusted, and dare he forget himself in devotion to the common welfare? If he feels that the forces within and without are working against him, it will be difficult for him to come to a decision. If, however, he comes to have faith in the unrealized potentialities within himself and to recognize that he will not be alone in his new devotion but can trust, and will have the support of, many others committed to like goals, he will gain courage to make the decision, even though it involves risk and sacrifice. Again the issue becomes basically religious. In making his decision will he find himself alone and helpless, or if his decision is in line with God's will for human life, can he count that God-given resources will be available in carrying out the decision, no matter what it costs? Does he have faith in God?

RELIGIOUS MANIFESTATIONS OF PERSONALITY PROBLEMS

While religious issues are involved in counseling, when it is basically carried on, it should be recognized that many problems which seem to be questions of religion turn out to be the religious manifestations of pervasive personality problems. For example, in the play *Life with Father* the autocratic, willful Mr. Day treats God—and even yells at him—in the same way he treats his wife, his children, and others with whom he comes in contact. To deal with his problem as if it were solely contempt for God would be to miss his basic personality pattern, and no solution of his relationship to God is possible apart from his relationship to others. If a personality problem with religious manifestations is dealt with solely as a religious problem, the danger is that religion will be used to alleviate the symptoms of difficulty but to continue, if not reinforce, the basic personality problem. For example, the question of God's providential care and direction in human life has exaggerated importance for an immature and dependent person. If in the counseling process he is led to accept God as one who will look after him like a superwise parent, he will be reinforced in his immaturity instead of helped to grow to maturity and at the same time to achieve a mature relationship to God.

TRANSFORMATION OF BASIC PERSONALITY PATTERNS

An individual in difficulty who comes for counseling may be one whose unsatisfactory attitudes and conduct patterns have become so basically a part of his personality structure that he seems powerless to change them. Where the difficulties are of long duration and deep seated, the individual should be referred to a professional counselor. If the difficulties are not too serious, a nonprofessional counselor can deal with them; although in all cases where changes in persistent and basic attitudes and conduct patterns are involved, it would be desirable for the nonprofessional counselor to have available a professional counselor with whom he may confer in case of need. In counseling with individuals with basic difficulties, it should be remembered that all such persistent attitudes and conduct patterns are purposeful—often unconsciously so—in that they serve the individual in various ways. However unsatisfactory they may seem to others, they are his ways of getting along in life, and he is dependent upon them. He is hot tempered or supersensitive, a fighter or a quitter, a rebel or a conformist, as the case may be, and has learned to get along in life in this particular way. Condemnation of his attitudes and behavior either makes him more aggressive in defense or causes him to sink deeper into ways of withdrawing, if he happens to be that type of individual. Only as he is approached positively and helped to find another way of negotiating life—a way in which he comes to have confidence and which he can use—can he or will he give up his undesirable style of life.

Choosing another way of life for an individual with persistent behavior patterns is more than an intellectual process. Intellectually a spoiled individual may admit that his ways of making life adjust to him and of getting his own way without reference to the welfare of others are undesirable, and that it would be better for him to adopt another way of meeting life; but emotionally he is still at the mercy of these undesirable habit patterns. Intellectually a counselee may see that his excessive childish dependence upon others and his inability to stand on his own feet are undesirable, but emotionally he is still immature and unable to act as an adult. Intellectually he may recognize that his aggressive or submissive attitudes toward anyone in a position of authority are unreasonable, and yet he still automatically responds in these ways. If the person in difficulty is a little child, particularly a child under six, it may be possible through counseling with his parents, or through arranging a substitute parent and family relationship in a church or other group, to provide for him the positive experiences in response to which these ways of negotiating life will be changed. But the older he is, the more impossible it is to adjust the life of which he is a part to his personality needs. He as an individual somehow has to be changed so that he can meet the circumstances of life in a healthy instead of an unhealthy manner. Fortunately this is possible in a counseling relationship. As the individual works through his basic problem with the counselor, actually something happens to him in his fundamental attitudes and conduct patterns through his experience in the counseling room. The possibility of personality transformation is particularly important for a distraught individual who is at the mercy of devastating and often forgotten experiences of the past. The opportunity to relive these distressing experiences in the security of the counseling relationship can release him from their grip and can result in the transformation of his emotional attitudes.

If basic personality patterns are to be changed in the counseling experience, it is important that the counselor shall not respond personally to the counselee. If, for example, he responds by counteraggression to the counselee's aggressive attitude toward him as representing authority, the counseling interview becomes just a repetition of the counselee's life experience and reinforces his difficulties. But if the counselor understands this aggression as aimed, not at him personally, but at what he represents to the counselee and can accept the aggression without responding to it, the counselee has a chance to release his emotion about authority and then to work on his attitude toward it. Correspondingly if to the very dependent immature individual who comes to the counselor asking to be told what to do, the counselor responds personally by giving advice, the counseling relationship just adds another experience of servile dependence upon others and reinforces his difficulties. If, on the other hand, the counselor rejects the counselee and tells him not to be a child but to make up his own mind, he only arouses fear or resentment. But if he can accept the counselee as an immature, dependent person, can give him assurance by his recognition of his need, and then can help him in the process of making his own decisions, the counselee can grow toward maturity in the counseling relationship. Counseling can furnish to the counselee experience in and through which he is changed and is better able to negotiate life. In such a process the religious counselor can help the individual to enter into a new and positive relationship to God.

DIRECTIVE AND NONDIRECTIVE COUNSELING

A main issue in counseling is between what has been called directive and nondirective counseling. Stated in this form, the issue is confused because unless the counselor is to be a wooden image, he will have some kind of influence upon the counseling process, whether or not he admits it. The issue is, in fact: What kind and degree of direction should the counselor give to the counseling process? The difference of viewpoint comes more with reference to the answer to the problem than it does in defining it. Most counselors would agree that it is not enough for the counselor to come to understand the problem and to tell the counselee what it is. The counselee must have time to understand and feel the problem for himself. Most counselors recognize that free expression is also important in releasing the feelings of the counselee and in enabling him emotionally to be able to deal with his problem. During this stage the direction of the counselor is in encouragement of expression by the counselee and in helping him to explore and define his problem for himself.

The main issue has to do with the part the counselor will take in determining the answer to the question. Some counselors give advice. They may say, "If I were in your place, I would do so and so," or "I think this is the best answer." Others try to furnish an answer on authority. They may use the Bible, or the authority of the church or synagogue, or the findings of psychology. Others may try by some form of persuasion to lead the counselee to accept and adopt the answer the counselor thinks is right. In the case given by Hiltner of the student who was debating whether or not to make a clean breast of his cheating, the counselor said, "There are many times in life when it hurts to do the right thing . . . , but you see that you've got to do it, don't you?" Others may use some form of suggestion, perhaps putting their persuasion in question form, but making the assumption on the side of the answer the counselor wishes. "Don't you think this is the right thing to do?" Whether in the form of advice or authority, persuasion or suggestion, the direction of the counselor is toward getting the counselee to accept and adopt the answer to the problem which he as counselor is convinced is the right one.

The so-called nondirective counselor is unwilling to try to determine the answer of the counselee, but he attempts to carry on counseling in such a way that the counselee has the emotional confidence and the guidance in his process of self-exploration which will enable him to come to his own answers to his problems. The counselor adopts this procedure for several reasons:

First, he believes that the only decision which will really be an answer to the counselee's problem and to which he can and will adhere in spite of difficulties is one that he has arrived at himself.

Second, he does not feel that he has the wisdom to make a decision for another person. He feels that he cannot say, "If I were in your place," because he cannot possibly put himself completely in another person's place. Therefore he does not trust his own answer to another person's problem. Nor as a religious counselor does he believe he has the wisdom to speak for God for another person's life.

Third, he feels it is unfair to make a decision for another person when he as counselor does not have to take the consequences of the decision, nor indeed can he take them. Temporarily for immature persons under his care he may make decisions, but only in areas where he can stay by them in carrying out the decisions. In the long run, however, he recognizes that each person has to live his own life and that he as counselor cannot keep on giving child care to the counselee.

Fourth, his desire as counselor is to get the counselee to the place where he is mature enough to live life for himself without dependence upon a counselor. He believes that such maturity will be achieved only as the counselee learns how to face situations for himself and to make his own decisions. Therefore, to help in the process of decision and to give him competence in it seems to the counselor equally if not more important than the particular decision which is being made.

GROUP COUNSELING

Group counseling is not different in principle from individual counseling. When carried on by an expert counselor, it involves a controlled situation like that which is obtained in individual counseling but differs in that several individuals are working out their problems with the counselor at the same time. In general it represents a professional type of therapy beyond the possibility of the nonprofessional counselor.[3]

There are three kinds of opportunity in religious education for counseling of the group type. First, it is at times possible in connection with the church or synagogue and its allied agencies to form intimate groups of individuals facing similar problems, in which there is a sufficient degree of intimacy among the group members that they trust one another and are free to express themselves without reserve. It is difficult to arrange a group where this degree of frankness is possible and desirable, particularly on personal problems. An individual cannot be sure that what he reveals about himself confidentially in the group may not be reported even unwittingly or be used against him often unconsciously outside the group. Therefore, usually group counseling in religious education will better be carried on in groups where the problems are discussed in the third person and without identification with individual members of the group. For example, where parents are considering their problems in dealing with their children, first-person discussion, in which mothers and fathers tell about their children and reveal their own practices, tends to develop attitudes of disapproval or approval and personal reactions of defense on the part of the group members. A third-person discussion—through case material, for example—gives opportunity for frank expression without the personal identifications. The same can be said of counseling on sex and marriage. First-person discussion results in revelations about sex attitudes and practices which are private matters and nobody else's business, and it also develops personal reactions of defense of one's self and approval or disapproval of others. The more personal and intimate the problem, the less is it appropriate to consider it in a group on a personal basis, and the more desirable it is to discuss it impersonally in the third person.

A second opportunity for group counseling comes in connection with children's, young people's, and adult groups in religious education. In such groups individuals manifest their personality strengths and weaknesses. An understanding group leader can so conduct the group that in its discussions, its planning, and its activities help is given on the problems of adjustment of the individual group members. Rudolph Wittenberg[4] gives an illustration of Barbara, a talented but "good" girl who always yielded to others and never asserted herself in a Sunday-school class. She was everywhere approved as such a fine member of the group, so co-operative and unselfish. A discriminating Sunday-school teacher saw that the group was losing the benefit of Barbara's potential ability, and Barbara herself had developed an exaggerated unselfishness. In the group experiences the teacher was able to make

[3] See Slavson, ed., *The Practice of Group Therapy*, for description of various types of professional group therapy illustrated with case material.

[4] *So You Want to Help People*, chap. xi.

sure that Barbara had a chance to take her legitimate part in the group's leadership and thus both to help Barbara and to increase the effectiveness of the group. The so-called disciplinary problems in a group give an excellent opportunity for the use of group-counseling principles. A wise leader can help individuals work out their problems in their relationships to him as leader. In such group leadership all that is said about individual counseling is pertinent. The leader must not respond personally to attacks upon him or efforts to win his favor, if positive results are to take place. He must recognize that the responses to him of blame or praise, resistance or co-operation, are not to him personally but to what he as leader represents to the group members. The group also must be conducted on a democratic participating basis so the group members have the opportunity to express and work out their problems.

A third opportunity for group counseling arises in connection with the life of the group as a group. Many decisions have to be made in a group: Who shall be members? Who shall be officers? How will its money be spent? Who shall take responsibility for this and that in the program? When these group problems are worked out, individual attitudes and feelings are expressed; and in the process of changing from an exclusive, self-centered group to a more inclusive, co-operative one, the individuals who are making these plans and decisions themselves are influenced and changed. Groups as groups may be used constructively to help the individuals in the group.

The Counselor and the Counseling Relationship

It must be evident from the discussion thus far that the relation between the counselor and the counselee is distinctively different from the ordinary relationships of life. In ordinary life individuals are accepted or rejected, approved or condemned, according to their attitudes and behavior. In counseling the counselee is fully accepted as he is, without praise or blame. In ordinary life an individual has to watch his step and be careful as to what he says or does, lest his words or his actions will get him into difficulty. In counseling he has freedom to express himself just as he feels and to uncover the secret things of his heart and life. In other words, in a counseling relationship there is hope that an individual may find his way because he has no need to guard or defend himself but can face his problem with complete frankness and without reserve.

The results described will not take place unless certain conditions are met: First of all, the counselee must have complete confidence in the counselor. The counselee must be able to express himself as if the counselor were not there—and yet more freely—because of the confidence which the counselor engenders. That the counseling interview shall be confidential is essential if individuals are to get at their real problems. The physical setting is also important. It should be in a room away from the pressures of life, where there is quiet and a sense of confidence is engendered by the very physical surroundings.

The character of the counselor is the most important factor in the counseling relationship. A counselor must be one who has learned how to find the answers to his own problems. Otherwise he will unconsciously be using the counseling relationship to work on his own difficulties. He cannot be an egocentric individual who lives life and its relationships in terms of the effect upon himself. If he is, he will unconsciously be using his relationship with the counselee for his own glory. His acceptance of the counselee, his understanding of him, his concern for his welfare, must be genuine. Unless he has real compassion, his lack of it will manifest itself unconsciously in subtle attitudes of contempt or condemnation which the counselee will feel, and the relationship will be broken.

RELIGION AND THE COUNSELING RELATIONSHIP

For the religious counselor his attitude in the counseling relationship is an expression of his religious faith. He has experienced a God who accepted him despite his human frailties and inadequacies, in whose presence he feels complete understanding and compassion, and in relation to whom he has found the confidence and the help for working out his own life problems. His God is like the father in the parable of the prodigal son, who had already forgiven and accepted his son before he could ask forgiveness. A counselor is not unmindful of the problems of justice; but he is, in the counseling relationship, not a judge attempting to administer justice, but a father concerned about helping the one who is in need. As counselor he manifests, not love in which the motive is to protect or enhance his own status, but love like unto that of God which has no concern but the welfare of the counselee.[5] In the relationship not only does the counselor provide for the counselee an experience of the kind of love he has seldom if ever found elsewhere in life, but he mediates the love of God and enables the counselee to experience the compassion and acceptance and love of God.

SUGGESTIONS FOR FURTHER STUDY

1. What, from your experience and observation, are the major types of situation and problem for which persons need individual or group counseling? For which of these problems is it true that individuals do not need to be at the mercy of immediate circumstances but can arrange for alternations from the traffic of life to explore their situations and problems? Why do individuals fail to do this?

2. Compare the counseling process as outlined in this chapter with aspects of

[5] See Lewis Sherrill, *Guilt and Redemption*, pp. 157-59.

religious education discussed in other chapters. Are the basic processes similar? Why, or why not?

3. Compare the process for nonprofessional counseling as outlined in this chapter with the description of professional counseling in Rogers' *Counseling and Psychotherapy*. In what regards is the process similar? In what regards dissimilar?

4. Is it true, as indicated in this chapter, that underlying issues of fundamental life purpose and basic confidence are involved whenever thorough counseling takes place? Why, or why not? Are these underlying issues basically religious? Why, or why not?

5. Which of the emotional factors discussed in the chapter are most important to be taken into account in counseling? Why do you believe these to be the most important? What other emotional factors, if any, should be added? Why do you think so? Has adequate recognition been given to these emotional factors in this discussion of counseling? What differences, if any, in the place given to the emotional factors would you consider desirable? Why?

6. Do you believe that the transformation of basic personality patterns is possible in and through the counseling process? If not, why not? If so, why? What is the role of the counselor in this transformation? What is the place of religion? Why do you think so?

7. Do you think that the counselee should have the opportunity of coming to his own answers to his problems? Why, or why not? If he is to come to his own answers, why does he need a counselor?

8. How is group counseling like, and how different from, individual counseling? Is it correct that group counseling in religious education should be conducted in the third rather than the first person? Why, or why not? Under what conditions and in what ways can group experience contribute to the solution of the individual personality problems of the group members? Why do you think so?

9. In what ways is the counseling relationship different from the ordinary relationships of life?

10. Which of the conditions for successful counseling as outlined in the chapter do you consider the most important, and which the least important? Why? What conditions, if any, should be added? Why?

11. Is it true that the religious counselor may and should manifest in the counseling relationship love like unto that of God? Why or why not?

BIBLIOGRAPH

Bonnell, John S. *Psychology for Pastor and People.* New York: Harper & Brothers, 1948.

Dicks, Russell L. *Pastoral Work and Personal Counseling.* New York: The Macmillan Co., 1949.

Elliott, Harrison, and Elliott, Grace Loucks. *Solving Personal Problems, a Counseling Manual.* New York: Henry Holt & Company, 1936.

Fosdick, Harry Emerson. *On Being a Real Person.* New York: Harper & Brothers, 1943.

Hiltner, Seward. *Pastoral Counseling.* New York and Nashville: Abingdon-Cokesbury Press, 1949.

Holman, Charles T. *Getting Down to Cases.* New York: The Macmillan Co., 1942.

Horney, Karen. *Our Inner Conflicts.* New York: W. W. Norton & Company, 1945.

Kemp, Charles F. *Physicians of the Soul—a History of Pastoral Counseling.* New York: The Macmillan Co., 1947.

Liebman, Joshua L. *Peace of Mind.* New York: Simon & Schuster, 1946.

May, Rollo. *The Art of Counseling.* New York and Nashville: Abingdon-Cokesbury Press, 1939.

Rogers, Carl R. *Counseling and Psychotherapy.* Boston: Houghton Mifflin Company, 1942.

Sherrill, Lewis J. *Guilt and Redemption.* Richmond: John Knox Press, 1945.

Slavson, S. R. *An Introduction to Group Therapy.* New York: The Commonwealth Fund, 1943.

————. *The Practice of Group Therapy.* New York: International Universities Press, 1947.

Wittenberg, Rudolph M. *So You Want to Help People.* New York: Association Press, 1947.

Chapter 16

NEWER TECHNIQUES IN TEACHING

MILDRED MOODY EAKIN

As a preliminary to understanding newer techniques in teaching, one needs to realize that a far-reaching change in our concept of teaching goals is under way. That the function of school is to transmit knowledge—the concept which for a long time has seemed to dominate—is still largely taken for granted. But growing significantly is another view, according to which the terms "change, growth, betterment" loom in the foreground as they did not used to. The teacher of arithmetic or geography, educators are saying, has not fulfilled his obligation to his group and to society in teaching these subjects only. Pupils as well as subjects are in his charge; he has persons to influence, not only materials to convey.

For those who are religious-minded this shift in emphasis should bring encouragement. Is it not a coming around to what has all along been our religion's point of view? At the same time the fact confronts us that church schools to a large extent proceed as if transmitting biblical material and doctrinal ideas was their main job, as if these materials and ideas would of themselves produce betterment. The new emphasis gives religious educators—maybe even more than it gives secular educators—something to think about.

And, as suggested in the opening sentence, there is a special reason why our thought needs to turn in this direction. In a discussion of techniques the "what" and "how" have to be prominent. But the "why" is basic and must also be kept in view. And the "why" of newer techniques in teaching is to be found largely in education's broadening vision—its new sense of responsibility for betterment. It is in no small measure because of this expanded outlook that improved techniques, better ways, are being sought. The church-school teacher will in some cases have to raise his sights—to see above and beyond what to him is most familiar—if newer techniques are to have for him their full significance.

TECHNIQUES FOR OBSERVING

Observing the pupils, not only en masse but individually, is a first requisite of good teaching. And since observations not recorded are in large degree lost, skill in recording needs to keep pace with facility at observing. This skill is not a thing acquired immediately, but it can be acquired.

A difficulty at the start is to avoid accumulating a lot of details—as to what one pupil and another have said and done—that add up to nothing in particular. What to seize upon as having special significance is the question. Perhaps an illustration will help in answering it. The other day, in one of my fourth-grade groups, Bruce was sitting near to Jean and heard her sigh in discouragement. She was working on a drawing. "What's the matter, Jean?" Bruce asked. "Maybe I can help." He did help and restored Jean's morale; then he went back to what he was doing. On another occasion, I remembered, Bruce had made a suggestion; then another pupil made a countersuggestion. "Oh, yes," Bruce had said, "that's better."

A number of incidents like that go far toward painting a picture of a youngster. They offer prime record stuff. Unfortunately space does not permit further illustrations, drawn from different types of behavior. A thing for the teacher to guard against is the tendency to give attention mainly to what troublesome pupils say and do. Not seldom is the passively "good" child the one most in need of careful observation and special help.

It need not take long to learn what sort of data, noted down in the running-comment record under a pupil's name, eventually yields a picture of the person. Sometimes it is better for the teacher to start by recording data on only one or two pupils. Having in this way got the knack, he can expand his record keeping to include every member of the group.

Expansion also in other directions is possible and desirable. Observations as to the effect or lack of effect on a pupil's behavior of what the teacher says and does can become a part of the record, as can what the individual's words and actions seem to signify as to inner feelings.

A further point is that data thus gathered needs to be considered in connection with information from other sources. Parents, public-school teachers, and fellow church-school leaders can often supply bits from the pupil's past history that are illuminating. Especially needed is comparison of data about an individual in the group with what the teacher knows or can learn about behavior patterns with their causes and consequences that are characteristic of this age group.

When data has for some time been accumulating in the running-comment record, the teacher can make good use of an outline consisting of simple questions under topic heads, for example:

Acceptance by the group:
    Is he generally liked? _____
    Is he a leader? _____
Relation to group work:
    Does he help in planning? _____ How?

Does he make suggestions? _____ What kind?
Does he consider the suggestions of others? _____ In what spirit?

Answers to such questions, from the record of observations and subject to revision, serve as an index to growth.

A different kind of method can be used to indicate how far the individual has gone in attaining desirable behavior goals.

Is accepted by:
Most members _____ None_____
A few members _____
Helps in planning the group work:
Usually _____ Hardly ever _____
Sometimes _____

This outline, like the other, will draw upon the recorded observations for the needed information.

When the leader has been with one group for some time and has become familiar with the interrelationships of the individuals in it, there is a form of graph which he can use with profit to picture those relationships. The graph is made up of small circles connected by single and double lines. A single line shows one-way popularity, so to speak: *D* likes to be with *A*, such a graph now before me shows, but *A* doesn't warm up to *D*—the single line connecting the *A* and *D* circles has an arrow pointing toward *A*. *D* is also drawn toward *C*, it appears, without return attraction in evidence; hence another single line, with arrow pointing *C*-ward. *D*, however, seems not to be hopelessly unpopular, since double lines without arrows connect his circle with those of *H* and *J*. According to the graph, *A* is the most popular pupil in the group: his circle is in a central position; of the eight lines running to it five are double lines; and of the three that are single, one— connecting *A* with *D*—points *A*-ward, as we have seen.

Such a graph makes readily available to the leader a kind of data that is important. The need to belong is a basic need. The urge to achieve belonging is back of many behavior difficulties. Group relationships offer to the individual one of his principal means of growth. Is he having a chance? Is he capable of utilizing the chance? Is something hindering? What? This and the other observation techniques can stimulate the asking of such questions and help the teacher work toward answers.

The techniques to yield good results will need to be used faithfully, persistently. Haphazard use is largely a waste of time. On the other hand, they should be used imaginatively. There is nothing sacrosanct about them. They are probably capable of improvement, certainly of adaptation. In general three good results may be expected to come from their use: (1) Pupils will stand out more as individuals. (2) Pupil behavior will be viewed more objectively and dispassionately. (3) The pupil can better be helped to understand himself.

Techniques for Planning

Planning for what? It may be for a session—what is to be done and how. It may be for a visit, a trip, an interview. It may be for the making of a worship screen, or an "annual," or a duplicated "newspaper" that will record things learned and insights gained in and through a unit of study. It may be planning for the carrying through of the unit as a whole, whether it extends through two or three sessions or through many weeks. It may be planning for improvement of group behavior. Objectives vary, but techniques likely to be effective in pursuing them are pretty much the same.

First and foremost is the fact that the planning—if we are thinking in terms of the newer techniques—is done by the group, not by the teacher alone. Observing, as we have seen, is a one-sided business—though pupils observe the teacher too, often shrewdly. Planning is at its best when everybody works at it. To many a teacher this is a hard saying, a frightening idea. Group planning can seem to spell teacher abdication, loss of control, chaos. This bugaboo aspect, however, should vanish upon closer scrutiny. Bulwarks against chaos are adequate.

There is, as an initial bulwark, the thing planned for—session, or trip, or whatever it may be. Planning for something definite need not go wildly astray just because a number of people are working at it. Another bulwark is the teacher's presence in the group. He is the most experienced member, and the opportunity and responsibility of guiding is his from first to last.

Are there other bulwarks? Yes; one other in particular: the pupils—their interest, if the thing planned for is, as it should be, within their range of interest; their ability to think, to form opinions and exercise judgment, to reach majority conclusions while safeguarding minority rights. This ability will vary with age, of course; it will also vary for other reasons. But at any age, from kindergarten up, pupils are much more capable of doing effective group planning than is generally realized. If they are slow at expressing themselves at first, their hesitancy may be due to the shock of surprise—when before did a teacher take them so seriously?

Granted, then, that group planning is feasible, is it also desirable? It is, for an array of reasons that can only be hinted at here. Drawing the pupil as fully as can be into the teaching-learning process, from the planning stage on, offers possibilities which the teacher who hasn't tried it may never have suspected. Last year, in the midst of a planning huddle, one of my juniors turned to me and said, "You and Becky certainly have lots of ideas." Seldom have I received a compliment that meant as much to me. It told me that I was one of the group, appreciated as others were for my contributions. Applying the democratic idea to school processes can be a thrilling experience. What otherwise might be a bored or clashing group with many frustrated members can be made into an alert and unified group that goes places and does things, with members growing with the doing.

What is the rationale of the group-planning technique? Perhaps mainly that participation gives the individual ego its chance, thus preventing frustration with its various annoying and sometimes ugly manifestations, and that with the frustration menace out of the way fruitful co-operation becomes possible.

For the teacher making first attempts at group planning a number of suggestions may be made:

1. Your role is that of moderator, as well as active participant. One thing that this means is that responsibility rests on you—as on no other member of the group—to keep in mind through all the planning just what it is for which plans are being made.

2. In what is being planned you must have real interest; in its worth-whileness you must have genuine confidence. Otherwise it will be a near miracle if the onward movement of the group's planning is more than lackadaisical.

3. You must be prepared, at the opening stage of group planning for something in particular, to stimulate pupil interest in that something. This is a necessary preliminary to the desired participation. In the choice of stimuli there is room for ingenuity. For example, ear appeal may need support from eye appeal.

4. Possible plans, ways that might be used in working toward the goal or goals in view, should also be in your mind when the planning begins—several ways, preferably. They should be thought-out plans which you can present persuasively, but not plans which you feel called upon to put through by whatever subtle means.

5. You should have confidence in the pupils' ability to plan, willingness not only to listen but to be convinced, open-mindedness to the possibility that a pupil's suggestion will be better than yours.

6. You should see that planning which eventuates in a real group decision, bringing the satisfaction of personal and group achievement to at least a majority of group members and frustration to none, can at one and the same time be good planning for the immediate objective and can also have importance of a farther-reaching kind—importance in relation to religion's life-enrichment and life-improvement goal.

Such are some principal things that need to be stressed. It may be added that group planning takes place mainly through discussion; hence books and articles which treat of discussion techniques competently will go far toward answering questions about details of group-planning procedure. But help from books and articles is best sought in connection with one's own experience.

Speaking of group-planning experience, one bit remains unforgettably in my mind. Fifth-graders and their leaders were planning an enterprise of making hymnbooks for a Southern mountain school from leaves out of discarded hymnals, supplemented by pictures and other materials. How should they organize the materials? Songs about the Bible should come first, one youngster thought. "Everything else comes from it," he said. This view won acceptance—firm acceptance, it was soon learned. When a little later an adult leader remarked, "Every real hymnbook has hymns of praise first," a pupil said, simply and crushingly, "We've already decided that."

TECHNIQUES FOR DOING

The use of activities in church schools at the present time can be described as mostly off-center. The value seen in "things to do" is mainly that they offer help to the teacher in his problems of holding pupil attention, keeping order, preventing situations from getting out of hand. Thanks to them he hopes to be able to salvage a few minutes of each session for having the lesson read and maybe talking about it to a passively listening group.

But with teaching time shortened, sometimes almost to the vanishing point, activities and teaching can appear to be competitors. "How am I to find time for the lesson if I use activities?" the worried teacher asks. The answer to this is that activities *are* the lesson, or, using a few more words, that activities rightly planned and carried through can constitute the main teaching-learning vehicle.

A thing that needs to be understood about lessons, and teaching, and activities—indeed about the very idea of school—is this: Experience is the real teacher—life experience—but its lessons are not neatly packaged, and therefore schools are needed. Life lacks pedagogical arrangement. So what we call activities are planned to yield experience of a special kind—a school kind, having, to be sure, a certain amount of artificiality as compared with life's experiences, but also having a condensation as compared with ordinary life that offers teaching advantages. School activities are, one might say, a form of art; and art is concentrated life, an epitomizing of one or another aspect of life which helps us in grasping its significance. Only as one understands this is he in a position to profit from study and experience in teaching by doing.

Whether carefully motivated and well-planned church-school action moves on to completed action, and to its hoped-for sequel in enriched and improved life, will depend on a number of things:

1. It will depend on how the teacher, if inexperienced in the guidance of activity programs, makes his first attempts with them. Let early attempts

be modest in scope; otherwise things can become chaotic. In a session starting as usual, place can be given, for example, to a picture interpretation in which the group participates though the leader has done all the planning. More diversified activities, group planned, can follow as readiness develops.

2. It will depend on the teacher's resourcefulness in marshaling aids to supplement those supplied in his teacher's book. Resource persons and materials are pretty certain to be available in the local situation. To get such aid calls for tact. Also, persons from whom aid is sought should be made to see that what is being done or planned for has other than a vague do-good character, that the good sought is specific and practical.

3. It will depend on how clear the plan of action is to each member of the group when responsibility is assigned and accepted. Opportunity for asking questions should be given and answers carefully made. Drawings, diagrams, charts, can sometimes be used helpfully. Each pupil should understand what he is to do.

4. It will depend on the teacher's alertness in seeing that pupil and thing to be done can get together without too great difficulty, and that they fit each other. Donald is to interview a minister in a near-by town about the program of a community house attached to the minister's church. Can Donald get there? How? Does he like to meet people? Can he converse freely? Is he observant? Is this a kind of assignment that will give him satisfaction, a sense of achievement?

5. It will depend on the recognition and use of group personality, so to speak, as well as individual personality. Group consensus is powerful and can indeed be overpowerful. Sometimes the crowd pulls the individual ruthlessly into its clutches, overruling his better judgment. Against this possibility the church-school leader may need to be on guard. But group consensus can also be wholesome, beneficent. Good technique calls for its use. The teacher's joy in seeing that an important lesson, implicit in what the group is studying and working at, is taking hold not only of individuals but almost in mass fashion is surely legitimate.

6. It will depend on the teacher's attitude toward group minorities, the interests of which can and must have due attention not only for fairness' sake but because outstanding values may be represented in them. When preliminary discussion has brought to light differing views that do not merge, the majority view can perhaps be acted on first, and one or more minority favored procedures followed subsequently. Or both majority and minority plans may be followed long enough to discover which seems to yield the greater satisfaction. In either case the leader's skill will count, but what will count even more will be his spirit, his freedom from any steam-roller tendencies. To lead is not to drive.

7. It will depend on how the time factor is dealt with. With short periods the experienced leader will do well to make a good deal of use of continuing

activities. This calls for fresh stimulus at the beginning of each session, but there are compensations. The through-the-week pause can result in fresh thinking and imagination being brought to bear on the enterprise, so that instead of losing momentum it gains cumulative force. In work with children long-continued effort is in any case undesirable. Whether the thing to be done calls for much time or little, care should be taken to assure that the time needed is available. If it is not available, an activity of more limited scope should be substituted. Hurried work has a poor chance of yielding good results.

8. It will depend, obviously, on leader's and group's staying qualities. For a group to see goals—to see them as interesting and worth making efforts to reach—is comparatively easy. To select routes—to agree upon ways of accomplishing the thing they have envisioned as worth accomplishing—calls for a greater exercise of energy and intelligence and imagination. To follow the routes purposefully and persistently—to translate plans into action and to push action to completion—is the third stage, and it is on success here that the whole enterprise stands or falls. Apart from completion, there is little ground for expecting that change in conception, in feeling, in attitude, in conduct, which is the ultimate test.

9. It will depend in the long run—this is the last and maybe the most important point—on the generating and channelizing of emotion that occurs within the various enterprises. Techniques are not usually thought of as being emotion charged. But human beings are emotional creatures; life experience which school activities try to epitomize is full of emotion; religion from long ago has been at home in life's emotional depths. Hence the church-school teacher who finds himself getting somewhere with techniques of doing may someday find himself and his group in an emotional atmosphere as keenly sensed as that of an old-time revival. The point for the teacher, of course, is not that he should try to induce emotion in any extraneous way, or that emotion is religiously valuable only as it assumes a form that is revival-like. The point is rather that he is in a situation which carries emotion within itself from its very nature—emotion with dynamic qualities available for life building. He may well hope and pray that he will not be found wanting as he tries to guide and use this power.

Techniques for Evaluating

Evaluation to be sound and helpful needs to stand in close relation to planning, to purpose. One of my groups—fourth-graders—recently visited an Episcopal church; and we leaders, in session by ourselves before meeting the children again, tried to evaluate the experience. It was not equal to that of last year, one of the leaders thought. But discussion brought out the fact that last year's visit to the same church was differently planned and had a different purpose. Then group interest was particularly in the Christian symbols to be seen in the beautiful church interior and in the liturgical service. This year the visit was made in the Christmas season, and the elaborately artistic reproduction of the stable-and-manger scene was the main focus of attention. The values in the two experiences were different, but both contributed to the objectives of the getting-acquainted-with-churches study.

Incidentally, something happened in the course of this last church visit which seemed to all the leaders to indicate progress toward a bigger, life-building objective. The minister, in talking to the children about the meaning of Christmas, stressed the Christian ideal of love and peace; and by way of contrast referred to strife between Jews and Arabs, non-Christian peoples. At this point a child in the group spoke up. She said, "We were fighting in a war too—not long ago." This group, visiting and studying about churches, had also visited a synagogue, studied about Jewish religion, become acquainted with Jewish people. And in following up this interest we had in mind, as the major objective, inoculation against the virus of anti-Semitism. The minister's comment, with its probably unintended implications, called forth evidence that the inoculation had some effectiveness—at least so we thought. Church-school leaders should view progress toward the narrower goals of a session, or unit, or project as having value also, and even more, what such progress contributes toward the development of a young life in Christian directions.

After a trip or other special experience a natural time for talking things over within the pupil group is in the following session. Children may be expected to speak first of what one and another member of the group did—maybe in praise, maybe in blame—and of incidental happenings that stand out in their minds. Talk about what "we" did may also be heard. How prominent this note is can be a measure of growth. At the proper moment the leader can bring about a shift to what the experience yielded in the line of plans made earlier and purposes then in view. Satisfaction from the achievement of goals or facing the fact of failure to achieve and probing for reasons why—these are among the important gains to be had from evaluation.

Thought about whether the experience contributed to making them better need never be forced upon children when evaluation is under way. Often, however, especially in group conversation of a reminiscent kind covering a series of related experiences, boys and girls who have been sensitized to the deeper values in attitudes and in deeds of fairness and considerateness will on their own initiative evaluate on this level. At such times alertness is perhaps what is most called for on the leader's part. Opportunity for a significant contribution may come, or little may be left for him to say.

That the group should have value-bearing experiences is the main thing. That members of the group should recognize the experiences as value-bearing and from time to time give expression to their sense of the value can also be important. Words by the leader probably bear most fruit when they operate, quietly and unaggressively, as a seconding influence.

SUGGESTIONS FOR FURTHER STUDY

1. As group leader, or observer with a group, try out the techniques of observation suggested in this chapter.

2. As leader of a study group try out the techniques for planning, doing, and evaluating suggested in this chapter. Note down, in a form usable by another teacher, what you discover about needed resources and where they are to be found in the community.

3. Examine a quarter's lesson materials in one or more series, considering what changes, if any, would be needed to adapt the materials to such teaching as is pictured in this chapter.

4. Familiarize yourself with "group dynamics" (see "Promise for Education of Group Dynamics"), and consider the applicability of this concept to church-school teaching or to other religious work with groups.

5. Acquaint yourself with the "workshop" concept and practice (see "Trends in the Workshop Movement"), and consider what it has to offer that is applicable to religious work.

BIBLIOGRAPHY

Baxter, Bernice, and Cassidy, Rosalind. *Group Experience.* New York: Harper & Brothers, 1943. Techniques for observation and group work with children.

Bradford, L. P., *et al.* "Promise for Education of Group Dynamics." Article in N.E.A. *Journal,* September, 1948.

Democratic Human Relations. National Council for the Social Studies, Yearbook No. 16, 1945. Practices in intergroup education. (Can be had from Bureau for Intercultural Education, 157 West Thirteenth Street, New York 11, N. Y.)

Dimock, H. S. *Rediscovering the Adolescent.* New York: Association Press, 1937. Observation techniques used in Y.M.C.A. summer camps.

Eakin, Mildred, and Eakin, Frank. *The Church-School Teacher's Job.* New York: The Macmillan Co., 1949. Has chapters on planning and carrying out activities.

Elliott, Harrison S. *The Process of Group Thinking.* New York: Association Press, 1928. Discusses techniques.

Group Processes in Supervision. Association for Supervision and Curriculum Development, National Education Association, 1201 Sixteenth Street, N.W., Washington 6, D. C., 1948. Deals with techniques of group planning, deciding, acting, evaluating.

Hartung, M. L. "Trends in the Workshop Movement." Article in *School Review,* December, 1946.

Kilpatrick, W. H. *Group Education for a Democracy.* New York: Association Press, 1940. A discussion of principles underlying the group-work concept.

Chapter 17

BUILDING FOR RELIGIOUS EDUCATION

JOHN R. SCOTFORD

A GROUP OF SUNDAY-SCHOOL TEACHERS from small-town and rural churches along the Saint Lawrence River were listening to a religious educator from Boston. "Twenty-five dollars is the least that *any* school should spend each year for its worker's library!" she exclaimed with enthusiasm. Her audience was distinctly uninterested. Probably not a school represented had an income of a hundred dollars a year—or had heard of a worker's library.

This mistake will be avoided in the pages that follow. They are not written "out of books," nor will they quote "authorities." Rather are they born of hundreds of conferences with churches in all parts of the country, where the question has been either "What can we do with the facilities which we now have?" or "What can we secure with the resources at our disposal?" Following the blueprints supplied by the religious educators of the past is impossible. The only feasible way ahead is achieved by compromise and accommodation. When this is done with intelligence and imagination, the results are surprisingly satisfactory.

Although the trend is toward fewer and larger churches, we need to remember that the average congregation has fewer than three hundred members, and that most church schools are attended by less than a hundred children. The fortunate church which must provide for greater numbers will also have more abundant resources and be in a position to secure expert advice. It would be a simple matter to outline minimum plans for facilities "which every church should have" that would cost at least half a million dollars under present conditions. This impulse will be resisted, and the other end of the scale will be the starting point.

First let us face a question of fundamental strategy. In former years it was assumed that the way to start a new church was to organize a Sunday school with the expectation that it would grow into an adult congregation. This procedure never worked as well as it was supposed to and today is quite ineffective. Investigation would show that the large Sunday schools of yesterday have not produced the strong churches of today. The fact seems to be that the people of a new community will avail themselves of a Sunday school as a convenience for their children without committing themselves to the enterprise in any permanent way; not until they themselves have joined an adult congregation is there the prospect of a strong church. Although enlisting the children and young people commends a church to a community, it is the service of worship which attracts and holds a permanent and financially responsible constituency. This can be corroborated in two ways: In the past many churches built the educational unit first, expecting to add a place for worship later. A surprising number are still struggling along in their "community building," except that not a few have died on the spot, or moved elsewhere and started over again. On the other hand, the Lutherans are currently the most successful of the major Protestant denominations in launching new churches, and they begin with a place of worship. Much evidence can be produced to show that it is a church service in a building constructed for that purpose which builds a successful congregation.

If this is so, the church should not be asked to accommodate itself to facilities designed primarily for the church school, but rather should the church school fit itself into the pattern of the church. This has been made easier by a shift in the ideals of religious education. The old Sunday school sought in varying degrees to secure decisions for Christ, to teach the Bible, and to recruit the membership of the church. These purposes expressed themselves first in the large auditorium suited to the uses of crowd psychology and then in small classrooms designed for intimate instruction and personal persuasion. Today the aim of religious education can be stated as the development of religious attitudes centering about the faith and life of the church. The school thinks of itself as a part of the church, particularly in its worship. This shift in emphasis has simplified the problem of housing the church school.

It is fundamental that any quarters used for religious education should command respect. Children are exceedingly sensitive to their physical environment. In church grownups are prone to commune with their memories while boys and girls live where they are and see what is in front of them. A disorderly room invites disorderly conduct; it can be argued that ugly churches produce quarrelsome congregations. Surprising results in the attitudes of both the young and the old can be achieved by simply clearing out the litter and getting rid of whatever distracts the eye. Before the first child puts in an appearance on Sunday morning, some brave person who fears neither the janitor nor the ladies' society needs to police the premises to make sure that everything is in order. This is just as important in a large church as in a small one, and oftentimes more difficult. The results in improved deportment are astonishing. When a room commands their respect, boys and girls will regulate their conduct accordingly.

Worship is receiving increasing stress in religious education. It is primarily a matter of the emotions. Ideas, liturgical forms, music, help to create it; but one of the prime conditioning factors is the place in which it is held, particularly with children and young people. Beauty in any form helps to establish an atmosphere which is conducive to worship, but it is not of itself sufficient. The room in which people seek to experience the presence of God should say something to them. It should possess an essential unity. Instead of the eye being drawn hither and thither by competing sights, it should be drawn in one direction. This implies a worship center which invites attention, and which gives meaning to all about it.

Here is an area where the ideal is difficult of achievement, but in which progress is easier than many think. We have inherited much ecclesiastical ugliness from our fathers, but there is no room so depressing that it cannot be measurably redeemed by the introduction of a worship center as a refuge from the confusion with which it may be surrounded. A church official tells of visiting a Western church, where he found a group of small boys "tearing the place apart." On returning for a second Sunday, he arrived before the boys and placed a cross and lighted candles at the front of the church, and this time the same youngsters came in on tiptoe and spoke in whispers. Order on one hand, with a touch of imagination on the other, will transform the atmosphere of most rooms.

Proceeding from these presuppositions, let us start with the irreducible minimum for a church, which is a single room.

A one-room church usually has both a small congregation and a small school, with the sense of intimacy compensating in some measure for the lack of numbers. The achievement of order, beauty, and an essential unity in a little church is relatively easy—it is the overelaborate auditorium structure of the nineties which poses the worst problems. If the adults can be persuaded to install a permanent worship center, this can serve for the church school as well. At its simplest and best this should consist of a dossall in strong color hanging in the middle of the front wall, with a communion table before it on which cross, candles, and possibly flowers may be placed. If this is not possible, the church school should set up a movable center, which may well be a triptych. This is a folding screen before which a table or stand may be placed for the display of various objects possessing beauty and religious significance. It has two virtues: it can be changed with the seasons and the church year and can easily be put away.

If a one-room church is to be used for the church school, two adjustments should be asked for: Flexible seating is highly desirable. Pews or benches are out of place in a small room; they are clumsy and oversize in comparison with their setting. Cathedral chairs, or even the folding variety, look better and are far more practical. If it is impossible to avoid the pews, they should be confined to the center of the room, with the corners, sides, and rear kept clear for classes. In the past all churches were oversold on pews; today new churches need to protect themselves at this point. It is far easier—and much cheaper—to bring in chairs when needed than to take out pews which are not needed. If possible, one corner should be set aside for little children.

Ample storage space in closets or cupboards will do much to overcome the limitations of the one-room church. If it must be used for a variety of purposes, a place to put away surplus equipment—from little chairs to the tables used for dinners—is essential. This calls for ingenuity but need not be expensive. It might be noted that an excellent way to seat the maximum number of people in the minimum space is to put them on the sturdy chairs commonly used for primary children.

The next step after a one-room church is a two-room church. Here an ideal may be suggested which may not be generally practical, but which is worth considering: The second room in a church may well be used for the kindergarten. The needs of the little child are quite different from those of older ones. They do not naturally sit still; it is their nature to move about. The rule is, the smaller the child the more space it requires. Four- and five-year-olds should have from twenty to thirty square feet apiece. Tables, chairs, windows, and toilets should be built to their scale. Pictures should be within their eye range. If possible, they should come and go through an entrance which is not used by larger children. Of all the groups which use a church they are in the greatest need of special consideration.

Little children offer the church its greatest opportunity for growth. In the years immediately ahead they will put the most severe pressure on facilities. The church is usually the first place outside of the home to which the child goes; the impression made is likely to be lifelong in its consequences. If something goes wrong, if the surroundings are depressing, a soul may be conditioned against the church; if the child is pleased with what happens, he will be predisposed towards the Christian faith. Not only that, but his parents will be drawn towards the church. With most families the moment of greatest susceptibility to the call of the Christian faith is when the first child starts to church school. If the relationship is a happy one, it is an easy matter to enroll them in the church.

Providing special facilities for little children can be defended on other grounds. They spend the entire session in one room. Oftentimes this room can be used for the care of children during the church service as well as at the church-school hour. A good room is an invitation for someone to start a weekday kindergarten, if the public schools do not have one, or a nursery school. These are highly appreciated services from which the church may profit financially in a small way.

It is probably asking too much to insist that the second room added to a church be used exclusively for little children. However, it can be designed primarily for this purpose and then adapted to other purposes without too much difficulty. Here, again, the secret of multiple use is the provision of adequate storage facilities. Changing things about requires work and costs money, but it is much cheaper than adding additional rooms.

When they expand beyond a single room, the natural impulse of most churches is to provide a general utility hall suitable for dinners, parties, sewing bees, and church-school classes. On the basis of economy this is generally placed in the basement. Here is a good place to face the question as to whether a church should expand vertically or horizontally—whether it should be a congregate structure with its various rooms as close together as possible, or whether it should be dispersed over a considerable area of ground.

The department stores have demonstrated that it is possible to make basements attractive by the use of an abundance of light, ventilation, and decoration. Yet there are fundamental objections to a church going under-ground. In some states, particularly Ohio, there are laws forbidding the use of educational purposes of any room with a floor more than three feet below the level of the ground, and more such enactments may be expected. The only alternative to a deep basement is to elevate the church itself, compelling those who would worship to climb to get into the house of God. With the current prevalence of weak hearts, this is objectionable and will become more so.

Economy is the prime argument for church basements. The cost per square foot of space secured by excavating under a church is undoubtedly less than it would be for the same space on the ground level; but the difference is not as great as is commonly assumed, and there are other factors to be considered. A building on two or more floors permits savings on the foundations and in the roof. Over against this must be put the cost of heavier footings for the walls and the space consumed by, and the cost of, stair wells. In many parts of the country it is possible to put a building with only one floor squarely on the ground with hardly any excavation at all, which is a most economical procedure.

The utilization of army barracks and chapels for church purposes is revealing some new and fascinating possibilities for the social and educa-tional buildings of the church, particularly in mild climates. The military usually build in a hurry, with an eye to reducing both cost and upkeep. To this end their structures are long and narrow, resting directly on the ground, and with the simplest of roofs. The churches which have taken them over have discovered in them two major virtues: every room has light and air on all sides, and what happens in one room does not interfere with what is going on in the others. Where the weather is not severe, the various rooms can be connected by porches or cloisters rather than by corridors, which reduces the cost. If there is a central building of churchly appearance to which the other structures are subordinated, the architectural effect can be pleasing. The Oneonta Church in South Pasadena, California, has built a "campus-type church," in which the various departments of the church school are housed in separate buildings connected by cloisters. This has many advantages over the congregate type of church, in which the voices of the various assemblies compete with each other, and in which it is often impossible to carry on more than one activity at a time. Obviously this sort of structure presents problems in a cold climate, and yet the differential in cost is likely to diminish with the increased use of concrete for floors, better insulation in the roof and walls, tighter windows which may utilize solar heat, and more flexible heating systems. While church basements will doubtless linger on, particularly in the crowded sections of our cities, the church of the future will be built on one floor and will extend over a large area of ground.

Some things may well be said about the use of the basements which we now have. Their greatest advantage is their general utility. They make good rumpus rooms and are well suited to nocturnal activities such as dinners, folk games, and other forms of recreation which need open floor space. They should not be used for little children for several reasons. If necessary, the basement can be assigned to the junior, junior high, or young peoples' groups with the minimum of objection. A basement should have a direct entrance from the street; it should not be necessary to climb up in order to climb down, as is often the case. The maximum of natural light should be made available. To increase the apparent height of the room the ceiling should be white with perpendicular lines stressed wherever possible. The windows should be brightened with gay curtains. Paint should be used lavishly. Knotty pine paneling can produce interesting effects.

Discussions with the pastors of churches having large buildings reveal that the most used rooms are the parlors and the chapel. Both are well suited to religious education. After a kindergarten and utility room they may well be the next rooms added to a church.

The church parlor owes its rise to the diminishing size of the American home on the one hand and the multiplication of small gatherings held under the auspices of the church on the other. Its dominating note should be a homey informality. The furnishings should be psychologically relaxing—their effect should be to put people at ease. Such a room is naturally congenial to the purposes of religious education. It is an excellent meeting place for informal study groups through the week and for young people's or adult classes on Sunday. The only adjustment needed is the setting up of additional chairs and, in some instances, the arrangement of a worship center. In one New England church the heavy furniture in the large parlor is pushed back on Sunday morning, and small tables and chairs for the primary department are brought in. Provided it is not dedicated solely to the women and kept locked up when they aren't using it, a parlor is a great asset to any church school.

The devotional chapel is the most recent addition to our Protestant churches and one of the most successful. The purpose is to provide a place where individuals and small groups may enter into an intimate type of worship, and where the services of the church which do not depend for their success on large numbers may be conducted. These chapels range in size from prayer nooks accommodating half a dozen people to miniature churches. The larger the church, the greater the need for such an auxiliary place of worship.

Chapels with a seating capacity of between fifty and a hundred are a great aid in religious education, as they permit a division in time and place between worship, and instruction, and discussion. In some churches the chapel is a place of pilgrimage where an occasional church-school service is held. More often the chapel service takes the place of the departmental assembly for at least two departments. A common arrangement is for one department to have its worship service in the chapel before the study period, while a second department assembles for study and then closes its session with worship in the chapel. This obviates the need for departmental assembly rooms. Juniors, junior-high groups, and young people may be cared for in this way.

To recapitulate: we have added to our one-room church special facilities for small children, a general utility room, a parlor or parlors, and a chapel. This will provide excellent accommodations for the beginners, the young people, and the adults. The juniors and junior-high groups are less well cared for; they may have to use the general utility room, which may be in the basement. The primary department is likely to be the area of greatest need.

Before a church goes beyond what has been outlined, it needs to face the possibility of having its school meet in double sessions. Today practically all small children are taken to and from the church school by an older person, usually in the family car. If the lower grades meet at the same time as the church service, the parents of the kindergarten and primary children are encouraged to attend divine worship. Such an arrangement increases the attendance at both the church and the church school, and it also permits a double use of many of the rooms. Its practicality depends upon the degree in which the various rooms are soundproof. In old buildings heated by hot-air furnaces a song which is sung in a remote corner commonly echoes throughout the building—and there is remarkably little that can be done about it. Remedial soundproofing is rarely satisfactory. In the future let us hope that our churches will be spread out horizontally rather than piled up vertically, and that the heating systems used will not be such as also to distribute noise. In churches which draw their constituency from large areas, the ultimate arrangement may be to have the entire school at the same hour as the church worship.

If a congregation has the need—and the means—to go beyond what has been suggested, the first step should be the provision of suitable quarters for the first three grades, which are commonly grouped together in the primary department. This calls for a large, sunny room, with alcoves if possible. Children of this age see more than they hear. Classes are usually small and can be separated by screens effectively.

Another specific need is for a nursery for children under four years of age. It need not be large, but it should be equipped with cribs, playthings, and toilet facilities. This room will have considerable utility during the week as a parking place for babies and small children while their mothers engage in various activities.

The next step in the development of an educational building should be the provision of classrooms to the extent to which they are needed and can be afforded. While sympathizing with the desire of generations of Sunday-school teachers to conduct their classes in separate rooms, let us put classrooms last rather than first in the list of priorities because of the experience of the churches during the last forty years. To provide separate rooms whose maximum use is for forty minutes a week for forty weeks of the year is utterly uneconomical. Anyone who travels about among the churches will find many small classrooms which are not used except for storage purposes. In many instances partitions have been torn out to make larger rooms; I know of no cases where large rooms have been divided up.

Separate rooms are most desirable for juniors, junior-high groups, and young people. These ages are gregarious. The tendency is to put boys and girls together, as in the day school, and to have larger classes with fewer but more competent teachers. The minimum room should accommodate at least twenty pupils and should possess some elements of beauty. Some schools are following the pattern of the day school and are grouping the children by grades rather than departments, with one or two grades to a room. Such a setup calls for a chapel and a series of rooms quite similar in size and arrangement to those in the better public schools. An excellent example of this can be seen in the Congregational Church of West Hartford, Connecticut.

Because few churches can afford separate classrooms, it does not follow that their educational work need be carried on amid the hubbub of the old-time Sunday school. A church of any size will have nooks and corners and accessory rooms which will permit classes to concentrate on their work. I have seen as many as eight classes going about their lessons in a church auditorium without noise or confusion. The room commanded respect, and the teachers knew their business.

After the first World War many churches plunged heavily in debt to provide gymnasiums, through which they hoped to reach and hold the rising generation. The experience of churches with gymnasiums is 80 per cent unfavorable. In a new community where school and Y.M.C.A. facilities are at a minimum, a church gym enjoys some years of popularity. In some underprivileged areas of our cities they are useful, while an occasional pastor or youth leader has enough personal magnetism to make a gym hum. On the other hand, most churches which have gyms would gladly be rid of them. Their cost is out of all proportion to the number of people served. For dinners they are cold and drafty; for speaking the acoustics are terrible. By nature they are almost incurably ugly. There is some tendency to use the space for other purposes, such as choir rehearsals, or to extend the balcony all the way across and to develop parlors.

Recreation undoubtedly has its place in religious education and in the youth activities of a church, but these needs can be more economically cared for through the provision of a rumpus room in the basement and the utilization of the facilities of the schools, the Y.M.C.A., and the great out of doors. (See Chapter 14.)

A belated recognition is at last being given to the place of color and pictures in religious education. The smaller the child, the more susceptible is he to external impressions. With him the use of bright colors can hardly be overdone. Throughout the building each room may well have a different color scheme, which adds variety and lends a sense of progression as the child is promoted from one to the other. The public schools have found that bright colors may become irritating after a time. Because the period of attendance is briefer, the church school can be more daring than the day school.

An increasing emphasis is being placed upon visual education. This should begin with the use of religious art, of which there is altogether too little available. The pictures used should be of the best quality, should be hung at the proper height for the different grades, and should be changed frequently. An interesting development of folk art is the painting of murals on the walls of church-school rooms. This is excellent, provided that they are not placed so that they must be looked at for long periods, and that it is understood they can be painted out when their usefulness seems to have ended.

The use of filmstrip, colored slides, and movies as accessories to religious education is enjoying a current vogue. The greatest difficulty is that most church-school activities are conducted in the daytime, while pictures can be projected effectively only in darkness. To exclude all light from most rooms in a church is difficult if not impossible. The answer seems to be to select the room which can be the most easily darkened and then do a real job of blacking out the windows with curtains or panels—or both. One room from which all light has been excluded is worth several that can be only partially darkened. (See Chapter 12.)

Religious drama is another medium for teaching which has its advocates. The experience of the churches is that any large investment in a stage or stage equipment is rarely justified. The actual use is far less than is commonly expected. (See Chapter 11.)

Anyone who travels about among the churches will be depressed by the large sums which have been invested in the past in facilities for religious education, such as Akron-plan auditoriums and rows of little classrooms, which have proved quite unusable. The question can properly be raised, "How can we know that the next generation will not want something radically different from what we are building today?" The answer is that we don't. Our fundamental quarrel with the past is that our predecessors assumed that they had the ultimate answer to the educational needs of the church and froze their plans in such a way that changes have proved most difficult. About the only thing which can be done with an Akron-plan Sunday-school building is to tear it down and start over again. We can protect ourselves against a similar error by building in such a way as to make future change as easy as possible. This means simple construction with level floors, and with no weight-bearing partitions. At present our prime need is room for little children. It is conceivable that in ten years the pressure may be on the high-school age. If our partitions are not too permanent, they can be shifted about to meet varying conditions without too much expense.

An additional warning should be given those who are now building. At the moment there is no generally accepted pattern for facilities for religious education. One result is that we have seen more foolish plans for parish houses than for any other type of church building. Not having specific requirements to which to build, architects are tempted to follow all sorts of whims. For this reason, plans for parsonages and educational rooms should be checked, double checked, and checked again with responsible denominational officers.

SUGGESTIONS FOR FURTHER STUDY

1. Which rooms in your present church receive the most use? Which the least?
2. What impression do you wish to create on the person who enters your church school for the first time? How would you go about securing it?
3. Younger children have a shorter "span of attention" than do older ones. What difference should this make in color schemes, windows, pictures?
4. What are the advantages and disadvantages of having worship follow the lesson period?
5. Should the pictures in a church parlor have sacred or secular themes?
6. What is the law of your state concerning: the doors of public buildings; the use of basement rooms for educational purposes; stairways in public buildings? Does your church conform to the state code?
7. In what ways is a single-story building economical? In what ways a building with multiple stories?
8. What proportion of the children beneath the age of twelve who attend your church school are brought by an older person?

9. What proportion of your church-school teachers regularly attend the Sunday-morning church service?

10. Is it possible to hold more than one meeting at a time in your church?

BIBLIOGRAPHY

Between 1929-1947 few buildings were constructed for religious education. Changing emphases in church life and the increase in building costs have outmoded nearly all that has been written on this subject in the past. We list the four recent books in this field:

Conover, Elbert M. *The Church, School and Parish House Building*. Chicago: International Council of Religious Education. New York: Interdenominational Bureau of Architecture, 1949.

Kramer, Jane. *Equipment and Arrangement for Children's Groups in the Church* (pamphlet). Boston: Pilgrim Press, 1946.

Leach, William H. *Protestant Church Building*. New York and Nashville: Abingdon-Cokesbury Press, 1946. A good discussion of mechanical features.

Scotford, John R. *The Church Beautiful*. Boston: Pilgrim Press, 1946. Contains chapters on "Housing the Church School," "Facilities for Social Life," and "Devotional Chapels."

PART III

Agencies and Organizations
for Religious Education

THE TOTAL CHURCH AS
AN AGENCY OF RELIGIOUS EDUCATION

DONALD M. MAYNARD

THROUGHOUT THIS STUDY Christian education has been thought of as that process by which individuals are brought to an understanding of, and commitment to, the Christian way of life. It has been recognized, furthermore, that commitment should be followed by that kind of guidance which will promote continued growth in Christian living and lead to recommitments on higher levels of Christian understanding and action. Therefore the meaning of the Christian way of life, its implications for personal and community living, and some of the methods and techniques by which individuals may be led to realize it in its fullness have been discussed in other chapters. In this section let us consider some of the agencies and organizations that have responsibility for achieving the aims and purposes of Christian education.

It is fitting that the first agency to be considered is the local church. After all, it is the only agency in a community that is primarily concerned with the moral and spiritual needs and interests of people. It is unfortunate, however, that in the minds of many—including altogether too many ministers—the educational work of the church is thought of in terms only of the church school, the youth fellowships, the vacation church school, and perhaps one or more additional auxiliary groups within the church. If the educational process is at work wherever the needs of individuals are being met, where people are learning, changing attitudes, engaging in meaningful activities, it is obvious that every aspect of the church's work is educational in character. It is the total church, not simply one or more of its auxiliaries, that is the primary agency of religious education.

This viewpoint is not new. In the symposium preceding this one, we find a plea for a consideration of "Every church a school in Christian living" and a corresponding emphasis upon the educational significance of all of the activities of the church.[1] During the intervening years this emphasis has been made again and again.[2] That an increasing number of

---

[1] Lotz and Crawford, *Studies in Religious Education*, p. 564.

[2] For example, see Munro, *Christian Education in Your Church*, chap. vi; Harner, *The Educational Work of the Church*, p. 19; Vieth, *The Church and Christian Education*, chap. iii; and McKibben, *Christian Education Through the Church*, Foreword.

ministers and laymen in the church have caught the vision of the total church as an agency of Christian education there can be no doubt. When they have done so, their churches present a unified approach to the task of meeting the needs of individuals. Their number is altogether too few, however. In church after church we find competing organizations that on the one hand are duplicating efforts and on the other are failing altogether to meet the specific needs of their constituency. We are reminded, furthermore, that these competing organizations tend to create divided loyalties and bitter rivalries among the church membership. Individuals develop concern for, and devotion to, not the church as a whole, but a particular auxiliary of that church. Consequently the impact of that church as a whole on the community is weakened.[3]

It should be noted, however, that the ministers and laymen of the local church are not alone responsible for this situation. This fragmentary approach is encouraged by the general boards of the denominations that bombard local church leaders with suggestions for study groups, social-action projects, devotional activities, and the like. That most of these suggestions are excellent cannot be denied. Coming as they do, however, from general boards that frequently are themselves competitive in character, without a unified approach to the local congregation, they tend further to confuse local leaders and to encourage duplication of effort. One example may suffice. Adult leaders in local churches of one denomination receive suggestions from at least three of the general boards of the church for the promotion of Christian family life. Each of these general boards has a corresponding board in the local church that is urged to promote vigorously its particular program. Is it any wonder, therefore, that in many local churches we find several auxiliaries competing for the time and attention of the membership, and that the task of Christian education is thought of largely in terms of a particular auxiliary rather than in terms of the total church program?

The Essential Over-all Planning Group

It has become increasingly apparent that the total church can function adequately as an agency of Christian education only as there is a general planning board for the entire church program. As such a board goes about its task, conceivably it might proceed as follows:

1. Make a thorough study of the needs and interests of the people whom it is to serve. The list of needs that grows out of such a study should include, not only the needs more or less common to all, but those that are peculiar to individual members of that church and community. For example,

[3] Harner, *op. cit.*, pp. 55-60.

those in a community on which tragic disaster has fallen during the year may be in special need of help in understanding how God works in the world, and how to deal with the problems of evil and pain. Other individuals may be facing doubts; some may be having difficulty in their homes or in other interpersonal relationships; and still others may be living smug, complacent, and selfish lives. A list of such needs will be extensive, but it is only as a church program is built with them in mind that it will become significant.

2. Make a study of the needs of the community. For example, there may be slum areas that should be eradicated, unwholesome working conditions in industry about which something can be done, increasing juvenile delinquency that can be prevented, graft and inefficiency in the police force that can be publicized, or taverns and nightclubs that degrade the youth of the city that can be cleaned up. How many children are there in the community who are not being reached by any church? In other words, let the church be aware of community needs as well as of the needs of its particular constituency.

3. Find out to what extent other agencies in the community are meeting some of the needs listed above—such agencies as the public library, musical and literary clubs, the Y.M.C.A. and the Y.W.C.A., the Scout organizations, the public school, and social agencies.

4. Evaluate the present program of the church to determine to what extent its various organizations are already meeting the needs discovered in the study in paragraph 2. To do this you will need to have a rather detailed description of the activities of each auxiliary and group in the church.

5. Make plans for the new year. It may be assumed that the program would provide opportunities for study, worship, fellowship, participation in social-action projects, training in leadership skills, growing insights into the meaning of stewardship, and support of the world-wide mission of the church. Provision likewise will be made for counseling individuals who need help. Significant community activities also will be projected.

The question arises as to which group in the church shall be given this responsibility for over-all planning. It has been suggested that in some situations it may well be given to the committee or board of education, which has on its membership representation from the many auxiliaries of the church as well as from the other boards. The weakness of such a plan is twofold: On the one hand, the fact that the board of education is simply one among many boards—such as the board of missions, or social action, or evangelism—gives the impression that missions, social action, and evangelism are not to be thought of primarily as educational enterprises of the church. On the other hand, the board of education—even though representatives of other Boards have membership in it—is likely to hesitate to "interfere" too much with the plans of these parallel boards. Nevertheless, if there is a spirit of co-operation and understanding among the membership of these various boards, such an organizational setup may be effective.

The other suggestion is that instead of a board of education or other boards in the local church, there should be one general planning board for the entire church that would be responsible for planning a program for all the age groups in the church. To be sure, auxiliary groups would be needed to carry out these plans, but the work of these subsidiary groups would be integrated into a total program of education that would prevent overlapping and inefficiency.

Shown opposite are Harner's diagrams for these two plans.[4]

EDUCATIONAL SIGNIFICANCE OF THE MINISTER'S TASKS

The realization that the total church is the primary agency of Christian education has many implications in addition to the need for an over-all planning group. For example, the minister becomes the chief educational leader. It is not necessary that he become an expert in every phase of Christian education, of course. His leadership, however, determines to a large extent whether or not the church becomes educationally minded and approaches its task with the needs of its constituency and community in mind. He needs to realize that a program becomes educational when it grows out of the needs and interests of the people. Consequently he must be on the alert to discover these needs and must be willing constantly to fashion a program that is based upon them rather than upon past procedures—or in conformity with the desires of certain influential persons in his church. He will be called upon to enlist laymen for specific tasks within the church. His approach to them and to all people should exemplify his understanding of human nature and of how people learn. It is as he shows an understanding of, and sympathy with, the educational work of the church that it flourishes and becomes vital.

The minister will realize, too, that his own responsibilities are a part of the total educational program of the church. He will think of his sermons, not as isolated messages given from week to week, but as contributing to that larger educational program. He will preach to people's needs and will deal with issues that are vital to them. The method by which he plans ahead for his sermons will be his own. What is important is that planning shall take place. There will be occasions when his sermons are in areas that are being studied in the church-school classes or by other groups in the church. There will be series of sermons that instruct, that inspire, that spur to action, and that give comfort. A wise minister guards against

[4] Ibid., pp. 65, 70. See also Vieth, op. cit., pp. 102, 104.

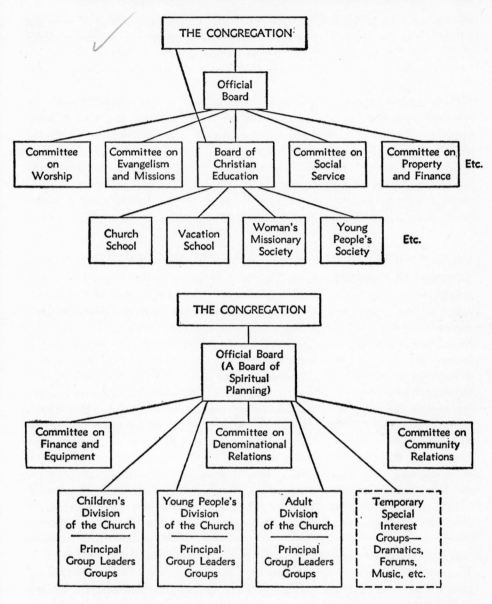

preaching too frequently on topics that have a particular appeal to him personally. For example, a minister who was especially intrigued by the contribution that religion can make to wholesome personality adjustment discovered that most of his sermons dealt with personality problems. It took a gentle chiding from some of his members to make him realize that he was not presenting them with a well-rounded gospel. The preacher needs to remember that his sermons are a vital part of the curriculum of religious education in his church. It is encouraging to discover that denominational leaders are gathering outstanding ministers into seminars to consider how sermons may be made more effective in the educational program of the church. (See Chapter 30.)

Only mention can be made of the educational opportunities of ministers and laymen as they lead boys and girls, men and women, to Christ. Educational evangelism is concerned not only with commitment but with the process by which the convert becomes acquainted with the full implications of the gospel for his own personal life and for society.[5] As the minister prepares boys and girls for church membership, as he administers the Sacraments, and as he counsels those in need,[6] he becomes a leader in the religious education program of his church.

EVERY PHASE OF PROGRAM EDUCATIONALLY SIGNIFICANT

It cannot be stressed too frequently that every activity of the church should be approached with the educational viewpoint. It should be remembered, for example, that the financial program has as its purpose not only the raising of needed funds but the development of intelligent givers who are imbued with the true sprit of stewardship. Those in charge of this part of the program therefore will consult age-group leaders before projecting any campaign to raise money that involves gifts from young and old alike. They will not follow the example of one official board that planned for such a campaign without asking for any suggestions from the leaders of children as to how the experience of giving might be made educationally significant for the children. Instead, they sent to these leaders small banks with the request that on a certain Sunday the children should put their offerings into them. No efforts whatsoever were made to give the children an insight into the purposes for which the gifts were to be used. In that same church a lad of fifteen remarked that the only letter he received from the church after joining it was one asking for his pledge. Such a letter may be appropriate, but in this case it gave the lad the impression that the church was concerned only with his financial contribution to it. The financial program of the church must be geared into the educational program if it is to avoid giving to many the impression received by this young man.

Mention could be made of the educational contribution that can be made by the choirs of the church; by the various organizations for men, women, and youth; by camping programs; and by the Christian family.

[5] See Chapter 6. An interesting symposium on "Evangelism and the Educative Process" may be found in *Religious Education*, May-June, 1948.

[6] See Chapter 15.

Consideration of most of these is presented in other chapters in this book. In fact, the philosophy underlying every chapter is based upon the conviction that the total church is the supreme agency for Christian education.

THE CONGREGATION TEACHES

It should be remembered also that the congregation of a church makes a very definite impression upon boys and girls not so much by what it may profess to believe as by what it actually is.

In the first place, the congregation as a whole performs a teaching function. For example, when it enters reverently into the spirit of worship on Sunday morning, when there is widespread participation in the various enterprises of the church such as the missionary and social-action projects, and when there is a contagious spirit of fellowship and good will pervading the membership, then boys and girls are led to feel that the church, and that for which it stands, is tremendously significant. On the other hand, should these characteristics not be true of a congregation, and should it be divided into warring factions, it is almost inevitable that young people lose respect for the church—a loss of respect, unfortunately, which may take in religion itself. Altogether too frequently also do we find young people disturbed and perplexed because the congregation does not seem to be sufficiently interested in their needs and spiritual welfare to provide them the resources necessary to carry on an effective program.

In the second place, individual members of a congregation are Christian teachers—whether they want to be or not—by virtue of the fact that they are members of the church. They are being watched by boys and girls and others to see whether or not they manifest in their everyday contacts the ideals they claim to possess. Children who feel that their parents have favorites, or are not fair to them, have difficulty in believing in the value of their parents' religion. Employees who find their churchgoing employers to be more concerned about profits than about the welfare of persons tend to become cynical about religion in general. It is not necessary to multiply examples, but it is important that we never forget that Christians are constantly teaching by what they are rather than by what they say.

Special chapters in this book consider the work of youth and adult organizations. The second half of this chapter therefore will be given to a consideration of the total church program of Christian education for children.

SUGGESTIONS FOR FURTHER STUDY

1. Work out a detailed plan for discovering the needs and interests of members of your local church.
2. Make a study of the auxiliary groups in your church and the specific per-

sonal and community needs they are meeting. Note duplication of effort and whether some needs are being met by several organizations, whereas other needs, are being met by none.

3. What are the educational possibilities in: (*a*) a meeting of the official board, (*b*) a banquet for men in the church, (*c*) the choirs, (*d*) a financial campaign, (*e*) a pastoral visit, (*f*) a family camp, (*g*) the administration of the Sacraments?

4. How would you go about developing an over-all planning group for your church? What are some of the obstacles you would encounter, and how would you overcome them? What would be some of the encouraging factors? Which type of organization suggested in this chapter would be best for your church?

5. What percentage of the membership of your church is active in some church enterprise? List ways by which more people may be enlisted in some activity.

6. Do the general boards of your denomination present a unified approach to the local congregation? How could such an approach be made?

BIBLIOGRAPHY

Beavan, A. W. *The Local Church*. New York: The Abingdon Press, 1937.

Cummings, Oliver de Wolf. *Christian Education in the Local Church*. Philadelphia: Judson Press, 1942.

Harner, Nevin C. *The Educational Work of the Church*. New York and Nashville: Abingdon-Cokesbury Press, 1939.

McKibben, Frank M. *Christian Education Through the Church*. New York and Nashville: Abingdon-Cokesbury Press, 1947.

Munro, H. C. *Christian Education in Your Church*. St. Louis: Bethany Press, 1933.

Smith, Henry G. W. *The Pastor at Work in Christian Education*. Philadelphia: Judson Press, 1935.

Vieth, Paul H. *The Church and Christian Education*. St. Louis: Bethany Press, 1947.

THE TOTAL PROGRAM FOR CHILDREN

ALICE L. GODDARD

CHILDREN'S WORK HAS BEEN THROUGH many changes since the first teacher gathered boys and girls into the church on Sunday afternoon. But, like those early teachers, literally thousands of men and women today are active in the religious education of children. Classes for children are an accepted part of almost every church's program, and many denominations have one or more staff members devoting full time to children's work. Many local and regional denominational and interdenominational church bodies have employed or volunteer leaders who carry children's work as a major responsibility.

Experience has shown that people learn by various methods; and teachers of children consider a lesson as a total experience which includes growth in knowledge, understanding, appreciation, and life experiences. Lesson plans include elements of activity and satisfying participation in Christian living. Leaders have come to appreciate the influence of every factor in a child's life, even the physical aspects of the church-school rooms. In many churches children's rooms have emerged from basements and dark hallways to bright, sunny locations where color contributes to feelings of joy and co-operative work and play. Children's work is increasingly emphasized as its importance is realized.

Much is still to be learned about the development of children. Not only are there wide variations within the same age group, but variations exist within the same child between his levels of physical, mental, and social growth. Leaders realize that experiences must fit the level of the child's development; and unless a child is ready, these experiences—however desirable they are in themselves—may be actually harmful. Also, rather than directing all children toward a preconceived pattern, teachers are considering children as individuals and attempting to provide experiences that will aid them in attaining the Christian growth of which each of them is capable. This necessitates acquaintance with each child's needs, background of training and experience, and a program based on this knowledge.

Leaders who concern themselves with the individual's religious development also consider all factors of the child's life. They study each phase of growth so they may understand the child as a whole person. They consider the effects of experiences in every situation at home, school, church, and elsewhere in the community and see the work of the church school in relationship. They know that satisfactory adjustments in every area of living are essential to Christian growth. These workers realize that insecurity is a detriment to religious development and plan ways of overcoming it. They study the desired objectives and give time and effort to the required planning to meet these goals. The degree to which church and church-school leaders have caught this vision of teaching helps determine the extent of the program and the quality of children's work in a church.

To develop the potentialities of each child to the fullest, it has been found necessary for boys and girls to be active in the planning, conducting, and evaluating of their own programs of work. Leaders have come to think, not of a lesson they are teaching, but of boys and girls with whom they are working co-operatively toward attainable goals. There is the realization that effective teaching necessitates a creative process at work within the child, not only that he may create and develop that which is creative within him, but as an essential to growth. Children must be helped to explore areas of Christian living and to evaluate their discoveries. Every good teaching program requires activities—whether they be study, discussion, service projects, handicrafts, writing, or expression of thought—which lead to wholehearted participation by the child and affect his development. A group of primary children, for example, could come to a deeper appreciation of the works of God as they express these thoughts in a "poem" on miracles.

It is a miracle
When dead leaves fall from a tree and bury deep in the earth and make it rich for other plants and trees.
It is a miracle—
That seeds and bulbs know when it is time to wake up and push through the ground.
It is a miracle—
That birds know when to fly south and when to come back again.
It is a miracle—
That tree buds know when it is time to change into leaves and blossoms.
It is a miracle—
That each year we can be sure of these things.
PRAYER: O God, we thank you for your miracles of growth and change. We are glad that we can depend on these miracles' happening every year. We thank you for the miracle of our minds that can think lovely thoughts. O God, we thank you! Amen.[1]

The time and length of the Sunday sessions vary with the church and the comprehensiveness of its program for children. In most of our churches the Sunday church school is in the morning, although many of the Canadian churches meet with their children for classes on Sunday afternoon. Many churches have Sunday church school with worship and classes and make no

[1] Ellen E. Fraser, from the *International Journal of Religious Education*, February, 1944, p. 32.

other provision for children. Some also have junior church, with officers and programs patterned after the general church organization. Many more—and this number is growing—use the expanded session, in which activities including study, service projects, worship, and training in worship contribute to a well-rounded program. With this plan boys and girls frequently participate in a portion of the worship in the church service.

Practices vary greatly regarding work during the week with children in churches, and very little except the Sunday work is done with those under the third or fourth grades. Leaders of these younger children frequently work with parents to plan activities at home. In many communities churches co-operate to provide weekday church schools and have no other regular weekday program for children. Several attempts have been made to build church-centered group work and club programs, but none has been developed to any great extent. Many of the character-building agencies with junior programs use churches as meeting centers. The degree to which these groups relate to the total religious education program depends on the leadership in the agencies and in the churches. Many churches realize the influence of these groups on children and insist that the leaders be carefully selected Christian persons and supervise this selection. In these churches the group work programs are planned as a part of the total church-school program. Other churches open their buildings and leave the supervision of leadership and program to the group-work agencies.

Although a large majority of church schools use the three-year grading plan there is a movement toward two-year grading in many primary and junior departments, beginning with the first and second grades. This has developed as a result of a growing understanding of the needs of children. Many smaller churches do not have rooms for complete grading of all of the work for children, and some of the denominations are providing written helps especially for these schools. Even in these churches every possible attempt is made to separate the younger children as much as possible and to arrange the program to provide for some graded experiences.

Vacation church schools, resident camping, day camping, and family camping provide summer opportunities for work with children and are growing in number. Vacation church schools are naturally the most popular of these and serve younger as well as older children. The widespread development of church camping is comparatively new and requires study. Day camping is sometimes erroneously confused with a vacation church school out of doors. Properly organized, day camping has a unique contribution to make to the religious development of older children. Resident camping is receiving attention in an effort to provide experiences suited to the junior child in keeping with church and camping standards. Family camping is being attempted by a few churches, with admirable results, and leaders are enthusiastic about its values. For younger children a family situation is the recommended type of camping.

Although many denominations employ staff persons with specific responsibility for missionary education, there is correlation between this and other phases of the program. Many lesson units have missionary emphases. The fine materials published for children by the Missionary Education Movement are used with entire departments. Church-school activities include service projects for missions. Worship, stories, and visual materials centering around missionary themes are a part of many programs. Leaders attempt to train all children to have an interest in, and to contribute to, missions as an important part of the work of the church.

The church has been active in the development of the nursery school movement and has provided housing for public and private nursery schools. Parents in a number of churches have organized co-operative nursery schools with a trained leader in charge, assisted by different parents. Most Sunday church schools have nursery departments planned to provide experiences on the child's level which will be the foundations for desirable Christian attitudes and habits. The increase of work with these younger children has opened up a developing area of specialized work in religious education.

There is great need for more adequate Christian education for children under institutional care of every type. Spasmodic attempts have been made in this field but this is a specialized area generally requiring co-operative effort, and much is yet to be done if the church is to fulfill its mission. Interest must be aroused, materials provided, and leaders trained to care for these boys and girls whose needs are exceptional.

Homebound, ill, or handicapped children are another group neglected by our churches except as a leader here or there arranges to work with parents of these boys and girls in a program of Christian education. This is an area of work needing study and effort and for which the church has a great responsibility.

With the increased emphasis on activity- and experience-centered teaching some have tended to minimize biblical and historical content. Consequently now there is concern that boys and girls, though they may be moral, are not motivated by Christian principles. Discerning writers of materials are giving considerable guidance to leaders in providing children with adequate knowledge of our Christian heritage without minimizing the importance of experiences leading to well-rounded Christian development. This trend naturally leads to an increased emphasis on meaningful worship.

Good music is used a great deal with children, with careful interpretation of words and music. Many denominations have printed hymnals for the various age groups with songs and hymns within the range of the religious and musical experiences of children. Churches have organized children's choirs, sometimes called junior choirs. These vary in the amount and kind of participation in the church service. In some they form a part of the processional and assist in the music of the church service of worship each week; in other churches participation is limited to less frequent intervals or special Sundays. Frequently the adult choir director assists in the training of these groups.

Many leaders use listening music to set moods for worship, work, or rest. Some churches have record players for this purpose. Endeavors are under way to provide more of a selection in this field and to furnish recorded children's songs suitable for church-school use.

Pictures and other visual materials are used to create moods, to impart information, to clarify ideas, and to enrich departmental and class work. Because of the lasting impression of things seen, discerning leaders select these with care. Projected materials are not recommended for use with very young children and often are no more satisfactory than nonprojected ones for older boys and girls. Dioramas, murals, flat pictures, models, and homemade movie scrolls all contribute to the learning process. Those which the children make for themselves have particular value.

Leaders are coming to realize more and more the place of children in the fellowship of the church and the importance of this fellowship in Christian development. This is already noticeable in planning which provides opportunity for groups of families including children to do things together in the church and in the general programs which consider children's interests. Children's Day is used by many churches to build an awareness of the place of children in the total church family.

A fine fellowship is enjoyed by children's workers on local, regional, and national levels. Many state and city councils have committees on children's work which hold frequent conferences or arrange for other programs with a resultant strong interdenominational group spirit. Some of these councils and also some denominations have loosely organized fellowships of children's workers.

Parents and leaders work together in many ways in the church school. Several denominations have prepared or are preparing curriculums by which home and church co-operate in the teaching process. Men are increasingly active in the work with boys and girls. There is a trend toward couples assuming responsibility with both the father and mother supervising and teaching even quite young children. Within the past few years three denominations have employed men as directors of their national children's work.

With the rise of the interdenominational movement the International Council of Religious Education constituted the Committee on Religious Education of Children, with membership from state councils and denominational children's workers. This committee has been responsible for co-operative planning, for the publication of leaflets and other materials including syndicated articles, for many common emphases in children's work, for service projects by and for children, for national and regional conferences on children's work, and for community efforts to improve conditions for children.

Members of the Committee on Religious Education of Children have worked closely with the World Council of Christian Education which concerns itself with the religious education of children around the world.

Efforts in child welfare vary from occasional programs in local churches to extensive national plans of child care and protection. Most denominations include some type of work in this field in their general planning and provide for it in their organizational structure. Sometimes this responsibility is related to home-missions boards working with migrant, underprivileged, remote, or other children not given adequate church care elsewhere. The Home Missions Council has been very active in fostering work with these groups. Some church bodies concern themselves primarily with legislative matters and the development of public conscience. Several state and city councils have been active in child welfare programs in their communities.

During the past the church has been responsible for many developments in organized public and private child welfare efforts; and many neighborhood houses, orphanages, and community centers are still church sponsored. Although some of the work originated by the churches has now been taken over by various agencies especially equipped for this, Christian education leaders generally agree that the church has a vital role to play in these efforts in the safeguarding of spiritual values.

Work with—and for—boys and girls knows no limits. The future promises much to those interested in the Christian education of children.

SUGGESTIONS FOR FURTHER STUDY

1. Make a case study of a small number of children of the same age to determine their various levels of development as revealed by school grades, responsibility in home tasks, reactions in church school, participation in organized groups, behavior in games and other play, and by other means. Study your teaching in the light of these findings.

2. Study the religious education programs of the various institutions for children in your community, particularly those giving detention or foster care of any type. If possible, arrange to give some time to working with children in one of these institutions.

3. Working with parents, and with the doctor if advisable, develop a program of religious education which you carry out with a homebound child. Keep a record of plans and results. Or supervise the work of another leader working with homebound children.

4. Study the relationship of the churches to the child-serving agencies in your community, and make any recommendations you think necessary.

5. Evaluate the program for children of your church as to adequacy of time, suitability to children's needs, child participation in planning and in creative efforts, home co-operation, and apparent outcome.

6. Discuss with a group of parents the needs of children, and determine ways home and church can work together.

7. Make a study of the curriculum of your denomination—or of some other denomination—to see where it meets the needs of children and conforms to the goals for the Christian education of children.

BIBLIOGRAPHY

Chaplin, Dora P. *Children and Religion*. New York: Charles Scribner's Sons, 1948.

Gesell, A. L. *Studies in Child Development*. New York: Harper & Brothers, 1948.

Gesell, A. L., *et al. The Child from Five to Ten*. New York: Harper & Brothers, 1946.

Gillet, Edith L. *At Work with Children in the Small Church*, Philadelphia: Judson Press, 1940.

Goals for the Christian Education of Children. Chicago: International Council of Religious Education.

Jones, Mary Alice. *The Faith of Our Children*. New York and Nashville: Abingdon-Cokesbury Press, 1943.

Lewis, Hazel A. *Planning for Children in the Local Church*. St. Louis: Bethany Press, 1933.

Odell, Mary C. *Our Family Grows Toward God*. New York and Nashville: Abingdon-Cokesbury Press, 1948.

Perkins, Jeanette E. *Children's Worship in the Church School*. New York: Harper & Brothers, 1939.

Roorbach, Rosemary K. *Teaching Children in the Small Church*. Nashville: Methodist Publishing House, 1943.

It is also recommended that reading be done on departmental methods of teaching and administration. See Bulletin 502, International Council of Religious Education, for recommended departmental books.

Chapter 19

THE HOME AND PARENT EDUCATION

WESNER FALLAW

IN SO SHORT A TIME as fifty years striking differences are seen in the American home. Fewer children, smaller living quarters, mobility, instability, 60 per cent of the families living in towns and cities of 2,500 or more population, and a steadily rising divorce rate leave the thoughtful observer wondering whether or not the American family may go the way of the clan. Certainly individualism is replacing familism as the dominant characteristic of the home.

When home life was mainly rural, with a relatively self-sufficient economy, the bearing and raising of children was profitable. Not so today in our industrial-urban order. Having a child costs money. Moreover, multiple-unit housing not only is insufficient to meet demands but is doubly difficult to find because owners often refuse to rent to families with children. Adults with nothing more annoying than a belled cat have preference in the renting of homes. Single-unit dwellings, even if available, are too expensive for the majority of families. Doubling up with relatives has been widely practiced for half a generation—in the depression of the thirties, during the late war, and until now. One need not experience this kind of living in order to know the mischief it reaps; slight imagination tells the story.

Children, youth and adults customarily go outside the family for education, religion, health care, recreation, and work. The traditional functions of the family have declined or vanished. Neither the family group nor the home base has remained magnetic enough to hold the interest of any given member of the family when he wishes to enjoy or enlighten himself. For many families eating out seems to have greater appeal than eating at home. And when people do stay at home, they bring in the world by way of radio, telephone, newspaper, comic book, magazine, and, more recently, television. Separately and together the modern family seems incapable of developing its own resourcefulness so that work, play, learning, and religion can be a family-group affair.

As familism with its demands of the group ahead of the individual abdicates before individualism, home life is put to the hard test of endurance in the face of the family in decline as an institution—and perhaps not yet in control of itself as a companionship affair in which interpersonal relations are democratically practiced.

The patriarchal family has no place in our society. And as the potential "cradle of democracy" the companionship family is confronted with its decisive hope for survival. Set down in an urban civilization, in which many or most of the decisions for living are made without regard to the moral law or a personal God, the family, like society, tends to be thoroughly secular. That is why it lacks motive power to learn the ways of democracy—conference, compromise, sharing, unselfishness, individual sacrifice. That is why the American family is today disintegrating as a social unit and spiritual matrix wherein persons might discover that individual freedom is derived only at the price of subordination of self to the common good.

The American home is generally the product of romantic love, which may be viewed as the product of physical attraction and excessive idealism that obscures the requirements of marital adjustment—individual subordination, financial obligations, household chores, and more. Romance is desirable as an initial cause for a man and woman taking the marriage vows; but the first cause needs quick deepening by open-eyed understanding that marriage means mutuality first, individuality only at length—marriage means children, and children mean group living, which is costly in work and time and devotion.

For the past few decades religious education, like social work and progressive general education, has emphasized that the home should provide unifying experiences so that personality development can be more assured than it is when divisive and fragmentary events are allowed to pull the person this way and that way, until he is an isolate, rooted neither in family nor society. Modern educators know the value of the growing person's having common experiences with his family—household improvement, hobbies, cultural and recreational activities. Social workers understand that emotional stability comes from a nice sharing of intimacies within the family, and from diligence in pursuing the ways of mutuality and co-operative living. And the religious educator knows it to be essential that persons find within the family support for moral conduct and guidance aimed at reverent living.

Burgess and Locke in 1945 listed "current long-time trends" of the family and expressed interest in observing whether they would continue:

Among these are:
(1) the declining birth rate,
(2) the consequent smaller size of the family,
(3) the increase in the proportion of the married to those of marriageable age,
(4) the decrease in the age at marriage,

(5) the increase in the proportion of all women and of married women gain-
fully employed,

(6) the decline in the historic function of the family—economic, educational,
recreational, religious and protective.[1]

To this list must be added the mounting tide of divorces. In 1890 there
were 16.2 marriages per divorce; in 1940, 5.7 marriages per divorce.[2] Today
there is about one divorce for every three marriages.[3] Ray Baber reported
in 1943 that the immediate future of the family was not bright, that, in
fact, the family was in for a difficult time but not destined for eclipse.
Improved parent education, among other services to the family, he viewed
as promising.[4]

Not only has marriage remained popular but the majority of couples
are married by ministers, frequently in the church. Over against a secularized social order this apparent sacred concept of marriage is heartening.
High-school and college courses on marriage and the growing interest
in parent education, fostered by the churches and sundry community
agencies, are additional cause for encouragement as the family's future
is considered. There is evidence that serious study of marriage and responsible leadership in courses on the family make for stabilized home life.[5]

The National Conference on Family Life, held in Washington in May,
1948, brought together representatives from 125 organizations concerned
with social, economic, educational, and religious issues that affect the
welfare of the family. Persons from labor and management, government
and volunteer agencies, constituted the first conference of this kind ever
held. Sections of the conference favored, among other things, public
housing, an increase in the number of homes for rent, wider training of
high-school students for marriage and family, and the securing of more
professionally trained counselors. The president of the United States was
called upon to appoint a commission to study marriage laws and divorce
procedures, along with juvenile courts and legal-aid provisions. The
conference has given impetus to the national movements committed to
strengthening the home.

The Commission on Marriage and the Home,[6] headed by Dr. Leland

---

[1] *The Family: from Institution to Companionship*, p. 750.

[2] Duvall and Hill, *When You Marry*, p. 365. Figures based on United States *Census*
information and the Lynds' *Middletown* (New York: Harcourt, Brace and Co., 1929).

[3] Zimmerman, *The Family of Tomorrow*, p. 2.

[4] "Marriage and the Family After War," *The Annals of the American Academy of
Political and Social Science*, Vol. 229 (1943), pp. 164 ff.

[5] Duvall and Hill, *op. cit.*, p. 422.

[6] Of The Federal Council of Churches of Christ in America, 297 Fourth Avenue, New
York 10, New York.

Foster Wood, has long served Protestant homes by means of conferences, guidance, and pamphlets of considerable merit.

In the field of family counseling the National Conference on Family Relations—of which Dr. Evelyn Millis Duvall is secretary—The American Institute of Family Relations, the Association for Family Living, the Child Study Association of America, and other agencies offer notable aid to American families.[7]

PARENT EDUCATION

The International Council of Religious Education, through which more than forty Protestant church bodies on the North American continent operate, views the family as "potentially the most important means of Christian education for all its members."[8] In the book *The Church and Christian Education*, Paul Vieth presents the results of a two-year survey of religious education made by sixty Protestant educators and other religious leaders. The committee of sixty calls for implementation of what the Council has been saying about the primacy of the home in Christian learning and living.

It will be no easy task to revolutionize the thinking and practice of Protestantism so that the cultivation of family religion shall become a major concern of the entire church. The enlistment of millions of parents in an effort to provide sound Christian education for their children and to continue in a process of learning throughout all the years of adulthood is an undertaking which will take all the resources of national agencies, denominational and interdenominational, as well as those in the local church. But it is doubtful whether any other effort will ultimately accomplish as much for the young and old and for the Kingdom of God.[9]

The slowness with which the churches have made bold to enlist parents for church-family education stems in part from skepticism about the interest and dependability of parents in Christian teaching, and in part from the ignorance of pastors and educational directors of how to train fathers and mothers to discharge jointly with church-school teachers the function of Christian education. Prior to teaching deliberately—systematically, effectively, and continuously—a parent must become a learner. Does he want to learn?

Adult education has made remarkable progress in America. The economic depression, the recent war, the present cosmic perplexity, have seen prolific adult interest in some kind of learning. A Gallup poll in December,

---

[7] For addresses of these and other agencies see Duvall and Hill, *op. cit.*, pp. 439-42.

[8] See *Christian Education Today: A Statement of Basic Philosophy*, p. 20.

[9] P. 186. The Bethany Press, publisher.

1944, "showed that 34 per cent of all adults wanted to continue their education. By July, 1947, this figure had grown to 41 per cent. Other surveys and spot checks indicate similar and widespread interest.[10]

It may be doubted that a formal series of leadership education courses, similar to those used with church-school teachers by the International Council and the denominations, would be successful with parents. A parent is seldom to be approached directly with the idea of educating him in theology, Bible, Church history, and teaching methods. Instead he is to be appealed to at the point of his greatest interest—his children.

For a stimulating and optimistic account of parental support of church and home education, Ernest Ligon's development of the Union College Character Research Project should be studied.[11] In the fall of 1948 the Presbyterian Church in the U.S.A. launched a curriculum, "Christian Faith and Life: A Program for Church and Home," based largely upon the importance of the home for Christian teaching. Other denominations are moving in the same direction. Whatever the worth of the programs just mentioned may prove to be, they do represent trends and make provision for training parents on the job. As a parent faces squarely his responsibility for guiding the growth of his child, he finds himself in need of religious education. This need motivates his learning.

Two reasons stand out that in a measure explain the readiness of modern parents—whether themselves in the church, or merely accustomed to send their children to the church school—to take seriously a local church's plan for church-family education: (a) the rising level of education in America, and (b) the religio-social heritage which is ours, and which has always maintained that the family is central in determining the kind of growth and behavior the child is to manifest. The early Hebrews insisted upon parental teaching of the young. Among the early Christians a man's entire household might accept the faith. In parts of colonial America parents were required to teach their children "letters, the catechism, and the capital laws of the country." [12] A hundred years ago New England thought was quickened by numerous reminders of the significance of the mother in teaching her children.[13]

If the church relies on parents' classes, couples' clubs, sermons on family living, and so forth, as instruments of parent education, disappointment is likely to follow—especially if promotional devices are employed, in

[10] Homer Kempfer, "Adult Education Is Growing," *School and Society*, September 11, 1948, p. 172.

[11] See especially *Their Future Is Now* and *A Greater Generation*.

[12] John S. Brubacker, *A History of the Problems of Education*, p. 581.

[13] See Anne L. Kuhn's *The Mother's Role in Childhood Education: New England Concepts: 1830-1860*.

contrast to the motivation for parent learning that comes from regular parent-teacher conferences on problems common to the two groups in their guidance of the child's religious growth. Systematic study is needed by parents as much as by teachers, but systematizing whatever procedure is to be followed should come after teachers and parents have met to assess their joint responsibility for teaching children. Parents as well as church-school teachers know quite well that most Christian education programs are puny affairs—if they do not know it, they need but ask the children. The force of this fact is sufficient to bring parents and teachers, under the direction of ministers and educators, into sessions for serious inquiry and investigation of what can be done to improve matters.

Increasingly, Protestant churches are holding periodic parents' nights, on which occasions helpful but generally limited education takes place. One need only attend a gathering of this kind to discover the absorbing interest which parents and teachers have in finding out what they can do together to improve religious education. Sessions of this nature are vital when they deal with specific boys and girls—what they say, do, and think about religious concepts, attitudes, and values. Moreover, beyond the occasional parents' night lies the monthly church-family conference. It is significant to the extent that it focuses upon the major issues confronting families today.

Sex practices on the current scene are a problem of first importance. Religious education of parents ought soon to face the data presented in the Kinsey studies of sex behavior. The first of a projected series of volumes offers a sharp challenge and an intriguing opportunity to persons concerned with Christian family living.[14] If it is true, as the Kinsey findings suggest, that one's social class is much more influential than church participation in determining sex behavior,[15] it follows that the churches must develop radically different ways of teaching both the physical and spiritual aspects of sex. Once parents and teachers determine to get at the roots of ineffectual religious education, they will find that their neglect of guidance in sex conduct contributes to personal guilt and fears, marital infelicity and family breakdown.

To say the least, a disturbing picture of the sex practices of the American male is presented by the Kinsey report. And despite the report's intimation that its data are of no value to the moralist and religious educator, conferences of parents and teachers, under the aegis of the church, are precisely

[14] Alfred C. Kinsey, Wardell B. Pomeroy, and Clyde E. Martin, *Sexual Behavior in the Human Male*.

[15] See Seward Hiltner's comments, "The Kinsey Report," *Information Service*, April 10, 1948.

the point of departure for initiating education designed to make the human body a fit temple for the Holy Spirit.[16]

From the conference stage parents and teachers can move toward a merging of their forces, so that they become a unified teaching order that meets regularly to consider general themes and particular problems in religious education.[17] When a father of a seventh-grade boy sits down with other parents of junior-high pupils and with their church-school teachers, he (a) becomes familiar with the content material being taught his boy, (b) hears how the teacher is conducting the class, (c) learns from other parents what they are doing to provide through-the-week Christian education that supports, extends, and makes fruitful the church's teaching. And if he is reasonably alert and ethically sensitive, the father may perceive that his life is negating the principles of Christ in so far as they might function in the life of his son.

Parent education of this kind presupposes that church-school teachers have experience, training, and poise equal to the task of guiding the thought of groups of parents. In other words, the teacher must first be an adult educator before he can do his best work with children or youth. That is high expectation of the teacher and calls for a new basis of selection and training.

Religious education of parents reaches genuine effectiveness when progress is made beyond the parent-teacher conference into short-term study groups under the best biblical scholars and educational specialists available. Study groups should evolve as parents recognize their needs for knowledge of content material and for developing competency in guiding the daily conduct of the young.[18] As a division of labor, the church will be responsible mainly for content teaching while the more difficult task of guiding the child's living of the Christian faith belongs primarily to the parents. Parents' training for this work should have begun when, as children themselves, their parents lived religiously. Their preparation for Christian parenthood should have been fostered when, as high-school and college students, they studied the meaning of Christian marriage. If the minister whom they consulted on the eve of their marriage did his job well, he initiated a process of counseling and church guidance which related

[16] Chap. 13, especially pp. 483-87, does show that sex practices among devout, active church participants are modified by religious codes. But for Kinsey and his associates, sex is a biological outlet, a drive which will always have expression in one form or another with a frequency determined by a particular individual's age, educational status, and class.

[17] For elaboration of this see Fallaw, *The Modern Parent and the Teaching Church*, chap. ix, "Unifying Home and Church."

[18] A significant program for teaching parents is that of the Myers Park Baptist Church, Charlotte, North Carolina. Dr. George Heaton, the minister, is developing church-family education to an advanced degree.

the couple to suitable group life in the church in preparation for the coming of children.

Parent education is especially timely when the children are small. Nursery education which includes guidance of parents in a church that is educationally thorough is one of the best points for inaugurating a plan that may grow into an inclusive church-family program.[19]

How the Family Teaches Religion[20]

The attitudes, values, and conduct of parents constitute the pattern for living by which the child fashions his early behavior. It is by imitation that the young child puts infancy behind him and moves toward the relative maturity of individuality. This is not to say that the child becomes a mere duplicate of a parent, or yet a composite of parents and older children in the family whose daily conduct he so closely observes and generally adopts. But it is to emphasize that a large part of the practices and customs of a given family constitute the raw material with which the growing child structures his life. Marian J. Radke's study of parental authority and the behavior of preschool children substantiates earlier findings of psychologists who hold that a child's behavior and values are taken directly from the overt behavior of his parents.[21] What he experiences in the home he reveals in his social relations outside the home. Not only so; his concepts of good and bad behavior are closely related to his experience in the home.

In the mid-twenties, Sonquist and Kerr, aided by Hartshorne and May in their work of the Character Education Inquiry, conducted a study which, though inconclusive, did establish reason to see that among eleven hundred children studied in grades 5-9, knowledge of right and wrong is definitely related to that of their parents.[22] At least, so far as these investigators could determine, the influence of parents ranked well above that of the children's friends, club leaders, public- and Sunday-school teachers.

Arthur Jersild finds that "the influence of religious training on children has not been studied . . . in a systematic manner."[23] He notes that "a study of the effects of religious instruction would . . . have to appraise the more

---

[19] For a number of years, work with children and parents at the First Church of Christ (Congregational) in West Hartford, Connecticut, offered an example of sound education. The program was developed by Mrs. Vincent J. Maramarco, former director of religious education.

[20] See Fallaw in *Religious Education*, January-February, 1948, "How the Family Teaches Religion," pp. 3-6.

[21] *The Relation of Parental Authority to Children's Behavior and Attitudes*, pp. 107-8.

[22] "Testing the Knowledge of Right and Wrong," *Religious Education*, October, 1926, pp. 539 ff.

[23] *Child Psychology* (rev. ed.), p. 419.

subjective phenomena denoted by such terms as peace of mind, relief from feeling guilt, hopefulness, the disposition to be forgiving and patient, and the like." [24]

Students of child behavior maintain that they do not know what factors in the child's experience actually cause him to be religious. It may be questioned that we shall ever know with scientific accuracy how a person becomes religious. The content of religion—knowledge of the Bible, church history, catechisms, creeds, the work of the church—is learned just as other kinds of information and facts are learned. Religious ceremonies are learned through participation. Both content and ceremony—ceremony meaning worship and other religious celebrations mainly of public nature—are confined, for the most part, to the church. And though content and ceremony are indispensable phases of religious teaching, they may be viewed as less significant than a contemporary incarnation of the God ideal.

Before religion, as value and conduct, is really learned, the spirit of Christ must be made flesh, must dwell in the learner. Content learning is an aid, not a guarantee, toward this end. Ceremony and celebration are aids, not guarantees, toward this end. This is why the function of parents as religious teachers is not so limited a matter as that of telling Bible stories, and going over next Sunday's lesson with the child, or hearing bedtime prayers, saying grace at table, or conducting hymn-singing.

Among the ways in which the family is to operate, as it seeks to assist the individual to incarnate something of the attributes of God, are the following:

1. The family must recognize the way that persons grow. Growth entails learning, which is modification of behavior. The child is no simple stimulus-response machine whose development lies along lines determined by his mentors. The unique endowments of the organism, the child, cast him in a dynamic role in which both heredity and environment are involved. The family as the initial environment that wields immediate and lasting influence may not be viewed as the sole determiner of the child's destiny. But the stimuli coming from this interaction of persons within the family do provide the developing person with necessary influences which cause his personality to grow or suffer retardation as the case may be.

Mental health is basic to the family's spiritual health. Religion is always more weighted on the side of emotion than on that of intellect. Religion entails devotion, attachment, feelings on the move. If any member of a family suffers emotional imbalance, he causes the family group to suffer the same. Emotionality mixed with religious bigotry, excessive religious verbalisms, puritanical restraints and fanaticism, is particularly destructive of personal and family growth. An overprotective parent fixates the child's

[24] *Ibid.*, p. 421.

loyalties so that he can neither mature nor experience the love of God. Possessiveness and egocentricity make an aberration of human relationships, thus destroying possibility of divine-human relationships.

Nature and nurture are inseparable; therefore no one can say just what part of a person's successful development, or failure to grow, is to be attributed to factors that inhere in the organism, and what part inheres in factors that arise from environmental conditioning. What we do know is that, other things being equal, the child tends to prosper as the family situation makes it possible for him so to do. And this is as true in spiritual terms—the divine-human relationships—as in the realm of dietary and health provisions. If the child is to gain, first, a concept of God and, second, a manifestation within himself, along toward maturity, of the God of Christ, he needs to find God in his own home, in his own father and mother.

2. The family that seeks to assist its members to develop godlike qualities will work with the church. It will function as a cell of the local church, an organ of the body of Christ. It will know that only as a cell is related to a living body can it survive, and only as the cell is alive can the body be healthy. For the fact is that the family needs the nourishment of the church, as a cell depends upon the body.

To the extent that the local church is itself a fellowship of persons gathered in the name of Christ will the family within that church learn to live as what it, too, essentially is: a fellowship of persons sharing life together. "The church and family serve and support each other." [25]

The family needs regular ministrations of the church as a worshiping community. It needs to join with the local church as one expression of the larger family of God, to explore the meaning and truth of religion, to encounter and investigate the compelling value contained in the Bible, to become energized so that high and noble service can be rendered in concerted fashion to meet the demands of suffering humanity.

Preparation for marriage, making a home, guiding children, facing pain, death, sorrow, and other major experiences and crises offer the church some of its best opportunities to serve the family. As God has caused the solitary to dwell in families, so he has enabled families to be in the Church. Family and Church belong together to the end that society may be impregnated with the spirit of God.

Summary

Homes today are beset by complex urban society. Children and adults go their separate ways, weakening or destroying the unity of the family.

[25] *Christian Education Today*, p. 22.

Yet marriage remains popular, and education for family life offers hope for preserving and strengthening the family as an educational agency in all important areas of life, including that of religion.

Parents and church-school teachers need to unite in order to nurture young and old in the Christian faith. Church-family education necessitates radically new thinking and practice on the part of clerical and lay leaders alike. The church that would train parents must begin at the point of their vital concern: their children. Adequate preparation of parents for guiding the religious development of their children entails genuine adult Christian education.

The family can inculcate the Christian religion in the young only as it understands how persons grow and as it works with the church as a cell of the body of Christ. The goal of church-family education is that of making the nature of the Christian God operative in the home, the church, and throughout society.

SUGGESTIONS FOR FURTHER STUDY

1. Discuss the significance of the family's having shifted its traditional functions to society.

2. Plan and experiment with several family projects that might provide companionship experiences.

3. Discuss the future of the family in light of its present status.

4. How can your church educate parents to teach religion in the home?

5. Wherein is home teaching inadequate that is confined to content materials and religious observances?

6. Develop a family council for the purpose of making religion function.

BIBLIOGRAPHY

Baber, Ray E. "Marriage and the Family After War," *The Annals of the American Academy of Political and Social Science*, 229 (1943), 164 ff.

Brubacker, John S. *A History of the Problems of Education.* New York and London: McGraw-Hill Book Co., 1947.

Burgess and Locke. *The Family: from Institution to Companionship.* New York: American Book Co., 1945.

Christian Education Today: A Statement of Basic Philosophy, International Council of Religious Education, 1940.

Duvall and Hill. *When You Marry.* New York: Association Press, 1945.

Fallaw, Wesner. "How the Family Teaches Religion," *Religious Education,* January-February, 1948, pp. 3-6.

———. *The Modern Parent and the Teaching Church.* New York: Macmillan Co., 1946.

Hartshorne, May, Sonquist, and Kerr. "Testing the Knowledge of Right and Wrong," *Religious Education,* October, 1926, pp. 539 ff.

Hiltner, Seward. "The Kinsey Report," *Information Service,* Federal Council of Churches of Christ in America, April 10, 1948.

Jersild, Arthur T. *Child Psychology* (rev. ed.). New York: Prentice-Hall, 1940.

Kempfer, Homer. "Adult Education Is Growing," *School and Society*, September 11, 1948, pp. 171-72.

Kinsey, Pomeroy, and Martin, *Sexual Behaviour in the Human Male*. Philadelphia: W. B. Saunders Co., 1948.

Kuhn, Anne L. *The Mother's Role in Childhood Education: New England Concepts: 1830-1860*. New Haven: Yale University Press, 1947.

Ligon, Ernest M. *A Greater Generation*. New York: Macmillan Co., 1948.

———. *Their Future Is Now*. New York: Macmillan Co., 1945.

Radke, Marian J. *The Relation of Parental Authority to Children's Behavior and Attitudes*. Minneapolis: University of Minnesota Press, 1946.

Vieth, Paul H. *The Church and Christian Education*. St. Louis: The Bethany Press, 1947.

Zimmerman, Carle C. *The Family of Tomorrow: The Cultural Crisis and the Way Out*. New York: Harper & Brothers, 1949.

Chapter 20

THE SUNDAY CHURCH SCHOOL

HARRY THOMAS STOCK

ROBERT RAIKES, PRINTER AND PROPRIETOR of the Gloucester (England) *Journal,* gave the Sunday-school movement its initial mighty impetus. A number of Sunday schools antedated the one he organized in Gloucester in July, 1780, but it was his zeal and success that won the support of such influential friends as George Whitefield and John and Charles Wesley. The plan was quickly copied in other cities, and in 1785 a Sunday School Society was formed, which in ten years distributed 9,200 spelling books, 25,000 Testaments and 5,300 Bibles to over a thousand schools which enrolled 65,000 pupils.

Four important characteristics of these early schools are worth noting. 1. The Gloucester Sunday school was a social-action project. Raikes had been an advocate of prison reform and naturally became interested in both the victims and causes of crime. All about him were boys and girls who worked twelve hours a day in factories, without a chance to go to school, and who spent Sundays on the streets. With the purpose of saving them from delinquency he gathered a group together on Sundays to provide the rudiments of education: reading, writing, arithmetic, and Bible studies. This "ragged school" was a short-period school that met on Sunday. Its curriculum was not a wholly religious one. The classes were for children of the poor only.

2. The first teachers were paid. But by the turn of the century this policy was abandoned, and teaching became a voluntary lay expression of social and religious interest.

3. The movement in England started and continued as a lay enterprise. The schools were not closely integrated within the life of the Church. Many clergymen opposed the experiment. When it spread to America, it received the vigorous support of most pastors, but in state and national Sunday-school associations laymen were more conspicuous than in any other phase of Protestant activity.

4. From the first, the Sunday-school movement crossed denominational lines and brought together local and regional workers in the most thoroughly interchurch program of Protestantism. For a century these organizations were undenominational rather than interdenominational; that is to say, they were not directly representative of the denominational "overhead."

In America

As long as a century before the Goucester school came into being, at least one Sunday school for children existed in New England, and during the decades that followed a number of others were organized. Some pastors found them convenient means of teaching boys and girls during the interim between the two services of worship. But there was nothing like a Sunday-school movement until the influence of the English society was felt in the New World.

Before the close of the eighteenth century Sunday schools were organized throughout the East; they were limited to religious instruction. The active interest of the Wesleys and Asbury put the Methodists squarely behind the plan, and workers in other denominations also participated enthusiastically. Sunday-school unions were formed in New York and Boston in 1816 and in Philadelphia in 1817. Out of the latter grew the most potent agency of Sunday-school extension, the American Sunday School Union, founded in 1824. As early as 1830 it was copied by denominational unions.

The time was propitious for a vigorous evangelistic crusade. After the War of 1812 thousands of Eastern families migrated to the new territories in the Middle West. For two generations the character of Protestant life was to be influenced by the shifting frontier. A great era of home missionary as well as foreign missionary endeavor began during the second decade of the nineteenth century. Hundreds of able young ministers set out to establish churches on the frontier. Wherever they went, they formed churches, Sunday schools, temperance societies, and colleges.

Influential as these denominational missionaries were, the undenominational Sunday School Union was the more zealous promoter. At its sixth anniversary it resolved that it would "within two years establish a Sunday school in every destitute place where it is practicable throughout the Valley of the Mississippi." Out of such schools grew churches later related to the various competing denominations.

The first national Sunday-school convention was held in 1832. It was decided that the schools should include persons of "all classes"; they were not for the poor and the unchurched alone. The second national convention, about eight months later, was not followed by another for twenty-six years. But this was to be the period of local, county, and state organization. The pattern was being set; the movement was undenominational in scope, it enlisted ministers and laymen, but lay leadership predominated, the regional undenominational organizations became more powerful than national denominational agencies. Sunday schools met and grew within the churches, but the regional associations were not responsible to ecclesiastical bodies.

National conventions were resumed in 1859. In 1875 the national convention became international; Canadian delegates were given official standing. It was not until 1887 that an administrative officer was employed. The International Sunday School Association had great vitality because multitudes of laymen gave freely of their time and money.

Although the denominations had published lesson materials for their Sunday schools, the ecclesiastical bodies did not take religious education seriously until the beginning of the twentieth century. When they began to employ specialized educational workers, these persons were drawn together for fellowship and mutual counsel. In 1910 such secretaries organized the Sunday School Council of Evangelical Denominations. This quickly challenged the nonofficial International Sunday School Association. Representatives of the two bodies conferred, and in 1922 they were merged into the International Sunday School Council of Religious Education, and later the words "Sunday School" were dropped. Its constituent bodies are the national denominational educational agencies and the regional interdenominational councils. The International Council is thus the representative agency of Protestantism in the whole field of religious education.

For All Ages

It is probable that many of the Gloucester boys and girls who worked all week were beyond the age which now divides the elementary and adolescent divisions. In the early days of the American movement there were often at least two groups within the schools, the "infant class" and the "senior pupils." When in the third decade of the nineteenth century Albert Judson was employed by the New York Sunday School Union to prepare sets of questions—lessons—for teachers, he provided three grades of questions. They were not recommended for clearly defined ages but were planned to serve different stages of mental development. During the expansionist era Sunday schools enrolled children, young people, and adults. In 1887 the Fifth International Convention formally recognized the Home Department.

In the early years of the present century a thoroughly departmentalized system was approved by the denominations through the International Council of Religious Education. The present system is as follows:

Nursery department, which includes:
  Nursery (or cradle) roll—birth to three years old
  Nursery class—three-year-olds
Kindergarten (or beginners) department—four- and five-year-olds
Primary department—six to eight years, grades 1 to 3
Junior department—nine to eleven years, grades 4 to 6
Intermediate (or junior-high) department—twelve to fourteen years, **grades 7 to 9**

Senior (or high-school) department—fifteen to seventeen years, grades 10 to 12
Young people's department—eighteen to twenty-three or twenty-four years
Adult department—those above the ages of the young people's department

The children's division includes all through the junior department; the young people's division is made up of those from twelve to twenty-three or twenty-four years of age; and those above this age are members of the adult division.

The matter of gradation and nomenclature needs to be restudied. A large proportion of American Sunday church schools have fewer than a hundred pupils, and strict adherence to a nationally determined organizational scheme is impossible for many of them. Moreover, many moderate-sized schools prefer to follow a two-year gradation for class sessions, and an increasing number of larger schools departmentalize on a two-year basis because of a greater homogeneity of interests than is possible under a three-year plan. The following organizational setup, therefore, prevails in many of the most effective Sunday church schools:

Nursery and kindergarten departments, as above
Primary department—six and seven years, grades 1 and 2
Upper-primary or lower-junior department—eight and nine years, grades 3 and 4
Junior or upper-junior department—ten and eleven years, grades 5 and 6
Intermediate or junior-high department—twelve and thirteen years, grades 7 and 8
Senior or high-school department—the four years of high school

A pressing problem arises in the years beyond high school. When does a young person cease to be a young person and become an adult? There is some support for the point of view that the church should recognize him as an adult when the state does. But it would be hard to draw the line at twenty-one in a day when national youth fellowships have become so strong, for many of the officers of these organizations are in the twenty to twenty-four age span, although the majority of members in local youth fellowships may be of the high-school age.

There has been an almost spectacular development of young-adult groups, largely outside of the Sunday church school. These are persons who are "on their own" economically. They seldom fit into a young people's department, and they are equally out of place with older adults. At present no satisfactory age lines have been drawn to determine when one becomes a young adult, and when young adulthood is at an end.

CURRICULUM DEVELOPMENT

The Sunday school was organized to be a teaching agency. Its growth was so rapid that the need of printed helps to guide lay teachers soon became acute. At least seven steps in the history of curriculum may be discerned:

1. In the colonial period the catechetical process prevailed. Early public and private schools were shot through with religion. The *New England Primer*, the greatest of the early textbooks for children—used in the church and in early day schools—was really a child's book on the Christian religion. The *Primer*, the Bible, and current catechisms were used in Sunday classes as well as on weekdays during the eighteenth century. The question-and-answer method was everywhere used, and successful "learning" consisted in the ability to give standard answers to the theological questions.

2. This was followed by a period of indiscriminate memorization of Bible verses. Public education after the Revolution was becoming more secular, as was the whole tenor of life. Day schools now had textbooks more appropriate to the educational purposes of the schools; religion found little place in many of them. The first three decades of the nineteenth century were prolific in the publication of new catechisms, but many of the lay leaders in the rapidly multiplying Sunday schools ignored them. The Bible was often their only reliance. Children were urged to memorize as many verses as possible—verses of their own choosing—and the Sunday session often consisted of little more than the recitation of scores or hundreds of ill-chosen texts. The habit of giving prizes for such memorization added zest and helped to give an illusion of success to the program.

3. Those most concerned for the future of the Sunday school and for a more significant type of Sunday experience decided that guidance should be offered in the use of Bible passages. The first efforts were in the direction of standardizing the selections to be memorized; all of the pupils in a school were urged to commit to memory the same verses. The more thoughtful men in the Sunday-school unions knew that something more was needed, and on January 1, 1825, the New York Association of Sunday School Teachers began a series of selected lessons for the next four months, on the theory that "all lessons in Sabbath Schools should be selected." The American Sunday School Union during the same year issued a card of lessons for the entire twelve months. This was the beginning of curriculum in terms of sequences of lessons. Nothing was provided for the pupils; the materials were for the guidance of teachers only. Soon denominational publishers issued their own sequences, and the rivalry between denominational and independent publishers began. So many varieties of lessons were offered the churches that the years between 1830-60 have been referred to as an era of the "Babel series."

4. In time a few prophetic leaders began to agitate for a national or international system of lessons—a uniform series. Through the persistence of such influential men as John H. Vincent and B. F. Jacobs the interest grew. When at the 1872 International Convention Jacobs introduced

his proposal for a single International Lesson Committee, it was overwhelmingly carried. The first committee consisted of five ministers from five denominations and five laymen from the same denominations. The work of this body has doubtless had a larger influence on the program of the Sunday schools than that of any other single factor. The committee continues at work today as The Committee on the Uniform Series of the International Council of Religious Education and produces outlines called "The International Bible Lessons for Christian Teaching."

The introduction to the annual series describes the present system:

> The outlines here presented are set up to include material for each Sunday of the year. This provides for a general weekly subject, with a basic Scripture block. . . . The outlines also include for each age group more specific suggestions for the selection of Scripture material for that group and a memory selection. A brief note is added to indicate to the editors and lesson writers the particular emphasis which the committee had in mind in making the selection.

The present uniform curriculum is an attempt to provide for some gradation within a uniform plan.

5. Although dissatisfaction with the defects of a uniform system had been expressed by various leaders, and Erastus Blakeslee had published his own graded materials when he failed to interest the International Lesson Committee, the real impetus toward a new type of course came from children's workers. The leader in this movement for materials more appropriate to the various ages within the school was Mrs. J. Woodbridge Barnes, Superintendent of the Elementary Division of the International Sunday School Association.

She called a graded-lessons conference, which was attended by age group workers and others. It proposed a closely graded series of courses from beginners through junior years. At this conference the needs of children of various ages were outlined; appropriate subject matter for courses was described; and progress was made toward the organization of the entire curriculum for the nine-year period. Representatives of this conference sought and obtained a meeting with the lesson committee and were so convincing that this committee agreed to recommend the plan to the next convention. At this 1908 International Convention the proposal for a closely graded system was unanimously approved. A strong syndicate, which included the Presbyterian (U.S.A.), Methodist Episcopal, Methodist (South), and Congregational boards, was organized to publish materials based on these outlines. They were also used by the Baptists as the basis for their "Keystone Series."

Thus a second system of lessons was available: one that offered a separate course for each age or grade, that conceived of church-school work as educational and not merely instructional or evangelistic, and that included some extrabiblical material.

Later a modification of the graded plan found acceptance in a number of denominations, and a third series had standing in the churches: the departmental or group graded. This grew out of the realities of Protestant life: Many church schools are small; they are capable of doing graded work and should have graded programs; but for such schools gradation needs to be on the departmental basis instead of by single ages or grades. All of the children in the primary department, for example, study the same lesson on a given Sunday—in one class or more—and in a three-year cycle this department covers much the same areas of experience and subject matter as are included in the three-year span of the closely graded courses. Outlines for closely graded and group-graded lessons are now prepared by the Committee on the Graded Series of the International Council of Religious Education.

6. Many churches have "shopped around" for lesson materials, often for no good reason. But a sound educational purpose has encouraged some of the larger and more progressive churches to choose courses from various sources during the present part of this century. This is a result of the "progressive education" movement, with its emphasis upon the project principle, local creativity, responsiveness to the emerging interests of pupils, and an unfettered and unstereotyped educational procedure. As ministers and directors of religious education were introduced to modern pedagogical theory and practice, they thought of the Sunday school in more thoroughly educational terms and sought to provide a true curriculum—something more than courses.

So the period of "homemade" curriculum was initiated. Sometimes they are quite fluid and flexible. In other cases competent local boards of education do what national curriculum agencies must do: they analyze the needs of the various age groups, determine what experiences should be introduced at each level, plan a three-year cycle, and seek the best available resources. Out of such experiments has come a trickle of books which are available to churches as electives. Much of this local curriculum making has been amateurish and not greatly significant, but in many churches the educational work has reached standards as high as those in public schools. And all of the rest of the churches have profited, indirectly, from this creative local effort.

7. In the middle of the twentieth century churches find it possible to choose among many materials. This is another Babel period. Most denominations publish uniform lessons, at least for young people and adults, and numerous independent publishers urge them upon the schools. Most of the larger denominations also issue closely graded or group-graded courses and

recommend them as preferable to the uniform. Large numbers of churches select materials from various sources.

It appears that the next step in curriculum development will be within the group- or departmental-graded sequences. Within the educational staffs of the churches there is a disposition to plan materials which will give greater unity to the work of the school, will bring the church and its school into more continuous unity of effort, and will relate the home and church in a common teaching task.

There is no desire to go back to the common subject matter which is characteristic of the uniform lessons, but the separate age-group courses in the graded plan can be so arranged that all departments are studying within the same general area during a quarter. For example, in any graded series some phase of the life and work of Jesus is studied in each age group during a three-year cycle. By bringing these courses about Jesus all together in the same quarter, churches can attain unification of interest and effort without uniformity.

By also taking account of the great functional and seasonal activities of the entire Church and denomination, and by relating those elements of "program" which are significant for children and young people to the church-school "curriculum," the church and its school unite more frequently in common endeavors, and the artificial distinction between "program" and "curriculum" does not arise. In International Council circles it is agreed that the home must become a primary teacher of religion, and various experiments are being made to develop a curriculum which is for both the church and the family.

Two denominations have released series of materials which include these characteristics—the Congregational Christians in 1947, and the Presbyterians (U.S.A.) in 1948. (See Chapter 8.)

PAST, PRESENT, AND FUTURE

During the twentieth century the old conception of the Sunday school has given way to a recognition of the Sunday church school as one means by which the church carries on an inclusive program of religious education. The emphasis now is upon the educational function of the church in developing Christian character and in fulfilling its mission in the contemporary world. The church must have a school or be a school. It is the task of this school to help persons of all ages to grow in the understanding, experience, and expression of the Christian religion. All persons within the fellowship and reach of the church need to be taught. In many ways and in many places the church tries to perform its educational function—in Sunday and weekday classes, in evening fellowships, in laymen's groups, and through a variety of specialized activities. Wherever the church by planned processes tries to educate people in the Christian religion, it is serving as a school; its school is in session. The Sunday church school is not an autonomous organization which takes its guidance from some outside source. It is the church at work; its mission is that of the church itself; its officers are elected by the church; its policies are determined by a committee or board of the church; and what goes on in the Sunday church school, the vacation and weekday church schools, and all the other educational agencies is part of a comprehensive and consistent program of Christian education.

The old Sunday schools fell far short of the educational standards of today. But they attracted and held multitudes of children and young people, and that alone was a significant achievement. Much of the teaching was of dubious quality. But they made God real, often fearsomely real; they introduced pupils to Jesus Christ, and hosts of them would not have known of him from any other source; they illuminated positive and negative aspects of morality and influenced countless lives for good; they made the church important in the lives of the younger generations and gave children and young people the experience of growing up within the fellowship of the church; they became the chief agency by which the church renewed itself numerically; they engaged multitudes of lay people in active Christian service and made it possible for them to grow mentally and spiritually as they carried on their work. There is still much that is trivial in the Sunday church school, but in many communities the Sunday educational program is of the highest quality.

Half of the people of America are still outside of the Sunday church school or any other religious education process. For many years enrollment had been declining. This may be accounted for, in part, by the low Protestant birth rate, the waning interest in adult classes in some denominations, the slight attention given to the home department, and the lack of the old evangelistic effort to bring the unreached into the schools. But during the middle of the fifth decade of this century the church began to recapture its sense of urgency; and this fact, together with an increased birth rate, has changed the direction of the attendance graph. Numerically the Sunday church school is in a healthier condition.

1. A major current trend is that of employing the creative contributions of progressive education in the communication of the faith and in furthering the mission of the church. There is a reaction against methods as ends in themselves. The person continues to be a central concern, but Christian education has two other aims: the progressive salvation of society and the extension of a vitalized Christian Church. Christian education is a means by which the Church seeks to fulfill its functions for persons and society. Christian education has no objectives of its own; its aims are those of a truly Christian Church. Education is the sound method by which the

Church bears its witness, interprets its faith, and carries on its varied work.

2. A second trend is a conception of religious education which goes far beyond the impartation or discovery of facts. Worship is as central in the modern church school as it is in the church itself. The curriculum for all age groups includes projects of social usefulness. The church school is more than a group of classes that study and discuss; it is a worshiping and serving fellowship. The church school is that, not only because its pupils may learn by doing, but because it is equally concerned to help its members to be Christian and to help fulfill the Christian mission in the modern world. Children and young people are not only being prepared intellectually for something in the future; they are engaged in study, worship, and service which are themselves religious experiences of primary significance.

3. Another hopeful portent is the effort to restore the home as a primary agency of Christian nurture. Something more basic is now envisioned than the old attempt to have parents prepare their children for the Sunday-morning session. The home and the Sunday church school are complementary media of Christian nurture, and church boards are beginning to realize that they must prepare high-grade materials for home as for class use. The more fruitful experiments are through family enjoyment of attractive booklets which help parents and children to share normal, satisfying experiences of reading, worship, play, and purposeful activities.

4. The perennial problem of the Sunday church school is that of adequate leadership. The elaborate systems of leadership education courses have helped to improve the skill of thousands of workers. But they have too often led to a mere bookish process of academic instruction. The better work has been done in demonstration classes, laboratory schools, and workshops. Such "learning-by-doing" projects are on the increase. New efforts are also being made to show pastors how to conduct monthly workers' conferences, in which both the subject matter and the teaching possibilities of current courses are explained. And Protestantism awaits the production of a collection of realistic visual materials which interpret religious pedagogy more vividly than the spoken or written word ever can.

5. It is reported that more projectors are owned by churches than by schools. This explains why so many commercial agencies are preparing slides, filmstrips, and movies for the church public. They are sometimes being offered as substitutes for printed curriculum materials. Unwisely selected and used in the church school, such resources are a dangerous fad which at once may make a "bleacherite" experience of the session and present ideas at complete variance with the faith of the church. But if church agencies will prepare printed and visual materials to supplement each other, will indicate clearly when and why and how the pictures are to be used, and will instruct leaders in their educational significance, such vivid clarity

and concreteness of interpretation will be given to the work of the Sunday church school as will make it doubly effective in its Christian mission.

It is more difficult than ever to grow a Christian generation. It cannot be done by the Sunday church school alone, no matter how efficient it may be. But with all of its defects the Sunday church school today is better prepared than ever before to make its unique contribution to the normal development of Christian character and to the leavening of our contemporary civilization.

SUGGESTIONS FOR FURTHER STUDY

1. Evaluate as objectively as possible the work of the Sunday church school which you attended as a child and young person.

2. Study the scope, sequences, and printed materials of the graded system issued by your denomination, and prepare a critique based on your study.

3. Give the arguments for and against the use of elective materials for an "average" church with which you are acquainted.

4. Secure from the International Council of Religious Education (206 South Michigan Avenue, Chicago 4, Illinois) copies of the bulletins which outline the Standard Leadership Curriculums. What are the values and limitations you see in the use of such courses for teachers?

5. List, in order of importance, the unique contributions that you think the Sunday church school should make in a comprehensive program of Christian education that involves, in addition, the home and the summer vacation school.

6. Offer some specific suggestions for conserving the values of the graded system and of developing a consciousness that the child belongs to something more than a class—the school as a whole, the church as well as the school.

7. Outline a plan for monthly workers' conferences, in which you try to do two things: (*a*) Give background information for the quarter's lessons. (*b*) Give practical help with reference to teaching methods.

8. What would you advise young parents of primary and junior children to do as means by which they would provide a normal religious education within the family?

9. Illustrate what is meant by this statement: "Religious educators have sometimes exalted methods as ends in themselves."

10. Suggest ways in which visual resources may be used as aids in a sound process of religious education.

BIBLIOGRAPHY

Bower, W. C., and Hayward, P. R. *Protestantism Faces Its Educational Task Together*. Appleton, Wis.: C. C. Nelson Publishing Co., 1949.

Brown, A. A. *A History of Religious Education in Recent Times*. New York: Abingdon Press, 1923.

Brown, Marianna C. *Sunday-School Movements in America*. New York: Fleming H. Revell Co., 1901.

Christian Education Today. Chicago: International Council of Religious Education, 1940.

Cope, H. F. *The Evolution of the Sunday School.* Boston: The Pilgrim Press, 1911.

Harner, N. C. *The Educational Work of the Church.* New York: Abingdon Press, 1939.

International Council of Religious Education Annual Reports.

Munro, H. C. *The Church as a School.* St. Louis: Bethany Press, 1929.

Vieth, P. H. *The Church and Christian Education.* St. Louis: Bethany Press, 1947.

———. *Improving Your Sunday School.* Philadelphia: Westminster Press, 1930.

Chapter 21

THE VACATION CHURCH SCHOOL

RUTH ELIZABETH MURPHY

THE LARGEST BLOCK OF TIME in which boys and girls are free to choose their
own activities is during the summer, when they do not have to go to school.
A child has about a dozen such free summers after he is old enough to work
in groups and before he begins to look for summertime jobs. Some children
go away to camps; others go out of town on vacation trips; but as a rule
these do not take the whole summer. And in most communities there are
many other children who never get away from home for more than a day
or two at a time. At any one period of the summer there will be found a
large group of children in most neighborhoods with somewhat more leisure
than they know what to do with happily.

For about half a century now the churches have realized that this free
time of boys and girls is a valuable resource for the teaching of religion.
It is time that can be used for concentrated teaching as is never possible during
the busy school months. Also there are many children who do not normally
go to Sunday church school, but who are willing to attend a school held at
the church in the summer if it has enough play elements to sound appealing.
Christian people, both lay and professional, have seen here an opportunity
to share their deepest convictions with boys and girls while at the same time
to give them guidance in wholesome activities. And so there has grown up
a very large movement concerned with the holding of summer vacation
schools of religion. Valid figures regarding attendance are difficult to secure,
but it seems likely that some five million boys and girls attend vacation
church schools each summer.

One minister who conducts a large community vacation church school
each year writes: "Nothing challenges me more than vacation church school
except the ministry, and if my choice were to be made again at an earlier
age, I'd choose the vocation of a Christian educator specializing in vacation
church school."

WHAT A VACATION CHURCH SCHOOL IS

A vacation church school is making the weekdays of vacation time count for
Christian teaching in the community. . . . It is a plan for using the freer summer
period for experiences in joyous everyday living with the boys and girls of the

260

community, thus discovering and sharing with them the Christian way of life.[1]

A vacation church school is a school which is held several hours a day, on weekdays, during a summer-vacation period ranging from two to six weeks. It is sponsored by a local church or group of churches. It is led by Christian persons, usually volunteer workers, who are striving to lead other persons, especially boys and girls, toward the goals of Christian education. Thus it is one of the Christian education agencies and has become a fixed part of the yearly educational program of many churches of all denominations.

Most vacation church schools are conducted for boys and girls from four to fourteen years of age. They are usually divided into four departments: Kindergarten (or beginners), four- and five-year-olds; primary, first, second, and third graders; junior, fourth, fifth and sixth graders; and junior high (or intermediates), seventh, eighth, and ninth graders.

There is a growing tendency to feel that a church school in vacation time is also a good opportunity for all the members of the family. In some rural areas the whole family brings a picnic supper to the church several evenings a week for several weeks. After supper they divide up for a vacation church school program. In other places the youth and adult programs are in the evenings, while the children come in the mornings.

In addition, a number of vacation church schools are held in connection with observation and laboratory schools where young people and adults are trained as teachers. The classes for the children are conducted by expert leaders, while those who are learning to teach are observing.

The program of the schools varies widely. The earlier pattern, still followed in many instances, included an opening session involving a certain amount of ritual, a game period, Bible study, handwork, worship, and special events. In accordance with the ability and training of the leaders more progressive methods of teaching are now being used.

WHAT HAPPENS IN A VACATION CHURCH SCHOOL

Perhaps the best way to describe what goes on in a vacation church school is to tell in detail the activities found in a typical school of four departments. There was a common general subject in all these departments. The leaders had chosen for this year as the area of study "Our Bible Heritage." There was also a common benevolence project—"a goat for Japan." The materials and activities, however, were graded.

Kindergarten Department (Beginners). The text was *Happy Times in Our Church*, by Elizabeth Shields. The early morning was spent in free play, using large blocks, housekeeping equipment, and other toys. Learning

---

[1] *The How of Vacation Church School*, p. 5.

to work in small groups and to take turns are forward steps at this age. As the piano was played softly, toys were put away, and the group gathered around the teacher on a large, clean rug. She sang a new song, "Every Morning Seems to Say," and told the story "Going to See Jesus." The boys and girls then "played the story." This was followed by a rest period, when the children lay down on newspaper mats. During a snack of crackers and milk a "thank-you" prayer was composed by the children and then used. The latter part of the morning included out-of-doors games and planning to make a gift for their room.

Primary Department. The text was *Child Life in Bible Times,* by Florence M. Taylor. School began when the first child arrived and started browsing at the book table and looking at the reading cards placed there. When the others came, they began to work in small groups. A picture of shepherd life was selected to go on the worship center table. Blankets were placed over a circle of chairs to make a shepherd tent. Newly made posters illustrating a new hymn were put up on screens.

Quiet music then called the group together in front of the worship center. The hymn "Lord of the Sunlight" was sung. The teacher told a favorite story, which was based on the building of the Hebrew tabernacle: "The Silver Bracelets." The offering plates—filled as the children entered— were brought forward, and a thanksgiving prayer was given for the opportunity of sending a goat to Japan to feed hungry children.

After worship the children went outdoors for some circle games, fresh air, and exercise. Coming in again, they grouped themselves informally around the teacher and decided to "play the story" they had heard, using the new tent they had made. This was most enjoyable and also helped the children to live the story in imagination. The dramatization over, they gathered around the piano and sang their favorite songs until it was time to go.

Junior Department. The text was *Discovering the Lands of the Bible,* by Lois Hazelwood. As soon as the boys and girls arrived, committees went to work. One was studying "resource cards" telling of places in Palestine, made according to directions given in the text. Another group was studying travel folders; a third was looking up Bible towns and stories in a Bible concordance. A fourth was arranging the worship center with lovely spatterprint cloth they had made several days before and with a picture of "Finding Jesus in the Temple."

Piano music called the group together for worship. A junior girl played the piano prelude. One group recited Ps. 122 in choral speech. "Tell Me the Stories of Jesus" was sung by all, and this was followed by a study of the picture on the worship center. The prayer used had been written by a group of girls and was given by one of them. It included a dedication of their gifts to buy a goat for Japan. The prayer hymn "O Master Workman of the Race" ended the service. Then the boys and girls went outdoors for games and later returned for work on their map of Palestine. They learned a new hymn and sang two favorite folk songs before leaving.

Junior-High Department (Intermediate). The text was *Our Living Book*, by Faye deBeck Flynt. The group had decided to dramatize "Letters by a Barred Window," a story in the text which told of Paul writing to Timothy. They divided the work, chose the cast, and worked on the play for the first part of the morning. Later the group in charge of the worship service completed their preparation for this, while another committee made plans for a farewell party to be given for the goat for Japan.

The department went into the church sanctuary for worship that day. The pastor had worked on the plans with the worship committee. The church organist played; the pastor spoke; and the boys and girls themselves carried through the rest of the service as they had prepared it.

After a game period outdoors there was guided study on the book of Acts, using the pupils' textbooks. Next, the boys and girls continued work, individually, on personal devotional books. They selected the hymns, poems, scripture verses, stories, or pictures which they liked best and put them in a book which they made for their own use. A brief planning session was held at the end of the morning.

One distinguishing characteristic of a vacation church school is its joyous spirit. Given a program at all adequate, children enjoy attending. There is a sense of freedom not found in most public schools, a sense of purposeful activity not found in unorganized leisure time, and a sense of informality not found in Sunday church schools. Since there is often more space to use than on Sundays, greater activity is possible also. "Fun" periods, involving outdoor play and trips, games, and sometimes motion pictures, are prominent features of the day's session. There is a chance to "make things" and to share what one has learned and made at a parents' meeting at the close. Teachers who have been through the schools are nearly always enthusiastic about them. They see children who are keenly interested in what they are doing, and who are developing daily in character and knowledge. "Those who have worked in it most intimately bear glowing testimony as to its value as an agency for Christian teaching, and emphasize its possibilities for future growth." [2]

A traditional feature of the vacation church school has been Bible teaching. With frequent sessions the material taught at one period is not forgotten before the next class meets, and it is possible for children to learn readily. There is time for Bible stories and dramatizations as well as for appreciation for Bible pictures. Some leaders in local churches have drawn up a comparative time chart between Sunday and vacation church schools to

[2] "The Study of Christian Education," Vol. III, *The Local Church Program*.

show that during one vacation church school children can learn as much as they can in a year of Sunday church school.

How Vacation Church Schools Got Started

During May and June, 1894, a Methodist minister's wife in Illinois held a four-weeks school, five days a week, in four departments, with a normal training division. In 1900 a Congregational minister in Elk Mound, Wisconsin, began a series of vacation religious day schools. In 1901 a Baptist executive secretary of the New York Baptist City Mission Society started some daily vacation Bible schools which were the beginning of a movement later organized into the International Association of Daily Vacation Bible Schools. This was originally under lay direction, as were the Sunday schools of the time, but councils of churches and denominations gradually took these schools into their Christian education programs. American missionaries started vacation church schools in the countries where they served.[3]

Although these schools are still known in the common parlance as "vacation Bible schools," the official name adopted by most national organizations is "vacation church schools." The close relation to other phases of the Christian education program is shown by the names "vacation church school," "weekday church school," and the "Sunday church school." That is, the "church school" may be held on Sunday, weekday, or during vacation. This also lifts up the importance of the responsibility the Church has for the vacation church schools.

Who Is Responsible for Vacation Church Schools?

If the vacation church school is the church's responsibility, it follows that the direction of the school comes under the groups in both the local church and the community which are responsible for the Christian education program. If every local church had a board of Christian education whose members truly valued the free time of its younger constituents during the vacation period, more, better, and longer vacation church schools would immediately be planned as an accepted part of the year-round program.

In each church a special vacation church school committee is appointed by the board of religious education or other authoritative body, or this responsibility may be given to some standing committee such as that of children's work. Their responsibilities are similar to that of a board of education for public schools. A high quality of leadership is, of course, greatly to be desired in the committee.

Some ministerial associations or alliances and most state, city, and county

[3] For a more adequate historical sketch see Bower and Hayward, *Protestantism Faces Its Educational Task Together.*

councils of churches and religious education have some committee which is responsible for the wider aspects of the vacation church school work, such as planning training enterprises for leaders, sponsoring community schools and schools in unchurched areas. The International Council of Religious Education has a Department and a Committee of Vacation Religious Education which are responsible for national and interdenominational aspects of this work. Most denominations give this responsibility to their national directors of children's work.

WHAT TYPES OF CO-OPERATION ARE POSSIBLE

Co-operation among churches is probably found as frequently in the holding of vacation church schools as in any other aspects of the church's work. Churches of a neighborhood or of a small community frequently combine their schools, making possible a wider choice of leaders and meeting places and also a more effective impact on the community.

In recent years this has led to more co-operation with other agencies in the community which also have good summer programs for children. Representatives of the various youth-serving agencies of the community, including the churches, meet and plan a "neighborhood summer program." This includes time for vacation schools, as well as for organized athletics, scouting programs, and so on. With such a calendar, youth-serving agencies avoid conflicts in dates and spread the programs for boys and girls more evenly across the vacation period.

There are many ways that good agencies concerned with the welfare of boys and girls can help each other in the summertime. In one Northern city the "Bookmobile" of the city library has made regular stops at the vacation church schools. In one state the state library loans religious pictures to such schools. Many community leaders are church members who gladly give their services on committees, in training enterprises, and in vacation church schools, as their time permits.

Vacation church schools also offer an excellent opportunity for co-operation between the home and the church. Mothers make up the largest group of vacation church school teachers and committee members. Parents are invited to "open-house" sessions and to the closing "sharing" program. Activities similar to those of the parent-teacher associations are possible. Usually, parents help with picnics, and trips, and special events. Teachers find it valuable to visit in the homes, especially in the homes of new children. Parents who learn in detail about the program of the school are then able to help their children carry on after school closes the interests started there. The preliminary planning for the successful vacation church school includes consulting with the families concerning the time period involved so that they will write the vacation church school into their family summer-time schedules.

What Leaders Are Needed

As in the case of any good school, the following workers are usually needed: an administrator, a head of each department, a teacher for every class, pianists, secretaries, assistants, and janitors. In a small vacation church school fewer leaders will be required, of course. The various things to be done are divided up among the leaders in accordance with their special abilities. Leaders of departments and teachers use the following types of activities: guided study, creative activities, and simple art work; directing group projects of a larger kind; leading recreation and singing; telling stories; and leading short worship services. Most important, the leaders must be able to guide the boys and girls into Christian ways of living and to confront them with the "good news" of the Christian religion.

Many ministers direct vacation church schools. A minister is the pastor of each child as well as of each board member in his church, but he does not have the opportunity to work with each child and therefore to get acquainted with him as a person. A vacation church school offers such an opportunity. Whether the minister can direct the school, serve during special periods, or visit only on certain days, it is valuable to have the boys and girls feel that they know him. In a community school all the ministers of the churches concerned may share in its leadership.

Usually when a church has a director of religious education, the director becomes the administrator of the school or of one of the schools in a community enterprise. When the pastor or the director is the administrator, it is possible more adequately to integrate the program of the vacation church school into the ongoing educational activities of the church.

How Leaders Are Trained

"Where can we get trained leaders?" This is the most often asked question concerning vacation church schools. The best answer is for each church to grow its leaders. If there is long-range planning for the total Christian education program of the church, which includes leadership education for all its phases, the matter is taken care of in the normal way. Local church and community leadership training enterprises will include courses in vacation church school materials and techniques.[4]

State councils of churches and regional denominational groups are increasingly coaching "leaders of leaders" who, after specialized training, con-

[4] The "Standard Leadership Education Curriculum" includes three courses on vacation church schools.

duct training enterprises for vacation church school leaders in smaller areas. Observation and laboratory schools are the most effective forms of training. Several cities use from five to ten Saturdays for training schools each spring. One- or two-day institutes, week-end clinics, a series of demonstration observation classes, and city or county-wide promotional rallies for vacation church school leaders are other methods used.

Well-trained leaders in the Sunday church school and church members who are public-school teachers easily learn to adapt their methods to the vacation church school program. Older young people may learn how to help in vacation church schools. These young people need to serve as apprentices to good teachers and to learn how to teach effectively before taking responsibility for a class.

The vast majority of the vacation church school leaders are volunteers. Some of them receive carfare or a small amount of pay to help cover extra expenses resulting from their absences from home while teaching. In a few places where schools are held in unchurched, underprivileged, or unusual situations, the leaders are employed by some outside agency. Often week-day church school teachers or Christian public school teachers are employed. In such cases it is important to have local persons help to integrate the work into the ongoing programs of the church or churches and to use the better-prepared leaders in the training of local church workers. One state council is using this method as a means of improving rural church leadership.[5] When schools are held for long periods, it usually becomes necessary to pay the workers. This is a legitimate charge upon the treasury of the church. "The requirements in training, experience and time . . . are so extensive as to make it desirable to provide compensation for the workers . . . if adequate and continuous leadership is provided." [6]

Sincere tribute is due to the devoted Christian workers who have given freely of their time, talents, and money to make possible the splendid Christian experiences which boys and girls have found in vacation church schools. It is the fine Christian quality of such persons, their enthusiastic interest and hard work, that have made these schools grow.

THE COURSE OF STUDY

The choice of a course of study for a particular department depends on many factors, such as: the purposes of the church people sponsoring the schools, the needs of the boys and girls, the other courses in Christian education which they have had, the teaching ability of the teachers, their

[5] See Stanley B. Hyde, "Reaching the Forgotten Ones," in the *International Journal of Religious Education*, April, 1947. See also Anna Laura Gebhard, "Give Us Trained Leaders!" *idem*, January, 1947.

[6] "The Study of Christian Education," Vol. III, *The Local Church Program.*

special training in teaching particular subjects, and the teaching resources available.

As in any teaching situation, it is most important for the leaders to understand their pupils and the ways in which they develop. What are the pupils' needs, interests, and possibilities? How do they learn? How do they grow as Christians? What can be expected at each age? How can they be trained to take proper responsibilities? How can individual problems be met? How can each pupil make his greatest contribution? Fortunately, the vacation school period is continuous enough and long enough for the leaders to get acquainted with the children individually and to guide them in their character growth and spiritual development.

There is a growing body of teaching materials which are of great assistance to the leaders in this work. Through the Cooperative Publishing Association the publishers of a number of denominations publish jointly vacation church school texts. These texts are based on outlines produced, again co-operatively, through the International Council of Religious Education.

These co-operative texts, as they are called, are developed in the areas of study described in the pamphlet, *Goals for the Christian Education of Children.* They are produced for the four departments—kindergarten, primary, junior, and junior high—and are planned for vacation church schools held during four to six weeks.[7] A few denominations, seeing the need for shorter texts, simpler presentations and less expensive format, have prepared their own vacation church school texts. Those of the Methodists and the Baptists have been widely used interdenominationally. A new ten-session series, which is suitable for small churches, is now in preparation by the Cooperative Publishing Association. Several independent commercial houses have also prepared vacation church school texts, but these are not recommended by most of the denominations or the interdenominational agencies.

WHAT TEACHING METHODS ARE USED

Any teacher's manual can become a taskmaster or a tool, according to the skill of the teacher. Using a text creatively is a part of good teaching. The co-operative texts mentioned here give simple lesson plans for the inexperienced teacher and also provide rich resources for those who can use them. They are built on "units of study," central ideas around which the guided experiences of the group cluster. Sometimes the study and activities of the whole school or department are centered around some imaginative idea which makes possible excellent learning situations.

For example, a visitor to one vacation church school was greeted in

[7] See *The How of Vacation Church School.* It contains a chart which shows the texts available in the various areas for the different age-group departments.

Palestinian style—with an offer to wash her feet! The "host" mentioned the hot, dusty road she must have been traveling and invited her into his "house," where she was given a fruit drink. The "house" was somewhat precariously made of folding screens with a plank across the top which supported a large box. Inquiry revealed that the box was the guest room on the roof. This dwelling was part of a Nazareth village where the council of elders ruled the synagogue school, showing how Jesus and his friends had read the Psalms from scrolls. Psalms had been memorized and copied on the scrolls by the boys. Another group pantomimed parables of Jesus which mentioned home or shop settings. The "temple-court committee" had charge of the care of the room used for worship. The boys and girls were imagining that they were living in Palestine in Jesus' day and entered into activities which combined study of Jesus' life and teaching with creative sharing of experiences in the group.

In another vacation church school, a visitor was greeted at the door by a small "policeman"—so indicated by the badge on his arm. He escorted his visitor to the "mayor," who presented the visitor with the "key to the city." Then the other "officers" were introduced: the street cleaners, the teachers, the mailman, and the other policemen. Covering one entire wall was a map of part of the real city in which the school was located. On it were indicated schools, homes, churches, libraries, stores, and many other institutions which were considered "worthy" to be in their city. At the bottom of the map, there were lists of certain other places to show that they were unworthy to be in the city.

A popular activity of older pupils is the preparation of "newspapers," usually coming out weekly. Choral presentations and dramatizations are enjoyed. Some schools have gone so far as to produce motion pictures, with the pupils serving as the cast for Bible plays. Through such imaginative experiences, Bible stories and vital religious truths are learned while the boys and girls are having actual experiences in Christian living together. Creative activities, made possible by the long, concentrated blocks of time, give an opportunity for each child to make a contribution to group activity. Where skilled leadership is present, there is a spirit of good will and religion which becomes an attractive aspect of daily living.

Out of such experiences in fellowship and sharing grow meaningful worship services. In these, Christian ideas of God, and the place of Jesus Christ in history, in life today, and in each individual life, and the meaning of Christian discipleship come to be understood and accepted.

Service projects of various kinds are increasingly used in vacation church schools. One town in Michigan had a *bon voyage* party in the park for the "belle"—a heifer bought by the vacation church school to be sent abroad. The vacation church schools of Birmingham, Alabama, in a recent summer gave $6,087 for relief and missionary work, in addition to making many gifts for local institutions.

Audio and visual materials and methods are being used where equipment is available, and where rooms can be darkened for projected pictures. There is time in vacation church schools for using these resources, but there is still much misuse of them. Most trained leaders of preschool children do not use films with them. However, with proper precautions there is a wide field opening up here as more suitable films and records become available. Since sound motion pictures can reproduce living situations, they have great possibilities for teaching. The present audio-visual materials are more useful for training leaders than for use with the pupils themselves.

Shorter schools have tended to eliminate the out-of-doors aspects of the vacation church school program, which is to be regretted. In longer schools there are often trips to places of interest, swimming parties, and hikes, which are a part of the joyous fellowship of the group. Even in short schools held in the city there should be provision for play out of doors and for trips to the parks. Summertime, after all, should not be wasted! Educational trips are also important at times. If one wants to teach a group of city children the twenty-third psalm or stories of Palestinian shepherds, and the children have never seen a sheep, a visit to a farm or a zoo may be a great asset in the learning process.

Country children are at an advantage in studying the Bible, since the rural background of the stories is familiar to them. They are also at an advantage because the pupils, teachers, church members, and neighbors are likely to know one another. There is usually a group feeling in the church, and the whole community is ready to support the program of the vacation church school if it is properly promoted. Each child is a person, even when very young, and has a recognized place in the life of the community. This gives him a sense of security and poise as he takes part in the activities of the vacation church school.

Most vacation church school texts show how to make adaptations for small churches where there are few children and leaders, and where indoor space and equipment are limited. Other factors, such as seasons for farm work which keep everyone busy, must be taken into account in planning schools in rural areas.

Good Administration

Many vacation church schools are successful in spite of poor administration because they have good teachers. Many others would succeed if there was a better understanding of the administrative factors involved. The teachers and pupils need the moral and financial support which are essential to all well-administered educational institutions.

. A successful school begins quite early with promotion among the officers of the church. A "climate of opinion" may be created by presenting the unique opportunities of this use of the summer. This will lead church boards to put the vacation church school into their accepted, year-round Christian education program and will make possible long-range planning over a period of years. Publicity must, of course, be geared to those for whom it is intended. Parents and church members will be stimulated to give wholehearted support to vacation church schools through one type of promotion, but quite another will be needed to appeal to the boys and girls.

Plans for vacation church schools include grading and grouping, adequate space and proper equipment, materials and supplies, calendars and schedules, finances and budgets. They also include leaders and the training of leaders, staff meetings and departmental conferences, supervision, standards, evaluations, and records and reports.

Such matters are items of concern for any school administrator, but there are certain special difficulties facing the vacation school leaders. How can they build a calendar for the school which will make possible the maximum participation of pupils and teachers when work, vacations, and conflicting programs must be considered? How can a three-hour-a-day program have balance and flexibility so that the children are not overstimulated and leaders overtired? How can leadership, time, space, and equipment be used to the best advantage? What plan of payment for leaders should be used? Should grading be done by ages or by last year's public school grades? How can one prevent too wide an age range in a small school or too big a group in a large school? How can supplies be bought most economically? What about janitor service to keep the rooms clean when they are used every day? When one considers the number of leaders who have solved all these problems so well that successful schools are the rule rather than the exception, he can only marvel at the energy and capacity of devoted Christian workers.

One place in which administration may be said to have broken down is in the matter of reports. Any work as valuable as this should be properly recorded and reported. Much fine work is unknown because it is not reported to denominational or interdenominational organizations.

On the local level, too, reports to the parents and to the churches concerned are important. These may be made in pictures as well as in written reports. Records and evaluations by staffs and committees make possible the improvements needed in long-range planning for vacation church schools.

THE VALUES OF THE SCHOOLS

The chief values of vacation church schools have been indicated throughout this chapter. They are a great boon to many city children who find in them friends, fellowship, and a new outlook on life. The cool churches are refreshing after playing in hot city streets. The happy, friendly atmosphere may be an illuminating contrast to crowded, unhappy homes. Partial records in one denomination in one summer showed that twenty thousand boys and girls had been enrolled in vacation church schools who had never before attended a church school of any kind. This shows the possibilities of the vacation church school as an evangelistic agency of the church.

There are also valuable effects accruing to the Sunday church school. New children are integrated into the year-round Christian education program of the church. More experienced, and often better-trained leaders are ready for winter service.

Many secular agencies are making a bid for the precious free time of boys and girls. The church was one of the first to offer a program which appealed to both children and their leaders. It must not relinquish this great opportunity to reach boys and girls with a unique type of education in the Christian way of life.

SUGGESTIONS FOR FURTHER STUDY

1. Visit a *good* vacation church school if possible, and write a description of the values you find there for boys and girls, for churches and the community.

2. Make out a "work sheet" for a vacation church school which contains a listing of all the things which have to be done when planning a vacation church school (see *The How of Vacation Church School*).

3. Make out lesson plans for the first two sessions for one department of a vacation church school. Include schedules.

4. (a) Write a description of the functions of the group, or committee, sponsoring a vacation church school. (b) Make out a proposed budget for a vacation church school. State the arguments showing the need for the various types of items, which could be used in presenting this budget to the church or churches who support the school.

5. (a) How can churches be stimulated to see the need for making better use of the vacation period for Christian education in the local communities? (b) How can community agencies concerned in the best welfare of boys and girls be stimulated to plan for "summer neighborhood programs" which would include the vacation church schools?

6. What co-operation can be developed between homes and churches on the vacation church school program?

7. How can the values developed through the vacation church school be conserved for the pupils and the year-round program of the churches?

8. Study and evaluate texts from the co-operative series, from the various denominational series, and from some commercial presses.

BIBLIOGRAPHY

Blair, W. Dyer. *The New Vacation Church School*. New York: Harper & Brothers, 1939. Rev. ed. The most complete description of various phases of this work.

Bower, W. C., and Hayward, P. R. *Protestantism Faces Its Educational Task Together.* Appleton, Wis.: C. C. Nelson Publishing Co., 1949.

Goals for the Christian Education of Children. Chicago: International Council of Religious Education, 1945. A basic statement. The co-operative series of vacation church school texts are being outlined under the "areas of study" which are based on these goals.

The How of Vacation Church School. Chicago: International Council of Religious Education, 1947. A practical guide for planning and administrating a vacation church school.

Ristine, Ethel. *The Vacation Church School.* New York and Nashville: Abingdon-Cokesbury Press, 1947. Plans and illustrations of a school in session.

"The Study of Christian Education," Vol. III, *The Local Church Program.* Chicago: International Council of Religious Education, 1947.

(The bibliographies listed under Part II, "Materials and Methods of Religious Education," of this book, should be used by those who are studying the work of the vacation church school.)

Chapter 22

THE WEEKDAY CHURCH SCHOOL

ERWIN L. SHAVER

IT IS NOT EASY TO GIVE a definition of a weekday church school which is applicable in all respects to the many programs classed under this general heading. In the pamphlet *Remember the Weekday to Teach Religion Thereon* we find this description, "A weekday church school is a school set up by the churches singly or in co-operation, in which the attending pupils are excused from their usual public school program, at the written request of parents, to go to a church or other building to receive religious education." [1]

ORIGINS AND BASIC PRINCIPLES

It is also difficult, if not impossible, to say with finality where and when the first weekday church school was established. There were a number of experiments which had a short and unfruitful existence. Two movements, however, which have had a continuous history and have set significant patterns deserve particular attention.

In 1912 the Mormons established in Salt Lake City their first "seminary"— a church-organized and church-supported high school using its own building located adjacent to the public school. It now offers courses in religion, fitted into the daily and weekly schedule of the public school, which are credited toward graduation. A report of the Church of Jesus Christ of Latter-day Saints for 1949 showed over 30,000 pupils enrolled in these courses in more than 100 seminaries. Since this first project in Utah essentially similar plans for offering church-supported credit courses in religion at the high-school level have developed in various states—particularly in Maine, North Carolina, North Dakota, Texas, Virginia, and West Virginia. Most of these programs, as differentiated from the Mormon plan, have been sponsored by the Protestant groups of the community on a co-operative basis. The classes have, in most instances, met in the public-school buildings.

The weekday religious education program which has had the widest recognition, and which has set the pattern for the great majority of weekday church-school systems, is that which began in Gary, Indiana, in 1914. It operated in co-operation with the elementary schools rather than at the

[1] Chicago: International Council of Religious Education, 1949, p. 4.

274

secondary level. It originated in a friendly protest made by the Protestant ministers of Gary that the public-school program so monopolized the child's day that there was almost no "good time" for church educational activities. Superintendent William Wirt graciously met the situation by offering to excuse those pupils whose parents requested it to take courses in religion offered by the churches on a time schedule staggered throughout the day and week. At first these classes met in the church buildings; later they were held in the public-school buildings.

These two major patterns and variations of them have one central concept—a program of religious education on the weekday, sponsored and supported by the churches, which is related to the pupil's everyday study program and is included in the time customarily set aside for his education. Weekday church schools have therefore based their programs upon five principles, each of which represents a new trend in religious education: (1) Education in religion must take place on the weekday as well as on Sunday. (2) Education in religion must be included in the everyday school program of the child and be related to his other learnings and experiences as closely as possible. (3) The contents and procedures used in teaching religion must be educationally acceptable. (4) The teachers employed must be as well trained professionally as those who teach the child in his other areas of learning. (5) The churches of all faiths can work together in conducting such an enterprise, and most of them can go so far as to carry on a common teaching program.

How Organized and Administered

Most weekday church-school systems have not attempted to include all grades, but most commonly operate classes for grades 4 through 6. A study reported by the United States Office of Education in 1941 showed that on the average weekday church schools enroll about two thirds of the public-school pupils in grades at the elementary level and about one third of them at the secondary level. It is not unusual, however, to find communities in which over 90 per cent of the public-school pupils, in the grades where the program is operated, are taking these courses.[2]

When pupils are excused for weekday religious education courses, there have been various time schedules. In a very few instances the entire public school, or certain grades, has been "dismissed"—that is, the public school is officially closed—and the children enroll in courses in religion or engage in play or other activities as their parents' desires, or their own, may decide. In such a plan of dismissal the individual parent does not present a request for excusal to the public-school authorities. In practically all of the known

[2] Mary Dabney Davis, *Weekday Classes in Religious Education*, p. 25.

weekday church-school systems the individual pupils are "released" from the public-school program on the basis of a request signed by the parent. Sometimes the plan calls for the excusal of all these children at the same time. In most instances a staggered schedule is arranged, so that pupils of various grades are excused at different hours throughout the day and week. This is a highly desirable plan, because it is then possible to employ full-time professional teachers, so essential to effective teaching.

In three fifths of the communities, according to the study previously quoted, the weekday classes in religion are held in near-by church buildings. In the remaining two fifths of the communities the classes have met in the public-school buildings as a matter of convenience.[3] This latter practice was banned by the opinion expressed in the Champaign case as constituting a definite "aid" to religion on the part of the public-school system.

Obviously weekday church schools cost money; for they not only employ professional workers in most instances but have other expenses—text and reference materials; teacher and pupil transportation costs in many situations; annuity pensions; building rental, heating, lighting, and custodial service; and various other items. Some communities manage to conduct a program on a nominal-cost basis, spending even less than a dollar a year per pupil. Others expend as much as ten or twelve dollars per pupil per year. If weekday church schools are to achieve and maintain an annual pupil expenditure commensurate, hour for hour, with that of the public school, this figure should approximate five dollars per pupil annually for each hour of religious instruction offered per week. This charge is entirely the responsibility of the churches; and no expenditure for any purpose, directly or indirectly, should be made from public funds. The best method of raising the budget is to prorate it among the churches on the basis of their ability to pay, as shown by their annual local-church expense budgets. Sometimes, either as a means of raising or supplementing this budget for the Protestant program, a community-wide campaign is conducted. Occasionally a portion of the costs is defrayed by tuition, a plan to be recommended only in the well-to-do type of community.

To classify weekday church schools according to "types" is not easy; for, as the United States Supreme Court discovered, there are many patterns, depending upon "various factors or combinations of factors" present in each local program. Attention should be called, however, to a grouping made on the basis of the degree of interchurch co-operation. In a small and decreasing number of communities it has been customary for each church to teach its own children. This plan has been labeled the "denominational type." In the vast majority of communities, and especially in those which have recently developed programs, there is a high degree of co-

[3] *Ibid.*, pp. 27-28.

operation among Protestant churches, resulting in a Protestant "community type" program, with a common course of study and teachers chosen without regard to particular church affiliation.

As the movement has expanded into other communities—especially the large industrial centers, with many denominations and faiths represented in the population—there has arisen the need for interfaith co-operation, and some kind of co-ordinating committee has been found a necessity. Each faith—Roman Catholic, Jewish, and others, as well as Protestant— is represented on such a committee. This committee plans for whatever common activities are necessary in maintaining the total project. Each faith conducts its own teaching program, the common Protestant program being one of these.

The Protestant community weekday church-school program is under the sponsorship of some local agency, preferably a council of churches or religious education. Ministers' associations or other agencies with limited functions do not have a sufficiently broad base for a successful and permanent program. The sponsoring body organizes a board or committee of weekday religious education, on which there should also be representatives of other interested groups—parent-teacher associations; public-school leaders, unofficially; leaders in community character-building agencies; and particularly laymen. This larger board appoints subcommittees—on personnel, on curriculum, on finance, on publicity and community education, and others as needed.

Weekday church-school teachers should be as well prepared as their public-school associates, with special training in Bible and other religious subject matter and in teaching methods. Every weekday church-school system should have a well-trained supervisor, either have its own if it is a large system, or share in the services of a district supervisor if it is a small system. Many state and local councils, and also the International Council of Religious Education, have adopted high standards for weekday teachers and supervisors. Needless to say these teachers and "helping teachers" should be individuals with a deeply Christian spirit and should possess well-integrated personalities.

What about the curriculum? The courses taught in weekday church schools vary considerably. Some communities and a few state councils of churches have developed their own curriculums—New York City and Virginia among them—but most weekday systems look to outside agencies to furnish them suitable courses. The Graded Series Committee, representing many denominations, prepares course outlines which the Cooperative Publishing Association follows in creating and publishing the curriculums known as the "Cooperative Series of Weekday Church School Texts."

WHY THESE SCHOOLS HAVE GROWN

Conservative reports give the number of communities conducting some kind of weekday church-school program as more than three thousand. Over two million children of all faiths are enrolled. With but a few and only partial exceptions all the religious groups in America have shared in conducting this new type of religious education program.

Since the close of World War II other countries also have become concerned—some of their own accord and some because of the stimulus of occupation forces—that some way be found to include religion in everyday education, to replace the older plans of state-church religious education at one extreme or a completely secularized public-school system at the other. In Germany, for example, a plan of weekday church schools similar to the American program is in operation. Inquiries are being made by both church and educational leaders in other countries, some of a confidential character for obvious reasons, but all of them indicating that religion must have a central place in education for democracy and for a peaceful world.

Why this extensive growth of weekday church schools? It is clear that this has not come about because of promotion. The International Council of Religious Education has had but one staff member directing this type of work. Only two denominational member agencies have full-time weekday directors, both very recent appointments. A few state councils of churches have established departments of weekday church schools because of the absolute necessity of giving educational guidance to this "grass-roots" movement. Definitely unpromoted, weekday church schools have sprung from the needs and desires of local communities as the religious-minded leadership—lay as well as ecclesiastical—has sensed and expressed them.

Among the major reasons for the growth of weekday church schools are these: There is an increasing awareness of the need for more and better religious education, especially so as we have become conscious of the critical world situation. The spiritual illiteracy of the "unreached half" and the postwar wave of juvenile delinquency are directing a particular challenge to the churches. The Sunday school, even at its best, both because of its limited time and its lack of adequate leadership and support, cannot do the job alone. Everywhere in life educational standards have risen—in the public schools, in community child-welfare services, in the programs of the character-building agencies. There has been a growing conviction on the part of many that religious education also must raise its educational sights, and that the church must take the teaching of religion more seriously. Movements in the public school for character and spiritual education are additional evidences that there is a need which must be met. Religion must be related more closely to everyday life, and therefore its teaching on the weekday as well as on Sunday is a logical corollary. Local leaders in our communities have become convinced that we cannot "get something for nothing" in religious education, any more than we can in other areas of life. Hence the appeal of a movement which puts religion on a par with the other subjects which boys and girls are expected to study. Finally, the movement has gained momentum because it has been successful at most of these points. Its very demonstration of them has brought to its support large numbers of our citizens who believe in the power of religion to undergird life.

Achievements of the Weekday Church-School Movement

While it may be somewhat early in the life of the movement to recount the achievements of the weekday church school, it has already shown some very positive results. One of its unique contributions is the fact that it has "reached the unreached" among the great body of unchurched and religiously untaught youth. When it is observed that one fourth of the pupils enrolled in weekday church schools on the average have come from this religiously illiterate group, we must agree that this is no mean result. This percentage is even higher in the case of Protestant interchurch weekday systems and in the neglected areas of our large cities and rural territory. With proper support and wise direction these schools can be made still more effective as evangelistic and home-missionary agencies.

For years many friends of the Sunday school and other church educational agencies have wished that they could have the use of persons definitely trained to teach religion, just as we insist on trained teachers for our public schools. In the weekday movement we have our answer, for in over half of the situations the teachers and supervisors have been professionally trained and are also persons of Christian experience and consecration. It is to be expected, therefore, that such leadership should teach the Bible and other religious subject matter skillfully. Weekday church schools have demonstrated this teaching effectiveness to the satisfaction of parents, of church leaders, and of citizens generally.

Another achievement of the weekday church-school movement is the degree to which it has brought together the three most important agencies which are responsible for the child's education—the home, the school, and the church. Each of these agencies is a "school" of character. Separately they have accomplished much. Working together, they can accomplish even more. In the community weekday church-school program we have a joint project of these three agencies—a uniting of efforts and purposes which has had the moral support and intelligent co-operation of all of them.

Few, if any, religious movements in America today have done more to bring the denominations and faiths together than have weekday church schools. When representatives of all the faiths in a community are willing to meet together to plan a total community program, and when Protestant churches of all creeds are willing to commit the instruction of their children to a common agency, something unusual has happened. Add to this inter-church co-operation the fact that children of all economic and racial groups are taught in the same class, and one finds a demonstration of unity which is rare in American church life.

An accomplishment which will be permanent, regardless of the future pattern for weekday religious education, is the degree to which it has emphasized both the educational method in the propagation of religion and the religious ideal in the development of American education. The contributions of the weekday church-school movement at these points can never be lost. After many years of gradual separation religion and education are again to be more closely related.

SOME LIMITATIONS OF THESE SCHOOLS

There are certain limitations in this kind of school of religion which should in all frankness be pointed out. Although it does give an hour or two of additional teaching time each week, it is quite probable that the future weekday church-school period of excusal will not exceed this amount. The friends of the movement have not intended to make this an "entering wedge" for more and more time.

Because of this limited period for class work, because of its reflection of public-school patterns, and for other reasons, the teaching program of the average weekday church school has been too largely confined to an information type of activity. Some of the better weekday teachers have overcome this limitation and have led their classes in undertaking very interesting projects, some within and some outside the classroom. But, like many Sunday-school teachers, others of them say, "We have so little time; we must teach the lesson!"

In view of the large number of individual pupils whom each weekday teacher contacts within a week—sometimes five hundred or more—there is not much opportunity for individual guidance and personal attention, although in time these teachers do come to know and do help many pupils. There is now a movement under way to limit the teacher's periods so as to allow more time for home visitation and personal help.

Another difficulty is that of correlating the weekday church-school program with the programs of other educational agencies working with children. To be sure, this difficulty is not confined to this type of school! It is the problem of every church educational agency and of the public school as well. Successful experimentation by resourceful teachers has demonstrated the possibility of correlation with public-school activities.

It has not been as easy in the case of correlation with local-church educational programs and curriculums because these are multitudinous in number and character. Correlation with home activities and problems is difficult largely because of lack of time and personnel, as we have noted. Nevertheless, in spite of these correlation difficulties, the future must see a greater integration of this new school of religion into a comprehensive, unified, and improved program of Christian education, furnishing on the average at least five hours of religious guidance each week throughout the year.

These limitations are thus not entirely fixed. Most of them can be overcome, at least to some degree. But they are difficulties which will have to be faced.

Problems Within the Movement

From the beginning weekday church schools have also struggled with certain other problems. The most serious and inclusive one is that of maintaining high Christian education standards. When it is recognized that this new type of school has deliberately set itself to the task of being a real school—second to no other in its goals, content, and methodology—it can be seen that the fulfillment of this purpose will be no mean achievement.

A more specific problem is that of enlisting, training, and holding a leadership both Christian in spirit and as well trained professionally as the child's other weekday teachers. In the face of a decreasing supply of professionally trained Christian educators and reluctance on the part of our Christian training schools to give attention to this dearth of trained leadership for the Church, the weekday movement has suffered seriously. It has had great difficulty in finding enough qualified teachers and supervisors, although local commmunities are ready and willing to pay them.

Similarly it has been hard to find suitable curriculum materials. The church publishing houses have hesitated to launch an extensive series of much-needed texts in view of the uncertainty as to their local use. The necessity of having some text materials for both pupils and teachers, local pride of creativity, and limited financial resources have resulted in a type of curriculum materials not too satisfactory. Projects are under way to relieve this current situation; and as the movement enters into a new stage of development, it is expected that rapid improvement will be made.

A problem which has only recently come to the fore is the tendency in certain areas for Protestants to divide their efforts. In setting up a community program of weekday church schools, we sometimes find the organization of one weekday system, more progressive theologically, by a council of churches, and another system, theologically more conservative, by other groups or organizations. This unfortunate division of the churches has not been caused by the weekday movement. The movement, nevertheless, has suffered from it.

This situation does suggest that still greater co-operation is one of the needs of the movement. We must look forward to an eventual pattern of one community weekday system so far as Protestants are concerned. Only to the degree that this is the case can weekday religious education succeed, for many of the factors which make for its effectiveness are based upon co-operative action.

Another problem of like character is the need for interfaith co-operation. With the spread of the movement into new territory, Roman Catholics and others have shown an increasing desire to make use of the plan. There has been a remarkable demonstration of willingness to work together in community planning and a commendable establishment of interfaith committees for this purpose. These co-operative activities are a positive and demonstrated refutation of the objection raised by some that weekday church schools "drive a wedge" between the faiths. There is, however, need for more practical community expressions of "inter-faith understanding," as one writer has pointed out.[4]

EXTERNALLY IMPOSED PROBLEMS

In addition to the problems which are largely internal in nature and origin, there are others which are due to outside conditions and factors. Some of these are of long standing; others are quite recent. These outside problems are the inevitable and welcomed evidences of an awakened public interest on the one hand. They are at the same time a decisive challenge to the strength of the movement and, if successfully met, will be the means of its establishment as a primary agency of Christian education for Protestantism.

There is the prior problem of discovering a legally "unexceptionable" pattern for released-time weekday religious education. The opinion of the Supreme Court in the Champaign case both helped and hindered this discovery. It helped in that it furnished a general principle: *the public school system must not be "used" by the churches to help them teach sectarian religion.* It hindered in that, as Justice Jackson pointed out, the members of the Court expressed this general principle "without laying down any standards to define the limits of our decision." Most churchmen and religious educators, and the vast majority of the American legal fraternity, are convinced that released time as a whole has not been invalidated. Only additional test cases will reveal "the various combination of factors which

[4] Isaac K. Beckes, *Weekday Religious Education: Help or Hindrance to Inter-Religious Understanding?* pamphlet (New York: National Conference of Christians and Jews, 1946).

may establish a valid 'released time' program," to use the words of Justice Frankfurter.

As a result of this opinion, a minority of the weekday church schools throughout the country had to make adjustments to their programs. Some of these had to find other places than the public-school rooms in which to house their classes in religion—churches, other buildings, homes, even "mobile classrooms" in busses and trailers. Some systems had to discontinue other forms of public-school "aid"—registration of pupils in the public school; promotion, control, and supervision on the part of public-school persons in their official capacities; reporting a grade in religion on public-school report cards; and practices of like character. In most of the systems the pattern of relationship between these classes and the public school was practically devoid of "entangling alliances," and these programs continued essentially as before. The adjustments made were not easy. It is believed that, having made them, the movement will be the stronger for being "on its own."

The status of the weekday church school is still to be established in the thinking of some persons. For the most part, those who have known of it have become its ardent supporters, as evidenced by the determined field reactions following the Champaign case decision. The denominational boards of Christian education, the legal fraternity, the rank and file of schoolmen, and the average citizen have cast strongly affirmative votes. In spite of this favorable attitude only now is the general public becoming aware of its extent and possibilities.

This problem of status suggests that there needs to be much more education of the local constituency with regard to the exact character and detailed plans for a program of weekday church schools. Much of the present difficulty, legal and otherwise, has come about because of misinformation and lack of information. For example, "teaching Bible in the public schools" has been unwisely used as a descriptive term in certain areas, in spite of warnings to the contrary. In the future there must be more field counseling based upon the experience of those who have conducted successful programs and the agreement of leaders as to what constitutes a desirable pattern for the country at large.

Again, the weekday church school, as its predecessors, the Sunday church school and the vacation church school, reiterates the challenging question, Will Protestantism become a "teaching Church"? For many reasons Protestants have tried to short-cut the evangelizing process, devising program after program and scheme after scheme to secure adherents quickly. Unlike certain other religious groups, they have been reluctant to organize a real *school* program—extending over a long period of years; with multiple contacts with its pupils; with a full-time, professionally trained, and vocationally consecrated leadership; with a comprehensive, integrated, and educationally sound curriculum—backed by an expenditure of funds commensurate with what they have been willing to spend for public-school subjects. Unless Protestants, now called upon again to face this fundamental question, say, "We will," they must continue to "muddle through" and must accept the consequences.

Certain Protestants now for the first time are coming to believe that the only answer to an undesirable situation is the establishment of parochial schools. The vast majority of Protestants, however, have always been loyal supporters of the public-school system. They have also looked upon the weekday church school as a practical alternative to a parochial-school system. Therefore, some of the opposition to weekday church schools on the part of friends of the public school would seem to be strategically shortsighted.

Another problem now presented to Christian educators is that of the relationship of weekday religious education to movements for teaching religion in the public schools. It is not within the scope of this chapter to discuss or evaluate these several other established practices and new proposals. Let it be said, however, that weekday church schools are neither a substitute for, nor an alternative to, any other program of teaching religion either on the part of the church or the public school. It will require the use of *all* of them to tip the scales in favor of individual and social righteousness in a day of "man's disorder." Conversely none of these other programs can take the place of that which has been effectively demonstrated in the weekday church-school movement.

In conclusion, the concept of teaching religion on the weekday, with serious intent and through the use of the best educational methods, is here to stay. The patterns for implementing this concept will be numerous and varied. The weekday church schools of tomorrow will accept and follow higher standards and will find ways of meeting their difficulties. Through the weekday church-school movement the public school has been challenged to give a larger place to religion in its program and will respond to the challenge. Americans—Protestants and those of other faiths alike—have been awakened by the weekday church-school movement to the seriousness of a national and world situation which can be remedied only by the seven-days-a-week teaching of the laws of God.

SUGGESTIONS FOR FURTHER STUDY

1. What is the present extent of the weekday church-school program? To what degree has it been affected by its new legal status?

2. How effective is the weekday church school as an agency of Christian education? In what ways is it meeting, or failing to meet, the goals set for it?

3. What is the legal status of the weekday church-school program? Is the re-

leased-time principle without the use of public-school buildings or other forms of aid accepted as legally valid?

4. Can the problems of providing adequate housing for weekday church-school classes and transportation where necessary be met successfully?

5. Will Protestantism accept the higher standards set for Christian education by the weekday church-school movement and give the increased moral and financial support which they presuppose?

6. How can a sufficient supply of teachers, supervisors, and directors, qualified for weekday church-school leadership, be assured?

7. What is the current status of curriculums for weekday church schools? How can the quantity and quality of text materials necessary for the weekday church-school program be provided?

8. How can the weekday church-school program contribute to a comprehensive, correlated, and effective program of Protestant Christian education?

BIBLIOGRAPHY

Of the following books and pamphlets, only those marked with an asterisk treat exclusively the weekday church school. The remaining books give only limited attention.

Bower, William C. *Church and State in Education.* Chicago: University of Chicago Press, 1944. See "Weekday Church School" in Index.

Choosing a Course of Study for Your Weekday Church School. Service Bulletin 620. Chicago: International Council of Religious Education, 1947.

*Davis, Mary Dabney. *Weekday Classes in Religious Education.* Bulletin 3. A survey made by the United States Office of Education, 1941.

Hauser, Conrad A. *Teaching Religion in the Public Schools.* New York: Round Table Press, 1942. Chap. XI.

Lee, Umphrey. *Render Unto the People.* New York and Nashville: Abingdon-Cokesbury Press, 1947. Pp. 85-86.

*Miller, Minor. *Teaching the Multitudes.* Bridgewater, Virginia: Beacon Publishers, 1944.

*Moehlman, Conrad H. *About the Church as Educator.* Pamphlet. New York: Hinds, Hayden and Eldredge, 1946.

*Moon, Alleen. *Planning for the Weekday Church School.* Nashville: Methodist Publishing House, 1942.

The Relation of Religion to Public Education. Section X, 1947. American Council on Education.

*Shaver, Erwin L. *Remember the Weekday to Teach Religion Thereon.* A pamphlet of forty-five questions and answers. Chicago: International Council of Religious Education, 1949.

Standards for Weekday Church Schools. Duplicated. Chicago: International Council of Religious Education, 1948.

Thayer, V. T. *Religion in Public Education.* New York: Viking Press, 1947. Pp. 78-79, 88-90.

Vieth, Paul H. *The Church and Christian Education.* St. Louis: Bethany Press, 1947. See "Weekday Church School" in Index.

Williams, J. Paul. *The New Education and Religion.* Association Press, 1945. Pp. 62-67, 115, 122-25, 171.

Consult also previous and current issues of *Religious Education, The International Journal of Religious Education,* and denominational religious education magazines for numerous articles on the subject of this chapter. An extensive listing of articles in these and other journals is included in a frequently revised *Bibliography for Weekday Religious Education,* issued by the International Council of Religious Education.

Chapter 23

THE YOUTH FELLOWSHIP [1]

OLIVER deWOLF CUMMINGS

THE DEVELOPMENT OF THE YOUTH FELLOWSHIPS represents a most significant trend in the history of the Christian Church. The name is already
a familiar one on church bulletin boards, in the local newspapers, and in
the religious press, though its use goes back only to 1936. Even so, it is not
clear to many that a major new development in the history of the Christian Church is taking place. There are far-reaching implications for the
Christian Church in this movement.

The youth fellowships have arisen because of an insistent demand to
unify and strengthen the ministry of the church itself, to and through
youth. This demand has come from local congregations, ministers, and
leaders. It has resulted in sustained and deliberate actions of responsible
boards and leaders in the various denominations, with the full support of
their constituencies. In some denominations there has been a long history
of youth organization prior to the present program. In others, the youth
fellowship is essentially the first denominationally distinct youth organization. Of great significance is the fact that the youth fellowships are founded
upon a new principle of approach to church youth organization—a principle as old as the New Testament. To understand the youth-fellowship
movement and the principle upon which it is founded it is necessary to
see it in the perspective of what was true before the youth fellowships
were created. Thus the true value of the present development may be
understood.

THE URGE TO ORGANIZE

It has been typical of the Christian Church during the last century and
a half that it has created many organizations. This has been a reflection
in part of the typically American urge to organize. It also reveals a tragic
lack of understanding, until recent years, that it is the mission of the church
itself to provide for the Christian teaching and training of children and
youth. The fact that the modern religious education movement is less than

[1] Part of the material in this chapter appears in my article in the *International Journal
of Religious Education*, April, 1948, and is used by permission.

two hundred years old is most significant. The church has tended to neglect until recent years its commission to teach. Likewise noteworthy is the fact that the dawning interest in Christian teaching and training expressed itself at the outset in a series of new organizations related to the church but not actually the church itself.

The story begins with the Sunday school. In 1780, when Robert Raikes, a Christian printer, became interested in teaching children to read the Bible, he started an organization which made use of the church for meetings but did not sense that Christian teaching was inherent in the very commission of the church.

The women's missionary societies were likewise organized to fill a need which was inherent in the church's commission. As early as 1812 Baptist "pious females" showed an interest in the "heathen." In 1814 the Presbyterian women organized their "Female Cent Society," a group of women who paid one cent as dues for missions. From such beginnings came the organized women's missionary societies.

At no point has the story been more confusing than at the point of organizations for young people. A forerunner among many organizations was Christian Endeavor, begun in 1881. This was followed by a number of denominational youth organizations of the society type. Among these were Epworth League, Baptist Young People's Union of America, The Luther League, Walther League, the Evangelical League, the Nazarene Young People's Society. But that is not all. Many other denominational and interdenominational organizations for young people were created to meet special needs. The Methodists, for example, at one time had two missionary organizations for girls, the Queen Esthers for home missions and the Standard Bearers for foreign. The Baptists had the World Wide Guild, a missionary organization for girls, and the Royal Ambassadors for boys. The Disciples and the Reformed Church both had girls' organizations. As each new need was discovered, a new organization was created—with typical American prolificacy. In this way the typical Protestant Church became greatly overorganized. The individual girl, for example, might be expected to establish membership in an organized Sunday-school class, the Christian Endeavor Society, a girl's missionary organization, the choir, and possibly also the Girl Scouts or Camp Fire Girls. Each organization had its officers, committees, projects, and meetings. In some churches there was confusion, competition, and overlapping. The struggle for loyalties left many young people bewildered. The tendency all too frequently was for loyalty to the Sunday-evening youth organization or a weekday club to become a substitute for loyalty to the church itself. Some of these organizations were nondenominational in character, often centering the loyalty outside the local church and beyond the direct control of the church.

THE NEED FOR UNITY

It was quite apparent that there was need for consolidation, in fact, for a fresh start in youth work. As early as 1925 Herbert Mayer, in his book *The Church's Program for Young People,* presented a general philosophy of a unified youth program. Through the International Council of Religious Education, leaders in the various denominations had been developing a new philosophy of religious education in which the need of persons and the central place of the church as an educational agency were prominent parts. The Sunday school had been broadened to become the church school; that is, *the school of the church.* The church had been encouraged to undertake its full teaching and training ministry through a church board of Christian education. A number of local churches had successfully experimented with a simpler and more unified pattern of youth organization to meet the varied needs of youth. Over a period of years steps were taken to bring about a basic change in the character of youth work. This process led to the creation of the youth fellowships. There was such an agreement on the philosophy of Christian education that the principle on which the new youth organizations were established became essentially the same in different denominations. Even more, the choice of the name "fellowship" by so many of the denominations, though the result of purely voluntary decisions, was an indication of a high degree of unity.

The first group to take the new name was the Congregational Christian Church, in 1936. They reached back into their history for a word with special significance and began to set up "pilgrim fellowships." Soon many others had acted along similar lines and had adopted the unified type of program classified under the term youth fellowship: Northern Baptist, Evangelical United Brethren, Protestant Episcopal, Presbyterian (U.S.), Church of God, Disciples of Christ, Presbyterian (U.S.A.), Methodists, Evangelical and Reformed, Church of the Brethren, United Presbyterian. The Baptist Young People's Union of America after fifty years of history went out of existence, with other Baptist youth organizations, in order to provide for the Baptist Youth Fellowship, organized 1941. The Epworth League and other Methodist youth organizations gave way to the Methodist Youth Fellowship.

In many cases the name of the denomination or a word related to its history is used as part of the organization name. In some denominations—for example, the Protestant Episcopal—the new youth movements have been created on what has come to be known as the fellowship pattern, even though the term "fellowship" is not applied nationally. For the most part, however, the deeply meaningful term "fellowship" is an important common element in the names applied to the youth movements of these denominations.

These denominations with a total membership of 20,000,000 people have at least 5,000,000 young people. In such denominations as the Methodists and Presbyterians (U.S.), practically 100 per cent of the churches having a youth organization are organized as youth fellowships under the denominational pattern. Most of the other denominations listed already have most of their churches using the fellowship program.

Besides these denominations there are another dozen denominations in the co-operative movement embracing well over 10,000,000 and serving another 2,500,000 young people which have denominational programs of their own comparable to the youth fellowship but using some other type of name. Among these are the United Church of Canada, the Lutheran bodies, and the Nazarene Church. These denominations have successful plans for a unified approach to their young people and expect the youth of their churches to co-operate directly with their denominational pattern.

Nature of the Youth Fellowship

Something new was added—the youth fellowship. This was not another one of a series of parallel organizations. It was and is a new departure in youth work. The basic premises upon which it is established are quite revolutionary though simple. The full implications of these principles for the total life of the church were not all clear at the outset. In the light of actual experience the realization grows that the church itself may find new vitality as a result of the application of these principles throughout its organizational life, with children, young people, and adults.

1. *The Basic Starting Point—Personality.* The youth fellowship in the local church begins with a concern for people—young people—as individual persons. This is in contrast to the older basis of competition of interests and the tendency to exploit young people for various purposes through separate organizations. The new approach recognizes the Christian emphasis upon the sacredness of human personality. It seeks to build one clear program of the church to meet the total spiritual needs of each age group of young people. It utilizes the various sessions or times of meeting of the youth fellowship to accomplish this purpose. The dangers of split programs and split personalities are thus reduced to a minimum. The values of a balanced life and a well-rounded view of Christian experience and action are accentuated. The youth organizational unit is a fellowship of personalities, regardless of the activity or time of meeting.

2. *The Central Loyalty—the Church.* The youth fellowship expresses its concern for youth in a central loyalty to the church of Christ. It is, therefore, but a subunit of the church. It is an inclusive body emphasizing the total task of the church. It is the visible expression of the church itself at the youth level. It is not limited to any one time of meeting or type of activity; but it embraces Sunday-morning, Sunday-evening, and weekday

groups and functions. It expresses itself through worship, study, fellowship, and service. The body of Christ—the Church—is seen as a living whole. The youth fellowship is but the youth division of the church, a functioning member of the body of Christ.

The practical expression of this is in the development of organizational units or departments of the church: the junior-high (or intermediate) fellowship, school grades seven, eight, nine; the senior-high fellowship, school grades ten, eleven, twelve; the young people's fellowship, beyond high school, whether students or employed. Each age-group fellowship elects one set of officers—or provides a youth council to co-ordinate the total program if there are subunits functioning with officers within the fellowship. These officers, with the help of the adult counselors named by the church, through the church board of Christian education, become responsible for building a complete program of the church for the age group involved. The degree of participation of students in local church fellowships varies with the different denominations. Some bodies have taken long strides toward an integration of student groups into the total youth-fellowship movement.

It is not surprising that the recent resurgence of emphasis upon the church should have met with enthusiastic response from young people trained in the fellowship movement. It is a noteworthy fact that many ministers and local church leaders have experienced new interest among young people in the total task of the church when the full implications of the fellowship idea have become clear to them. In certain denominations there have been developments of far-reaching import, resulting from the efforts of young people to apply the fellowship idea through a concern for the world mission of the church.

3. *The Heart of Christian Experience—Fellowship.* The youth fellowship is an embodiment of the central experience of the Christian life—fellowship. It is therefore more than a youth organization or movement—it has all the dynamic potentialities of the early Christian church as a living fellowship. The hunger for fellowship among youth is but an echo of the struggle of mankind to find meaning in life through fellowship with God and others of his creatures. The true nature of the church itself is found in fellowship with God, in Christ, and with others in his service. In so far as the youth fellowship emphasizes its function as a fellowship, it is like a cell in the body of Christ—a living, growing, functioning organism. It is at this point that the youth fellowship offers hope for the renewal of the church. Fellowship cells of spiritual power, devoted to Bible study, worship, mutual sharing, service, and witnessing may become the means of restoring to the church its previously demonstrated power to transform society by the quiet but revolutionary process of changing human lives in

small-group relationships. The fellowship concept is valid for children and adults as well as for youth.

Points of Strength

There are many points of strength appearing in the present programs of the denominational youth fellowships. A recent survey covering various developments in the youth program of the Protestant denominations of the United States and Canada has been made.[2] This survey contains such observations as the following under the heading "Points of Strength in Present Program":

Numerous service projects where youth have handles to express their Christian convictions (heifer project, soap sharing, work camps, voluntary service, cattle boats, peace caravans, etc.).

Trend of youth to deepen spiritual roots in prayer cells.

Development of a Christian sense of vocation in the young people.

A growing awareness among our leaders of the uniqueness of the Christian faith calling for greater consecration and devotion to the business of being a Christian.

More youth responsibility being developed through commissions.

Young people becoming more aware of Christian tasks through the church. The summer conference program is the greatest instrument in bringing about this awareness.

Simple and more flexible organization for the local church.

Program based upon young people's needs, rather than denominational structure.

A National Council setting the pace for the whole church. Youth representation upon official church boards. Coordinated programs and activities from national to local.

The Disciple Plan (or spirit) arising out of a real experience of 12 young people on our National Executive Board is the spiritual heart of our Youth Fellowship. It expresses itself in many types of dedicated discipleship (day by day service in the local church and community, short term service projects, and vocational discipleship in all occupations).

A real sense of fellowship has developed among the youth of our churches. Commission type organization from national to area to local level is developing well-balanced programs and leadership among young people themselves. The Youth Fellowship in its total program is geared to the total program of the denominations. At the same time it has been one of the denomination's best instruments for the development of the ecumenical spirit.

The unifying of the total youth activity program in a local church under one organizational pattern. The training of youth leadership through actual partici-

[2] Under the auspices of the Youth Department, International Council of Religious Education, Isaac K. Beckes, Director.

pation in planning and program. Opportunities for putting Christian ideals and principles into practical experience through laboratories of social action.

It is evident on the basis of these observations and many other developments that a new vitality is being felt among the youth of the Christian Church. Due allowance must be made for the slowness of human nature to adopt new ideas and for difficulties in getting the fellowship idea established, particularly among adult leaders raised on a different philosophy of youth work. It still is true that a major shift in the direction of church work with youth has taken place among the Protestant denominations. This shift, once started, has taken place with great rapidity and on a far-reaching scale. A major factor of strength is in this latter fact. In the local community among the churches of various denominations as well as in the denominational conferences and in interdenominational gatherings, young people can talk a common language and be understood. They are already experiencing a new sense of solidarity and are finding enlarging loyalties within their denominations and in ecumenical relationships.

A word of caution should be offered. The fellowship plan is a perfectionist ideal which loses nothing of its soundness because, like the Christian life, it may not be achieved in all its fullness in every situation. Success must be measured in terms of progress made toward the goal, from year to year. Certainly the situation is a vast improvement over the previous one; already great progress has been made. Many of the difficulties arise because of the carry-over in some churches of a philosophy of Christian education for children and adults inconsistent with the new fellowship principle. A thoroughgoing application of this principle in all phases of the life of the church should open the door to new horizons of achievement.

Types of Activity

The youth fellowship permits and encourages a wide variety of activities. The major functions of the church in its teaching and training ministry are provided for in sessions held at different times on Sunday and during weekdays.

The most far reaching of these sessions in terms of numbers is the Sunday church school, with its traditional emphasis upon study of the Bible and Christian truth. The youth fellowship becomes the young people's division of the Sunday church school, with age-group departments and graded classes as far as numbers permit. Adults continue to serve as teachers and advisors of the fellowship classes and department activities, assisted by young people. The attempt is increasingly made to enlist more actively the leadership of the youth officers and committee chairmen. This is done through the recognition of these officers in class and department activities, in the teaching of the lesson, in preparing and conducting worship services and devotional experiences, in increasing attendance, in hospitality, and in the carrying through of projects arising out of the class study and discussion. Emphasis upon Bible study becomes an important project of the youth fellowship.

Practical difficulties are faced in churches which do not have graded departmental rooms for fellowship purposes in connection with the Sunday church school. Under such circumstances it becomes necessary to place even larger dependence upon the evening meeting for the training of members in the building and conducting of programs. However, there are some churches which have made large use of young people in the conducting of sessions of the "main school."

The fellowship principle of respect for personality applies to the spirit in which Christian teaching is undertaken and to the methods employed. The class becomes a fellowship, with the teacher sharing rather than imposing his will. The discussion method rather than the lecture method encourages freedom of expression and personal development.

The Sunday-evening meeting—in some cases a week-night meeting is substituted—has traditionally occupied a large place in the interest of young people. The youth fellowship seeks to maintain and enlarge this place without limiting the fellowship to this one session. This meeting furnishes a unique training ground for the development of youth leadership. Many thousands through the years have learned the basic skills of the Christian life in connection with such sessions. These skills include how to pray in public, how to take part in a meeting, how to plan and conduct worship sessions, how to lead fruitful discussions and effective meetings, how to plan and carry through youth projects. The demand of youth groups is more and more for worth-while content in these programs and discussions, and likewise for meaningful action resulting from the discussion.

In the new study of group dynamics there is justification of the importance of church youth meetings as proving grounds for spiritual democracy. The spirit of Christian fellowship, involving respect for the opinions of all and care to avoid domination by a few, adds a plus factor to good discussion techniques. When there is conscious waiting on God through prayer and Bible study and there is active sharing in group insights, the youth meeting becomes more than a discussion club—it is a true cell of the body of Christ. There is great hope for the Christian Church if the springs of spiritual power and of democratic action may be released through youth groups of this type.

The weekday activities of the youth fellowship are, or may be, greatly diversified. They may be coeducational or segregated, group or individual. They may vary widely to meet the needs of junior-high and senior-high age young people and of employed youth and students; and may be influenced by the nature of the community, either rural or urban, highly scattered or concentrated.

A recurring element in the program of many churches is the weekly "youth night," in which varied activities are involved, usually including those of a recreational nature. Some churches have launched an extensive program of craft and hobby interests. Work nights and "fix-things-up" parties have been surprisingly popular during war days and since. Some groups have provided special study classes, others fellowship-cell sessions, devotional breakfasts, music-appreciation hours, and gymnasium groups. Activity is by no means limited to the church building. It includes homes, recreational and cultural centers, and places of interest in the out of doors.

Development of the youth-fellowship movement has been paralleled by a recent trend on the part of the character-building agencies, such as the Boy Scouts, Girl Scouts, Camp Fire Girls, Y.M.C.A. and Y.W.C.A., toward more emphasis upon the church. The "God and Country Award" of the Boy Scouts of America and the *Protestant Manual on Scouting* are examples of this. Without changing its character as a nonsectarian organization the Boy Scouts of America has endorsed plans which make it possible for church-sponsored troops to relate their programs much more directly to the church and to its other youth activities. Somewhat similar developments have taken place in other agencies—the Girl Scouts, Camp Fire Girls, Y.M.C.A. and Y.W.C.A. In essence these developments look toward the recognition of the weekday club group as an activity of the fellowship. Though there are elements of confusion for those participating in these organizations and for their leaders, there are real advantages in the closer identification of these groups with the church as the central institution of the spiritual life. Some denominations have taken steps to develop a weekday boys' program of the fellowship and girls' program of the fellowship, so as to claim the advantages of specialized activity as well as of coeducation.

An encouraging evidence of the creative force at work within the youth fellowships is the extensive list of projects sponsored nationally by the various denominations for use in local groups and listed in the survey previously mentioned. The list includes such typical projects as the following: brethren volunteer service (a year of service on a maintenance basis); pen pals to European youth (a letter-writing project); soap drive for relief; support of denominational mission program; use of "Lenten Devotions for Young People"; sponsorship of youth week; summer service projects (in America and overseas); overseas caravans (traveling teams visiting churches, camps, schools, and cultural centers); relief and reconstruction projects (work camps and many other activities); volunteer service program (enlistment for a limited period of specialized service); Bible-reading program (reading lists, study suggestions); church loyalty crusade ("Let's go to church"; Let's roll up our sleeves"—manual work; "Let's

apply for jobs," in the church); "New Friends for Christ" program
(youth evangelism week ends, visitation, "fellowship events," and so on);
"Adventure in Living and Giving" (Adventure in Friendship—interracial.
Adventure in Service—community. Adventure in Giving—youth budget);
Christian community program (survey, study, and concrete action); hope
chests for relief (blankets, clothing, shoes, and so on); coaching clinics
(combined retreat, planning and training session); discipleship internes
(subsistence service in youth evangelism for one year); youth visitation
evangelism; "Friendship Frontiers"; book-of-the-month Bible study.

An important development of the youth fellowship has been the summer
youth caravans, which have taken advantage of the availability of time in
the summer for special service of young people in teams selected and
trained for specific tasks. The first Methodist Youth Caravans were trained
and sent out in the summer of 1939. By the summer of 1948, 699 Methodist
caravans, with a total personnel of 3,323, had served approximately 12,500
churches in nearly 90 annual conferences. The caravan plan with various
adaptations has been widely used by many of the denominations. In some
cases colleges have furnished specialized training as part of their curriculum
and have issued credit for the work done on the field. The character of
the program has varied—in some cases the primary emphasis has been upon
youth work, in others upon vacation church school activities, evangelism,
recreation, interracial and other social action projects; sometimes a combination of these. The program has been extended to include overseas
activities, visiting camps, churches, schools and cultural centers, and assisting in religious activities.

A comparatively recent development in the history of the church is the
work camp, the winter or summer service projects in which young people
volunteer their services to meet special needs. These projects have grown
with great rapidity from the initial impetus supplied by the Friends Service
Committee and such bodies. Most of the denominational youth fellowships
are participating in such enterprises. These activities are fresh expressions
of the missionary spirit of the Christian gospel. The projects often include
manual labor, worship, fellowship, and spiritual ministries in, or related to,
a living situation shared in common. However, there are many variations.
Some put primary emphasis upon work with people, while others emphasize
manual labor. Some projects are rural, others in large or small cities, and
still others in summer camps.

LEADERSHIP OF YOUTH

The crucial problem of the youth fellowship, as of all church work, is
leadership. The fellowship idea will not work itself. It must have leaders
who understand it, believe in it, and who will give themselves with ability

and dedication to make it work. This means youth leaders of youth and *main* also adult leaders of youth. Without the latter it seems quite likely that *purpose* there will not be the former. In the survey previously referred to the one problem listed in practically every report was leadership.

Adults who believe in the church and in youth must commit themselves with true devotion to the task of discovering, encouraging, and training young people. The leadership concern should begin with the minister, who himself must be deeply interested in youth and in the discovery and training of leaders for youth. The minister and the church officials will find it advisable to enlist some of the most capable members of the congregation for this highly challenging and thrilling work.

Among the qualifications needed in adult leaders are: a radiant personal faith, the capacity to encourage and inspire youth, the ability to share in the building of a worth-while program through group action, a good sense of humor, a fertile imagination, and capacity for growth.

The resources for a leader of youth are many and varied. They include textbooks on psychology, the Christian faith, the problems of today's world, and effective methods of church work with youth. Fortunately there is a rich supply of publications in the field of curriculum, such as Bible study, worship, vocation, personal and social action. The Standard Leadership Education curriculum supplies a range of courses and textbooks for training. This curriculum is supplemented by various new aids for informal training, such as manuals, flip charts, and slides. Leaders who are willing to accept the call of God to serve as counselors and teachers can find sufficient help if there is the willingness to undertake the task with sincere purpose. New friends of youth are needed in nearly every community who will come to feel that their call to serve through the youth fellowship is a true part of their lifework.

The ultimate test of effectiveness of the adult leadership of youth is its ability to draw forth the latent capabilities of the young people themselves. The best leader of youth is, not the one whose programs are most efficient, but the one who helps to produce young people who themselves are good examples of the Christian life, and who are able to take leadership responsibilities. Inherent in the fellowship idea are great possibilities for a co-operative approach of adults and youth to the life of the church, an approach in which young people will learn how to function effectively as churchmen and will find increasing satisfaction in the service of God through his Church.

ECUMENICAL POTENTIALITIES

At first glance the youth-fellowship movement has seemed to some to be a resurgence of denominationalism. This is because it has taken the form of the development of youth organizations with denominational names.

However, to fail to see the implications of the movement for interdenominational co-operation is to fail to understand its true nature. The primary emphasis of the movement is upon the church. It is therefore quite natural that since the churches are denominational in character, they should have created many denominational materials and projects for their youth fellowships. There has, however, been a marked disposition of the youth fellowships to co-operate with each other. The very fact that there has been such similarity of philosophy, structure, and program has tended to encourage a larger sense of unity. The awareness of denominational differences has been the basis for a more realistic approach to ecumenical activity.

The experience of fellowship, when it is truly Christian, has the quality of inclusiveness. This sense of belonging to the whole family of God and this eagerness to join hands with others in a comradeship beyond denominational, racial, and national boundaries is characteristic of the youth-fellowship movement.

There have been many wholesome evidences of co-operation of the youth fellowships in the United Christian Youth Movement. Through this body they are uniting in the sponsorship of youth week, in annual program emphases, the support of community Christian youth councils, and regional and national conferences. Through the Committee on Religious Education of Youth of the International Council of Religious Education the representatives of forty Protestant denominations and the various character-building agencies are developing common plans to serve the needs of youth through co-operative action and mutual sharing. Large interest has been revealed by young people in recent ecumenical conferences and in the development of the World Council of Churches. The youth fellowships were well represented in the Oslo World Christian Youth Conference and the Youth Section of the Amsterdam meeting. They have shared in plans for relief and reconstruction and for the exchange of persons. Much co-operative activity has already been initiated. The future offers many elements of challenge. The ceiling is unlimited.

SUGGESTIONS FOR FURTHER STUDY

1. Consider what changes may be necessary in children's work and adult work if the youth fellowship approach to organization and program is to become church-wide.

2. Review the flexibility of the fellowship idea and its suitability for small and large churches.

3. Develop a co-ordinated calendar for a year for the young people of a local church including emphases, projects, and special events.

4. Explore the present situation in a given local community to discover actual patterns of church youth work and the degree to which community co-operation is practiced.

5. In what ways can the youth fellowships advance the ecumenical movement?

BIBLIOGRAPHY

Beckes, Isaac K. *Young Leaders in Action*. New York and Nashville: Abingdon-Cokesbury Press, 1941.

Finegan, Jack. *Youth Asks About Religion*. New York: Association Press, 1949.

Harner, Nevin C. *Youth Work in the Church*. New York and Nashville: Abingdon-Cokesbury Press, 1942.

Hayward, P. R., and Burkhart, R. A. *Young People's Method in the Church*. New York: The Abingdon Press, 1933.

Trueblood, Elton. *Alternative to Futility*. New York: Harper and Brothers, 1948.

Wood, Violet. *In the Direction of Dreams*. (Stories of volunteer service.) New York: Friendship Press, 1949.

Chapter 24

THE CHRISTIAN EDUCATION OF ADULTS

HARRY C. MUNRO

THE CHURCH'S CURRICULUM of Christian education for adults consists of all the activities and enterprises which the church provides, uses, or recognizes for the purpose of contributing to the religious growth and welfare of men and women and the moral and spiritual improvement of group life. Hence a church program for adults will include worship; preaching; study groups; service enterprises; social fellowship; activities of social reform, improvement, or reconstruction; athletics and other recreation; and all influential activities of societies, clubs, and movements affiliated with or recognized by the church.

This quotation from Book 4 of the adult section of the *International Curriculum Guide*, a basic and widely influential document developed interdenominationally to guide in program building, indicates how broad the scope of adult religious education is conceived to be. In practice the program includes five principal elements, each of these being interpreted in a broad and inclusive sense:

a) *Worship*, including both public worship in the church and its auxiliaries, and provisions for private and family devotions.

b) *Study*, including not only class work but also guided reading, sermons, lectures, and all provisions for increasing the knowledge, understanding, and insights of the learners.

c) *Service*, including stewardship, volunteer leadership in the church or as a Christian in other agencies, and activities of social action or social reconstruction.

d) *Fellowship*, consisting of the social life of the Christian group, recreational activities, and enjoyment of the life of the "beloved community."

e) *Evangelism*, including the extension of Christian fellowship to surround unchurched persons, witnessing for Christ, and seeking to bring others into a "saving experience of Christ" and membership in his church.

Some of these experiences are provided chiefly by the church in its corporate life, such as public worship and sermons. The great majority of them, however, are provided through the various study, fellowship, and service groups which develop as auxiliaries of the church. All these groups, and not merely the so-called classes, contribute to the Christian education of men and women. They arise because many of the religious needs of adults and many of the tasks in which they necessarily engage as Christians cannot be provided by the congregation as a whole, particularly if it is large. These auxiliaries are, therefore, essentially the church itself functioning through the only type of organizational life fitted to carry certain essential functions. This point of view needs wider recognition both to improve the working relationship of these groups to one another and to the corporate church, and to insure more careful supervision of their work on the part of the church's responsible executive, the minister.

In all but the smaller churches, the corporate congregation as such is too large and formal for most types of effective adult education. Participation in the corporate public worship and a sense of identification with the whole congregation is an important part of essential educational experience for adults. But most of the learning which should be under way in the life of the Christian man or woman will be best provided through the smaller, more specialized groups of the church. The fact that the minister is responsible for, and identified with, the corporate congregational experiences, while these group activities are chiefly under lay leadership, causes the minister greatly to overrate the relative importance of his share of the program and to underrate the significance of this group life. Many ministers even consider these groups more or less of a nuisance because they sometimes seem to become competitors for interest and loyalty with "the church" itself.

Two principal changes are needed in order to improve the provisions made for adult Christian education by the typical church. Both of them involve a retraining of the ministry and a redefinition of the minister's job on the part of the congregation to enable him to render them the most needed service. One change is to make a much more educational use of the preaching program. This requires an opportunity for the listeners to do something else with the sermon ideas they hear than merely to listen to them. Related discussion, experimentation, problem solving, and reflective thinking would make these sermons really educational in outcomes. This involves a close relationship between the preaching program and the group life of the church. The second change is for the minister to be expected to accept the same professional responsibility for the quality of experience which is under way in every fellowship, study, and service group of the church that he does for the public worship program. Such a constructive educational supervision rendered by the church's professional leader, the only one usually competent to do it, would greatly increase the educational effectiveness of the church's group life. There is a dichotomy which divides the church's program into two categories—in one of which the activities are almost wholly determined, carried out, and dominated by the church's professional leader; in the other of which the activities are almost wholly determined, carried out, and dominated by lay leaders without training and with a minimum of professional guidance. Such a dualism prevents the church as a whole from being anything like the effective adult-educational agency which it might be. It is of the greatest importance that these "auxiliaries" of the church, which constitute its best setup for education, should come to be recognized as the church itself functioning in its most effective educational capacity.

Obviously other chapters deal with some of the most important aspects of this whole adult program, such as worship, family life, and educational evangelism. Here we will major in the study, service, and fellowship functions of the church's adult group life.

Changing Concepts

The present adult generation is conditioned by a social and cultural environment which is changing with unprecedented rapidity and complexity. This fact results in changing concepts which drastically affect the church's program for adults. It is necessary at least to outline these changes as a background for understanding current adult religious education. The changes are due largely to the development of modern science and the consequent technological changes which condition our modes of living and our modes of thinking.

The intellectual climate has been changing rapidly because of the dominance of the scientific method and viewpoint in general education and in vocational life. Increased facilities of communication and travel have banished isolation and set the individual at the crossroads of the world's intellectual traffic. This has vastly increased the possibilities for richness of life, but also for confusion and frustration.

Because of both the wider range of influences to which we are subjected and also the critical-mindedness of a scientific attitude, moral codes are changing, many old taboos being freely surrendered. Social pressures have rendered some untenable. For instance, the Christian virtue of thrift has, under some conditions, become "hoarding," while scruples against some forms of self-indulgence are "intolerance." Alcoholism is not sin; it is a disease. Seminakedness is not indecency, but scruples against it constitute prudery.

The emancipation of woman into a status of equality with man is profoundly affecting the pattern of family relationships as well as the economic situation. This and the decline of religious sanctions render the family increasingly unstable. Democratic ideals in family life find our generation in a confusing transition between the authoritarian pattern and something akin to domestic anarchy.

An industrialized and specialized economy with urbanization and suburbanization of living conditions, brings about a complexity and a fragmentizing of life into many relationships which create tensions and call for different roles. The result is a disintegration of personality with nervous tensions and strains which result in widespread nervous disorders.

These changes have altered the nature, function, and scope of education, with most important changes in the concept of adult education. Whereas education was once the occupation of youth, equipping each person with the required knowledge and skill to live in a stable, predictable world, the best education can do now is to enable each person, at whatever age, to live resourcefully and efficiently in the present. The future is so unpredictable that the best preparation for it is rich and skillful living in the present. This makes the school much more a part of real life. But it means, by the same token, that education must be lifelong. Since one cannot be fitted out in youth with all the needed adjustments for later life, those adjustments have to be made "on the job," as life is being lived. Hence the necessity of lifelong or adult education.

If education is guidance in adjusting oneself on the job to his environing world, then experience under enrichment and guidance becomes the real curriculum. Subject matter is just one instrument in the process. This means that the total community educates. Indirect learning is often more important than direct learning. The aims in terms of personal growth and character are often defeated by the patterns of social or economic life within which the person must live. This means that education becomes concerned, not only with effecting desirable changes in persons, but also in bringing about basic social reconstruction. The school sets out to build a new society. The church, through the education of the young, sets out to achieve the kingdom of God on earth.

These changes necessitate a new concept of adulthood. If a rapidly changing world requires adults to continue learning throughout life, can they make good? Does learning ability continue unabated throughout life? Research says, "Yes, for all practical purposes." If the learning powers are kept active and in use into adulthood, their decline is negligible. Failure to continue education throughout life is due more to laziness or lack of motive than to loss of ability.

Furthermore, continued growth from level to level of achievement during adulthood is the only alternative to regression back into immature forms of behavior. One goes "stale on the job" in his vocational life unless he is finding ever new interests and achievements in his work. The "dangerous forties" are the price of marital relations which have not far outgrown the scope of honeymoon love. A backward-looking religious experience will become ever thinner and less relevant to daily living.

Of major concern to our purpose are the changed concepts of adult religious experience. Instead of expecting religious experience and behavior to follow a fixed or standardized pattern, we should recognize great variety.

And the validity or potency of one's religious experience seems to depend less on its form or behavior patterns than on its relevancy to one's wants, or basic values, or purposes. While one's religious experience is a product of the co-operation of human and divine forces, its character and content seem to be largely determined by education and social environment. Consequently the religious life is largely under human control.

Preoccupation with otherworldliness or the future life has been largely supplanted by this-worldly concerns. Otherworldliness persists chiefly in our hymns only. Also the neat categories of "saved" and "lost" have become decidedly blurred, and with this a greatly decreased "passion for souls." The sense of sin and guilt characteristic of adult religion of an earlier day has become "maladjustment" or a "neurosis." For the more sensitive and serious-minded has come the social gospel, with a deep concern to make the teachings of the prophets and Jesus the basis for a thorough reconstruction of society into the kingdom of God. Account must be taken, however, of the recent challenge to these trends made by the Barthian "theology of crisis," which has become widely influential in American religious thinking. While not dominant, it doubtless constitutes something of a corrective to the earlier trends.

Of major significance for the Christian education of adults is the formulation during the last generation, on the part of many of the great religious bodies, of the social implications of the gospel of Christ. This new "doctrine of the kingdom of God" recognizes that personal religion is not something apart from economic, social, and political relationships; but it is both achieved in, and limited by, them. It isn't a matter of producing better persons first and trusting them to develop a better social order. Nor is it a matter of first building a Christian society and through it producing Christian persons. Neither can wait for the other. Any success in either goal carries the other with it. Delay or defeat in either also obstructs the other.

This identification of the personal and the social goals of Christianity has chief significance at the adult level. To be sure, we have been thrilled at "Christian Youth Building a New World." We have seen civilization marching forward "on the feet of little children." If it were only that simple and easy! The world is controlled by adults. Christian youth can't build a new world as long as adults don't want one. And as rapidly as youth crosses the bridge into adult responsibilities, youth is assimilated, by those very responsibilities, to the existing adult ideals and patterns. Only as two generations work together can real social improvement be made. At the present time there is a vast gap between the religious thinking and living of the rank-and-file church membership and those doctrines of social reconstruction which their denominations have written in the book. The supreme task of adult education in the church today is to close that gap.

THE UNITED CHRISTIAN ADULT MOVEMENT

Aware of the conditions and trends already noted, the executives responsible for national leadership in the religious education of adults in the various Protestant denominations began about 1935 to consider together a major attack upon their problem. They worked at first through the Committee on Religious Education of Adults of the International Council of Religious Education and the Adult Work Professional Advisory Section of the Council. They at once felt the need, however, for the collaboration of other types of executives who were projecting programs into the local church: missionary secretaries, social-action secretaries, stewardship specialists, and general executives; as well as for the counsel of selected pastors.

The committee and section called a conference of carefully selected personnel representing all these groups to meet for ten days at Lake Geneva, Wisconsin, July 27 to August 8, 1936, to face the need for some kind of grand strategy in the churches' work with men and women. Out of this conference came the preliminary outlines of what came to be called the United Christian Adult Movement. Further study and experimentation during the year and a second national conference in 1937 developed the plans into definite form and began the preparation of the guidance materials. The movement was defined in part as follows:

The United Christian Adult Movement is a voluntary fellowship of Christian forces serving in the field of adult work, and united in an international emphasis upon education and action in personal, social, and world relations. The purpose of the movement is to make the life and teachings of Jesus the practical basis for living; to increase the effectiveness of the church through adult education; to provide a means for the voluntary co-operation and participation of denominational, interdenominational, and other Christian agencies in the field of adult education in one united approach; to furnish a channel through which the co-operating groups can share their experiences, leadership, and materials.[1]

The movement developed a "program of worship, study, and action, in seven areas of adult experience, to be carried out in a setting of Christian fellowship." The seven areas are a basis, not for organizing adults, but rather for determining the scope and content of the essential program experiences which should be provided. The areas are as follows:

a) *The Bible in Life:* The Bible is still a best seller, revered but neglected, "the Book nobody knows." An intelligent, mature, historical conception of the Bible is needed, as well as a working mastery of its contents, to provide a discriminating use of its teachings in studying and working in the other areas.

[1] From the *Report* of the U.C.A.M. Adult Conference (Lake Geneva, 1937), p. 11. Used by permission of the International Council of Religious Education.

b) Personal Faith and Experience: The Christian faith as intellectual conviction, as healthy-mindedness, as inner experience of relationship with God through meditation and prayer, and as personal practices in such matters as stewardship, witnessing for Christ, and Christian interpretation of vocation, is an essential experience for growing adults. It is their necessary qualification for Christian living in the various areas.

c) Christian Family Life: The increasingly recognized importance of the family in all Christian education and the confusion and difficulty in achieving Christian family life today make this one of the most vital areas of adult education and experience.

d) Church Life and Outreach: The practice of intelligent and skillful churchmanship is as rare among lay men and women as it is desperately needed. The church's own continuous self-criticism and reconstruction for its task in a rapidly changing world depend upon a higher level of churchmanship than is usually achieved.

e) Community Issues Calling for Christian Action: Christian social concern is too often long range and theoretical. In this area the Christian man power of neighboring churches is expected to come to grips intelligently and constructively with what needs to be done in their own community to promote the religious growth of all its people and to make social relationships support rather than defeat what the church seeks to achieve.

f) Major Social Problems: Social pronouncements of religious bodies have formulated Christian objectives in many of these problem areas. It remains to make these doctrines rank-and-file convictions and to mobilize Christian forces in making them realities.

g) World Relations: The world mission of Christianity is clearly the evangelization of all peoples. But this cannot proceed apart from the achievement of world peace, a stable international order, and co-operative economic and cultural relations among the peoples of the world. These goals, with the achievement of a sense of world citizenship on the part of the individual Christian, demand a heroic program in this area.

The first major program provision in putting this plan into operation was the development of a comprehensive study curriculum in terms of courses in the several areas. This "Learning for Life" study program, as it is called, is set forth in U.C.A.M. Bulletin 410, with brief descriptions of some sixty courses and a listing with annotations of the recommended texts for them. The bulletin is revised biennially to take advantage of the latest text material as it appears. A few texts have been especially prepared for certain courses. For others there have not been satisfactory texts. The program is promoted on the elective principle, though a cycle arrangement of courses is suggested to provide a balanced and comprehensive curriculum.

A dozen bulletins or program guides have been developed to carry the various features of the movement. These are listed in the Bibliography.

The movement has been furthered through summer regional conferences, through occasional national conferences, and through the circulation and use of its bulletins and conference reports. By far its largest influence, as was to be expected, has been through the adult-work programs of the various denominations. These have carried the viewpoints, objectives, and ideals of the movement through innumerable conferences, conventions, and institutes, through curriculum and promotional materials, and field counseling projects. While this has usually been under denominational labels, it has nevertheless given a needed unity and mutual support throughout the adult work of Protestantism. And of course the thoroughgoing nature and purposes of this movement are of long-range rather than immediate significance. The movement shows at least what the Christian education of adults aims to be and may someday actually become.

THE LAG IN PRACTICE

It must be recognized that the actual program of adult religious education in local church and community lags far behind the envisioned United Christian Adult Movement, even more than a decade after its inception. Instead of adult education constituting the advancing front of the whole Christian education movement, it seems almost to be covering the church's retreat before rampant secularism.

The church's adult-study program, if indeed it can be called study for anyone but the teacher, still consists largely of uniform lessons. As used, these make a superficial, unhistorical, and fragmentary approach to the Bible. Few uniform-lesson classes could pass even the simplest examination over their textbook, to say nothing of showing intelligence, skill, and satisfaction in using it. In the effort to be "practical" and "apply" the lesson to life, most uniform-lesson teachers base superficial homilies on random texts which do utterly nothing except to confirm existing prejudices and foster spiritual pride. Systematic elective courses, even with the "Learning for Life" plan available, have made painfully slow headway.

The church's rank-and-file members are largely unaware of the social pronouncements of their own denominations and about equally blind to the crucial issues with which they deal. The relevance of personal religion to economic, political, and vocational behavior is seen only in very superficial ways. In fact, an actual popular referendum on many of these ideals, if made to the whole church membership, might result in a negative vote to about the degree that the members understood what was really involved.

On the other hand, the largely inherited "faith" of many of these men and women has almost no relevance to the problems, confusions, and frustrations of their daily living in a rapidly changing and increasingly complex social environment. Consequently their religious convictions are not the source of their driving power. Their feelings, concerns, and values are related to social, economic, and even aesthetic experiences which lie outside the narrow range of their religion. This accounts for the low vitality and the limited motive power of their religious life.

While united fellowship and action of neighboring Christians at the community level is desperately needed, inherited denominational prejudices are effective deterrents, and these prejudices are fostered rather than exorcised by the denominational label on nearly everything religious which they hear, read, or experience. Of course, promotion gets better response under this label than without it. We have the kind of people our past programs have developed. But how soon shall they be ready to respond to a truly ecumenical appeal on the local level unless their denominational leaders undertake the responsibility of re-educating them through making a united approach in some of the concerns and activities which are really central and important?

What are some of the reasons for this lag at the adult-education level? One difficulty is that the major attention in the whole religious education movement has been given to work with children and youth. This is because they are more responsive, less "sot in their ways," and easier to work with. Also, of course, "they are the church of the future." We forget that before they become the church of the future in terms of controlling it, they will have been assimilated to the existing adult type. Directors of religious education are usually expected to work chiefly with children and youth. Field directors in religious education cannot give time and promotion to summer adult conferences because they are already loaded with youth conferences and vacation-school work. Curriculum investments in the children's and youth field are large, their deficits frequently being paid out of the profits from the adult uniform-lesson business. The situation is rapidly improving, but we are reaping the results of the tardiness of that improvement.

Ministers are the church's principal adult educators; and if they were trained and skilled as real educators, adult work could soon take its proper place as the cutting edge of the church's advance. But their job is not interpreted as one of adult education, and they are not trained in educational techniques. Many ministers now in training are getting ready to serve a generation that is already gone. Their training has too little relevance to the kind of changing world in which they must work.

Many of the church's members have been brought into their nominal church relationship through superficial types of evangelism which involved no adequate commitment of themselves to Christ and his cause. They constitute dead weight rather than power in the church's task. They did not accept church membership as a real discipleship, so have little interest in their own spiritual growth. Their desperate need for vital adult Christian education is quite unfelt.

There is very inadequate co-ordination of the various programs of study, missions, evangelism, service, and social action projected into the local church by denominational and interdenominational agencies. Consequently they are accepted on an elective principle, if at all, and do not constitute the mutually re-enforcing elements of a true adult-education program.

The recognition of this lag, and some of the reasons for it, does not overlook real progress that is being made, particularly at certain points, as will be noted later. This analysis is an attempt at an honest view of the situation with definite indications as to the needed next steps. Some such plan as the United Christian Adult Movement is overdue. What is needed is to appropriate it and use it.

Promising Developments

Space limitations prevent any survey of the multiform lay activities and organizations in the various denominations which constitute current Christian education of adults. Only a few trends can be recognized. Over most of the country the large adult Bible class of near congregational proportions seems much less prevalent than formerly. Its doubtful value as a real educational agency means that its decline has not been a serious loss. It did little that the church congregation as a whole could not have done better anyway. It should be replaced more widely than is being done by a genuine Bible-study program of study-group size, using study methods not possible in the corporate congregation.

Women's work is tending increasingly toward a unified organization in the local church, in which a "woman's council" becomes the co-ordinating center for work of various types in smaller, sometimes specialized groups. This usually makes for a more balanced program and closer co-ordination with the church as a whole.

Men's work as such has been much more spasmodic and varied in type and is far less prevalent than organized women's work. This is probably due chiefly to the fact that the most active men of the congregation usually find a place of service and fellowship in the official board of the church, from which women are all but excluded. There are, however, in some denominations vigorous men's work organizations under way, usually being chiefly means of fellowship.

The widespread use of visitation evangelism among the churches in recent years has been a significant activity of laymen and usually of laywomen as well. In some of the denominations this pattern of evangelism has largely replaced traditional types. The laboratory training of the lay workers for this task has been a significant type of adult education.

Survey work in the National Christian Teaching Mission revealed the fact that the church the country over has failed most signally at the young-adult level. The great majority of churches find their responsibility list of unchurched young adults to be relatively greater than that of any other group. This seems to be due to the fact that young adults have fallen between the youth program and the adult program, neither of which meets their very special need. An accurate basis for identifying these persons on the basis of the experiences of transition from youth to adulthood is replacing the former artificial and inaccurate age-group designation. The six identifying "transition experiences," any three or four of which indicate young adulthood, are: leaving school, self-support, marriage, leaving the parental home, voting age, and discharge from military service. These experiences involve drastic readjustments in which religion should be a vital factor and help. They create certain hungers, such as that for new fellowships to replace those of youth, which should be met in the church program. *Young adulthood* is that period in life during which these adjustments are under way. It varies in length and comes at various ages. A group selected on the basis of the recency of these experiences and helped to develop a program to guide in the adjustments involved receives the church's effective and successful service. On this new basis several denominations have developed excellent materials and have a vigorous young-adult movement in full swing. This means much for the future of adult education.

Of great significance also is the new recognition that home and church are partners in Christian education, and the curriculum should recognize this by being designed for joint use in home and church. Some of the new materials are giving almost as much attention to the home as to the church. This trend may be revolutionary and is probably the only realistic approach to parent education.

Recognition is increasingly given to the strategic importance of the later years of life, in which the leisure of retirement creates both the opportunity and need for a vigorous program for older adults. They have almost unlimited service potential if they can be guided and motivated to keep growing.

The new program of "fellowship evangelism," treated fully in Chapter 6, is one of the bright spots in the adult education picture.

The trend toward regarding the total church as an educational enterprise, likewise treated elsewhere, has great significance as adult education. There are forums, schools in Christian living, family camps, adult and young-adult camps and institutes, all of which point the way to new possibilities and agencies of adult work. It is probable that some of the goals and ideals of the United Christian Adult Movement will sooner find their embodiment in some of these newer patterns of work than by a reconstruction of the more stereotyped and traditional agencies and programs.

SUGGESTIONS FOR FURTHER STUDY

1. Secure the adult work materials of your own denomination and appraise them in the light of this chapter.

2. Investigate the provisions being made for young adults as here defined by three or more near-by churches; also for persons of retirement age.

3. Explore the "social pronouncements" of your own denomination.

4. Try introducing the "Learning for Life" study program into some adult class.

5. Interview three ministers regarding the program of adult education in their churches, and check against the presentation in this chaper.

BIBLIOGRAPHY

Barclay, Wade Crawford. *The Church and a Christian Society*. New York and Nashville: Abingdon-Cokesbury Press, 1938.

Bulletins of the U.C.A.M. Chicago: International Council of Religious Education.
   401. *Adult Program Guide*, 1940.
   402. *Adults in Action*, 1938.
   403. *Group Work With Adults Through the Church*, 1938.
   404. *Personal Religious Living*, 1939.
   405. *Christian Action on Social Problems*, 1939.
   410. *Learning for Life*, 1940, and later editions.
   411. *Adult Projects in Study and Action*, 1940.
   412. *Schools in Christian Living*, 1939.
   415. *Young Adults in the Church*, 1945.
   423. *Home and Church Work Together*. 1940.
   Looking Ahead in Adult Work, 1946 conference report.

Westphal, E. P. *The Church's Opportunity in Adult Education*. Philadelphia: Westminster Press, 1940.

Zeigler, Earl F. *The Way of Adult Education*. Philadelphia: Westminster Press, 1938.

Special Interest or author in both?

Chapter 25

AGENCIES OF RECREATION
AND GROUP SERVICES

PAUL M. LIMBERT

IN EVERY URBAN COMMUNITY in America and, to a more limited extent, in rural areas there are voluntary associations of boys and girls and older youth that must be taken into account in any comprehensive review of religious education. It is difficult to find a designation for these organizations that is wholly satisfactory. Frequently they are called "character-building agencies." But this title does not mark them off sufficiently from the home, the school, and the church, which also build character; nor do young people join these organizations consciously for the sake of developing their own character. A designation much in vogue currently is "group-work agencies." But group work is a method that may be used in a variety of settings, and the term does not apply accurately to all aspects of the program of these agencies. More satisfactory is the term "youth-serving organizations," used by the American Youth Commission to describe any agency "where activities are devoted wholly or in substantial part to advancing the welfare of young persons." But the majority of the 320 organizations so designated by the commission are composed largely of adults who serve youth, whereas our concern in this chapter is with organizations comprised primarily of youth members. So let us use the somewhat cumbersome but more accurate term "agencies of recreation and group services."

What significance do such agencies have for religious education? To what extent may they be considered allies of the churches? What distinctive contributions are they making to the religious experience of youth?

Our attention will be focused on a small number of these movements which profess a specifically religious purpose and welcome close co-operation with churches. But this is by no means to rule out the importance of other agencies whose objectives coincide with the goals of religious education at many points. Any organization that seeks to develop good health, good comradeship, and good citizenship is an ally of the religious educator. Usually these leisure-time agencies provide a setting favorable to the functioning of religion in concrete terms. Conversely, the weekday activities of a church-sponsored youth group are very similar in type and purpose to those which are under the auspices of a recreational agency.

Secular Agencies

Boys' Clubs of America. Among the agencies that make no effort to deal with religion directly is the Boys' Clubs of America. The policy of this organization toward religious instruction is typical of a great many private and public organizations, such as settlement houses, Four-H Clubs, community recreation centers.

Boys' Clubs of America are a rather loose federation of clubs for boys between eight and twenty-one years of age. These clubs are located in low-income areas and centered around a building which provides facilities for sports, crafts, and other forms of recreation. Membership is open to boys without restriction of nationality, race, or religion.

The earliest Boys' Clubs were the outgrowth of a religious liberalism that deliberately ruled out all denominational teaching or worship. In a report printed in 1881 it was said that the founders of the organization saw something to be done that is commonly left outside of church work. They agreed that "no work distinctly and in name religious should be undertaken."

The relation between the Boys' Club and the churches is cordial and friendly, but all religious instruction is left to the home and the church. It is feared that any attempt to give religious instruction through the club would have a divisive effect.

Four-H Clubs. These are organized ordinarily through high schools in small towns or rural districts and are conducted by the extension service of the United States Department of Agriculture in co-operation with the state colleges of agriculture. County extension agents, together with supervisors and specialists of the extension services of the state agricultural colleges, assist the local volunteer leader in conducting the various Four-H Club activities.

Four-H objectives include helping rural boys and girls to develop desirable ideals and standards for farming, homemaking, community life, and citizenship. The activities include tours, demonstrations, exhibits, social and recreational activities, homemaking and agricultural projects. Since these clubs are an extension of the public-school system, there is no explicit religious content or purpose; yet Four-H Clubs constitute in many rural areas an important group service for church young people.

Agencies with Explicit Religious Purpose

There are five national agencies for recreation and group services that give religion an important place specifically in their programs and that provide in various ways for religious ceremonials and instruction: Camp Fire Girls, Boy Scouts of America, Girl Scouts, Young Men's Christian Associations, Young Women's Christian Associations. These five organizations are related to the Committee on Religious Education of Youth of the International Council of Religious Education through what is now called the Youth Agency Advisory Committee. These organizations have units in other countries. In the United States alone they have a total membership of about 3,500,000 boys and girls between nine and twenty-one years of age.

Even among these five agencies there are some important differences in policy and practice regarding religion. It is important to examine each separately before attempting any generalizations.

Camp Fire Girls. Camp Fire Girls is the oldest girls' organization in America, originating in 1910. The purpose of the organization is "to perpetuate the spiritual ideals of the home and to stimulate and aid the formulation of habits making for health and character." In becoming a member of a Camp Fire group, a girl states: "It is my desire to become a Camp Fire Girl, to serve God and my country, and to follow the Law of the Camp Fire which is—'Worship God, Seek Beauty, Give Service, Pursue Knowledge, Be Trustworthy, Hold on to Health, Glorify Work, Be Happy.' "

The words "Worship God" were inserted in the constitution in 1942. Since that time there has been more stress than formerly on church-sponsored groups. Separate pamphlets are published describing the relation of Camp Fire Girls to the Protestant Church, the Catholic Church, and Jewish synagogues and centers. In these publications the policy of the movement is stated as follows:

Close co-operation between Camp Fire Girls and the Church is mutually beneficial. Church sponsorship adds the religious emphasis to the Camp Fire programs, gives the group continuous leadership and good supervision, provides a meeting place and a host of interested friends. Camp Fire gives to the Church a varied and interesting character-building program for its girls.

Since the program is for girls of all races and creeds, the girl's training in her particular religious faith is left to her parents and church leaders. Local Councils are directed to schedule all community-wide activities in public buildings to which girls of all faiths may come.

When a Camp Fire group is organized and sponsored by a church, its activities are to be closely integrated with the local church program. The minister or priest is to be the spiritual leader of the group. The girls are awarded honors for service to the church. Some religious requirements may be added for progression in the Camp Fire program. It is asserted that the Camp Fire law is deeply rooted in the Christian-Judaic ethic.

Boy Scouts of America. The Boy Scouts of America have the largest boys' membership of the privately supported youth agencies in the United States, numbering more than 1,500,000 members between seven and eighteen years of age. This movement, unlike the Boys' Clubs, builds no club houses of its own. Scout troops and Cub packs are sponsored by organizations in the community that provide meeting space and help to supply leadership. Great emphasis is placed on outdoor activities and a camping program.

Religious attitudes and relationships are recognized as a basic element of the Boy Scout program. As a part of the Scout oath or pledge the boy promises, "On my honor I will do my best to do my duty to God and my country and to obey the Scout Law." The last item in the Scout law stresses religion: "A scout is reverent: He is reverent toward God. He is faithful in his religious duties and respects the convictions of others in matters of custom and religion."

Included in the Constitution of the Boy Scouts of America is this paragraph on religious policy:

The recognition of God as the ruling and leading power in the Universe, and the grateful acknowledgment of His favors and blessings are necessary to the best type of citizenship, and are wholesome things in the education of a growing boy. No matter what the boy may be—Catholic or Protestant or Jew—this fundamental need of good citizenship should be kept before him. The Boy Scouts of America, therefore, recognizes the religious element in the training of a boy, but it is absolutely non-sectarian in its attitude toward that training. Its policy is that the organization or institution with which the boy is connected shall give definite attention to his religious life.

The sponsoring institution operates its own Scout troop. The Scout movement provides a general program, trains Scoutmasters and maintains Scouting standards; but when a church undertakes to sponsor a Scout troop the officials of the church have full charge of this unit. Scouting does not attempt to provide religious training in its own name but turns this responsibility over to the churches.

In line with this policy a National Protestant Committee on Scouting and a Catholic Committee on Scouting have been established. The Lutheran churches also have a special Committee on Scouting. In each case official sanction is given to the Scouting movement, and a separate manual is published describing the values of a church-centered troop and outlining the procedures to be followed.

In the Protestant manual the emphasis is placed on integrating the Scouting program into the church's total program of Christian education. The pastor is to be registered as a member of the troop committee and as chaplain of the troop. Each church may decide whether its troop shall be limited to boys affiliated with this church or open to other boys of the neighborhood. The great majority of Protestant church troops are of the latter sort. Among the policies suggested for church troops, several are worthy of special note:

a) Troop church policies are drawn up in consultation with the pastor or his representative and are approved by formal action of the church board or committee on religious education. These policies are to cover overnight camps and week-end hikes to avoid conflict with other phases of the church program.

b) A program of study and worship is provided for the boys in the troop who belong to the sponsoring church; boys from other churches are directed to their own churches for religious training.

c) Special training is to be given by the pastor to the troop committee and Scoutmaster in what the church expects of its troop.

The Protestant manual includes a chapter dealing with religious programs at camp, religious services for Sea Scouts, and grace at meals, in forms accepted for common usage in camps where Scouts of diverse religious groups are present.

There is a chapter also on religious projects outlining the standards to be met by Protestant boys as they progress through the several ranks of Scouting. Provision is made for a special church-Scout badge known as the "God and Country Award." These standards include regular attendance at Sunday school, regular Bible reading and personal prayer, knowledge of the books of the Bible, a specified number of hours of assigned personal service to the church.

The Catholic manual *Scouting for Catholics* bears the subtitle "Adding the Supernatural." The Catholic philosophy of Scouting is indicated by the following quotation:

The Program does not supplant the Church, home, school, or other agency, but supplements them and is so conducted that there is a proper co-ordination as far as Scouting is concerned. Scouting is a program, well conceived and well serviced, of boy activities, done in the spirit of a splendid moral code which is essentially Catholic as far as we are concerned; and Scouting can become for us and our boys one of the means of eternal salvation. "Christ builds the supernatural upon the natural." It is entirely within our province to use this Program as a means to an end and not as an end in itself. We can, and indeed we must, supernaturalize the movement according to our Catholic teaching in order to justify our official adoption of Scouting.

Although Scouting has been organized in Catholic parishes since near the beginning of the movement in America in 1910, a nation-wide plan was not developed until 1933. Diocesan Scout chaplains have been appointed in practically all dioceses. The Catholic Committee on Scouting is advisory to the Boy Scouts of America and has the responsibility of promoting and guiding co-operative contacts with the Catholic Church. Each troop has a priest as chaplain, whose duty it is to keep in personal contact with each Scout, to preside at investiture ceremonies, and to prepare a religious program as part of the troop's participation in the program of the parish.

In a chapter entitled "Adding the Supernatural" the Catholic manual shows how all Scout functions can be enhanced with a religious atmosphere. An approved Catholic investiture ceremony is outlined. A candidate is expected to make a half-hour adoration before the Blessed Sacrament, meditating upon his duty as a Scout, before presenting himself for acceptance as a Tenderfoot. There is an annual Council spiritual rally for Catholic Scouts in a body and in uniform. It is recommended that Holy Communion be received on the second Sunday of every month in uniform in a body.

A set of religious standards is drawn up for Catholic Scouts at each level of advancement. These standards center around knowledge of rituals, the sacraments, and other Church doctrines. The *Ad Altare Dei* Cross is an award for special advancement in Catholic Scouting.

Girl Scouts. Girl Scouts, Incorporated, parallels the Boy Scouts of America in many ways in its development and general purposes, but this movement has its own distinctive program designed to make girls from seven to eighteen resourceful and well-balanced individuals and responsible citizens. Founded in 1912, this organization now includes in its membership about 900,000 girls.

Special publications are issued defining the policy and program of Girl Scouting for Protestant, Catholic, and Jewish girls. A statement of religious policy is included in the Constitution:

> The Girl Scout organization is a character-building agency open to girls of all faiths. The force behind Girl Scouting, which gives life and meaning to every activity, is a spiritual one.

This official policy receives further amplification in the following two paragraphs:

> The Girl Scout organization, in carrying out its program, does not attempt to assume the prerogative of the church and parents in giving religious instruction. Instead, it encourages girls to be reverent and loyal to their own religion and helps them to carry out the religious teaching already received. It also helps each girl to respect, understand, and appreciate the religious convictions and practices of others.
>
> For example, in a camp where girls of various faiths and denominations are present, counselors are provided, insofar as is possible, representing the major faiths, and arrangements are made for each girl to attend services in her own church if at all possible. If there is no church near the camp of the denomination of a particular girl, her parents are so informed before her application for camp is accepted. Menus in camp are planned to meet religious requirements, and the Sunday program is in keeping with the day.

The religious program of Girl Scout troops is not spelled out in as great detail as in the Boy Scout manuals. It is suggested that the ethical and spiritual standards expressed in the Girl Scout promise and laws are very similar to those taught in Protestant and Catholic churches, and that the troop leader or pastor can provide for many natural interpretations and applications. It is assumed that creedal instruction will be taken care of in other parts of the church program and not introduced into the troop. Considerable stress is put on community service and the development of useful skills. There is little emphasis on badges or awards. Special investiture ceremonies are suggested for troops in Catholic and Protestant churches.

There are Protestant, Catholic, and Jewish Girl Scout advisory committees. For the Jewish girl the following paragraph may serve to summarize the point of view:

The synagogue, the Jewish center, and the Jewish organization are vital and important factors in the community life of today. They play a significant role in the life of the individual Jewish girl, helping her round out the positive influences of home and community. The Girl Scouts, the sponsoring group, and the Jewish girl come together to build a troop in which Jewish interests and values are enhanced by the ideals of Scouting. Jewish girls find in Scouting real-life opportunities for putting into practice the democratic ideals that are an integrated part of their training in our society.

Young Men's Christian Associations. Y.M.C.A.'s differ in several ways from Boys' Clubs and Boy Scouting. The Y.M.C.A. movement is a complex organization which covers a wide age range and includes, in addition to the well-known community associations, work with college students, soldiers and sailors, and railroad men. The Y.M.C.A. movement is much older, dating back to an origin in London in 1844. Its work is carried on in many cities through centrally located buildings, frequently well equipped with recreational and educational facilities. Yet to an increasing extent its program is decentralized throughout the community and is organized in co-operation with schools, churches, and other existing organizations.

The religious policy of the Y.M.C.A. differs also from any of the agencies dealt with earlier in this chapter and is less easily defined. The Young Men's Christian Association is an outgrowth of the Protestant Evangelical movement. It was established by young laymen of the Protestant churches. For many years active membership and the privilege of holding office were restricted to members of Protestant Evangelical churches, even though some Catholics and many who were members of no church were served by the Y.M.C.A. from its beginning in America.

Throughout a large part of these hundred years the Y.M.C.A. has been recognized as an important ally of the Protestant churches and as a center for types of activity that could not be provided in the average small church. The Y.M.C.A. played an important part in bringing churches together; it functioned as an interchurch agency before the formation of councils of churches. Nevertheless, the Y.M.C.A. movement always maintained its identity as an independent organization of and for Christian youth, paralleling and supplementing the work of the churches at home and abroad.

The early Y.M.C.A.'s were avowedly and devoutly religious. As the program expanded in the latter part of the nineteenth century to include many educational and recreational activities, the Christian purpose of the movement was stressed consistently. A fourfold program developed—religious, educational, social, and physical. Bible-study classes and evangelistic meetings were common. The accepted objective was to lead young men and boys to Jesus Christ. The Y.M.C.A. pioneered in conducting leadership-training classes for Sunday-school teachers. It took the lead also, around 1900, in organizing boys' camps, boys' clubs, and older boys' conferences.

In the last three decades the religious program and point of view of Y.M.C.A.'s have undergone modification for a variety of reasons. Direct evangelism gave way to an educational approach that sought to relate the Christian purpose of the Association to all aspects of the program and to lay stress on informal expressions of religion. The Protestant churches became more zealous in religious education and leadership training and were less willing to delegate these functions to the Christian Associations. Meanwhile the constituency of the Y.M.C.A. was much less homogeneous in religious background than in earlier days; in some sections of the country Catholic youth comprise a large portion of the membership. Also, the Y.M.C.A. took an important part in the development of Community Chests and councils of social agencies, with the result that it came to be popularly regarded as a social agency rather than a religious organization.

As the depression of the 1930's deepened, however, and as a second World War developed, the pendulum swung back toward a renewed concern about the C in the Y.M.C.A. A program survey in 1941 revealed that Bible study, devotional periods, and special religious observances are still sponsored by a large proportion of Y.M.C.A.'s. Whereas it had been assumed by some leaders that all activities within the Y.M.C.A. are religious, more attention is now being given to the conditions that must be fulfilled if Christian values are to be achieved. Associations think no longer of "religious work" as one department among many of the Y.M.C.A. program but of a Christian emphasis that ought to pervade all activities and relationships of the association. Only a handful of Y.M.C.A. workers are now designated as religious-work secretaries, but increasing attention has been given to preparing every Association secretary to carry his share of responsibility for religious leadership.

The stated purpose of American Y.M.C.A.'s, as adopted by the National Council in 1931, is: "The Young Men's Christian Association we regard as being in its essential genius a worldwide fellowship of men and boys united by a common loyalty to Jesus Christ for the purpose of developing Christian personality and building a Christian society."

Y.M.C.A. Boys' Work. There are approximately one million members of American Y.M.C.A.'s under twenty-five years of age. The latest formulation of the purposes of boys' work in the Y.M.C.A., adopted in 1944, includes three major objectives:

1. To become healthy, well-balanced and responsible citizens
2. To learn how to live together as members of our democratic society and to work unitedly for the common good
3. To grow in their understanding and love of God and in their loyalty to Jesus Christ

Since each Y.M.C.A. has a large degree of autonomy, there is great variation locally in the boys' work program. Yet nation-wide patterns in boys' work are developed through the recommendation periodically of major program emphases and the adoption of common nomenclature for work with different age groups. The Eighth North American Assembly on Work with Boys in 1947 approved seven major program emphases:

> Christian Experience—Values—Faith
> World Citizenship—World-mindedness
> Interracial and Intercultural Understanding
> Youth Status—Participation—Responsibility
> Education for Family Living
> Sex Education
> Education for Health

Y.M.C.A. workers with boys are urged to relate all of these program objectives to the Christian purpose of the Association. The first of these emphases, however, is regarded as basic. In more detail it calls for:

> Helping Younger Boys and Youth of High School Age:
> Develop a Christian faith to hold to and live by
> Understand what it means to be a Christian in daily living
> Grow as Christians and take part in building a Christian society
> Identify and become loyal to Christian values

Although there is still considerable variation in terminology among associations, there are "four fronts" officially in Y.M.C.A. boys' work: Father and Son "Y" Indian Guides, Gra-Y Clubs for grade-school boys nine to twelve years of age, Junior Hi-Y Clubs for boys twelve to fourteen, and Hi-Y Clubs for boys fifteen to seventeen. Some Associations have similar clubs for high-school girls called Tri-Hi-Y. (About 10 per cent of Y.M.C.A. membership nationally is made up of women and girls.) Each of these groups includes a religious emphasis in its statement of purpose; each has its suggestions of appropriate rituals for initiating new members and installing officers.

Two paragraphs from a Hi-Y manual indicate the flexibility of approach to religion in Y.M.C.A. groups:

There is a wide range of opinion about the place of religion in the Hi-Y. A few clubs have taken the stand that the organization's chief purpose is to furnish the setting for periods of devotion and Bible teaching. They consider that these two activities are essential to religious growth and therefore rightfully within the province of the Hi-Y. At the other extreme are the clubs, equally small in number, that consider it unnecessary to include any religious observance or teaching whatever in their programs. They believe that they can develop moral character and democratic behavior without such aids.

The religious function of Hi-Y lies somewhere between these two extremes. The test of a boy's religion is not how much religious information he has but rather how he behaves, what sort of attitudes he has, around what values he centers his major loyalties. His behavior, his attitudes, and his sense of values, he learns through his daily experiences and contacts with his fellows, both young and old. Therefore his Hi-Y Club can provide through its varied activities a splendid opportunity for these religious learnings to take place.

In many communities Y.M.C.A.'s have carried on their boys' work in close relation to the churches and have sought to aid in training church leaders for more effective work with their own groups. There is at present a trend toward less reliance on building-centered Y.M.C.A. program and more emphasis on neighborhood-centered group work in co-operation with home, school, and church. The 1947 Assembly on Y.M.C.A. Work with Boys urged further decentralization:

A decentralized boys' work program, making use of the Four Fronts terminology offers an effective means of re-establishing a more creative relationship with the churches which most Associations have always held in theory but seldom demonstrated. The fact that the "purpose" of the Y.M.C.A. is similar with that of the church, that the church offers less institutional problems than the schools, and that through its group work program the "Y" can make a real contribution to the character development of the boy members of a church are valid reasons for attempts to create more workable relationship between local churches and the Y.M.C.A.

Young Women's Christian Associations. The Y.W.C.A. movement developed in the latter quarter of the nineteenth century with special emphasis on work with students and with young women in cities away from home. There was little work for girls during these earlier years, except as a few "student clubs" were formed in high schools after the pattern of college associations. The Y.W.C.A. co-operated in founding the Camp Fire Girls.

Until 1918 girls' work in the Y.W.C.A. was carried on largely through Camp Fire Girls and the Girl Scouts. In that year the Girl Reserves came into being, growing out of a conviction that the Y.W.C.A. needed a teen-girl program of its own.

One of the important reasons for organizing the Girl Reserve program was a desire for a more definite Christian basis. This religious emphasis represented an effort to carry on everyday living according to Christian ideals. It was expressed through the importance given to "Spirit" as one side of the Blue Triangle, and in the extensive use of Christian ceremonials in the new organization. An early formulation of Girl Reserve standards called for: "Friendliness, fair play, acceptance of individual responsibility, loyalty, clear thinking and speech, reverent understanding of God as it shows in work and worship, participation in local service activities and the task of interpreting the Social Ideals of the Churches."

In the 1930's leaders in the Y.W.C.A. saw the need of more attention to the religious purposes of the movement and a clearer statement of the Christian philosophy of the associations. This concern led to the adoption in 1934 of a new statement of the purpose of the Young Women's Christian Association: "To build a fellowship of women and girls devoted to the task of realizing in our common life those ideals of personal and social living to which we are committed by our faith as Christians. In this endeavor we seek to understand Jesus, to share his love for people, and to grow in the knowledge and love of God."

Girls' workers in the Y.W.C.A. continued to seek to make religion a functional element in the entire program, to stimulate discussion of religious questions, to lead to appreciation of the religious background of others, and to provide meaningful worship experiences in clubs and conferences. There has been no concerted effort, however, to organize Girl Reserve groups in churches or to relate the Y.W.C.A. to the churches in any way comparable to the Y.M.C.A. approach. It should be noted also that the Y.W.C.A. has seldom entered the field of work with younger girls but has concentrated its efforts on the fourteen-to-eighteen-year range.

In 1946 a new name was adopted, Y-Teens, taking the place of the Girl Reserve designation. There has been no substantial change in the nature of the program. About 500,000 girls under eighteen years of age are included in Y.W.C.A. activities.

Student Christian Associations. One of the most significant nonchurch programs of religious education is to be found in the student work of the Young Men's and Young Women's Christian Associations. Although beyond the scope of this chapter, the work of Student Christian Associations, organized nationally under the National Intercollegiate Christian Council, is worthy of special study. The Y.M.C.A. and Y.W.C.A. pioneered in developing voluntary Bible-study groups in colleges, in conducting student summer conferences, in promoting personal and vocational guidance under Christian auspices. Seldom has there been so effective a synthesis of personal and social aspects of prophetic Christianity as in the Student Christian Association movement.

Summary. From this review of community agencies of recreation and group services it should be clear that it is difficult to make generalizations regarding their approaches and contributions to religious education. A few observations by way of summary may be profitable:

1. Most of these agencies, of which the Boys' Clubs and Four-H Clubs are an example, make no explicit reference to religion in their statements of purpose or formulation of program. References to religion in these agencies are general, indirect and occasional.

2. The Scouting organizations and the Camp Fire Girls include religion explicitly among their objectives and have well-organized national channels for the promotion and expansion of church-centered groups. It is assumed that religious instruction is the prerogative of the church. There is strict avoidance of any control over the religious program on the part of the youth organization, and a studious effort to keep free from affiliation with any single religious movement. It is assumed that the religious objective of Scouting can be detached from the normal troop program and dealt with separately.

3. The two Christian Association movements have an explicit Christian purpose which they seek to integrate into the entire program of the organization. Both are in the Protestant tradition, although independent of official denominational or interdenominational affiliation. The Y.M.C.A. has been more closely related historically to the churches than has the Y.W.C.A., and this association is reflected in close co-operation with the churches in boys' work in many communities. The Y.M.C.A., however, does not turn over the control of its religious program completely to any church. It assumes that growth in religious experience should take place at many points, whether under church auspices or not. Both Y.M.C.A. and Y.W.C.A. assume that every professional worker should share in carrying out the Christian purpose of the Association. Their difficulty lies particularly in knowing how to make an effective explicit approach to religion in groups of diverse religious backgrounds.

4. All of these agencies may be regarded in varying ways and degrees as allies of the churches in religious education, broadly conceived. The club or Scout troop to which a youth belongs may be the most determinative of all character-forming influences at a certain stage of development. A larger measure of understanding and co-ordination is called for if the resources of all these agencies, along with the churches and the schools, are

to be utilized fully for an inclusive program of religious education in the community as a whole.

SUGGESTIONS FOR FURTHER STUDY

1. What are the advantages and disadvantages of an indirect approach to religion such as that followed by Boys' Clubs and Four-H Clubs?

2. What proportion of Boy Scout and Girl Scout troops in your community are sponsored by churches? What differences in philosophy and practice regarding religion appear in troops sponsored by Catholic and Protestant churches?

3. What opportunities and difficulties are faced by the Y.M.C.A. and Y.W.C.A. when they seek to carry out their Christian purposes in groups made up of boys and girls from diverse religious backgrounds?

4. To what extent is any effort being made in your community to interrelate the churches and the agencies for recreation and group services in order to achieve a more co-ordinated program of religious education?

BIBLIOGRAPHY

Atkinson, R. K. *The Boys' Club*. New York: Association Press, 1939.

Chambers, M. M. *Youth-Serving Organizations*. Washington: American Council on Education, 1941.

Kurtz, Russell H., ed. *Social Work Year Book, 1947*. New York: Russell Sage Foundation. Articles on "Boys' and Girls' Work Organizations" and "Youth Services."

Vance, Catherine S. *The Girl Reserve Movement of the Young Women's Christian Association*. Bureau of Publications, Teachers College, New York, 1937.

Wiley, S. Wirt. *History of Y.M.C.A.–Church Relations in the United States*. New York: Association Press, 1944.

Pamphlets available from agency headquarters:

Camp Fire Girls, Inc., 16 East 48th Street, New York City.

Boy Scouts of America, 2 Park Avenue, New York City.

Girl Scouts, Inc., 155 East 44th Street, New York City.

National Council of Y.M.C.A.'s, 347 Madison Avenue, New York City.

National Board of Y.W.C.A.'s, 600 Lexington Avenue, New York City.

Chapter 26

THE COMMUNITY AS A UNIT
OF RELIGIOUS EDUCATION

HELEN MARIE EDICK

ACCEPTANCE OF RELIGION has been a part of the process of acculturation and has played an important role in conditioning the individual. From early times religion has been intimately bound to group mores and ideals. It has come into being in its varied forms as it has been selected and set apart as "the authority." This has seemed to remove the medium of control from the group where it originated to an outside source which we of the Judeo-Christian tradition have called "God." In him we have embodied the moral and idealistic aspects of our living. In matters where right or wrong decisions were to be made, the criterion of judgment was placed outside the group in a supernatural being embodying the "Good," whose word was the higher law.

Through this long process some values have been lost. The main one is the recognition of the importance of the community or group in the molding of standards of living and right conduct. Placing the authority in an outside source has resulted in our ignoring the power of community pressure to *change* modes of living and to mold character. We have failed to take advantage of one of the ways in which God is at work in the world: namely, through activity within the world in the process of interaction between individuals and groups. The value of the community as a power to develop or change character has been lost, and the sense of our individual responsibility as a part of the group authority has diminished. In our search outside the group for the source of a criterion for right conduct we have let the group progress more or less as it would, or through the religious convictions of a few individuals down the ages: men and women who have given their lives to raising the level of standards of conduct.

The church as a fellowship is a part of the community, a part of the group authority which changes living and molds character. However, it is only *one* of the forces and has not yet asserted itself to its potential stature nor assumed its full strength as a power to improve the quality of living so as to make it more like the Supreme Being in whom it believes and around whom it organizes its teachings. If God is *in* and *of* the activity which is ever present in his universe, then this power must be harnessed, if his kingdom is to be realized. This kingdom can be realized only as relationships between people who live and work together become more godlike. If it is to be a reality it must function in *all* associations which people have with each other. The kingdom will be realized in such measure as this living produces results for all mankind and arouses concern for the welfare of all of God's children.

Man learns and gains from the community; he also contributes to the learnings and gains of others. What he contributes is determined by his character; thus it becomes imperative for the church to build good characters, adequate to the task of building the kingdom of God, if such a kingdom is to be established. It is imperative that we recognize the importance of the community as a unit of religious education if we are to work with the forces already in operation. The church, a part of the community, must begin with the best of the forces at hand if it is to change disinterested citizens into dynamic workers to establish the rule of God among men

The Educational Process

A knowledge of what the community has to offer is the starting place. It consists of groups of people bound together for specific purposes—to secure food, clothing, housing, security, recreation, or some of the many things which have become necessary to physical and mental health. A study of the community will show what it holds to be of worth, what its supreme values are, the *quality* of its religion. Therefore some communities will show forth higher standards, and others will be satisfied with relatively low ones.

Once it has learned the values to be found within the community, the church must discover and plan how it can best use these existing values. How can the church harness these forces and make them allies in its program of religious education? How can the church determine the quality of education which the community is continuously providing? How can that quality be made a religious one? Life and learning are intimately related. Learning implies that education—a change in behavior—has taken place. Religious, like secular, education can take place only in actual life situations. This means that religious education is gained at other times than the hour or two on Sunday morning or in the weekday class in religion. It is not confined to the church. It is taking place in home and school and in hundreds of community contacts. It is taking place wherever human relationships are being experienced and in the many conflict situations which occur daily. The religious education of the church will improve the quality of living only as it enters into the lives of the people and influences their relationships.

The Community as a Means of Religious Education

The church may utilize the community in the formation of a definite plan for a program of religious education designed to improve the quality of living. This must touch all ages. It must be implicit in the total program, for each activity contributes to the religious education of the people. The responsibility of the church extends beyond its doors out into the community. We must recognize that the church is but one agency in the community and in the whole character-molding scheme of community setup. The church, along with other character-building agencies, has always assumed that it was in the business of building better character. Since it is now more widely recognized that character is formed in the varying organizations which make up daily living, a greater responsibility than ever before is placed upon the church. It should raise the level of community life by improving community organizations and also by contributing specific programs of religious education.

In the early days of our country the church was the center of the community, and many of the needs of the people were met by and through the program of the church. The church acted on occasions as the basis of community government, the dispenser of charity, and the means whereby education was provided. Social life centered around it. During the past century the church has lost many of its powers and at the present time remains as a guardian of spiritual values and, in the case of the Christian Church, the chief means for teaching Jesus' way of life. The church has become separated from other agencies and set apart because of its unique function. Sometimes the church has become a disorganizing force rather than an organizing one. This is especially true where denominations are strong and divergent in their theological and organizational principles. Such differences have prevented or hindered community organization and created factions controlled by groups whose loyalties were not religious. They have caused us to lose sight of fundamental things. Each group pulled its own way, even while many held values in common. We are still faced with rivalry, not only among the major divisions of the Church—Jewish, Catholic, and Protestant—but among small groups of Protestant denominations operating in communities hardly able to support one. The need for community organization and co-operation should be faced by the church if it is to utilize the educative power of the community to mold and change behavior. Education does not take place apart from a situation; neither will religious education take place outside the setting where life is lived naturally, for religion and living are closely bound together. The church through the widening of its horizons must see the community as a character-building agency. It must so relate itself to the community that it will make full use of its power to influence action, to raise standards, to offer leadership, to educate and co-ordinate religion and life. If the church is to be an organizing force or a force that contributes to community advancement, it must develop community loyalty. This will be obtained only through close and sympathetic integration of community and church. The recognition of local needs and interests, co-operative participation in projects to improve community conditions, the building of attitudes toward people which will develop into concern for their welfare—these will make the church accepted as an agency at work in and with the community. Many people must feel this impact to recognize the worth of the church in their own lives. A more intimate relation with the community will enable it to act as a guidepost showing the way to racial and religious appreciation and a feeling of brotherhood.

The church may widen its horizon without infringing on the duties or prerogatives of other organizations. It may participate in everyday affairs without lowering its standards or compromising itself in any way. The Protestant church has a contribution to make as it works on community problems with other groups not definitely religious. In this way the church's ideals may very well permeate those of the community. In one community the church took the initiative in uniting several women's organizations of the community to provide better movies for children. Pressure was brought to bear upon the local theater. In a short time the management provided wholesome, educational motion pictures, suitable for children and at a special performance once a week. The organizations secured the co-operation of parents, and children were glad to have their own performance.

The city offers a more complex situation. Most community organization is according to specific interests without too much attempt at bringing the various interests together either for co-ordination or co-operation. Some interaction takes place between groups, but there is an insufficient amount to make much impact. We cannot minimize the work of the Council of Churches or the Council of Social Agencies in larger communities. The councils are co-ordinating primarily, but they often provide impetus for investigation and a stimulation to social action of real value. In larger places there are a host of organizations especially concerned with character building or service projects of some kind. These groups need to be co-ordinated for more concerted effort, and what organization is better adapted for this work than the church?

No program can be offered which will fit every town or meet individual community needs. Each community has its own problems. But fortunately, each has within its constituency some means for meeting and solving these problems. The community-minded church is the logical organization to take the initiative in this. Some type of survey will reveal existing conditions. These facts should be made known to the organizations in the community. If this has been well done, united action will follow. To secure the co-operation of all existing agencies a representative committee should estimate what each agency may be expected to contribute in time, money, influence, interest, or pressure. Once the plan has been formed and the forces rallied to execute it, the hard work begins, but the load is lightened by the realization that all are working together for a winning cause. As the group mind is greater than the individual mind, so is the strength derived from concerted effort far greater than any single group can summon.

The church at the head of, or working side by side with, such organized forces lends more than leadership, valuable as that may be. It lends a spiritual impetus which should remind us of the zeal of the early Christians, who had a message for the whole world. Some may wonder if the church will be compromising or "watering down" its purpose when it joins a number of more secular groups working for ends that may be temporal. No one who thinks of religion and life as inseparable will object to the church's leading the way to better living.

In its attempt to give a spiritual emphasis the church has often duplicated community activities, enlarging its program to hold its young people or adults. It has added gymnasiums, bowling alleys, craft rooms. These resources may not be available in some communities unless the church provides them. But better co-ordinating of community organizations might reveal other needs which the church could better fulfill as a part of its community responsibility and thereby avoid duplication of leisure-time programs. Most communities today have a number of organizations and attractions bidding for the time and effort of the same people. In such a case the church finds the loyalty of its members divided or given to secular groups. Better community organization would prevent the duplication of camping and recreational facilities and spread the provision for leisure-time recreation over the entire year. A better understanding of purposes and aims of many organized groups might reveal to each that they are working for the same ends and that co-ordination would be of greater value than the existing competition. Working together, church and community groups would inevitably come to recognize the splendid qualities of leaders in groups other than their own and see the contribution made to the life of the community by organizations which heretofore they had known little about. Recognition of the worth of personality, the activity of God at work in and through people irrespective of their religious affiliation, may be lifted to the height of a religious experience for those who understand.

THE CURRICULUM AND THE COMMUNITY

The need for keeping subject matter and the more abstract aspects of learning close to the daily experiences of those whom we would educate was suggested earlier. Let us now take a look at the possibilities for teaching

as they relate to the community. These possibilities have to do with curriculums and will include some teaching of a more formal nature.

Verbalization plays little part in the education of the nursery and kindergarten child. His vocabulary is limited, and his past experience is small.
If he is placed in a situation where he learns to associate with his contemporaries, where he has the guidance of an intelligent and understanding
adult trained for the work, he will establish better relationships in everyday
contacts than if left to his own devices. Such opportunities help him to
understand the meaning of his experiences revealing to him the inevitability
of cause and effect. These experiences begin his induction into the larger
community life. The smaller community of the home expands to the larger
community of the nursery, the kindergarten, and the church school. For
a few hours a week he may experiment with better ways of getting along with
his peers in situations which make for him a satisfying community experience. The wise church will parallel these experiences with comparable
learning experiences for the parents. Consistency must be established in
handling the child and helping him to interpret his experiences so that he
may continue to learn religiously in his home during the intervening days.
The church must help parents to see the necessity of continuing religious
education day by day in the home if permanent changes in behavior are
to take place, and if religion is to function in moments of crisis. Parents
need to see that the verbalization which formed so large a part of their
own religious education has failed in most cases to provide either the
impetus to, or the authority for, Christian living today. A look at our
present world situation causes us to doubt the adequacy of the former
methods of teaching religion.

The kindergarten child's community experience will widen again as
he enters the public-school world. There he finds new people, new situations, new experiences. He comes up against many new standards which
cause him to question, and which may cause conflicts in his thinking and
behavior. Constant interpretation must be provided, with opportunities
for him to weigh values in the light of what his religion teaches. For his
religion will be founded upon the values he holds supreme. On those values
he should instinctively make his daily choices. Sunday work in the church
school must be strengthened by better methods of teaching and through
the best materials for its curriculums. Parent education should be continuous. Such education ought to give parents help where they need it, to
meet their growing needs, and to help them to a better understanding of
the program of the church and its teachings. It must challenge them and
impress them with their responsibility as a part of the fellowship.

Since it is possible here to begin some teaching of a slightly formal nature,
we should scrutinize the curriculum of the kindergarten department of the
average church school. What opportunities for community understanding

and appreciation does it give? If we operate on the principles of learning given us through the best educational and psychological research of today, we will look with some disfavor on some of the so-called "units" of study being used in many of our church schools which allow only a few sessions for their development. Understanding of the community and an ultimate assuming of one's responsibility toward it does not come by spending a week or two each on a few obvious helpers like the farmer, the policeman, the postman, or the fireman. A much wider group of workers must be known and appreciated. Longer time needs to be spent in certain areas where interdependence is a vital factor, where the young child may learn to see that we all need each other. His world or community must be enlarged, not merely through the consideration of isolated people for study from week to week, but through an understanding of how we all work together to have concerns for each other. One kindergarten group spent a whole church-school year in a study of people who were involved in helping us obtain our food. Any brief statements given by the teacher were amply enlarged upon by good story material week after week. Opportunities for dramatic play which centered around dozens of experiences were given to the children. These were built around relationships they had had with people who produce food. There were weekday trips to the farm, the grocery store, the dairy. Good visual aids in the form of a few selected slides were used from time to time to make the study more vivid. The children prepared some food for their own consumption so that they might know more about the work involved in the home. Before Christmas they shared in the celebration of Jesus' birthday by making cookies to take to a home for aged couples.

During the past quarter of a century the world of the primary child in our country has enlarged tremendously. To his school experience has been added travel made simple by new methods of locomotion and, obligatory in some cases, by the economic pressures of our culture. The movie and the radio have brought other parts of the world close, and the last war years have given the child vicarious experiences as members of his family and their friends have lived in other parts of the world. Social studies during the primary years in the public school attempt to give the child a better understanding of his more immediate world, the local community. Inclusive as they may seem to be in some communities, they are often rather superficial. They cannot include many of the implications which the religious education program of the alert church will provide if Christian values are to be instilled. It hardly seems sufficient to know some of the problems as they exist in a community or among groups of workers unless one is to go further and consider how these conditions came to be and what may be done to improve them. A plan for improving the undesirable state of affairs must follow. The church should interpret situations in the light of what it believes about Jesus' teachings and life. The ideals held by the church, which have come to it largely through its understanding of Jesus' message, must become more than wishful thinking. If we believe in brotherhood, it must be more than a statement of faith; it must become a living reality, existing between peoples in their daily relationships. For the primary child it is important that he learns more than the fact that there are other people of various races or nationalities. He needs to know other facts which the school may or may not teach. Basic in our religion is a belief in the brotherhood of man under the fatherhood of God. The meaning of the word "brotherhood," with all of its ramifications, needs to be understood in terms of how we treat other people and what concerns we hold for them.

Helping the primary child to an intelligent understanding of community problems in the light of true brotherhood would call for more emphasis on how we as one small group or as individuals are related to the situations we find through observation and research. How are we affected by what goes on in the community day by day? There are roots from our economic setup which go deep into the homes of the community. It is necessary to keep the attention of the primary child close enough to home so that his experiences may be real and so that we may be certain he sees the *meanings* of what he is asked to consider in terms of living realities.

However, there are many problems of more than community significance which should be considered. What happens in one part of our country leaves its mark in many other parts. Once the problem is recognized, suggestions for meeting it should be made. What is it possible or advisable to do under the circumstances? As members of the larger community, how responsible are we? Problems centering around housing, securing of food, provisions for safety on the streets, adequate recreational facilities through well-organized playgrounds, may be close to home for the primary child. He may be affected directly or may know others in the community who are. Other problems centering around work may seem a bit more removed although they are related. One group of children learned about the problems of the miner. Another group learned what it meant to be a migrant. Still others became aware of the conditions under which employees of a local mill worked day after day. Such studies have rarely been made by children, yet the problems they reveal may be understood by the primary-age child. He is old enough to become aware of existing conditions and to form an attitude, if nothing more, about the rights and wrongs of such conditions.

Understanding does not come without adequate time for consideration. A part of each church school year might well be spent in a short-time study of the community and its problems. In ten or twelve weeks a considerable amount might be learned about one problem. If this does not work in, one large block of time during the primary years might be taken for definite community study. This might occur during the church vacation-school period or for as much as half of the church-school year. Some materials at this age level have been published which could be used as guides for such a venture. There is a crying need for more materials of this nature.[1]

Junior boys and girls are practical, realistic, fair-minded. They possess a strong sense of justice. These characteristics enable them to face many of our problems as they are, once they have been presented to them. The social studies of the public schools inform children of problems in various parts of the world. However, little more than factual knowledge is given. The church may build upon this knowledge, interpreting these facts in the light of what we believe about living as brothers and God as the Father, and according to the teachings of Jesus. To the Christian the problem is greater than an apparent inadequacy in our economic planning. It has to do with the worth of an individual in the sight of God and our evaluation of him in society. It should make us determine our responsibility if we are truly working for the kingdom of God. Does it matter how we treat people, how we let them live? Is there any personal or community responsibility if we let people go hungry in a world where there is plenty; if we let people die of disease when there is information and means to prevent it; if well-qualified people cannot find an opportunity to make their contribution to our community living because of the color of their skin?

In a church school where possibilities for religious education throughout the community receive some emphasis, each year a plan similar to that for the primary department might be used in departments in the upper grades. If such a plan has not been in operation, perhaps one of the junior years might be spent in a comprehensive study of what it means to live and work in our country.[2] Such a study should be related quite closely

[1] See Lulu Doyle Baird, *Our Daily Bread* (New York and Nashville: Abingdon-Cokesbury Press, 1937); Florence Martin, *Living in Our Community* (St. Louis: Bethany Press, 1935); Helen Sweet and Sophia Fahs, *Exploring Religion with Eight Year Olds* (New York: Henry Holt & Co., 1930); Esther Freivogel, *All Around the City* (New York: Friendship Press, 1938), *A Primary Teacher's Guide on the City* (*idem*, 1938); Jeanette Perkins Brown, *Joe Lives in the City* (*idem*, 1938). There are other units published by the Friendship Press which have to do with our relationships with others. These should be considered.

[2] See Edna M. Baxter, *Living and Working in Our Country* (New York: Methodist Book Concern, 1938). This study is exceedingly valuable. However, it should be brought to date in the light of changing conditions. New resources are needed. See also Mildred Moody Eakin, *Exploring Our Neighborhood* (New York: Abingdon Press, 1936); Thelma Burdick and Josephine Gifford, *Making a Better Neighborhood* (Boston: Beacon Press, 1935). It is significant to note that no studies have been made in this area, or at least none have been published under church auspices, since 1938. All the resources listed were published from 1935 to 1938.

to the immediate community if facilities are available. However, the problems of the larger community must not be ignored just because their counterpart is not in our own backyards. We are all affected in one way or another by what goes on in areas where fuel is provided, foods are raised or manufactured, and various kinds of equipment are made. Strikes and the problems of organization for co-operative bargaining are always before us and often affect our living more or less vitally.

Bible verses may become alive by an understanding of what they mean in terms of human relationships. If the Bible is to be of value to any growing child, it must be understood in terms of today's living and in terms of the relationships we have with people in modern situations, in terms of the worth we place upon each human being. The junior child is able to grasp some of the implications of the life and teachings of Jesus with better understanding than is the primary-age child. He needs to know more than the *facts* of Jesus' life. He must see what *meanings* the facts of Jesus' life have for us who live two thousand years after he did. The memorization of the Beatitudes must be brought to life by application of their effectiveness in specific situations today. They will have meaning only as they become a part of the living of people; and our living is in and of a community, where the interdependence of people is an indisputable fact.

The youth groups of the church and the church school, beginning with junior-high age and extending through the senior-high departments, offer another foundation on which we may build. Junior children see things realistically. They will be candid with us if given the opportunity. The maturing adolescent becomes more idealistic—longing for a better way of doing things, a better world order. Impractical as some of these ideas may be, they frequently offer a valuable point of departure for the study of improving things as they now are. Youth has a desire to do something about existing conditions which is linked with an idealism sufficient to move mountains if harnessed to that end.

Much of the restlessness of the teen-agers is occasioned by the lack of real work to do.[3] Modern living has become so automatic that there are no chores for the young people to do. Many of our so-called activities for this age group are mere play acting; they are substitutes for the real thing. It is true that the lives of youth are filled with numerous activities which fill their time. However, real work, if sufficiently challenging, can make these activities seem undesirable. Here and there throughout our land there has been a little effort to harness this idealism of youth to their ability to see through and into problems because of their straightforward way of getting at things. Some attempts have been made by public educa-

<hr>

[3] See Howard Mitchell Bell, *Youth Tell Their Story* (Washington: American Council on Education, 1938).

tion. A few have been made by church groups or with the aid of church organizations.[4] While these are but a drop in the bucket, they show what can be done. Once youth have studied the community activities in the way of assets and liabilities, they will have some basis for evaluating the work of their town. They may then plan improvements and changes. Good work experiences for these young people must follow such a study. Work experiences would offer two advantages: They would give the person a chance to identify himself with a problem in a real way, for he would be working to discover facts, to improve conditions. They would satisfy his urge to be a part of a going concern, to be recognized as one whose help is of value in the world of labor. Surely the problems of living in a world only nominally at peace are just as challenging as those in a world at war. Cannot work to make a peaceful world be as thrilling as work to aid a war effort?

The Sunday afternoon or evening programs of the church offer excellent opportunities for such religious education. To accomplish worth-while results, real effort should go into this project. Using only the weekly topics and short-time units of study put out by many of our denominational boards is hardly adequate to give clear insights. Spending a week or even four weeks in considering our responsibility as a citizen, or as a Christian, will not prepare us to be responsible or Christlike. Such short-time study will be of a vicarious nature and will not lead the youth into any firsthand knowledge of the existing conditions about which he is urged to be responsible.

Many a good youth cause has been lost because of lack of understanding or sympathy in the home. This indicates that we need parent education which parallels what is being taught to children and youth all along the way. In many cases the problem is found in the home itself and must be faced there before many changes can occur in the community. Parents must know how to use the home situation as the miniature community. There problems should be faced and solved to train the young people to solve those in the larger community. They must see the community in relation to what it offers youth in the whole process of acculturation. How is the community molding character, and what kind of character is being formed? Will the next generation settle back, cognizant of the problems of our world, yet lethargic in their attempts to meet and conquer them? If the quality of our living is to be improved, we are the ones who must improve it. It can become better only when the character of the people becomes stronger. Character is formed in daily living situations and in the total community, not in any one segment of it. If we fail to

[4] See Jean and Jess Ogden, *Small Communities in Action*. Note especially the chapter "Putting Christianity to Work," the story of the Christian Youth Association in Kingsport, Tennessee.

take advantage of the way in which character is formed, we by implication at least, seem to indicate that the task is not of importance.

There are many things that the church must do for these young people in its program of religious education. We need constantly to press back into the meanings involved. What does a program with such opportunities mean in the light of our Christian heritage? As young people mature physically and mentally, they ought to mature socially and spiritually according to Christian standards, according to values which should be paramount for them, and which should form the basis for their conduct as Christian citizens.

A balance of subject matter is also needed. Long time units of study on the community should occur in right proportion to that which seems, on the surface, to be of a more religious nature—Bible, missions, church history, and so on. Such studies should be pursued for part of each year, so that the young people will not get too far away from a knowledge of the actual situation in which character is formed and in which they grow religiously. While the transcendence of God in the world will be recognized and acknowledged, his immanence needs to be taught and discovered again and again as his activity is seen in the lives of people who plan and work for a better world order. God must be realized in the interaction of people.

It is necessary for us to face the innumerable changes that a community must make to solve its problems, but we must also see what the community has done and what it contributes to our daily living for both our comfort and enrichment. Some appreciation of those who have worked for us in the past should be developed. Our communities are filled with living monuments of their labors. They are rich in what has been given by men and women of vision and consecration. Appreciation and gratitude need to be developed just as surely as the challenge to the present members to be a real part of the on-going work of such a community.

In summary, then, four factors need to be recognized in the consideration of the community as a unit of religious education.

1. The community is a vital force in the molding and building of character and provides learning situations through which the quality of our living may be improved. It must be remembered that the church is a part of the community and as such serves as a part of the control.

2. Closely allied to the first is the understanding of how learning takes place and how behavior is changed. We must understand what is involved in the process of *education* in order that we can see how much more is involved in the process of *religious education,* where so many teachings deal with intangibles.

3. The church should build its religious education program around existing strong points in the community. It should lead existing agencies in

organizing for definite character-building efforts and for improved standards and higher ideals.

4. Better curriculums must be developed and used in the church if the problems of our living are to be solved. Such curriculums must be developed from living situations and may be used as guides for other churches and communities where leadership needs stimulation and help.

SUGGESTIONS FOR FURTHER STUDY

1. Trace the growth of morals and standards of conduct among early peoples. Note ways in which the accepted patterns of behavior become the codes of ethics and religious precepts of the future. See Dewey and Tufts, *Ethics* (New York: Henry Holt & Co., 1938).

2. What changes in the history of our country have tended to set religious education apart from the community and to place it as a responsibility of the church? See V. T. Thayer, *Religion in Public Education* (New York: Viking Press, 1947).

3. How should you help lay leaders in the church to a better understanding of the values to be derived from the community as a unit of religious education? How should you use them to organize and co-ordinate community activities?

4. Do some research on what is being done by groups of people to face the problems of the community as a part of one's responsibility as a Christian. Note what is being done by such groups as the American Friends Service Committee, and Fellowship House in Philadelphia.

5. What evidences are there that the church is working on preventive measures in the field of delinquency?

6. Develop a piece of curriculum for a specific age group and in a definite situation which is designed to help those involved to a better understanding of one problem in a community. Include a workable plan for its alleviation. List definite activities which would give experiences for Christian growth.

BIBLIOGRAPHY

Blackwell, Gordon W. *Toward Community Understanding.* American Childhood Education, 1943.

Dubois, Rachel Davis. *Build Together Americans.* New York: Hinds, Hayden and Eldredge, 1945.

Educational Policies Committee. *Education for All American Youth.* Washington: National Education Association, 1944.

Hanna, Paul. *Youth Serves the Community.* New York: D. Appleton-Century Co., 1936.

Hartshorne, Hugh, *et al. Community Organization in Religious Education.* New Haven: Yale University Press, 1932.

Herriott, Frank. *Christian Youth in Action.* New York: Friendship Press, 1935.

———. *A Community Serves Its Youth.* Montclair, N. J.: Montclair Printing Co., 1933.

Ogden, Jean, and Ogden, Jess. *Small Communities in Action.* New York: Harper & Brothers, 1946.

Watson, Goodwin. *Action for Unity.* New York: Harper & Brothers, 1947.

———. *Youth After Conflict.* New York: Association Press, 1947.

Chapter 27

CAMPS AND SUMMER CONFERENCES

ELIZABETH BROWN

SUCH SIGNIFICANT AND RAPID developments are taking place at this time in the field of camps and summer conferences that it is difficult to prepare a statement that will be applicable for a long period. On the other hand, any volume dealing with Christian education today would be incomplete without consideration of this important phase of the church's program. Moreover the present state of experimentation and change lends interest and presents intriguing possibilities for further exploration.

This chapter is limited to the following questions: What are the nature and function of both camps and summer conferences as related to the larger program of Christian education? What are the differences between camps and conferences? What are some significant trends? What are some basic guiding principles? What are some problems and fields for further exploration in relation to each of these two agencies?

A GLANCE BACKWARD

A historical approach to the subject would make an interesting study within itself. The untiring "circuit rider," the "brush arbor," and the "all-day meeting with dinner on the ground" are all familiar pictures in the panorama of the early church in this country. The traditional camp meeting was not only a significant forerunner of our present church camp and conference program, but it is recognized as an antecedent of the organized camping movement of America.

One type of camp, which antedates the genesis of organized camping as generally accepted, is the religious camp meeting. These gatherings were not always of the "revival" type; quite often their purpose was recreational—a desire to escape from everyday routine for a time and to enjoy the simple life out-of-doors. There was a "boarding tent" for those who wished to share a community table, and a tent or "tabernacle" where the religious programs were carried on. This is folk history, rich in color and interest, and it is also a legitimate part of the history of organized camping.[1]

[1] Robert Rubin, *The Book of Camping* (New York: Association Press, 1949), pp. 2-3.

The organized camping movement of America, however, involves more than simply out-of-door experiences. "Since the time of Moses people have camped out along the banks of streams, by the shore of lakes and in the mountains, but camping as an organized, co-operative way of living, is a comparatively recent movement and is distinctly American in its origin." [2]

Although a variety of camps sponsored by youth-serving agencies and individuals have constituted the organized camping movement of this country for more than half a century, the church was late in entering the field on any broad scale. There are exceptions, such as a camp sponsored as early as 1880 by the Rev. George W. Hinkley for his parish on Gardners Island, Wakefield, Rhode Island, according to Carlos Edgar Ward in *Organized Camping and Progressive Education.*

The Beginning of Youth Summer Conferences. The terms "institutes," "conferences," and "assemblies" have various interpretations in different denominations. Since there is no uniformity in terminology as it relates to specific types of gatherings, use will be made throughout this chapter of the term "summer conference" to designate all such summer meetings for youth and adults. It is recognized that the term "conference" has a wider implication as related to many year-round meetings, but the term "summer conference" is used here in a more limited sense.

With the flourishing of the youth movement in the early years of the new century a summer program for youth developed which was destined to play an important role in Protestantism. Such meetings were known variously as "conferences," "institutes," and "assemblies" and were held at summer-conference grounds such as Lake Chautauqua, which had been in use since 1874 as a summer center for Christian instruction, on college campuses, and at camp-meeting grounds. An example of the latter type was the Des Plaines Institute near Chicago in 1906. "There was some hesitation among the good brothers who controlled the camp ground over letting the young Methodists come on it for any such purpose, and when the lease was finally signed it contained the stipulation that no games or other recreational features should be permitted." [3] The result was an arrangement with a farmer for the use of an adjoining cornfield as a play field.

The purpose of such early meetings was stated in the *Epworth League Handbook* as follows: "While not lacking in spiritual and inspirational features, it should be chiefly a school for face-to-face, heart-to-heart drill in methods of Christian service, in addition to the study of themes which

[2] H. W. Gibson, "The History of Organized Camping," in *Camping Magazine,* January, 1936.

[3] Paul Hutchinson, *The Story of the Epworth League* (New York: The Abingdon Press, 1927), p. 98.

are closely identified with the Epworth League departments, while the fundamentals of such life and work must be emphasized and illustrated."

An interdenominational summer program was started at Lake Geneva, Wisconsin, in 1914 under the direction of the International Sunday School Association. This program has been continued under the International Council of Religious Education.

Although the program at Lake Geneva in 1914 is sometimes referred to as the beginning of the church camping movement, and various denominations have reported camps for seniors and young people through the years, it is generally conceded by denominational leaders that these so-called "camps" were for the most part conferences or institutes held in camping situations.

The summer conference program, both denominational and interdenominational, has taken on tremendous proportions, involving hundreds of thousands of youth and adults each season. As suggested elsewhere in this chapter, however, results must be measured in terms of less tangible but more important criteria than numbers. Recreation not only legitimately takes place within the geographical bounds of the site but is recognized as an important factor in the present-day program of worship, fellowship, study, and service. Young people carry an increasingly larger part in the planning process. The implications of good educational procedures and principles of counseling and group work for the summer conference program are recognized in the training program of the several denominations.

Present Developments in Church Camping. Generally speaking, the church camping movement as we know it today has developed within the past twenty-five years or less. It is an outgrowth of the summer program for youth which has been described but is characterized by the basic elements common to the larger camping movement of America. It seems to have come about in this way: Although the summer conference program was started largely for youth of middle and later teens and often included adults as well, intermediates were gradually included. It soon became apparent that the program was unsuited to these younger boys and girls. The result was the development, by various denominations, of a program specifically for early adolescents. For example: "The period from 1920 to 1930 saw a continued growth of the camping movement within the Church of the Brethren. . . . During the period of expansion age-group camping came to have a significant place. Intermediate boys' camps were started in the late twenties with intermediate girls' camps soon following." [4]

Camp Cheonda was developed by the Methodist Episcopal Church South on the outskirts of the Lake Junaluska Assembly ground and opened in 1925 with camping periods for early and middle teen-age boys and girls.

[4] Raymond Peters, *Let's Go Camping* (Elgin: Brethren Publishing House, 1945), p. 15.

Following the prevalent pattern of private and agency camps, there were separate periods for boys and girls respectively. From 1931 to 1941 this camp operated as a training center for camp leaders of the denomination throughout the Southeastern states, with the Cheonda intermediate camp providing a laboratory situation.

Meantime, camps for intermediate or junior-high boys and girls were developing in various parts of the country under the direction of several of the major denominations. These camps were conducted on sites rented from state parks and various other agencies and on church-owned camp and conference grounds. Although some of them started for boys and girls separately, they soon became predominantly coeducational in nature, in keeping with the organizational pattern of the local intermediate or junior-high groups in the various denominational church schools or youth organizations.

Although a relative newcomer in the field of camping, there is one phase in which the church-sponsored camp is pioneering: that of co-ed camping. . . . Such a camping group makes necessary more preparations, more planning, a broader program and above all, a more efficient and able leadership. However, these added responsibilities are more than compensated for by tremendously increased opportunities of service to an age group that gets all too little guidance today.[5]

From the beginning most of these camps followed the prevalent "camping" pattern, with small cabin groups, a trained staff, and a relatively small total attendance; on the other hand, in an effort to meet the eager response of both church and home, camps rapidly multiplied their numbers and in a few instances followed, for a time, something of a "conference" or "institute" pattern of older youth, meeting at conference sites or on college campuses. Generally speaking, however, the intermediate or junior-high camp as it has developed out of experimentation and evaluation marks the beginning of a new agency within the Christian education program of Protestantism.

The movement spread like wildfire—at last the church had found something which "clicked" with the early adolescent boy and girl. The result was not only a rapidly expanding camping program but a stimulation of interest in the junior-high program of the church as a whole. "Perhaps more than any other one factor, camping has dramatically spotlighted the Junior High or Intermediate age youth—those 'younger youth' who are so often forgotten or lost in the shadow of the older group. Camping has helped to reveal to church, home, and society some of the amazing potentialities wrapped up in these awkward 'tween-teens.' "[6]

[5] Clifford Dahlin, *Church-Sponsored Camping* (Minneapolis: Lutheran Augustana Synod, 1947), p. 4.

[6] *Intermediate Camps* (Dayton: Evangelical United Brethren Church, 1949-50), p. 6.

Although camping has a peculiar appeal for the adventuresome early adolescent, the church camping program of today and of the future is not confined to any age group. For several years some denominations have provided camps for junior boys and girls, and the day camping movement of the church which is just emerging is particularly suitable to these younger boys and girls—a day camp is held at a site within easy transportation distance of one or more local churches. Boys and girls go home each night and usually have breakfast and the evening meal at home. The duration is from ten days to a period of several weeks.

In addition to the widespread "conference" type of program described above for seniors, young people, and adults, a variety of camping experiences is in the picture for the future including trip camps, week-end camps, work camps, hostels, and family camps. The church, as well as other agencies, has experienced within the past few years an unprecedented period of expansion in physical facilities. Many new camp sites are being developed, and various improvements are being made on existing sites. Although some sites are being developed as conference centers and will serve the needs of both camps and conferences, camping needs are being taken into account. For example, on some of the larger conference grounds of several hundred acres areas designated specifically for camping are being developed. On some sites one of the most attractive areas is being reserved for pioneer camping and for future development.

In spite of the rapid development it is evident that the camping program of the church is only in its infancy. The program of the future will center increasingly in the local church and community. Such a program will not displace but supplement the present program now projected on sites which serve a larger territory, such as a presbytery, conference, or district. Simple camping facilities, probably starting with a day-camp location, will be developed co-operatively by several local churches within a community and will be used by small groups throughout the year. Or community sites will be developed and used co-operatively with other agencies. Many large churches will come to think of a camp site as a normal part of its plant for Christian education work. Many of the new sites for district, conference, and area use will have a group of buildings constructed for year-round use by local church groups.

THE DIFFERENCE BETWEEN A CAMP AND A CONFERENCE

It has been pointed out that the term "summer conference" is used in this chapter to apply to a variety of summer meetings for seniors, youth, and adults, such as conferences, assemblies, and institutes, and that these latter terms have different connotations for various denominations. The common purpose, however, is for training, enrichment, and fellowship.

Basic elements are worship, recreation, study, counseling, and service projects including an emphasis on world friendship. Conferences are held on college campuses, assembly grounds, conference centers, and camp sites. Many leaders feel that a college campus is preferable to a camp site for the holding of a summer conference which emphasizes training.

A camp sponsored by the church has been described as

an actual twenty-four hours a day experience of Christian group-living in the outdoors, shared by campers and counselors alike. In this unique camp community the tools of living become people, nature everywhere about you, the common experiences of the day, the heritage of your camp, your Bible, the skills you find in your hands—all these and many more! Camp is not just the absence of school and chores. Camping is an opportunty for living at its best.[7]

The characteristic elements that, blended together in the right proportion, constitute an organized camp include (1) persons, (2) outdoor life, (3) living in groups, (4) a camp community, (5) leadership and conditions designed to satisfy personal needs and interests and to stimulate wholesome personal, social, and spiritual development. The program of the organized camp consists of the experiences that are *indigenous to group living in the out-of-door setting.* This distinguishes an organized camp from a conference, institute, convalescent home, athletic, or other type of program that may be conducted in an outdoor or "camp" setting. The process of living together in groups out of doors is the major content of the camp "curriculum"—not discussion, instruction, training, or recreation imported in the outdoor setting.[8]

Thus the problem for seniors, youth and adults is, not one of deciding between a camp and a conference because one is better than the other, but rather of recognizing the inherent values in each and utilizing which-ever best meets the needs of a group at a particular time. For example, one denominational bulletin describes types of summer opportunities suitable for young adults including week-end conferences, workshops, conference-wide assemblies, and camps, and offers the following suggestion:

The conference council . . . should take the initiative in developing the plans for a summer conference-wide meeting. They should review leadership needs of the young adults in their conference on the basis of the developments that have taken place in the last year. They should explore problems such as these: What helps do these persons need? What type of meeting will best train these persons? What activities and experiences will give Christian motivation to the aims we seek? What major emphases should be made?[9]

[7] Rodney Britton, *Adventuring into Friendship* (Philadelphia: Judson Press, 1948), p. 6.

[8] Hedley Dimock, ed., *Administration of the Modern Camps* (New York: Association Press, 1948), p. 22. See also Betty Lyle, *Camping—What Is It?* (American Camping Association).

[9] Robert Clemmons, *Planning Summer Conferences with Young Adults* (Nashville: General Board of Education, The Methodist Church, 1948).

It would be unfortunate if camping suddenly should be substituted for the present summer conference program. Training, which is an important element in the summer conference, is an essential part of the year-round program for seniors, youth, and adults. It may be provided, of course, other than in the summer agency.

A camp for a group from a single local church or from several neighboring churches usually is preferable to a camp serving a wide territory, since the temptation in the latter is to enroll too large a group. Intriguing possibilites are week-end camps, trip camps, family camps, day camps for boys and girls, work camps for youth and adults, involving not only work on the grounds and the equipment but also a program of worship, recreation, and fellowship.

Camps rather than summer conferences are suitable for boys and girls of intermediate age and younger. Training should be for adult leaders rather than for the boys and girls themselves. The importance of carry-over values from camp into the local church is recognized. Such results are an outgrowth of informal experiences of doing and living in camp rather than of the type of training which is appropriate to older groups.

The interaction of camps and conferences is evident. It has been pointed out that the camp stemmed to an extent from the conference program. As the church-sponsored camp, in turn, developed a distinct pattern in harmony with the contemporary organized camping movement, certain values became apparent. Some of these have been incorporated into conference programs—and rightfully so. Examples are: an increased emphasis on counseling, recognition of small-group experiences as contrasted to the mass approach of the early conference program in some denominations, utilization of group-work procedures, recognition of the implications of "community" in the everyday life of the group, importance attached to incidental learning and a concept of program which includes the total camp day rather than a few segregated experiences such as "classes," "worship services," and the like.

The paragraphs which follow further interpret the camp and conference programs and suggest some basic guiding principles. Space does not permit attention to details of administration, program and standards. These are dealt with in other books and manuals, some of which are listed in the Bibliography.

Some Unique Values in Camping[10]

Camp leaders often express surprise at the ease and rapidity with which changes come in the lives of campers. The camp affords continuity of

---

[10] Adapted from the leaflet *Camping in the Program of Christian Education* (Nashville: Methodist Board of Education), in which I collaborated.

experience in a controlled environment. Countless opportunities for learning by doing are written into the very nature of camping. Likewise, in camp learning through experience is speeded up because of the camper's readiness to learn. This camper readiness is assured.

In their zeal to take full advantage of the situation leaders often overcrowd the program. But the camp is only a part of the larger Christian education program. Some things can be learned best in a local church situation; others can be taught more meaningfully in camp.

The following are factors in camping which present unique opportunities for learning:

1. Camping affords a laboratory for Christian living. The meaning of the teachings of Jesus may be made real in hour-by-hour life situations. Ability to live as Christians is tested and interpreted in the lives of both leaders and campers in the variety of everyday experiences and relationships.

A camp in which there is a conscious effort to establish a Christian environment with provision for effective individual and small-group guidance offers unique opportunities for Christian growth and for each camper to take the next step in his personal religious growth.

2. Camping is living out of doors. Camping means more than for Johnny to come home with a list of twenty-three trees which he has identified at camp. It is an opportunity to awaken within the camper a sense of wonder, a chance to make real to him the meaning of God's laws at work in the natural world.

Aware of God's creative power in the physical universe, the camper not only is awakened to his responsibility for conserving natural resources for mankind, but may be inspired to work with God in his ever unfolding purposes for human beings. Camping opens new doors to wholesome interests and lifelong hobbies, a welcome antidote today to artificial and deadening varieties of commercialized recreation.

3. Camp affords experiences away from home. Many young campers make rapid strides in the achievement of self-reliance and dependability through such simple experiences as looking after their own things, doing their part in cabin duties, and getting to places at the right time.

4. Camp provides a means for deepening and expanding Christian fellowship. Camping is a natural for fostering Christian fellowship within a group as responsibilities are shared and as they work, play, and worship together. When members of a local church group go camping together, this fellowship, once established, undergirds the ongoing program in their church.

5. Camp makes possible an experience in democratic living. Implicit in camping are many experiences in small groups. In cabin groups, quest and discovery groups, and committees campers and leaders together undertake and carry through activities which they recognize as significant to the life

of the camp community. Thus camping affords the best laboratory we know for democracy.

Quest groups for intermediates and discovery groups for juniors refer to a plan whereby campers and leaders divide into several groups for exploration of some problem or phase of Christian living appropriate to a camp situation. There is a central theme with subdivisions. The quest or discovery groups are not limited to one period such as a class but may find expression in various ways. There is purposeful participation on the part of campers through research, reading, committee activities, discussion, evaluation, and the employment of such mediums as nature lore, drama, music, crafts, and the like for sharing with the larger group. Resources are the out of doors, the leaders, the Bible, and other selected printed materials.

Likewise camping may provide a climate which encourages mutual understanding and appreciations between campers, not only of different races and nationalities, but of varying social and economic backgrounds. Camp leaders today hold in their hands a mighty potential for the development of world community as concepts of democracy come alive in day-by-day group experiences in the camp community. Leaders concerned with Christian values may make of camp an experience in group living on a Christian level—a Christian community in action.

Summer Conferences—What Kind?

Each season we listen to enthusiastic reports of summer conferences telling of joyous good times, expanded horizons, and deepened Christian convictions. In the months that follow many local youth groups take on life as new ideas find hands and feet. Only the years can tell the story of some decisions affecting human relationships, lifework, problems, and covenants with God.

But we need also to reflect upon less glowing reports which would scarcely be chosen for promotional material in next year's folder.

What makes the difference? How may we more fully realize the potential values in the summer conference program? Too often we have measured results in terms of numbers. The questions below will be helpful in the evaluation of your summer conference program.

1. Were objectives clearly defined? List evidences of progress or failures in achieving them.

2. Were leaders chosen from the standpoint of their adaptability and willingness to participate in the total program rather than from the standpoint of contributing at a few "spots" such as classes or worship?

3. Was there provision for youth participation in preliminary planning as well as day-by-day procedures? (In situations where a denominational

youth organization is functioning in the territory to be served, the summer conference may be one of the projects in the year-round program, the adult advisors working in their usual capacity.)

4. Was there understanding of responsibilities on the part of leaders? What training or other means were used such as correspondence, bulletins, suggested books, bibliographies? Was there a preliminary joint meeting of the staff and youth council?

5. Were there democratic procedures in the day-by-day program as well as in preliminary planning? Organizational structure does not guarantee democracy. Some tests are: Was there mutual trust between youth and adult leaders? Was there respect for all persons irrespective of color, economic background, profession, or position in the conference? Was there a sense of responsibility as well as initiative and purposeful participation on the part of individuals and small groups, for example in committees or interest groups functioning during the conference?

6. Were there adequate preregistration and registration plans? Was attendance limited to an effective number? Was there overcrowding in sleeping quarters? Dining room? Sanitary facilities (one shower to ten to fifteen persons; one lavatory and one toilet to each ten persons)? Classrooms and other program space?

7. Was there complete understanding (written agreement recommended) with the management as to: fees; condition of grounds and buildings at opening and closing; bedding to be furnished; daily cleaning of buildings, including toilet facilities; trash disposal; use of health center, first-aid materials, recreational equipment; fire insurance; minimum sanitary and health requirements; and so on?

8. Did the dining-room situation contribute to health and to a relaxed, happy atmosphere? Was the food adequate and attractive? Was there a plan of table service initiated at the opening meal by having hosts and hostesses instructed and assigned to each table? Was there absence of boisterous and outmoded "We-Are-Table-Number-One" songs?

9. Was there time in the daily schedule and on the closing day for putting grounds and buildings in order? Was there a plan and an understanding of specific responsibilities? Were grounds and facilities left in as good or better condition than found?

10. Was there, on the part of both adults and youth, a recognition of the implications of Christian citizenship in the conference "community" such as co-operation in matters of schedule, rest hours, and so on?

11. Did counseling arise naturally out of co-operative living and work between adult leaders and youth, or were "counseling periods" set aside which seemed artificial and unrelated to the rest of the program?

12. Was specific help given through classes, experimentation, committees,

and counseling for more effective Christian living and work in the church, home, and community?

13. Were health and safety measures observed in the total program? Water-front safety regulations? Fire protection? Adequate sleep (nine hours, seniors; eight hours, older youth and adults)? Adequate food? Registered nurse on grounds? Pure water supply? Insurance (health and accident protection, also comprehensive liability)? Sanitary condition of buildings and grounds?

14. Was the co-operation of the local church encouraged? Was promotion adequate? Was it attractive, and did it accurately interpret the program to pastors, parents, and adult workers as well as to young people? Were there follow-up efforts?

Interdenominational Co-operation

It is significant that in the early days of camping for intermediates and juniors, there was sharing of experiences and materials through the respective age-group committees of the International Council of Religious Education.

A nation-wide "Conference on Camps and Conferences" at Toledo, in the fall of 1946 marked a milestone in interdenominational co-operation. Eighteen denominations participated as well as official representatives from many youth-serving agencies of the nation. As an outgrowth of this conference work is going forward on printed materials, visual-education helps, leadership courses, study conferences, and training conferences dealing with specific aspects of both camps and conferences.

Relation of Church Camping to the Larger Camping Movement

Church-camp leaders have profited by the hard-earned experiences of leaders of many types of camps through the years. They now have many opportunities to contribute to the larger camping movement of America. The American Camping Association represents, from an organizational standpoint, the camping movement in America. There is no such organization or movement in which "summer conference" leaders find a place.

Generally speaking there is evidence among camp leaders of America today of a concern for spiritual values in the camping program. This is significant at a time when public-school camping is on the increase, and when colleges and universities are including courses in their curriculums. Church-camp leaders should be ready, not only to give leadership at such points as worship, but to help in developing a philosophy in which spiritual values are recognized and integrated into the larger camping movement.

The church can help by maintaining high standards in its own camp program. Church-camp leaders are encouraged to co-operate with other camp leaders, beginning on a community basis. On a national level there is a co-operating relationship between the Committee on Camps and Conferences of the International Council of Religious Education and the Church Relations Committee of the American Camping Association. The latter is interfaith in its membership.

SUGGESTIONS FOR FURTHER STUDY

1. What opportunities do you see in camp for counseling with individuals and small groups? (See Chapter 15; also resource materials on camping. Illustrate in terms of camper experiences.)

2. A church in an industrial area is considering a day camp for its junior children. Provision already is being made for juniors in the annual vacation school. Would you advise both? Why, or why not? (Read Chapter 21; also resource materials on day camping in the Bibliography of this chapter.)

3. What values and possibilities do you see for day camping in a small town with three or four churches of different denominations? List the requisites. Outline various possibilities for an interdenominational or community approach. (See Chapter 26; also day-camping resource materials of this chapter.)

4. A promotional folder is needed for a camp. Make a list of items which should be included. What purposes should such a folder serve? List.

5. Thousands of leaders are working each season in church-sponsored camps. What types of training should be provided? What training opportunities do you know of already available? (See Chapters 16 and 31.)

6. Several hundred colleges and universities are now offering courses in camping. To what extent are such courses needed in departments of religious education in church colleges and universities? What are some related courses which are helpful? With what specific aspects of camping should a camping course deal? (See Chapter 28.)

7. Evaluate a specific summer conference, indicating whether you were there as a leader or young person. List the positive and negative reactions in separate columns.

8. What are the implications of the present discovery and quest group approach to camping for juniors and intermediates, respectively? For the senior and older-youth camps of the future? How will the latter differ from summer conferences?

9. What procedures would you suggest for evaluating a church-sponsored camp? List some questions or measuring rods for evaluation. Reread the section "Some Unique Values in Camping."

10. What uses can you see of the Bible and other resources of our religious heritage in an informal camp situation? Illustrate. Make a list of basic resource materials for an intermediate camp. In the light of the section "Some Unique Values in Camping," with what areas of experience should we seek primarily to deal in camp as related to the year-round Christian education for a given age group?

11. What are some values to church-camp leaders in meetings and co-operative training efforts with camp leaders of other agencies? What contributions might be made? What aspects of training might be done co-operatively? What aspects separately for church as well as other agencies?

12. What are the implications of the rapid spread in the camping movement for world community?

BIBLIOGRAPHY

Although some of the materials listed in this limited Bibliography are applicable both to conferences and camps, many are designed for camp leaders only. Few such helps are available for conference leaders, since there is no movement beyond the church comparable to the camping movement. Many of the books listed elsewhere in this volume, such as those dealing with the laws of learning, group work, and counseling will be helpful. Bibliographies and current program helps, standards, lists of suggested courses for conference, camp quest and discovery group materials, and the like may be requested from your denominational headquarters and from the International Council of Religious Education, 206 South Michigan Avenue, Chicago 4, Illinois.

ADMINISTRATION AND LEADERSHIP

Baxter, Bernice, and Cassidy, Rosalind. *Group Experience—the Democratic Way.* New York: Association Press, 1945.

Carlson, Reynold. *Day Camping for Your Church.* Philadelphia: Judson Press, 1948.

Dimock, Hedley, ed. *Administration of the Modern Camp.* New York: Association Press, 1948.

Graham, Abbie. *Working at Play in Summer Camps.* New York: Woman's Press, 1941.

Going Camping with Junior High Boys and Girls. Chicago: International Council of Religious Education, 1944, rev. ed. 1949.

Jobe, Mabel. *The Handbook of Day Camping.* New York: Association Press, 1949.

Lyle, Betty. *Camping—What Is It?* Chicago: American Camping Association, 1947.

Marks of Good Camping. Published for American Camping Association. New York: Association Press, 1941.

Ott, Elmer. *So You Want to Be a Camp Counselor.* New York: Association Press, 1946.

When Juniors Go Camping. Chicago: International Council of Religious Education, 1947.

CAMPCRAFT, NATURE LORE, AND GAMES

Carlson, Reynold. *Nature Lore Manual.* New York and Nashville: Abingdon-Cokesbury Press, 1945.

Downer, Marion. *Discovering Design.* New York: Lothrop, Lee & Shepard Co., 1947.

Hammett, Catherine. *Campcraft ABC's.* Girl Scouts, Inc., 155 E. 44th St., New York, N. Y., 1941.

Program Helps for Camp Leaders. Pleasantville, N. Y.: Rafter Crafters, 1947.

Stevens, Bertha. *How Miracles Abound.* Philadelphia: Judson Press, 1941.

Vinal, William. *Nature Recreation.* New York: McGraw-Hill Book Co., 1940.

HEALTH AND SAFETY

Is Your Camp Protected Against Accident? Chicago: American Camping Association, 1941.

Kaiser, Clifford. *Group Feeding*. New York: McGraw-Hill Book Co., 1946.
Safety-Wise. New York: Girl Scouts, Inc., 1945. Catalogue No. 19-502.
Suggested Standards for Camp Nursing. Chicago: American Camping Association, 1944.

SOME OTHER PROGRAM HELPS

Harbin, E. O. *Fun Encyclopedia*. New York and Nashville: Abingdon-Cokesbury Press, 1940.
Pease, Dorothy. *Altars Under the Sky*. New York and Nashville: Abingdon-Cokesbury Press, 1942.
Sawyer, Ruth. *The Way of the Storyteller*. New York: Viking Press, 1942.
Smith, H. Augustine, ed. *The New Hymnal for American Youth*. New York: Fleming H. Revell Co., 1930. For intermediates, seniors, young people.

Chapter 28

RELIGIOUS EDUCATION IN CHURCH COLLEGES AND THEOLOGICAL SCHOOLS

EDWARD R. BARTLETT

TYPICAL OF THE PURPOSES for which many of the Protestant church colleges in America were founded is this statement appearing in the *DePauw University Bulletin*, taken from the Indiana Conference report of 1832.

Deeming, next to the religion of the Son of God, the lights of science best calculated to lessen human woe and to increase the sum of human happiness, and having learned from observation and information that, where superior schools and colleges are neglected, ordinary schools are almost universally in a languid state, and many persons live and die without any education, we, therefore, report that a seminary or college, under good literary and moral regulations, would be of incalculable benefit to our people, and recommend the establishment of such an institution.

While the establishment of higher education in New England prior to the Revolutionary War was specifically related to the preparation of ministers, and subsequently of men for other professions,[1] here is evidence that early in the nineteenth century denominationally established colleges were to serve the broad purpose of enriching community life through education in the arts and sciences as well as in religion.

In carrying out their objective in education the denominations have exercised varying degrees of control of the institutions. In one group may be placed those who believe that "the mission of the Christian Church through higher education is an integral and strategic phase of her missionary enterprise."[2] Usually direct supervision of the staff appointments, curriculums, extracurricular life, and public relations on the part of the denomination through official representation is to be found.

A second group comprises the major number of church-related colleges. These do not "undertake to offer even elective courses which interpret the peculiar doctrine of the denominations to which the colleges are related.

[1] See Samuel Brown, *The Secularization of American Education* (New York: Columbia University Press, 1912), chap. 1.

[2] J. Arthur Heck, "The Church in Higher Education," *Christian Education*, June, 1939, p. 370.

They do not teach creeds. The sectarian spirit largely has been eliminated." [3] Expressed positively, they regard themselves as engaged in liberal education defined as "not a training for a specific skill [but] the living of life itself. Education in this sense is harmony with nature and with God. [It includes] worship which teaches the spirituality implicit in the mainsprings of life and being." [4] These schools have denominational affiliation with little direct supervision of the academic program by the denomination.

Some institutions founded under denominational auspices subsequently have passed from any administrative relationship with the Church. Economic crises sometimes have induced this change, new benefactors, whether individuals or corporations, having made severence of denominational bonds the condition of granting their support. In most cases curricular offerings in the field of religion have not been reduced.

But whether to develop professional religious leaders, to fulfill the missionary responsibility of the Church, or to provide a liberal education constituted the motivation for their establishment, church-related colleges in the twentieth century only with difficulty have maintained their religious orientation. Among the reasons for this fact are:

1. The rise of tax-supported institutions of higher education, whose curriculums were oriented to science and economics rather than to religion, offering strong competition for students.

2. The establishment of standards for degree-granting institutions in terms of amount of endowment, buildings and equipment, size and adequacy of library, education and experience of the faculty. Although it was not necessarily true that colleges having their curriculums organized about religious interests and values would fail to qualify, frequently schools which relied upon denominational support were unable to meet even the minimum standards.

3. Expansion of the curriculum to include courses demanded by the changing industrial and social order, together with the growth of the "elective" system in arranging students' programs of study. Not only did religious courses suffer from comparison with "practical" offerings, but the concept of a basic liberal education which controlled the earlier classical curriculum, with religion as an integral part, was no longer widely accepted.

4. Finally, the fact that few courses in religion were in the curriculums of teacher-training and graduate schools, from which the faculties of the church-related colleges must be secured. While few institutions would require that staff members be recruited from a given denomination, it is

[3] Robert Kelley, *The American College and the Social Order* (New York: Macmillan Co., 1940), p. 267.

[4] *Coe College Courier* (Cedar Rapids) March, 1948, pp. 23-24.

reasonable to expect that a staff of a Christian college have some grounding in the content of the Christian religion. Lacking this, colleges in which the faculty exercises considerable power in shaping the curriculum probably will fail to provide for objectives that are much different from those of state-controlled schools.

This last consideration raises the question of how a "religious" objective differs from the other objectives of a college curriculum.[5]

Recently, marked attention has been given to social values in describing the functions of higher education. First among the basic outcomes listed by the President's Commission on Higher Education is this: "To develop for the regulation of one's personal and civic life a code of behavior based on ethical principles consistent with democratic ideals." Commenting on this purpose the report continues: "Many colleges have tended in recent decades to concern themselves with the intellect alone. They have left to other agencies or to chance the students' spiritual and ethical development." [6]

If this is viewed as one of the aims of educational institutions generally, the question whether a "religious" objective is held solely by the church college is indeed pertinent. Dean Frank G. Lankard of Brothers College of Drew University, a denominational institution, points out the distinction:

> We regard religion as being so vital and creative in democracy and culture that we want our entire educational program to be carried forward in an atmosphere which is friendly to and surcharged by vital and creative religious ideals. We conceive of our entire program as a reverent search after truth in a setting where a vital religious faith is recognized as being the greatest motivation to the highest and noblest living.[7]

Where this objective is accepted, religion is not represented primarily by a regular series of courses, whether directed toward exploration or indoctrination, but it is the frame of reference from which the entire curriculum derives meaning. Under this concept the curriculum of the church-related college is oriented to religion quite as definitely as in the eighteenth century, when church colleges were assuming the task of higher education for this nation. It is also manifestly organized around an order of value which differs from that about which the state or secular institution plans its curriculum.

[5] See Harrison Elliott, "Religion in Higher Education—a Syllabus," *Religious Education*, January-February, 1942, pp. 12 ff.

[6] "Establishing the Goals," in *Higher Education for American Democracy* (Washington: Government Printing Office, 1947), I, 50.

[7] In C. F. Sitterly, ed., *The Building of Drew University* (Cincinnati: Methodist Book Concern, 1938), p. 234.

Objectives of College Religious Education

As interpreted in this chapter, religious education includes all offerings in religion, academic and extracurricular, since these are intended: "(1) to guide students in discovering an orderly, ethical, purposeful pattern which undergirds experience, and, (2) to develop insights and skills which will aid students in creating a more nearly Christian social order." [8]

Among the purposes to be served by the academic courses are the following: (1) Providing a factual background in the field of religion which in substance and scholarship is comparable to that available in other disciplines; (2) assisting the student to develop a Christian philosophy of life through the interpretation of biblical and other religious source materials; (3) developing interests and skills which will make effective laymen in the church and community to which the college graduate goes; (4) laying the foundation for subsequent graduate study on the part of those planning to enter Christian vocations professionally.

It should be noted that course work alone will not enable a college to meet the obligation to the denomination of which it is a part. The role of the administrative officer in determining the extent to which religion is at the center of the curriculum cannot be too strongly emphasized. The attitude may be expressed in published statements. More important is the record of day-by-day decisions in matters of policy and program. When the record indicates a concern for religious values in contrast to strictly secular considerations, the entire program of religious education is strengthened.

Describing the modern campus scene, Arthur L. Frederick lists the following provisions for the religious orientation of college students in addition to the academic program: (1) Campus-wide organizations, such as the Council on Religious Life, the Young Men's Christian Association, and the Young Women's Christian Association, whose programs may be inter-denominational, may follow a general institutional pattern, or may be developed out of specifically local needs; (2) the college chapel, attendance being voluntary or required, the program conforming to a service of worship or following the plan of a general assembly; (3) the Religious Emphasis Week, with speakers brought in to vitalize campus religious life; (4) student organizations, national or local in sponsorship, conducted on a denominational basis and more or less closely related to the work of the churches in the community. Favorable or unfavorable attitudes of faculty members toward religion, expressed in classroom or in informal groups, are noted as having a marked bearing upon students' religious interests. Student

[8] See Bartlett, "What College Graduates Should Know About Religion," *Christian Education,* October, 1941, pp. 39-46.

experience in these various relationships should aid in developing standards of values essential to effective living.[9]

COURSES IN RELIGION

Religious education as an academic discipline may be defined as courses which provide the theory and techniques necessary to understanding the processes by which human relationships may be modified in accord with religious values. Usually such courses are regarded as presenting a "practical" approach to religion as distinguished from the philosophical, historical, or aesthetic approach. Such a distinction, however, appears to be artificial when personality is regarded from the organismic point of view, since theory and skills become intermingled in the outcomes of behavior.

In a survey of thirty-five liberal arts colleges of The Methodist Church in 1932 "an astounding variety, both in the areas of the field which are covered and also in the nomenclature of the courses themselves," was discovered, indicating that little agreement existed as to what constitutes the subject matter of courses in religion. Probably little more of a concensus would be found today. F. W. Reeves and others reported that seven eighths of the course titles were not duplicated in the catalogues of more than two colleges, and only six titles were common to more than one fourth of the colleges. These are: history of religion, Old Testament history, philosophy of religion, life and teachings of Jesus, psychology of religion, and curriculum of religious education.[10]

A similar problem of classification was noted by Gould Wickey and Ruth Eckhart in their survey in 1935 of 768 institutions of higher learning, 334 of which were Protestant church-related colleges. They found 2,388 courses offered in the field of religion by the latter group, the largest number in any one discipline being 11.2 per cent in religious education and the smallest, .9 per cent in apologetics. This survey lists 27 categories, courses most frequently appearing, in second, third, and fourth rank respectively, being Old Testament, 10 per cent; New Testament, 8 per cent; life and teachings of Jesus, 7.5 per cent. All biblical courses together account for 40 per cent of the offerings in religion.[11]

The position of courses in religious education in this survey reflects the shift in emphasis toward a functional concept of education early in this century. Impetus was given this trend by two men prominent in the public-

---

[9] "Religion on the College Campus," in *Religious Education,* July-September, 1941, pp. 145-52.

[10] *The Liberal Arts College* (Chicago: University of Chicago Press, 1932), pp. 204-5, 419-20.

[11] "The National Survey of Courses in Bible and Religion," *Christian Education,* October, 1936, pp. 9-45.

school field, Walter Scott Athearn and George Herbert Betts, as they challenged the teaching of the Bible and other courses in religion simply as a body of factual material.

Support to religious education courses also came from the rapid development of weekday religious education programs in the period 1920-34, with the resulting demand for teachers and from the increased interest of denominational boards in the services of laymen in the local church. Adverse factors since 1935 include the following: (1) release of professional leadership in religious education from local church positions during the depression period of the '30's; (2) preoccupation with curriculums related to national security in the '40's; (3) the absence of a well-defined policy regarding the objectives of departments of religious education and the relation of either departments or courses to the programs of the denominations.

Whether viewed from the standpoint of professional course work or of the orientation of students to religious values, religious education makes a vital contribution to the church-related college program. Indeed, in a recent study, Merrimon Cuninggim well supports his thesis that on the American college scene "secularism is past and administrative responsibility for religion is increasingly being recognized." [12]

ADMINISTRATIVE PROBLEMS

Earlier two underlying aims of the college program in religion were suggested: developing a Christian life philosophy, and developing competency to contribute to a Christian social order. How is the curriculum to be organized and administered to achieve these ends? Among the alternatives confronted are the following:

1. Offering course work in religion in separate or combined departments, or placing emphasis upon the religious approach or content available in all the disciplines. Prevailing practice is to offer religion in departments of Bible, religion, philosophy, philosophy and religion, or religious education. This conforms to the familiar academic pattern but is under criticism because unless courses are required, only a segment of the student body becomes informed in this field.

Recent trends toward general education in the first two college years are producing a restudy of the departmental organization of course work in religion with a view to securing a closer integration of religion with the other disciplines and a more adequate appreciation of the place of religion on the part of a larger number of students.

One modification of this approach is the proposal made by the curriculum committee of the National Protestant Council on Higher Education that

[12] *The College Seeks Religion* (New Haven: Yale University Press, 1947), p. 3.

departments of economics be provided with data which would make possible a creative Christian appraisal of contemporary economic theory, practice, and organization. Elsewhere comes the suggestion that since Jeans, Eddington, and other physical scientists make a religious interpretation of the universe basic to their technical treatment of phenomena, these underlying concepts become a part of the offerings in the division of science.

2. Requiring the study of religion or making all courses in the field elective. The study made by Wickey and Eckhart reports required courses in 82.2 per cent of the 334 Protestant institutions, and among a dozen reasons advanced in support of the requirement states: "Students need the knowledge obtained in such courses, which would not be elected if not required, because of pressure from professional schools, other departments and the spirit of the age." Although the figures are not comparable, Cuninggim reports that 149 church-related and independent colleges out of 702 institutions listed in *American Colleges and Universities*, 1940 edition, require courses in religion for graduation, comprising 60.3 per cent of those possessing departments of religion. Acknowledging the difficulties met in prescribing such courses for all students, he concludes that "as long as the study of religion is altogether elective, the college will not be taking seriously its desire that religious illiteracy be abolished." [18]

3. Back of these and other problems is the question whether the purpose of the college in the field of religion is to prepare professional and lay leadership or to be primarily concerned with the religious basis of students' lives. If the former, stress will be placed upon separate departmental organization, courses which develop skills as well as those providing a foundation in theory, a continuing study of the needs of churches and other areas in which religious vocations are found, and the criteria by which professional and lay leadership is to be evaluated. If the cultural aim predominates, attempts will be made to discover the religious content and implications of each of the academic disciplines, to provide opportunity for extracurricular experience in church and campus projects in religious activities, to encourage through lecture, discussion groups, and other means the development on the part of each student of a life philosophy based upon religious considerations. Whichever is chosen, in the majority of situations both types of religious education probably will be made available.

AIMS OF THEOLOGICAL EDUCATION

The aims of theological education vary in accord with the ecclesiastical and doctrinal character of the denomination to which the school is responsible. Broadly expressed, while most communions have a body of beliefs,

[18] *Ibid.*, appendix iii, pp. 280, 305.

practices, customs, and forms of worship which each seeks to perpetuate, some place greater emphasis than others do upon indoctrination, defined as the propagation of approved ways of thinking and acting. The minister who is being educated is, from this point of view, one who seeks the acceptance of those beliefs and practices supported by the authority of his church.

A different approach is that which is primarily concerned with bringing persons and groups to establish standards of conduct, concepts of value, and goals of living in the light of the Christian tradition. Education for the ministry under this concept will place greater stress upon the modification of present social institutions and the techniques by which the resources of the Christian faith may be brought to bear upon individual and social growth.

Whichever of these emphases appears to be primary in the seminary program, both have the ultimate purpose of developing a professional leadership for the parish ministry or some specialized phase of Christian service.

It is becoming apparent, however, that a graduate school of religion has an additional obligation similar to that of schools of engineering or medicine. Not only must students become qualified as general practitioners or as specialists, but the relation between established truths and new situations must be explored, principles developed to take account of newly discovered physical and social data. Research is essential in theological education, not only in such fields as textual criticism, church history, or psychology of religion, but also in the role of Christianity in economic, intercultural, and other aspects of human relationships.

From the Edinburgh Conference came the suggestion that "theological colleges or seminaries . . . should make provision in the curriculum for instruction of the future ministry in all that pertains to the drawing together of the various Christian communions [including] instruction in the doctrines . . . of other communions." [14] Chairs of church history, liturgics, symbolics, and missions should deal with the history and work of all branches of Christendom. The merit of the conference recommendation is clear in view of the shifting political and cultural boundaries in the twentieth century. But churches today need to be aware, not only of those of other denominations, but even more of a world oriented to secular considerations. To understand the forces now at work, and to bring about a new alignment in which the goals of Christianity determine a nation's course requires something beside grounding in the tradition of one or more denominations.

The opinion-poll approach to determining the aims of seminary education is employed in a study of the seminaries in the Northern Baptist

[14] Leonard Hodgson, ed., *The Second World Conference on Faith and Order* (New York: The Macmillan Company, 1938), p. 336.

Convention by Hugh Hartshorne and Milton Froyd. Assuming that "the theological curriculum is either an accidental accumulation of courses or it is based on definite ideas regarding the job for which it is supposed to prepare," they asked a representative group of 411 ministers two questions which would indicate what the seminaries' aims should be. The questions were (1) What are the responsibilities of the local church? (2) What are the tasks of the minister?

The four statements regarding the local church obligations upon which there was closest agreement were:

1. To reach the unchurched with religious education and evangelism
2. To provide opportunities for public worship for all ages
3. To constitute itself a Christian community of old and young, providing for all the opportunity to share in creative Christian living as a group through sharing of responsibility and control of the life and work of the church
4. To adjust its program to the specialized needs of the community as rural, industrial, foreign, suburban, et cetera

Among the possible tasks of the minister in aiding churches to fulfill their responsibilities, the one on which there was closest agreement being listed first, are the following:

1. Bringing persons to Christ and to personal commitment to the will of God as disclosed in Christ
2. Getting people to support the world mission of the church
3. Helping parents to build Christian homes and provide Christian nurture for their children
4. Providing education in the beliefs and practices of the Christian faith
5. Developing faith in God and in the resources of the universe [15]

Here is a promising basis for a sharper definition of purpose by schools of theology. Analysis of needs which ministers must meet, of services they must render, and of the nature of the knowledge and skills necessary to effective performance of these tasks will bring the curriculums into much closer relation to current living.

A Functional Approach to Curriculum Building

In the past theological education has been more directly concerned with the dissemination of bodies of information and mastery of this material than with the development of competence in making spiritual values effective in human behavior. This emphasis upon knowledge, as differentiated from knowledge in relation to goals of human endeavor, has characterized

[15] *Theological Education in the Northern Baptist Convention. A Survey,* pp. 33, 36, 38.

liberal arts education in general, to which education for the ministry has been closely related. The criticism made by Hartshorne and Froyd that "basically the theological curriculum is a liberal arts curriculum with some trade school practices added" [16] is essentially sound.

It is understandable that in some quarters there is no disposition to change the existing pattern of courses, save to adopt techniques from clinical psychology, social group work, and other fields which may contribute to practical theology. The aims of some denominations are best achieved in this pattern. Elsewhere a genuine effort to integrate the so-called applied courses and the content courses is evident. The point of view is well expressed in a report presented by Frank Grebe to the American Association of Theological Schools in its 1948 biennial meeting.

Training in the various aspects of the ministry should, in the judgment of the Joint Committee, be of a kind which will develop both understanding of what is to be done and competence in carrying on their function . . . . Knowledge of the practical work of the ministry will not result in competency however if mastered theoretically apart from its actual use. Competency cannot be assured unless knowledge and its uses, theory and practice, are firmly interrelated.[17]

THE PRESENT CURRICULUM

Organized in various divisional patterns, the theological curriculum today includes the following fields: the Hebrew-Christian revelation (Old Testament and New Testament), theology and philosophy, church history, comparative religion and missions, practical theology (homiletics, worship, pastoral work, evangelism), religious education and psychology, Christian and social ethics.

An analysis of the offerings in seminaries of the Northern Baptist Convention reveals that

the pattern . . . reflects the aim in emphasizing traditional subject matter (58.6 per cent) and practical theology (19.1 per cent) which with religious education and psychology (13.6 per cent) comes to 32.7 per cent. The expressed aim of social information, however, is represented by only 3.8 per cent of the offerings and the aim of understanding human nature and its remaking is represented by only a small part of the 13.6 per cent assigned to religious education and psychology.[18]

In a period when economic and political issues depend so greatly upon world understanding, these seminaries present "other religions and missions

---

[16] *Ibid.*, p. 214.

[17] "The Training of the Minister as Teacher," *Sixteenth Biennial Meeting of the American Association of Theological Schools, Bulletin 18,* June, 1948, pp. 125-33.

[18] Quoted in Hartshorne and Froyd, *op. cit.*, p. 179.

in 4.9 per cent of the total courses." Probably these figures reflect the current situation in most of the schools of theology in this country.

Progress is evident, however, in relating classroom work to contemporary life. Some schools require from one summer to an entire year in a supervised field experience before completion of the three years' course. Catalogues in increasing numbers are listing courses which include rural and urban projects; the introduction of representatives from the areas of politics, agriculture, labor, and management in the discussion of social ethics; and the inclusion of clinical experience in courses on pastoral counseling.

New Demands upon Religious Leadership

Traditionally "the ministry" has meant the pulpit and pastoral ministry. With the multiplication of specialized forms of service in the Protestant Church it would seem desirable to speak of "ministries"; and after providing a common background for all forms of professional religious work, to make provision for such specialization as the following vocations, among others, might require: educational ministers, including directors of religious education, age-group specialists for denominational and interdenominational work, and teachers in religious fields in colleges and training schools; ministers of music, whose technical preparation in composition and in instrumental and choral music would be basic to the theological-school program; pastoral ministers, with specialization in rural work, industrial relations, military chaplaincy, minority-group services, institutional service, including prison, mental hospital, and juvenile delinquents' school chaplaincies; missionaries; writers and journalists for various forms of mass communication, press, radio, and screen, and also for production of denominational literature.

Not only must the parish minister be able to preach effectively, to develop an educational institution, to organize a congregation for fellowship and philanthropy; but increasingly his church is recognized for what it is, a civic institution concerned with the interests of the public schools, business and industry, the civic and social life of the community. The effect of this is to lay upon the seminary the need for discovering ways by which the vitality of the Christian religion may be communicated through the mechanisms of community organization. Unless this is accomplished, the congregation will tend to fulfill its religious obligations within the orbit of its fellowship and to have little effect upon the economic and social developments of the community.

Trends in Religious Education in College and Seminary

The inclusion within a single chapter of the fields of college and theological school is itself indicative of an important trend. The religious maturity of layman and minister alike is today viewed as the outcome of a continuing process in which educational programs at each academic level contribute to progressive understanding and maturity. The insistence on the part of theological schools on the fact that preprofessional undergraduate work should not include courses in religion is changing to concern that orientation to religion, as to science, philosophy, and other disciplines, be of such quality as to afford a sound basis for advanced study.

Despite some thirty years' effort to standardize the requirements for professional workers in the church, in particular for directors of religious education, the status and duties of these persons are still not clearly defined. This fact as much as any other is responsible for the varied preprofessional course offerings in church colleges. A number of denominations are providing for conference between field, college, and seminary officers which eventually should result in an integration of leadership education programs.

Another trend is an increasing interest in bringing the techniques of research to bear upon questions such as these: What are the factors in personality and preparation which make for success in the pastoral and other ministries? How are basic and related needs in church and community being met by ministers, and to what extent are college and seminary curriculums concerned with these needs?

Finally, a confused social order needs to know its spiritual resources and their bearing upon the practical problems of daily living. An increasing sensitiveness on the part of educational institutions to their obligation to develop persons possessing this essential knowledge and skill is evident.

SUGGESTIONS FOR FURTHER STUDY

1. Compare the purpose for which the institution with which you are most familiar was established with the aims of two other colleges in the same state, state controlled, denominational, or privately supported. Do the different objectives appear to be carried out in the curriculums of each school? What major differences in purpose may be noted?

2. What elements of strength and of weakness are to be found in requiring all students to enroll in courses in Bible or religion? Upon what criteria is your judgment based?

3. How would the religious values existing in the following fields of study best be expressed in a classroom course: English literature, geology, physics, American history, economics, sociology?

4. What forms of guided experience and study should be found in the college program of persons who are to be effective laymen in a local church?

5. If a job analysis were made of the work of an urban or rural minister, what would appear to be the essential fields of study his seminary should provide? By what criteria is this selection made?

6. Based upon evidence in the current press, in what areas of human need do ministers appear to be doing the most effective work? What college and seminary programs will most adequately prepare persons for these services?

BIBLIOGRAPHY

Armentrout, James. *Effectiveness of Presbyterian College Programs in Developing Leadership for Religious Education.* Yale Studies in Religion, No. 10. Philadelphia, 1936.

Calhoun, Robert. *The Place of Religion in Higher Education.* Hazen Pamphlets, No. 2. Haddam, Connecticut: Edward W. Hazen Foundation.

Cuninggim, Merrimon. *The College Seeks Religion.* New Haven: Yale University Press, 1947.

Hartshorne, Hugh, and Froyd, Milton. *Theological Education in the Northern Baptist Convention. A Survey.* Philadelphia: Judson Press, 1945.

Hartshorne, Hugh; Stearns, Helen; and Upham, Willard. *Standards and Trends in Religious Education.* Part II. New Haven: Yale University Press, 1933.

May, Mark, *et al. The Education of American Ministers.* 4 vols. New York: Institute of Social and Religious Research, 1934.

Merriam, Thornton, *et al. Religious Counseling of College Students.* Series IV. Student Personnel Work, No. 4. Washington: American Council on Education, 1943.

Morse, H. N. "The Integration of Education for the Christian Ministry," *The Sixteenth Biennial Meeting of the American Association of Theological Schools, Bulletin 18.* June, 1948. Pp. 93-124.

Shedd, Clarence. "The Movement of Religion in American Higher Education," *Journal of the American Association of Collegiate Registrars,* October, 1945.

———. *Proposals for Religion in Postwar Higher Education.* Hazen Pamphlets, No. 11. Haddam, Connecticut: Edward W. Hazen Foundation, 1945.

White, Goodrich C. "The Liberal Arts Ideal and the Christian College," *Association of American Colleges Bulletin,* March, 1946.

Chapter 29

RELIGIOUS EDUCATION IN TAX-SUPPORTED COLLEGES AND UNIVERSITIES

EDWARD W. BLAKEMAN

IN THE DEVELOPMENT of higher education in the United States the state-type of college and university arrived late. Harvard College at Cambridge, Massachusetts, was 150 years old before the University of North Carolina at Chapel Hill first taught classes, in 1795. However, the debate out of which the concept emerged was carried on chiefly in Virginia between Thomas Jefferson and others, where Albermarle Academy, predecessor to the University of Virginia, had given courses of instruction before it was absorbed by the University of Virginia at the time of its founding by the state in 1819. The University of Georgia at Athens was chartered in 1785 but did not open its classes until 1801. The University of Michigan at Ann Arbor was not chartered in its present form until Michigan became a state in 1837, though its predecessor, the Catholepistemiad, or center of universal knowledge, had existed in Detroit as the beginning of a public-school system since 1817. Michigan, therefore, was one of the early group. On its central building, Angell Hall, is carved the notable sentence from the Enabling Act of the Northwest Territory: namely, "Religion, Morality, and Knowledge being necessary to good government and the happiness of mankind, schools and the means of education shall forever be encouraged (A.D. 1787)." Today all of the states have state universities or state colleges, or both, or have educational institutions adopted and subsidized by the state.

The support of these institutions traditionally is from taxation, the initial grants having been made in the Morrill Act, passed by Congress in 1862. Each member of that body received thirty thousand acres of land for the establishment of colleges of agriculture and mechanical arts, which institutions were to be started by 1874. This impulse and certain later grants of smaller proportions gave public education a prior right within the participating commonwealths across the entire continent.

THE PROBLEM DEFINED

A fair picture of the curricular status of religion within the tax-supported center of learning can be obtained by reporting upon one large university within each of fifteen representative states. In the state institutions used in the sampling procedure below, courses in religion are part of the liberal arts curriculum, except in Illinois, Iowa, Montana, Texas, and Virginia. There the ecclesiastical bodies supplement the university programs by creating foundations, schools, or Bible chairs in which teaching faculties offer courses and the students taking such courses offer them for "credit" within the university concerned.

CURRICULAR RELIGION IN CERTAIN STATE CENTERS[1]

University	Courses	Hrs.	Affiliated	Courses	Hrs.
U. of California (Berkeley)	17	72			
U. of Colorado	24	65			
U. of Georgia	10	55			
U. of Illinois	5	17	Foundations	12	24
State U. of Iowa			School of Religion	19	68
U. of Kentucky	8	38			
U. of Louisiana	6	24			
U. of Massachusetts	6	21			
U. of Michigan	20	59			
U. of Montana			School of Religion	4	14
U. of Nebraska	16	38			
Col. of The City of N. Y. (A City, not a State U.)	8	27			
Pennsylvania State	17	50			
U. of Texas	12	48	Bible Chairs	12	36
U. of Virginia	3	9	School of Religion	17	49

PATTERNS OF RELIGIOUS EDUCATION IN STATE CENTERS

There are several approaches where state and church converge on the question of religion as an academic subject of study.

1. Religion as a phase of culture is customarily presupposed. Religion by its very nature is an inclusive orientation and therefore calls for treatment by each of the major disciplines—history, literature, philosophy, sociology, and so on. Hence this curricular method aims to give the needed scope to religion. It has the advantage of offering a challenge to the faculty of each department and, eventually, to each professional college to treat religiousness and spiritual experience in its own way. This is the prevailing pattern in state centers. D. D. Parker in a survey[2] conducted in 1946 reported that Ohio State, one of the stronger land-grant colleges which has become a university, offers the "English Bible" in the Department of English, "Crusades and The Reformation" in the History Department, and in the

[1] See Blakeman, "A Realistic View of Religion in State Universities," *Religious Education,* November-December, 1948, p. 356.

[2] "Religion at Land Grant College," *Religious Education,* March-April, 1947, pp. 80-85.

Philosophy Department, eleven courses of specific religious interest. The University of California at Los Angeles offers

Greek New Testament	Medieval Latin Literature
Early Middle Ages	Civilization of Later Middle Ages
Renaissance, Reformation and	The Founding of Christianity
Overseas Expansion	History of Church Music
Oratory Literature	History of Greek Thought
Philosophy of Religion	Medieval Philosophy (Christendom)
Psychology of Religion	

A refinement of the "phase of the culture" plan is used at the four universities—University of Michigan (Ann Arbor), University of Indiana (Bloomington), University of California (Berkeley), and the University of Kentucky (Lexington). These centers list a "Degree Program in Religion and Ethics," or an "Area of Concentration in Religion." A faculty committee to administer this program is drawn from the various departments, but there exists no department of religion, as such.[3]

2. The affiliated college is a second form of administration. In Columbia, Missouri, and Grand Forks, North Dakota, are church colleges especially designed to complement, not to duplicate, the state curriculum. The economy of such a situation was first developed on this continent by the state and church co-operating at the University of Toronto. Certain Christian colleges for many years have enrolled, housed, and taught religion to students who at the same time were enrolled in the provincial university. Like aims are entertained at Columbia and Grand Forks. Exponents of this plan aim to strengthen the state university at its weakest point. At the undergraduate level the plan enables a faith or denomination to enroll its students in the state university for their core curriculum in general education. Duplication is avoided.

The disadvantages are that (a) it divides the academic situation among many controls, tends to place a burden on administration, and raises the question of state-Church entanglement or "establishment"; (b) it relieves the state university of a rightful responsibility for religion, a phase of culture.

3. An interfaith school of religion constitutes a third system. The state university of Iowa at Iowa City has a School of Religion which is now completing its twentieth year. Its director and its Jewish, Catholic, and Protestant faculty are selected and supported by a board of trustees representing the university and the churches. The School of Religion was incorporated in 1928. The articles were revised in 1939 with a clause in Article VI reading as follows:

[3] See "Developing an Indigenous Religious Program at a State University," *Religious Education*, April-June, 1941.

provided that in no case shall the number of members representing the University exceed the number representing the religious denominations.

Members of this corporation shall be elected hereafter by the Board of Trustees subject to the approval of the religious denomination or the University, respectively, which they shall represent, said approval to be given in whatever manner the respective denomination or University may decide.

According to Article I in the Articles of Incorporation, the objectives of the school are (a) to provide courses that will help students gain a wholesome view of religion and increase their interest and efficiency in religious activities; (b) to provide graduate courses and advanced degrees for those desiring to qualify for the highest leadership; (c) to create an expectancy for men and women to choose religious callings and to begin their preparation for such work; (d) to assist the churches and synagogues of Iowa in their approach to their own students by making it possible for the Catholics, the Jews, and the Protestants to maintain professorships at the university; (e) to combine the scholarly ideals of the university and the religious ideals of the church so as to produce an atmosphere conducive to faith. Wise leadership, wholesome participation by many faiths, and high-grade teaching for two decades, without having witnessed formal objection before the courts of the state, have brought to this school a steady growth in numbers and influence. In 1947-48 the curriculum was pursued as a whole or in part by twelve hundred different students, the course registration climbing to two thousand. The courses offered at Iowa City are:

Introduction to Religion (2 sem.	Hebrew Language (2 sem.)
Christian Origins (2 sem.)	Jewish History and Literature (2 sem.)
The Protestant Faith (2 sem.)	Life Motive (2 sem.)
Life Problems	Catholic Church from 1500
Religion of Mankind	Little-Known Religious Groups in
American Religious Groups	America
Religion in the Americas	Seminar in Interfaith Relations
Reading in Religion (2 sem.)	Research in Religion (2 sem.)

Now let us move away from this idea which we have called the interfaith school of religion to the next pattern, a pattern which more nearly resembles the church of the average community than it resembles a college. We refer to a plan which stops short of interfaith or interchurch methods.

4. Ecclesiastical foundations offer a plan extensively used. In many state centers, as at the Universities of Illinois, Montana, Texas and Kansas, certain religious bodies have stationed teaching ministers. Each such campus church (faculty-student congregation), located adjacent to the state college or university, has a "Bible chair" or "foundation" incorporated and supported by that ecclesiastical body as the campus agency. Each chair or foundation

offers courses as illustrated in the previous table on *Curricular Religion* on page 366. But the central feature is a church. Campus pastors as well as these religious teachers are chosen and maintained, not by the congregation of the community, but by a board of trustees, the education board at the state level, and the religious body at the general or national level. The development of the ecclesiastical or denominational method of religious education at the state centers is significant, first, because it serves large groups of students according to the tradition concerned, and, second, because it engages church and state in given concrete problems as to the spiritual need of students.

STUDENT PATRONAGE

The task of religious education in state centers as well as in independent and church-related institutions was defined specifically in 1936-37 when the enrollment by religious affiliation was reported in an elaborate survey by Gould Wickey.[4] Another report during the year 1946-47 as part of an extensive study [5] makes a comparison possible. In a given forty-five institutions from twelve states selected to fairly represent both various types of colleges and a widely scattered distribution, the enrollment increased 68 per cent in ten years—48,712 to 82,104. The changes also carry a slight shift in the ratio of student enrollment by denomination.

DENOMINATION AFFILIATIONS IN AMERICAN COLLEGES

	1936-37	*1946-47*
Methodist	18.4%	17.4%
No Preference or No Information	14.7	13.8
Presbyterian	12.5	11.2
Catholic	12.4	13.1
Others	10.9	13.8
Baptist	8.5	8.0
Episcopal	6.9	6.8
Congregational Christian	6.8	5.6
Hebrew	4.6	4.6
Lutheran	4.3	5.7
	100.0%	100.0%

A major issue comes to light here as we ask how well the religious pursue curricular religion, how seriously students concentrate on the intellectual

[4] "A National Survey of the Religious Preference of Students in American Colleges and Universities, 1936-37," *Christian Education*, October, 1937.

[5] See Blakeman, "The Administration of Religion in Universities and Colleges," *Religious Education*, March-April, 1947.

side of religion, and how effectively the religious education serves the whole.

If it is assumed that religious knowledge has a definite value for the culture and the nation, it is fair to conclude that the greater the registration in religion, the more the service to our society. The following table shows what might be expected, namely: In the 200 institutions, the 102 colleges in the three states had 571 course registrations for each 1,000 students. That is, only half took even one course in religion. In the case of the church-related colleges, of which there were 66, we found 985 course registrations in religion per 1,000. However, in the 25 public colleges there were but 84 registrations in religion per 1,000.

Then we found in the junior colleges—71 in all—in these states that there were but 29 registrations in religious courses per 1,000 students. In arriving at these facts the nine church-related junior colleges rose to 530 registrations in this field per 1,000 students; while the public junior colleges—51 in all— dropped to less than one (0.7) registration for every 1,000 students. Therefore, the 58,819 public junior-college students were farther from a religious education by means of courses than students in any other type institution.

CURRICULUM AND STUDENT REGISTRATION IN COURSES OF RELIGION AND COURSES OF RELIGIOUS INTEREST, 207 INSTITUTIONS IN THREE STATES—PENNSYLVANIA, ILLINOIS, AND CALIFORNIA—FOR THE ACADEMIC YEARS 1941-42

Type of Institution	Number	Affiliation	Hours Of- fered	Hours Re- quired	Reli- gious Regis- tration	School Enroll- ment	Religious Registration Per 1,000 Students
University	14	Church-related	800	89	8,872	27,684	320.3
	7	Private	604	1	3,808	45,383	84.6
	6	Public	305	0	1,950	48,015	40.6
Total	27		1,709	90	14,630	121,082	120.9
College	66	Church-related	3,530	546	28,965	29,446	985.2
	11	Private	409	20	4,330	7,707	562.3
	25	Public	119	6	2,109	24,922	84.3
Total	102		4,058	572	35,404	62,075	571.0
Professional and Techn.	7	Private	23	0	101	10,075	10.0
Junior Colleges	9	Church-related	284	41	1,655	3,126	530.4
	11	Private	22	6	30	1,847	16.6
	51	Public	2	0	40	53,846	0.74
Total	71		308	47	1,725	58,819	29.3

RELIGIOUS AGENCIES

Courses and other formal exercises are not the only routes to a religious experience at the student level. Chapels, churches, Bible classes, devotional meetings, Christian group conferences, as well as choirs, deputations, and pastoral leadership offer opportunities to grow religiously.

The faculty and students within the Universities of Virginia and Michigan in 1858, when those state universities were young, created Student Christian Associations.[6] Fostered later by the Young Men's and Young Women's Christian Associations, this movement spread rapidly to other student centers.

On the state campus, either college or university, will be found a central building—home of the Y.M.C.A. and Y.W.C.A., or possibly rooms set aside for their agencies by the institution. An executive secretary or perhaps two —one for the women and the other for the men—will serve the students. This work, being in the control of laymen, is projected and carried forward chiefly by members of the faculty and alumni.

A single paragraph from a recent joint statement of these faculty-student associations sets forth their objectives rather succinctly:

THEREFORE, We seek to find meaning in life through selfless devotion to God,

We seek to understand ourselves through an analysis of our motives and behavior in the light of God's truth, in order that we may conduct ourselves at all times in accordance with His will.

We emphasize the importance of knowing people as people, not just as members of different races or as persons with different backgrounds.

We seek friendship and understanding among people who differ from us in background, culture, belief and experience.

We work for better social and economic conditions to the end that the growth of all persons may be possible.

We seek to use to the fullest the God-given energy and potentiality within us to fulfill these goals to which we have pledged ourselves.

The associations conduct training colleges for secretaries, vast intercollegiate conferences, international assemblies of student leaders, and short-term coaching efforts for lay student leaders. The associations publish some of the most educative literature designed to teach adults and have persistently held their leadership for more than half a century.

Also, the Christian movement, at the time youth are emerging from provincialism, relates each campus group to students at adjoining universities. It also relates them to religious movements across the country. In seeking high ideals they mature by means of Christian hopes, common cause, and concerted action. These associations provide a "field" of activity of real educational significance. Hence an education service of great merit is performed by the religious agency.

The following outline introduces the lines of responsibility which faculty and students have worked out for themselves in the colleges and universities of the Pacific region. The advisory boards from campus to campus confer

[6] C. P. Shedd, *Two Centuries of Student Christian Movement*, pp. 94-100.

once a year, and there is an annual training conference at which faculty and students discuss their religious activity using four major divisions: (*a*) Christian Heritage, (*b*) Personal and Campus Affairs, (*c*) Social Responsibility, (*d*) World Relatedness. The outline will show the lines of responsibility of a voluntary type whereby campus committees assume responsibility and study the dynamic relation of a Christian group to the culture.

THE UNITED STUDENT CHRISTIAN COUNCIL IN THE U.S.A.

Membership in the World's Student Christian Federation

The Annual Meeting delegates are as follows:

STUDENT VOTING DELEGATES:

27 student voting delegates: representing student Y.M.C.A. and Y.W.C.A.

36 representatives of church student movements. At the 1948 meeting these places were allocated as follows: Methodist, 6; Lutheran, 6; Northern Baptist, 4; United Student Fellowship (Congregational Christian, Evangelical and Reformed), 5; Disciples of Christ, 3; Evangelical United Brethren, 1; Episcopal, 4; Presbyterian U.S., 3; and Presbyterian U.S.A., 4.

2 students from the Student Volunteer Movement

2 students from the Interseminary Movement

NONSTUDENT VOTING DELEGATES:

6 faculty and local staff, of which two thirds are to be faculty selected by Y.M.C.A. and Y.W.C.A.

10 faculty and local staff appointed by church movements

18 executive secretaries from the agencies

6 members-at-large selected by the U.S.C.C. Executive Committee U.S.C.C. officers and executive secretary

Chairmen of Standing Committees may be invited to attend the annual Council meeting as voting delegates, if not otherwise provided for.

NONVOTING DELEGATES:

10 local and regional staff may be invited by the executive committee. Some persons who may assist in committee work, or on U.S.C.C. projects as advisers, may also be invited for specific purposes.

The following fraternal delegates are invited without vote: Executive Secretary of the United Christian Youth Movement, Youth Secretary of the American Section of the World Council of Churches, Secretary of the Commission on Recruitment for the Ministry of the Federal Council of Churches, a staff and student representative of the S.C.M. of Canada.[7]

[7] Parker Rossman, *Ecumenical Student Handbook*, p. 108.

GREAT COMMUNIONS ARE ALERT

Inasmuch as each religious denomination finds at the state university or college as many of its sons and daughters as attend its own college in the state, its board of education follows its students to each campus. Thus there has now developed, since the beginnings between 1900-15, a vast network of socio-religious agencies known as chapels, foundations, and campus pastorates, in which students are central. Each unit begins with an aggressive local congregation, a zealous alumni or a farsighted committee in the state concerned. It grows by campus leadership, student loyalty and denominational support. Frequently a subsidy to the campus constituency from the congregations afar, plus support from the parents, becomes the guarantee of a strong campus group and a continuing program for students.

Baptists, Catholics, Congregationalists, Disciples, Episcopalians, Jews, Lutherans, Methodists, Presbyterians, Reformed, and Unitarians have developed specific foundations or educational boards which function parallel to the Student Christian Movement of the Young Men's and Young Women's Christian Associations. Therefore, ecclesiastical bodies through their boards of education create at each state college or university a series of agencies.

These denominational agencies established for religious education are certain to become, in some measure, competitive or at least disconcerting, unless the college or university concerned can assume the obligation of co-ordination. If the university can assign certain socially constructive faculty persons to the boards in control of religious agencies and hold them responsible for an academic conduct of the activities, the work will strengthen faith and complement the tax-supported institution. The Christian associations are sufficiently flexible to receive such faculty advisors, and frequently they become the one solidarity able to express and teach a value system which will challenge growing young scholars.

The Protestant denominations also function in state centers through campus pastors or local pastors specifically subsidized. At its national level the denomination names a university secretary to supervise these student units. This university secretary travels from campus to campus to supervise his campus pastors and to visit the faculty leaders who help students of the denomination in group thinking. Every unit attempts a statement of purpose and program. To illustrate the Protestant objectives, here is the statement published by the Congregational Board in 1945-46.

The *Christian Student Fellowship* of Congregational students is engaged in all of its college and university units in the study and discussion of the following statement:

Believing that we as students have been brought to a watershed of history by the release of nuclear energy,

Believing that the initial use of this energy reveals the inevitable result of secular leadership and power,

Believing that our own heritage, stressing freedom disciplined by fellowship, has a heightened relevance to this new age, and

Believing that now, as always, the Word of God provides life's only guide and power, we affirm our faith:[8]

Then follow five affirmations of God, Christ, the Bible, Church, and the kingdom of God. Thus the students and faculty of one great communion recorded its Christian faith and conviction.

A similar comment might well be made on the Jewish groups. A Jewish writer says:

The American way of life is a definite spiritual outgrowth of the Hebraic-Christian emphasis on the worth of the individual and the challenge of human brotherhood. A vital Jewish and Christian life will help to make democracy work, and what is equally important, will extend its hopes and aspirations to coming generations.

The Hillel Foundations [organized across the nation to serve Jewish students at great centers are] representative of the entire Jewish community. . . . In their creative history of a quarter of a century, the Foundations have provided at least a partial dynamic answer to a question which for many still remains clouded in intellectual dialectics. Hillel, to paraphrase many of our creative Jewish thinkers, believes definitely that Judaism is a "Way of life." Hillel further affirms that to be an effective Jew, one must share and participate in all phases and facts of Jewish heritage.

.   .   .   .

Hillel's basic pattern on the campus is thus truly non-denominational within the framework of Jewish traditions. All Jewish students may belong to and participate in Hillel as their "Jewish home away from home." There are no creedal requirements or subscriptions to a specific pattern of either belief or action. Students come to the Foundation as members of an old, historic group with a sense of a common past, a common fate and a common destiny.

The Jewish calendar itself is the background and framework upon which this year-round Hillel program is built. With the fall High Holydays as a dramatic opening, students are reminded on the very threshold of academic life of the role of the individual in religion. Rosh Hashonoh and Yom Kippur speak of the universal disciplines of judgment, repentance and atonement. Young people in the Holyday liturgy are taught to see life as a training ground for conscience and not merely as a vehicle for material acquisition and educational advancement.[9]

The Newman Club federation functions for Catholic students in four hundred student centers, many of them state colleges and universities. Their national chaplain, Frank McPhillips, writes:

[8] Ralph D. Hyslop, former University Secretary.

[9] Harry Kaplan, "The Hillel Foundation as Educator" (in "Religion at the College Level"), *Religious Education*, March-April, 1947.

With few exceptions they all bear the name "Newman Club," and all have the common purpose of strengthening the Catholic student's faith by providing spiritual, educational, and social advantages. In most large universities there are full-time chaplains assigned to the work, and there is established, in effect, a student parish. In almost all clubs there is a Catholic center of some kind, either a house that is set aside for the use of the students, or the local parish makes some of its facilities available for the students. They are encouraged in the practice of the Faith, and through discussion groups and Religion classes, come to learn a better appreciation of moral and dogmatic teaching.

When each of the several ecclesiastical bodies sends its respective campus pastor—rabbi, priest, or director—to the state campus to shepherd his flock and to make a contribution to the spiritual life of the university, a general federation becomes essential at that university. The Christian associations usually lead in efforts to bring about such correlation.

The United Religious Work developed at Cornell [10] is one of the oldest and strongest centralized agencies. Its building, Barnes Hall, erected by alumni on the University Campus accommodates all official and voluntary religious groups. The pastors as well as the association's staff have offices in this building. An inspiring, vital, spiritual comradeship prevails month after month in this Cornell religious center.[11]

THE ADMINISTRATIVE STRUCTURE

The final and crucial question for the religious educator at a state college or university is upon centrality. Whose task is it to correlate and select goals, to bring about unity of purpose on basic truths, and to administer many programs as one education? Whereas the chaplain and chapel are central at Yale, Princeton, Chicago, or Stanford, and at such colleges as Williams in Massachusetts, Lawrence in Wisconsin, or Texas Christian, a state center officially must get on without that center. The First Amendment to the Constitution, while definitely guaranteeing freedom of worship, likewise restricted the use of public funds for any religious sect. Such disestablishment may have become more thorough than was intended, but the situation so stands. Within the state college or university the staff of the institution alone can assume leadership. How, then, may unity be attained? At Cornell the reply is made by means of the Cornell United Religious Work. This developed, by stretching the former Y.M.C.A. and Y.W.C.A. to dimensions which embrace the Jew and the Catholic as well as all Protestants and others, to perform the function of centrality. An alumni

[10] Cornell is not a state university but an independent one, whose Colleges of Agriculture and Home Economics are subsidized by the state.

[11] M. C. Towner, *Religion in Higher Education* (University of Chicago Press, 1931), pp. 264-84.

board fosters the program, finds the budget, employs the executive officer, owns property, and meets the expenses.

Other efforts to reach an administrative unity and yet to preserve the diversity of the several faiths have been variously attempted. At Ohio State University, a university co-ordinator of religious activities has been named by joint action of the university and the religious agencies.

Also, the University of Minnesota recently created a similar office, reported as follows:

In September, 1947, the Regents of the University of Minnesota voted to create the position of Coordinator of Students' Religious Activities, to become a functioning agency of the Office of the Dean of Students. The position carries with it the faculty rank of associate professor. As a symbol of public interest in this pioneering work, interested churchmen in St. Paul and Minneapolis agreed to contribute to the University sufficient funds to defray the expenses of the program during its first two years. The Dean of Students, acting in cooperation with the directors of religious foundations on campus, selects the coordinator. Functioning as directors of these twenty-one organizations are thirty individuals, nearly all full-time workers, who work cooperatively on the campuses as the Minnesota Councils of Religion. During a typical week of the academic year, more than 150 regularly scheduled meetings, study groups, and worship services are held.[12]

There are five movements of national scope designed to create coherence from university to university, or to conduct training conferences for campus religious leaders and to challenge both educators and churchmen with the religious task before higher education: (*a*) The United Student Christian Council of the United States of America, 347 Madison Avenue, New York City; (*b*) The Commission on Higher Education of the Religious Education Association of the United States and Canada, with headquarters at 20 Jackson Boulevard, Chicago, Illinois; (*c*) The National Council for Religion in Higher Education, 200 Prospect Avenue, New Haven, Connecticut; (*d*) The Edward W. Hazen Foundation, New Haven, Connecticut; and (*e*) The National Association of Chaplains and Directors of Religious Life, 200 Prospect Avenue, New Haven, Connecticut.

SUGGESTIONS FOR FURTHER STUDY

1. What sort of budget should be necessary at a state teachers' college to create a department of religion and to produce lay teachers of religion? Is the institution aimed to be as effective in religion as that college now is in teaching? How should history and literature of religion be taught? What curricular courses? What practice? What supervision? What incentives?

2. In what particulars do the approaches of the faiths and denominations to a state university strengthen or weaken the pattern of campus-wide participation

[12] Henry E. Allen, "Religious Coordinator at Minnesota," *Higher Education*, 5:3, 33.

in religion? Include the three objectives: (*a*) creating a system of values for the whole faculty-student body, (*b*) the function of religion in the culture, and (*c*) the need of spiritual solidarity as a phase of the learning process as well as the ministry to persons and the constituencies involved.

3. How can the features embodied in the three documents (the Bill of Rights enacted by the British Parliament in 1687, the Bill of Rights enacted by the Convention of Virginia in 1776, and the first ten amendments to the United States Constitution) be made specific for the use of an administrator of a public junior college in your own state?

4. What would be the social and religious value to a state university of a completely integrated religious program such as Princeton or Yale can attempt? In that system are chaplain, chapel, curricular studies, a Graduate School in Religion, religious counseling, voluntary Christian associations, dormitory units in religious discussion, churches about the campus, and freedom to use any of the university facilities for religious education groups.

5. Outline a system of religious education performing the following functions to be co-ordinated if the university regents and the ecclesiastical bodies in the state concerned should agree to foster and support a plan:

a) Curricular instruction

b) Research in religious education in arts college, each professional college, graduate school

c) An interfaith center accommodating Jews, Catholics, Protestants, and others

d) A comparative religion enterprise for Eastern faiths

e) Pastoral leadership by each major sect

f) A correlated socio-religious program such as Cornell enjoys

6. What would be the preparation for religious leaders in state colleges and universities in (*a*) the personal characteristics, (*b*) the academic preparation, and (*c*) the professional experience?

7. Outline a plan which would merge religious counseling in the general counseling with a view to the attainment of a more effective therapy.

BIBLIOGRAPHY

Blakeman, Edward W. "Administration of Religion in Universities," *Religious Education*, March-April, 1947.

———. "Developing an Indigenous Religious Program in a State University," *idem*, April-May, 1941, pp. 67-76.

———. "Religion at State Universities," *idem*, April, 1930.

Bond, Charles M. "College Student Attitudes Toward Some Basic Christian Values," *idem*, April-June, 1940.

Brumbaugh, A. J., ed. *American Universities and Colleges.* 5th ed. Washington: American Council on Education, 1948.

Calhoun, Robert L. *The Place of Religion in Higher Education.* Hazen Pamphlet No. 2. New Haven: Edward W. Hazen Foundation, 1942.

Campbell, James M. "The Catholic Contribution to the American College." Roy J. Deferrari, ed., in *Vital Problems of Catholic Education in the United States.*

Cole, Luella. "Moral and Social Attitudes of College Students," in *The Background for College Teaching.* New York: Farrar and Rinehart, 1940. Chap. VII, pp. 169-98.

Cuninggim, Merrimon. *The College Seeks Religion.* New Haven: Yale University Press, 1947.

Elliott, Harrison S. "Syllabus on Religion in Higher Education," *Religious Education,* January, 1942, pp. 5-21.

Hale, Lincoln B., Hartshorne, H., *et al. From School to College.* New Haven: Yale University Press, 1939.

Kaplan, Harry. "The Hillel Foundation as Educator," *Religious Education,* March-April, 1947, pp. 70-73.

Lampe, M. Willard. "Teaching Religion in a State University," *Christian Education,* April, 1938, pp. 219-24.

Nash, Arnold. *The University and the Modern World.* New York: The Macmillan Co., 1944.

Parker, Donald Dean. "Religion at Land Grant Colleges," *Religious Education,* March-April, 1947, pp. 80-85.

"Religion at the College Level" (symposium), *Religious Education,* March-April, 1947, pp. 65-105.

"Religion in Higher Education" (symposium), *Religious Education,* November-December, 1948.

Rogers, Carl A. *Counseling and Psycho-Therapy.* New York: Houghton Mifflin Company, 1942.

Shedd, Clarence. "The Agencies of Religion in Higher Education," *Religious Education,* September-October, 1943, pp. 287-98.

———. *The Church Follows Its Students.* New York: Association Press, 1937.

———. *Two Centuries of Student Christian Movements.* New York: Association Press, 1934.

The State and Sectarian Education. Washington, D. C.: National Education Association, Research Bulletin, Vol. XXIV, No. 1, February, 1946.

Swinton, Roy S. *An Introduction to the Teaching of Engineering Ethics.* Ann Arbor: Edwards Brothers, Inc., 1948.

Van Dusen, Calhoun, and others. *Church and State in the Modern World.* New York: Harper and Brothers, 1937.

PART IV

Directing Religious Education

Chapter 30

THE EDUCATIONAL MINISTRY
OF THE CHURCH

NEVIN C. HARNER

FOR THE PURPOSES of this chapter all the Protestant congregations of America can be divided into two groups: those in which the *pastor* must assume full responsibility for the direction of religious education, and those which employ a *director* of religious education. Unfortunately, these two groups are by no means equal in size. The former outnumber the latter many times over. But the two situations are so markedly different that they must be given separate treatment.

THE MINISTER WHO IS HIS OWN DIRECTOR

This caption fits the case in the overwhelming majority of American churches. The minister is the sole professional full-time servant of the congregation. Aside from the devoted efforts of laymen and laywomen, freely given out of the margins of their time and energy, whatever is done to promote worthy religious education within the parish must be done by him. If he fails to do it, it will remain undone.

The discharge of this major responsibility involves five main functions:

1. He must interpret the privilege and task of religious education to the entire congregation. The rank and file of the membership may not fully realize that the very fact of having their names on a church roll obligates them willy-nilly to the work of Christian nurture; and, as a result, the necessary moral and financial support for a vigorous program of religious education is not forthcoming. Here the minister's part begins. Through occasional sermons he can lay seriously upon their hearts the inescapable duty of every religious fellowship to advance its members—young and old—in the nurture and admonition of the Lord. When church-school teachers and officers stand before the congregation for a service of installation, he can characterize these leaders as being merely the representatives of the whole body for the discharge of a mission which belongs to all. On Children's Day or Youth Day he can point to these immature members of the Christian community as being the church of tomorrow, whose zeal in the future will depend upon what the mature members do in the present. In meetings of officials and in pastoral contacts he can uncover the same vistas—not riding a hobby, but

merely helping people to see what it means to belong to a continuing religious fellowship.

2. He must visualize the congregation's program of religious education as a whole and organize it as a unit. In many churches a great deal of splendid work is carried on within the field of religious education, but in a disorganized and uncorrelated manner. It would seem almost that we may have taken too literally the scriptural injunction not to let our right hand know what our left hand is doing. As a result, some things are done two or three times, while others are not done at all; and a few good people wear themselves out keeping the wheels turning. Here again the minister steps in. He may have to initiate the group process of study and planning which will fit this part to that part, and adapt the whole to the deep needs and high interests of the congregation; and he must help to make the process intelligent and to keep it vital. Normally some sort of clearinghouse is needed to accomplish this result—some board, or council, or cabinet, or committee, of which he is an ex officio member and within which he makes his own distinctive contribution.

3. He must vitalize the major educational agencies within the congregation. We come now to the actual business of religious education, the places where teaching is done and growth takes place. If the several agencies are not living up to their possibilities, someone must step in to bring new life and to introduce new procedures. It may be that a new lesson series is needed, or a program of broader gauge, or the inauguration of audio-visual aids. Very often it is the minister who must provide the initial impetus for the new development; but he does this not alone. Rather he proceeds by welding the active leaders into a creative group who enjoy being together, learn to evaluate their work, and acquaint themselves increasingly with good methods and materials.

Sometimes the minister finds himself stymied in his approach to one or more of these agencies by a long-standing tradition of their independence. Indeed, his overtures may be heartily resented. This is particularly prone to be the case with the Sunday church school. Such a situation requires much tact and patience, a long-term program of educational co-operation with the leaders, and perhaps a gradual change of personnel.

4. He must procure, train, and inspire leaders. No other of the minister's functions in religious education strikes so close to the heart of the matter as this one—the development of an adequate corps of under-shepherds of the flock. There comes to mind the instance of a venerable pastor, who, despite the heavy preaching and pastoral duties incident to a congregation of fifteen hundred members, was concerned over a prospective vacancy in the kindergarten department of his church school and was casting about for someone to fill it. Promising leaders must be found, challenged to devote themselves to the work of religious education, sent to summer camps, trained

in leadership education classes and workers' conferences, and advanced in their leadership from one level of difficulty to another until they are workmen who do not need to be ashamed. Some of this devolves inevitably upon the minister in many churches. And there is nothing to which he can devote his time with a larger expectation of spiritual fruitage.

5. He must participate directly at necessary and strategic places in the program of religious education. All that we have considered thus far is at least one step removed from the persons for whom our religious education efforts exist. It affects them vitally, but through the medium of organizations, plans, and leaders. In addition, the minister who is his own director will find himself again and again taking the final step which brings him into face-to-face contact with individuals and groups. He may be called upon to teach a class in the Sunday church school—although many ministers would prefer to be relieved of this responsibility. In certain denominations he will have a church membership class to teach each year. He may become the official or unofficial counselor of the youth fellowship. It may develop that there will be no vacation church school unless he is the principal or no parents' class unless he is the teacher. Some of these tasks he cannot avoid, and some he would not if he could.

Let us consider the pastor's church-membership class—an institution which is traditional in some communions and only occasional in others. The considerations opposing this practice are, first, the conviction that entrance into full church membership should involve primarily a definitive experience rather than a series of lessons, and, second, the hope that our whole program of Christian education will soon be so adequate in scope and quality that a separate class will be unnecessary. On the other hand, the point can be made that even those who undergo a definite experience need careful study both to prepare the heart for such an experience and to work out its many implications afterwards. Furthermore, even if our total program should become fully adequate—which it is far from being as yet—a pastor may well prize this special opportunity to become intimately acquainted with each oncoming generation of church members and to live his life into their own. At all events, the practice seems to be growing rather than diminishing at the present time.

Do these five functions, taken together, constitute too formidable an assignment? Do they seem to ignore the fact that the average minister has to preach, and to visit his people, and to administer the affairs of his church, and to take part in community activities? They are indeed a heavy assignment. No minister can perform them all in any one period of time. They require adequate seminary training, and hard-won experience, and continuous reading and practice. They may require also some careful budgeting of the minister's time and the maintenance of a proper balance among his various responsibilities. He may, for instance, have to hold only one service a Sunday instead of two, or to limit his involvement in community affairs, in order to do justice to his role of educator. It is a matter of investing time and energy where they will bring the largest results for the church and for the kingdom of God.

The Minister Who Works with a Director

When a director of religious education is added to the staff of a church, the pastor is not thereby relieved of all responsibility in this field. Some burdens are indeed removed from his shoulders, and some obligations from his conscience, because they are being cared for by another person. But as shepherd of the flock he cannot be indifferent to any of the means by which any of his charges, young and old, grow in spiritual grace.

The first function mentioned above—namely, that of interpreting to the congregation its corporate educational duty—still remains in large part. He alone can perform it fully. Unless his precept and example lead the way to a lively sense of educational obligation, the congregation will not follow; and the director will find the ground cut from beneath his feet.

The second function—that of visualizing and organizing the congregational program of religious education as a whole—still needs him. The director may well assume the initiative at this point, as we shall see later. But in most instances the minister is still better qualified than anyone else to see the congregation's life steadily and see it whole. His panoramic view of the present situation and his intimate knowledge of past traditions may often help a board or council to avoid dangerous reefs and anchor finally in an ampler harbor.

As for the other three tasks, he will not have to give them the time which would be demanded if he were proceeding alone; but the contributions he is prepared to make are still essential. For example, when the choice or construction of a new curriculum for the church school is in the offing, his help and guidance may be desired by all. Or when some new undertaking which costs money is under discussion, his support may tip the balance in its favor. Likewise, there are some prospective leaders whom he can challenge more effectively than anyone else; and some workers' conferences or leadership classes which he can teach better than anyone else. And when it comes to direct participation in the teaching-learning process, a minister will scarcely want to give that up entirely—even though he has a paid staff of fifty persons. At the very least, he will want to stand before the children of his congregation on occasions when he can fit best into their life and work—or his young people, or the parents, who so largely shape the homes of the parish. In all these respects he will probably do less than he would otherwise, but what he does is just as invaluable as ever.

Furthermore, something new has been added to his allotted duties—the necessity of working with the director sympathetically and intelligently. The program of a congregation is never twofold; it is always a unity. In closest conference and collaboration the minister and director share their hopes and aspirations for the congregation they serve. The lay leaders, too, enter into this process of conceiving, weighing, and executing plans. When the final result emerges, it is the product of teamwork. The point is that the minister is an essential member of the team. A director expressed in writing not long ago how much it meant to know that the minister was at hand, and on the side of the angels, and ready to talk and to be talked to.

There is one more essential for a smooth-working relationship between pastor and director. Particularly if the director is a man and ordained—but to a lesser degree in any case—a clear-cut understanding of respective spheres of initiative and responsibility is necessary. Otherwise, there will be a borderline area within which misunderstanding and irritation can arise. The minister, therefore, should take pains at the outset to work out with the director a fair, clear, and mutually satisfactory division of labor.

THE EDUCATIONAL APPROACH TO THE MINISTRY

If the basic insights of religious education are true, they are just as true for preaching, and pastoral work, and the conduct of a church-board meeting as they are for the church school and the youth fellowship. People are precisely the same at eleven o'clock on Sunday morning as they are at nine-thirty. They have the same needs, cherish the same interests, grow in the same way. In the broadest and truest sense of the term, there is an educational approach to everything a minister does in the discharge of his high calling.

This does not mean at all that the church service is to be cast in the form of a glorified church-school class, or that pastoral contacts are to be burdened and corrupted with a weight of psychological or pedagogical jargon. Perhaps it means simply that a minister will approach everything he does with persons foremost in his mind, and with a sound understanding of what they are like, and how they develop in the Christian life.

According to this view of the matter, when he comes to the preparation and delivery of a sermon, he will raise a number of person-centered questions in his mind. Who are these people whom he is about to face? How old are they? What perplexities and difficulties are they undergoing? In what are they interested predominantly? What is the exact texture of the course of their day-by-day experiences? At what points should the Christian gospel be fitted to their lives? What do they need primarily in order to move forward in their discipleship? Is it clearer thinking? Or hard facts? Or a clarification of some of the basic realities of the Christian faith? Or a more direct confrontation with God as he has made himself known in Jesus Christ?

To approach preaching in this way is quite different from coming at it primarily in terms of biblical texts, or a set pattern of scriptural lessons, or the books from which the minister has profited recently. All of these will be used faithfully, and the invariable backdrop for the whole process will be the unchanging gospel; but the orientation will be toward living persons whom the preacher names over one by one and desires to serve.

In pastoral work the same questions will arise. The parishioners will stand out boldly as flesh-and-blood individuals—some young, some old; some educated, some well-nigh illiterate; some rich, some poor; some well, some ill; some riding high on the crest of the wave, and some depressed by misfortune, temptation, failure, or disgrace. As he goes to them, or they come to him, he will individualize them in his mind. And the best resources of religion and psychology with which he can equip himself will be mobilized for their benefit and focused upon their respective lives.

Even the conduct of an administrative meeting can be handled in an educational or a noneducational manner. For here, too, persons are involved—both within the meeting and beyond it. The latter may consist of the constituency of this particular church, or certain citizens of the immediate community, or peoples of different race and skin color at the other end of the nation or of the world. Whoever they are, if they are allowed to move silently in and out of the meeting, it will be redeemed from the mere turning of administrative wheels and lifted to a higher plane. As for the people within the meeting, they too are important. Is this coming together an occasion of growth for them? Are they given a chance truly to participate? Are their contributions welcome, even though inconsequential and perhaps ill informed? Are they stimulated to think? Are they given experience in weighing issues and making far-reaching decisions? Do they glimpse increasingly, as the meeting wears on, the larger purposes which are at stake? Do they give themselves in ever-growing measure to these purposes and find happiness in so doing? In short, are they better and abler men and women when they go out than they were when they came in?

This same logic can be applied to the conduct of corporate worship, or the processes of evangelism, or anything else which falls within the purview of a minister's profession. With or without a director a good minister never ceases to be an educator.

THE TASK OF THE DIRECTOR OF RELIGIOUS EDUCATION

It is a significant day for a congregation when it first calls a director to assume primary charge of the more explicitly educative aspects of its work. But in many instances neither the congregation, nor the minister, nor the director is altogether in the clear as to what the new staff member is expected to do. This is especially true in a church's first venture with a director. Just what is his—or her—work? Probably a fair answer can be found in terms of the same five educational functions which have been suggested previously for the minister:

1. He will interpret the privilege and task of religious education to the entire congregation. To be sure, if the relationship with the minister is what it ought to be, the director will not perform this function alone; but much of it will fall to his care. As he gets to know the key members of the church, both in and out of office, he will find occasion to offer them carefully chosen readings dealing with pertinent phases of religious education and the congregation's responsibility for it. Under his guidance children and young people will prepare programs to be given before the whole church body, in which the educational mission of the church is brought forcefully to the attention of all. He will make many talks before various congregational groups and before the congregation itself. He will conduct personal conferences with the lay leaders of the church in which their sense of the educational imperative will be sharpened and refined. And when he visits homes, he will do so as a walking representative and embodiment of the church's educational task. One test of his success at the end of five or ten years is whether or not the members of this religious community are more alive now to their educational responsibility than they were when he came.

2. He will visualize the congregation's program of religious education as a whole, and organize it as a unit. Here the director assumes the leading role. In all probability he will not be the chairman of whatever board or council serves the purpose of unified planning. Rather he will be its guide and inspiration, its resource leader, and its executive officer. His business it is to help this responsible group gather up in mind all the existing organizations or units within the church, note carefully what they are doing for the several age groups, detect overlappings as well as omissions, ferret out points of tension, and lead the way gradually and peaceably toward a more coherent and comprehensive program. One tested device for catching up as many people as possible in this process of study and analysis consists of establishing commissions to study this or that aspect of the total problem, so that the wisdom of all will be drawn upon and the thinking of all enter into the building of the program.

Needless to say, the accomplishment of this task requires a person who is as wise as a serpent and as harmless as a dove. The director must have a clear picture of the general objectives of religious education, and the particular objectives to be pursued within this church during the next few years —without foisting his own conception upon his co-workers. He must be acquainted with what is being done in other congregations—without parading this knowledge overmuch. And above all he must be alive to the vested interests, the hallowed traditions, and the personal likes and dislikes which walk as softly as ghosts through the corridors of the average church, but materialize suddenly and furiously when they are aroused.

3. He will vitalize the major educational agencies within the congregation. Here too the director carries major responsibility. He is a fertile source of suggestions for curriculums, programs, and plans. As the occasion requires, he must come forward with a helpful response to demands ranging all the way from a story to tell in next Sunday's class period to the blueprints for a new educational building. In a meeting of lay workers, he is the catalytic agent in whose presence the group is more closely knit and more educationally effective than it would be without him. In group meetings as well as in individual conferences, he is the incarnation of the faith that something better is yet to be. He is a walking library, a team worker and team inspirer, and a steady antidote to discouragement. In a very real way he is the "alternative to futility."

In the performance of this function the director may not hold any official positions at all within the several educational agencies of the congregation. For example, it is possible that in certain situations he may be elected superintendent of the Sunday church school; but a competent layman should probably occupy this post, if one is available. Similarly, the director may find it necessary to become official counselor to a youth fellowship; but again it is probably better to place a layman in this office, if a suitable one can be found or trained. Precisely because of his tenuous relationship to the ongoing agencies of the church, the director may find his entrance partially blocked into organizations with a strong tradition of independence. For this reason, and also because his basic educational philosophy requires it, he needs to cultivate the difficult art of working with and through people. As he comes to be known, loved, trusted, and respected, some of these obstacles will disappear from his path, and he will be free to live the best that he knows and is into one agency after another.

4. He will procure, train, and inspire leaders. A considerable share of the director's time and energy will be channeled into this task, because in the final analysis the better day in religious education waits not so much upon equipment or programs as upon people. Consequently he will cast about for the most advantageous ways of taking hold at this point. He will be on the lookout for young people and even children who show the promise of leadership and will see to it that they are sent to summer camp and given assignments matched to their growing powers. He will become a personal friend of the leaders now in service. He will probably settle into the responsibility of planning workers' conferences and leading many of them. He will block out classes of leadership education and teach some of them. He will build up a workers' library and—what is more!—try to get it used. Most important of all, he will devote most of the hours when programs are being carried out to the supervision of the leaders of such programs—without ever using

the word "supervision." Rather by friendly interest and demonstrated competence he will earn the role of a second mind and heart at work in every situation of leadership. At first he may have to take the initiative in securing conferences with individual leaders. Ideally in time the leaders will largely seek him out of their own accord.

5. He will participate directly at necessary and strategic places in the program of religious education. For the most part a director of religious education, like all directors, works largely behind the scenes and does not appear at all while the play is in progress. But sometimes he steps out on the stage as an actor. Both the play itself and the director's own life would be impoverished if he did not do so. As has already been implied, he will probably be wise to avoid overloading himself with regular offices and teaching positions. This is scarcely the way for him to make his best contribution; and, besides, laymen and laywomen should be drawn into the work as fully as possible. This principle by no means stands in the way of his becoming superintendent of a vacation church school or teacher of a weekday class in religion. It does raise serious doubts as to the wisdom of his taking a class regularly in the Sunday church school. But there will be many times when he will appear as the leader of a worship service, the director of a recreational program, or the teacher of a group for one session or a unit of several sessions. The pupils need these sporadic but carefully planned contacts with him. He himself needs them for the good of his own soul. And, without being labeled as such, they can become useful demonstrations of materials and methods to the advantage of the lay leadership of the congregation.

PROBLEMS OF THE DIRECTORATE AS A PROFESSION

At the time this is being written, the chief problem is to find enough qualified persons to meet the insistent demand from every quarter. We may venture to hope that the demand will continue unabated, but that the supply will slowly rise to meet it.

Beyond this, there are a number of ambiguities and difficulties which perplex directors as well as their associates. One is the tendency of many churches to request a person who can fill a combination of positions: director and secretary, director and parish visitor, director and organist or choir director. Should this tendency be discouraged or met realistically? How successful can any one person be in combining two different jobs? On the other hand, may it be that this is the only way whereby many congregations can secure a measure of professional direction for their programs of religious education?

Another problem concerns the relationship of the director with the pastor and the congregation. To whom should a director be responsible? To the pastor? To the official board? Or to the congregation itself?

Still another concerns the director's status in the denomination. Unless he is ordained, his standing may be poorly defined. He is neither minister nor layman but something in between. How shall his name be listed in the year-book of the denomination? Shall he have the privileges of voice and vote in denominational gatherings or not?

A final problem is the uncertainty which often surrounds the director's tenure of office. When a financial recession occurs, will the church's first retrenchment consist of scrapping the office which he holds? If the minister leaves for another pastorate, is the director automatically expected to resign also? Or, if his work has been satisfactory, can he anticipate remaining to become the senior staff member of the church?

Difficulties such as these are inevitable in any new profession, and the directorate is no exception. But it is only in proportion as they are solved reasonably well that this relatively new branch of Christian service will attain the stature and render the contribution of which it is capable.

SUGGESTIONS FOR FURTHER STUDY

1. On the basis of the above-mentioned fivefold outline, prepare a detailed job analysis for the religious education activities of the one of the following that interests you most: (*a*) a minister who is his own director, (*b*) a minister who works with a director, (*c*) a director of religious education.

2. Interview a minister or a director of religious education to ascertain: (*a*) his present activities in the field of religious education, (*b*) his proposed activities, (*c*) the chief problems or difficulties he is facing.

3. Outline the seminary training that would best fit a minister for the performance of his religious education tasks.

4. Outline the course of training, undergraduate and graduate, that would fit a director for his profession.

5. Prepare an outline for a sermon which you would regard as being soundly educational, and tell why you regard it as such and wherein it differs from one that is noneducational.

6. Discuss the directorate as a profession—its accomplishments to date, its future prospects, its chief advantages and disadvantages in the eyes of a possible candidate, the qualifications needed to succeed in it, and so on.

BIBLIOGRAPHY

Chave, E. J. *Supervision of Religious Education*. Chicago: The University of Chicago Press, 1931.

Eakin, M. M. *The Pastor and the Children*. New York: The Macmillan Company, 1947.

Edwards, R. H. *A Person-Minded Ministry*. Nashville: Cokesbury Press, 1940.

Harner, N. C. *The Educational Work of the Church*. New York: The Abingdon Press, 1939.

Lindhorst, F. A. *The Minister Teaches Religion*. New York and Nashville: Abingdon-Cokesbury Press, 1945.

McKibben, F. M. *Improving Religious Education Through Supervision.* New York and Nashville: Abingdon Press, 1931.

Munro, H. C. *The Director of Religious Education.* Philadelphia: Westminster Press, 1930.

———. *The Pastor and Religious Education.* New York: Abingdon Press, 1930.

Nelson, J. O., ed. *We Have This Ministry.* New York: Association Press, 1946. Especially chaps. 2, 4, and 11.

Palmer, A. W. *The Minister's Job.* Chicago: Willett, Clark and Co., 1937.

Shaver, E. L. "Directors of Religious Education—a Survey," *Religious Education,* XLI (1946), 345-75; XLII (1947), 3-27.

Smith, H. G. W. *The Pastor at Work in Christian Education.* Philadelphia: Judson Press, 1935.

Chapter 31

THE EDUCATION OF LAY AND PROFESSIONAL RELIGIOUS EDUCATION LEADERS

HERMAN J. SWEET

TRAINING FOR CHRISTIAN SERVICE is an integral part of Christian education. It is Christian education oriented toward a more purposeful and creative sharing of the Christian life. It is Christian nurture with emphasis upon being *and* doing, learning *and* serving, seeking *and* sharing.

Christian education aims to produce persons with a life worth sharing and with the desire to share it. On this foundation leadership training builds the skills for more effective sharing. Christian service training seeks to nurture growing persons in the Christian life, increasing their knowledge of the will of God and of the mind of Christ; deepening their experience; spiritualizing their attitudes, appreciations, hopes, and purposes; and strengthening their faith; with the specific purpose of developing skills in sharing this knowledge and experience creatively with other growing persons. It seeks to put tools in the hands of workers.

Christian service training perceives of the teacher or leader as being himself "within the process." He also is a student and a learner. Only growing persons can help others to grow. Only lives changed and still being changed change other lives. Only those who have known the joy of discovery and continue to find fresh each day the joy of new discovery can open the eyes and stir the souls of others. Therefore, leadership education must help persons to grow themselves. "If it does not happen to the teacher, it will not happen to the class." Hence, there is the futility of merely lecturing teachers on how to use creative methods, and the absurdity of talking about pupil participation in a class where little or no real participation is possible—to persons who are given no opportunity to experience group participation in purposeful learning.

The qualities of good teaching and the creative factors in activities which are desired in work with pupils must be present in the process by which the teacher learns to teach or to conduct activities. "Learning by doing," "experience centered"; these are as valid and necessary in teacher education as in the education of children. And they have their foundation in the experience of the teacher, as well as in his theories about educational procedures. Christian service training should help persons to take those

392

qualities of human living so fruitfully and often unconsciously used—so naturally and intuitively used—in the best parenthood, in creative friendships, and in good neighborliness, over into the class or group where growing persons seek to share their faith, and their knowledge, and their experience of the Christian life with other growing persons.

HISTORICAL BACKGROUND

It may be generalized that the demand for training of leadership in Christian education roughly paralleled the rise of the training for public-school teachers in America. Between 1839-60 twelve state normal schools were established, four of them in Massachusetts. In 1847 the Rev. D. P. Kidder appealed for normal schools for Sabbath school teachers. That appeal was frequently repeated by church leaders in the years following without great response. The struggle for improved Sunday-school curriculums began in the early 1880's and continued throughout the century, issuing in the uniform lessons and the beginnings of grading. This is a story by itself, not to be outlined here, but it did have a bearing on the demand for leadership training. In 1831 *The End and Essence of Sabbath School Training* was published by Crocker and Brewster of Boston. It attacked the memorization system of teaching and proposed improved lesson outlines. In 1839 *The Teacher Taught* was published by the American Sunday School Union. These and other publications had far more to do with simplified outlines of content than with what we would describe as methods today, but they were pointing the way. By 1860 Dr. John H. Vincent of The Methodist Church was persistently calling for teacher education, especially for teachers' institutes such as were being used by the public schools, and he was carrying forward experiments of his own. The first twenty years after the Civil War saw great advances. The uniform lessons were launched in 1873 amidst a great wave of enthusiasm for teacher training; and the Chautauqua movement, which began as a lay-training venture by church leaders, was started in 1874.

These efforts were more largely concerned with content and its organization than with skills in teaching. One might even say that they were efforts to organize and systematize a body of knowledge so as to make it readily handled, or "transmitted," by persons of limited education and little teaching skill. This is not to imply that there was not much good teaching. It might be worthy of secular educators today, with their often overinflated estimates of educational advance, to recognize that in those early years Sunday-school teaching was at least on a par with most public-school teaching and often pioneering in ways that contributed to the advance of public education.

It may be pointed out here parenthetically that whereas these early attempts at improvement were concerned largely with better ways of selecting, organizing, and handling content, there came a time when training was too largely absorbed in methods. The older movement did not make the mistake of contributing to the divorce of education and evangelism, a breech only now being healed. Nor did the early Christian education movement make the mistake of assuming that a person with information and adequate skills could effectively teach the Christian faith regardless of personal experience or commitment.

The Situation Today

With all the development in leadership education in recent years, the need for training is still tremendous. The lag in face of recognized need and tremendous effort is one of the scandals of the church. With the steady secularization of life in America, with millions of children and youth not receiving any systematic religious training, with a large majority of nominally Christian adults virtually illiterate as to the essentials of the faith they profess, the church has scarcely more than dabbled in leadership training. In the face of great progress in secular education the church has talked much and done far less than should have been possible. Whether this lag is due to lack of deep conviction or largely to the volunteer nature of church leadership, one cannot say with conviction. There are well over two million Sunday church-school teachers in the United States. It is estimated that there is one-third turnover each year, making an average tenure of office of three years. The vast majority of these workers have not been reached effectively by anything but the most elementary or informal training if at all. They take up their work without training and often give it up in discouragement.

But there is a brighter side. Concern for better leadership is widespread and deepening. Use of standard leadership courses is again being increased. There is evidence that more and more local churches are making an effort to train their workers. Ministers are coming from seminary with a better appreciation of the value and necessity for a trained lay leadership and with better skill for training that leadership. A wider variety of training methods and techniques is being developed. Boards of Christian education seem to be no longer seeking to meet the popular demand for a curriculum which, as one executive defined it, "can be used effectively by untrained teachers who are unwilling to study, with pupils who are absent 50 per cent of the time," but are rather challenging the churches with the demands of curriculums which can be effectively used only by a consecrated and trained leadership.

There is a renewed emphasis upon the meaning and value of an enlightened lay leadership. Lay movements, especially among men, are noted in many denominations. The training of women in churchmanship is an increasing concern of the great women's organizations of the major denominations, once almost exclusively devoted to missionary endeavor. Protestant youth movements have steadily increased the breadth and effectiveness of their leadership training efforts in terms of the total program of the Church.

TRAINING ON THE JOB

Leadership training is always going on. Wherever persons are creatively engaged in any enterprise, they learn by experience. There is at the disposal of the church not only a vast amount of native ability and talent but a great reservoir of skills that have been developed in everyday vocations. For instance, many public-school teachers and persons who have had public-school experience are serving our Sunday church schools. A large number of parents who have developed teaching and counseling skills in the process of rearing their own families are serving the church. This great potential is used far less effectively than might be for lack of adequate guidance on the job. People learn best by doing. The best possible leadership training is properly supervised experience. In-service training is receiving an increasing amount of attention in the field of secular education, and a considerable literature has been developed. There is evidence that guidance on the job has increased manifold in recent years. Allowing for the great increase in professional and semiprofessional directors of Christian education, and for the increased skills in this regard of many younger ministers, perhaps a still larger factor is in the increase of departmental superintendents. Whereas the general superintendents have been absorbed for the most part in general administration, an increasing number of departmental superintendents are able to guide their teachers in the teaching process.

Still the church is slow in using the well-developed techniques of supervision. Teachers are still left to struggle through without help in lesson planning, without the simplest direction in class or group procedures, and without guidance in finding and using resources. Lethargy and lack of vision are the chief reasons. There is scarcely any excuse for failure to use resources readily available to the church in most communities today.

The *workers' conference* is a time-honored method of leadership development. A vast amount of effort has been expended in an attempt to universalize and improve the workers' conference. Much has been written about it, many leaflets and pamphlets prepared. No one can say what proportion of our churches regularly conduct effective workers' conferences. It is safe to say that a vast number do not. The old "business meeting" still obtains in many places, valuable for fellowship, and perhaps a democratic administrative device, but largely ineffective in improving educational standards or in building morale. The good workers' conference should be a balanced program of fellowship, deep spiritual cultivation, and practical helps for the job to be done. Experimentation in public-school teacher education has shown that people grow most rapidly as they are helped to accomplish more effectively the job immediately before them and to solve present urgent problems.

In recent years there has been a rapid expansion of an effective type of training called the *lesson preview*. These may be quarterly, monthly, or weekly. Workers gather on a local church or area basis for a presentation of the curriculum by experienced leaders. Previews may include a survey of the general plan of the lesson series, a review of the needed resources, specific helps in lesson planning, and a demonstration class session in more or less detail. This type of training is proving to be most effective and should be widely extended. It is especially effective for use by denominations on an area basis in promoting the effective use of their own respective lessons but is also an excellent means of leadership growth in the local church when used either on the weekly, monthly, or quarterly plan. Aimed at the more effective handling of the teaching program immediately at hand, it seems practical to the workers. It promotes advance preparation and the wider use of resources. It makes available to the less experienced the greater training and experience of others in the group. It tends to prevent discouragement and failures on the part of new teachers who do not know how to tackle their job. The preview is, in fact, a short institute directed specifically to the task of improving the teaching of the series of lessons immediately ahead, but it has many by-products and should be greatly extended as a means of training.

The *Standard Leadership Education Curriculum* was developed by the denominations co-operating in the International Council of Religious Education. During the quarter century and more in which the leadership curriculum has evolved, it has performed a notable service. Hundreds of thousands of workers have received some training through the medium of standard courses. It is estimated that nearly three million standard-course credits have been granted; and these probably represent about half of the number of persons who have taken courses, since experience indicates that normally one half or less take the courses for credit. Perhaps the most notable service of the leadership curriculum has been to hold before the church generally the ideal and necessity of a better equipped lay leadership.

The Standard Leadership Curriculum comprises First, Second, and Third Series Courses, leading in various combinations to marks of achievement in the form of Certificates of Progress. Third Series Courses are not widely used. In the First and Second Series there is a total of more than 150 courses, covering the whole range of church work, both in content and method. Courses are approved for inclusion in the standard curriculum through official action of the member denominations acting through the

International Council. Denominations are free to use the courses as they wish while complying with the common policies as to requirements. Denominational leadership education programs range all the way from the few basic courses promoted by some denominations to the more than two hundred courses in the comprehensive program of one major denomination. There is now a tendency among groups in the Council to promote a basic-training program for all workers, consisting of a few selected courses, and to encourage local churches to adopt this minimum standard of basic training.

The interdenominational use of the standard curriculum is administered through the Leadership Education Department of the International Council of Religious Education. After several years of experimentation—beginning with the designation of a First Standard and an Advanced Standard Course in 1910, followed by a three-year training course outlined in 1916-17 and adopted by the International Sunday School Association, on through many changes—the Standard Curriculum of Leadership Education was approved by the Council in 1936 in essentially its present form.

A peak year in number of standard schools under interdenominational auspices was 1936. There were 677 schools accredited, with about 3,000 classes and 35,000 course credits, indicating an enrollment of about 75,000. In the same year the denominations using the standard curriculum granted 120,000 credits. World War II seriously affected leadership schools in both number and enrollment, but a healthy postwar expansion of standard classes and credits is being noted, in spite of the evident expansion of various less formal types of training. Accredited interdenominational leadership schools averaged well over 600 per year for more than ten years prior to 1948. The number of accredited classes under denominational auspices runs into many thousands each year.

Reference should be made here to two systems of accredited training other than the international standard curriculum. One is the highly successful training system of the Southern Baptist Convention. Through their own extensive leadership training curriculum and by means of their training unions, the Southern Baptists have reached hundreds of thousands of leaders. The program has been highly evangelistic and promotional in nature, but it has been steadily improved in methods and materials. It is still highly "book centered." Credit may be obtained by reading a prescribed textbook and answering a set of questions on the reading. Southern Baptists may co-operate in interdenominational schools using the international standard plan but receive credit from their own board only if they read and report on the Southern Baptist text for the corresponding course.

Another leadership training system, in use in nondenominational community schools supported largely by fundamentalist churches, is that of the Evangelical Leadership Training Association. In 1945 the Evangelical

Leadership Training Association claimed more than a hundred accredited schools and employed a full-time executive secretary. The system receives promotional support from the National Association of Evangelicals. It has been the means of providing training opportunities on a community basis to churches which do not readily co-operate in schools under church council auspices.

The *laboratory school*, in which student teachers work with children under careful guidance of experienced instructors, has proved to be a highly effective means of training. Akin to it is the observation-practice school, which is also very effective, and in which workers observe a skilled teacher at work, participate in planning and evaluation, and participate to some extent in the learning activities of the group. Success seems to depend upon the following factors: leadership proficient in teaching adults as well as children, proper selection and preparation of the student teachers or observers, full democratic participation of all in planning and in evaluating the process, a strong spiritual or devotional motivation, and emphasis upon serious study and thorough preparation. Perhaps the best single tribute to the laboratory school is the fact that so many older and experienced teachers point to their first laboratory-school experience as a turning point in their lives, both in personal religious growth and in educational insight and practice.

Dozens of good laboratory and demonstration schools are now held each year, principally in the summer, under both denominational and interdenominational auspices. Some continue for one week, others for two weeks, the two-weeks school being preferable. Laboratory experience is still largely confined to work with children, although some experiments have been made with junior-high and even high-school age groups. Fortunately a high standard seems to have been established for such schools, and they have developed slowly because of scarcity of instructors of proved ability, able both to handle children and to guide adults. It should be kept clear that in the true laboratory school the student teachers actively participate in teaching activities under expert supervision. In the demonstration type students watch the expert teacher at work with the children. In both types participation in the planning and plenty of time for evaluation following each session are highly important.

The designation *workshop* has been applied loosely in recent years to all sorts of conferences, institutes, committee meetings, and other educational activities. However, there are outstanding characteristics of the workshop approach to teacher education as it has been developed by public-school educators and as it is being adapted for use in training church workers.

The workshop gives intensive consideration to practical problems that have arisen from the daily functioning of the teaching job. It seeks to provide flexible and informal working conditions, active sharing by workshoppers in developing plans for individual or group study, and easy access to a wide range of resources—in terms of staff, books, and other aids to learning. The usual schedule consists of meetings of small discussion groups organized around the specific interests; free time for individual work, for conferences, and for recreation; and general meetings and individual work in the evenings. A prominent feature in many workshops is a definite period set aside for informal work in the arts or crafts. It is usual for participants and staff members to make a point of living together and to foster informal contacts of all sorts. A significant consequence of the working plan is that emphasis tends to develop on organic relationships so that participants are stimulated to think in terms of the whole child, the whole curriculum, and the whole situation in which they work, rather than in terms of narrow specialization or isolated functions.

Reading has always been one of the ways of leadership development. There has been a vast production of religious education literature in the Protestant Church in the last twenty-five years. However, the consuming public has been relatively small. Here, as with the training courses, they have not been able to carry over into practice a significant amount of what they have read. In this respect there seems to be considerable improvement in very recent years. Church-school magazines have been improved and the circulation increased. There has been great interest in the development of church libraries and the promotion of reading courses. Several good library manuals are available, and publishers regularly furnish suggested lists of materials for workers' libraries. It must be admitted that much literature designed to help lay workers in the church has been written in terms too academic and professional to meet the need of the average volunteer worker except in guided study, but there has been a vast improvement in this regard in the past ten years.

TRAINING OF GENERAL CHURCH LEADERS

We are in a period of new emphasis upon evangelism and are constantly reminded that the church is far more than an institution or an organization. At the same time there is growing recognition of the fact that the church must use organization and institutional means, and that it ought to do so far more effectively. Many sins have been committed against the true meaning and spirit of the church in the name of efficiency, yet the church must be held accountable for bad stewardship in the wasteful use of time, talents, and material resources for the cause of Christ in the world. Consequently there has been a growing demand for the careful training of church officers and the leaders of all church groups. As an institution subject to the same demands of group life as are secular organizations, the church uses and sometimes exploits the native abilities and acquired skills of church members. It is in transforming these abilities and skills through training and supervision until they achieve the true social purposes and spiritual ends of the church that the church begins to transcend its mere institutionalism.

Officer-training courses are now available in most denominations and are being vigorously promoted. Many churches require all new officers to take some training, at least a course of reading. Development of denominational councils of laymen and of laywomen has been a spur to such training. Schools for the training of leaders in women's work have begun to develop along somewhat broader lines than the older schools of missions which have been of great training value among churchwomen for many years. The idea that the church is simply another institution which can be run by the pooled marginal thought and effort of lay leaders who are immersed in secular pursuits is giving way to a concept of the church as distinctive in mission and method, demanding policies, techniques, standards, and procedures suited to its nature and its mission.

OTHER LEADERSHIP NEEDS

The vast expansion of vacation religious education is a great challenge to the development of leadership. The number of junior and intermediate camps has increased by leaps and bounds. Whereas the camps and conferences may depend quite largely upon volunteers, their success will rest ultimately upon well-trained professional supervision. Where they are well managed by skilled leaders, these camps have proved to be one of the finest mediums for highly effective religious education. We know that the value of youth camps and conferences depends largely upon the quality of adult leadership. We know that we are pressed to find sufficient good leadership now for our existing conferences. The problem will become more insistent unless our training program is enlarged. It is obvious that the demand for vacation-school teachers and leaders will continue to increase rapidly. Here again the church is faced with disappointment in a great opportunity if it is not able to furnish good educational leadership.

In the field of youth work in the local church it is becoming apparent that much more emphasis should have been placed upon the training of adult counselors of youth. In all the years that we have concentrated upon the young people themselves, we have neglected to enlist and train a sufficient number of adult counselors. Consequently, many a youth program in the local church has failed for lack of adult participation.

Another area for leadership that seems to be developing is that of family counseling. The new interest in the Christian family and in adult education has opened up an opportunity for family counseling of which we are not now able to take full advantage.

Perhaps one of the greatest opportunities for Christian education in the Protestant Church today is in the use of volunteer field workers— those people in the community or in the area who are able to furnish expert leadership and guidance to a number of local churches where such leadership is lacking. These volunteer or part-time workers are sufficiently close to the situation in the community or area to furnish an indigenous leadership. Vast numbers of our churches will never be able to employ professional help other than the pastor. The need is urgent for the development of volunteer workers who may be available, under denominational direction, to give assistance to leaders in local churches. Through this method we might revitalize the life of many a local church.

There is also a need for the training of instructors for leaders' classes, for workshops, and for laboratory schools. The demand for tested laboratory-school teachers exceeds the supply, and the demand is growing. Laboratory-school teaching calls for peculiar talents and training under careful guidance. We must intensify our efforts to provide an adequate supply of persons competent for such teaching.

PROFESSIONALLY TRAINED CHURCH WORKERS

There is a great lack of professionally trained workers in the Protestant Church. Directors of Christian education, weekday-school teachers, camp leaders, church social workers, deaconesses, teachers in church schools and church colleges, are not only in short supply but on the whole are inadequately trained. The church has shown less initiative in recruiting and training for the church at home than it has shown in selecting and training missionaries for the foreign field. Whereas the missionary has had status and security to a degree, the professional worker in Christian education has had to confront inadequate recognition, poor salaries, and almost a total absence of job security. A great deal more attention must be paid to the development of professional workers in Christian education. This means, explicitly, that the church must speedily change its traditional pattern so that these workers, mostly women, may have status and security in the church which they do not now enjoy.

One of the most hopeful signs is the development of colleges of Christian education in connection with seminaries, with the full support of denominational bodies. The recruiting of sufficient candidates remains a serious problem but is showing marked improvement. A master's degree in Christian education, based on two or three years of graduate study, is coming to be an accepted standard for local church directors of religious education. However, there are many serving successfully without this amount of training. In 1946 there were approximately twelve hundred full-time directors of Christian education serving local Protestant churches in the United

States. Since then there has been a steady increase. While the demand has drawn some inadequately trained persons into service, the higher salaries and greater acceptance of the profession have attracted persons of training and experience in other fields who are able to serve the church well. It is still uncertain what changing economic conditions might mean for professionally trained directors, but it is not likely that they will be as drastically affected as in the depression of 1930-40. They have a much more secure place in the life of the church today.

CONCLUSION

Given the Protestant principle of volunteer lay service in the church, leadership development will always remain a major problem in Christian education.

We need to understand the dynamic relationship which exists between a vital program which is really meeting human needs and the natural, spontaneous leadership potential thrown up by such a program. The church looks for leadership that can perceive and guide the creative functions by which the family of the church, with spontaneity, but in ordered fashion, brings the riches of Christ and his kingdom to bear on human life. It is no longer a question only of improving the Sunday school, or setting up a new youth program, or launching a program of parent education. It is a question of how to revitalize the total church as a fellowship so that it is redemptive in quality. It has been said that the leadership education problem is a continuous problem, and that is true, but there is an immediate need of gigantic proportions. We must develop an adequate educational philosophy in line with a Christian view of man, which takes full account of modern scientific findings.

SUGGESTIONS FOR FURTHER STUDY

1. Collect a number of denominational leaflets concerning leadership education and evaluate them from the standpoint of effectiveness in motivating lay leaders to seek training.

2. Work out in detail a five-year leadership development program for a local church.

3. Survey the churches of your community to learn what policies and standards are in use in the selection of leaders, what training procedures are carried out, and the apparent relationship between training and program effectiveness.

4. Canvass a selected list of volunteer church workers by questionnaire or preferably by interview to learn what their interest seems to be in obtaining further training and what kind of training they desire.

5. Study the use of audio-visual methods in leadership education in the church.

6. Study the training programs for volunteer leaders as carried on by numerous social agencies, such as Red Cross, Scouts, Y.M. and Y.W.C.A., to see how these

compare with the churches in effectiveness in recruiting, degree of training, turn-over, quality of leaders, and so on.

BIBLIOGRAPHY

Bower, W. C., and Hayward, P. R. *Protestantism Faces Its Educational Task Together*. Chicago: International Council of Religious Education, 1949.

Brown, Arlo Ayres. *A History of Religious Education in Recent Times*. New York: Abingdon Press, 1923. Chap. VI. Contains Bibliography of early training aids.

Educational Bulletins No. 501 and 502. Chicago: I.C.R.E.

The Improvement of Teacher Education. Commission on Teacher Education. Washington, D. C.: American Council on Education, 1946.

Overstreet, H. A., and Wilkinson, Bonaro. *Leaders for Adult Education*. New York: American Council for Adult Education, 1941.

A Philosophy of Leadership Education. Department of Leadership Education. Chicago: I.C.R.E., 1950.

Prall, C. E., and Cushman, C. L. *Teacher Education in Service*. Washington, D. C.: American Council on Education, 1944.

Chapter 32

EXPERIMENTATION AND RESEARCH

ROSS SNYDER

WILLIAM JAMES's *Varieties* remains the classic American study of religious experience. Nothing since has equaled its fruitful combination of reference to the concrete along with striking hypotheses within a general theory. Following James came E. D. Starbuck's study of the conversion experience. He secured 192 documents from individuals whose report was guided by a printed questionnaire. In 1936 Anton Boisen contributed *Exploration of the Inner World*, a story of his own struggle back to an integrated personality, interpreted as essentially a religious struggle. Unfortunately we have few other significant studies of the inner meaning of the religious experience. With the present religious interest in faith and the existential person, combined with a turning in psychology toward the personal, we have new tools and new concern for such studies. In the meantime most research moved in other directions.

A type of study widely quoted in religious education circles of the early 1930's was the Character Education Inquiry. It was a direct study not of religion but rather of character traits—deceit, helpfulness, co-operativeness, persistence, and self-control. Much of the interest in church circles was due to the evidence that there existed no significant correlation between the amount of knowledge of the Bible and high performance in these traits. Today the study would be criticized on its major approach and conclusion. It seems clearer now that these traits are definitions by adult society rather than the kind which function in children's personalities. Further, a study of such traits fails to uncover the fundamental dynamics operating—the concern of present-day psychology. Stealing, for example, is, not a dynamic trait in a child's personality, but rather *a symptom* of some pushes and pulls, fears, anxieties, and goals that exist in the child. The conclusion of the study that behavior is specific to situations is now also questioned. Present interpretation tends toward the hypotheses that a child's behavior is largely a function of the group to which he belongs and is consistent with his own particular motivations and general personality organization.

Ernest Ligon's character project has carried on something of the general-trait theory characteristic of the Character Education Inquiry. However, he combines it with an endeavor to change the character behavior of the children involved. And these assumptions, which were characteristic of various character-education projects in the late 1920's and early 1930's, are in his case enriched by a certain amount of Christian philosophy of life and an enlistment of the parents in the effort to pattern children in the traits set up by the project.

Another endeavor in the general field of study and research of religious growth might be termed the measurement movement. In the latter half of the 1920's many people felt that the day was at hand when the religious growth of a child could be examined scientifically, and that great progress would come because of such measurement. Tests of biblical knowledge were proposed, such as the Northwestern University test and one published by the Westminster Press. Even though these tests came along at the time of a general movement toward the historical interpretation of the Bible, they placed almost all their emphasis upon the testing of isolated facts. They dealt very little with testing the religious insights of the child, and testing the historical understanding necessary to see the biblical message and character in historical context. Perhaps this defect, combined with the depressing evidence revealed by them and their lack of correlation with specific lesson materials, was sufficient to cause the gradual withering away of this movement to measure biblical knowledge.

At the end of the 1920's Ernest Chave worked with L. L. Thurstone to develop attitude scales by which religion could be measured in individuals. Significant among these were the scales of attitudes toward the Church and toward God. These scales never realized the hope and promise of the work that brought them into existence. Part of the difficulty was that the question still remained, "What do you do once this test is administered?" It was not very clear how the results could be used as a basis for action about anything. Secondly, the attitude scales themselves were somewhat ambiguous in revealing what the person really thought and felt about the matter at hand. More recently Ligon has been developing a personality profile of fifty-nine character traits.

Basic Approaches in Future Research

Modern research and experimentation in religious education will probably build itself upon the following six trends in present-day research in personality and group life.

1. We will be concerned with studying the total personality functioning in realistic situations. Some of the most significant insights into the nature of personal life and its reconstruction have come from studying men under stress—in psychotherapy, in group dynamics, tension situations such as industrial and intergroup relations, men in internment and concentration camps, men at war, parents living twenty-four hours a day with children.

At least in the field of religion what is active when men are under stress and strain is what we want to study.

This trend tends to throw out "pink-tea" paper and pencil tests and questionnaires. It recognizes the latter for what they are—illustrations of the verbal behavior of the people being studied.

2. We will study process—that is, something in motion from one point to another. "Immigrant," transition experiences give a chance to see better what is really operating. There is no longer a high regard for what might be thought of as a static, descriptive cross-section study. The height of ambition would be a long-term study of the religious experience and development of a representative sample of people.

3. We will endeavor to understand the dynamics rather than to get a picture of symptoms and external phenomena. To illustrate from the Hartshorne and May study, stealing is a symptom behavior. To establish that a boy steals tells nothing of the motivation. The dynamics of stealing in any specific instance may be, for example, a desire for love, or hostility toward parents and society, or intense desire to be accepted by a group, or a settled image: "This is the kind of person I am." It is these dynamic motivations that we must understand, because it is these with which religion must deal rather than with just the symptoms. To illustrate further, research will be concerned with the meaning and the "why" of a child's learning Bible verses. What function this behavior performs in the self-economy of this child will be considered. In method this concern would seem to lead away from questionnaires and nose-counting into an endeavor to combine a study of behavior with some method of getting below the purely verbal level into the subjective life of the individuals. This trend means studying fewer persons and groups but studying them with deeper penetration. Collecting statistics on the superficial factors in a large population has a place but not a major one.

4. We will study from within the process as a participant servant—and will enlist and train all other participants in co-operative scientific method. Increasingly there is evidence—particularly from the work of Carl Rogers and Kurt Lewin—that the behavior of an individual is always in terms of the situation as *he* sees it, not as some observer sees it. From this follow some interesting conclusions about methods of experimentation and research—particularly in the field of religion.

For one thing, we can no longer say that the external observer knows what the situation is for the child, or anyone else. The situation may be perceived by him, not as one involving deceit, but as a situation in which very unfair demands are made upon him. It is this latter situation, therefore, within which he reacts. No situation or action can be understood except from *within* the internal frame of reference of the experiencing person.

Therefore we need to bring into our observation and analysis of any situation the people involved in it. Their perception of the situation and its effects is necessary for any adequate interpretation and understanding of the experiment.

Further—through sad experience—researches have discovered that it does little good to pile up great amounts of data by external observers. For it is the people who are being studied who must change and act responsibly. It is they who must do something significant about the matter being studied. But only when the people who must act have been involved in study itself—the study is a part of a goal seeking on their part—will the results of the study get into the bloodstream of action and group life. And from studies in learning it is beginning to be seen that the most effective content for any person's learning is the data of his own immediate experience as he looks at it and analyzes it with the help of important ideas. To do this results in more fundamental and personal learning than to study the case records of other people.

We may identify three forms of this type of "research from the inside"—the participant observer, the participant servant, and the self-analyzing group.

Many of our most important insights into personality and its reconstruction have come from participant servants. The psychotherapist's major purpose is to help people in distress, but at the same time he is discovering important ideas about the nature of persons and developing a theory—a total theory about personality and its therapy. The participant-servant research role would be particularly appropriate for the religious leader, who by Christian impulse attempts to understand the internal frame of reference—the self-situation—of each person. As ministers become skilled in pastoral counseling and as the vocation of religious counselor grows, significant data should come from the field of religion.

The self-analyzing group is in some measure an extension of the participant-observer role. The total group, instead of just one participant, is looking at the process of its immediate common life. This is very potent, provided the members are objective and a skilled leader helps in the analysis. The staff of the Group Dynamics Center at the University of Michigan has developed a number of techniques.

5. Instead of starting out just to examine things and to find out what happens, contemporary method often involves first setting down some hypotheses. These are to be subjected to testing. We see if we can predict. This is partly because we are no longer satisfied just with descriptive studies. We are concerned with helping something happen in our world. Also we are clear now that our thinking is always within some assumptions. It is better if these are known. We know also that once we have the data, facts do not speak for themselves; the human mind is always involved in the perceiving and interpreting.

For example, there is no longer so much concern just with determining whether or not people like sermons or what sermon they liked best. It is more important to get a fairly clear-cut hypothesis about what dynamics within sermons and the total situation make for useful sermonizing—for example, that consciously cherished ideals, precisely defined, arise only when contrasting and alien beliefs meet—then try it out and see what happens. In the social sciences the work of Kurt Lewin for group climates stands out as genotype of such experimentation.

6. Finally, the emphasis today in all research and experimentation is upon a team attack. People in the field of religious education need to come together and to map out the most strategic points of attack for experimentation and research, the most strategic ideas and methods to be tested, and where such experimentation could be done. What follows in this chapter is partly aimed toward this goal.

Anyone who studies the activities of the ministers and churches of our country from this standpoint of experimentation and research is struck with the pitiful amount of significant activity. There is not enough original constructive work and scientific study of religion operating in contemporary life. Do we really have a *profession* of religious leadership? Necessary evidence of a profession is that it is vigorously carrying on significant experimentation and research, precise in its design and criteria, communicated in professional journals and in professional meetings. On the whole the professional journals and meetings of people in the field of religion are given over to either exhortation or descriptive statements of what some person is doing. Usually what this person is doing is imitating a general trend, something that he has read about, or frontier work done by another profession. There is very little that can be called experimentation and research in religion. And that which exists is in too many cases unclear about a basic hard-hitting idea and usually limited to the descriptive level. Ministers and directors of religious education today can regain some professional self-respect and standing among other professions if a few discover something significant to be done in advanced experimentation and research; and all of us discover some action research that we can do.

A minimum experience in action research could be one of the disciplines of each seminary's fieldwork department. And what if one requirement for graduation from a theological seminary would be evidence on the would-be minister's part that he had been a responsible agent in someone's conversion experience? Or at least in some enterprise in which people discover the discrepancies between what they think they do and what they do.

Around each seminary and school of religious education we need field studies, clinics, and demonstration centers of new and better ways of doing things with tested evidence to submit. By clinic and demonstration center is meant a church or religious enterprise in which people training for religious leadership could intern, knowing that they would be surrounded by people who know their field and who are doing something significant —just as an intern in a medical clinic knows.

AREAS OF FRONTIER EXPERIMENT

We need the application of the best inventive genius within the church to shape up frontier experiments which will yield knowledge of the approaches just listed and bring new constructive force into the life of the church. These frontier experiments will be action accompanied by the study which will enable us to see what is going on.

1. We will have many diverse projects based upon the family as a unit of religious growth. In most cases they will bring families into a joint partnership with the church, toward the development of self-directing family groups in which all members are learning simultaneously. A central part of such projects will be "boot training" for parents in religious interpersonal relations, in worship, and in theologizing. The nursery school of the Family Life Project at the Glenview Community Church, Glenview, Illinois, would be genotypical of such projects. In co-operation with the Chicago Theological Seminary a plan for twenty-five family groups has been put into operation. One center of the program is a morning nursery school for three- and four-year-olds, meeting six days a week. Only family groups who enroll for the total program are included in the project. The fathers and mothers of the project grow by observation in the nursery school and individual conferences with the director and by working together in two series of parents' meetings each year. The parents' meetings are organized in three sets of sixteen parents, meeting in homes one night a week for a unit of six successive weeks. Observation and study of these various activities are made by the director and include wire recordings of some parent meetings. It is expected shortly to move up through the church school with this design for helping families grow simultaneously in religious faith and functioning.

As more and more people trained in the field of religious education become parents—and as more married students are in our schools—we may expect more firsthand reporting of the Christian family group as it functions in today's world.

2. Another field in which there is such widespread interest that we can confidently expect some important projects is the area of counseling. Perhaps the most significant developments will be in family counseling and group counseling. The project reported above is based upon such assumptions.

In the field of marriage counseling we have now arrived at the point where counseling in regard to physical sex need not be the most important contribution of the minister. Ministers can go on into experimenting with the best ways of counseling in terms of the religious interpretation of the meaning of the marriage relationship. We can study better ways by which people who are looking toward marriage can discover deeper insight into their own meanings of the nature of love, the nature of being a person, the intention of a Christian to live as part of a group. On a long-term basis they can acquire fresh skills in religious interpersonal relations—including handling conflict.

The ability of religion to match itself against the characteristic anxieties, hostilities, and "market personalities" of our culture will be evidenced in individual and group counseling with adults. And the time has arrived when the church must produce something in the field of handling inter-group tensions. We are called upon to develop some project religiously more significant than preaching sermons on the brotherhood of man and the fatherhood of God and exchanging pulpits one Sunday during a year. There have been sufficient psychological studies of the ethnocentric bigot that we may expect the construction of a barometer of bigotry potential, so that we may be able to catch in growing children the beginning of this type of sickness of human personality. But all of this will be of little effectiveness unless we can discover how to deal with the adult bigot; or, even more important, how the church deals with the cults of bigotry. We need records of how in a local church a person with this affliction, or a group of persons so inflicted, are released from their desire to be impervious to other people and to maintain a fictitious superiority.

Now that men of theology are turning their attention to interpreting the process of therapy and counseling we can expect to see some projects which make clear the special religious process in counseling. This may have its clearest application in counseling young people whose major feeling tone is that of the hunted and of meaninglessness. Some counseling education which restores an aliveness and a sense of an open end to life is needed. And measuring ourselves against the popularization of disintegrating sex standards and behavior, we need some careful frontier experiment in the religious interpretation and integration of sex in human life. Preferably these projects will be worked out with young people and with parents.

3. The emergence of Kurt Lewin's theory and the group dynamics movement has opened up a range of possible projects in the life of the church. Man's persistent hunger for intimacy, for thinking through meanings, for being understood by other significant people, can be met by various face-to-face groups within the church. By group is not meant an organization or a collection of people brought together to hear someone talk, but an interacting group of persons—possibly not more than fifteen—who "together are a field of power," for a short or long time. We need

considerable experimenting in fellowship groups, cell groups, instrumental groups, and therapy groups. Growing understanding of group processes and dynamics will make possible new procedures in church committees, conferences, workshops, and camps. Youth groups and Sunday-school classes can study their own functioning as a team and as persons.

To think of the church as an organismic fellowship points immediately to the task central in the fate of a church—growing indigenous leadership. There have now been sufficient experiments in retraining foremen in industry, in retraining recreational leaders and other community leaders, that some confidence of success could be held, if clear-cut projects could be established for lay training. These new leadership-growth projects will have religious depth and will couple the best insights of present education theory with counseling and group-dynamic procedures. Regional workshops and an American equivalent of the Iona Community Center and the Sig Tuna effort on the Continent are further possible experiments and sources of study of the religious growth of adults.

These group tools and experimentation have considerable to suggest what could be done in denominational colleges to prepare college students for future leadership in the church.

4. A major task for experimental research is the whole developmental approach to religion in personal life. Development gradients and maturation patterns of religious growth from birth to old age need to be described. This involves studying the life tasks of each stage of development and the persistent problems of human life as they express themselves in characteristic forms for each age group. The problem is complicated because such a study is always of some *particular* religion. This particularity is escaped only in more general maturation-level tests, such as applying the Dale Readability Formula to determine the school-grade reading difficulty of a story, church-school quarterly, or book.

It is impossible to indicate here even the contours of research necessary for establishing such a picture of life tasks critical in the religious growth throughout life. At present we depend upon general studies of human growth and development. A few hints may show where some of the fruitful fields lie for study in the field of religion.

A critical life task of the first few years of life is the growth of love power and conscience. What goes on in a Christian home that helps this happen well? We need to understand better—all through the life of children—the growth of conscience, which can partly be expressed as what they expect themselves, what they think parents and teachers expect of them, and what will happen when they don't live up to these expectancies. It has been indicated already that the self-concept—that is, a person's feeling and idea about himself—is one of his most precious possessions. It is particularly touchy and vulnerable during adolescence. What is the religious community doing to the self-concept? Recent psychotherapists have pointed to the market personality and failure to find meaning in work as the life-tasks defeats of the adult of our time. A preliminary study opening up the new concern of the church's ministry to old age has been made under the direction of the Department of Pastoral Care of the Federal Council of Churches.

It is very important that the critical points of development be understood by people teaching children in the church school and living with them in the home. If for instance the ages nine to twelve are still mistakenly conceived of as the golden age of memory, then we will treat youngsters quite differently than if we understand that the critical life task during this period is to establish such personal identifications and achievements that a secure status and role among one's peers is possessed.

Whatever study is made must be, not only of such specifics, but within an endeavor to study *religion as a whole*—if such can be done. "Total religion" is dependable trust in a God whose nature is being increasingly understood. Total religion is also the establishing of selfhood and falling in love with it in one's own existence and that of other people. What are the developmental levels of religion thus defined? Also today we will want to study the negative—the anxieties, sins, and sin operative in Christians and non-Christians of all ages. For these must be brought into the open, with something significant done with them, or else any teaching is but a mask behind which these sicknesses go on.

5. Likewise the time is ripe for new and extensive experimentation in communications. We need to establish communication centers, possibly in connection with schools and seminaries, where all of the old and new arts of communication can be assembled into an effective battery of all-out witness by the church. We are but at the threshold of the possibilities of radio and television as a means of communicating the gospel—particularly with planned collaboration of group activity in the local churches. For example, the correlation of a series of radio programs with an effort of the community churches to train leaders in civic righteousness, or a children's television program correlated with the church-school program.

A whole new concept of the resources for teaching in a church school is now upon us. No longer are we limited to a cheaply printed lesson quarterly. The teacher can now expect that the material for teaching any unit will include a movie, a series of radio transcriptions, an excellent reading book, and "comics."

In seminaries we may confidently expect the appointment of teachers who will make the communication of the religious life via mass communications a full-time study. We can have both theory and research going on into how man can preach to the people *not* in the churches of our time, as well as to an assembled congregation. Both will involve discovering how to communicate to the "unconscious" of the listeners.

The church also has a responsibility to the general culture to set up certain criteria by which it can explore the motifs of the comic, the motion picture, the radio and television programs, so that those motifs may be examined for their fundamental effect upon human personality and our possibilities of living together as a democracy in America.

This leads us to certain important experiments in teaching ideas and beliefs. Ideas and faith have reassumed a central importance in religion. For the church and church school of our time we need new vigorous effort at teaching fairly clear-cut ideas and concepts: yet in such a way that they do not leave untouched—in fact, hide—the real motives of the person.

The church is suffering from a lack of self-definition, and of what a Christian is and God is doing. When the role of any group is unclear and when its self-concept is fuzzy, then we can expect no important action from the group. In a study of the Poston Internment Camp, A. H. Leighton found evidence that human groups cannot effectively carry out acts for which they have no underlying systems of belief. In industrial research, Elton Mayo found that workers could not persist in action for an end which they could not see. How important it would be to find out at what points the people of a church find themselves lacking an underlying system of religious belief which enables them to function with a certain amount of confidence.

A most important experiment and study needed for our time is this—an attempt to put into operation a nonsectarian theistic theology which could be used as a part of a fundamental philosophy of education in a public school. It would have to be one that does not use sectarian symbols. If this cannot be done, then we must experiment with evolving some kind of nonlegalistic morality which will be the motivation matrix and design of democracy.

6. Now that psychotherapy has revealed to us something more of the operation of the human psyche and the general journey which it follows in releasing itself from anxieties and adhesiveness, we can more effectively pattern worship services which can be of significant help. We are rather well over the attempt to prettify the services. We are now ready to ask ourselves what kind of services do more than just remove the blemishes. What kind actually purify the blood stream of the worshipers? We can now be better physicians of the soul, through the kind of group worship and extended periods of meditation and retreat which follow the fundamental strategies now being discovered of the self's course of healing.

SUGGESTIONS FOR FURTHER STUDY

1. What are the process conditions for a religiously disciplined and productive face-to-face group? (One hypothesis to be tested is—"at least one person who

gives understanding to the ideas and feelings of the other members.") How do people best discover and appropriate these processes? What happens under various hypotheses on how persons acquire a concept of love that is not just romantically superficial, but of Christian depth?

2. Under what conditions are persons best able to become aware of their sins (ill health and adhesions of the inner personal core)? Of the basic assumptions with which they perceive the world and themselves? How best can you help them change their perception of themselves and of their life space? (Their actions are determined by *their* perceptions; perception is a strategic point: their perception of self is central in their personal dynamics.)

How best can you lead groups into release from *group* sins and world of assumptions? In examining the group self-concept and its discrepancies? (For the individual exists largely within social groupings whose perceptions and patterned energies are determinative.)

3. Within what personal climate and activity do people best fall in love with selfhood—in themselves and all other people?

How do specific religious practices and beliefs "solve" the persistent human hunger for status and role? The prevalent feeling of being among the hunted, the conscripted, the depersonalized? The lack of a clear-cut cause to live for? What conscience structure and dynamics fit with a Christian democratic social order (as contrasted with a fear-producing authoritarian one)?

4. What is the experience content, at various developmental periods of life, of the paradigmatic experiences of the Christian?

5. Through what human channels does growth in faith come? In the face of the anxieties and frustrations of immediate experience and of being a social minority, how can you build morale for the long-range assumptions of religious faith?

6. What is total sequence of the "always becoming of a Christian"—the attraction-conversion-training-participation in group action and thinking, falling and rebirth—as revealed in the life story of individuals and groups? Study the typologies of the "becoming a Christian process"—à la revivalist, Kierkegaard, Bushnell, biblical theology, fellowship group, and so on.

7. What evidence is there of the role of religious ideas in the choices, behavior, integrity of people (for example, a Christian concept of what it means to be a person)? When and how are theological ideas grown and appropriated in such a way as not to become an ideology in the Marxian sense? (The real motives impelling the person's actions remain unknown to him and untouched by the ideas.) What new experiments have there been in the teaching of Christian myth, biography, meaning of history, as carriers of the Christian message "all put together"?

8. How is Christian life communicated via mass communications? What conditions are necessary if people are to listen to, and accept, distasteful truth? Under what personal conditions does the spoken or written word become God's word to us? What motifs and feeling tone are communicated to children through present-day comics, movies, and radio?

9. How is the Christian ethos operating in our culture—in family, work, and intergroup life? To what degree is contemporary literature a revealing account of the state of the people with whom we work? Out of what matrix of family functioning does "the feeling tone" of the Christian movement come to pervade a home?

10. How does a religious movement begin and develop?

BIBLIOGRAPHY

(Many of these are selected for method rather than as reporting research in the field.)

Allport, Gordon. *The Use of Personal Documents in Psychological Science.* Bulletin 49. New York: Social Science Research Council, 1942.

Helping Teachers Understand Children. Washington: American Council on Education, 1945.

Hendry, Charles. *Scouting for Facts.* New York: Boy Scouts of America, 1944.

Hoslett, S. D. *Human Factors in Management.* New York: Harper & Brothers, 1947.

Kluckhohn, Clyde, and Murray, H. A., eds. *Personality in Nation, Society, and Culture.* New York: Alfred A. Knopf, 1948.

Leighton, A. H. *The Governing of Men.* Princeton: Princeton University Press, 1945.

Lewin, Kurt. *Resolving Social Conflicts.* Studies in experimentally created autocratic and democratic groups. Iowa City: University of Iowa Studies in Child Welfare, XVI (1940), No. 3.

Ligon, Ernest. *A Greater Generation.* New York: Macmillan Company, 1948.

Lippitt, Ronald. *Training for Community Relations.* New York: Harper & Brothers, 1949.

Maves, P. L., and Cedarleaf, J. L. *Older People and the Church.* New York and Nashville: Abingdon-Cokesbury Press, 1949.

Newcomb, Theodore. *Readings in Social Psychology.* New York: Henry Holt & Co., 1947.

Pearse, I. H., and Crocker, L. H. *The Peckham Experiment.* New Haven: Yale University Press, 1945.

Williams, Robin. *The Reduction of Intergroup Tensions.* Bulletin 57. New York: Social Science Research Council, 1947.

JOURNALS

American Journal of Sociology, L (1945), 279-83.
Human Relations, Vol. I, Nos. 1 and 3.
Journal of Consulting Psychology, June, 1949.
Journal of Social Issues.
Religious Education.
Sociatry, June, 1947.
Sociometry, February, 1947.

PART V

Agencies for Co-operation in Religious Education

Chapter 33

CITY AND STATE COUNCILS OF CHURCHES AND RELIGIOUS EDUCATION

JOHN W. HARMS

THERE ARE 40 STATE COUNCILS and 672 city and county councils for inter-church and interdenominational co-operation among Protestants in the United States.[1] According to the best records available, 227 of these councils have budgets and employed staffs, ranging from a few thousand dollars and one part-time employee to the Protestant Council of the City of New York, with an annual budget of $266,000 and 52 employees; Los Angeles, $167,000 and 55 employees; or Chicago, $147,000 and 31 employees. The movement has grown rapidly during the last thirty years, especially the last ten, and expenditures probably range from $3,500,000 to $5,000,000 annually.

These councils of churches and religious education are the embodiment of two fundamental ideas. They are primarily an ecumenical fellowship of local churches and local denominational bodies in cities, counties, and states. They are a product of the rising ecumenical spirit in Christianity. Without them ecumenical relationships would be largely confined to national or world denominational bodies and would not become a very large part of the common experience of local congregations and the rank and file of Christians.

At the same time the councils are organizations for what may be called functional Christian unity. They represent the practical work which the churches and denominations can do well or at all only when they work together. They are a recognition of the fact that together churches of Christ have corporate tasks of leadership and service in the corporate life of cities, counties and states.

As a result of this functional unity the churches and denominations together are bringing an increasingly effective Christian influence to bear upon

[1] According to data provided by the Inter-Council Field Department, a joint agency for the co-ordination of field work representing the Federal Council of the Churches of Christ in America, The Foreign Missions Conference of North America, the Home Missions Council of North America, the International Council of Religious Education, the United Council of Church Women and the United Stewardship Council. Several of these organizations are now in the process of uniting as the National Council of the Churches of Christ in the United States.

The word Protestant is used because it seems to be the best term available to indicate the main body of non-Roman Catholic churches.

American life. They are demonstrating that there is an inherent unity in Protestant and orthodox Christianity at the community level which can be expressed in practical work without sacrificing freedom.

THE COUNCIL SYSTEM AND ITS ORIGIN

This system of city, county, and state councils[2] has evolved through three phases: (1) nonecclesiastical or quasi-official Sunday-school co-operation led largely by lay people; (2) the rise of the new religious education movement and of official denominational programs for its promotion, and the rise of official co-operation among local churches and area denominational bodies; and (3) the period of reorganization when these separate movements were brought together into today's unified councils.

1. *The Period of Nonecclesiastical Sunday-School Co-operation.* The Sunday-school movement gave birth to the first form of institutional co-operation on the local or city and state levels among Protestants in America. In the strict official sense as the term is used today it was, not interdenominational, but nondenominational or at best quasi-interdenominational co-operation, because the Sunday schools were usually outside of ecclesiastical control. Hence they were not restrained by the denominational hesitation about, and even antagonism to, official interdenominational relations which characterized this early period. From about 1790, when the First Day or Sunday-School Society of Philadelphia was organized,[3] until about 1908-10 Protestant co-operation at the city and state levels remained almost exclusively on this nonecclesiastical or quasi-interdenominational basis.

The New York City Sunday School Union was organized in 1816, and Philadelphia followed in 1817. The American Sunday School Union, later the International Sunday School Association, was organized in 1824 [4] under the sponsorship of city Sunday-school unions, and the first national convention was held in 1832.

The unions were led in the main by lay people and often served as centers of united Protestant action in evangelism and social welfare for children. Pioneer missionaries from the unions went up and down the land establishing Sunday schools, many of which were the beginnings of strong denominational churches. The American Sunday School Union spent $60,000 in two years, 1930-32, establishing Sunday schools in "every destitute place . . . throughout the Valley of the Mississippi." [5] The Maryland Sunday School

---

[2] The term "council" will be used to designate federations of churches, as well as councils of churches and religious education.

[3] See Arlo Ayres Brown, *A History of Religious Education in Recent Times*, p. 49.

[4] *Ibid.*, p. 50.

[5] *Ibid.*, p. 56. Quoted from *Experiences and Missionary Labors of Stephen Paxson* by his daughter, B. Paxson Drury (American Sunday School Union, 1882), p. 29.

Union, organized in 1846, reports that from 1864 to 1891 it alone organized 1,404 Sunday schools, 952 in Maryland and 452 in the neighboring state of Virginia. Also, at about the same time seven child-welfare organizations and institutions grew out of encouragement, if not actual sponsorship, given by the Maryland union.

County conventions began in 1846, and out of them came large numbers of permanent county and state Sunday-school organizations beginning about 1856. By 1910 every state and province in the United States and Canada was organized, and 2,541 of their 3,254 counties had organizations. More than 53,000 conventions of all kinds were held in 1910.[6]

2. *The Rise of Official Interdenominational Co-operation.* With the turn of the century, the denominations began to take a more vital interest in their educational functions. Denominational leaders were usually associated with the more scientific and professional approach to Christian education and were increasingly dissatisfied with the simple and somewhat rigid practices of the Sunday-school associations. Association leadership tended to resist these changes—for example, the adoption of graded lessons—while denominational leadership advocated them with a crusading zeal. In 1910 they organized the Sunday School Council of Evangelical Denominations, and thus there were two over-all organizations for Sunday-school work, each developing programs for local schools and offering specialized services and leadership to them: the Sunday School Council, controlled by the denominations, and the International Sunday School Association, with its state, county and city auxiliaries, not under ecclesiastical control.

Conflict was the inevitable result, and not until the international association and the council were united into the International Council of Religious Education in 1922 was it resolved. The outcome dramatized the place that the denominations were to have in the future of co-operative Christian education in America. It was also a triumph for (1) the idea of official interdenominational as contrasted with nondenominational co-operation, and (2) the new religious education movement as contrasted with the nonprofessional practices of the earlier Sunday schools.

However, another phase of the developing ecumenical movement had been emerging—namely, official interchurch and interdenominational co-operation. The American Evangelical Alliance, organized in 1876, was active in promoting city and state branches principally for evangelism. The new social-welfare movement among the churches produced local organizations which, together with local chapters of the alliance, organized the National Federation of Churches and Christian Workers in 1901. This was the forerunner of The Federal Council of the Churches of Christ in America,

* *Organized Sunday School Work in America,* 1908-11. Report of Thirteenth International Sunday School Convention, San Francisco, June 20-27, 1911 (Chicago: International Sunday School Association, 1911), p. 150.

organized in 1908, the first organization for co-operation among the denominations on the highest ecclesiastical level.

The Greater New York Church Federation, now a part of the Protestant Council of the City of New York, traces its origins to one of these early movements in 1894 and 1895. An earlier effort was the Interdenominational Commission of Maine, organized in 1890. The Connecticut Council of Churches emerged in 1899. By 1910 many of the major cities and a few states had one or another of these newer forms of co-operation.[7]

Local interchurch organizations did not always survive. In most communities they had a slow and uncertain growth. Baltimore, for example, was not able to establish successful interchurch co-operation until 1919, after numerous discussions and two failures—one organized in 1887 and the other in 1910.

But with the Federal Council of the Churches of Christ successfully launched and competent field service beginning in 1919, the idea gained ground and church federations began to grow rapidly.

3. *The Period of Merger Into Unified Councils.* Beginning in 1922, the year of the merger of the International Sunday School Association and the Sunday School Council of Evangelical Denominations, city and state associations began to reorganize into councils of religious education. Denominational leadership took its place in the reorganized councils and became a dominant influence in shaping their policies and programs.

Some cities effected mergers at once: for example, the Cook County (Illinois) Sunday School Association became the Department of Christian Education of the Chicago federation in 1924. Rochester probably preceded Chicago, and others followed. Church federations were growing in numbers and strength, and the problems of relationships between them and religious education organizations called insistently for solution. Then came ten years of depression with their struggle to survive. Two co-operative organizations in the same community looked like rank extravagance to hard-pressed churchmen who had to raise the money.

Connecticut led the procession of states that merged their councils of religious education and councils of churches as the depression deepened. Illinois, California, Massachusetts, New York, Nebraska, and Maryland-Delaware followed. In 1938 there were twelve comprehensive state councils of churches, seven of which were the result of mergers, and five were councils of religious education that had expanded their functions into a council of churches.[8] The two professional organizations of employed executives representing the church federations and the councils of religious education joined to form the Association of Council Secretaries in 1940.

[7] See E. B. Sanford, *Origin and History of the Federal Council of the Churches of Christ in America*, pp. 146-47.

[8] See William Clayton Bower and Percy Roy Hayward, *Protestantism Faces Its Educational Task Together*, p. 193.

By 1948 thirty-eight states had comprehensive councils of churches and religious education. Only one had both a council of religious education and a council of churches. City organizations merged, too, although in 1948 there remained fifty-nine city councils of religious education with employed executives. These were usually found in communities where there were no federations of churches.

The depression hastened this merger process, but the decisive factor was not economics but the soundness of the idea that Christian education is a central function of the Christian strategy. It belongs, therefore, at the center of Protestant organization for community action. It was the final triumph for the plea of the old Sunday-school movement that Christian education is one of the churches' most important functions.

TOWARD A PHILOSOPHY OF COMMUNITY RELATIONSHIPS

With these major organizational problems now largely worked out, council leadership is giving its attention more and more to the important questions of council functions and to the place of Christian education in them.

Parallel to the rise of denominational concern for Christian education has been the development of denominational-wide Christian education programs and services and leadership to local churches. Hence, one after another, the direct services of the old Sunday-school associations to local Sunday schools have largely been assumed by the denominations.

This conflict between denominational and interdenominational Christian education functions has not been fully resolved, but the trend is for the councils to relinquish direct services to local churches, except where the denominations specifically request otherwise, and for councils to find their distinctive role in relationship to the churches' corporate mission to the corporate life of the community. This has raised two basic questions in relation to council functions: (1) What are the corporate functions of Protestantism in community life? (2) What is the role of Christian education in this total community task? The first of these questions remains more or less unanswered, although the Association of Council Secretaries has given it a great deal of attention. The second problem has had considerable attention by the Christian educational forces of America, with significant results for the whole council movement as well as for the specialized function of Christian education. In February, 1947, after two years of intensive work, the International Council of Religious Education adopted a statement on "The Community Approach to Christian Education," [9] prepared by its committee for the restudy of Christian education. The problem was again considered

*Chapter VII in *Study of Christian Education*.

by the national Conference on Community and Religious Education in Columbus, Ohio, December, 1947.[10]

The fundamental question of these pioneer studies is whether or not there are any valid Christian sanctions for including the corporate life of individuals as it is lived in the community within the sphere of the church's responsibility. Is life so constructed that the community is an inescapable part of it? And if so, do the churches have a responsibility for only a part of life or the whole of it? The International Council's committee answered these questions with a series of affirmations[11] that provide a tentative outline for a "theology of community," an undertaking which it is hoped the theologians will complete:

1. "The community concern of the churches is rooted in the nature of personality."

2. "The community concern of the churches is rooted in the structure of social relations." Biologically, culturally and psychologically, social relationships are essential to the very existence of human life. They are a part of the basic structure of life. Personality, the traditional concern of Christianity, in and of itself is an abstraction. There is no personality without social organization.

3. "The community concern of the churches is rooted in the nature of God." The spiritual basis of the churches' community responsibility is grounded in the character and purpose of God: (a) The love of God, which seeks the good of all men through his work as Creator and Redeemer. (b) The fatherhood of God, which makes men members of one human family. (c) The immanence and transcendence of God in history as well as nature, which places all social arrangements under his judgment, and compels men to seek the kingdom of God in human relationships.

4. "The community concern of the church is rooted in the application of the Christian ethic to life." The individual's institutional relationships in addition to his face-to-face relationships require the application of ethical principles. For the Christian these decisions must be made in the light of Christian principles.

5. "The community concern of the churches is rooted in the nature and mission of the Church itself." The churches are themselves a community of interest and purpose dedicated to the realization of God's community within the larger geographical community. The churches deal with the great issues of evil, sin, guilt, and salvation. To do this successfully they must

[10] For a full report on this conference see T. T. Swearingen, *The Community and Christian Education* (St. Louis: Bethany Press, published for the Cooperative Publishing Association, 1949).

[11] *Study of Christian Education*, pp. 11-19.

proclaim "a Gospel that is as relevant to the nature of community as it is to the nature of the individual." [12]

This work of the International Council represents the first official effort to formulate a basic philosophy for interchurch and interdenominational functions in community life. It is a first long step toward the development of a philosophy of community relationships for Protestantism.

ORGANIZATION AND PROGRAM

Before we consider the basic principles of council organization and program, it is important to understand that there are serious limitations inherent in the nature of the relationship which the denominations have with one another through the councils. Furthermore, the extent of their commitments to interdenominational co-operation vary greatly from community to community, from local church to local church, from denomination to denomination, and often within denominations themselves.

In the area of faith and order the denominations insist on complete sovereignty when they become members of councils—that is, they always retain the right to determine matters having to do with the internal organization and administration of their local churches, including the supervision and guidance of Christian education activities.

On the other hand, the denominations are recognizing more and more that they have corporate Christian functions in the area of life and work on the community level which they expect to perform through councils. However, even in the area of life and work, as in the area of faith and order, they reserve the right to make any decision or to enter into any activity which they individually may determine, regardless of the consequences for local interdenominational co-operation, and it must be said that they exercise that right regularly.

Under these circumstances a realistic and meaningful concept of the nature of a council of churches must reflect accurately the nature of the relationship among the co-operating churches and denominations, expressing both its limitations and possibilities.

The partnership idea seems to meet these conditions. Therefore, a council of churches may be called a partnership of local churches and denominations for the purpose of accomplishing certain aspects of their common mission in the area of life and work on the community level. Generally speaking, the functions committed to the partnership are twofold: (1) co-ordination of denominational activities in the interest of bringing the total resources of the churches to bear upon given problems without wasteful competition, and (2) corporate or united functions which are recognized

[12] *Ibid.*, p. 16.

as beyond the ability of any one local church or denomination to accomplish by working alone.

The partnership concept calls for a few simple operating principles which are being used more and more, and are in general advocated by the Inter-council Field Department.[13]

First, city and state—and local or county—councils should be created by official action of the member local churches and denominations. In other words, councils are the local churches or the denominations in fellowship and corporate action.

Second, the governing body of the council and the membership of the committees directing all of the major program function should consist mainly of official representatives of the churches and denominations so that policies and program planning will be done jointly.

Third, the member bodies—local churches and denominations—should accept responsibility for financing their councils.

Fourth, adequate provision should be made for the direct official participation of lay people, young and older men and women, and ministers. Also, individuals who have special competence but are not directly appointed by member bodies should be enlisted both in program planning and in financing.

Program Functions. The International Council's Committee on the Community Approach to Religious Education found that there are nine basic council functions for Christian education.[14] These are expressed in various ways through the council and its several groups, youth, women, laymen, and ministers, as well as functional committees for these specific purposes.

1. Community-wide fellowship and sharing of experience in Christian education.

2. Ecumenical education.

3. Active concern in the churches and in the community for public education.

4. Developing public opinion favorable to Christian education.

5. Co-operative efforts to reach all the people with Christian education through: (*a*) weekday religious education; (*b*) summer-vacation religious education; (*c*) audio-visual education, including radio; (*d*) community surveys; (*e*) annual or periodic community visitations; and (*f*) community-wide emphases on religious education values.

6. Community co-ordinating councils of character-building agencies.

7. Educational undergirding for effective community social action.

[13] See Church Co-operation Series, Pamphlet No. 2, "How to Organize a Local Council of Churches and Religious Education."

[14] For a more extended statement about these functions see *Study of Christian Education*, pp. 240-46.

8. Religious education needs of public or private institutions for care of unfortunate people.

9. Collective "self-service" activities to strengthen the religious education program of local churches themselves. For example, (*a*) community leadership training schools, conferences, and institutes, (*b*) co-operative laboratory schools, (*c*) employment of community directors of community education for service directly to local churches.

Program Organization. Some councils have committees for each specific program function, regardless of its general classification. For example, instead of a Christian education department or committee there will be committees on children, youth, and adult work; leadership education; vacation church school; weekday religious education; audio-visual education; and other functions. These stand alongside an array of committees on comity, evangelism, radio, ministry in institutions, social action, social service, and others. Each committee is responsible directly to the council or its governing body. Those who favor this type of organization believe that it insures more readily that Christian education will be integrated into the total work of the council.

Other councils have organized each major function into departments with committees in each to take care of its specialized functions. For example, there will be a department of Christian education with the usual committees, responsible to the governing body through the department. The advocates of this type of organization hold that it provides a higher visibility for Christian education, and that anyhow the integration of Christian education into the total life of the council will take place only when special administrative attention is given to it.

A third type of organization which is being used by a few councils— for example, Chicago, Dayton, and Cincinnati—recognizes two basic types of structure within the council. One is known as personnel divisions, which include the women's organization (council of church women), ministers (ministerial association), youth (united Christian youth fellowship), and laymen. Sometimes there are other personnel groupings, such as Sunday-school superintendents or choir directors and organists. The second group of activities are the functional departments, such as Christian education; social service; citizenship education and action (social action); ministry in institutions; church development and comity; research and planning; radio, publicity, or public relations; and evangelism. These functional departments are the basic program thrusts or the strategy of leadership and service of the united churches, while the personnel divisions are the channels through which the personnel resources of the churches are mobilized and related to these basic program functions.

Relationships to National Organizations. Local, city, and state councils are autonomous organizations and maintain friendly, co-operating, and sometimes a constituent relationship to national interdenominational organizations. County and city organizations are usually constituent members of the state councils, which in turn are members of the International Council of Religious Education. No provision is made by the Federal Council of the Churches of Christ for the membership of city or state councils of churches. It does provide for representatives of city and state councils of churches to be members of its executive committee and of the council itself, but these representatives have to be approved by their respective denominations before they are accepted as members after their nomination by the Association of Council Secretaries. The proposed National Council of the Churches of Christ in the United States will permit one representative from each state council which meets certain requirements and ten people to represent all city councils. Councils as such will not be members.

The United Council of Church Women has local constituent or state units, which are usually the women's divisions of the corresponding geographical council. The United Christian Youth Movement, administered by the International Council of Religious Education, provides for local and city units through state youth organizations. These are known as youth councils or, more recently, united Christian youth fellowships, and they usually are the youth divisions of the corresponding geographical council.

Probable Trends in the Future

What is the future of Christian education in local or city and state councils of churches? As the history of these organizations clearly shows, community organization for Christian education has just emerged from a period of revolutionary adjustment. It went through two major reorganizations and a devastating depression within twenty-five years. A movement with less vitality would surely have been destroyed. However, councils are here to stay. They will increase in strength and importance, and their development may be expected along the following lines:

1. There will undoubtedly be a deepening of the churches' and denominations' sense of mission to community life, and Christian education will play an increasingly important part in this development. More and more the work of councils of churches will be conceived in terms of the corporate responsibilities of Christianity, and the denominations may be expected to look to them for service and leadership in this field.

2. Christian education may be expected to conceive its function in terms of the total task of the churches in community life and to perfect its techniques for realizing this integration of the educational function into the other specialized functions of the councils: for example, in relation to evangelism, social action, fellowship, and other council functions.

3. Christian education will undoubtedly continue its recent efforts to recapture the interest of lay people in its goals and program for the children, youth, and adults of the community and for community life itself.

4. Christian education forces, denominational and interdenominational, may be expected increasingly to work together in grounding the community concerns of the churches in the educational programs of the local churches. Corollary to this will be the larger and larger dependence which the councils will place upon basic educational processes in projecting their social-action programs.

5. Christian education in councils will give a large place to a concern for public education in all its aspects but especially on teacher motivation and enlistment, educational ideals and goals for the community, and character education.

6. Christian education in councils will probably make larger and larger use of modern mediums of communication, especially radio and other audio-visual aid methods. This probably will be one of the specialized functions where the councils will be called upon to give direct local church service.

7. The councils may be expected to play an increasingly important role in the ecumenical movement. The World Council of Churches will undoubtedly depend more and more upon them for its relationship to American life. Ecumenical education will surely have a large place in the councils' future programs.

8. Finally, the budgets and staff for Christian education in councils will probably be enlarged as council programs stabilize and Christian education is more and more closely related to their distinctive role in community life. There will undoubtedly continue the trend toward the integration and uniting of denominational Christian educational fieldworkers into united staffs to provide more comprehensive field service to local churches and communities on an interdenominational basis.

These developments may or may not take place, depending upon what happens in local, national, and world affairs, but they are clearly discernible trends in the history and in the life and practice of the council movement at the present time. In any event, the councils will continue to be laboratories of ecumenicity at the grass-roots level of life in which a practical, functional unity among the churches of Christ is being fashioned. This new functional unity has in it the power to transform classic Protestantism in America from one of the most divisive factors into one of the potentially most unifying factors in the community.

Thus they may be expected to make their contribution, along with the national and world councils, to the fuller realization of Christian unity and to the achievement of a New Christianity which will provide the spiritual undergirding that freedom and democracy so desperately need.

SUGGESTIONS FOR FURTHER STUDY

1. What is the place of Christian education in councils of churches, and what should its relationship be to other functions such as evangelism, comity, radio, ministry in institutions, social action, social service, publicity?

2. What Christian educational functions properly belong to the denominations or local churches, and what belong to councils of churches and religious education?

3. What is the significance, if any, of councils of churches for the ecumenical movement and the ultimate goal of Christian unity?

4. What is the difference, if any, between the idea of ecumenicity in the local community and in the world relations of the churches?

5. In the light of latest developments in Christian education as you understand them now, what changes should be made in the "Probable Trends" on pages 428 and 429?

BIBLIOGRAPHY

Bower, W. C., and Hayward, P. R. *Protestantism Faces Its Educational Task Together.* Chicago: International Council of Religious Education, 1949.

Brown, Arlo Ayres. *A History of Religious Education in Recent Times.* New York: Abingdon Press, 1923.

Church Co-operation Series, entitled "Forward Together," a series of pamphlets about the organization and program of city, county, and state councils of churches, prepared by the Intercouncil Field Department, 297 Fourth Avenue, New York City.

McFarland, Charles S. *Christian Unity in the Making.* New York: Federal Council of the Churches of Christ in America, 1948.

Sanford, E. B. *Origin and History of the Federal Council of Churches of Christ in America.* Hartford: S. S. Scranton Company, 1916.

Swearingen, T. T. *The Community and Christian Education.* St. Louis: Bethany Press, 1949.

Vieth, Paul H. *The Church and Christian Education.* St. Louis: Bethany Press, 1947. Summarizes *Study of Christian Education* (Chicago: International Council of Religious Education, 1947, a copyrighted duplicated publication). See entire volume, but in connection with this study refer to the full text of chap. vii, "The Community Approach to Christian Education," in the latter document.

Chapter 34

THE INTERNATIONAL COUNCIL
OF RELIGIOUS EDUCATION

ROY G. ROSS

THE SIGNIFICANT PLACE of the International Council in the total movement for religious education in North America can best be understood as one views its services on the background of its objectives, its organizational purposes, and its basic relationships to its member agencies and, through them, to innumerable local churches and communities.

The ultimate objectives of the Council are to be found in the eternal purposes of the Christian gospel in relation to the spiritual needs of growing persons of all ages. The latest formulation of these objectives is based on a first draft made in the year 1930 and revised ten years later.[1] This formulation was the result of long consultations, through which leaders of the council's forty denominations worked together. Through the years these objectives have been a guide for hundreds of programs in religious education, and they have been a primary factor in drawing the denominational boards closer together in both their separate and co-operative activities.

ORGANIZATIONAL PURPOSE AND FUNCTION

The purpose and the function of the Council as set forth in the 1948 revision of the by-laws are as follows:

The purpose of the International Council of Religious Education shall be as specified in the Charter granted by Act of Congress: "To promote organized Sunday school work, to encourage the study of the Bible, and to assist in the spread of the Christian religion."

In pursuance of its purpose as stated in its Charter, it shall be the function of the International Council of Religious Education to serve as an agency of the churches of North America through which they may engage cooperatively in mutual helpfulness toward maintaining and developing the most effective program of Christian education and through which their leaders in Christian education may (a) enjoy the inspiration and self-education which come through fellowship, (b) share convictions, ideas, and experiences, (c) evaluate their current

[1] See *Christian Education Today.*

plans and practices, (d) cooperate in examining areas of needed service, (e) carry on cooperative research, (f) carry on activities for enrichment of their denominational programs, (g) plan together religious education activities of a community nature, (h) cooperate in developing a public mind favorable to the conduct of Christian education, (i) unite in carrying on certain designated aspects of their work, (j) conduct joint experimentation in needed new fields vital to Christian education, (k) provide a means whereby two or more denominations may join in common endeavors of their choice, (l) organize and assist councils of churches or of religious education at each geographical level, and (n) join in such other plans and activities as may seem wise and helpful.

. . . .

The International Council is the agency of only those denominations which are historically known as evangelical in nature. It is the medium through which they carry forward such tasks as they wish to undertake on a cooperative basis. It has no control over its member denominations but is instead controlled by them. It does not presume to pass upon the tenets of the faith of its member groups. It accepts without further tests of membership the persons whom they have chosen as their trusted leaders.

Each member denomination determines the areas and the extent of its participation in the Council's work. It also decides the use which it will make on behalf of its constituency of the products of this cooperative process.

The experience of the years has demonstrated that, through a council which operates on these policies, denominations of widely differing background can achieve an amazing degree of cooperation. Through the years, the extent of this cooperation has steadily enlarged as they have had opportunity to investigate the scope of the concerns, convictions, and loyalties which they share.[2]

The Council's Program

The council's program provides for innumerable services which the council's member agencies deem to be essential to a successful religious education movement, and which can be carried on most effectively interdenominationally. These services fall into three primary categories:

1. *Services to Member Denominations.* This category of services can best be explained by a few illustrations:

The local church needs curriculum materials for its Sunday church school. Such materials are prepared by their respective denominational editorial staffs. In the majority of cases, outlines are used which have been prepared co-operatively through the International Council. The council maintains two regular committees for this purpose. Through one committee denominational editors work every year on uniform-lesson outlines; through the other, on varied types of graded-lesson outlines. Between the years

1942-45 a special curriculum committee produced the *Curriculum Guide for the Local Church*, which was issued in 1945.

Local churches need structures, programs, curriculum materials, plans for accrediting instructors, and plans for certifying progress in the task of training leaders for various types of Christian service. In some cases they work separately and obtain these services through their respective denominational boards; in other cases they join with other churches and work through their local agencies for co-operation. They oftentimes do not realize that most of the standard leadership training services of North America, whether rendered through denominational boards or through local and state councils of churches, are along lines which were worked out co-operatively through the International Council. On the basis of these plans approximately 135,000 credits are issued annually by the forty member denominations, while approximately 39,000 credits are issued directly by the International Council of Religious Education or through its member state councils and related city councils.

Another illustration of this type of co-operation is found in the youth field. Most of the larger and medium-sized denominations and several of the smaller ones maintain denominational youth fellowships as media for advancing Christian education among the youth of their local churches. These fellowships have become the most dynamic and dependable force in youth work in North America, especially within the last decade. However, it is recognized that while youth need these vital media for fellowship, inspiration, program planning, and leadership education within their denominations, they also wish a sense of fellowship with all Christian youth who are working at like tasks through other denominational agencies and through extrachurch, Christian-education, and character-education organizations. Therefore the youth leaders and the officers of thirty-nine denominational youth agencies and sixteen general youth organizations, such as Christian Endeavor, Y.M.C.A., and Y.W.C.A., have banded themselves together in the United Christian Youth Movement of North America. Through this movement they plan occasions for fellowship and interchange of experience, the outlining of common emphases, the training of leaders for community co-operation, the National Youth Week observance, and a score of other activities. This movement is guided and staffed through the International Council of Religious Education.

Many of the denominational educational leaders have decided that there are field services for both local church and community aspects of Christian education which can most effectively be carried on co-operatively. Therefore, from time to time, they pool their personnel and financial resources in projects such as the United Christian Education Advance, the National Christian Teaching Mission, and the regional children's work conferences.

In 1947-48 thirty children's work leaders from eleven denominations, in addition to interdenominational agencies, joined in holding regional training conferences throughout the United States and Canada. Through these conferences 2,740 children's specialists were given training for assisting in local church and community leadership enterprises in their several areas.

These were planned and administered by the Committee on Religious Education of Children through the Department of Children's Work of the International Council of Religious Education.

The most dramatic co-operative field enterprise of a quarter-century is the National Christian Teaching Mission, which has as its objectives the following:

To help teachers become more clearly aware of their evangelistic responsibility and opportunity; to provide them guidance and inspiration and to bring them to a more vital personal Christian experience;

To discover, through a religious census, the unreached and unchurched of the community;

To bring under the influence of Christian teaching all those not now receiving it;

To win to Christ as Saviour and Lord and to membership in His Church all those reached and taught.[3]

Through this medium of co-operation, leaders of many denominations are making an impact for Christian education on increasing numbers of North American communities which is gaining continent-wide attention. A conspicuous example—though not a unique one—of its success was found recently in a West Coast city where 7,500 callers brought in over 300,000 prospect cards for distribution to the churches of that city. These callers were from 122 churches of 21 denominations and were led by a corps of 81 guest leaders under the leadership of the Director of Educational Evangelism of the International Council of Religious Education and a team of seven associate directors whose services were loaned by the denominations in which they have staff responsibility.

2. *Services on Behalf of Member Denominations.* In addition to services which have such direct relationship to member denominations, the Council renders some services on behalf of its constituent bodies and with their consent rather than directly through them. These also are too numerous for detailed delineation in this chapter.

a) A first group is addressed to the developing of a climate favorable to religious education. It includes a lesson syndication service to daily and weekly newspapers, the administration of three national observances— namely, National Youth Week, National Christian Family Week, and Religious Education Week—a regular service of press releases on news regarding

[3] Literature of the Department of Educational Evangelism, I.C.R.E.

significant happenings in Christian education, hundreds of local-station or national-chain radio broadcasts, and for two years the maintenance of a daily broadcast promoting Sunday-school attendance over as many as 167 stations at the peak.

b) A second group of such services is related to guiding community enterprises for Christian education, such as weekday schools of religious education, community vacation church schools, and special projects in underprivileged areas. Here there is need for organizational plans, program plans, textbooks, and administrative standards, which no one denomination alone can provide. In providing them the council sustains a direct relationship to local community enterprises comparable to that which a denominational educational board sustains to its local churches.

Such services are planned by the educational leaders of many denominations who come together nationally to help devise patterns and services which will facilitate the community co-operation of their local churches.

c) One of the most significant interdenominational services of the past quarter-century has been the attempt to provide the English-speaking world with a translation of the Bible which will help persons of all ages to the fullest possible understanding of the message of the Scriptures. Since 1929 a committee of America's foremost scholars has been at work on this prodigious task. Their task was outlined by the International Council as follows:

We record the conviction that there is need for a version which embodies the best results of modern scholarship as to the meaning of the Scriptures, and expresses this meaning in English diction which is designed for use in public and private worship and preserves those qualities which have given to the King James Version a supreme place in English literature. We, therefore, define the task of the American Standard Bible Committee to be that of revision of the present American Standard Edition of the Bible in the light of the results of modern scholarship, this revision to be designed for use in public and private worship, and to be in the direction of the simple, classic English style of the King James Version.[4]

On February 11, 1946, the New Testament section of the Revised Standard Version was released to the public and was received with widespread acclaim, with the rest of the Bible to follow about six years later.

3. *Joint Program Undertakings.* In keeping with the trend toward unified program planning by local churches and both regional and national denominational agencies, the International Council attempts to integrate its activities carefully with those of other interdenominational agencies. Among the enterprises which are now jointly sponsored or administered by two or more councils, including the International Council, are the following: (*a*)

[4] Minutes of Board of Trustees, I.C.R.E., February 12, 1937. Used by permission.

National Christian Teaching Mission; (*b*) Inter-Council Committee on Christian Family Life; (*c*) Committee on Town and Country; (*d*) Joint Commission on the Urban Church; (*e*) Washington Office; (*f*) Committee on Cooperative Field Research; (*g*) Committee on Planning and Adjustment of Local Inter-Church Relations; (*h*) Inter-Agency Committee on Child Welfare; (*i*) United Christian Youth Movement; (*j*) United Christian Adult Movement; (*k*) Inter-Council Field Department; (*l*) Protestant Film Commission; (*m*) Protestant Radio Commission.

All of these joint enterprises are worthy of special consideration by the student of present-day all-Protestant structures and programs. Comment will be confined to four of them.

The United Christian Youth Movement was organized in the year 1936. It now has a staff of six persons and an annual operating budget of over $50,000. Most of its functions were stated earlier in this chapter. In addition, it serves as the avenue for linking the Christian youth of America into the World Youth Commission, which has been developed under the joint sponsorship of the World Council of Churches and the World Council of Christian Education.

The Inter-Council Field Department was organized in 1939 as a means of co-ordinating the field services of the several interdenominational agencies and thus enabling each of them to serve the field more effectively. The department carries on field research; compiles information regarding existing services for use of local and territorial leaders; promotes interdenominational programs and structures; counsels state and city councils regarding structures, programs, and personnel; synchronizes field schedules; and renders innumerable other services. Its members are the officially appointed representatives of the several councils. Its staff are persons from these councils who are assigned to field administration and service.

The latest of the joint enterprises are the Protestant Radio Commission and the Protestant Film Commission. These agencies are different from the others in the fact that their memberships root back directly into the participating denominations as well as into the interdenominational agencies. In each case, however, the councils have turned over their programs, budgets, and staffs to the commission in order to make possible more complete unification of efforts. In each case it is hoped that the new commission will be able to accomplish a more complete co-ordination of denominational interests, programs, and support. Also, it is expected that unification will make possible more effective relationships with the respective industries.

THE COUNCIL'S STRUCTURE

The Council has at this writing a working family of ninety-nine full-time employees, including twenty-seven staff persons who man the following departments of work: General Administration, Educational Administration and Research, Children's Work, Young People's Work, Adult Work and Family Education, Vacation Religious Education, Weekday Religious Education, Lesson Studies, Leadership Education and Church-School Administration, Educational Evangelism, Ecumenical Education, International Journal of Religious Education, Audio-Visual and Radio Education, Field Administration, Promotion and Finance, Newspaper Lesson Syndication, English Bible, Financial Development, Public Relations, Business, and Literature Service.

The International Council was organized in 1922 as a merger of the International Sunday School Association and the Sunday School Council of Evangelical Denominations. It operates under a charter granted to the International Sunday School Association in 1907 by special act of the United States Congress. While the present organization is only twenty-seven years old, it has its rootage in the oldest tradition in interdenominational co-operation in North America. Its oldest program enterprise—namely, the work of its uniform lesson committee—dates back over seventy-five years.

The structures of the Council for maintaining this interdenominational service at first seem intricate. However, they are necessarily so in view of the extensive and varied services which it performs. These structures include the following:

1. *Thirteen educational committees*, through which member agencies determine the services which they want to obtain through the Council and make plans for united efforts. These committees are made up predominantly of the staff members of constituent agencies with portfolios in their respective areas of service. Their combined membership totals approximately seven hundred persons.

2. *Seventeen associated sections*, all except one of which are composed of professional leaders in the several fields of religious education service. They are autonomous groups, each of which prepares its own by-laws, elects its own officers, and prepares its own programs.

The by-laws of the I.C.R.E. require that the statement of purpose and function for each section shall provide for—

a) Suggestions and recommendations to the Council in the areas of their respective interests for the guidance of the Council on matters of policy, program, and procedure.

b) Mutual fellowship and the sharing of experience in their respective fields which may or may not be a concern of the Council.

A few changes have been made through the years in the roster of associated sections. At present the authorized groups are as follows: Adult Work, Children's Work, City Executives' Section, Directors' Section, Editors' Section, Denominational Executives' Section, Lay Section, Leadership Education, Missionary Education, Pastors' Section, Professors' Section,

Publishers' Section, Research Section, State and Regional Executives' Section, Vacation Religious Education, Weekday Religious Education, Young People's Work Section and Commission.

The combined membership of these associated sections is approximately 1,600. The annual attendance at meetings varies from 1,100 to 1,500.

The sections have their meetings simultaneously during the second week of February each year. Through a joint program committee they plan two or three general sessions of all. Occasionally there will be joint meetings of two sections. Most of their programs, however, run parallel.

The International Council has found these associated sections of great value to its work. They are a fertile source of new ideas and they provide an extraordinary avenue for fellowship.

3. *The International Quadrennial Convention,* an institution of the Council primarily for local church leaders, has a tradition dating back to 1832. Through more than a century such conventions have proved valuable avenues for—

a) Encouraging local church and community workers.

b) Developing among them a sense of mission.

c) Providing a sustaining fellowship with a great host of other such workers.

d) Developing interest in, and understanding of, proposed new enterprises and activities.

e) Creating a public opinion in the convention city and state, as well as throughout the two nations, favorable to Christian education.

According to the by-laws of the International Council, the Convention is a delegated body composed of the officers, members, and staff of the Council, the members of standing committees and associated sections, and delegates chosen by the state and provincial councils and by the denominational boards which are constituent members of the Council, on such numerical basis as the Council may determine.

At the International Quadrennial Convention held at Des Moines, Iowa, July 23-27, 1947, over 7,500 persons were in attendance. The next convention is dated August, 1950, at Toronto, Canada, as part of the World Convention of the World Council of Christian Education.

4. *The Commission on Educational Program* is the Council agency which, according to the Council's by-laws, guides and co-ordinates the work of the Council's program committees and carries such other responsibilities as may be assigned to it by the Council. In practical operation the Council looks to this Commission for the following:

a) Review, co-ordination, and guidance of all routine work of the various educational committees of the Council.

b) An analysis of emerging questions of educational policy with recommendations thereon.

c) Recommendations for the development of new educational programs to be carried on by the Council.

d) Recommendations of procedures for dealing with major educational problems so as to carry out effectively the will of the majority of us member agencies.

The Commission is composed of chairmen of all standing and special committees, twenty members-at-large, all directors of educational departments of the I.C.R.E. staff, and four ex officio members.

5. *The Board of Trustees* is the Council's agency for handling matters of business, budget, investments, financial promotion, public relations, and personnel. This board consists of thirty-five members elected by the Council, plus four officers of the Council who serve ex officio.

The board co-ordinates and guides the work of the Council's business and properties committees. During the interim between meetings of the Council, it is empowered annually to act for the Council.

6. *The Council* itself is the final authoritative body to which the Commission on Educational Program, the Board of Trustees, and the standing committees report. It represents the member agencies in final determination of philosophy, policy, and program. The Council is composed as follows: (*a*) 224 representatives of denominational boards of Christian education; (*b*) 151 representatives of accredited state councils of churches and religious education; (*c*) 20 convention-elected members; (*d*) 18 members-at-large; (*e*) 17 representatives of Associated Sections; and (*f*) 17 members of approved Related Agencies (without voting power).

The Council's Basic Philosophy

Though the Council does not presume to determine the educational philosophy nor the theological foundations of its member agencies, it must necessarily have a basis for those program undertakings which it administers on behalf of these agencies.

Within the past fifteen years two committees have formulated statements for the guidance of the Council staff and committees. The first of these statements was entitled *Christian Education Today*, which was adopted by the Council and published in 1938. It was prepared by a committee of fifteen persons, all from within the membership of the Council. This statement proved to be very helpful.

Approximately five years later a number of considerations indicated the wisdom of a thorough restudy of the program of the Council. Among those considerations were:

a. Conditions precipitated by the war, taking account of the necessary adjustments in the program of Christian education to meet the needs of the new situation and of men and women returned from military and defense services.*

b. The need of a considered statement as to the place of theological and other concepts in Christian education.

c. The educational opportunity and responsibility presented by the forth-coming publication of the new Revised Version of the English Bible.*

d. The place of the educational program and of the educational method in the total program of the church, the home and the community.

e. The urgent need of new ways of serving the unreached part of the constituency.

f. The need of plans for securing a more adequate lay and professional leadership.

g. The incorporation of the ecumenical Christian ideal in the program of Christian education and the conscious participation of the International Council in the world-wide movement in Christian education.

h. A definition of the functions of the inter-church agency of Christian education and of its committees and other groups.

i. The basic issues involved in accepted organizations and patterns of work.[5]

A committee was authorized at the annual meeting of 1944 and began its work that fall. This Committee on the Study of Christian Education, in contrast with the preceding committee, was composed of persons both within and outside the field of professional Christian education. It included laymen, local pastors, local directors of religious education, college and seminary teachers and administrators, biblical and theological scholars, in addition to editors, religious education board executives, publishers, and general ecclesiastical leaders.

The Study of Christian Education was carried on through eight sections. These sections had assignments on (*a*) theological and educational foundations, (*b*) local church program, (*c*) family, (*d*) leadership, (*e*) curriculum, (*f*) community approach, and (*g*) structure and functions of agencies.

The committee addressed its reports to the Council rather than formulating them with the thought of Council adoption. They were, however, given appropriate consideration by the Council itself and by those bodies of the Council which function in the respective areas of responsibility. They were wholeheartedly received in the annual meetings of 1946, 1947, and 1948, and were referred to the staff and educational committees as guides for their future efforts. Most of the changes which were recommended in the report on structure and functions of agencies were adopted in 1948, and many of the recommendations regarding program are already in force.

* These responsibilities were later assigned to other committees of the Council.

[5] *Yearbook,* 1944, International Council of Religious Education, p. 108. Used by permission.

The results of the Study were brought to a much larger audience through a more popular interpretation which was prepared by the chairman at the request of the Council.[6] The report in this form has had a far-reaching influence upon the leaders of the churches and upon the lines of activity in the organizations which they serve.

PIONEERING FOR A NATIONAL COUNCIL OF CHURCHES

Beginning in 1940, the International Council, through its officially appointed representatives, has worked with representatives of other interdenominational agencies in preparing the way for a National Council of the Churches of Christ in the U.S.A. After three years of study, a report was made to the participating agencies recommending the structural basis for such a council, submitting a proposed constitution, and recommending that a constituting convention be held as soon as the Planning Committee deemed that a sufficient number of the participating organizations had taken action, this in no case to be less than six of the eight which participated in the preparation of the report.

The preamble of the proposed constitution read:

In the providence of God, the time has come when it seems fitting more fully to manifest the essential oneness of the Christian churches of the United States of America in Jesus Christ as their Divine Lord and Saviour, by the creation of an inclusive cooperative agency to continue and extend the following general agencies of the churches and to combine all their interests and functions.[7]

The objects of the National Council, as stated in the constitution, were:

1. To manifest the essential oneness of the cooperating churches in spirit and purpose for the furtherance of their common mission in the world.
2. To carry on such work of the churches as they desire to be done in cooperation.
3. To continue and extend the work of the interdenominational agencies named in the Preamble, together with such additional objects and purposes as may from time to time be agreed upon.
4. To encourage devotional fellowship and mutual counsel concerning the spiritual life and religious activities of the churches.
5. To foster and encourage cooperation between two or more communions.
6. To promote cooperation among local churches and to further the development of councils of churches in communities, states, or larger territorial units.

[6] See *The Church and Christian Education.*

[7] *The Closer Relationships of General Interdenominational Agencies,* report of the Committee on Further Procedure, composed of representatives of eight interdenominational agencies (rev. ed., April 25, 1944, p. 9). Used by permission of the Planning Committee for the National Council of Churches.

7. To establish consultative relationships with National Councils of Churches in other countries of North America.
8. To maintain fellowship and cooperation with similar Councils in other areas of the world.
9. To maintain fellowship and cooperation with the World Council of Churches and with other international Christian organizations.[8]

As of March 1, 1949, actions have been taken on the report by all of the eight agencies whose representatives helped to draft it. Five agencies have given it final approval. Two others have approved, subject to ratification by their own member agencies. In both cases the ratification requirements have been met and final official actions are assured. The Foreign Missions Conference has disapproved the report.

The International Council of Religious Education approved this report, subject to ratification by a majority of its member denominational boards and by a majority of its member state councils. At the time of the 1949 annual meeting a sufficient number of ratifications had been received to meet this condition. However, final action was postponed until 1950 in order to give time for preparing the necessary legal actions and in order to secure the concurrence of an even larger number of the Council's member agencies.

In the meantime, representatives of the several councils have worked through a Planning Committee for the National Council of Churches on the tasks of outlining by-laws, proposed policies, and procedures for bringing the new agency into being. The proposed constituting convention was scheduled tentatively for November or December, 1950.

With the organization of a National Council of Churches, we shall have the type of national structure in the United States which is the logical outcome of a policy which makes religious education an integral program function of the church vitally related to all its operations.

Executive Leadership

Through its twenty-seven years of existence the Council has had but two general secretaries—I am the second. Hugh S. Magill was its first executive, coming to this position from a distinguished career as Field Secretary of the National Education Association and serving for a period of thirteen years. I have served the Council since 1936, coming to this position after eleven years with my denominational board, first as youth director and then as executive secretary of the Department of Religious Education.

[8] *Ibid.*, pp. 9-10. Used by permission.

SUGGESTIONS FOR FURTHER STUDY

1. What trends in the basic educational philosophy of the religious education movement are indicated by the statements found in the curriculum guide (1929), *Christian Education Today* (1937), and the report of the Committee on the Study of Christian Education (1947)?

2. Is the International Council of Religious Education truly an interdenominational organization? If so, what factors in its policies and structure make it so? If not, why not?

3. How is the International Council of Religious Education related organically and functionally to its member denominations? What is the merit of such relationships? Are relationships equally vital and effective in research and program planning on the one hand and in administration and promotion of field enterprises on the other?

4. To what extent is the religious education movement integrated with the total work of the church on the national interdenominational level? What are the present definite evidences of integration? What are the prospects and implications of the proposed merger of interdenominational agencies to form the proposed National Council of the Churches of Christ in the U.S.A.?

5. Is the scope of interdenominational work growing? How rapidly and in what particular areas? What new departments of work have been added in the International Council during the past decade, and what longer established departments have expanded their work?

6. What policies are followed and what organizational patterns are used to build interdenominational bridges of understanding among local church leaders while preserving the values of their denominational fellowships?

7. What are the values of associated sections which account for their persistence and steady growth during the past quarter-century?

8. What has been the trend with respect to lay participation in the national interdenominational work of religious education during the past half-century? Was it ever necessary to minimize the place of laymen in this movement in order to obtain complete interdenominational cooperation? What contributions can laymen make to the movement which are not now being made? Will laymen be disposed to have an increasing part in the Council's program under present organizational plans and policies?

BIBLIOGRAPHY

BOOKS

Bower, W. C., and Hayward, P. R. *Protestantism Faces Its Educational Task Together.* Appleton, Wisconsin: C. C. Nelson Publishing Co., 1949. Pp. xi, 292.

Swearingen, T. T. *The Community and Christian Education.* St. Louis: Bethany Press, 1949.

Vieth, Paul H. *The Church and Christian Education. Idem,* 1947. P. 314.

Yearbook of the International Council of Religious Education. Chicago: The International Council of Religious Education. Published annually, 1924 ff.

PAMPHLETS AND BROCHURES

Christian Education Today, a Statement of Basic Philosophy. Chicago: The International Council of Religious Education, 1940. P. 40.

Curriculum Guide for the Local Church. Chicago: International Council of Religious Education, 1946 (revised). P. 93.

Plan Book, American Cooperative Christianity. New York: Friendship Press; 1947. P. 96.

Ross, Roy G. *What Is the International Council of Religious Education?* Chicago: International Council of Religious Education, 1944. P. 8.

REPORTS

Report of the Committee on the Study of Christian Education. 8 Vols. Chicago: International Council of Religious Education, 1947. (Duplicated.)

    I. *Christian Education, Yesterday and Today.*
    II. *Theological and Educational Foundations.*
    III. *The Church Program.*
    IV. *The Curriculum of Christian Education.*
    V. *The Family.*
    VI. *Leadership.*
    VII. *The Community Approach to Christian Education.*
    VIII. *The Structure and Functions of Agencies of Christian Education.*

Report of the Committee on Religion and Public Education. Chicago: International Council of Religious Education, 1949. P. 10. (Duplicated.)

PERIODICALS

International Journal of Religious Education. Chicago: International Council of Religious Education. (Monthly except August.) 1924 ff.

Chapter 35

THE RELIGIOUS EDUCATION ASSOCIATION

ORVILLE L. DAVIS

MUCH OF THE IMPROVEMENT in religious and moral education as a scientific movement has been stimulated by the Religious Education Association. This representative fellowship of pioneering religious leaders and educators began in response to an urgent need. Acquaintance with the purpose, spirit, method and achievements of the R.E.A. is of real value as a basis for an understanding of the direction and need of the religious education movement today.

The R.E.A. may be defined as a voluntary, interfaith association or fellowship of men and women interested in the improvement of religious and moral education. It has sought to hold consistently to the threefold purpose: "To inspire the religious forces of our country with the educational ideal; to inspire the educational forces of our country with the religious ideal; and, to keep before the public mind the ideal of moral and religious education and the sense of its need and value." [1] Stated more concretely, the purpose has been to analyze significant issues, to stimulate, to promote, to inspire, to assist. It undertakes no work being done by other agencies but functions as a clearinghouse and center for constructive analysis and useful information related to the cause of religious and moral education. Thus is brought to focus the "deep sense of our national need of a great emphasis upon moral and religious education and upon the inter-penetration of educational and religious ideals." [2]

THE TASK DEFINED

Significant changes during the nineteenth century helped to bring to focus the need of this new movement. Among these were the divorcement of the American public school from religious education, the accelerated development of training for Sunday-school teachers, a wave of enthusiasm for Bible study and instruction, the waxing and waning of supreme emphasis on "conversion," a felt need of the gradation of pupils, the improvement of teaching methods, conflict between the promoters of historical method

[1] "Purpose of the Convention" (1905), *Religious Education*, April, 1906, p. 2.
[2] H. C. King, "A Forward Look in Religious Education," *Idem*, April, 1907, p. 9

in Bible study and the aggressive conservatives, increased knowledge of growing persons because of developments in the study of child psychology, and changes in the theory of education.

Under the active leadership of President William Rainey Harper of the University of Chicago, the "Council of Seventy" of the Institute of Sacred Literature sought to promote the historical study of the Bible and related sacred literature and to improve religious and moral education. Included among the 1,259 charter members of the R.E.A. were oustanding representative leaders such as Edward Scribner Ames, James B. Angell, Nicholas Murray Butler, George A. Coe, John Dewey, Frederick B. Eiselen, William Rainey Harper, Shailer Mathews, William F. McDowell, Francis G. Peabody, and Walter Dill Scott. They were deeply concerned about the inadequacy of biblical instruction in the Church and the decrease, almost to the vanishing point, of religious instruction in the public schools.

A "decalogue of needs" was published to "brief" prospective members of the R.E.A., outlining a program

(1) To endeavor to define the true relation of religious and moral instruction with the instruction of history, science, literature and other subjects in the public school; (2) to seek to show how to correlate religious and moral instruction with the instruction of history, science and literature obtained in the public schools; (3) to present and apply the established results of modern pedagogy and Bible study as related to religious and moral training; (4) to indicate the proper place of the Bible in religious and moral instruction and set forth the general and specific methods of using the Bible for this purpose; (5) to show the necessity and method of gradation of pupils according to age, capacity and attainment and of graded method for them; (6) to indicate how this new, higher ideal can be worked out in the churches and in other agencies; (7) to seek to create a graded curriculum embodying the larger substance and better methods of moral and religious education commensurate with current biblical, theological, ethical, psychological and other scientific knowledge; (8) to recommend for the study of the Bible, religion and morality in ancient and modern times the best available sources as judged by the new ideal, and to promote further preparation of materials in the field; (9) to seek by all possible means to accomplish adequate training of moral and religious teachers, pointing out how to get and use needed knowledge, the necessary qualifications for teachers in training, and the best methods to serve them; (10) and to seek to unite in common work all individuals and agencies laboring for this high ideal.[3]

Organization and Program of the R.E.A.

With great hope the R.E.A. held its first convention in Chicago, February 10-12, 1903. Religious education was henceforth to mean more than Sun-

[3] *A Call for a Convention*, Bulletin No. 1, R.E.A., August, 1903, pp. 5-6.

day-school reform. Involved was the entire educational program of the Church and all other responsive agencies. The comprehensiveness of the first convention keynoted a pioneering program which year after year has sought to focus the vital issues of the time, such as the relation of religious and moral education to general education as conditioned by modern psychology and the historical study of the Bible; education in and through the family, youth societies, and associations, and other community agencies; and the development of a better organized curriculum. Dean Frank K. Sanders of the Yale University Divinity School, stated the flying goal: "To reach and to disseminate correct thinking on all general subjects relating to religious and moral education."

Originally the plan was to federate all religious educational forces of the continent under the ablest leaders. In order to cope with the complex task as envisioned by the founders, the R.E.A. undertook a sweeping program; and the organization fairly bulged with officers, committees, and activities. The first two decades (1903-23) were a period of organizational expansion. Not only did it weather the stormy years of the First World War, but it continued to establish new bridgeheads for the movement. For seventeen years (1906-23) Dr. Henry F. Cope, as general secretary, demonstrated amazing versatility in executive, editorial, and promotional activity. For example, it was reported that in 1908 there were 52,000 who attended 208 conferences. In a period of five years a large share of 307 textbooks in the field were written by members of the association. However, organizational and program changes were made in accordance with newly discovered needs.

The R.E.A. was recognized as a strong unifying agency and was appropriately called "an epitome of work." What at the beginning of the century had been dubbed "the harmless hobby of academic theorists" became a practical organization with a dynamic program. This included the application of scientific method in religious education, the stimulation and construction of more adequate building facilities for Sunday and weekday programs, the standardization of Bible departments in colleges, encouragement of the use of the Bible in accredited high schools, making various kinds of helpful surveys such as that by Walter S. Athearn, who was concerned with the co-ordination of educational agencies in the Church.

After the death of Cope in 1923, the question of continuance was raised. Typical of its functional emphasis and practice, the R.E.A. ordered a thorough investigation of itself to discover if it had outlived its usefulness. For this the services of the Institute of Social and Religious Research were secured. As a result the Institute reported, in 1927, the R.E.A. as a "professional organization of high value, a forum of free discussion, a meeting place for educators of all faiths, a common ground for character education, and an opportunity for pioneer inquiry and experimentation," thus confirming the policies already in practice as an independent organization for fellowship and service.

In the third decade the association was concerned largely with world affairs and the way "in which every national group may expect to realize its own essential aspiration within a system of mutuality." This program involved the integration of missionary education into the normal process of religious education, the criticism of all literature to eliminate subtle appeals to social and national prejudice, a more general acceptance by all religious bodies of the principles and policies currently avowed by leading exponents of the missionary enterprise, conserving religious devotion and eliminating partisanship, a resolute effort to promote in each locality the study of such objectives as the principles and methods of developing world-mindedness (helping teachers in their work with children, youth, and adults), organizing the church school to see the problems concretely, and how to overcome factors which militate against world-mindedness. It was agreed to get down to facts; to teach the conception of society which was in harmony with the Judeo-Christian tradition; to work especially through the unchurched families; to make all possible contacts with children and foreigners; to note honestly the unchristian attitudes found in the Bible, especially in the Old Testament; and to make every effort to improve the attitudes of adults.

With the support of the Institute of Social and Religious Research and the co-operation of such agencies as the newly established International Council of Religious Education "a research extraordinary" was launched under the direction of twelve specialists. The findings were published by Hartshorne and May (1928-30) on familiar themes: studies in deceit, in service and self-control, and in the organization of character. This well illustrated the persistent interest in the scientific approach as a truth-finding basis for religious and moral education.

In the last fifteen years there has been a deep sense of responsibility for the discovery of ways and means of developing integrated and socialized personalities and the problem of placing the knowledge in hand at the disposal of those who need it. The R.E.A. has been particularly sensitive to the need of understanding the relation of religion to the social, economic, and political situation and has sought diligently to suggest solutions. Much emphasis has been given to the responsibility of religion operating through the educational agencies of the community in meeting social and individual problems with concentration on "religious experience in an unstable world." By 1937 the sharp contrast between democracy and totalitarianism became more and more alarming. Studies of what happens to religion in such situations were carefully made under such themes as "education and authority in the church and state" and "what liberty does religion require?" Since 1935, the R.E.A. has operated under entirely voluntary leadership with a greatly simplified program. Weathering the "rough waters" of economic depression, reorganization was effected under the leadership of Hugh Hartshorne, E. J. Chave, H. S. Elliott, and H. S. Dimock, and the fellowship continued to function. By a vigorous editorial program through the official journal *Religious Education*, emphasis has been given to social, economic, and political issues and their effect upon American morale. However, such basic problems as those arising from the philosophy of experimentalism, the tensions created by differences between progressive religious education and current theology, the alcohol problem, and the relations of church and state, particularly the problems involved in religious education in the public schools, have been investigated and publicized. Consideration has been given consistently to character education on all levels of life from the elementary school through the university and for adults.

Principles and Policies

From this brief survey of the rich and varied experience of the R.E.A. certain tested principles and policies of value emerge. The foresight of the founders is attested by the fact that the principles and policies outlined by them are still applicable and challenging. These progressive religious educators have been neither faddists nor mere academic dreamers.[4]

1. From the beginning there has been the threefold tone quality of scientific, universal, and co-operative spirit. Diligent effort has been made to secure the best available scholarship for the purpose of integrating religion and education. The principle of ecumenicity has been the very breath of the fellowship, broadening out from evangelical Protestants to an interfaith movement. Co-operation has tended toward the breaking down of provincialism and the avoiding of sectarian, denominational, or partisan competition and duplication.

2. The threefold purpose of imbuing education with the religious ideal, imbuing religion with the educational ideal, and publicizing the progress as a public service has appealed to religious educators.

3. The effectiveness of such a voluntary fellowship of scientifically minded pioneers is seen in the creative policy and activity which has come from being organizationally independent and from having the much needed freedom for functional emphasis and unity.

4. Recognition of the Bible as the primary source book for religious education, keeping in mind scholarly thoroughness, has led to a constructive interpretation of the historical setting of our Judeo-Christian heritage.

5. A keen sense of the social responsibility of religion has prompted

[4] For a more detailed statement see Davis, "History of the R.E.A.," *Religious Education*, January-February, 1949, pp. 41-54.

emphasis on the family, church, school, and other community agencies as interrelated factors contributing to personality and character development.

6. Because of the recognized central importance of growing persons there is a constantly felt need of exploring their nature, nurture, and rights, thus demanding redefinition of the educational process in accord with psychological discovery along with reorientation in method.

7. Rising from this is the improved philosophy that sound education is, not a fragmentary, but a unifying process involving all factors, inherited and environmental.

8. The pioneering, missionary spirit as related to progressive religious education demands the functional emphasis by which changing need is critically examined, and by which is produced the kind of organization and program which serve co-operatively and avoid duplication of effort. Outcomes of such a working principle are notable in a unified local church program, as well as in the fields of missionary service.

9. Research of the highest quality as a basic policy is the only sound basis for an adequate organization and program as seen in the many research projects sponsored or stimulated by the R.E.A.

10. Conferences, conventions, consultations, correspondence, and publications have provided the principal channels for the expression of these principles and policies.

Contributions to Religious Education

Since 1903 the R.E.A. has consistently sought to demonstrate the functional approach. This is seen in the use of scientific method to discover and to serve need. Noting that religion and education had drifted apart, the R.E.A. endeavored to reunite them. Secular education without religious and moral education has been considered fragmentary. Religion without the developed insights, techniques, and other values in the process which we call "education" has been considered both inadequate and inefficient. The study and use of the Bible being more or less haphazard, more critical scholarship has been applied to it. With such worthy concerns the R.E.A. has served as a critic and publicity agent.

Emphasizing the functional approach, this group of pioneers has stimulated and fostered several investigations of current needs and has pursued solutions for them. New outposts have been won. New methods have been discovered and used, even though the basic policies have not been changed. For example, the R.E.A. has sought the answer to the question of how to improve the co-operation of orthodox and liberal Christians, orthodox and liberal Jews, and unchurched idealists. This has demanded organizational flexibility and mobility.

Concerned more with the *facts* than the *theories* of inspiration, the R.E.A. has helped to discover and emphasize the values of experience as found in extrabiblical sources. Hence the careful examination of religious facts of experience recorded in sacred literature and the need of discovering more effective ways of bringing it into vital contact with experience in the home, church, school, community, state, and international relations. From such an emphasis comes the demand for teachers in the local church school better trained in biblical interpretation and in the study of the nature and nurture of growing personality.

The changing of the concept of education as formal discipline or the mere acquisition of knowledge to the concept of education as a social process with heredity and environment as interrelated factors has been given considerable emphasis. The growing personality has been placed in the center of importance by making better use of the laws of learning and growth. This has led to more intelligent use of the findings of psychology, sociology, and other specializations related to religious experience; also to an awareness of the ever-recurring need of research. A more intelligent gradation of pupils and curriculums has come in consequence.

Emphasis upon the co-ordination of educational agencies in the local community has been one of the contributions of the R.E.A. This tends toward a better understanding of the need of the improved co-operation of educational forces of the church and state involving world-wide neighborliness and the ecumenical movement. In this connection it is helpful to find an example of the practice of the cardinal principles of organization, such as (1) basing the organization on discovered need, (2) maintaining the spirit and practice of unity, (3) practicing flexibility occasioned by the real need, (4) simplicity, and (5) the effective placing of responsibility.

One of the most significant contributions of the R.E.A. has been through its interfaith fellowship because of interest in the enrichment of *all* education by religious experience and the enrichment of religion in different groups by the process of progressive education. Introducing one issue of the journal, in which appeared a symposium on "The Community in America—Problem and Opportunity," Leo L. Honor wrote as follows:

Catholics, Protestants and Jews have engaged in cooperative efforts in many areas of endeavor. Usually, however, such cooperative effort is made possible through each group's restraining itself from emphasizing its distinctive outlook upon life and through its concentrating upon aspects of religion which are common to all religious groups, or else through the temporary lack of identification on the part of the cooperating individuals with the respective groups to which they belong.

In the Religious Education Association, the three groups are carrying on a much more significant experiment in intergroup cooperation. Each group is encouraged to work with the others on a problem of common interest while each group remains fully conscious of its own peculiar pattern of religious living. Unity is attained without any sacrifice of distinctiveness. What is more, the problem to which this common effort is directed pertains to the very field of human endeavor in respect to which the cooperating groups have differed in the past, . . . and shall continue to differ in the future. This presents an experiment in democracy at the point of its highest significance.[5]

EDITORIAL SERVICE

The editorial achievements of the R.E.A. have been significant. In the official publications can be found the record of important conferences and conventions, the presentation of various points of view as found in group discussions of experienced leaders, and the findings of research and survey. Of particular historical significance are the three volumes of proceedings of the early conventions: *The Improvement of Religious Education* (1903), *The Bible in Practical Life* (1904), and *The Aims of Religious Education* (1905). In the journal *Religious Education* from 1906 can be found the record of the principles, policies, organizational developments and changes, as well as a wide range of articles, symposia, syllabuses, and book reviews of value in the study of the movement. The short Bibliography at the end of this chapter is offered to suggest sources for further study either about the R.E.A. as such, or of the principles and methods presented by writers who have been associated in the work of the organization. In addition there have been a large number of publications by many others who have been inspired and stimulated by the R.E.A.

Of special interest and value for an analysis of current trends are the symposia and syllabuses published in *Religious Education*. They contribute to a better understanding of the vital issues and the present task of religious education. For example, one of the severest, and to some extent justifiable, criticisms of the religious education movement has been the accusation that it has lacked proper emphasis on *religion*, that doctrinally it has floundered in confusion, seeking to "save souls by techniques and a process."

As a corrective for any such shortcoming it is profitable to study the religious philosophy underlying the movement as presented from time to time in the journal, especially during the past ten years. Attention has been called to the *religiousness* of religious education: that it needs a theology, that there is a theology relevant to it, and that there are observable facts of experience where theology and education meet. "The Real Problem of Religious Education," by E. B. Homrighausen[6] and numerous other articles through the decade, have called attention to theological trends, the need of restudying the religion of childhood and youth, religion on the college

[5] *Religious Education*, XL (1945), p. 192.
[6] *Ibid.*, January-February, 1939.

level, the resources of the religious community, and religious education for adults.

Reports of regional and general meetings and other editorial contributions of the association through the years provide reliable source material on many vital issues confronted by the educational agencies of the Roman Catholic and Protestant churches and the Jewish synagogues. Particularly notable are symposia, containing as many as ten articles each, on such themes as the religious resources of the college (1942); the significance of religious education for psychiatry and psychology, with emphasis on clinical methods in the training of ministers; education in the postwar world (1943); the alcohol problem; community tensions and intercultural education; the family in transition; education for citizenship; character education in the church school (1944); education for the Christian ministry; religious education in rural America; religion and race in education (1945); progress in weekday religious education; biblical scholarship and religious education; intercultural comity; sources of vitality in the religious community; contributions of psychology to religious education (1946); a survey of directors of religious education; spiritual forces to undergird the United Nations; religion at the college level; religion in public education; ongoing projects in religious education; character education; emotions in religious education (1947); the public schools; considering the children; evangelism and the educative process; religion in higher education (1948). In addition to the symposia there have been many stimulating articles dealing with growing persons on the various levels of experience, and on methods by which to minister to their needs. Various useful Bibliographies have been prepared, as, for example, that prepared by Edward W. Blakeman on religious education and the public schools.[7] Critical book reviews in each issue of the journal also add to the resources by which one may keep abreast with the movement in general. Plans are now under way for the preparation of syllabuses for the use of local chapters of the association in the following areas: Religion in Public Education, Religion in Higher Education, and Interfaith Co-operation in Religious Education.

The Association Today and Its Services

Service to the cause of religious and moral education has been the motivation of the R.E.A. Shaping its organization and program to currently discovered need, it has consistently practiced the principles of simplicity, adaptability, and democratic procedure. Effective pioneering—the concentration upon vital issues and their solutions—has been and still is the consuming interest. Thus, acquaintance with the present organization and program is

[7] XLIII (1948).

of value to those who are interested in reports of current trends and the prophetic utterances of present-day leaders.

The present organization consists of the following offices under voluntary leadership: honorary president, president, three vice-presidents, treasurer, and recording secretary. The standing committees are as follows: executive, editorial, finance, and central planning.

The R.E.A. seeks to perform its functions through three channels: the bimonthly journal *Religious Education,* national and regional meetings held somewhat irregularly, and the four standing committees. Special committees are created for work in special areas needed. At present there are eight regions, each having a director: California, Florida, Kentucky, Michigan, Missouri, New England, New York, Texas. Membership in the association includes a subscription to the journal.

Summary

For forty-five years this volunteer, interfaith association has served as a clearinghouse for useful information and opinion based upon the experience of leaders imbued with the scientific and ecumenical spirit. Avoiding duplication in its organization and program, the R.E.A. has kept on the frontiers, blazing trails in progressive religious and moral education and keeping before the public the vital issues involved in the enrichment of education by religious experience and the enrichment of religion by the process of education. Free from institutional emphasis and entanglements, as well as from partisan bias, the association has held an important place of leadership in objective, friendly, reverent, constructive criticism by which the values of religious and moral education may be conserved and new pathways may be discovered.

The R.E.A. continues on the assumption that as long as men are free there is need of pioneers. The statement of Laird T. Hites, who for several years served as editor of *Religious Education,* expresses the spirit and purpose of the present association:

We are seeking, with all that is in us, to develop a philosophy adequate to the needs of men and women who are religious educators in the larger sense, who are interested in developing wholesome religious personalities in children, in youth, in adults—and in the social whole.

In the midst of a rapidly evolving society, a developing science, a questioning of every standard that is old and authoritative, some group of fearless and penetrating minds must continue to formulate and reformulate that philosophy. They must question relentlessly. They must be free . . . to criticize *themselves and each other,* and through joint effort to discover more truth.[8]

[8] *Ibid.,* XXXIII (1938), p. 194 Italics mine.

Progress in education reveals unexplored areas, unreached goals, unfinished tasks. The R.E.A. seeks to serve the cause of progressive religious and moral education.

SUGGESTIONS FOR FURTHER STUDY

1. What are the implications of the *purpose* of the Religious Education Association for religious and moral education today?

2. Make a critical study of the stated principles and policies of the R.E.A. and list the agencies in your local community to which they may or may not be applied.

3. What areas of religious and moral education need an independent association of pioneers imbued with the scientific and ecumenical spirit today?

4. What are similarities and dissimilarities of Jewish, Roman Catholic, and Protestant education?

5. Choose one of the outstanding past or present members of the R.E.A., such as George H. Betts, William C. Bower, Ernest J. Chave, George A. Coe, Harrison S. Elliott, or Hugh Hartshorne, and prepare a report on his contribution to religious education.

6. Choose one of the emphases listed in the section of this chapter dealing with the editorial achievements of the R.E.A., such as "the religious educational resources of the community" or "religion in higher education," and prepare a report based on your findings in the journal *Religious Education* through a given period of at least five years.

BIBLIOGRAPHY

Brown, A. A. *A History of Religious Education in Recent Times.* New York: Abingdon Press, 1923.

Cope, H. F. *Organizing the Church School.* New York: Doubleday, Doran & Co., 1929.

Davis O. L. *History of the Religious Education Association.* Unpublished master's thesis. Evanston: Northwestern University, 1933. This chapter contains material from this unpublished thesis.

————. "A History of the Religious Education Association," *Religious Education.* January, 1949. This chapter contains material from this article.

Elliott, H. S. *Can Religious Education Be Christian?* New York: Macmillan Company, 1940.

Lankard, F. G. *A History of the American Sunday School Curriculum.* New York: Abingdon Press, 1927.

Lotz, P. H., and Crawford, L. W. *Studies in Religious Education.* Nashville: Cokesbury Press, 1931.

Murphy, A. J. *Education for World-Mindedness.* New York: Abingdon Press, 1931.

Religious Education, Official Journal of the R.E.A., 20 West Jackson Boulevard, Chicago 4, Illinois.

Chapter 36

THE UNITED CHRISTIAN YOUTH MOVEMENT

ISAAC K. BECKES

As OFFICIAL CHURCH MOVEMENTS GO, the United Christian Youth Movement is comparatively new. Its formation was the definite result of a series of important meetings in 1934: the February 7-14 meeting of the Committee on the Religious Education of Youth of the International Council of Religious Education; the Conference of National Leaders in Youth Work at Pittsburgh, March 26-28, under the auspices of the Joint Committee on United Youth Program, representing eleven national agencies concerned with youth work; and the Christian Youth Council of North America on June 26-July 1, a gathering of youth and adult leaders representative of denominations, state councils of churches and religious education, and national agencies. The plans for a new united youth program projected at this meeting were the natural outcome of almost a decade of prayer, study, and experimentation by youth leaders in an effort to find an acceptable plan for interdenominational action. These leaders were on untried ground in their labors to build an interdenominational youth program representative of the churches; and it would have been surprising, indeed, if the plans they made should not have needed considerable adjustment later. The United Christian Youth Movement today is not the creation of a few months of planning or of a few men's imagination. Rather it is the result of twenty-five years of experience and of the aspiration and work of literally hundreds of leaders, both youth and adult.

Actually, the new united youth program outlined in 1934 bore the title "Christian Youth Building a New World." The words "United Christian Youth Movement" do not appear in that sequence until 1935. Furthermore, this new united effort was designed more as a program than a movement. Nevertheless 1934 was a decisive year in the development of a new united youth movement. Its leaders were conscious of being at a crucial moment in Christian youth work.

Since 1934 the philosophy, program, and organization of the movement have undergone repeated adjustment in order to clarify and make more effective its place as the instrument of united youth action. Matured and strengthened as the U.C.Y.M. is today, it is still an emerging movement.

Paramount since 1934 is the concern that the movement become an instrument of united action among young people.

The United Christian Youth Movement is a movement of the youth of the Christian churches and related agencies who are joined together by a common belief in Jesus Christ as Lord and Saviour through whom they are united in the fellowship of his Church. Because of their unity in Christ, they face together the problems of Christian youth today, seeking to express their witness in Christian action at the local, state, national and world levels.[1]

Thus was the U.C.Y.M. defined in 1948. Although since 1934 the movement has been redefined as its purpose clarified, it still operates in the same mood of complete Christian dedication as was expressed by its founders as they wrote, in "A Statement of Christian Commitment," their reaffirmation of faith in Jesus Christ as Lord and Saviour, confessed their responsibility for contemporary human tragedy, described the Christian enterprise as they understood it, and concluded with the following paragraph:

We recognize something of the magnitude of the (Christian) enterprise. It demands new individuals and a new society. It calls upon individuals to abandon petty and selfish aims and to lose themselves in glorious adventure. But we have faith in youth and their leaders, that they will respond to that call. We are not alone. Divine resources flow through us and human fellowship sustains us as we give ourselves to that task. He that loses his life shall find it. For us there is no alternative: to this cause we give ourselves, and call upon all those of like purpose to share with us.[2]

Background and Organization of the U.C.Y.M.

To a major degree, the development of the United Christian Youth Movement is the result of two emerging streams of emphasis in youth work. These emphases had been challenging existing patterns of youth work with increasing success over a period of at least a decade and a half prior to 1934.

The first of these emphases grew out of the conviction among youth leaders that young people themselves, below the age of twenty-five years, should have a real share in the shaping of their programs at all levels—local, state, and national. Certain denominational youth departments led the way in this new emphasis upon youth's place in planning and policy making, and the pressure was soon applied at the interdenominational level.

In September, 1937, the Director of Young People's Work for the International Council of Religious Education made a statement to the Administra-

---

[1] *Minutes* of the Committee on Religious Education of the International Council of Religious Education, Chicago, October 1948, Exhibit J. *Minutes* of the Committee on the United Christian Youth Movement, Kalamazoo, Michigan, September 5-8, 1948, Appendix D.

[2] *Minutes* of the Conference of National Leaders in Young People's Work, Pittsburgh, March 26-28, 1934, pp. 7-8. This Statement of Christian Commitment was revised and adopted also by the Christian Youth Council of North America, June 26–July 1, 1934.

tive Committee of the Committee on the United Christian Youth Movement in which he stated, "Previous to 1926, there had not been any agency representing young people themselves in the development and promotion of the interdenominational youth program through the International Council.[3]

The director's statement went on to review the activity which had resulted in the formation of the Committee on the United Christian Youth Movement, tracing it back to a meeting in Birmingham in 1926, where a plan of organization was projected for a Christian Youth Council of North America that would bring together representative young people and their leaders from denominations, state councils of churches and religious education, and national agencies.

This council was a paper organization until 1930, when it met in Toronto, where provision was made for consultation and co-operation in planning with the Committee on Religious Education of Youth of the I.C.R.E. in the interim between quadrennial meetings.

In June, 1934, at the third meeting of the Christian Youth Council of North America the new united program was presented to the youth representatives of the churches and agencies of the International Council and the Joint Committee on United Youth Program. It met with immediate and enthusiastic response. The next important step was the calling of the Christian Youth Conference of North America—held at Lakeside, Ohio, in 1936. This larger conference was called "because of the need of bringing a larger group than the membership of the Christian Youth Council [of North America] to consider the development and promotion of the United Christian Youth Movement." In reality, the Lakeside meeting of 1936 was the occasion for the launching of the Christian Youth Building a New World program and the United Christian Youth Movement.

The second of these major trends leading to the formation of the U.C.Y.M. was the emphasis upon denominational responsibility for youth work. This emphasis involved all phases of the churches' program, not youth work alone. This trend was an essential factor in bringing about the organization of the International Council of Religious Education in 1922, combining the interests of the International Sunday School Association and the Sunday School Council of Evangelical Denominations. It has been a decisive factor in changing the interdenominational movement from the hands of interested and consecrated individuals to official representatives of the church bodies.

The effect of this trend toward denominational responsibility for interdenominational agencies upon the United Christian Youth Movement is

[3] Percy R. Hayward, *Minutes* of the Administrative Committee of the Committee on the United Christian Youth Movement, New York, September 18, 1937, p. 1.

pointedly described in the report of the Committee on the Religious Education of Youth to the Commission on Educational Program of the I.C.R.E. in 1938:

In summary, this report stated that when the movement was organized, it was thought the widest possible representation would be secured by setting up a governing committee representative of eleven youth agencies,[4] but by 1938 certain weaknesses in this plan had appeared. Primary agencies such as the national church bodies and state councils of churches and religious education were not directly represented in the Committee on the U.C.Y.M. Because these groups were not represented, it was difficult to get satisfactory youth attendance at important planning sessions, and the meetings in which young people did participate—Christian Youth Council of North America and Christian Youth Conference of North America—were not directly related to the Committee on the U.C.Y.M., which made the policy decisions.

Furthermore, while the International Council provided executive leadership for the movement and in the public mind was held responsible for all its activities, the movement was not actually responsible to the I.C.R.E.[5]

These viewpoints were largely those of the denominational leadership. They resulted in the adoption of the plan of organization which greatly enlarged the Committee on the U.C.Y.M. by the inclusion of representation from both state councils and denominations. Administratively, the movement was related directly to the I.C.R.E. through the Committee on the Religious Education of Youth, and thereby came under the full direction of the Boards of Christian Education of the denominations. Both the Christian Youth Council of North America and the Christian Youth Conference of North America were administratively related to the Committee on the U.C.Y.M., thus ending the confusion and overlapping which grew out of parallel programs sponsored by the Committee on the Religious Education of Youth of the I.C.R.E. and the Joint Committee on the United Youth Program.[6] In 1945 the Christian Youth Council of North America was eliminated entirely from the plan of organization in favor of a major annual meeting of the Committee on the United Christian Youth Movement for purposes of policy and program making.[7]

[4] Young People's Work Professional Advisory Section, Missionary Education Professional Advisory Section, Committee on the Religious Education of Youth, Federal Council of Churches, International Society of Christian Endeavor, Missionary Education Movement, Home Missions Council, University Commission, Student Christian Movement, Young Men's Christian Association, Young Women's Christian Association.

[5] See *Report* of the Committee on the Religious Education of Youth to the Educational Commission, February 10-11, 1938, pp. 6 ff.

[6] See *A Plan for Organization of the United Christian Youth Movement*, Minutes of the Meeting of the Committee on the United Christian Youth Movement, February 4-6, 1938, pp. 11 ff.

[7] *Minutes* of the Meeting of the Administrative Committee of the Committee on the United Christian Youth Movement, June 27-29, 1945, New York, Exhibit C.

Throughout the past decade, the young people themselves and the denominational youth fellowships have played an increasingly important part in the development of the movement, and the movement has become firmly established as the official united youth agency of the churches. The movement continues to report its activities through the Committee on the Religious Education of Youth to the International Council for administrative approval.

Matters of program, policy, and finance are handled by the Committee on the U.C.Y.M. This committee meets once each year and is comprised of four youth representatives and one adult from each national church body; two youth representatives and one adult from each state council and national, or international, youth agency; the national officers of the movement; the chairmen of the seven regional conferences of the U.C.Y.M.; commission chairmen; and such other desirable persons as may be recommended by the staff.

An Ad Interim Committee, consisting of one youth representative from each national church body, state youth council, and national or international agency, the national officers and regional chairmen of the U.C.Y.M., and the chairman of the Committee on the Religious Education of Youth, meets once each year to conduct the interim business of the movement. The Executive Committee, which includes the national chairman, the national secretary, the financial secretary, the eight regional chairmen, and the chairman of the Committee on the Religious Education of Youth, acts in an advisory capacity to the staff.

PHILOSOPHY AND OBJECTIVES OF UNITED ACTION

United youth action recognizes that certain areas of the Church's ministry to youth belong in the local church and does not attempt to duplicate them, but the churches must join hands to provide a total ministry to the youth of any community. Christians, young and old alike, have an obligation to work together for the salvation of their communities and their world. The reconciliation of man to God is, not a competitive process, but a sharing process that involves right relationships between man and God and man and his brother. Christians may disagree in interpretation, but they cannot break relationship with each other in their cause of spreading the gospel and remain in the Christian context.[8]

With such interpretation of the Christian task in mind, the Committee on the United Christian Youth Movement adopted and submitted to the

[8] For a full statement of the basis for carrying on the work of the U.C.Y.M. see *Christian Youth in Cooperative Action* (Chicago: United Christian Youth Movement, 1945).

Committee on the Religious Education of Youth a revised Statement of Christian Commitment in 1948.

We believe:
  That Jesus Christ is Lord and Saviour of Mankind.
  That the Unity of the Christian fellowship is in Christ.
  That God wills the ecumenical movement among the churches.
  That God is calling all Christian youth to a united witness of prayer, study, and
    action today.[9]

This statement of conviction reflects clearly the growing consciousness of participation in the maturing ecumenical movement among the churches. It takes co-operative action at the youth level out of the realm of expediency or individual interest and places it in the category of a basic Christian affirmation.

Likewise the Committee on the U.C.Y.M. in 1948 prepared a revised statement of objectives committing the movement to:

Be a channel for the ecumenical movement at the youth level expressing unity in
    Christ and the presence of his person in a fellowship of power.
Be a movement of cooperation among young people of the Christian churches,
    state and provincial councils of churches and religious education, national youth
    serving agencies, and national interdenominational agencies in the United States
    and Canada.
Develop national programs and projects as shall express the united concern of
    youth among the churches and agencies.
Guide state and community councils of churches in the development of united
    youth action.
Train young people for leadership in ecumenical action.
Provide opportunity for Christian young people to share their best experience in
    planning strategy and program for a united attack on the problems of our time.
Give youth inspiration and insight into contemporary problems that lead to
    constant commitment to Christ and his Church.[10]

This statement of objectives summarizes recent efforts to define clearly the areas of united action. A divided Protestantism makes the need for an expression of unity in Christ basic to all united action that will have sound and permanent appeal to Christian young people. In a century of youth movements there is obvious need for youth to have a channel for a united witness. Young people from the different churches need experience and inspiration which comes from sharing in common tasks. The development of activities which will make for a united youth witness is now the accepted responsibility of the United Christian Youth Movement.

[9] *Minutes* of the Committee on the Religious Education of Youth of the International Council of Religious Education, October 4-6, 1948, Exhibit J.
[10] *Ibid.*, p. 9.

More urgent even than a united witness has been the need to discover a strategy for community co-operation. The Christian community is the strategic unit for Christian planning. The ministry of the churches to youth is not complete until they provide a program of action that will reach all the youth of the community with the Christian gospel. Only when such community action is taken can the inroads of secularism be halted and Christian truth be made central in community life. Planning a total ministry to youth in a community is not within the prerogative of any one church or denomination. This area, too, is now recognized as clearly within the responsibility of the U.C.Y.M. and its state and local youth councils.

The development of local church programs is left entirely to the youth fellowships and youth departments of the national church bodies. As the church youth and their leaders plan together in the Committee on the U.C.Y.M., effort is made to correlate the community and local church programs into one united approach. Upon the denomination rests the burden of support to united community action, and upon the local united youth council rests the obligation to help local churches build an effective ministry to youth within the various denominational contexts.

As the years have passed, the areas of responsibility for the churches and agencies within the movement have become clearer. Competition for constituency has declined, and the sense of fellowship in a divine mission has increased. Through the first decade there was constant emphasis upon the fact that the U.C.Y.M. was a movement, not an organization. Today there is general recognition that there can be no movement without organization, and the early fears of building an overhead organization that would compete with the denominational youth fellowship have been replaced by confidence in the U.C.Y.M. as an agency for united action on the part of all who understand its philosophy and objectives.

THE PROGRAM FOR UNITED ACTION

The United Christian Youth Movement conceives its task broadly as the building of a total Christian ministry for youth in the United States and Canada. Such a statement should not be taken to imply that all the functions and activities necessary to an effective Christian ministry to youth shall be carried forward by the staff and committees of the movement. A major part of such a ministry must necessarily be carried on by the national church bodies and agencies co-operating within the U.C.Y.M. structure; but the welding together of all these constituent groups into a sense of unity in the name of Christ, the carrying forward of those functions which can be completed only through a representative agency, and the motivating of churches and agencies to greater effort in behalf of young people—these are the functions of the program of the U.C.Y.M. Broadly these functions fall into four categories.

The first includes activities carried forward in relation to world Christian agencies. For many years, because of its relation to the International Council of Religious Education, which is one of the members of the World Council of Christian Education, the U.C.Y.M. has been related to the youth activities of that body and has organized delegations for such conferences as that held in Havana in 1946 with Latin-American youth.

With the development of the Youth Department of the World Council of Churches the U.C.Y.M. has served as the channel for clearing the various problems of relationship between that body and the youth of the churches. It has been the administrative channel for providing the church delegation for the world-youth conferences held in Amsterdam in 1939 and in Oslo in 1947. It has co-operated closely with directors of the Youth Department of the World Council in providing a channel of ecumenical education.

The second of the broad program categories has to do with the representation of the interests of Protestant youth in such agencies as the Youth Division of the National Social Welfare Assembly, with the youth activities in which young people are concerned,[11] and with the provision of foreign travel facilities for students each summer. There are also numerous projects carried on by church agencies in which the interests of youth must be represented, such as the various conferences on vital Christian issues sponsored by the Federal Council of Churches of Christ in America.

Successfully maintaining such relationships involves considerable effort and expense, but they are unavoidable if a Protestant Christian witness is to be made in national activities of signal importance to youth, and if the spiritual and moral needs of youth are to be included in total church strategy. Before the emergence of the United Christian Youth Movement no agency could effectively represent the interests and needs of Protestant youth. On some occasions the absence of such a channel for united expression at the national level has had grave consequences for the Church's ministry to youth.

A third program category includes the sharing of experience, common planning, and joint programming. The Committee on the U.C.Y.M., the Ad Interim Committee of the U.C.Y.M., the Christian Youth Conference of North America, the Youth Service Commission, the Young People's Section of the I.C.R.E., the Committee on the Religious Education of Youth, and numerous informal consultations—all are channels for the building of Christian fellowship and programs at the youth level.

Not only do these committees and commissions serve the needs of national church bodies and state councils for studying their common tasks;

[11] White House Conference on Family Life, in 1948; Attorney General's Conference on Juvenile Delinquency, 1947; Four-H Clubs.

but they offer opportunity for national church agencies, such as the Federal Council of Churches, Home Missions Council, Missionary Education Movement, Student Volunteer Movement, to bring their specific concerns into the total planning for youth work.

In recent years there has been some effort within the U.C.Y.M. to redefine the relationship of such agencies as the Y.M.C.A. and Y.W.C.A. to the churches. There is a growing conviction among national leaders that closer co-operation between these two agencies and the churches may result in a far more effective service to youth. Increasing effort is being made to more clearly define these areas of co-operation. There is also a strong belief that church leaders have not, in past years, either at the national or local level, given the kind of broad, understanding leadership to these organizations that would make effective relationships with the churches possible.

Another kind of joint planning done within the structure of the U.C.Y.M. is the consultation given to such youth agencies as the Boy Scouts, Girl Scouts, and Camp Fire Girls. Because of the need for club programs thousands of units of these organizations have been organized in local churches. The programs of these clubs, as related to the churches, contain religious elements. These character-building agencies must look to some national church agency for guidance in the development of the religious aspects of their programs and in establishing relationship to the churches. Experience has demonstrated that individual denominations cannot effectively deal with the problems of policy in relation to such national agencies. Some channel of united Protestant negotiation is necessary to prevent confusion, opportunism, and misunderstanding.

The Youth Service Commission will serve as a final illustration of activity in sharing and joint planning. Voluntary service has become an avenue of challenging youth activity. Work camps, caravans, institutional service units, and numerous other types of activity have been organized over the past decade to meet the desire of young people to give themselves in sacrificial Christian service. In the Youth Service Commission some thirty agencies sponsoring voluntary-service projects share experiences and plan together. Through the commission they have jointly published *Invest Your Summer*, an annual annotated listing of practically every voluntary-service project available. *Invest Your Summer* circulates by the tens of thousands each summer and is in itself an important evidence of the value of joint planning.

The fourth program category includes the development of united youth action at the state and community levels. Since the chief purpose of the state youth council is to organize co-operation among Christian youth in the local community, most of the programming is on that level.

The objectives of united youth action in the community will vary somewhat with the need, but in general they may be summarized as follows:

1. To unite Christian forces in providing an effective ministry to all the youth of the community.

2. To provide a channel whereby the youth of the churches become aware of their unity in the fellowship of Christ.

3. To provide certain services to local churches which may best be provided at the community level, and which will be in harmony with the structure of the denominational youth program, such as consultation in developing an effective youth program, leadership training, guidance in using program resources inherent to the community itself.

4. To provide a channel whereby the needs of youth in the community may be under constant study, so that the churches may have accurate knowledge of those needs and how they may be met.

5. To undertake youth projects which can be effective only through united action, such as radio programs, religious-emphasis weeks, youth-week celebrations, services of ecumenical worship.

Most U.C.Y.M. publications are written to help local communities develop programs of united action. Chief among these program publications is the *Annual Emphases Manual*, specifically designed to help local united youth councils in building co-operative projects. The "Youth Action Series" provides detailed guidance for action in specific areas of major concern.

Through the national staff—national and regional officers—substantial field consultation is provided for both state and local U.C.Y.M. councils. Because of the inability of many state councils of churches to provide staff leadership for youth work the Committee on the United Christian Youth Movement has recommended, and the International Council of Religious Education has approved, the establishment of regional offices to give field service under the state councils of churches. The first of these offices was opened at Springfield, Massachusetts, in January, 1949. Others will be provided as finance permits.

One of the important services of the U.C.Y.M. to state and local communities is the holding of seven regional conferences where key young people are given training in the philosophy, purpose, and method of co-operative youth action. When the U.C.Y.M. was first organized, the Youth Department of the International Council had been conducting three International Camps. These camps had been in existence since the beginning of the camp-and-conference movement in the churches. In the early days of denominational camp and conference programs, the International Camps were important centers of experimentation; but as the denominational programs matured, they were of declining importance. It was only natural therefore that these three camps should become the training centers for leadership in the new united movement, where they could render a unique and needed service. By 1940 the transition in the program of the International Council Camps was complete, and during the ensuing years four more have been added. Some twelve hundred young people are trained annually for leadership in united youth program in these regional conferences.

An important asset in dramatizing the importance of Christian youth work in general and united action in particular is the national Youth Week celebration. This celebration has received wide support in local churches and communities and involves a variety of activities. An important part of the Youth Week observance in recent years has been the Parshad Youth Week awards, given in recognition to Christian young people who have rendered outstanding service in the local church and community. These awards are in the nature of four-year college scholarships. Twenty-five young people have received Parshad scholarships in the last four years.

Since the beginning of the movement the young people of the U.C.Y.M. have been greatly interested in social issues. This interest has been expressed in several ways. The Youth Action Series of publications gives attention to the most pressing of these issues. Programs of study have been a continuing part of the U.C.Y.M. program. From time to time the Secretary for Social Action has made presentation to Congressional committees on matters of importance to young people. These presentations are made in behalf of those constituent groups within the movement who wish such presentations made, and who have taken definite action on the issue involved.

Recently social-education seminars have given young people guidance in making their Christian leadership effective on social issues. These seminars have dealt with a variety of problem areas, taking young people where they may get firsthand knowledge of the issues involved. Seminars on world order have been held in connection with the United Nations organization; seminars on understanding national government have been held in Washington, and on state and local government in numerous communities. Intergroup retreats have proved exceptionally valuable as a means of bringing interracial and interfaith groups together for extended periods of fellowship and study.

In Conclusion

A most important factor in the advance of the United Christian Youth Movement has been the maturing of the denominational youth fellowships. The first of these fellowships was organized in 1936; and through the early years of the U.C.Y.M. denominational youth programs, too, have undergone major reorganization. As these denominational programs become stabilized, they are able to give more leadership to co-operative activity. The clarification of the unique contribution of the movement has helped greatly to build confidence and support. Finally the provision of increasing financial support on the part of co-operating national church bodies, agencies, and interested individuals makes more effective staff service possible.

Many problems still confront the movement in achieving its ultimate potentialities. Some problems, such as lay leadership, are inherent in the general youth situation in the churches. Lack of staff leadership at the state level is a major hindrance to the expansion of united activity. Inadequate understanding of community church leaders of what constitutes a total ministry to youth results in indifference, ineffective leadership and planning, in the local church and community. Finances for the program of a united youth movement will be a continuing problem for years to come, if plans are carried forward commensurate to the needs of Christian youth.

Nevertheless, the United Christian Youth Movement continues to be a growing, emerging movement. No one who understands its development doubts that there will be changes in its programs and organization in the years to come. On the other hand, few leaders who have an understanding of the problems of ministering to contemporary youth in the name of Christ question that there must be a great united movement of the Church's youth dedicated to the Christian fellowship as the instrument of divine reconciliation among men. The United Christian Youth Movement is well on the way to becoming that united movement; and, given consecrated support, adjustable as its program is to the needs of the future, it can expand its present service to the youth of the Church beyond our present comprehension. In the words of the founders of the U.C.Y.M., "For us there is no alternative: to this cause we give ourselves, and call upon those of like purpose to share with us."

SUGGESTIONS FOR FURTHER STUDY

1. Using *Christian Youth in Cooperative Action* as a guide, list the specific factors which differentiate the community program of united youth action and the youth program of the local church.

2. Make a study of the youth programs of the churches in your immediate community, and estimate the needs of youth which the churches have not effectively met. On the basis of these what are the various elements that would be included if the churches were to join hands in providing a total program for young people?

3. Make a survey of the various organizations besides the church and school which are serving young people of the community. What is the relationship between these programs and those of the churches? Are the churches helping these organizations to understand fully their responsibility for the spiritual and moral development of young people?

4. If there is a United Christian Youth Council in your community, make a study of its organization and program. If there is no such Council, with the help of *Christian Youth in Cooperative Action* draw up an effective plan for such an organization.

5. Using the *Guide for Interdenominational Youth Action* as a resource, outline a program of united youth action for your community. Review your plan with

several ministers and lay leaders to discover what possibilities and problems they see in it.

BIBLIOGRAPHY

Bower, W. C. and Hayward, P. R. *Protestantism Faces Its Educational Task Together;* Appleton, Wisconsin; C. C. Nelson Publishing Company, 1949. Chap. VI.

Christian Youth in Cooperative Action. Chicago: United Christian Youth Movement, 1947.

Guide for Interdenominational Youth Action. Chicago: United Christian Youth Movement (Annual Emphases Manual for Community Action).

Our Healing Ministry. Report of the Christian Youth Conference of North America, 1944. Chicago: United Christian Youth Movement.

United! Committed! In Christ! Report of the Christian Youth Conference of North America, 1948. Chicago: United Christian Youth Movement.

"Youth Action Series." Chicago: United Christian Youth Movement.

Christian Youth in Cooperative Action, 1947.

Christian Youth and the Economic Problem, 1944.

Christian Youth and Interfaith Cooperation, 1944.

Christian Youth and Interracial Understanding, 1946.

Christian Youth Preparing for Marriage and Home Life, 1945.

Christian Youth in Missions and Reconstruction, 1946.

Christian Youth and Political Responsibility, 1948.

Christian Youth and the Rural Task, 1946.

Christian Youth and World Order, 1944.

Helping Other Young People to Be Christian, 1948.

Chapter 37

THE WORLD COUNCIL OF CHRISTIAN EDUCATION

FORREST L. KNAPP

CONTEMPORARY DEVELOPMENTS have prompted in many persons a desire for a fuller understanding of the ecumenical organizations. This chapter is a response to that desire. It deals primarily with the World Council of Christian Education, but it touches briefly upon several other bodies.

THE BEGINNING OF THE WORLD COUNCIL OF CHRISTIAN EDUCATION

The Sunday-school movement was begun in 1780 by Robert Raikes, a publisher in England. There had been Sunday schools prior to that date; but Raikes, having aggressiveness and a newspaper, initiated a movement by spreading the news of his own school in Gloucester. One hundred years later astonishing growth had taken place. There were thousands of Sunday schools in Britain, Europe, and North America; and missionaries were planting them in many other parts of the world.

Not long after the movement was started, the leaders of different Sunday schools began to form Sunday-school associations in local communities, and then county, state, and provincial associations were established. The Sunday-school leaders and teachers naturally wanted to share their enthusiasm and get help from one another. By 1880 there was in England the National Sunday School Association; in the United States and Canada, the International Sunday School Association; and similar associations in several countries of Europe and even in India. These local, county, state, and national associations were having local, county, state, and national conventions, from which tremendous inspiration was derived. More than that, they were helping to train teachers, and the national associations were helping to provide lesson materials—two of the basic essentials for all good schools.

Then some of the North American and British leaders said it was time to have a world's convention, and so they held one in London in 1889. The reports presented to the convention reveal something of the status of the Sunday-school movement at that time. Almost phenomenal growth had taken place in England and Wales, there having been an estimated increase from 250,000 Sunday-school pupils in 1785 to 5,733,325 in 1889, with a total of

7,399,685 being given as the number of teachers and pupils in the United Kingdom. On the continent of Europe the movement was still in the beginning stages; but there were some large schools, such as one in Berlin with 1,300 pupils in 80 classes. The estimated total for the continent was 1,080,266 pupils. Canada was reported as having 522,342 pupils, and the United States, 9,455,535. In India the movement had been under way for some fifteen years. Other countries were seeing the beginnings of Sunday schools through the efforts of missionaries, but the number which had been established around the world is not known.

The 1889 Convention was a great event, and in it seeds were sown which grew into the World Council of Christian Education.

The Development of the Council

Two significant decisions were made in the 1889 Convention:

The first was to hold another convention in St. Louis in 1893. That led to others: London, again, in 1898; Jerusalem, 1904; Rome, 1907; Washington, 1910; Zurich, 1913; Tokyo, 1920; Glasgow, 1924; Los Angeles, 1928; Rio de Janeiro, 1932; and Oslo, 1936. Durban, South Africa, was chosen for 1940, but the war intervened. Toronto was the choice for 1950. These world's conventions brought together more persons across the lines of nation, race, and denomination than came together in the same period under any other auspices in the interest of world-wide Christian education.

The second decision in the 1889 convention was to provide money to send a missionary to India to be secretary of the thirteen-year-old India Sunday School Union and to write lesson materials and to train teachers. That action led to one of the most important developments in modern Christian education. The leaders of the World's Sunday School Convention set out with unquenchable missionary zeal to help every country in the world by forming and undergirding national Sunday-school associations to provide lesson materials, to train and inspire teachers, and to promote Christian teaching. Through the conventions themselves, and by means of the travels of officers and other representatives, the idea was conveyed to many parts of the world that through national, interdenominational co-operation the Sunday school could be promoted, teachers could be trained, and lesson materials could be provided. To understand how important this undertaking was, you should imagine yourself in a country where no one was promoting Sunday schools or other such institutions, no one was training teachers, and no one was preparing lesson materials.

Go to any major part of the world today and you will find work under way which was started as a result, in significant measure, of what happened back there in 1889: China has a National Committee for Christian Religious Education; South Africa has a National Sunday School Association; Brazil has a Confederation of Evangelical Churches; Mexico has a National Evangelical Council; and so on around the world. In time fifty-five countries were being served by such bodies.

Brazil provides a good illustration of how this development took place. In the Washington Convention in 1910 the two or three delegates from that country were asked by the general secretary of the World's Sunday School Association why they did not form a Sunday-school union. When they returned, they put his suggestion into effect. Soon the new union began publishing teacher-training materials and providing other helps for the young Sunday-school movement. Then the demands upon the Union became too great for volunteer leadership. Requests were sent to the World's Sunday School Association for a full-time secretary, and in 1920 Herbert S. Harris was provided. He led vigorously forward. After a while the union expanded into the Council of Religious Education. Rodolfo Anders became Harris' assistant; and then later Harris withdrew, and Anders, a native of Brazil, took over. Later the Council of Religious Education merged with another body to form the Confederation of Evangelical Churches. Through all the years since 1920 the World's Association has supplied annual grants-in-aid, as local Protestant resources are insufficient, but at the same time there has been expanding strength and widening service within Brazil.

This story could be paralleled in numerous other countries. Only the details would differ; the principal lines of growth, with stimulus and help from the World's Sunday School Association, are essentially the same.

Speaking of the World's Sunday School Association, let us go back to Rome, 1907. To meet world-wide needs, a permanent organization was required. Quadrennial conventions with committees functioning in between were not enough. Therefore the World's Sunday School Association was formed. The association's first substantial budget was adopted in 1910 when the Washington Convention raised nearly $75,000 for three years. By 1928 the Association had changed its form somewhat and had become a federation composed of national, interdenominational Sunday-school associations and councils of religious education.

Then came the latest change. Sunday-school leaders had seen long before that the Sunday school was not enough. Other institutions and agencies—young people's societies, daily vacation Bible schools, and weekday schools developed. The World's Association was asked to help them. And so in August, 1947, the name of the World's Sunday School Association was changed to World Council of Christian Education to show the full breadth of its responsibility and program.

Such an organization, world wide in scope, may seem far removed from the local church and its members. In one sense the distance is long, and yet there is a clear line from the one to the other. Take a local church in the

United States, for example, which is part of one of the many co-operative communions or denominations. The denomination has a board of Christian education. That board of Christian education is a member of the International Council of Religious Education, and it in turn is the American-Canadian constituent organization of the World Council of Christian Education. In other parts of the world there are other member organizations, each with its roots in the local church and community: The Department of Christian Education of the Canadian Council of Churches, the India Sunday School Union, the Congo Protestant Council, the Korea Council of Christian Education, and others in other countries.

The World Council of Christian Education is a *council* of *councils;* but each member council, or association, arises out of denominations or local churches and Sunday schools. The World Council helps the national councils and associations in serving the local churches in their respective countries.

The Council Today

An effective and democratic form of organization on a world scale may be fairly easy to conceive in theory, but in the presence of facts regarding distances and travel costs, the task is difficult. It is impracticable to have frequent meetings of representatives from all over the world.

The governing body of the World Council of Christian Education is known as the Assembly. It is composed of official representatives of the constituent organizations of the World Council plus the officers and a few members-at-large. It is expected to meet every four years. Between meetings of the Assembly, its functions are discharged by a small Board of Managers. Much of the work of the council is done by two committees, the British Administrative Committee and the North American Administrative Committee. The necessity of having such committees, composed of persons drawn largely from only two geographical sections, results from the fact that members of the assembly are so widely scattered, and from the inescapable fact that a large proportion of the financial resources of the council come from Britain, Canada, and the United States. But through the travels of the secretaries and the extensive correspondence which they carry on, the counsel of leaders in many countries is enlisted.

The present and projected program of the Council may be summarized in eleven points. This eleven-point program does not include all the worldwide services that are needed in the field of Christian education, but further expansion may be possible in the future.

1. Field visitation by the secretaries to encourage and strengthen national, interdenominational organizations for service in Christian education. Again and again, in both the World Council of Christian Education and in other bodies, it has been demonstrated that nothing can take the place of personal

relationships and personal counseling. Plans have been approved for supplementing the work of the secretaries in the headquarters offices by regional secretaries.

2. Grants-in-aid to national, interdenominational organizations which cannot enlist adequate resources from within their own constituencies.

3. Audio-visual aids. The following are the main elements of the program: (a) formulation of the principles of using visual aids in Christian education; (b) evaluation of audio-visual aids and equipment for use in Christian education, in co-operation with other bodies; (c) counseling of its member units in the setting up of a program of service in visual aids, and in incorporating visual aids into their curriculum; (d) training of specialists in visual aids for nation-wide interdenominational service; (e) research to determine the needs in visual aids and to find ways to meet them; and (f) general promotion of the use of visual aids in religious education through its member units.

4. Study and research. The World Council of Christian Education is carrying on its study and research in close co-operation with the International Missionary Council and the World Council of Churches through a Joint Commission on Christian Education. The first project was a study of church youth work around the world.

5. Sponsoring the World Fellowship in Christian Education, including the publication of the quarterly *World Christian Education* as a medium for the exchange of experience and ideas.

6. Helping in the indigenous preparation of curriculum materials. The importance of this help is recognized by those who realize how few countries have leaders with thorough training and experience in the preparation of curriculum materials for conditions in those countries.

7. The training of teachers and other leaders. In order for us to have well-prepared teachers and other leaders in religious education, there are four inescapable requirements: (a) curriculum materials for teacher training, (b) a plan for organizing and promoting training opportunities, (c) a sufficient number of teachers, and (d) a strong emphasis in theological schools and elsewhere upon the pastor's task in religious education. In most countries these needs are very far from being met. The World Council of Christian Education seeks to use every channel to help in correcting that condition.

8. Children's work. The number of well-trained specialists outside the United States, Canada, and Britain who are rendering nation-wide interdenominational service in children's work is distressingly small. The World Council of Christian Education is expanding its service in this field.

9. Youth work. Unless the Church captures and holds the youth of today, what hope will there be for the world of tomorrow? In many countries there is appearing an unprecedented interest on the part of the churches

in youth work, and that interest ought to be fed and guided with the best experience and help to be found anywhere. The World Council of Christian Education is widening its service for this purpose.

10. Travel and study scholarships. The policy has been established of providing scholarship aid to enable selected persons to advance their preparation for nation-wide, interdenominational service in Christian education.

11. Conventions. The council continues the practice of holding World Conventions on Christian Education. These conventions have brought together thousands of persons across the lines of nation, race, and denomination, helping not only to promote Christian education, but also to lay the foundations for recent ecumenical developments.

OTHER ECUMENICAL BODIES

The International Missionary Council, which had its beginning in 1910 in the first World Missionary Conference in Edinburgh, has shown strong interest in Christian education. This interest was especially manifest in the Jerusalem Conference in 1928. The second volume of the reports was given wholly to Christian religious education. The following paragraph from that volume has been quoted many times and has had wide influence:

Religious education in the Christian sense includes all efforts and processes which help to bring children and adults into a vital and saving experience of God revealed in Christ; to quicken the sense of God as a living reality, so that communion with Him in prayer and worship becomes a natural habit and principle of life; to enable them to interpret the meaning of their growing experience of life in the light of ultimate values; to establish attitudes and habits of Christ-like living in common life and in all human relations; and to enlarge and deepen the understanding of the historic facts on which Christianity rests and of the rich content of Christian experience, belief, and doctrine.

The World's Young Women's Christian Association, the World Alliance of Young Men's Christian Associations, and the World's Student Christian Federation, three parallel ecumenical bodies, are carrying on a great deal of Christian education, even though their work is not always so labeled.

The World Council of Churches, youngest and yet in nature most comprehensive of the ecumenical organizations, is in principle concerned with Christian education, although its development of a program in this field is yet to take place. In its First Assembly, held in Amsterdam in 1948, it approved certain criteria which should be applied in considering a church's application for membership. One of them states that the church "should have an established program of Christian nurture and evangelism." The 1937 Oxford Conference on Life and Work, a forerunner of the Council of

Churches, issued a valuable statement on "Church, Community, and State in Relation to Education."

Many persons have asked this question: What is to be the relationship between the World Council of Christian Education and the World Council of Churches? The ultimate answer is not known, but co-operation on certain projects of mutual interest is under way. Moreover, the First Assembly of the Council of Churches approved the following item, which was presented by one of its committees:

The Committee express admiration for the work of the World Council of Christian Education and recommend that the World Council of Churches welcome cooperation with the World Council of Christian Education in the field of Christian education, and further recommend that the World Council of Christian Education be included among the organizations invited to send representatives in a consultative capacity to the Assembly.

What the future holds for any of these organizations cannot be known in advance. None should outlive its usefulness. But so long as the task of the Church of Christ is unfinished, there will be need for ecumenical fellowship and service in Christian education.

SUGGESTIONS FOR FURTHER STUDY

1. Compile information regarding the participation of your denomination in the task of extending and strengthening Christian education beyond the national boundaries. In seeking data, you might: (a) Write to the chief officer of the denomination asking if the denomination as a whole has taken any action pertaining to this subject, and especially on the subject of support of any of the ecumenical bodies in its work in Christian education. (b) Ask your denominational board of Christian education what responsibility, if any, it carries for world-wide service. (c) Ask your denominational board of foreign missions what it does to advance Christian education in the countries in which it serves. You might ask for information about the participation of your denomination in the World Council of Churches, the International Missionary Council, and the World Council of Christian Education.

2. Make an analysis of one year's issues of each of the following quarterly periodicals, considering what is being done by the respective world organization to advance Christian education: ,

World Christian Education, published by the World Council of Christian Education.

International Missionary Review, published by the International Missionary Council.

Ecumenical Review, published by the World Council of Churches.

BIBLIOGRAPHY

Because of the nature of this chapter, there is no thoroughly satisfactory bibliography to accompany it. However, persons interested in the latest information about the work of any of the world organizations mentioned in the chapter might write to its American headquarters for current descriptive leaflets or pamphlets. Those who wish to read more widely are referred to the following, which, although in most cases out of print, are in some instances available in libraries:

The Churches Survey Their Task. Report of the Conference at Oxford, July 1937, on Church, Community, and State. London: G. Allen & Unwin, 1937.
Faith and Order. Report of the Second World Conference on Faith and Order, 1937. New York: Macmillan Co., 1938.
Religious Education. Vol. II of the reports of the Jerusalem Meeting of the International Missionary Council, 1928, New York, 1928.
Reports of the World Sunday School Conventions from 1889 to date.

PART VI

Wider Perspective of Religious Education

Chapter 38

THE RELATION OF CHURCH AND STATE

RAY GIBBONS

THE RELATION OF CHURCH and state is coming into sharp focus in American life, especially in the field of education. The need of the public schools for increased support, the serious inequality of educational opportunity among the several states, and the alarming illiteracy revealed by the selective service program have accelerated efforts to secure federal aid to education. Recent decisions of the United States Supreme Court—approving the payment of bus transportation to parochial-school children from public tax funds, in the Everson case; and the disapproval of weekday religious education conducted in public-school buildings on "released" time, in the McCollum case—have aroused new interest in the meaning of the First Amendment. The formation of a new organization called "Protestants and Other Americans United for the Separation of Church and State"; the publication of a statement by the Roman Catholic bishops, November 21, 1948, on *The Christian in Action,* which favored "free co-operation between government and religious bodies"; and the issuance of a statement by twenty-seven Protestant leaders, *Christianity and Crisis,* on July 5, 1948, which approved "co-operation, entered into freely by the state and church and involving no threat to the religious liberty of any citizen"—these have high-lighted Catholic and Protestant views on the relation of church and state. Obviously that relationship is still in flux and has become a subject of current controversy. The determination of the pattern for the future presents a problem which deserves the earnest attention of schoolmen and churchmen, statesmen and religious educators.

HISTORICAL BACKGROUND OF CHURCH AND STATE IN AMERICA

The early colonial churches in America were established churches. They were supported by taxes. Church attendance was compulsory. Only church members could vote and hold public office. Religion was considered a community responsibility.

There was a strong pressure toward religious uniformity in the early period. The Puritans in New England and the Anglicans in Virginia were alike in their suppression of Baptists, Catholics, and Quakers and also in their rejection of each other. Puritans were banned in Virginia and Anglicans in Massachusetts. Pennsylvania, Rhode Island, and Maryland, when it was predominantly Protestant, generally practiced toleration, but discriminated against Catholics. New York and the Carolinas recognized the Church of England but were generally tolerant of all faiths.

Several factors early began to undermine the establishments. In order to secure more colonists the proprietors offered inducements of religious liberty to other than established churches. Puritans were settled in Anglican New Jersey and the Carolinas and Presbyterians in Anglican Virginia. The Carolinas and Rhode Island wrote religious toleration into their charters as early as 1663, and Virginia followed suit subsequent to the English Revolution of 1689. Roger Williams and William Penn preached and practiced toleration as a matter of principle. The establishments were further weakened under the pressure of deism and the "Great Awakening" which invigorated the newer, dissenting sects. The forms of establishment remained, but the heart had gone out of it by the time of the Revolutionary War.

The Revolution hastened disestablishment, especially in the South. The Virginia constitution of 1776 included a clause on "the free exercise of religion" and finally dissolved the last bonds of establishment through Jefferson's bill of 1786. State after state followed suit, concluding with the dissolution of the last bonds in Massachusetts in 1833. The process was uneven but in one direction. Separation was the result of state by state accommodation to the changing culture patterns rather than a sudden consensus of conviction or the act of the federal government.

The newly formed federal union was generally favorable to religion and appointed chaplains for the Congress and for the army. The Congress did what it could to encourage religious freedom. In the Northwest Ordinance of 1787 it forbade interference with any person in that area "on account of his mode of worship, or religious sentiments." In the Constitution it prohibited religious tests for "office or public trust under the United States." In the First Amendment to the Constitution the Congress laid upon itself the prohibition, "Congress shall make no law respecting an establishment of religion, or prohibiting the free exercise thereof." At the time, this amendment applied only to the federal government and did not affect the five states which had established churches. It was not until a century later that these protections were extended to the several states—long after these states had disestablished their churches and granted freedom of religion to all faiths. Both the federal and state governments continued their favorable attitude toward religion in general. Disestablishment did not mean either indifference or hostility toward religion but, rather, encouragement without partiality.

RELIGIOUS FREEDOM IN PRACTICE AND THEORY

In view of the foregoing history we are led to conclude that the American pattern of "separation of church and state" is the practical result of political necessities. It is a way of accommodation to a situation in which we have many differing religious faiths and some persons of no particular faith at all. If the pattern is unique, it is because the problem to be solved was unique. Other countries have maintained religious freedom under other forms of church-state relationships. These facts should relieve us of the necessity of defending the present pattern as necessarily the best, or of transforming a practical solution into a universal, unchanging principle. The principle is not "separation" but religious freedom. Separation must be judged by its service to that principle.

A common-sense definition of the American "separation of church and state" means that the state may not establish or favor any one religion or interfere with the free exercise of any religious faith, except to safeguard public order and morals. No "establishment" of religion means no state or federal financial support to any religious institution, no compulsory church attendance, and no religious test for a public office. It means no preferment of one religion above another, since this might be considered a kind of halfway establishment. The "free exercise" of religion includes the right to worship, attend, participate, support, proselytize, and publish the faith of one's choice. It does not condone practices which disturb the peace; nor does it permit licentiousness, blasphemy, polygamy, or the violation of public health provisions.

Some carry separation to its logical extreme and define it as the estrangement of church and state, not only as institutions, but as spheres of influence. Such radical separation means that the state will not favor religion in any form, and that religious influence will be divorced from every sphere of public life, such as education. The United States Supreme Court has stated in the Everson case that it is the purpose of the First Amendment "to create a complete and permanent separation of the sphere of religious activity and civil authority by comprehensively forbidding every form of public aid or support for religion." Some hold that this would make the tax exemption of church property unconstitutional, and others that it should lead to the withdrawal of state support of chaplains in the armed services and civic institutions.

The state which has gone the furthest in carrying separation to its logical limit is Russia. Article 124 of its Constitution reads: "In order to insure to citizens freedom of conscience, the church in the U.S.S.R. is separated from the state, and the school from the church. Freedom of religious worship and freedom of antireligious propaganda is recognized for all citizens." Separation has not been carried to such limits in the United States. Here the state has been well disposed toward religion. When action was brought against a church because it had brought a minister from England under contract to be its rector, Justice Brewer rendered the opinion of the Supreme Court saying, "No purpose of action against religion can be imputed to any legislation, state or nation, because this is a religious people. . . . These and many other matters which might be noticed add a volume of unofficial declarations to the mass of organic utterances that this is a Christian nation." [1] The state is still favorably disposed toward religion. The sharp differences of opinion arise over whether or not a more complete separation of spheres of influence of church and state would promote the general welfare.

FREEDOM FOR RELIGION

The Papal encyclicals have protested against the separation of the Church from education, proclaimed the role of the Church as teacher, and maintained the right of the Church to regulate the schools. Said Pope Leo XIII:

To exclude the Church, founded by God Himself, from the business of life, from the power of making laws, from the training of youth, from domestic society, is a grave and fatal error. The Church of Christ is the true and sole teacher of virtue and guardian of morals.[2]

Pope Pius XI developed this position in *Christian Education of Youth.*

First of all education belongs preeminently to the Church, by reason of a double title in the supernatural order, conferred exclusively upon her by God Himself; absolutely superior to any other title in the natural order. . . . To be this [that is, a fit place for Catholic students] it is necessary that all the teaching and the whole organization of the school, and its teachers, syllabus and text-books in every branch, be regulated by the Christian spirit, under the direction and maternal supervision of the Church.[3]

Where this is not possible in the public schools, separate parochial schools are established in order that religion may play its proper role in relation to education.

The Roman Catholic feels there is a measure of justice in his desire to have the state support parochial schools, if it can be done without violating religious freedom. Pope Pius XI stated in *Christian Education of Youth,*

In other countries of mixed creeds . . . a heavy burden weighs upon Catholics, who, under the guidance of their Bishops and with the indefatigable cooperation of the clergy, secular and regular, support Catholic schools for their children entirely at their own expense. . . . If such education is not aided from public funds, as distributive justice requires, certainly it may not be opposed by any civil

---

[1] Church of the Holy Trinity *vs.* U.S. 143, U.S. 457 (1892).

[2] *Immortale Dei* (1885). *Principles for Peace. Selections from Papal Documents* (Washington, D. C.: National Catholic Welfare Conference).

[3] Washington: National Catholic Welfare Conference, 1930.

authority ready to recognize the rights of the family, and the irreducible claims of legitimate liberty.

Protestant churches vary among themselves in their views on the relation of religion to education. Some claim to be the true and sole teachers of faith and morals, and some establish their own parochial schools wherever possible. They have not usually sought state support for such schools, but frequently they have accepted indirect aid of many sorts. Generally Protestants reject the idea that any one church has the sole authority to teach faith and morals. Their emphasis upon freedom has resulted in great variety and widespread toleration. Justification by faith emphasizes the unmediated, direct communication of God and man without dependency upon any intermediary institution. God calls men to freedom. He makes men free, not only from their own past and their former sin, but also from dependence upon an authoritative interpretation of truth by the institution of the church. To be fully free toward God a man must be free from present sin, free to fulfill his present moral obligations. Such freedom requires religious freedom, freedom of association, and freedom of education and action. By and large Protestantism stands for the freedom to obey God according to one's conscience and rights of others to do the same.

Protestant principles teach that both church and state are created by God. The one is not supernatural and the other natural. Neither the church nor the state has any superiority because of its origin.

The church is a voluntary fellowship of believers who engage in worship, religious instruction, propagation of their faith, and service to society. In order to achieve its purpose it must be free to assemble, to formulate its own creeds and ordinances, to regulate its own household, to teach, publish, and proselyte, as long as these activities do not infringe upon the rights of others or endanger civil order. In fulfilling its function it has a certain responsibility to the state: namely, to erect and maintain moral standards. At times this will mean support of the state when it is right and condemnation of the state when it is unjust. The church's only weapons are moral suasion, conscientious objection, and, in the last analysis, martyrdom.

The nature of the state is to exert power and to compel service to establish and maintain order within and without the state. Maintenance of order within the state includes promotion of such things as public welfare, education, health. The state alone can levy taxes and compel attendance at school. The state safeguards freedom of religion, encourages the church in the performance of its functions, and gives equal treatment to all sects and faiths. The state rightly demands obedience of the church and its members to the laws of the state in the interests of maintaining order.

The tension between church and state arises because both claim the loyalty of men. The church claims final authority in matters of faith and morals—

authority, not for the visible church, which is the human fellowship, but for the invisible kingdom of God, to which the visible church itself must give its obedience. The state claims final authority in matters of order and security, not for the government, but for the people, to whom the government itself is answerable. The state must resist the claim of the church to rule as a theocratic state; the church must resist the claim of the state to rule as a pagan church—that is, totalitarianism. Both are subject to God and responsible to him for their conduct.

To summarize: Church and state are "separate" in the sense that each respects the autonomy of the other; they are "inseparable" in that each contributes to the fulfillment of the other.

Protestant theory has a rather direct bearing upon education. It emphasizes the importance of religion in education as strongly as Catholicism, but it does not believe in the exclusive possession of truth by any one church. To attain the truth requires freedom of inquiry, freedom from the control of any church or state. Protestantism is not content with a purely secular education which produces a kind of freedom without faith, or a church-controlled education which produces faith at the expense of freedom. Rather it seeks a kind of religious freedom which includes both faith and freedom. It has sought to relate and supplement public and religious education in many helpful ways. When this becomes impossible and religious freedom can be safeguarded only by separate church schools, it establishes parochial schools of its own. In a totalitarian state, for example, it would be necessary, for conscience' sake, to establish separate schools. The principal effort of Protestantism, however, is directed toward free, public education, with religion supporting, surrounding, and co-operating with it to the end that religious freedom may be increased and flourish. The First Amendment puts two prohibitions upon the state, "Congress shall make no law respecting an establishment of religion, or prohibiting the free exercise thereof." A long series of court decisions has clearly defined the meaning and scope of the "free exercise" part. "In this country the full and free right to entertain any religious principle, and to teach any religious doctrine which does not violate the laws of morality and property, and which does not infringe personal rights, is conceded to all." [4] The Supreme Court has repeatedly quoted Thomas Jefferson's favorable comment upon this "free exercise" clause in which he refers to it as a "wall of separation." Wrote Jefferson:

Believing with you that religion is a matter which lies solely between man and his God; that he owes account to none other for his faith or his worship; that the legislative powers of the Government reach actions only, and not opinions, I contemplate with sovereign reverence that act of the whole American people which declared that their Legislature should "make no law respecting an establish-

---

[4] Watson *vs.* Jones, 13 Wall. 699 (1871).

ment of religion or prohibiting the free exercise thereof," thus building a wall of separation between Church and State.[5]

The state is prohibited from interfering with the "free exercise" of opinion, but in the realm of actions it may limit "free exercise" in order to safeguard the general welfare.

Recent Supreme Court decisions have also interpreted the first half of the First Amendment, "respecting an establishment of religion," in the light of Jefferson's "wall of separation." In the Everson case the court held that it was not unconstitutional for New Jersey to permit the payment of bus transportation to children attending parochial schools using money derived from tax funds, but that "no tax in any amount, large or small, can be levied to support any religious activities or institutions, whatever they may be called or whatever form they may adopt to teach or practice religion," since that would be an "establishment" of religion. New Jersey had not breached this wall. Bus transportation, the court decided by a 5-4 decision, was not aid to religion or a religious school, but general welfare legislation. The benefits of such legislation must be distributed equitably without regard to one's faith or lack of it.[6] In the McCollum case, however, the Supreme Court decided (8-1) that weekday religious education on "released" time conducted in public school buildings *was* an "establishment" of religion. It was a form of aid to religion and therefore unconstitutional, even though the aid was very slight and impartially given to all faiths. In these cases Justice Black interpreted the prohibition against "establishment" as meaning:

1. Neither a state nor the Federal Government can set up a church.

2. Neither can pass laws which aid one religion, aid all religions, or prefer one religion over another.

3. Neither can force or influence a person to go to or to remain away from church against his will or force him to profess a belief or disbelief in any religion.

4. No person can be punished for entertaining or for professing religious beliefs or disbeliefs, for church attendance or non-attendance.

5. No tax in any amount, large or small, can be levied to support any religious activities or institutions, whatever they may be called, or whatever form they may adopt to teach or practice religion.

6. Neither a state nor the Federal Government can, openly or secretly, participate in the affairs of any religious organizations or groups, and vice versa.[7]

Some authorities on the Constitution hold that points 2 and 5 go beyond any previous interpretation of the First Amendment, since they allow no aid to "all religions" even if given impartially. Edward S. Corwin, formerly

[5] Reynolds *vs.* United States, 98 U.S. 164 (1878).
[6] Everson *vs.* Board of Education, 330 U.S. 1 (1947).
[7] People of Illinois *ex rel.* McCollum *vs.* Board of Education, 333 U.S. 203 (1948).

Professor of Jurisprudence at Princeton University, comments, "The historical record shows clearly that the core idea of 'an establishment of religion' comprises the idea of *preference;* and that any act of public authority favorable to religion in general cannot, without falsification of history, be brought under the ban of that phrase." [8] Does this interpretation of the First Amendment make all forms of co-operation between church and school unconstitutional? For example, does it threaten released-time programs when not conducted in public-school buildings? Is the tax exemption of church and parochial school property a form of aid to all religion which is unconstitutional? Is the release of an hour a week as much of an aid to religion as the payment of bus transportation to parochial schools? Would not the cessation of all aid to religion in effect deny some people the right to worship and endanger the "free exercise" of religion? Do not the two clauses of the First Amendment impose limitations upon each other so that neither the prohibition against establishment nor "free exercise" are absolutes? Is there not a wide area for functional interaction between the poles of "establishment" and "free exercise" in which church and state can co-operate without setting up an established church or endangering the free exercise of religion? If a line should be drawn between church and state to prevent establishment of a religion, who should decide where it should be drawn? The Roman Catholic Church? The Protestant Churches? The Supreme Court? The public schools? The American public? In the interests of religious freedom is it better to define the boundaries of the respective spheres of church and state once and for all or to maintain an area for interaction and experimentation in forms of co-operation? What are the possible results if either the state or a church takes an intransigent position?

Church-State Relations in the Field of Education

The earliest American practice was to support church schools with public tax funds, but the trend was toward supporting only public schools by taxation. In the middle of the nineteenth century New York City withdrew tax support from any school which taught or practiced "any religious or sectarian doctrine." State after state followed suit until it became universal practice to use tax funds for public schools only. Either by provisions in their constitutions, state legislation, or court decisions the states have all limited tax funds to public-school use. As the Supreme Court declared in the Everson case, "No tax in any amount, large or small, can be levied to support any religious activities or institutions, whatever they may be called or whatever form they may adopt to teach or practice religion." Other schools, private and parochial, may be maintained separately, for the state

---

8 "The Supreme Court as National School Board," p. 681.

has no power "to standardize its children by forcing them to accept instruction from public teachers only." [9] But such permission does not imply public support, other than the tax exemption granted to all educational institutions. Many services which incidentally or indirectly aid the schools, such as school lunches, health programs, educational aid like the GI grants, scholarship assistance, bus transportation, and nonreligious textbooks, have been classified as "welfare" and must be given to all children without discrimination as to their religion. "It [the state] cannot exclude individual Catholics, Lutherans, Mohammedans, Baptists, Jews, Methodists, nonbelievers, Presbyterians, or the members of any other faith, because of their faith, or lack of it, from receiving the benefits of public welfare legislation," said the Everson case. There are now eighteen states which permit the payment of bus transportation to children attending parochial schools, and five may provide nonreligious textbooks for children of parochial as well as public schools. The latter was declared constitutional by the Supreme Court.[10]

Since the Supreme Court has distinguished between direct aid to schools and welfare services to children regardless of the school they attend, it is good to keep the distinction in federal legislation and administration. The school lunch program and the health program were not incorporated in bills to aid education as such. Some of the bills to further federal aid to education have followed states' rights and included aid for welfare services. Others have specifically excluded health services and bus transportation. At the present time efforts to extend bus transportation payments from federal funds to all forty-eight states, or to forbid the use of federal funds for bus transportation in the eighteen states which now permit such use, have both been unavailing. Present practice is to permit the states to determine whether bus transportation and nonreligious textbooks shall be granted to children attending parochial schools. The Supreme Court decisions permit, but do not require, such action by the states.

It is within the power of the states to compel the attendance of children at some school—public, private, or parochial—for a certain minimum number of hours per year. "Released time" substitutes attendance at a parochial school for all the hours of the week or at a weekday school of religious education for one hour a week. Under certain conditions the children may attend religious festivals and celebrate religious holidays. The Supreme Court decided that the use of public-school buildings for religious education on released time was a violation of the First Amendment in the Champaign, Illinois (McCollum), case, but it has not as yet ruled specifically upon the use of released or "dismissed" time.

[9] Pierce vs. Society of Sisters, 268 U.S. 510 (1925).
[10] Cochran vs. State Board of Education, 281 U.S. 370 (1930).

The reasons given by the court for arriving at its decision have been more disturbing than the final decision rendered. The Roman Catholic bishops stated in a public release on *The Christian in Action*, "We feel with deep conviction that for the sake of both good citizenship and religion there should be reaffirmation of our original tradition of free co-operation involving no special privilege to any group and no restriction on the religious liberty of any citizen." A group of twenty-seven Protestant leaders issued a statement in *Christianity and Crisis* to the effect that "co-operation entered into freely by the state and church and involving no special privilege to any church and no threat to the religious liberty of any citizen should be permitted. As Protestants we desire to affirm this interpretation of the American doctrine of separation of church and state, and protest against the interpretation that has been formulated by the Supreme Court." On the other hand, some Protestants, Jews, and others welcomed the "wall of separation" metaphor applied to the "establishment" portion of the First Amendment. To them it seemed to secure religious freedom rather than to endanger it.

Many forms of religious observance and instruction are practiced in public schools. At this point we are interested only in the problem these programs raise for church-state relations. Twelve states prohibit religious instruction of a sectarian nature. No state constitution prohibits the use of the Bible, but the courts differ as to whether the Bible is sectarian or not. Some states prohibit teachers from conducting religious exercises in the public schools; some prescribe reading of the Bible, while still others permit the use of the Bible, the Lord's Prayer, and the teaching of the Ten Commandments. Most courts have upheld the validity of Bible reading on the grounds that its contents are largely historical and moral, but a few have held that reading the Bible violates the religious freedom of non-Christians. In general, non-sectarian exercises have been permitted when they do not infringe on religious freedom. Thus far the willingness of religious groups to adopt common-sense, tolerant attitudes has aided the process of finding workable solutions. Intransigence on the part of any religious group or the desire to press "separation" to its logical end jeopardizes these programs and furthers the secularization of public education.

Neither American experience nor court decisions have completely crystallized the relations of church and state or built a "wall of separation" which is fixed and immovable. The First Amendment does not define separation with precision but rather defines the limits as no "establishment" on the one hand and no interference with "free exercise" on the other. It does not mean that the state is opposed to religion or neutral toward God. It does not mean that the church must avoid political activity or withdraw from the field of education. Rather it permits a wide area for interaction. Church and state are free and independent institutions, but they are both subject to God's laws and may co-operate with each other in discerning and obeying these laws. Their spheres of influence partially overlap each other, as, for example, in education.

Much yet needs to be done to clarify the Protestant position on religious freedom. It is not merely defensive. It is not based upon secular sources. It is derived from firsthand religious experience of God and the nature of salvation. Historically it has contributed greatly to the growth of religious freedom and free public education. It can yet make a unique and significant contribution to the future of American society and its system of education.

The future patterns of church-state relations in education will be determined by the attitudes and actions of many parties and groups in American society. Intransigent positions on the part of the churches or state will impede solutions. Substitution of slogans and metaphors for careful thought will delay the process of accommodation. Construing practical solutions as if they were absolute principles will complicate the problem. More positively genuine efforts of Protestants, Roman Catholics, Jews, school administrators, and religious educators to find solutions which are mutually agreeable and conform to American practices of toleration and religious freedom will do much to further the interests of public education and will help promote relations of church, state, and education.

SUGGESTIONS FOR FURTHER STUDY

1. What are the arguments for and against federal aid to education? What groups line up in support of, or in opposition to, such legislation?

2. What is the present practice of your state in regard to bus transportation, nonreligious textbooks, and other services paid to parochial-school children from tax funds? What do you consider desirable policy in regard to these and other welfare services?

3. Discuss the implications of the McCollum decision on the program of weekday religious education. What are the effects in your city and state?

4. What attitude do Protestants, Catholics, Jews, humanists, and others have toward current programs of weekday religious education? How do school administrators view the program?

5. What specific programs of co-operation between the churches and the schools are in effect? What would be possible and advisable?

6. In what sense is the United States a "Christian," "non-Christian," "religious," or "nonreligious" nation?

7. What do you consider essential parts of a Protestant program of church-state relations in the field of education?

BIBLIOGRAPHY

Barth, Karl. *Church and State*. London: Student Christian Movement, 1939.

Brown, William Adams. *Church and State*. New York: Charles Scribner's Sons, 1936.

The Christian in Action. Statement of the American Roman Catholic Bishops.

National Catholic Welfare Conference, 1312 Massachusetts Avenue, N. W., Washington 5, D. C., 1948.

Corwin, Edward S. "The Supreme Court as a National School Board." Reprint from *Thought*, Fordham University Quarterly, XXII (1948).

Everson vs. *Board of Education*, New Jersey. 330 U.S. 1 (1947).

Federal Aid—Imperative. National Education Association, 1201 Sixteenth Street, N. W., Washington 6, D. C.

Gibbons, Ray. "Protestantism and Public Education," in *Social Action*, February 15, 1949. Council for Social Action, 289 Fourth Avenue, New York 10, N. Y.

Greene, Evarts. *Church and State*. National Foundation Press, 143 N. Meridan Street, Indianapolis, Indiana.

Hocking, William. *Man and the State*. New Haven: Yale University Press, 1926.

Keehn, Thomas. "Church-State Relations," in *Social Action*, November 15, 1948.

Kingberg, Frank. *A Free Church in a Free State—America's Unique Contribution*. Indianapolis: National Foundation Press.

McCollum vs. *Board of Education*, Champaign, Illinois. 333 U.S. 203 (1948).

"Statement of Twenty-Seven Protestants," in *Christianity and Crisis*, July 5, 1948. 600 West 122nd Street, New York, N. Y.

Waite, Edward. *Jefferson's "Wall of Separation": What and Where?* Minnesota Law Review, April, 1949, pp. 494 ff.

Chapter 39

THE RELATION OF RELIGION
AND PUBLIC EDUCATION

J. PAUL WILLIAMS

THE DIVORCE BETWEEN RELIGION and the public schools in the United States was an experiment. All through colonial times, and for fifty years after our birth as a nation, the teaching of religion was considered to be a major function of all schools—public as well as private. Secular education was the creation of politicians in the middle of the nineteenth century in an effort to resolve the conflict among the churches over what type of religion should be indoctrinated at public expense. The Trinitarians fought the Unitarians; the Catholics fought the Protestants. The politicians, though they were convinced of the necessity for religious instruction, saw no solution to the problem except to take out of the schools—or to almost take out—any instruction in the traditional religions. This secularization of education placed the burden of teaching religion on the churches and the homes.

This solution has seemed so firmly a part of public policy in this country that until about a decade ago educators assumed the finality of the divorce between religion and the public schools. Recently, however, dissatisfaction on the part of many religious leaders with the situation has brought the problem back into focus. These leaders are motivated by a variety of convictions and are by no means in agreement. Most prominent among the reasons advanced for disapproval of the present arrangements for religious education are the following.

1. Secularism in the schools: The politicians did not intend to establish an antireligious school, and most contemporary public educators do not intend to maintain one. Nevertheless, the net effect of the present system, it is contended, has been unfavorable to the traditional religions. It has left the impression that religion is divorced from real life, that maturity of religious experience is possible without serious study, that knowledge of religion is not essential to a rounded education. Moreover, while the public school has prevented Jews, Catholics, and Protestants from indoctrinating their views, it has often granted naturalists and humanists freedom to indoctrinate their views under the guise of teaching philosophy, logic, science, or even literature.

2. The weakening influence of the traditional religions: Religious leaders

debate the present strength of the churches and synagogues. Many scholars point to increasing membership rolls as an evidence of waxing strength: at the beginning of our life as a nation only about 5 per cent of the population were active church members; by 1890, about 22 per cent were members; today over 50 per cent are members. Other scholars aver that, in spite of this favorable growth, church membership means less, clergymen have less prestige, and churches have less influence than in former generations. Many who view the situation pessimistically find the root of the difficulty in the large portion of the population which receives no systematic instruction of any kind in religion. This proportion is frequently estimated at 50 per cent.

3. Widespread moral laxity: The extent of crime in the United States is a common observation. Antisocial acts—falsehood, graft, bribery, overcharging, dishonest advertising, lewdness, racial discrimination, warmongering— are an equal cause for comment. Many observers hold the opinion that one major cause of this moral laxity is inadequate instruction in religion, that is, ineffective efforts to reach the basic moral judgments of individual persons.

4. Disagreement on basic social values: Society, it is averred, is at basis a spiritual entity, a set of values which are held in common, and which are believed to have ultimate sanctions. But there is much disagreement—so runs the argument—on what values are basic to American life. Our societal standards are a frequent subject for debate. Youths soon learn that they cannot take at face value the moral preachments of their elders. Even loyalty to democracy is sometimes called into question: as a whole our people have little understanding of democracy as an ultimate ideal, and there is much conduct predicated on antidemocratic principles. Since religion deals with basic values, it is contended that the integration and vivification of social ideals demand more effective religious education.

5. The threat of radical social action: Some of the persons who are dissatisfied with the present manner of providing for religious education are opposed on principle to any major social change. They think of religious education as a conservative force and as a bulwark against communism and socialism; fascism seldom figures in their writings.

Before presenting five proposals which are seriously advanced in answer to the question "How should responsibility for teaching religion be allocated among American institutions?" let me comment on a number of factors which affect all the proposals.

1. It is frequently supposed that state and national laws prevent any kind of religious instruction in public education. This supposition is in error. A few states actually require a limited amount of religious instruction—usually reading daily a passage from the Bible without comment. Almost universally the laws proscribe the teaching of "sectarianism," not of "religion." These two terms are not necessarily identical in meaning.

Some of the proposals advocate the indoctrination of sectarianism and thus assume changes in the present laws. Making such proposals is of course entirely proper; legal enactments, including constitutional provisions and Supreme Court pronouncements, are not infallible.

2. The term "teach" is used in two different ways. Usually it is equated with the term "indoctrinate." More and more, however, teaching means giving students the resources by means of which independent decisions can be made. Some of the proposals assume the first definition of the term, and other proposals assume the second.

3. The term "religion" is used in different ways. Some thinkers insist on the ordinary dictionary definition. Religion for them is what goes on in the churches and synagogues; it is always characterized by belief in a personal God, in petitionary prayer, in immortality, and so on. Other thinkers consider this point of view as "naïve and arrived at after an insufficient view of the data." There are religions, say such persons, which are not theistic—for example, early Buddhism. Thus, a person's religion is considered to be whatever he believes about the nature of the universe and its ultimate demands on human beings. Under this definition such things as hedonism, nationalism, communism, are thought to be the religions of some people.

The definition assigned to the term "religion" must be closely watched in appraising the various proposals listed below.

4. Advocates of all the proposals contend that they believe in freedom of religion. However, conceptions of what freedom of religion consists of vary greatly. Historically, freedom has meant in America the protection of the rights of parents and sects, rather than of children; children have often been the objects of spiritual coercion. Some of the proposals imply objections to this historic practice and seek to protect children from violations of their religious freedom.

Moreover, freedom can be denied by inaction as well as by action; lack of provision for experience with religion is as much of a denial of freedom as is insisting on a specific type of experience.

Also it should be noted that Roman Catholics use the word "freedom" in a sense almost exactly opposed to the ordinary American usage. Catholic usage is predicated on the assumption that Catholic theology is perfect, infallible, the Truth. Catholics use the term "freedom of religion," but mean by it a social situation in which persons are free to believe the Truth, Catholic dogma, and are prevented from believing Error, religious teachings contrary to Catholic dogma.

5. The amount of effort necessary to bring about conduct in line with given religious ideals is often grossly underestimated. Of course, religion can be "taught," in the sense of gaining information, with about the same ease as any subject of comparable complexity—though the complexity of religious knowledge is frequently underestimated. But when it comes to

gaining the level where religion becomes a vital factor in living, many impressions are essential, and they must be continued over an extended period. One hour a week is clearly inadequate. Teaching religion—in the sense of helping a growing person to achieve a life orientation—is probably the most difficult teaching anyone can undertake.

The five proposals for allocating responsibility for religious teaching will be presented in the order of the increasing involvement they suggest of the state in the teaching of religion. One very live option—weekday religious instruction on released time—will not be discussed since a full chapter is devoted to the topic in this volume. (See Chapter 22.)

1. Keep Things as They Are

Aside from persons who are constitutionally against any and all change, opposition to proposals to make religion part of the public school curriculum comes from four major groups.

a) One group is afraid that the members of some one church might get control of the school and run it in their own interest. In the past the schools in a good many sections of the country have been dominated by a Protestant or a Catholic bias.

In answer to this objection, it is said that no doubt sectarian domination of the schools is a danger, but that it is not as serious a danger as the threat of religious vacuum. Religious disintegration furnishes the opportunity for the totalitarian demagogue. When the barometer really drops, hurricanes follow.

b) Another group wishes to keep things as they are because it is thought—sometimes unconsciously—that the public school in this country has a Protestant bias, a bias which is favored. Wherever this supposition is true, freedom of religion is of course not a reality. Moreover, such Protestant teachings as may be in the public school are not of sufficient strength to warrant the assumption that strong Christian character will result from them. Also, if the schools of certain sections are Protestant, then we must expect that the schools of other sections will be Catholic. Sauce for the goose is sauce for the gander. And our great cities are more and more dominated by Roman Catholic groups.

c) Another group which wishes the present arrangements maintained is composed of persons who are opposed on principle to the traditional religions: atheists, humanists, antichurchmen, secularists. They think that the present situation is unfavorable to the continuance of the traditional religions, and they rejoice. Christianity and Judaism are, from this point of view, a liability; they represent "superstition," "otherworldliness," "gullibility." The sooner society can slough off "religion" and adopt the ways of "science" the better it will be for all of us.

No attempt to present the answer to this antireligious point of view can be undertaken here.

d) The major group which wishes to preserve the present divorce between religion and the public schools avows a deep concern for religion but asserts that its teaching should be the concern of homes and churches, not of public institutions. This group says the churches should get busy and make of their schools really respectable educational institutions operating in the nearly 150 hours a week when the public school is not in session. Our American division of labor between church and school, it is contended, has worked remarkably well; we have in the United States as virile a set of churches as is to be found anywhere in the world. Giving them state support through public education would probably have the same effect that state support has had in Europe, where in spite of, or because of, public financing, interest in the traditional religions is considerably less than it is in America.

Persons who oppose this point of view argue that however virile American churches are in comparison to those of other nations, American churches are not strong enough to maintain the religious life of their members in the face of a public school which is secular, and which takes an overwhelming amount of a child's vitality. Americans are in fact ignoramuses religiously, especially Protestants and, to a lesser degree, Jews—the Catholics who are informed religiously are the ones who have attended parochial schools. We must not force the churches, say many persons who oppose the status quo, to choose between a secular public school and a parochial school. Moreover, state support of a church, as in parts of Europe, has a very different psychological effect than state support of a school, which in turn gives to the church certain services, even as certain services are given by the school to other institutions: government, industry, commerce, the theater.

2. Indoctrinate Nonsectarian Spiritual Values

The religious needs of society—as over against the needs of individuals—can be served, contend some writers, by the indoctrination in the public schools of those values which are basic to our culture. These values are sometimes called "spiritual," at other times, "ethical," and at other times "democratic." The thesis is that the teaching of the basic moral obligations—honesty, generosity, bravery, the Four Freedoms, the Bill of Rights, the rights of minorities and of the majority, the responsibilities of living in a democracy—must not be left to the haphazard activities of homes and churches. Too many parents are inadequate as teachers. Too many people have no contact with the churches. Too many churches are concerned about other matters.

One group which espouses this point of view is motivated by an effort to preserve essentially the present setup. Many of them are humanists who distrust the churches and believe that a counterproposal is the best way "to keep the church out of the schools."

Another group believes that any society "is at basis a spiritual entity," assumes that democracy—the democratic *ideal*—should be the basis for American society, and proposes that democracy be religiously indoctrinated in the public schools. To public-school men who say, "Why, we're doing that already," this group replies: Democracy is no doubt taught in the public schools as a political system, but two things must be added to public-school practice before teaching will reach the depths of religious conviction. One of these is metaphysical sanctions—that is, the installation of the firm belief that democracy is part of the basic law of the universe, is the way of life which if pursued will bring to human beings greater happiness than any other way of life. The other thing which must be added is worship—that is, the periodic glorification, individually and by groups, of the ideal of democracy. Worship in this sense is used to refer to the integration and vitalization of life which follows contemplation of the ideal, rather than to refer to the adoration of an object.

Serious objections are raised on semantic grounds to the proposal to teach democracy as religion. It is averred that such usage of terms is contrary to all custom and thus is confusing. In reply protagonists of the point of view assert that words do not count if we can have the reality, and that the kind of convictions which are sought are more like those aroused by the historic religions than by any other social force. Therefore, the use of traditional religious terms is desirable in order adequately to communicate meanings.

Another objection to the proposal is that if democracy is religion at all, it is religion at a very cool temperature, merely a highest-common-denominator kind of religion. No significant experience of religion is possible, according to this objection, except through experiences of a deeply sectarian nature, for the real heights of religious experience are attainable only through fellowship with persons dedicated to some sectarianism—many would say, "Dedicated to *my* religion." In reply humanists who are for the proposal would deny the value of traditional sectarianism. Theistic protagonists would reply by agreeing that the "religion of democracy" is not deeply significant from the personal point of view, since it leaves out so much of what is precious in historic Judaism, or Catholicism, or Protestantism; but these protagonists assert that the proposal nowhere implies that religious experience should be limited to the religion of democracy. Freedom for the promotion of sectarian education remains.

3. Teach Religion Objectively

Though the public schools are prevented by law from indoctrinating sectarianism, they are not prevented by law, in the opinion of many students, from *describing* the religions. The term "objectivity in teaching" is usually intended to mean the presentation of the truth without personal bias; this usage is borrowed from the physical sciences, where it is assumed that all competent and unprejudiced observers will agree as to the facts. Objectivity in this sense is obviously impossible in fields where there is sharp disagreement as to the facts. However, not only is objectivity in the sense of accurate descriptions of the *opposing* points of view possible; it exists in much of the teaching of controversial material in our schools and colleges. Thus most of the teaching of economics and politics is predicated on a serious effort to be objective; likewise many classes in religion at the more advanced levels are taught objectively.

Persons who advocate teaching religion objectively in the public schools point out that a proper function of the schools is to introduce the child to the whole culture. Making religion the only major aspect of culture not described in the school results in a serious crippling of the student's understanding. He gets a warped view of the forces which produced his society and of its essential nature.

Some of the advocates of this proposal think that religion should not be studied as a separate subject in elementary schools. These persons believe that at this level religion should always be integrated with other studies. Such an integration, they contend, will result in less divorce between religion and life. Other persons, however, contend that as long as subject matter generally is departmentalized, religion will get little attention unless it too is treated as a subject.

Objectors to the proposal point out that mere knowledge of religion is not what is needed. Vital religious experience demands much more than information. Advocates of the proposal would reply that knowledge is the place to begin. Knowledge of the religious possibilities would put Americans in a position to go on and develop religion as an effective individual and social experience through the help of homes and churches. If homes and churches could build on a foundation of religious information, they would be in a position to succeed more frequently in the difficult task of mediating vital religious experiences.

Other objectors contend that the sects would not permit their children to hear anything but derogatory appraisals of other sects. No doubt this judgment is a correct estimate of the situation in some communities. However, the judgment does not apply to all communities. At present the effort to teach religion objectively would not be universally feasible; nevertheless it could be experimented with widely.

4. INDOCTRINATE THE CORE OF THE TRADITIONAL RELIGION

It is contended that 90 per cent of America belongs to the three major faiths. Some students contend that the common core of belief held by this overwhelming majority should be indoctrinated at public expense. Some writers even go so far as to assert that *Christianity* should be indoctrinated at public expense, since they claim that this nation is a Christian country and quote from Supreme Court decisions and the slogans on United States coins to prove it.

Against this proposal it is asserted that only half of the American people are actually church members and that there are a large number of agnostics and atheists. Indoctrinating belief in God, the value of prayer, the necessity for churches, and similar dogmas is a denial of the liberty of persons who do not believe in Jewish or Christian teachings.

The reply to this objection is that the welfare of the overwhelming majority cannot be sacrificed in order to preserve the supposed liberty, the idiosyncrasy, of a few.

5. PUBLIC SUPPORT OF SCHOOLS CONTROLLED BY THE CHURCH

Many Catholics—though not all—and a few Protestants hold the position that the state should provide the schools but turn their operation over to the churches.

Catholics would say that all education belongs by divine right to the Church. She possesses the Truth and alone is capable of presenting it without error to children. The state has the right of taxation, by means of which adequate support of the schools can be assured and equitably distributed. The Church has the right and responsibility of conducting schools in which religion is the chief object of study. Persons opposed to this point of view would deny that any one Church has the whole of truth and would deny the definition of freedom implicit in the argument.

Protestants who favor this proposal are impressed by the difficulty of teaching religion and think that any scheme would be inadequate which does not provide for saturating ordinary educational experiences with religious and spiritual instruction. Such persons hold that a series of denominational school systems would not destroy religious freedom, since the operation of such a system would be open to all major sects.

The opposition to this line of thought contends that the unity of the nation and good will among the sects would be destroyed by such a series of competing school systems. Moreover, efficiency would be reduced and expense increased by the resulting small classes, duplication of overhead, and multiplication of building and transportation facilities.

CONCLUSION

These six proposals—including weekday religious instruction on released time—do not exhaust the possibilities. Many students of the problem conclude that the effective teaching of religion will require a variegated approach. They assign responsibilities to various institutions: homes, church schools, public schools.

Surely it is probable that no effective solution of the problem of teaching to the general public anything as subtle and complex as religion—in the sense of life orientation—can be found apart from the utilization of the resources of many institutions. The home has the supervision of many hours of living and is an effective laboratory for putting theory into practice; but left to itself the home will teach haphazardly and in amateur fashion. The church has a rich heritage and has shown the capacity to mediate the preciousness of sectarian faith, but it has not shown the capacity to give breadth of spiritual insight. The public school has pedagogical skill and contact with most of the population, but as now constituted the public school lacks the capacity to lead children to the depths of religious experience. If these observations are accepted, it is clear that no one institution should be saddled with the obligation of teaching religion to all the population.

The keep-things-as-they-are policy will surely land us in deep trouble. We are confronted by a clear and present spiritual danger, the danger that America's commitment to the democratic ideal is not sufficient to stand up in the face of continuing world revolution. As a nation we must come to realize the spiritual nature of the problem and to realize that courageous action is mandatory.

The temptation is to settle on solutions which propose too little, too late. The extreme difficulty of teaching religion—of reaching primary motivations —has not been grasped by the average churchman or schoolman. The problem is not going to be solved by relegating religion to the odds and ends of time, or by providing in the curriculum a new course or two. It is comparatively easy to get enthusiastic backing for solutions which do not cost too much in time, or money, or readjustment. Many an American community has thought it could dispose of the problem by hiring a new teacher.

But the problem is too basic for any such casual handling. Education in spiritual values is the most important education a child ever gets. Only by bringing all our educational skill and the resources of all our institutions to bear on the problem can we hope to preserve liberty of personal belief, secure depth of religious experience, and ensure religious faith in the democratic ideal.

SUGGESTIONS FOR FURTHER STUDY

1. Are there any religious values which you think must be shared by all Americans? If so, what values? What makes them *religious* values? If you think there

are no such values, are there *spiritual* values on which you think all Americans should agree? Or *ethical* values?

2. What do you mean by "Freedom of religion": (*a*) Freedom *from* religion? (*b*) Freedom for the individual? (*c*) Freedom for parents and sects? (*d*) Freedom from any state control over churches and synagogues? (*e*) Some other statement?

3. In your judgment what should be the role of sectarian religion in public life? In personal life? Is sectarian disagreement necessarily bad? Is sectarian faith good or bad? Always? Under what circumstances?

4. Should the family play a different role in teaching religion than in teaching politics? Economics? Health?

5. How would you assign responsibilities among American institutions for bringing the American people to "maturity" of religious experience?

6. Which of the foregoing proposals—or what combination of proposals—do you think best for your community? For the majority of American communities?

BIBLIOGRAPHY

Brubacher, John S., ed. *The Public Schools and Spiritual Values.* New York: Harper & Brothers, 1944.

Harner, Nevin. *Religion's Place in General Education.* Richmond: John Knox Press, 1949.

Hauser, Conrad. *Teaching Religion in the Public School.* New York: Round Table Press, 1942.

Pius XI. *Encyclical Letter on Christian Education of Youth.* Washington: National Catholic Welfare Conference, 1930.

The Relation of Religion to Public Education—The Basic Principles. Washington, D. C.: American Council on Education, Committee on Religion and Education, 1947.

Thayer, Vivian. *Religion in Public Education.* New York: Viking Press, 1947.

Williams, J. Paul. *The New Education and Religion.* New York: Association Press, 1945.

Chapter 40

JEWISH EDUCATION IN AMERICA

ISRAEL S. CHIPKIN

JEWISH EDUCATION, like all education, is a progressive process towards self-realization and social salvation. Jewish education, like all religious education, stresses quality, meaning, and destiny in human existence. If education is life, Jewish education has, historically, been a way of life for the individual Jew and for the Jewish community. Through emphasis on informed self-discipline Jewish education became the process and the promise whereby the individual Jew developed a sense of self-worth and an appreciation of his neighbor, and whereby the Jewish community achieved fortitude and creative existence.

The attainment of *wisdom* is a primary value of the Jewish educational process. But what is the essence of wisdom? "The beginning of wisdom is the reverence of God" is a Hebrew proverb taught to very young Jewish children. Behavior and inspiration are, as Jewishly conceived, essential attributes of knowledge. Hence the pursuit of learning is identified with the study of Torah, which includes not only knowledge of original religious texts but also all inspired learning and discussions which lead to virtuous conduct, peace, the love of fellow man, and the love of God. Learning and conduct, culture and custom, become integrated to form the personality of the individual and to give distinctive character to the community. Jewish education, the study of Torah, therefore became traditionally the religious preoccupation of the individual Jew and the basic obligation of the Jewish community.

It is this sacred tradition, "the study of Torah," which has preserved the Jews through the centuries and which in turn they have preserved to date. The institutions of learning which they developed during the ages varied in form and character with the *Zeitgeist* and with the conditions in the countries in which they lived. The content of Jewish education, or of Torah, expanded with the progressive recording of three thousand years and more of Jewish history, with the accumulation of Jewish writings in Hebrew and other languages, and with the development of Jewish religious law and practices. So that today this content represents an extraordinary store of knowledge, including languages, literature, history, religious philosophy, customs, and ceremonies. It is in the spirit of this sacred tradition that Jewish education as a process must transmit this accumulated knowledge to the individual Jew and to the Jewish community in America. In so doing, it has also a strictly American function. It must so transmit the Jewish heritage as to integrate the Jew with the great American culture, to fortify the foundation of American democracy, and to contribute to the spiritual welfare of all American citizens and their communities.

THE AMERICAN JEWISH SCHOOL SYSTEM

Structure. The structure of the Jewish educational system in America reflects in large measure the facts and influences of the American environment. Nearly all Jewish children of school age attend the public schools. These children receive their Jewish education in Sunday schools or in supplementary weekday schools which hold classes after public-school hours. Only about 2 per cent of Jewish children in the whole country attend the all-day schools which correspond to private or parochial schools.

Half the enrolled pupils receiving a Jewish education attend the supplementary weekday afternoon schools, five, four, or three times a week.

To the elementary and secondary schools should be added Jewish educational summer camps, Jewish educational activities in synagogue centers and in Y's and Jewish community centers, colleges of Jewish studies for youth and adults, teacher-training schools, communal bureaus for Jewish education, national agencies and organizations for Jewish education, rabbinical seminaries, a training bureau for communal workers, Jewish universities for higher Jewish learning and for secular studies.

Pupil, Teacher, and School Distribution. A partial picture of the organizational structure and the extent of the American Jewish school system can be noted from the distribution of pupils, teachers, and school units among the several types of schools.

According to the 1948 figures the Jewish population in the United States is more than 4,500,000.[1] The number of Jewish children of *elementary*-school age—6 through 14—is estimated at 600,000 plus. Of this number over 238,000, or 39.6 per cent are reported attending some type of Jewish school.[2] This percentage is larger in small communities and smaller in large communities and represents the actual attendance at a particular date. It is estimated that close to 80 per cent of the 600,000 children will have attended a Jewish school sometime during their elementary-school career, but only one to three years.

The number of Jewish children of *secondary*-school age—15 through 18—is estimated at more than 311,300. Of this number more than 14,400, or

---

[1] Ben Seligmann and Harvey Suddos, "Jewish Population Studies in the United States," *The American Jewish Yearbook* (Philadelphia: The Jewish Publication Society of America, 1948-49), Vol. 50.

[2] Uriah Z. Engelman, "Educational Review of the Year," *idem.*

4.6 per cent, were reported attending some type of Jewish school. Of the 14,400, 45.8 per cent were in afternoon weekday schools, 39.4 per cent in Sunday schools, and 14.8 per cent in all-day schools.

Of the total enrollment in all types of Jewish *elementary* schools 43.8 per cent are to be found in afternoon weekday schools, 49.1 per cent in Sunday schools, and 7.1 per cent in all-day schools. The afternoon weekday schools whose language of instruction, besides English, may be Hebrew or Yiddish—7.3 per cent—can be classified according to the number of days which the children attend them. Of these pupils 34.2 per cent are reported receiving instruction five days per week; 27.4 per cent, four days per week; 22.3 per cent three days per week; and 16.1 per cent two days per week. These figures do not include children who attend "released-time" classes which meet once a week on weekdays. There is probably a total of about 10,000 such Jewish pupils throughout the country.

As for teachers in these schools, it is estimated that their total number is 9,845, of whom 6,034 teach in Sunday schools, 2,906 teach in afternoon weekday schools, and 905 teach in all-day schools. And as for school units, their total number is estimated at 2,745, of which 43.1 per cent are Sunday schools, 52.3 per cent are in afternoon weekday schools, and 4.6 per cent are all-day schools.

TYPES OF SCHOOLS AND THEIR DESCRIPTION[8]

These several types of schools differ from each other in the required number of days and hours of pupil attendance, in the emphasis on their respective subjects of study, and in the auspices under which they are conducted.

The Sunday School. The common characteristic of the Sunday schools is their one-day-a-week session, usually on Sunday mornings, although there are a few which may meet on Saturdays. Most Sunday schools offer an average of two hours per week of instruction. Part of this time is devoted to classroom work and part to assemblies. Such schools usually meet thirty to thirty-five Sundays a year and provide a total of sixty to seventy hours of instruction per year. The course of study in these schools lasts from six to eight years. While this type of school is usually identified with the reform synagogue or temple, we find many such schools conducted under the auspices of the Conservative or Orthodox synagogues. As a type of school it is a definite reflection of the American environment and partially influenced by the example of the Protestant Sunday school.

The course of study in the Sunday school depends upon the auspices

[8] See *Types of Jewish Schools in America* (New York: American Association for Jewish Education, 1948).

under which it is conducted. The language of instruction in all of them is English. In the Reform Sunday school the emphasis is on preparation for life in the synagogue; and the studies include Temple worship and ceremonies, festival celebrations, religious or ethical teachings, biblical stories and selections, some Jewish history, and some current events, a little Hebrew, participation in charitable and civic activities, and preparation for confirmation. The teachers in these schools are most often those who teach or have taught in public schools.

The All-Day School. In contrast to the Sunday school, there is the all-day school, sometimes referred to as "parochial" because it offers religious as well as secular studies and is in session during public-school hours. Actually it differs from parochial schools. It is not a parish school or a "church" school, since there is no central or over-all "church" in Judaism. It is called "Yeshivah Ktanah" or "lower" academy of learning, in contradistinction to the traditional European higher academies of learning. These schools have two sets of teachers, one for Hebrew and the other for English subjects. They are usually conducted and supported by a local membership society, which elects its own school board. Parents contribute either dues or fees, and donations are collected for scholarships. In a sense a Yeshivah is a private school but is charitably or communally supported. It reaches a very limited number of Jewish children who receive intensive instruction which helps to prepare them for higher Jewish studies and religious leadership.

The Yeshivah or all-day school meets five days a week, six or more hours per day. Allowing for vacations and holidays, it is in session, except for extraordinary cases, about thirty-eight weeks per year and offers an average of twelve hundred hours of instruction per year.

The individual schools included under this type vary among themselves in daily schedule, in language of instruction, in emphasis on the subjects of study, in controlling auspices.

Most of the all-day schools are conducted under Orthodox auspices. They emphasize strict Orthodox observance of ritual law and a very thorough knowledge of original biblical and Talmudic sources. They begin their day with Hebrew prayers and continue with their religious studies during the first half of the school day. The secular or English subjects follow in the afternoon. Since many of the leaders and teachers in these schools have brought with them the traditional practices of European Yiddish-speaking Yeshivoth (Talmudical academies), they continue to teach the original Hebrew and Talmudic sources by means of Yiddish translation. The parents of many of these pupils still use Yiddish at home.

There is another group of Yeshivoth where Hebrew as a language is important and is used in the teaching of biblical and Talmudic texts. As for the secular subject matter, it is taught in English in all schools and follows the prescribed course of study of the local state department of education.

There is also a group of schools which, using modern pedagogic methods, offers Hebrew and English studies alternately throughout the day. The intensive character of the instruction in these schools is preserved, but the integration of subject matter and bicultural experience become added purposes. Most of the parents who send their children to this school do not want to burden them with a two-school schedule and program, which practice becomes necessary if they must attend an afternoon school in addition to a public school. In some instances the teachers in this type of school are selected because of their special training to teach both English and Hebrew subject matter. Some of these schools stress Hebrew and a conservative or moderate approach to religious observance. Others, sponsored by organized Yiddish-speaking labor groups, stress Yiddish and a more radical or secular approach in their interpretation of religious customs and ceremonies.

The all-day school is a relatively new phenomenon in the Jewish school system. While there had been a few Jewish private schools under religious auspices in New York City, Chicago, Philadelphia, before the rise of the American public-school system, and even one or two at the turn of the century, 80 per cent of the existing all-day schools have been established since 1945. For this reason many of them do not yet have a full eight-year course of study. More than 70 per cent of the pupils in these schools are boys.

Foundation School. There is one school in the latter group that is worthy of special mention. It is called the "Beth Hayeled" (House of the Child). It was established in 1939 by Ivriah, a Jewish women's organization in New York City, as a progressive experimental school in bicultural education for early childhood and was conceived as a foundation school for the education of the American Jewish child. It includes the usual nursery, kindergarten, and primary grades. It admits the child at the age of three and holds him to the age of eight or nine, during which time it prepares him for transfer to grade three or four of the public school and for continued Jewish studies in the afternoon Hebrew weekday school. In addition to setting a pattern for a new type of school, it has also developed a curriculum of bicultural experiences for young children, and it has become an observation and practice school for students in teacher-training schools in New York City. The "graduates" of this experimental school were found to have made good social and scholastic adjustments in their subsequent attendance at both the public and the afternoon weekday religious school.

The Afternoon Weekday School. Between the all-day school with its intensive program and the Sunday school with its very rudimentary program, there is the afternoon weekday school with its extensive program.

It is commonly known among Jews as the Talmud Torah (the study of the Torah), an institution dating back to Talmudic times and maintained as a religious obligation by Jewish communities in Palestine and the Diaspora, particularly for children of the poor. It was brought to this country from Eastern Europe together with the one-room school, Heder, and its private teacher. The latter proved a failure; but the Talmud Torah became the popular, the democratic, or the community school.

In Eastern Europe it was an all-day school. Here it is a supplementary school which meets during weekdays after public-school hours. For Jews the Sunday school is historically a new type of institution. For religious schools in America the Talmud Torah is a new pattern and an outstanding contribution.

The Talmud Torah is most often found under community auspices and is generally Orthodox or Conservative in religious point of view. There is a growing number of them under congregational auspices, and some two-day-a-week schools belonging to Reform temples.

While the majority of Talmud Torahs still offer 5 days, 7½ hours per week, and 38 weeks of instruction, some offer more and some less. In other words, while most pupils in the afternoon weekday schools receive about 285 hours of instruction per year, there are some who receive as much as 400 hours per year, and others as few as 150 hours per year. These figures compare with 60 to 70 hours per year in the Sunday school, approximately 1,000 hours per year in the Yeshivah.

The more orthodox schools usually require the longer hours of attendance and offer a six-year course of study. Some Talmud Torahs prescribe a five- or three-year course. In the latter case the elementary-school course may be supplemented by a three-year junior- or senior-high school course, depending upon the age the children enter the school. The vast majority of the pupils in these schools remain only two or three years. Most of them enter at the age of nine or ten or just before confirmation—age of thirteen. The late afternoon and evening hours—4 P.M. to 7 or 8 P.M.— have proved difficult both for pupils and for teachers, and the subject matter or methods of instruction unattractive. It is these difficulties which have influenced the schools to experiment with a variety of schedules.

Secondary Schools. Enrollment in the Jewish secondary schools is about 5 per cent of the number of pupils in the Jewish elementary schools and is growing. So is the number of high-school classes. In a number of cities local central agencies in Jewish education have set up high schools for the few graduates from Talmud Torahs. Language and literature electives are offered. Their schedules call for two to five days of attendance and from four to ten hours of instruction per week. The course of study is usually about four years; and the subjects of study include the original classic sources, such as the Bible, Prophets, commentaries, the Talmudic text, medieval Hebrew literature, modern Hebrew literature. Hebrew is used as the language of instruction. In addition there are, naturally, courses in history, including American Jewish history; in Palestine, ancient and modern; in Jewish philosophy and sociology; in current events; and the usual extracurricular activities. There are afternoon weekday high schools where English is the language of instruction, but the Hebrew language and literature and classical sources are major subjects of study. There are also high schools sponsored by the labor groups where, in addition to Hebrew texts, the Yiddish language and literature and the growth of the labor movement are important subjects of study.

The Sunday schools also have their respective high-school departments which may require from two to four years' attendance. The language of instruction is English. The studies include more comprehensive courses in history, religion, literature, and Hebrew and are a continuation of the elementary-school program.

The most intensive course of study—four years—is, of course, that offered in the high-school departments conducted by the all-day schools. The subjects of study and the language of instruction in these schools are continuations of those taught in their respective elementary schools. The graduates of these schools usually acquire a very thorough knowledge of biblical, Talmudic, and medieval classic sources. Many of them continue their studies at rabbinical schools.

Summer Camps. In recent years a number of summer camps have been opened where children as well as student teachers are encouraged to continue their Jewish studies. Conducted entirely in the Hebrew or Yiddish languages, the educational program in these camps is very similar to that of other camps. In the camps attached to teacher-training schools, bureaus of education, or national educational agencies, part of the day is used by student teachers and campers to continue their Hebrew or Yiddish studies, and the rest of the day is for usual camp activities. In some instances Hebraic studies during two months of summer have proved equivalent to two semesters in afternoon classes.

Vacations and Holidays. Except for the winter holidays, vacations and holidays in the Jewish schools usually follow the calendar in the public schools. To them are added the Jewish holidays.

CONTENT OF STUDIES

Ideological Differences. In presenting the several types of schools described above, attention has been called to schedule, curriculums, and ideological differences among them. In the area of Jewish religious education four ideological groups have been mentioned: the Orthodox, the Conservative, the Reform, and the Laborites (or Yiddishists). Their respective designations and distinctions are the product of the American Jewish experience, even though they may have historical roots in European Jewish communities.

The Orthodox group carries forward and emphasizes the traditional points of view and practices derived from rabbinic interpretation of Talmudic law and codified in the Shulchan Arukh.[4] That code was until recent years the basic law and spiritual sustenance for the individual and the community in most Jewish settlements all over the world.

The Conservative group still respects the traditional codified laws; but it accepts a more historical and modern view toward revelation, the books of the Bible, and toward the interpretation of traditional customs and ceremonies. This group, in a sense, is the center between the Orthodox and the Reform, or Liberals.

The Reform group developed in this country under the influence of rabbinical leaders who came here about the middle of the nineteenth century from Germany, where as a result of the Emancipation a movement was started to westernize Judaism. In America this movement found its expression in the Pittsburgh platform of 1885, which called for a complete break from traditional codified laws, customs, and ceremonies, a modern scientific view toward revelation and the Bible, the substitution of English for Hebrew prayers, and the negation of aspirations for a return of exiles to the land of Israel. In 1937 a new platform was adopted in Columbus, Ohio, which restored a more favorable attitude toward festival ceremonies, the Hebrew language, and the land of Israel.

The Laborite or Yiddishist group has its origins in the East European struggle for the political, economic, social, and religious emancipation of the masses. Retaining in this country the language of the masses and many of their folkways, they have sought to modernize Jewish cultural values and to emphasize the social-justice ideals of the Jews through adherence to socialist doctrine. Today their common attitudes toward religious values and traditional customs have been modified as have their interpretations of some aspects of socialist doctrine.

Subparty divisions are to be found within each of the four groups listed here, and these internal differences are reflected within the respective types of schools as previously described.

Common Elements. Despite ideological differences among these groups, there are nevertheless historical, cultural, and social bonds which unite them organically. These appear in the curricular programs of their respective schools. The space limitations of this chapter do not permit a detailed discussion of these separate programs. Their organic or communal rela-

4Joseph Karo (1488-1575).

tionships are briefly presented here through the listing of seven common elements,[5] to be found in all of their several programs:

1. "Torah" represents the accumulated and expanded spiritual treasure of the Jewish people through the ages in all parts of the world. It begins with the Pentateuch and continues through the literary, religious, cultural, institutional, and ethical contributions of the Jews in all countries and in all languages. That is why it is frequently referred to as a guide to the Jewish way of life.

2. "Personal Jewish living" implies the application of Torah to personal behavior. It means the acceptance of obligations to one's fellow man and to God. Traditionally a Jew was expected to achieve salvation through the performance of mitzvoth, commandments, of the Torah. It demanded of him obedience to the moral law and observance of Jewish customs and ceremonies. It called for practicing the Jewish way of life.

3. "Hebrew" is the unique, the classic, the national, and the holy tongue of the Jewish people. It has become the language repository of the age-long experience and the cultural expression of this people. Its treasures have been translated into many languages, and the literary excellences of the other peoples have been translated into Hebrew. In the school it is required for the learning of prayer, as well as for reading the Bible or a modern Hebrew newspaper.

4. "The Jewish people" involves the affiliation and identification of every individual Jew. There is a historic and fateful relationship between the individual Jew and his people everywhere, a mutual responsibility. Knowledge of the past and present of the Jewish people is a necessity for intelligent exercise of individual or group responsibility toward the welfare and survival of individual Jews or of the Jewish people.

5. "The land of Israel," like the Hebrew language, has played a unique role in Jewish history, literature, and tradition and in Jewish aspirations for a return to the homeland after centuries of enforced wandering in unfriendly lands. Its rehabilitation has become a special interest and obligation of Jews in the present era everywhere after the fate imposed on them by Hitler, his predecessors, and his successors.

6. "The American Jewish environment" is a distinctive element of the curriculum of the American Jewish school. It requires of the individual Jew familiarity with the history and development of Jewish settlement in America, participation in its institutional and communal welfare, sharing in its cultural and spiritual contributions to American democracy, and the

[5] Supervisors of the several types of Jewish schools met under the auspices of the Jewish Education Committee of New York City in 1944 and formulated a list of "Common Elements" to which they could subscribe. This is reported in the *Jewish Education Magazine*, November, 1945, by Dr. A. M. Dushkin.

preservation of the equal status of the Jew as an American against anti-Semitic and un-American influences.

7. "Faith" in a loving God and "in the divine purpose making for the improvement of the world and man, involving the human obligation to strive toward a better, more informed, democratic world order." This faith has kept the Jews alive for centuries and inspires them to participate in all progressive and international efforts of humanity toward individual and national self-fulfillment.

No special significance attaches to the order in which the curricular-content elements have been listed here. They are all interrelated and reappear in all the subjects studied. The amount of time, the emphasis or interpretation, given to each or all of them are determined by each school. Two assumptions underlie these common elements and relate all schools to each other in what may be termed very broadly a common program. All the schools seek the continuity of Jewish life, regardless of the changes they promulgate. All of them permit some adjustment or change to environment, regardless of method of interpretation. Thus we find a program of organic unity allowing for dynamic diversity of approach to fundamental values within Jewish and American life. This program is in itself a product of, as well as a contribution to, American ideals of democracy.

Methods. The method of instruction varies from the formal to the progressive within each type of school. Each school is in complete control of its own methods, textbooks, and curriculum. Stress on memorization and use of classical or original texts are greatest where the more formal methods are used. In the less formal schools the curricular activities include music, dramatics, arts and crafts, current events, trips. Practically all the schools include such extracurricular activities as festival celebrations, Sabbath services, school assemblies, and participation in some fund-raising for charitable purposes. Many of the schools have club activities, student organizations, school paper, parent-teacher organizations, and participation in community activities.

YOUTH AND ADULT EDUCATION

The Jewish Center. In addition to the formal education offered by secondary schools and colleges for Jewish study, there is a host of informal educational activities offered in schools, synagogues, Jewish centers, and Y.W. and Y.M.H.A.'s. Education is an organic process in which the formal and informal are integrally related.

The Jewish center, a communal institution—sometimes under synagogue or school auspices—is by far the most inclusive and the most developed in the conduct of these informal activities. These Jewish centers are affiliated with a national agency called the Jewish Welfare Board. This body reports that in 1947 there were 314 centers with a participating membership of 458,000. Of these 37 per cent were adolescent and young adults; 37 per cent adults; and 26 per cent children.[6] While some of these centers offer formal class instruction in Jewish or general subject matter, their primary activity directed by trained leaders is group work. Many of these activities are associated with Jewish events, festivals, and community experiences. Frequently these activities are stimulated through country-wide projects initiated by the Jewish Welfare Board, such as Jewish Book Month, Jewish Music Month, or Jewish History Week. The Jewish Welfare Board, incidentally, provides all centers with program material and personnel services. A number of the Jewish centers also house Sunday schools or afternoon weekday schools and conduct summer camps in the city or the country.

Jewish Youth Organizations. In addition to the activities just mentioned, there are a number of national Jewish youth organizations—male, female, or both—whose affiliated groups meet locally in a Jewish center, in a synagogue, or in a school.

These national youth organizations are in most cases the youth divisions of the national organizations, religious, Zionist, Hebraist, Yiddish, or philanthropic in character. They and their affiliates usually stress their respective ideologies and purposes as well as their own youth interest through a variety of social, intellectual, communal, and charitable activities.

Adult Institutes for Jewish Studies. In Judaism formal study for its own sake has been regarded as a religious obligation and a revered form of relaxation. All through the ages adults were encouraged to spend some time in the morning or in the evening in individual or group study. This practice is reflected in the contents of the daily prayer book, which is replete with chapters and verses from the Bible and Talmud. The holiness of the Sabbath is enhanced through the study of biblical and Talmudic portions. The synagogue itself has been called the Beth Hamidrash, the house of study.

In this country adult study groups may be found in synagogues and in Jewish centers. In some communities, synagogues and centers have cooperated with local central agencies for Jewish education to establish adult institutes for Jewish study for students sixteen to sixty, which offer a variety of formal graded courses in Jewish subject matter including history, Hebrew and Yiddish languages, religion, and contemporary life. There are no specific entrance requirements, but there are graduation and attendance requirements for those who seek certificates or diplomas.

[6] *Yearbook, Jewish Social Work, 1947* (New York: Council of Jewish Federations and Welfare Funds, 1948), p. 49.

Colleges of Jewish Studies. For graduates from secondary Jewish schools there are colleges of Jewish studies where they may continue their Jewish studies on advanced levels during the evenings, while attending secular colleges during the day. Upon completion of three or four years of studies in these Jewish colleges, students either transfer to teacher-training schools, to rabbinical schools, or to social workers' schools. Many of them become professional or lay leaders in charitable, educational, or communal work. Colleges of Jewish studies, of which there are about a dozen in the country, are currently conducted under the auspices of local bureaus of Jewish education or higher institutions of Jewish learning. They may also have schools or departments for teacher training or adult studies.

Teacher-Training Schools. In 1949 there were approximately ten teacher-training schools in the country. Seven of them were accredited institutions with high admission and graduation requirements, offering four- or five-year courses of study. These schools require their students to continue their Jewish content studies and to take method courses to enable them to teach the elementary and kindergarten classes of the Jewish school. Courses in general psychology and educational theory are pursued by the student at a general academic college. Some teacher-training schools offer B.S. degrees, and others have postgraduate departments leading to higher degrees. The total number of teachers graduated from all these schools in 1948 was only about a hundred, reflecting, in a measure, the war conditions of preceding years when male students were drafted.

Institutions of Higher Learning. At the pinnacle of the Jewish educational system are the institutions of higher learning. They include the graduate schools and rabbinical seminaries, which train rabbis, teachers, scholars, communal workers. In New York City there is the Jewish Theological Seminary, with its several departments, its world-renowned Jewish library, and its famous radio program known as the "Eternal Light." It has a Los Angeles branch known as the University of Judaism. This seminary represents Conservative Judaism in this country, and its national affiliates are the United Synagogue of America and the Rabbinical Assembly of America.

There is also the Yeshiva University, with high school, college, rabbinic, education, and communal service departments. The undergraduate college department offers courses in both secular and Jewish subject matter. This institution represents the Orthodox point of view in this country. With it are affiliated the Union of Orthodox Jewish Congregations of America, other Orthodox agencies, and the Rabbinical Council of America. Another rabbinical Orthodox college is located in Chicago, known as the Hebrew Theological College. In New York City there are some all-day schools which have rabbinical departments.

The Reform ideology is represented by the graduate rabbinical institution in Cincinnati known as the Hebrew Union College and by the Jewish Institute of Religion in New York City. These two institutions have recently been merged. In New York City this merged institution conducts a School of Religious Education, which trains teachers and supervisors for Sunday schools. These institutions are affiliated with the Union of American Hebrew Congregations and the Conference of American Rabbis.

In Philadelphia there is the Dropsie College for Hebrew and Cognate Learning. It is a nonpartisan graduate institution for the training of Jewish scholars and advanced students. Through its Department of Education it trains educational directors for central agencies in Jewish education, research workers, and authors.

In New York City there is a graduate-training bureau for executives in Jewish communal work, nonpartisan in character. The only nonsectarian general undergraduate college in this country under Jewish auspices is the Brandeis University, which was opened in the fall of 1948 in Waltham, Massachusetts. It includes Jewish content courses in its curriculum.

The Yiddishist group has teacher-training schools; but in the field of higher learning it is perhaps best represented by "Yivo," the Yiddish Scientific Institute in New York City, brought over during the early days of the Hitler regime from Vilno, Poland. It has a number of research workers engaged in Jewish historical and sociological studies. With it are affiliated a number of the Yiddishist laborite groups in this country.

TEACHERS

The teacher is the most important factor in the Jewish school. He must love children and love Judaism. In addition to a general college education he must have received a good Hebrew and Yiddish education. He must be familiar with the classic and modern literature in these languages. He must know original sources as well as the history, religion, philosophy, and contemporary life of his people. In his daily behavior he must practice Judaism in his relations between man and man, man and nation, man and God. In the science of pedagogy he must know American theory and practice as well as its application to the Jewish school.

While the expected qualifications of the Jewish teacher—male and female—are many and high, economically and socially his status is below that of the public-school teacher. In most cases he teaches more hours than does the public-school teacher, and his teaching task itself is more taxing. His pupils come to him at the end of the day, when they are tired, and the subject matter he teaches is foreign and burdensome to them.

Relatively recently teacher organizations and central communal agencies in larger communities have begun to make some provisions for salary scales, tenure of office, health insurance, and pensions. They have also instituted in-service courses, supervision, and opportunities for advancement. As standards rise, there is hope that more qualified personnel will be attracted to the profession, to produce more effective results and also to overcome the present lamentable shortage of Jewish teachers.

BUILDINGS AND FINANCES

While there are still too many Jewish schools housed in synagogue vestry rooms or in poor makeshift buildings, there are in many cities excellent school buildings either under communal or congregational auspices, and their number is growing.

It is estimated that the current annual expenditures for Jewish education in the United States is $15,000,000. This money is contributed by parents, individual donors, and Jewish Community Chests. The costs vary with the type of school. In the Sunday school it is about $25 to $40 per child per year. In the afternoon weekday school it is about $125 to $150. In the all-day school, it is about $400 to $650.

CENTRAL AGENCIES FOR JEWISH EDUCATION

In 1949 there were about forty local communal central agencies for Jewish education commonly known as bureaus of Jewish education. Two of them are regional or state-wide in scope. They are local service, co-ordinating, and promotional agencies. Their functions are wide and varied. They provide scholarships for poor pupils or budgetary grants to individual schools. They help provide teachers and to supervise instruction. They offer curricular guidance and textbook materials. They seek to improve methods and to advance standards in all aspects of school life and activity. They conduct the central communal school or a group of associated schools. They conduct interschool activities and encourage school graduations. They conduct the central high school, an adult school for Jewish study, a college for Jewish study, and in-training courses for teachers. They conduct enrollment campaigns and collect tuition fees. They have Jewish libraries for teachers and the public and act as sources of Jewish information.

They are supported from central communal fiscal agencies called Federations of Jewish Charities or Jewish Welfare Funds. Their governing boards are usually representative of the individual schools in the community and of the community at large. While encouraging co-operative effort and community planning, the ideological autonomy of each affiliated school is respected. The programs of these bureaus offer a healthy example of democracy in action.

In addition to central agencies for Jewish education, there are national agencies. The Reform and the Conservative groupings each have a National Commission on Jewish Education. The Orthodox have a national body known as "Vaad Hahinukh Haharedi." Some of the all-day schools have a national body known as "Torah Umesorah," and some of them are affiliated with a particular Hassidic group. All of these agencies seek to promote locally and nationally their own types of schools, prepare textbooks or teachers for them, provide them with curriculums and sometimes supervision, occasionally even with funds. They hold national conferences for teachers, principals, and lay leaders of their respective groupings.

There are two national professional bodies. The National Council for Jewish Education includes bureau executives, supervisors, principals, authors, and college personnel of all groups. The National Federation of Hebrew Teachers includes Hebrew teachers, but not Yiddishist or Sunday-school teachers. These professional organizations hold national and local conferences for discussion of common interests. They publish pedagogic magazines and encourage research, experimentation, and planning.

The American Association for Jewish Education is the representative body of the several local central agencies for Jewish education, whose presidents together with other communal lay leaders constitute its Board of Governors. The association is their national service and co-ordinating agency. Its primary purpose is to help raise the standards of Jewish education through a program of communal responsibility and communal planning for Jewish education. It operates through several departments, which include research, information and publications, personnel, pedagogic and curricular materials, community organization, consultation, and promotional activity. It is supported by contributions from individuals and local Jewish Welfare Funds. The association has been very effective in organizing local bureaus for Jewish education, in obtaining communal support for them, and in assisting them educationally. It sponsors a national Board of License which helps to set up local boards of license, qualifications for teachers, and standards for teacher-training schools. It supports the professional organizations. It provides fellowships and co-operates with Dropsie College, the Training Bureau for Jewish Communal Work, and other institutions in the training of executive leadership in Jewish education. It also co-operates with existing national agencies operating in the field of Jewish education. It publishes research bulletins, pedagogic bulletins, promotional literature, and a periodic *Jewish Education Newsletter*. It corresponds in large measure to the Office of Education in Washington. Its relationships with all local and national agencies are voluntary and advisory.

CURRENT TRENDS

The development in American Jewish education during the past ten years have revealed progress toward the intensification of the program of studies, the organization of the structural system, the advancement of professional standards, and acceptance of community responsibility and programs.

Toward the intensification of the program of studies we have seen the phenomenal growth of the number of all-day schools, the progress in early childhood education, increase in the number of high schools and schools for adults, the continuation of Hebrew studies in summer camps, and the Jewish culture programs in the Jewish centers. In many congregations the higher classes in the Sunday schools have been transferred to the afternoon weekday departments, and pupils desiring participation in public confirmation exercises are required to attend such classes for a minimum of three years. The establishment of the State of Israel has stimulated more natural motivation and interest in much of the subject matter taught in the Jewish school.

Toward the organization of the structural system of American Jewish education there have been added to the several types of elementary and secondary schools the Foundation school, the preschool grades, the Hebrew-speaking and Jewish educational camp, the college and adult institute of Jewish studies, the central agency for Jewish education, locally and nationally.

Toward the advancement of professional standards in American Jewish education there have developed local boards of license and a national co-ordinating body for all of them. Qualifications for the certification of teachers have been intensified. Central agencies for Jewish education have set up codes of practice for teachers' employment and welfare. Supervising and executive positions and opportunities for advanced training, research, and experimentation have grown in number.

Extraordinary progress has been made toward the development of democratic community responsibility and community programs in Jewish education. The number of local central agencies in Jewish education has more than doubled in this decade. The aggregate financial support from central fiscal agencies for local Jewish educational programs has increased fourfold. In the national scene, ideological agencies have improved their own programs, standards, and activities. The American Association for Jewish Education has developed its intensified program of community services and pedagogic standards, and helps to co-ordinate the efforts of local and national agencies toward the organization and improvement of the American Jewish school system as an organic part of the cultural and religious life of America.

Outstanding Problems

While progress has been made in the areas indicated, many problems still remain unsolved. Only some of them can be listed here. The problems of schedule and double schooling still persist. In the case of the afternoon weekday school there is a noticeable tendency to reduce attendance, thus affecting the quantity and quality of instruction.

Still another problem which the afternoon weekday school must solve is its holding power. Too many of its pupils remain for only two years. How much subject matter can be offered in a two- or three-year course of studies? Should the elementary school be followed by a junior-high school? How can methodology and textbooks be improved, and what place in the curriculum should be given to experience and activities? How can audio-visual aids be applied to Jewish schools and teachers be trained to use them?

Questions of methods, textbooks, and orientation apply, not only to the afternoon weekday schools, but to all types of schools. How much of the past is related to the present? What is the relationship of the Jewish classic tradition to American democracy? What is the relationship of Israel to America and to other peoples of the world?

Another problem is the relationship of the Jewish school to the Jewish center. How shall the formal be integrated with the informal, the classroom with the clubroom, the emphasis on individual personality with that on group work?

This problem is also related to that of co-operation and co-ordination among the several types of schools in a community. Despite efforts of local bureaus of Jewish education, competitive habits still prevent common efforts and better mutual appreciation among schools and agencies.

In the area of community effort there is still no satisfactory solution to the problem of finances or to the problem of organizing Jewish educational endeavor in the rural district and in the small community. There is also the problem of finding and cultivating lay leadership.

Finally, there is the lack of educational personnel. This includes teachers, supervisors, executives, research workers. When and how shall qualified young people be attracted to, trained, and retained for professional growth and creative spiritual activity in American Jewish education?

SUGGESTIONS FOR FURTHER STUDY

1. What are the objectives for Jewish education in America?
2. What changes in structure, schedule, curriculum, or methods should the afternoon weekday school make in order to hold its pupils a longer period of time?

3. How can the general and specifically Jewish subject matter in the all-day school be better integrated?

4. How can the school, the center, the synagogue, the home, and the community council develop an integrated service program for the benefit of the individual child, especially in the small community?

5. How can audio-visual aids be applied to the Jewish school and subjects? What are current audio-visual aid practices in the Jewish schools?

6. What contributions can Jewish education make to American cultural life, and what contributions can American life make to Jewish education?

BIBLIOGRAPHY

JEWISH EDUCATION

Berkson, Isaac B. *Theories of Americanization.* New York: Teachers College, Columbia University, 1920.

Chipkin, Israel S. "Twenty-Five Years in Jewish Education," *American Jewish Year Book, 1937.* Philadelphia: Jewish Publication Society.

Dinin, Samuel. *Judaism in a Changing Civilization.* New York: Teachers College, Columbia University, 1933.

Gamoran, Emanuel. "Jewish Education in the United States," in Lotz and Crawford: *Studies in Religious Education.* Nashville: Cokesbury Press, 1931.

Honor, Leo L. "Jewish Education in the United States," in *The Jewish People, Past and Present,* II, 151. New York: Central Yiddish Culture Organization (C.Y.C.O.), 1948. Also other articles on Hebrew schools, Yiddish schools, Yeshivoth, and the Jewish Way of Life in the same volume.

Jewish Education Magazine. New York: National Council for Jewish Education, 1776 Broadway, New York 19, New York.

HISTORY, RELIGION-LITERATURE

Grayzel, S. *History of the Jews.* Philadelphia: Jewish Publication Society, 1947.

Kaplan, M. M. *Future of the American Jew.* New York: Macmillan Co., 1948.

Edidin, Ben M. *Jewish Customs and Ceremonies.* New York: Hebrew Publishing Co., 1941.

Steinberg, Milton. *Basic Judaism.* New York: Harcourt, Brace & Co., 1947.

Jung, Leo. *Israel of Tomorrow.* New York: Herald Square Press, 1946.

Schulman, Samuel. *Jewish Ethics, Jewish Traits,* No. 4. Cincinnati: Union of American Hebrew Congregations, 1909.

Chapter 41

ROMAN CATHOLIC RELIGIOUS EDUCATION

EDWARD J. HEFFRON

IN THE SCHOOL YEAR 1947-48, the Catholics of the United States maintained: 221 universities and colleges, with 220,226 students; 338 seminaries and scholasticates, with 23,701 students; 377 schools for nurses, with 30,331 students; 2,432 high schools and academies with 506,397 students; 8,248 elementary schools with 2,274,840 students. The total number of youths under Catholic instruction, including those attending special religious instruction classes, those in orphanages and protective institutions, was put at 4,138,695.

American Catholics pay their full share of taxes for erection and maintenance of public schools, including state universities and normal schools, and are entitled to use them, like other citizens, without cost. Why, then, do they willingly and gratuitously undergo the very considerable sacrifice which must be entailed by support of such an elaborate educational apparatus?

Many non-Catholics must find this a perplexing business. If they ask whether Catholics object to anything that is being formally taught in the public schools, they will be told that in general they do not. If they ask how much time is spent in the formal teaching of religion, they will learn that it is hardly more than could be pieced together by a combination of released time, Sunday school, and religious vacation school. In 1947-48, the number of public-school pupils attending such special Catholic instruction classes was 1,078,436.

If such an inquirer finds it difficult to comprehend why Catholics make such tremendous sacrifices to maintain separate schools; if he begins to wonder whether the separatism may be not merely a concomitant of such schools but their very end and purpose, his bewilderment is understandable.

The fact is, however, that one can never understand Catholic schools unless one understands the whole system of Catholic values, the Catholic outlook on life.

WHY CATHOLIC SCHOOLS?

Catholics believe that man is a being composed of matter and spirit; that he was created by God for an eternity of happiness in heaven; that this earth is but a proving ground, and that the manner in which he conducts his life here will determine whether he is to enjoy that eternity of happiness or to suffer an eternity of loss; that he has inherited a fallen nature, which while it does not make him guilty of actual sin in itself, makes him prone to evil; that God, the Second Person of the Blessed Trinity, became man in order to reveal to him the way of salvation and to make available to him the means whereby his fallen nature might be elevated and thus made fit for heaven.

Catholics are not singular in these beliefs, of course. Most Protestants believe them, too. But if others wish to understand Catholic education, it is important that they grasp the fact that this is not merely an ancient formulary to which Catholics give honor and respect, but that all Catholics believe every word of it *literally*.

To the Catholic, then, the only ultimately important thing is the salvation of his immortal soul—not because he is selfish, but precisely because he believes that is the task God set him to, the only task he set him to. Of course, one of the conditions for saving his soul is that he shall be unselfish—that he love God with all his heart and soul and his neighbor as himself. Again, this belief is not unique to Catholics; but it *is* Catholic belief—universal Catholic belief.

Accordingly the Catholic believes that it is much less important whether he becomes a great doctor, a great statesman, or a great scientist, than that he becomes a simple saint—that is, one who saves his soul. He believes that God wants him to develop those talents he has given him; but whereas he can often be uncertain whether God meant him to be an artist or an artisan, he can never be uncertain that God meant him to be a saint.

Some modern people, truly religious, seem almost to think that it is man's *first duty* to make the most of his temporal talents—in a moral and honorable way, of course—and that his salvation will accrue as a sort of by-product. The Catholic would hold that such a person was confusing ends with means. The result is that well-disposed non-Catholics have sometimes thought that Catholics deprecated secular education. If to regard it as a means and not an end is to deprecate it, they do.

Thus if the only college available to a Catholic boy or girl were known as a hotbed of atheism or immorality, the parents of such a youth might well prefer to have their son or daughter forego a college education altogether than to endanger his or her faith. No doubt many Protestant and Jewish parents would feel the same.

But the public schools are not generally hotbeds of atheism or immorality. Hence the fair-minded non-Catholic may still wonder why Catholics don't save themselves these burdensome sacrifices by sending their children to the public schools, taking care of their formal religious instruction through released time, Sunday schools, and so on.

There are two things to be said about this. In the first place, Catholics do not feel that children can be expected to esteem very highly any branch of education which their elders deem worthy only of after-hours attention. If children are taught the three *R's* five days a week on a very businesslike nine-to-four schedule, and the fourth *R* is left for catch-as-catch-can treatment on Sunday, or for one hour a week of released time, or for after-school attention—when, still worse, it must infringe upon what they are entitled to regard as normal playtime—they are not likely to think that catechism is as important as the alphabet and the multiplication table.

But there is a more serious objection. Religion is not simply one department of education any more than it is one department of living. To expose the child to one "Christian" or "Jewish" period a day, and to seven or eight wholly secular periods, is to encourage the kind of thinking—the Catholic says—that results in "Sunday Christianity" or "Sabbath Judaism."

To the Catholic the world has never been the same, and never can be the same, since Christ was born in Bethlehem; and this revolutionary historical fact affects *every aspect* of living and of learning.

If the Catholic child were to get a half-hour of catechism in the morning and to hear nothing more about religion the rest of the day; if Ned in the primer were simply to count apples as any good little pagan boy might do, but never make a visit to a church, never say his prayers, and never mention God or his Guardian Angel or the saints; if the geography teacher were to seem oblivious of the fact that Lourdes means something in France, Guadalupe in Mexico, and Fatima in Portugal; if the history teacher were unmoved by what John Sobieski did at Vienna and Don John at Lepanto, or regarded Mary as a bloody murderess, Elizabeth as Good Queen Bess; if the English teacher assigned *Westward Ho* as required reading, without comment; if the science teacher gave the common version of the Galileo story but did not see fit to comment on Pasteur's profound faith—if these and a thousand other things happened, day after day, but nothing was said or done of any apparent religious or spiritual significance outside the daily thirty-minute catechism class, Catholics would not feel that their children were getting a well-rounded education. Even assuming their children could be given this half-hour of catechism each day in the public schools, they would not be satisfied—and, of course, under the McCollum decision even that is impossible.

CATHOLIC VIEW OF LIFE

Catholics are not willing to regard religion as simply one of the subjects in the curriculum—they think it should permeate the whole course of study. As long as it does not, they cannot feel that they have discharged their most important obligation to their children; that is, to give them the best possible equipment for their lifelong battle against the unbelief and the temptations of the world.

The informed Catholic acknowledges such an obligation in conscience entirely apart from any urging by the Church, but he is supported in his thinking by the highest authorities. Pius XI, in his encyclical *Divinis Illius Magistri*, says, "It is necessary that all the teaching and the whole organization of the school, and its teachers, syllabus and textbooks in every branch, be regulated by the Christian spirit"; and as a consequence he says that "the frequenting of non-Catholic schools, whether neutral or mixed, those namely which are open to Catholics and non-Catholics alike, is forbidden to Catholic children, and can be at most tolerated, on the approval of the Ordinary [bishop] alone, under determined circumstances of place and time, and with special precautions." This position is made a part of the declared law of the Church in Canon 1374.

This may seem a harsh view to many non-Catholics, who may wonder to themselves, "Do the Catholics think we are leprous?" But this will happen, if it does, only because they are trying to understand a Catholic view from a non-Catholic viewpoint.

The Catholic believes that Jesus Christ, true God and true Man, established a Church and declared that "the gates of Hell shall not prevail against it"; and, again, "Behold I am with you all days even to the consummation of the world."

It is therefore a logical necessity, not merely an arrogant preference, for the Catholic to believe that this Church is infallibly correct in its official, binding teachings on faith and morals—and, by the same token, to believe that any other Church or system, in so far as its teaching deviates from what is taught by this divinely established Church, is in error.

The Catholic believes that this divinely established Church is the Catholic Church, and that it teaches what Christ came on earth to teach—the fulfillment of the Law, all that man needs to know to save his soul.

Catholics are human beings. They develop *esprit de corps*, certain clannish prides and rivalries and jealousies, the same as other men. It may sometimes seem to non-Catholics that this is the main explanation—nay, the only explanation—of the Catholic's wholehearted allegiance to his Church and of his fierce concern lest the faith of his children be disturbed by premature contact with non-Catholic views.

But this is a misunderstanding. The Catholic wants his children to associate in brotherly love with their fellows and to know as much as they can of the world about them, but he wants to be sure that they have a sufficient understanding of their own faith before they come up against other faiths.

THE "SEPARATISM" OF SEPARATE SCHOOLS

Some honest non-Catholic Americans nevertheless deplore the existence of Catholic schools. They see the public school as the cradle of democracy, an institution which provides "a valuable and indispensable democratic experience for American children of all nationality backgrounds, races, and religious loyalties, thus providing a unifying process that strengthens the civic life of the nation." Such a person distrusts separate schools precisely because they are, in his view, separatist.

It is sufficient for the Catholic case to point out that there is no reason why the argument for a single school system should stop with the schools. It is an argument for a monolithic educational apparatus; but if it has any validity at all, it is equally valid as an argument for a monolithic state. If it is desirable to exclude the "separatism" of separate schools, why not the "separatism" of separate religions? Or of separate workingmen's organizations? Or of separate political parties? Or of separate state sovereignties?

The Catholic holds that the right to the education of children belongs to three societies, the family, the state, and the Church. The Church's claim lies in the supernatural order and derives from Christ's injunction: "All power is given to me in heaven and in earth. Going therefore teach ye all nations . . . , teaching them to observe all things whatsoever I have commanded you."

A single system of common schools would—at least under the McCollum decision—exclude the Church from any share in the greater and most important part of the educational process, relegating it to a second-rate position "after hours." But while this argument is sufficient, it is unnecessary to maintenance of the Catholic case for separate schools. The Catholic prefers to argue that case on the basis of the respective rights of the state and its citizens.

RIGHTS OF PARENTS

Thomas Aquinas says: "The father according to the flesh has in a particular way a share in that principle which in a manner universal is found in God. . . . The father is the principle of generation, of education and discipline and of everything that bears upon the perfecting of human life."

Pius XI, in *Divini Illius Magistri—Christian Education of Youth*—speaking of the three societies, to which the education of children is entrusted, wrote:

In the first place comes the family, instituted directly by God for its particular purpose, the generation and formation of offspring; for this reason it has priority of nature and therefore of rights over civil society. . . . The family therefore holds directly from the Creator the mission and hence the right to educate the offspring, a right inalienable because inseparably joined to the strict obligation, a right anterior to any right whatever of civil society and of the State, and therefore inviolable on the part of any power on earth.

Nevertheless, as the Pope points out,

The family is an imperfect society, since it has not in itself all the means for its own complete development; whereas civil society is a perfect society, having in itself all the means for its peculiar end, which is the temporal well-being of the community; and so, in this respect, that is, in view of the common good, it has preeminence over the family, which finds its own suitable temporal perfection precisely in civil society.

Pius XI goes on to explain this:

It is the duty of the State to protect in its legislation the prior rights . . . of the family. . . . It also belongs to the State to protect the rights of the child itself when the parents are found wanting either physically or morally in this respect, whether by default, incapacity or misconduct. . . . The State can exact and take measures to secure that all citizens have the necessary knowledge of their civic and political duties, and a certain degree of physical, intellectual and moral culture . . . necessary for the common good.

He adds,

However, it is clear that . . . the State should respect the inherent rights of the . . . family concerning . . . education, and moreover have regard for distributive justice. Accordingly, unjust and unlawful is any monopoly, educational or scholastic, which, physically or morally, forces families to make use of government schools, contrary to the dictates of their Christian conscience, or contrary even to their legitimate preferences.

In the case of Pierce *vs.* Society of Sisters (1925), the Supreme Court of the United States held: "The fundamental theory of liberty upon which all governments in this Union repose excludes any general power of the State to standardize its children by forcing them to accept instruction from public teachers only. The child is not the mere creature of the State; those who nurture him and direct his destiny have the right coupled with the high duty, to recognize and prepare him for additional duties."

STATE AID TO RELIGIOUS SCHOOLS

If religious schools have the right to proceed without undue molestation from the state, many would hold that they are deprived, by the same process of reasoning, of any claim to state support.

The Catholic view is not that the state has no right to say anything about Catholic schools. On the contrary, Archbishop McNicholas has noted that,

As the custodian of the common welfare, [the State] wisely insists on compulsory education . . . , setting standards of education and supporting in large measure the schools of our country. If the family or parents can not or will not discharge their duty in educating children, then the State . . . must assume parental responsibilities, [but] always having due regard for the faith of parents. When the State assumes parental obligations, when it establishes . . . schools, as it must do in a modern world in order to assure suitable education for a country blessed as ours is, it can not endow itself with arbitrary powers. . . . Usurped totalitarian powers in education, if not checked by freedom of education, will inevitably lead to a Fascist State in all functions.

What the Catholic holds, therefore, is something like this:

It is lawful for the state to lay down reasonable requirements for schools.

It is lawful for the state to compel parents to send their children to such schools as meet these requirements.

In so doing, however, it is bound both morally and legally, by Pierce *vs.* Society of Sisters, to honor the legitimate conscientious scruples of such parents.

It is right and lawful for the state to assist parents in fulfilling its compulsory education laws by building and maintaining schools, by giving grants-in-aid, or by providing custodial services, and so on.

It is right and lawful for the state to use tax monies for such assistance.

But in the interests of distributive justice it should assist all parents indiscriminately who send their children to schools which meet its requirements.

This seems exorbitant to many non-Catholics. Some say that if all Americans were of one faith, there could be no objection to tax-supported religious schools. They might even go so far as to admit that if Americans were divided among only a few religious groups, it would be practicable for the state to provide confessional schools for the several faiths, as is done in England, Scotland, and elsewhere. But there are literally hundreds of religious groups in the United States, they point out, dozens of them in many small towns; and even if it were possible to support hundreds of confessional-school systems over the country as a whole, the average town obviously couldn't support dozens. Hence the only solution, they say, is to make all schools nonconfessional, *a*-religious.

Further, it seems to be assumed that *a*-religious schools are a direct and necessary outgrowth of American constitutional democracy, that the public school as we know it is as basically a part of our institutions as our courts. If the Catholic parent feels that he must have Catholic schools for his children, well and good—let him have them. But let him not expect the community to assist in their support, any more than it does in the support of ecclesiastical courts.

What this argument overlooks is that ecclesiastical tribunals have not been erected to subserve a legitimate purpose of the state, enjoined by statute, whereas Catholic schools do subserve such a purpose, with acknowledged adequacy, and do enable those who use them to meet an obligation enjoined by statute in the only way their consciences permit, and in full accord with their constitutional right, even their "high duty," as declared by the Supreme Court in Pierce *vs.* Society of Sisters.

The problems man encounters in life are not the blacks and whites he met in the textbooks of his youth—they are frequently mostly gray. Yet it often happens that the only way to keep from losing sight of the main lines in a complicated chiaroscuro is to draw back and to take a careful squint at its simple elements.

And it is the simple fact that the Catholic parent is paying for the education of his children in a manner that fully meets the requirements of the state educational authorities, that satisfies compulsory education laws, and that has the blessing of the Supreme Court; and at the same time he is paying his full citizen's share for the education of his non-Catholic neighbor's children.

He doesn't have to do both, of course; he is free under the law to ignore his obligation in conscience—what the Supreme Court in the Pierce case calls his "high duty"—and to send his children to the public school. But that is obviously only a Hobson's choice. As the late Monsignor George Johnson said,

When the State passes compulsory education laws and thus forces parents to send their children to school, it is up to the State to aid parents to provide schools that square with the dictates of their consciences. Not to do so is an invasion of religious liberty. *The principle of "take it or leave it" cannot be invoked here,* as it might in the case of a road, or a sewer, or a water main. For education does not come into the competence of the State as these things do. "The child," in the words of the Supreme Court of the United States, "is not the mere creature of the State. Those who nurture him and direct his destiny have the right coupled with the *high duty,* to recognize and prepare him for *additional obligations.*" (Italics mine.)

RELIGIOUS EDUCATION AND THE STATE

Another argument for refusing state aid to religious schools is that this would violate "the traditional doctrine of Separation of Church and State." This argument received powerful support from the Supreme Court in the Everson and McCollum decisions, though only in so far as the argument applies to school costs proper, not as it applies to so-called custodial services— bus transportation, textbooks, and so on—exempted in the Everson case and in the earlier Cochran case.

As long as this rule of law stands, Catholics have no disposition to flout it. But the Supreme Court does not profess to be infallible, and Catholics are not alone in thinking it was very fallible in these decisions. There is nothing unpatriotic or unconstitutional or undemocratic about continuing to say so, or about continuing to hope that another case involving the same issues may come before the court, and that the court may then see fit to modify its 1947-48 views.

In the Everson case, the court held that the clause in the First Amendment, "Congress shall make no law respecting an establishment of religion"—made applicable to the states by the Fourteenth Amendment—erected a wall of separation between Church and State. This meant, it held, that "Neither a State nor the Federal Government . . . can pass laws which aid one religion, aid all religions, or prefer one religion over another." In the McCollum case, this principle was used to strike down a released-time arrangement in Champaign, Illinois.

The phrase "a wall of separation between Church and State" does not of course appear anywhere in the Constitution. It was a phrase used by Thomas Jefferson, and not in the debate on the First Amendment, for he was at that time in France. As Justice Reed, a non-Catholic, remarks in his McCollum dissent, "A rule of law should not be drawn from a figure of speech."

The question is, what did those who moved this clause of the First Amendment and those who adopted it mean by the language of the clause? Those who maintain that it goes beyond a mere prohibition of an "established church," in the clear historical meaning of that phrase, rely largely on Madison and Jefferson—who, as noted, was in France.

Edward S. Corwin, Professor Emeritus of Jurisprudence at Princeton University, and a non-Catholic, after reviewing the historical evidence says: "I sum up Madison's and Jefferson's attitude, therefore, not as demanding that public-supported education should be exclusively secular and admitting no religious elements, *but that no public authority should give a preference to any religion or any denomination.*" [1]

In his *Commentaries*, the great constitutional authority, Joseph Story—another non-Catholic—declares:

Probably at the time of the adoption of the constitution, and of the amendment to it, now under consideration, the general, if not the universal sentiment in America was, that Christianity ought to receive encouragement from the state, so far as was not incompatible with the private rights of conscience, and the freedom of religious worship. An attempt to level all religions, and to make it a matter of state policy to hold all in utter indifference, would have created universal disapprobation if not universal indignation.

[1] "The Supreme Court as National School Board," *Thought*, December, 1948. Italics mine.

What the Congress meant or did not mean when it adopted the First Amendment—proposed in 1789, adopted in 1791—may be gathered from what was said in the Northwest Ordinance which was passed by the Continental Congress in 1787 and re-enacted by the Congress of the United States in 1791. Article III of that Ordinance provided that, "Religion, morality and knowledge being necessary to good government and the happiness of mankind, schools and the means of education shall forever be encouraged."

Everson-McCollum Inconsistencies

Corwin makes two strong points against the McCollum opinion. The Supreme Court there held that the two chief unconstitutional elements in the Champaign released-time program were (*a*) that public property (school premises) was used for religious instruction, and (*b*) that the police power (the Illinois compulsory education law) was used to "recruit" children for such instruction.

As to the former point, Corwin refers to the Lockport case—Saia *vs.* New York—decided three months after the McCollum case, in which the Supreme Court held that it was unconstitutional for that municipality to forbid the unlicensed use of sound equipment, by a Jehovah's Witness, to amplify religious lectures in a *public* park. He remarks that "the Court seems to feel a strange tenderness for *outré* religious manifestations which contrasts sharply with its attitude toward organized religion."

As to the latter point, he observes that in the Pierce case—affirmed in Everson-McCollum—the court held that attendance at a qualified religious school satisfied all legitimate requirements of compulsory education laws, and asks: "Can it be said that the Oregon compulsory school law, or that any State compulsory school law, does not aid in 'recruiting' pupils for parochial schools?"

In an article in the *Lawyers Guild Review* Leo Pfeffer offers an able defense of the McCollum majority opinion. But in his honesty he gives the case away. He writes:

It may be that Justice Rutledge was historically incorrect in stating: "The Amendment's purpose was not to strike merely at the official establishment of a single sect, creed or relgion . . . ; the object was broader than separating church and state in this narrow sense. It was to create a complete and permanent separation of the spheres of religious activity and civil authority by comprehensively forbidding every form of public aid or support for religion."

Possibly, in the words of Justice Reed: "The phrase establishment of religion may have been intended by Congress to be aimed only at a state church."

But the precise intent of the framers and adopters of the First Amendment, while interesting, is not decisive. . . . The generation which adopted the Amendment expressed as a basic principle of American democracy the broad concept of separation of church and state. The evolution of that concept did not end in 1791. It is a continuing evolution, and *each generation must interpret the meaning of separation for itself in the light of its conception of American democracy and the enlightened political thinking of the day.*[2]

Apart from the fact that no one has taken any adequate steps to discover how *this* generation interprets the meaning of separation of Church and state, least of all the Supreme Court, and apart from the inherent difficulties of determining whose political thinking is "enlightened," there remains the question as to whether such a change of interpretation would be a mere evolution, an explication of principles previously implicit, or whether it would be a revolution, the addition of new principles never previously intended, explicitly or implicitly; and if the latter, whether the Supreme Court has the constitutional power so to amend the Constitution.

Not a few of those who support the McCollum decision seem to think that the American religious school is a Catholic invention, more or less. As a matter of fact, nearly all of the early American schools were religious schools, and it was only under the fight led by Horace Mann in the latter part of the last century that they largely ceased to be. Yet even as to Mann, Raymond Culver writes in his authoritative work, *Horace Mann and Religion in the Massachusetts Public Schools:* "He took a firm stand against the idea of a purely secular education, and on one occasion said he was in favor of religious instruction 'to the extremest verge to which it can be carried without invading those rights of conscience which are established by the laws of God, and guaranteed to us by the Constitution of the State.' At another time he said that he regarded hostility to religion in the schools as the greatest crime he could commit."

This problem is not peculiarly Catholic. In 1948 an organization was founded called Protestants and Other Americans United for Separation of Church and State. Its declared purpose was to resist what it regarded as Catholic attempts to encroach upon separation of Church and state. One of the organizers was Charles Clayton Morrison, retired editor of the *Christian Century.* Here is what Morrison, writing in 1946 on "Protestantism and the Public School," thought of our present school system:

Protestantism has been greatly weakened in its inner character by this kind of education. Unlike Catholicism, the Protestant churches . . . have given to the public school their consistent and unreserved devotion. The result is that their own children have been delivered back to their churches with a mentality which is not only unintelligent about religion but relatively incapacitated even to ask the questions out of which religion arises, to say nothing of answering them the way religion answers them. This result must not be thought of in terms of children only. For these children have become the adult membership of Protestant

[*] May-June, 1948. Italics mine.

churches. The mentality of the entire body of American Protestantism has thus been fashioned under the influence of the secularized public school.

This is powerful testimony, coming from an acknowledged adversary, and should make it clear why Catholics are determined to maintain their own separate schools, whatever the sacrifice.

Is Catholic Education "Professional"?

Not a few honest men and women tend unconsciously to disparage Catholic education. They think of the teachers in the public schools as professionals and incline to regard the priests, brothers, and nuns teaching in Catholic schools as zealous, well-intentioned amateurs. In earlier days this was undoubtedly true, in some measure, but it was probably true in just about the same measure as it was of the Hoosier schoolmaster and his contemporaries.

Today teaching in a Catholic school is just as truly a profession as teaching in a public school. The thousands of teaching nuns, brothers, and priests—and thousands of laymen and laywomen, too—are not mere amateurs. They undergo the same training, take the same tests, qualify for the same certificates—and in the same subjects—as teachers in the public schools.

And what is the daily schedule in a Catholic school? Some seem to think that it is largely taken up with catechism and other *ex professo* religious subjects. Not at all. Catechism is important, very important; but it doesn't take much time each day. For the most part, the daily schedule in a Catholic school would pretty well parallel the schedule in the neighboring public school. Where a secular subject impinges upon a religious truth or a historical religious fact, the point is brought out, in a natural way—not in such detail as to impede the pursuit of secular learning. The point is that secular learning occupies vastly the greater part of the school day—but secular learning taught *sub specie aeternitatis*.

Those who fancy it is otherwise have obviously not pondered the fact that students in Catholic schools hold up their end very well in city, state, and national spelling bees, essay contests, history competitions, science awards, that they meet the entrance requirements for state universities, that they do all right in civil service examinations and the rest.

Organization of the Catholic School System

In the 1947-48 school year there were 101,944 full-time teachers in Catholic schools. Of these, 372 were scholastics (that is, those on the way to the priesthood); 3,445 were brothers (that is, men who had dedicated their lives to religion but with no expectation of becoming priests); 6,779 were priests (devoting their full time to teaching); 11,396 were laymen and laywomen; and 79,952 were sisters.

As the United States is divided into states, with a state superintendent in charge of education in each of the 48 jurisdictions, the Catholic Church here is divided into dioceses (and archdioceses), with a diocesan superintendent of schools supervising each of the 124 jurisdictions. His function is to oversee the general Catholic educational effort, to co-ordinate and in some measure standardize courses of study, and to work for the improvement of the whole undertaking all along the line.

Most Catholic elementary schools and some secondary schools are parochial institutions. They are built and supported by the people of the respective parishes. They are staffed largely by nuns of the teaching orders. Usually the pastor or one of his assistants occupies a position comparable to principal in the public system. The diocesan authorities establish standards for all the schools in the diocesan system, and the diocesan superintendent supervises their implementation.

Most secondary, and a few primary, schools are operated by "communities" of nuns, priests, or brothers, independently of any parish. These schools are dependent on tuition and gifts.

Many bishops have established high schools to serve several parishes or a whole city. They are supported by the parishes which they serve and are a regular part of the diocesan system.

Most Catholic colleges and universities are operated by orders of priests, nuns, and brothers and are supported by tuition and gifts. A few bishops have established their own diocesan colleges, supported by tuition and contributions from all the parishes of the diocese.

The Catholic University of America, Washington, D. C., is maintained by tuition, gifts, and an annual contribution taken up in all the parishes of the country.

The bishops of the United States have set up a Department of Education in their national organization, the National Catholic Welfare Conference. And the Catholic educators have set up their own organization, the National Catholic Educational Association. Some of the orders—Jesuits, Franciscans, and so on—have their own educational associations. The Director of the N.C.W.C. Department of Education is usually general secretary of N.C.E.A. Both N.C.W.C. and N.C.E.A. have their headquarters at 1312 Massachusetts Avenue, N. W., Washington 5, D. C. Information on Catholic education is available there on request.

SUGGESTIONS FOR FURTHER STUDY

1. Do Catholics regard the public schools as evil in themselves, or as good, but not good enough, in view of their omission of the fourth *R*? Discuss.

2. Do Catholics hold that the parent or the state has the primary responsibility and right over the education of children? Discuss in light of democratic and

totalitarian principles, especially doctrine of Pierce *vs.* Society of Sisters (Supreme Court of U. S.).

3. Why do Catholics hold that integral education must include education of the whole man, that education without religion is incomplete? Explain.

4. Why do Catholics say that a "humanistic" or "democratic" education is not necessarily a satisfactory "religious" education? What does this mean?

5. Is Catholic teaching on authority in religious matters incompatible with democracy? Is the idea of divine revelation compatible with democracy? Is the doctrine of parental authority? Distinguish and explain.

BIBLIOGRAPHY

Burns, James A. *Catholic School System in the United States; Its Principles, Origin, and Establishment.* New York: Benziger Brothers, 1912.

Cunningham, William F. *Pivotal Problems of Education*: An Introduction to the Christian Philosophy of Education. New York: Macmillan Company, 1940.

Deferrari, Roy, ed. *Essays on Catholic Education in the United States.* Washington, D. C.: Catholic University of America Press, 1942.

————, ed.: *Workshop on Philosophy of Catholic Higher Education.* Proceedings of the Workshop. Washington, D. C.: Catholic University of America Press, 1948.

Hovre, Francis de. *Catholicism in Education.* A positive Exposition of the Catholic Principles of Education. New York: Benziger Brothers, 1934.

Leen, Edward. *What Is Education?* New York: Sheed & Ward, 1944.

McGrath, Sister Mary Bernard. *The Compatibility of Catholic Schools and Democratic Standards.* Washington, D. C.: Catholic University of America Press, 1948.

McGucken, William J. *Catholic Way in Education* (Religion and Culture Series). Milwaukee: Bruce Publishing Co., 1934.

MacLellan, Malcolm A. *Catholic Church and Adult Education.* Washington, D. C.: Catholic University of America Press, 1935.

Maritain, Jacques. *Education at the Crossroads* (Terry Lectures, 1943). New Haven: Yale University Press, 1943.

Pope Pius XI. *Christian Education of Youth (Divinis Illius Magistri),* Encyclical Letter. Washington, D. C.: National Catholic Welfare Conference, 1930.

Redden, John D., and Ryan, Francis A. *A Catholic Philosophy of Education.* Milwaukee: Bruce Publishing Co., 1942.

Chapter 42

THE DEVELOPMENT OF RELIGIOUS EDUCATION IN OTHER COUNTRIES

ERICH F. VOEHRINGER

THE EVENTS AND EXPERIENCES of the two world wars have shaken, not only the economic and political, but also the spiritual foundations of practically every country in the world, and have left deep marks on the development of religious education. In many places churches, schools, and meeting halls have been destroyed, as well as the textbooks and other teaching materials and the printing presses which were needed to replace them. Thousands of the younger leaders, and often some of the best and most promising, were killed in the war. Whole populations were uprooted and scattered, and with them the organizations which had served their spiritual needs. Is it any wonder that in the face of such experiences many religious education workers have succumbed to a sense of frustration, a doubt in the efficacy of all education, of all human efforts to better this world? Some have become tired and weary, physically by privation and hardships, spiritually by disappointment and shame at the apparent failure of the Church. The progressing secularism of our civilization has led some of our theologians to state flatly that we are in the post-Christian era, at least as far as the Western nations are concerned, that Christianity has passed its peak, is fighting a losing battle of retreat.

On the other hand, many have been awakened to a keener realization of the importance of the task of Christian education, to a sense of urgency in view of the appalling disintegration of human values, to an eagerness to use the newest and best means at our disposal, and to join hands and forces across boundaries of race and nation in sincere co-operation with all who have the same burden and the same goal.

It is impossible, of course, in one chapter to give anything like a complete picture of religious education around the world. All we can hope to do is to point out certain conditions and trends in some countries of special interest.

LATIN AMERICA

The situation in Latin America is marked by the predominance of the Roman Catholic Church, which regards Protestant work as an unwanted competitor. The extent to which this feeling is put into action depends largely on the local situation, ranging from guarded tolerance, as in the Dominican Republic, to actual persecution, as in some parts of Mexico and Colombia.

Interdenominational co-operation among Protestants has been widespread and effective, especially in the field of literature production. As a result of the Latin American Congress in Montevideo in 1925, the Committee on Co-operation in Latin America undertook a comprehensive project, in which different countries were given responsibility for the production of various curriculum materials which were then to be used throughout the Spanish-speaking area. No such program for so many different countries has ever been undertaken anywhere in the world.

There is also a strong desire for fellowship and co-operation among the Protestant young people, who in most countries are forming interdenominational youth organizations. These are united in the Latin American Union of Evangelical Youth, which grew out of the first Evangelical Youth Congress in Lima, Peru, in 1941, and now has member organizations in Argentina, Bolivia, Brazil, Chile, Colombia, Cuba, Ecuador, Mexico, Puerto Rico, and Uruguay. Let us select a few representative countries.

In *Puerto Rico* Protestant educational work has been marked by an unhampered freedom to expand and by a fine spirit of interdenominational co-operation. The Committee on Christian Education of the Association of Evangelical Churches is arranging interdenominational training courses for Sunday-school and vacation church-school teachers, young people's conferences, institutes of music, and similar projects. The committee decided to initiate a special program of audio-visual aids, with a rental service of films and slides. The Sunday schools with a total enrollment of sixty thousand pupils are the most influential agency of Christian education, besides some seventy vacation church schools, thirty-one Protestant day schools, and about two hundred young people's societies. In Puerto Rico, as in most Latin American countries, there is a Union Seminary, in which several denominations co-operate in the training of the clergy.

In *Mexico* religious education of any kind is forbidden in all day schools, whether private or public. Though there are a few private schools of Protestant origin, no religion is being taught in them. The Protestant Churches therefore have to concentrate entirely on the Sunday school and vacation church schools for the religious training of their young. There is a Sunday school in every church, mostly including all ages from infants to adults. In some rural communities the Sunday school is more important than the church service or may replace it altogether. Vacation schools are held in many churches, either in July or in December, for one to four weeks. Besides Bible teaching and hymns, the curriculum includes health and hygiene, manual work, games, and sometimes reading for illiterate adults.

Even Catholic children are eager to attend these schools; in some places they make up as much as 50 per cent of the enrollment. The teachers in Sunday and vacation schools are all volunteers with varying degrees of training. Efforts are made to improve their training in courses and institutes. The Department of Christian Education of the National Evangelical Council is concerned with service in this field and also, in connection with the above mentioned scheme, with the preparation of Sunday-school lessons which are issued bimonthly with a circulation of twelve thousand in all Spanish-speaking countries and the southern part of the United States.

In *Argentina* the old law of 1884, which prohibited religious education as part of the official school program but permitted it on school premises after school hours, was abolished in 1947. The new law provides for compulsory religious education in the Roman Catholic faith in all schools. Pupils may be exempt from attending these classes by personal application on the part of the parents, but there is so much moral pressure that few dare to avail themselves of the exemption. For Protestant schools, therefore, the situation is very difficult. The same is true of Peru.

In *Brazil* the World Council of Christian Education assisted in organizing and developing a strong Council of Religious Education, which later shared in forming the Confederation of Brazilian Evangelical Churches.[1] The Sunday-school lesson materials which are prepared and published by it are issued quarterly in 125,000 copies. A new task has been added by the opening of the public schools, primary and secondary, to religious instruction, by government decree of 1947. The churches must provide teachers and literature for these classes if they want to avail themselves of this opportunity. The Brazil Council has a special committee to deal with this whole problem, the question of teacher training, the preparation of curriculum, and the publication of textbooks.

Perhaps the most outstanding feature of Christian education in Latin America is the excellent day schools which nearly all major denominations are conducting in many centers of population. In the field of the education of women, which had been almost completely neglected before, Protestant schools have been particularly progressive and pioneering. There are, all told, about nine hundred Protestant schools in Latin America; from 20 to as high as 80 per cent of their pupils come from Catholic homes. The influence of these Christian schools and the contribution they are making reach far beyond the limits of the Protestant Church into the community and the state. Their graduates fill leading positions in public life. The example of their educational methods has often served to raise the standards in state schools for the entire country. Some years ago a person no less than the president of the Republic of Brazil, although a Roman Catholic, sent his

[1] See Chapter 37 on "The World Council of Christian Education."

children to one of these Protestant schools and paid it a high tribute by saying that people who attend such a school become more "industrious, honest, and truthful, improved in manners and personal appearance, and . . . better citizens and members of the community." [2]

Protestant forces in Latin America are, generally speaking, exerting a far greater influence than their small numbers would warrant, not the least being the beneficial effect on the Roman Catholic Church itself, which is forced to greater effort and better methods of religious instruction in its own fold through the competition of the Protestants.

ASIA

In Asia, Christianity has taken deep roots through the devoted efforts of the missionaries. Here, on the background of old, indigenous cultures, the younger churches have attained greater maturity than elsewhere and have produced more leaders who are able to interpret the new faith to their own people and to make a real contribution to the Christendom of the world.

The fact that *Japan* is in a period of transition from the old imperialism to a new democracy is reflected in the religious education situation. The new constitution under the guidance of the American occupation authorities follows the American philosophy of complete separation of Church and state. Religious education is forbidden in all public schools. This regulation of course affects Buddhists and Shintoists as well as Christians, who constitute only 0.5 per cent of the entire population. Private schools may have a religious program and instruction only if it does not interfere with the secular teaching work of the school. No educational institution which is not operated and controlled by the government may receive any financial support from public funds. This means that Christian day schools have a hard struggle and that most of the education in the Christian faith will have to be done by the churches themselves. However, the educational work of the churches is still largely undeveloped. The Sunday school, being regarded as something foreign, declined during the war years. In Japan the Sunday school had always been more of a lay movement with little encouragement from the clergy, who, having had no practical training in religious education in the seminaries, looked upon it with suspicion as an exponent of Western civilization. Now the Sunday school is being revived, and its great possibilities are being recognized. There is a rush of children and young people to the church schools as never before, and in some districts tuition fees are being charged to cope with the abundance of applicants.

One must consider also that one third of all Protestant church buildings

---

[2] W. Stanley Rycroft, *On This Foundation*, p. 130. Used by permission of Friendship Press.

in Japan were destroyed during the war, and that public buildings, such as schools, which were formerly used for religious instruction in some places, are now ruled out by the new constitution. It will be one of the chief tasks of the Christian churches in Japan—and by no means an easy one—to provide the physical conditions, as well as the literature and teacher-training facilities for a comprehensive educational program. For this purpose the Kyodan—the Church of Christ in Japan, comprising about 75 per cent of the Protestants—and the other Protestant denominations, such as the Lutherans and Anglicans, have organized the Japan Council of Christian Education.

A full-time youth secretary has been appointed to consolidate the beginnings of youth work in various parts of the country, though youth work in our sense of the term is hampered by the fact that the Japanese custom does not know coeducational enterprises, and the Japanese churches in general have no social activity programs.

It is to be hoped that the new Christian University, being established near Tokyo as a gift of American Protestantism, will also mark the beginning of a new day in religious education in Japan.

There is no country where the ravages of war have caused more suffering and dislocation, and where the forces of Christian education have had greater difficulties to face and obstacles to surmount, than *China*. Yet, in spite of this, and perhaps even because of it, it is in China where these forces have rallied to greater effort, and where we find more interdenominational co-operation and more enthusiasm in the field of religious education than in most countries. In the National Committee for Christian Religious Education in China nine denominations and four other organizations, such as the Y.M.C.A. and the Y.W.C.A., co-operate. It carries out a vigorous program in all branches of the field, with special attention to the Christian home, children's work, youth work, leadership training, and rural education. From its inception in 1931 this committee has been remarkably active and fruitful. Among its publications are a closely graded Sunday-school series, a group-graded Sunday-school series, a curriculum for nonschool children, courses for young people, worship material, hymns, a series for lay training, books on the Christian family, and others. At the same time the Religious Education Fellowship was founded. It now has a membership of over eight hundred church workers and teachers, enthusiastically supporting the work of the N.C.C.R.E. A monthly bulletin and annual conferences unite the members in spirit and work.

The emphasis on the Christian home as the primary agency of religious education is characteristic of China, where the family plays such an important part. The National Christian Council here has a special Committee for "Christianizing Homes," which co-operates with the N.C.C.R.E.

The China Christian Educational Association, another agency of the National Christian Council, concerns itself with Christian high schools and colleges, which have made a great contribution to Chinese life. They have been particularly hard hit by the vicissitudes of war. There is nothing in the history of Christian missions comparable to the exodus of the colleges and universities, which fled before the Japanese armies; faculty and student body, with books, apparatus, and all, started out on boats, wagons, push-carts, and foot, to set up shop again hundreds of miles inland. After the surrender of Japan they returned to their campuses, often to find their buildings in ruins. Bravely they started to reconstruct, when they were faced with another threat, the civil war and the communist advance. This time the situation was different. Not a national enemy intruding from the outside, but a part of their own people was advocating a new government and order of society, so they decided to stay and render their service as long and as best as they could. For the time being the communists seem to adopt a tolerant attitude. Christian schools and colleges are allowed to function under certain restrictions. However, what the future will bring is very uncertain.

The development of Christian education in the *Republic of the Philippines* is similar to that in the United States, having been modeled after our system during the twenty years of American rule. The interdenominational Philippine Islands Sunday School Union, founded in 1911, became the Philippine Council of Religious Education in 1918; this in turn was merged with the Philippine Federation of Evangelical Churches as its Committee on Christian Education. An idea of the work of this committee can be gained by looking at the list of its eight subcommittees: (1) curriculum, (2) leadership training, (3) adult work, (4) young people's work, (5) children's work, (6) vacation and weekday religious instruction, (7) special days, and (8) Christian homes. Lately a department of audio-visual aids has been added, with plans for a nation-wide program, including a radio station.

The declaration of independence in *India* and the establishment of national governments in separate dominions, Pakistan, India, Ceylon, and Burma, is likely to have far-reaching consequences for Christian education in this part of the world. For the time being, government support of schools under private auspices, including Christian schools, has been continued, but all sorts of restrictions are being imposed by provincial authorities on schools accepting such aid. In one instance a Christian school in India was requested to have 50 per cent non-Christians on its faculty and in the student body as a condition to receiving the grant. Such a policy may result eventually in many changes in such institutions or even in a reduction of Christian day schools. Much thought is being given by the Central Board of Christian Higher Education of the National Christian Council to this entire question. Conditions with reference to education are not yet settled. In any case, more responsibility will rest upon the educational institutions of an exclusively religious character. The India Sunday School Union, which has for many years successfully furthered the spread of the Sunday school in India, is planning to enlarge and intensify the work and to make the Sunday school the vital educational agency of the churches.

India has progressed more than any other of the younger church areas in the use of audio-visual aids and mass communication mediums. There are two religious-film libraries with several hundred films and filmstrips for interdenominational use. The National Christian Council has a special Committee on Audio-Visual Aids, which is wide awake to the possibilities of these new means. Under its auspices institutes on audio-visual aids are being held for the training of local church workers and for production and experimentation. Plans are under way for a great expansion of this work, with full-time field secretaries specially trained in audio-visual techniques and with mobile units carrying motion-picture and still projectors, generators, public-address systems, and record players, to cover eventually all parts of India. Beginnings have been made in the local production of audio-visual aids—films, filmstrips, slide sets, and flannelgraph materials—which are much better suited to the background and cultural level of the audiences than imported American and British productions. Attention is being given to the use of radio, and native personnel is being trained in the preparation and broadcasting of religious radio programs. The density of population in India lends itself particularly well to an intensive use of these means, and the future should bring great results.

Moslem Countries—the Near East

In Moslem countries Christian education is facing a very difficult situation. Indigenous Christian minority groups—mostly of the Eastern Orthodox confession—have arrived at a more or less tolerable mode of living by keeping to themselves and avoiding any active propaganda. Though religious liberty is officially included in some of the constitutions—Turkey, Iran, Iraq—it is regarded simply as the right of an adult to believe as he wishes and to worship his own God; except in Iran it does not include the right to teach one's religion to others if that religion differs from the state religion, that is, Islam. There is a strong public feeling, sometimes crystallized into legislation, that it is a crime against the community to teach any religion other than Islam, especially to sick people—in Christian hospitals—taking advantage of their helpless situation, and to children, even if their parents or guardians should give their consent.

Christian educational institutions must be exceedingly careful not to do anything that might look like propaganda for their faith. It may be dangerous for a Christian teacher to answer a Moslem pupil's question on religion, even outside of school hours. In *Turkey* and *Iraq*, Christian schools are forced to accept government-appointed teachers in history, geography, and civics, whose prescribed salary—usually much higher than those the insti-tuition can pay their Christian teachers—must be paid by the school. In *Egypt* a law demands that instruction in Islam and a place of worship must be provided by Christian schools for their Mohammedan pupils. On the whole, Christian minorities and missions are allowed to conduct their own schools; but they must conform to government regulations in curriculum, textbooks, standards of examination, especially in the teaching of Arabic and of local history and geography. Religious instruction may be given to the Christian pupils but may not be offered, even on a voluntary basis, to Moslem students.

Still Christian schools in general are popular and have no lack of students. The Christian personalities of the teachers and the Christian spirit permeat-ing the entire life of the schools do not fail to make an impression and are recognized and valued as important factors in character training, even by Moslems.

Christian children going to public schools may be excused from Islamic teaching, but no provision is made for their instruction in the Christian faith. Often they have to take part in study and memorization of the Koran. As Friday is the general Moslem holiday, attempts are made in some places, for example in Egypt, to have "Friday Schools" instead of "Sunday Schools" to provide Bible instruction.

The strongest interdenominational agency in this area is the Bible Lands Union of Christian Education, serving Syria, Lebanon, Palestine, Trans-Jordan, Cyprus, and Iraq. It carries on a vigorous program in support of the Sunday schools and other forms of Christian education. It is a hopeful sign that both the churches of the West, through their missionary establish-ments, and the ancient orthodox churches of the East are co-operating in this union, by which all are benefited.

There is a renewed interest in religious education in the Eastern Orthodox Churches, which are engaging in new programs of work among children and youth, and are applying new methods of teaching and evangelism. In *Greece* there are now over 1,000 Sunday schools of the Greek Orthodox Church, with no fewer than 150,000 children. Over 1,000 students are among the volunteer teachers, who have to attend study groups for two to three hours a week during one year before they are permitted to teach. The religious brotherhood "Zoe" (life), made up largely of educated laymen with some theological training and license to preach, has been very active in giving Christian instruction to children and adults, with special atten-tion to workmen and farmers.

GREAT BRITAIN AND BRITISH COLONIES

England may serve as an example of a country where the forces of Christian education are rallying bravely in the face of secularization and the economic and spiritual upheavals following the war. Here we find a system which avoids both extremes: complete separation of state and Church, and the exclusive recognition and support of one Church only by the state.

One of the outstanding contributions England made to religious education was the Sunday-school movement, which was founded in 1780 by Robert Raikes, a wealthy Gloucester businessman, who collected ragged, illiterate children from the streets on Sundays to teach them the Bible and the fundamentals of learning. Today the Sunday school in England is still one of the most important factors in the Church's educational program. After some years of decline in enrollment and interest, there has been a decided upward trend since the middle forties. In 1946 it was estimated that there were about 2,900,000 pupils in the Sunday schools of England and Wales, over half of them—about 1,642,000—belonging to the Free Churches, and the rest to the Anglican Church. The total enrollment comprises about 42 per cent of all children of Sunday-school age, as against 40 per cent in 1943, and 47 per cent in 1938. Since there is also religious instruction in the day schools, covering Bible-story and memory work, the Sunday schools can concentrate more on the task of building Christian character and preparing for active church membership.

The National Sunday School Union is giving careful attention to teacher training and lesson materials. Westhill Training College in Birmingham is the center of teacher training, providing specialized courses with practice schools and sending out teams of leaders to conduct courses for teachers in various districts. The British Lessons Council is furnishing two distinct sets of lessons for Sunday schools to fit different local situations:

1. The Standard Graded Courses, dated and issued annually, with lessons grouped on a topical basis—Bible, Christian biography, history of the Church and of missionary enterprise—in three grades, primary, junior, and senior.

2. An all-Bible course, undated, with material chosen from the same area of the Bible but with different lessons for each age group.

The family church course is a new experiment which is aimed at bringing about a closer integration of the Sunday school, the home, and the Church. In this course special emphasis is given to the great Christian festivals and their celebration by the church, leading up to a united worship of all departments with the congregation, thus drawing the children, many of whom come from homes with no church connection, into a more vital relationship with the church. Lessons about the local church, its history, work, and personnel, are intended to strengthen this bond still further.

In recent years a great deal of experimentation in new methods and means has been going on. Greater emphasis on worship, on the self-teaching and project method, on audio-visual aids has improved the attractiveness and efficacy of the Sunday school. Flannelgraph materials are furnished by the National Sunday School Union and others in connection with lesson materials. The religious motion picture and filmstrip as teaching aids are widely advocated. Such film series as "Two Thousand Years Ago" and "The Life of St. Paul," produced by Religious Films, Ltd., have been pioneering in this field and have provided excellent tools for the teaching of biblical background and history.

A special feature of British Sunday-school life is the scripture examinations, which are conducted annually on a nationwide basis by the National Sunday School Union, and which are very popular among the boys and girls.

In addition to the Sunday school, religious instruction is offered in both government and private schools. The Sunday-school movement was already well under way when in 1870 the Education Act established community schools for the whole country, including nonsectarian Bible instruction in the curriculum. The Education Act of 1944 provides that in addition to regular classes in religion the school day in every state-aided school shall begin with collective worship. In the same act local school authorities were charged with drawing up, in consultation with the various church groups, adequate syllabuses for "undenominational" religious instruction. The Apostles' Creed is not regarded as being distinctive of any particular denomination and may be included. The religion classes are taught by members of the school staff, who in connection with their professional training were given special courses in religious education. There is, and always has been since 1870, a "conscience clause," which opens the possibility for parents to have their children exempt from religion classes or to make other provision for their religious instruction. Approved private schools such as church schools and church training colleges are given financial support by the state.

Youth work has received more and more attention by the churches during recent years. The state recognizes the importance of Christian youth work to the extent of providing training facilities and monetary assistance, irrespective of denominational allegiance. In the Church of England youth clubs and guilds for boys and girls are often regarded as the continuation of the Sunday school, which largely takes care of children under the age of thirteen. Also, in the Free Churches there are thousands of congregations who have their youth clubs, many with full-time paid leaders.

These clubs are an important factor in reaching unchurched youth and bringing back many who have drifted away after quitting the Sunday school. In one club of a Methodist church only two of seventy-five members came from church-affiliated homes. A well-rounded program, including sports and social activities, draws the young people into a Christian fellowship which is of supreme importance in these decisive years.

The Church of England has its own Central Council for Education under the chairmanship of the Archbishop of Canterbury. Much emphasis is placed on courses or institutes in which small groups of people such as Sunday-school teachers and youth leaders get together for a period from two days to three or four weeks for special training. In "family schools" parents and children may combine holiday with study. Most dioceses have special residential conference houses for this purpose.

The situation in *Scotland* and *Northern Ireland* is similar to that in England, though flavored by its special historical and national background. The abiding influence of Calvinism, with its emphasis on education, is responsible for the fact that the teaching of the Scriptures has occupied a prominent place in the life of the Scottish school ever since the sixteenth century. *The First Book of Discipline*, by John Knox, has always been the impetus and inspiration of the Christian education program.

In the *British colonies* conditions are marked by the same sympathetic attitude of government authorities toward Christian education. Missionary societies as a rule are carrying on an extensive educational program, and in many colonies the mission day schools provide by far the largest part of all education. In these schools religious education is naturally given a prominent place in the school curriculum, covering Bible stories, memory work, hymn singing; and in the upper grades Christian doctrine, as well as general and local church history, with the result that, for example, an African school child, though perhaps from a non-Christian family, may know far more about the Bible and Christianity than the average American Sunday-school pupil. Under this system we usually find the institution of the "teacher-preacher," which is typical of many a mission field or young indigenous church. This means that the teacher in charge of the village school is at the same time the preacher of the local congregation on Sundays, in addition to being responsible for catechetical instruction of new converts and for other church duties. An ordained pastor, who resides at a larger center and is the overseer of an entire district with several villages, comes around from time to time to inspect the school, to check the records, and to administer baptism and Holy Communion. We have here the closest possible connection of school and church, where an able, conscientious leader can mold a village, young and old, into a real Christian community.

The British Colonial Government in each territory gives considerable financial support, called grants-in-aid, to the missions for their school work, without making any distinction as to the national or denominational origin of the mission. The only condition is that the mission schools must meet a certain standard, set by the government, in curriculum, equipment, and teacher qualifications. These grants cover the salaries of local teachers and of missionaries engaged exclusively in educational work, and in some cases even building and equipment costs, especially of secondary schools.

This assistance is, of course, of great help to the missions and enables them to carry on and expand their educational work to a degree which otherwise would be impossible. On the other hand, there are also certain dangers in this arrangement, as it tends to secularize the educational work of the Church. When the government school inspector visits a mission school to check its efficiency, he is naturally concerned only with the secular subjects. This easily creates the impression with pupils and teachers that religious subjects are of little importance. In fact, often many, if not most, of the graduates of the higher grades and secondary schools are lost entirely to the Church. The office of a mission-school supervisor in many places counteracts this tendency.

Another outgrowth of the grant system is the fact that the salaries of teachers, as fixed and supported by the government, are often higher than those which the missions or local churches can afford to pay their pastors. Since pastors are recruited mostly from the ranks of the church-school teachers, you have the anomalous, and sometimes very difficult, situation of an advancement to a higher and more responsible position with a con-comitant reduction in salary. To keep their schools as nurseries of Christian character and of active church membership is one of the chief problems of many a younger church under a colonial government, sympathetic though it may be.

In such lands, where the weekday school under Christian auspices pro-vides religious education, it is sometimes thought that there is little need for Sunday schools, or vacation church schools. Some churches, therefore, have no special provision for the Christian education of the young besides the weekday school, while adult education, at least as far as new converts are concerned, naturally receives careful attention in missionary countries. A two-year course of instruction to prepare for baptism is not uncommon, though the length of time varies in different missions. After baptism there are frequent meetings for adults, such as daily morning devotions in the chapel, evening Bible study or prayer meetings, which are used for further education.

Literacy campaigns as conducted by Frank C. Laubach according to his method of using picture charts are a potent factor in Christian education, because in many areas the only available literature for the newly-literates to read is the Bible and Christian tracts.

The great problem in Africa, as in other countries where primitive cul-tures clash with the influx of Western civilization, is the disintegration of the moral standards and economic bonds of the old tribe and the resulting emancipation and uprooting of the individual. Christian education is called

to provide guidance in this period of transition, so that the younger generation may find new standards and values in the Christian faith, may find a new spiritual home in the Church and become adjusted in a positive way to a new cultural situation which has come to stay.

CONTINENTAL EUROPE

Turning to Continental Europe we enter the battleground upon which the conflict between the ideologies of today is most bitterly fought, and where Christian education is most intimately drawn into this conflict and often finds itself in the front line of battle. Conflicting systems of thought are contending for the souls of men, especially of the younger generation, which has witnessed the downfall of a civilization in blood and ruins. Nationalism and nihilism, communism and capitalism, are offering their lures. Christian education is faced with a task as never before among a people whose hearts have been plowed deeply by suffering and despair, whose seeking for truth is more earnest or whose skepticism more ingrained, because they have had the sobering experience of utter disillusionment. Christian forces have the bread of life which alone can truly satisfy this hunger; but it must be offered in new ways, or else the old forms, where they still exist, must be filled with new life and meaning.

It is only natural that youth work should receive special attention under a situation like this. The Y.M.C.A. and Y.W.C.A. and similar youth organizations in Europe have a strongly evangelistic character and are much more closely related to the Church than in the U.S.A. Youth camps are becoming increasingly popular with a well-rounded program in which devotions and Bible study hold the center. Full-time youth workers and nationwide church youth organizations have contributed much to expand and strengthen this work. Projects of practical Christian service are playing an important part in youth work and are of real value where homeless children, people living in ruins, hunger, unemployment, and poverty abound. The French "Cimade" (*Comité Inter-Mouvements auprès des Evacués*) is a shining example of this kind of practical Christianity. In this movement all French Protestant youth organizations are co-operating in the task of alleviating the manifold sufferings brought about by the German occupation, the war itself, and the aftermath of the war, through personal self-sacrificing service in concentration camps, in industrial centers, to youth, to displaced persons, without regard to nationality, creed, or political adherence.

Another field which had long been neglected by the churches of Europe, and which now receives widespread attention, is that of adult education. The failure of the Church to understand the common man and his needs has resulted in a wholesale estrangement of the masses. The socialist and communist movements in Europe therefore have been largely anti-Christian. To make Christianity meaningful again in the lives of the people in factory and street is the deep concern of present-day Church leaders. The Sigtuna Foundation in Sweden since 1917 has been offering a fellowship of work and study to young adults, as well as special study conferences where ministers and laymen of all walks of life can meet. Other institutes with similar concerns were founded elsewhere: the Johannesstift in Berlin, Germany; the Church-and-World Center in Driebergen, Holland; the Iona Community in Scotland; the Cluny Community in France. The Evangelical Academies in Germany are a large-scale attempt to bridge the gulf between the Church and the secularized public, especially the working classes, by lectures and week-end discussion conferences on vital topics of the day in the light of the Christian faith.

The problem of state and Church is ever present in European countries with its bearing upon religious education. Solutions are attempted in different ways ranging from a state Church, with religious instruction obligatory in all schools, to an antichurch state, with no religious instruction permitted in any school. In Roman Catholic countries the Catholic faith is taught in the schools. It is compulsory in *Spain, Portugal,* and to some extent *Italy,* voluntary in *Poland, Belgium,* and *Czechoslovakia.* Belgium and Czechoslovakia provide also state-supported instruction in the Protestant faith by Protestant teachers where desired. A similar situation exists in some predominantly Protestant countries, where both Protestant and Catholic instruction is offered in state schools, each Church body taking the responsibility for, or the supervision of, the instruction in its own faith. This is the case in *Germany*—the three Western zones—*Switzerland,* and *Holland.*

The *Scandinavian countries,* which are almost exclusively Lutheran, likewise have religious instruction in all schools, with the possibility of exemption. The instruction thus given may be more or less perfunctory in many instances, but the churches are realizing the great need and the great opportunity and are seeking ways for providing better teacher-training facilities and for making these classes more fruitful and evangelistic. Especially in *Finland* this goal has been attained to a remarkable degree. Special catechetical instruction by the pastor in preparation for confirmation, usually for two years, when children reach the age of adolescence, is common in all Lutheran countries. It is based on that classic of religious instruction, the *Small Catechism* by Martin Luther. Instead of the American type of Sunday school, there is usually a "Children's Service," a regular church service for children of all ages with group instruction, in place of the sermon. The clergy is trained at state universities, which have a theological faculty, and theological degrees are on a level with those of other branches.

France is the only one of the Western European countries which bars religion from the schools and offers "moral training" instead. The different

Protestant denominations therefore are emphasizing Sunday-school work and are co-operating in the French Sunday School Association.

The states in the Russian orbit are adopting more and more the communist pattern of secularism in schools and restriction of the educational activities of the churches. Here the state tries to control all schools and excludes all religion from them; this is the case in *Yugoslavia, Bulgaria, Rumania, Hungary*, as in the *Soviet Union*. In the *Russian Zone of Germany*, when religious education was taken out of the school building and curriculum, the Church rose to the occasion and provided instruction after school hours by voluntary teachers. When permission for the printing of only one religious textbook was given, the Church authorities created a masterpiece by combining in one volume the main Bible stories of the Old and New Testaments, an introduction to the origin and history of the Bible, 150 Bible verses for memorization, 92 hymns, selected prayers, the catechism, an explanation of the liturgy and of Christian symbols, and a brief Church history. When only 400 students, all from the working classes, were permitted to study theology, the churches trained thousands of lay catechists and evangelists. In other countries in the Eastern orbit, the Church is showing similar resourcefulness and heroism against great odds.

Finally one should mention, as a bright sign of promise, a new and singular venture in Christian education, the Ecumenical Institute at Bossey, near Geneva, Switzerland. Under the auspices of the World Council of Churches this institute is dedicated to the study and teaching of Christian truth and all its implications in our age, with special emphasis on the laymen's aspect and contribution. To its courses and conferences, held the year around, come students and teachers from many countries of the world. An idea of its comprehensive scope can be gained by a look at some of the items on one year's (1947) program: a course for young pastors and theological students (with participants from seventeen different countries and lecturers from ten countries); a meeting of leaders of laymen's associations and institutes; youth leaders' course; group of leaders active in political life; conference of Christian university teachers; meeting of World's Student Christian Federation; course for Christian educators; conference of Christian doctors; Bible-reading fellowship; course for laymen.

This spirit of ecumenical fellowship and co-operation in Christian education is growing more and more and is bringing new help and hope to those who are engaged in the task, given by Christ, to "teach all nations."

SUGGESTIONS FOR FURTHER STUDY

1. Study the problem of religious education in public schools. Give reasons pro and con. Compare the various measures existing in different countries and solutions attempted.

2. In what countries has religious education been influenced by the American system? How does this show itself?

3. In what parts of the world have political changes in recent years affected religious education? In what ways?

4. What are the special problems of the younger churches in religious education? What attempts are made to solve them?

5. Why should there be interdenominational co-operation in religious education? What patterns of interdenominational co-operation have been developed in various countries?

6. Contact foreign students or missionaries of your acquaintance about Christian education in their respective countries. Compare their systems and methods to our own. What can we learn from each other?

BIBLIOGRAPHY

GENERAL

Bates, Miner Searle. *Religious Liberty, an Inquiry.* New York: International Missionary Council, 1945.

World Christian Education. Quarterly magazine. World Council of Christian Education, 156 Fifth Avenue, New York, N. Y.

LATIN AMERICA

Rycroft, W. Stanley. *On This Foundation.* New York: Friendship Press, 1942.

ASIA

Gregg, Alice. *China and Educational Autonomy.* Syracuse: Syracuse University Press, 1946.

NEAR EAST

Morrison, S. A. *Religious Liberty in the Near East.* New York: World Dominion Press, 1948.

EUROPE

Horton, Walter. *Centers of New Life in European Christendom.* New York: World Council of Churches, 1948.

Leeson, Spencer. *Christian Education.* New York: Longmans, Green & Company, 1947.

Professional Life as Christian Vocation, by the Ecumenical Institute. Geneva: Oikumene, 1948.

Chapter 43

PROTESTANTISM'S STRATEGY FOR RELIGIOUS EDUCATION

ARLO AYRES BROWN

PROTESTANTISM IN AMERICA is committed to the principle of separation between Church and state. It wholeheartedly supports the public schools of the United States. However, this separation cannot prevent churches from co-operating with the state, or citizens from seeking to improve the quality of public education for their children. How far can Protestantism go in co-operation with public education? What can our churches do by themselves and unitedly to give the total education of our children the Christian quality which we believe is so essential to our democratic way of life?

Roman Catholics believe in parochial schools. Should we join this movement? Possible decisions by the Supreme Court of the United States might make this necessary, but that is both improbable and undesirable. On the other hand, we cannot surrender to secularists who say that every reference in education to religion is sectarian and hence should be eliminated from all public education. It should never be forgotten that in a democracy such as ours majorities have rights as well as minorities and that tolerance must be a two-way road.

The principle in our Constitution of no state Church and no religious discrimination must be preserved, but the state does not try to get along without the co-operation of the churches in normal peacetime and leans heavily upon them in great emergencies. The armed services would not think of having their young men and women go without the benefit of religious sanctions and the counsel of chaplains who must be fully ordained by some church.

USO, which rendered such conspicuous and invaluable service to those in uniform in World War II, was an organization through which citizens of all faiths co-operated with the government on a volunteer basis. It was organized by the leaders of the Protestant, Catholic, and Jewish faiths; and the programs were carried on through such agencies as the Y.M.C.A., the Y.W.C.A., the Salvation Army, the National Catholic Community Service, and the National Jewish Welfare Board.

The most difficult problem for education in the United States is to devise effective means for the co-operation of all the teaching and other welfare agencies in a community so as to develop the highest type of growing citizens.

It is clearly recognized that Protestant forces must develop to the fullest possible extent the educational resources over which they exercise a reasonable amount of control. We cannot blame public education for teaching failures in the churches. No device can be a substitute for good teaching. The training of parents, teachers, and other leaders must be basic to any strategy for Protestantism in religious education. How to make such teaching so interesting that it will successfully compete for a part of the time given to recreation or significant organizations like the Red Cross is one of the most serious problems confronting our educational leaders.

Home, church, community—these are units of society with which Protestantism carries great weight. On the state, national, and international levels she has schools, colleges, universities, and other institutions rendering high-grade educational service. None of these levels can be ignored, nor can their influence be minimized, without serious impairment of the total program. We will consider religious education on the community, the national, and the international levels.

RELIGIOUS EDUCATION ON THE COMMUNITY LEVEL

Someone has said that we have no theology in community terms. The individual, family, and church—even the world at large—have been treated in detail by theologians. Perhaps it is too much to ask our theologians to think in terms of community, but some thinking must be done, or the churches of Christ will fail. Community standards of morals, of amusement, of vocation, also of family life, to mention just a few, often oppose the ideals of the churches and defeat much of their effort. Those faithful in church attendance and loyalty constitute a wholesome leaven, in some places more wholesome and uplifting than in others, for Christian people have been known to think of life in much narrower terms than the teachings of Jesus about the abundant life. But even where the leaven is at its best, it is not strong enough. Fortunate suburban churches together with some in the smaller cities and towns may set a wholesome pattern for living which is generally accepted by the community, but even under the most favorable conditions enough has not been accomplished to make the community truly Christlike.

Someone may say, "Why should Protestant Churches worry about the whole community? Let them improve themselves by developing better educational programs within their own walls and particularly on Sunday." Such counsel sounds plausible but spells defeat. If Christianity does not influence the way a person works and plays, how can our civilization be made to express the ideals of Jesus Christ and of the Hebrew prophets who preceded him?

EDUCATION IN THE HOME

The Church has a unique opportunity in the home, for most of the families of the United States are established by the sanctions of the Church; their children are christened or baptized by some church; and when death comes, each member of the family is buried under the auspices of the Church. All through life in one form or another even those indifferent to religion are apt to seek guidance and comfort from religious agencies. Newer curriculums and other educational instruments designed to arouse interest and to increase the effectiveness of religious teaching in the family circle are significant steps in the right direction. If these programs are promoted with persistence and skill, progress in religious education should be certain.

EDUCATION IN THE LOCAL CHURCH

The movement to improve religious education within the local church or under its auspices has gained momentum for more than a century. If results have been disappointing, it should be kept in mind that this is a characteristic of human life. Achievement may be great, and yet people fall far short of their goals. Think how long the race has tried to achieve enduring peace. Ages ago prophets sang of a day when nations would "beat their swords into plowshares and their spears into pruninghooks." How many instruments have been devised to bring about such a day! The latest of these is the United Nations, for whose success we work and pray.

Human nature does not perfect itself easily. Men do not want war, as a rule, but their passions and desires produce conditions which make wars inevitable. As individuals and as nations they are inclined to want others to give to them benefits which they are unwilling to share. They expect others to discipline themselves while they give greed, lust for power, and hate a free rein.

Religious education is one of the instruments for the improvement of the race. It is unique in that it uses divine sanctions and calls upon supernatural aid. But the religious training which it tries to inculcate makes clear that men must be worthy of divine aid and work with God if the kingdom of God is ever to come on earth.

Education embraces every aspect of life. It has been defined as "the progressive reconstruction of experience." Religious education attempts to develop in growing persons a sense of values based upon a world view which thinks of God as the ultimate reality creating and guiding his creatures. The Christian view of life, based upon the life and teachings of Jesus, ascribes to

God not only moral perfection but the spiritual attributes of a Father as human beings know fatherhood.

To think that the Protestant churches can control enough time on Sunday, even if used with maximum efficiency, to develop the knowledge, attitudes, and skills necessary for successful Christian living is to indicate a very narrow view of the responsibilities and possibilities of a growing person. A statesman of this century wisely remarked, "An increasing complexity of life is the price we pay for an advancing civilization." Although we may strive to live simply and to stress only the essentials, complications confront us on every hand. The word of Scripture, "None of us liveth to himself, and no man dieth to himself," was true when uttered and becomes more compelling as a principle of life in our machine age. Hence the Church must perfect its Sunday program. The morning and evening services of worship with music, liturgy, and a sermon which inspires through teaching as Jesus and Paul did; the Sunday church school with its one hour or more of instruction and worship; Sunday-evening forums for youth and other age groups—these and other Sunday religious activities have very great possibilities. They have been standard patterns for a long time. Anyone who underestimates what they have accomplished would be a superficial student of religious movements. They are capable of being made still more effective.

In addition to the Sunday resources for religious training most commonly used, the possibilities of storytelling and good reading at home in the family circle should also be stressed. Nevertheless all of these, even if developed to maximum capacity, are not enough. One cannot be secular in thinking and action for six days of a week and get enough religion on the seventh to motivate and guide his action. Increased attention should be given to improving our Sunday teaching program. Some have thought that because volunteer and little-trained, if not untrained, teachers are no match for the professional teachers in our public-school system, the Sunday church school has seen its best days. Possibly it has lost some of the glamour it had when so many aspects of community life centered about the church, and the Sunday school was the most popularly attended church gathering in the week. The effort to make the Sunday school more like a school and less like an inspirational mass meeting has improved educational content with some loss of popularity.

However, the one hour or more of worship and instruction in a Sunday church school has very great possibilities still to be realized. Competition for time even on Sunday is increasing, but the opportunity for parents and children to assemble for learning more about their religion in proper age groupings cannot fail to make a strong appeal. Parents have great interest in what vitally concerns their children. Make the Sunday-school-hour program interesting as well as helpful to these children, and a considerable number of parents will gladly teach classes or go into older groups for religious study. Professionally trained directors of religious education can be of unusual help in making available to a church the best materials and techniques for education. Financially strong churches may increasingly look to paid teachers, professionally trained, to supervise some of the departments or to teach classes, but as the writer sees it, the Sunday church school will always place great reliance upon the volunteer teacher. Under proper guidance these volunteers can be trained to render increasingly effective service, while their example and personal interest in their young pupils will be another element of teaching strength. A great teacher has wisely said, "All good teaching is the sharing of experience." Few readers can fail to think of volunteers with little pedagogical training who have enriched growing lives by such sharing.

WEEKDAY RELIGIOUS EDUCATION

However, Sunday programs of religious education are not enough. In the first place, there is a time limit upon what the churches can rightfully ask their members to do on Sunday. The Sabbath was decreed as a day of rest. Worship and study are helpful ways of renewing one's spirit, but life is geared to such a fast pace that workers everywhere are asking for increased time for recreation. The ten-hour day and six-day week for workers have long ceased to be the usual schedule. Farmers at certain seasons pay little attention to the clock, while many in professions, business, and industry work without much thought of the time being consumed. Nevertheless, the general demand of society for more leisure time is being granted and without serious loss of production except in times of emergency.

Another reason why religious education cannot all be given on Sunday is the very nature of this education. Habit formation is an essential part of religious training. Right attitudes toward one's playmates and neighbors of whatever race or creed are also desired objectives. An adequate program of religious training requires weekday as well as Sunday time. This is why correlation with the public school program is so essential. It need not involve the use of public-school property, compulsory attendance by public-school authorities, or any form of public-school supervision, but it does require mutual understanding and co-operation on the part of all the teachers who are guiding the development of growing lives.

Some form of weekday church schools seems to be necessary in the best interests of the children themselves, their parents, and the community of which they are to be citizens. This judgment does not necessarily imply criticism of the public-school system. Like all educational systems it too is conscious of failure to achieve its high goals. It would not be a human institution if this was not true. Great progress is being made by public education in adapting its programs to meet the needs of individuals.

Since these needs are so varied, partial failure is to be expected, but the degree of failure is constantly being lessened by experimentation with newer methods and materials.

RELIGIOUS MATERIALS IN PUBLIC-SCHOOL CURRICULUM

Since so many children come out of homes with religious backgrounds, it will create tension if any public-school teacher insists that all religious materials and references are sectarian and therefore taboo. The protagonists of this theory are propagandists for another view which might also be labeled "sectarian"—namely, secularism or atheism. For example, to study European history of the Middle Ages and leave out the influence of the Roman Catholic Church, together with other religious movements, is as unscientific and biased as to study the winning of the West in the United States and omit all reference to the place of pioneer preachers and churches in the development of the cultural life of our great country.

We must think through a way of treating religious subjects adequately on an interfaith basis in the public-school curriculum or the propagandists of atheism and materialism will win the day. At present they are very much in the minority but are very vocal and gaining ground by misusing the slogan "democracy" as if democracy were a way of government in which small minorities have all the rights and can prevent majorities from doing what they think is in their best interests.

The recent study[1] made by a commission appointed by the American Council on Education points the way to a solution of this important problem. But patient study, experimentation, and mutual interfaith tolerance will be necessary to chart a course of action for communities of mixed races and creeds. In the last analysis much will be left to the judgment of the individual teachers, who should be carefully trained for this responsibility.

On the community level a wise strategic program for Protestantism should include both Sunday and weekday programs. Primary responsibility for Sunday teaching will rest with the local church. Improvement of curriculums and methods, together with the use of audio-visual aids and other newer mediums, is not a proper subject for this chapter. Various aspects of this subject are treated elsewhere in this book. The point, however, is that the Sunday programs of religious education, despite time limitations, have achieved much in the past and have even greater possibilities for the future. Any effort to play down these possibilities will be shortsighted. As weekday church-school programs improve, we will be faced, not with an "either-or" proposition, but with "both-and." Even

[1] *The Relation of Religion to Public Education, the Basic Principles.*

when Protestantism uses all of her educational resources wisely, she will still have less than enough to mold life according to the Christian pattern. She will need to join forces with Catholics, Jews, and those of other religious faiths if the goal of human brotherhood in "one world" is ever to be realized. A community training school for Protestant workers in religious education is also highly desirable.

Weekday church schools, including vacation schools, will require a high degree of interdenominational co-operation to be at their best. Such co-operation makes possible the use of the best teachers and educational equipment of a community for all who wish to avail themselves of the opportunity. With resources pooled and a reasonable budget, teachers can be paid enough to assure their regular attendance, training, and supervision. The lack of enough money is responsible for much of the poorer teaching both on Sunday and during the week. This is a condition which exists at all levels of education, secular as well as religious. However, the lack is much more serious in the field of instruction in religion on the lower levels where income from taxes, tuition, or endowments is not usually available. On the upper levels tuition and endowment income may be expected.

The nature of these weekday church schools will vary with community sentiment and need. One pattern of released time, that of using public-school property for religious classes, has been declared unconstitutional by the United States Supreme Court. Other patterns are now being tested in lower courts. Whatever the outcome, it is inconceivable that the Supreme Court will ban all forms of co-operation between the public school and the churches. Logically that would lead to banning all forms of co-operation between government and religious organizations. However, the use of public-school supervision over attendance, curriculum, and teaching may be banned without too seriously handicapping the weekday church-school movement. Public-school pupils have schedules which close at noon or soon thereafter, at 3 P.M., and at 4 P.M. The compulsory-attendance hours can be regulated by the community or state but not by the federal government unless on the basis of financial grants.

CAMPS AND INSTITUTES

Camps and institutes for young people, conducted under denominational and interdenominational auspices, have long enjoyed popularity as an opportunity to combine religious training and recreation. They have been described in a previous chapter of this book. Since they are effective instruments of religious education, their continued development seems to be assured.

OTHER AGENCIES

Other elements in a community program of religious education should include the activities of the United Christian Youth Movement, which may be especially effective in developing projects of interracial and interfaith co-operation. The zeal of youth for world-mindedness and ecumenical Christianity is also a great potential asset. The possibilities of community welfare projects, under the auspices of a united Protestantism, are almost without limit, and many of the most difficult problems confronting our world today must first be solved on the community level. On an interfaith basis Boy Scouts, Girl Scouts, Four-H clubs, and other organizations render effective service in character building.

RELIGIOUS EDUCATION ON THE NATIONAL LEVEL

While basic religious education is on the family, local-church, and community levels, the program goes much higher. Through the past century public education in the United States has expanded and improved its system from the lowest grades through the graduate and professional schools of the university. In the course of this expansion the Protestant churches have adjusted their programs so as to serve unmet needs. Once they had many schools for children in the grades, with even more attention concentrated on the high-school work. Some of these institutions are still strong, especially where adequate endowments have been built up. But more than one academy or high school under church auspices has given way to the public high school when the latter's plant and teaching became adequate for the community. Today Protestantism in America maintains a relatively small number of schools on the primary and secondary levels; but she is strong in her colleges, theological schools, and universities. At present, church-related junior colleges have a field of unique service. How long this will last nobody knows, for public education is expanding in this field as rapidly as adequate funds can be supplied by taxation for the whole community system, and sometimes before the funds are adequate. Large cities either have or want standard four-year colleges. Smaller cities aspire to such also or at least to a junior college. Various commissions, including President Truman's,[2] have encouraged this development in order to raise the intellectual level and improve the skills of as many citizens as possible.

Much has already been achieved in uniting Protestant forces for the promotion of religious education on a national scale. In addition to strong programs of denominational boards co-operative programs of large sig-

[2] *Higher Education for American Democracy*, report of the President's Commission on Higher Education.

nificance are also making good headway. Among these are those of the
National Christian Teaching Mission, the Committee on Town and
Country, the Protestant Film Commission, and the Protestant Radio Com-
mission. The new National Council of the Churches of Christ in the United
States of America, when organized, will face an unusual opportunity for
constructive service through more united effort.

RELIGION IN HIGHER EDUCATION

It is to be expected that enrollment in public institutions of higher
learning will increase more rapidly than in private and church-related
institutions, but the quality of education provided by the latter constitutes a leaven vital not only to the ongoing of the Christian movement but
to the perpetuation and improvement of our democratic way of living. This
has often been affirmed by leaders in all walks of life. One of the major
tasks of Protestantism is to strengthen and improve the quality of this
leaven. Church-related and other privately endowed institutions of higher
learning are free to teach religion as competently as the funds of the
institution and student demand will permit. Training for citizenship is one
of the recognized major goals of these institutions. It is not too much to
expect that training for Christian citizenship and for competent participation in the Christian movement will be a goal of church-related colleges
whether they are Protestant or Catholic. Catholics give more attention
to this aspect of their educational work than Protestants, and it is an
important source of their strength. Any farseeing strategy for Protestantism will include increasing emphasis on the training of citizens to use
their religious resources wisely and effectively. A soundly based Christian
philosophy of life is only a beginning toward this end. The attainment of
some skills for responsibility as parents, teachers, and leaders in community
welfare projects is a reasonable objective.

Protestants will have little difficulty in finding colleges and universities
with strong programs for the teaching of religion in its various aspects.
As far back as 1921 a joint committee of the Religious Education Association, the Council of Church Boards of Education, and the Sunday
School Council of Evangelical Denominations worked out a suggested
college major or field of concentration for those desiring to prepare for
work in religious education.[8]

Many colleges have used the suggestions, making proper adaptation to
meet their own situations. The four-year college can lay a good foundation
for the development of skill as a parent, a teacher, or a worker in some
other capacity in the local church. If professional training and status are

---

[8] See Brown, *History of Religious Education in Recent Times*, pp. 246 ff.

desired, one should lay a foundation in the college and build upon this in a graduate school. Yale University, through the leadership of Dean Weigle and his colleagues, has made a conspicuous record in the training of men and women for professional careers in religious education. Many other institutions have their graduates with Ph.D. and M.A. degrees earned in this field in positions of responsible leadership around the world.

This graduate training is usually given by a university which has in its organization, or affiliated with it, a strong theological seminary. For nearly forty years these seminaries have been developing capable departments of religious education along with departments of Bible, theology, Church history, and other subjects. It is clearly recognized that in Protestantism the pastor must be the chief teacher and educational leader in the local church. By the very nature of his office he is a teacher as well as a preacher and pastor. That he is as competent in this field as he should be in order to discharge successfully his educational responsibilities is more than the most optimistic can affirm. Several partial excuses for this situation can be cited. In the first place, the minister might well say with Paul, "Who is sufficient for these things?" In the second place, even if he has the necessary knowledge and skills, he is not apt to have time to make the educational work of his church as effective as it should be.

Many speakers have proclaimed, "If our theological schools would only give to religious education the attention which it deserves, this problem would be solved." The solution is not so simple. The seminaries should do more and better work in this field. But unfortunately religious education is only one of the many fields of study competing for a student's time, and the usual three years of graduate study required for the B.D. degree is not long enough to do much more than introduce men and women to the subjects which they study. These programs are better adapted to prepare preachers and pastors than to develop teachers, and even for these vocations the training is just a beginning. A four-year program leading to the B.D. would, it seems, better meet the total need of the young minister than the present one of three. In some seminaries many students elect to take the degree in four years. However, training for the profession of teaching or administering educational responsibilities requires additional classroom study and research. Protestants can learn from the Roman Catholics the advantage of taking time enough to train leaders for specific tasks. To produce more great teachers for our colleges and universities, more preachers and administrators of outstanding ability, more directors of religious education with spiritual insight and creative skill as well as knowledge, would be worthy objectives in any program for the advance of the Christian movement through Protestantism.

Some denominations have also developed programs of religious education for students in state universities and other tax-supported institutions.

At the present time these for the most part center in the local church and are stronger in their emphasis on social activities than in teaching with academic credit. However, the movement has already accomplished much and has still greater possibilities.

In viewing the total picture of Protestant religious education one should see also the part played by related organizations under Protestant auspices; such as the Y.M.C.A., the Y.W.C.A., and the Religious Education Association. It is beyond the scope of this chapter to describe such agencies.

THE INTERNATIONAL LEVEL

The agencies doing significant work in religious education on the international level are many. The Sunday school has long been promoted in practically every land which has Christian churches. Boards of foreign missions of the Protestant denominations have used this instrument in local churches. The World's Sunday School Association, now called the World Council of Christian Education, has rendered effective service, and its program should be greatly expanded.

The World Council of Churches was organized in Amsterdam in August, 1948. The place of religious education in this council has yet to be defined, but in a short time it should have a very significant place. As a factor in promoting mutual understanding and good will among the nations it is indispensable.

While much is being accomplished by Sunday schools in the "younger" churches, the most effective and intensive work in religious education has been done in institutions from the elementary to the university level. Education has been a major factor in developing the Christian forces in lands served by missionaries. The rise and effectiveness of able leaders in the younger churches constitute one of the most brilliant chapters in the history of the Christian movement.

Protestantism has developed a strong system of educational institutions for the spread of Christ's teachings and the development of his followers around the world. Their influence on behalf of interracial understanding and good will has been incalculable, and they should be greatly strengthened if we wish to hasten the day of world peace.

This is not the place to discuss the detailed organization and work of great denominational boards of education and of other boards with educational responsibilities. Some of these have large staffs of experts in particular fields. Others have a smaller but highly trained personnel. The amount of literature which they send out is enormous, including the lesson materials which are prepared by additional staffs and sent to the churches through boards of publication. The writer of Ecclesiastes was right when he said, "Of making many books there is no end," but the record of earlier ages has been far eclipsed in our modern day. Unfortunately, literature by itself will not Christianize our civilization, but it helps, and one of the most crying needs of the younger churches abroad is their lack of adequate Christian reading material.

Boards of Christian education multiply their strength and avoid much duplication of effort by creating and working through such councils as the International Council of Religious Education and the World Council of Christian Education. These have been described in previous chapters of this book. Their strength is growing, and the outlook for Protestant advance is all the brighter because a merger of several of the greatest interdenominational agencies serving on the national and international levels is in prospect. It is hoped that in the near future the Federal Council of Churches, the International Council of Religious Education, the Home Missions Council of North America, the Council of Church Boards of Education, the Missionary Education Movement of the United States and Canada, the United Stewardship Council, and the United Council of Church Women will all—or most of them—become parts of the National Council of the Churches of Christ in the United States of America. The new organization will give as much autonomy and freedom of action to the constituent groups as possible but should achieve much through greater unity and less duplication of effort.

SUMMARY AND CONCLUSIONS

Protestantism's strategy for religious education, then, should perfect what she is using and constantly experiment for the improvement of materials and methods. She cannot afford to discard useful instruments because they fall short of perfection, or to give all of her attention to these instruments and neglect newer mediums for instruction. The churches must realize the dimensions and content of their educational task, which is nothing less than the perfection of human character with divine aid. That this may take millenniums should not discourage us, for it is the glory of Christ's gospel that the achievement of godlike character and a Christlike society is its goal. However, if we are wise we will be impatient with our slow progress and improve our workmanship as rapidly as possible, for we have no guarantee of the time at our disposal.

We could not neglect major units of society if we would. The family, church, community, nation, and the world all play a large part in the education of a growing child, and the citizens whom they help to develop must improve civilization if it is to endure. The task is complicated, and we may give up in despair. On the other hand, ours is a religion of faith, called in its Scriptures "good news." It has accomplished much and should ultimately attain its ends. The Christian, wherever he is, must take hold with the tools available to him. Others will help him improve his workmanship if he will avail himself of this help.

In the last analysis leadership education in its many forms is the place to concentrate attention in preparation for any advance. Literature for this purpose is useful, but it needs enrichment. New books dealing with the philosophy of Christian education and other aspects of Christianity applied to education should be produced in the near future. As far back as thirty years ago I was pleading with a dean in a great university to introduce courses in religious education. The dean was sympathetic but puzzled. "What will the young people study? What are the books in this field?" These were pertinent questions. They were answered then, and the literature on the subject has been expanded since. However, such a task as Protestantism faces in education constantly needs rethinking. We must fight battles of the future, not struggle over dead issues.

The following challenges are offered as not beyond the realm of possibility:

1. Protestants Unite! While a greater degree of united effort is going on in the field of religious education than in any other activity of the Christian churches, this is not enough, and we do not have unlimited time. Secularism has not yet engulfed us, but it is still a rising tide fraught with the utmost peril. To turn it back requires more than denominational zeal and efficiency can produce. While we recognize the necessity for co-operating with other agencies of good will if we are to produce the "one world" of our dreams, Protestantism has responsibility for a great share of this task. A more closely knit Protestantism than we now have is not optional but a prerequisite to success. For example, the use of new equipment and techniques, such as audio-visual aids, requires much more money and many more trained workers than any one denomination can provide. Illustrations of the necessity and possibilities of such united action are many. Among these are the International Christian University in Japan, the Protestant film and radio commissions, and a program of adequate weekday religious education.

2. Give increasing attention, not only to developing in growing lives a faith based upon adequate knowledge of the Bible and other religious materials, but also to forming attitudes and habits which will help to solve such pressing problems as social justice, interfaith, intergroup, interracial, and international tensions.

3. Improve the tools which religious education has successfully used in the past. Education is a long, slow process, and short cuts often fail to reach the goal. However, improvement must be greatly accelerated to meet the present world crisis.

4. Make much larger use of Christian higher education for the training of teachers and specialists in many fields, including research.

5. Let workers in religious education prove themselves worthy of their calling by developing a sacrificial spirit as well as knowledge and skill, keeping in mind the master Teacher, of whom it was said, first in derision, but with profound truth, "He saved others, himself he cannot save."

"Go . . . teach" was our Lord's command, accompanied by a promise of divine aid. Our civilization in Christendom owes much of its idealism and freedom to the effort of Christians to carry out this command. It should ring in our ears with even more compelling tones in the years immediately before us.

SUGGESTIONS FOR FURTHER STUDY

1. What are the latest developments in the relations between Church and state in the field of religious education? What forms of co-operation seem most promising?

2. How much recent progress has been made in the improvement of Sunday programs for religious teaching? Is there any truth in the criticism that religious education devotes too much attention to the purely informational aspects of teaching and too little to other factors in character building?

3. What are the principal types of weekday church schools in the United States, and which seem to hold the greatest promise for the future?

4. Study some of the best community-wide programs in religious education. What are some of their strongest and weakest features?

5. What are the colleges and universities doing to train for Christian leadership on the community, national, and international levels? Appraise the achievements and possibilities of this movement.

6. How may denominational boards of Christian education improve their efficiency?

7. What are some of the major educational tasks which will confront the National Council of the Churches of Christ in the United States of America, if and when organized?

8. Appraise the achievements and possibilities of religious education as a force in developing Christian unity around the world. What are its principal agencies, and what progress are they making? How should religious education be related to the program of the World Council of Churches?

BIBLIOGRAPHY

Barclay, Wade Crawford. *The Church and a Christian Society*. New York: Abingdon Press, 1939.

Bower, William, and Hayward, Percy. *Protestantism Faces Its Educational Task Together*. Appleton, Wisc.: C. C. Nelson Publishing Co., 1949.

Brown, Arlo Ayres. *A History of Religious Education in Recent Times*. New York: Abingdon Press, 1923.

Higher Education for American Democracy. A report of the President's Commission on Higher Education, New York: Harper & Brothers, 1947.

Johnson, Alvin W., and Yost, Frank H. *Separation of Church and State in the United States*. Minneapolis: University of Minnesota Press, 1948.

Lotz, P. H., and Crawford, L. W., ed. *Studies in Religious Education*. Nashville: Cokesbury Press, 1931.

The Relation of Religion to Public Education, The Basic Principles. Committee on Religion and Education, American Council on Education, Series 1, Reports of Committees and Conferences, April, 1947, Washington, D. C.

Schofield, Charles E., ed. *The Church Looks Ahead*. New York: Macmillan Co., 1933.

Vieth, Paul H. *The Church and Christian Education*. Published for the Cooperative Publishing Association. St. Louis: Bethany Press, 1947.

Appendix

I.

A SELECTED BIBLIOGRAPHY
OF RELIGIOUS EDUCATION

LEONARD A. STIDLEY

A BIBLIOGRAPHY IS of necessity elective because "of making many books there is no end." And a bibliography in religious education is doubly selective because both religion and education are extensive fields. Because this Bibliography is selective, an explanation of the factors which determined the choices of books may be clarifying.

My purpose was to choose those books which a worker in the field of religious education would find helpful both in an orientation to the present functioning in the field and also as a guide to the understanding of the requisite skills in religious education. More emphasis was placed upon the skills than upon the nature of religious education, although these two cannot be separated. There are more books upon the former and less upon the latter.

Religious education could readily be labeled Christian education in this Bibliography because of the groups for which it is intended. But because of the emphases in education it is preferable to retain the term "religious education."

In addition to these general factors there were at least six more determinative factors in selecting the Bibliography:

1. The books chosen were published comparatively recently, and largely since the close of World War II—although a few of the standard texts of a longer period were included.

2. Many basic books went out of print during World War II. The checking of books in print reduced the Bibliography considerably. This factor points to the need of either reprinting "standard" texts or else calling for new ones.

3. Many high-grade books are excluded because of denominational emphasis.

4. Books in certain areas in the field of religious education were omitted because of lack of space—for example, peace education and organization by age groups.

5. Certain areas are represented by only a few books—for example, Curriculum and Research and Measurement.

6. Because of the limitations of space it was deemed advisable to use more inclusive divisions in the Bibliography. As a result a broad spread of books is found in certain divisions and hence some overlap—for example, Nature of Religious Education. The classification will assist somewhat in alleviating this problem.

In one of the final sections of this Bibliography a list of Bibliographies in religious education is given. To those persons who want books covering a more extensive area these Bibliographies will serve as a resource. Of course, many of the books include commendable Bibliographies.

A number of books have been marked with an asterisk. These books may serve as a nucleus of a small working library.

CLASSIFICATION

I. Nature, Principles, and History of Religious Education

1. Nature of Religion and Religious Education
2. Principles and Objectives of Religious Education
3. History of Religious Education

II. Religious Growth and the Learning-Teaching Process

1. Moral and Religious Growth
2. The Learning Process
3. The Teaching Process
4. Character Education
5. Group Work and Group Dynamics
6. Counseling
7. Leadership Education

III. The Home, the Family, and Religious Education

1. Books for Parents
2. The Church and the Home
3. Sex Education

IV. Organization and Administration of Religious Education

1. Organization in Local Church
2. Religious Education and the Public Schools
3. Weekday and Vacation Church Schools
4. Camping
5. Rural Church
6. Religion in Higher Education
7. Building for Religious Education

V. Curriculum for Religious Education

VI. Methods in Religious Education

1. General Consideration of Methods
2. Age Groups
   a. Children
   b. Youth
   c. Adults
3. Use of the Bible in Religious Education
4. Stories
5. The Arts and Religious Education
6. Drama and Pageantry
7. Play and Recreation
8. Discussion
9. Audio-Visual Aids
10. Music
11. Handwork
12. Evangelism
13. Missionary Education

VII. PRAYER AND WORSHIP
   1. Nature of Prayer and Worship
   2. Prayer and Worship for Age Groups

VIII. RESEARCH AND MEASUREMENT

IX. BIBLIOGRAPHIES
   1. General
   2. Religion in Higher Education
   3. Religion and the Public Schools

X. SELECTED MAGAZINES FOR THE TEACHERS AND THE CHURCH-SCHOOL LIBRARY

CLASSIFICATION

I. NATURE, PRINCIPLES, AND HISTORY OF RELIGIOUS EDUCATION

1. Nature of Religion and Religious Education

Boisen, Anton T. *Exploration of the Inner World: A Study of Mental Disorders and Religious Experience.* Chicago: Willett, Clark and Company, 1937.

Bushnell, Horace. *Christian Nurture.* New Haven: Yale University Press, 1947.

Christian Education Today: A Statement of Basic Philosophy Developed Co-operatively by Protestant Evangelical Forces of the United States and Canada Through the International Council of Religious Education. Chicago: International Council of Religious Education, 1940.

Coe, George Albert. *What Is Religion Doing to Our Consciences?* New York: Charles Scribner's Sons, 1943.

Eakin, Frank, and Eakin, Mildred Moody. *Let's Think About Our Religion.* New York: Macmillan Company, 1944.

Edwards, Newton, and Richey, Herman G. *The School in the American Social Order.* Boston: Houghton Mifflin Company, 1947.

Elliott, Harrison S. *Can Religious Education Be Christian?* New York: Macmillan Company, 1940.

Fitch, Robert E. *Preface to Ethical Living.* New York: Association Press, 1947.

Harkness, Georgia. *Understanding the Christian Faith.* New York and Nashville: Abingdon-Cokesbury Press, 1947.

Horne, Herman Harrell. *The Philosophy of Christian Education.* New York: Fleming H. Revell Co., 1937.

Jacks, Maurice Leonard. *God in Education.* London: Rich and Cowan, Ltd., 1939.

Johnson, F. Ernest. *The Social Gospel Re-examined.* New York: Harper & Brothers, 1940.

Johnson, Paul E. *Psychology of Religion.* New York and Nashville: Abingdon-Cokesbury Press, 1945.

Johnson, Raymond B. *What Is Happening in Religious Education?* Boston: Beacon Press, 1948.

Knight, Dunlap. *Religion: Its Functions in Human Life.* New York: McGraw-Hill Book Co., 1946.

Leeson, Spencer. *Christian Education.* New York: Longmans, Green & Co., 1947.

Man's Disorder and God's Design. An Ecumenical Study Prepared Under the

Auspices of the World Council of Churches. New York: Harper & Brothers, 1948.

Moehlman, Conrad. *The Church as Educator.* New York: Hinds, Hayden and Eldredge, 1947.

Moore, John M. *Theories of Religious Experience.* New York: Round Table Press, 1939.

Niebuhr, Reinhold. *The Nature and Destiny of Man.* New York: Charles Scribner's Sons, 1941.

Smith, H. Shelton. *Faith and Nurture.* New York: Charles Scribner's Sons, 1941.

Sperry, Willard L. *What We Mean by Religion.* New York: Harper & Brothers, 1940.

*Vieth, Paul, ed. *The Church and Christian Education.* Published for Cooperative Publishing Association. St. Louis: Bethany Press, 1947.

Wieman, Henry. *The Source of Human Good.* Chicago: University of Chicago Press, 1941.

2. Principles and Objectives of Religious Education

Barclay, Wade Crawford. *The Church and a Christian Society.* New York: Abingdon Press, 1939.

Bower, William. *Christ and Christian Education.* New York and Nashville: Abingdon-Cokesbury Press, 1943.

Chave, Ernest. *A Functional Approach to Religious Education.* Chicago: University of Chicago Press, 1947.

DeBlois, Austen, and Gorham, Donald R. *Christian Religious Education: Principles and Practice.* New York: Fleming H. Revell Co., 1939.

Harner, Nevin C. *The Educational Work of the Church.* New York, Abingdon Press, 1939.

Myers, A. J. William. *Religion for Today.* New York: Association Press, 1941.

Price, John M., et al. *A Survey of Religious Education.* New York: Thomas Nelson & Sons, 1940.

3. History of Religious Education

Bodein, Vernon. *The Social Gospel of Walter Rauschenbusch and Its Relation to Religious Education.* New Haven: Yale University Press, 1944.

Bower, William C., and Hayward, Percy. *Protestantism Faces Its Educational Task Together.* Appleton, Wisc.: C. C. Nelson Publishing Co., 1949.

Brubacher, John. *A History of the Problems of Education.* New York: McGraw-Hill Book Co., 1947.

Butts, R. Freeman. *A Cultural History of Education.* New York: McGraw-Hill Book Co., 1947.

Eby, Frederick, and Arrowood, Charles. *The History and Philosophy of Education, Ancient and Medieval.* New York: Prentice-Hall, 1946.

Kinloch, T. F. *Pioneers of Religious Education.* New York: Oxford University Press, 1939.

Kuhn, Anne. *The Mother's Role in Childhood Education: New England Concepts, 1830-1860.* New Haven: Yale University Press, 1947.

Myers, A. J. William. *Horace Bushnell and Religious Education.* Boston: Manthorne and Burack, 1937.

Sherrill, Lewis J. *The Rise of Christian Education.* New York: Macmillan Company, 1944.

II. Religious Growth and the Learning-Teaching Process

1. Moral and Religious Growth

Breckenridge, Marion E., and Vincent, E. Lee. *Child Development.* Philadephia: W. B. Saunders Company, 1944.

Crawford, John E., and Woodward, Luther. *Better Ways of Growing Up.* Philadelphia: Muhlenberg Press, 1948.

Dickerson, Roy. *Understanding Myself.* New York: Association Press, 1942.

Fox, Henry. *The Child's Approach to Religion.* New York: Richard R. Smith, 1930.

Gesell, Arnold. *The First Five Years of Life.* New York: Harper & Brothers, 1940.

Gesell, Arnold, and Ilg, Frances L. *The Child from Five to Ten.* New York: Harper & Brothers, 1946.

Kunkel, Fritz. *My Dear Ego.* Boston: Pilgrim Press, 1947.

*Manwell, Elizabeth, and Fahs, Sophia. *Consider the Children—How They Grow.* Boston: Beacon Press, 1940.

McLester, Frances Cole. *A Growing Person.* New York and Nashville: Abingdon-Cokesbury Press, 1942.

Sherrill, Lewis J. *Understanding Children.* New York: Abingdon Press, 1939.

Thorburn, Marjorie. *The Spirit of the Child.* London: G. Allen & Unwin, 1946.

2. The Learning Process

Allport, Gordon. *Personality: A Psychological Interpretation.* New York: Henry Holt & Co., 1937.

Burton, William H. *The Guidance of Learning Activities.* New York: D. Appleton-Century Company, 1944.

*Gates, A. I., *et al. Educational Psychology.* Rev. ed. of *Psychology for Students of Education.* New York: Macmillan Co., 1942.

Hilgard, Ernest. *Theories of Learning.* New York: Appleton-Century-Crofts, 1948.

Prescott, Daniel. *Emotion and the Educative Process.* Washington: American Council on Education, 1938.

Riolin, Harry, and Shueler, Herbert. *Encyclopedia of Modern Education.* New York: Philosophical Library, 1943.

Zachry, Carolyn, and Lighty, Margaret. *Emotion and Conduct in Adolescence.* Progressive Education Association. New York: D. Appleton-Century Co., 1940.

3. The Teaching Process

Dewey, John. *Experience and Education.* New York: Macmillan Co., 1939.

McLester, Frances Cole. *Teaching in the Church School.* New York and Nashville: Abingdon-Cokesbury Press, 1940.

Murray, Alfred. *Psychology for Christian Teachers.* New York: Round Table Press, 1938.

Overstreet, Bonaro. *How to Think About Ourselves.* New York: Harper & Brothers, 1948.

Sherrill, Lewis J. *The Opening Doors of Childhood.* New York: Macmillan Co., 1939.

Slattery, Margaret. *A Primer for Teachers.* New York: Harper & Brothers, 1942.

*Staff of the Division on Child Development and Teacher Personnel. *Helping

Teachers Understand Children. Washington: American Council on Education, 1945.

Torgerson, Theodore. *Studying Children.* New York: Dryden Press, 1947.

Wieman, Regina. *Does Your Child Obey?* New York: Harper & Brothers, 1943.

Winn, Ralph. *Encyclopedia of Child Guidance.* New York: Philosophical Library, 1943.

4. Character Education

Betts, George. *Foundations of Character and Personality.* Indianapolis: Bobbs-Merrill Co., 1937.

Jones, Vernon. *Character and Citizenship Training in the Public Schools.* Chicago: University of Chicago Press, 1936.

Kunkel, Fritz. *Character, Growth, Education.* Philadelphia: J. P. Lippincott Company, 1938.

Kunkel, Fritz, and Dickerson, Roy. *How Character Develops.* New York: Charles Scribner's Sons, 1940.

Ligon, Ernest. *A Greater Generation.* New York: Macmillan Co., 1948.

——. *The Psychology of Christian Personality.* New York: Macmillan Co., 1935.

——. *Their Future Is Now.* New York: Macmillan Co., 1939.

McLester, Frances. *Achieving Christian Character.* Nashville: Cokesbury Press, 1937.

5. Group Work and Group Dynamics

Baxter, Bernice, and Cassidy, Rosalind. *Group Experience: The Democratic Way.* New York: Harper & Brothers, 1943.

Blumenthal, Louis. *Administration of Group Work.* New York: Association Press, 1948.

*Coyle, Grace. *Group Experience and Democratic Values.* New York: Woman's Press, 1948.

——. *Group Work with American Youth.* New York: Harper & Brothers, 1948.

Group Planning in Education, 1945 Yearbook. Washington: Department of Supervision and Curriculum Development of the National Education Association, 1947.

Hendry, Charles, ed. *A Decade of Group Work.* New York: Association Press, 1948.

Kilpatrick, William, and Van Til, William, eds. *Intercultural Attitudes in the Making.* New York: Harper & Brothers, 1948.

Lewin, Gertrude. *Resolving Social Conflicts, Selected Papers on Group Dynamics, 1935-1946.* New York: Harper & Brothers, 1948.

Slavson, Samuel. *An Introduction to Group Therapy.* New York: The Commonwealth Fund, 1943.

Trecker, Harleigh. *Social Group Work.* New York: Woman's Press, 1948.

Vickery, William, and Cole, Stewart. *Intercultural Education in American Schools. Proposed Objectives and Methods.* New York: Harper & Brothers, 1943.

6. Counseling

Boisen, Anton T. *Problems in Religion and Life.* New York and Nashville: Abingdon-Cokesbury Press, 1946.

Bonnell, John. *Psychology for Pastor and People.* New York: Harper & Brothers, 1948.

Dicks, Russell. *Pastoral Work and Personal Counseling.* New York: The Macmillan Co., 1944.

Fosdick, Harry Emerson. *On Being a Real Person.* New York: Harper & Brothers, 1943.

Hiltner, Seward. *Religion and Health.* New York: The Macmillan Co., 1943.

Holman, Charles. *Getting Down to Cases.* New York: The Macmillan Co., 1942.

Kemp, Charles. *Physicians of the Soul.* New York: The Macmillan Co., 1947.

Kunkel, Fritz, and Gardner, Ruth. *What Do You Advise?* New York: I. Washburn, Inc., 1946.

Merriam, Thornton, *et al. Religious Counseling of College Students.* American Council on Education Studies, Series VI, Number 4, April, 1943. Washington, D. C.: American Council on Education.

*Rogers, Carl. *Counseling and Psychotherapy.* Boston: Houghton Mifflin Co., 1943.

Schindler, Carl. *The Pastor as a Personal Counselor.* Philadelphia: Muhlenberg Press, 1942.

Wise, Carroll. *Religion in Illness and Health.* New York: Harper & Brothers, 1942.

7. Leadership Education

Connor, Miles. *Leadership in Religious Education.* Baltimore: Garland Press, 1947.

Milhouse, Paul. *Enlisting and Developing Church Leaders.* Anderson, Ind.: Warner Press, 1946.

Sanderson, Dwight. *Leadership for Rural Life.* New York: Association Press, 1940.

Shaver, Erwin. *The Workers' Conference Manual.* New York: Abingdon Press, 1938.

(For Standard Leadership Curriculum of Leadership Training Publishing Association consult your denominational publisher.)

III. THE HOME, THE FAMILY, AND RELIGIOUS EDUCATION

1. Books for Parents

Beaven, Albert. *The Fine Art of Living Together.* Rev. ed. New York: Harper & Brothers, 1942.

Bro, Margueritte. *When Children Ask.* Chicago: Willett, Clark & Co., 1940.

Dunbar, Flanders. *Your Child's Mind and Body.* New York: Random House, 1949.

Ellenwood, James. *It Runs in the Family.* New York: Charles Scribner's Sons, 1942.

———. *Just and Durable Parents.* New York: Charles Scribner's Sons, 1948.

———. *There's No Place Like Home.* New York: Charles Scribner's Sons, 1939.

Foster, Robert. *Marriage and Family Relationships.* New York: The Macmillan Co., 1944.

Groves, Ernest. *Conserving Marriage and the Family.* New York: The Macmillan Co., 1944.

Wood, Leland, *et al. What the American Family Faces.* Chicago: Eugene Hugh Publishers, Inc., 1943.

2. The Church and the Home

Carrier, Blanche. *Church Education for Family Life*. New York: Harper & Brothers, 1937.

Cope, Henry. *Religious Education in the Family*. Chicago: University of Chicago Press, 1915.

Duvall, Evelyn, and Duvall, Sylvanus. *Leading Parents Groups*. New York and Nashville: Abingdon-Cokesbury Press, 1946.

Fallaw, Wesner. *The Modern Parent and the Teaching Church*. New York: The Macmillan Co., 1946.

Goldstein, Sidney. *Marriage and Family Counseling*. New York: McGraw-Hill Book Co., 1945.

Groves, Ernest. *Christianity and the Family*. New York: The Macmillan Co., 1942.

Odell, Mary Clemens. *Our Family Grows Toward God*. New York and Nashville: Abingdon-Cokesbury Press, 1949.

Sherrill, Lewis. *Family and Church*. New York: Abingdon Press, 1937.

———. *Understanding Children*. New York: Abingdon Press, 1939.

Sweet, Herman. *Opening the Door of God*. Philadelphia: Westminster Press, 1944.

*Taylor, Florence. *Their Rightful Heritage: Home and Church Working Together for the Christian Nurture of Children*. Boston: Pilgrim Press, 1942.

Wiegman, F. W. *Christian Happiness in the Home*. St. Louis: Bethany Press, 1947.

Wieman, Regina. *The Family Lives Its Religion*. Creating the Family and the Creative Family. New York: Harper & Brothers, 1941.

———. *The Modern Family and the Church*. New York: Harper & Brothers, 1937.

(There is pamphlet material on the church and the home from the denominational departments of family life.)

3. Sex Education

Bibby, Cyril. *How Life Is Handed On*. New York: Emerson Books, 1947.

———. *Sex Education. A Guide for Parents, Teachers, and Youth Leaders*. New York: Emerson Books, 1946.

Dickerson, Roy. *So Youth May Know*. Rev. ed. of *Sex Education for Youth*. New York: Association Press, 1948.

Duvall, Evelyn, and Hill, Reuben. *When You Marry*. New York: Association Press, 1945.

Geddes, Donald, and Aimee, Enid. *About the Kinsey Report*. New York: New American Library, 1947.

Kinsey, Alfred, *et al. Sexual Behavior in the Human Male*. Philadelphia: W. B. Saunders Co., 1948.

Levine, Milton, and Seligman, Jean. *The Wonder of Life: How We Are Born and How We Grow Up*. New York: Simon and Schuster, 1940.

Popenoe, Paul. *Building Sex Into Your Life*. Los Angeles: American Institute of Family Relations, 1944.

*Strain, Francis. *Sex Guidance in Family Education*. New York: The Macmillan Co., 1942.

———. *Teen Days: A Book for Boys and Girls*. New York: D. Appleton-Century Co., 1946.

(For pamphlets on sex education, including parents' guides, write to the Publications Service, American Hygiene Association, 1790 Broadway, New York 19, New York, or to your state board of health.)

IV. Organization and Administration of Religious Education

1. Organization in Local Church

Beaven, Albert. *The Local Church: Its Purpose and Program*. New York: Abingdon Press, 1937.

Crossland, Weldon. *How to Build Up Your Church School*. New York and Nashville: Abingdon-Cokesbury Press, 1948.

Cummings, Oliver de Wolf. *Christian Education in the Local Church*. Philadelphia: Judson Press, 1942.

Desjardins, Lucille. *Building an Intermediate Program*. Philadelphia: Westminster Press, 1939.

Harner, Nevin. *Youth Work in the Church*. New York and Nashville: Abingdon-Cokesbury Press, 1941.

Jones, Philip. *The Church School Superintendent*. New York: Abingdon Press, 1939.

*McKibben, Frank. *Christian Education Through the Church*. New York and Nashville: Abingdon-Cokesbury Press, 1947.

2. Religious Education and the Public Schools

Bower, William. *Church and State in Education*. Chicago: University of Chicago Press, 1944.

Brubacher, John, ed. *The Public Schools and Spiritual Values*. New York: Harper & Brothers, 1944.

*Committee on Religion and Education: *The Relation of Religion to Public Education: The Basic Principles*. Washington: American Council on Education, 1947. (*Studies*, Series I, No. 26.)

Dawson, Joseph. *Separate Church and State Now*. New York: Richard R. Smith, 1948.

Harner, Nevin. *Religion's Place in General Education*. Richmond: John Knox Press, 1949.

Hauser, Conrad. *Teaching Religion in the Public School*. New York: Round Table Press, 1942.

Mattox, Fount. *The Teaching of Religion in the Public Schools*. Nashville: Bureau of Publications, George Peabody College, 1948.

Moehlman, Conrad. *School and Church: The American Way*. New York: Harper & Brothers, 1944.

Norton, John, and Lawler, Eugene. *Unfinished Business in American Education*. Washington: American Council on Education, 1946.

O'Neill, J. M. *Religion and Education Under the Constitution*. New York: Harper & Brothers, 1949.

Parsons, Wilfred. *The First Freedom*. New York: Declan X. McMullen Company, 1948.

Thayer, V. T. *Religion in Public Education*. New York: Viking Press, 1947.

Torpey, William. *Judicial Doctrines of Religious Rights in America*. Chapel Hill: University of North Carolina Press, 1948.

*Williams, J. Paul. *The New Education and Religion*. New York: Association Press, 1945.

3. Weekday and Vacation Church Schools

Blair, Winfrey. *The New Vacation Church School*. New York: Harper & Brothers, 1934.

Eakin, Mildred Moody. *Getting Acquainted with Jewish Neighbors*. New York: The Macmillan Co., 1944.

Miller, Minor. *Teaching the Multitudes*. Bridgewater, Va.: Beacon Publishers, 1944.

Nelson, William. *Vacation Bible School Handbook*. Cincinnati: Standard Publishing Co., 1942.

(For the "Cooperative Series of Vacation and Weekday Church-School Texts" write your denominational publisher. Also consult bibliographies on Religion and the Public Schools under IX.)

4. Camping

Dimock, Hedley, and Statten, Taylor. *Talks to Counselors*. New York: Association Press, 1939.

*Ledlie, John, and Holbein, Francis. *The Camp Counselor's Manual*. New York: Association Press, 1947.

Ott, Elmer. *So You Want to Be a Camp Counselor*. New York: Association Press, 1946.

Peters, Raymond. *Let's Go Camping*. Elgin, Ill.: Brethren Publishing House, 1945.

5. Rural Church

Lindstrom, David. *Rural Life and the Church*. Champaign, Ill.: Garrard Press, 1946.

Schlingman, Edward. *Good Times in the Rural Church*. Philadephia: Christian Education Press, 1947.

*Smith, Rockwell. *The Church in Our Town*. New York and Nashville: Abingdon-Cokesbury Press, 1945.

Wintermeyer, Herbert. *Rural Worship*. Philadelphia: Christian Education Press, 1947.

6. Religion in Higher Education

Blakeman, Edward. *The Administration of Religion in Universities and Colleges: Personnel*. Ann Arbor: University of Michigan Press, 1942.

Cole, Stewart. *Liberal Education in a Democracy*. New York: Harper & Brothers, 1940.

*Cuninggim, Merrimon. *The College Seeks Religion*. New Haven: Yale University Press, 1947.

Gross, John. *Education for Life*. New York and Nashville: Abingdon-Cokesbury Press, 1948.

Hartshorne, Hugh, ed. *From School to College*. New Haven: Yale University Press, 1939.

Nash, Arnold. *The University and the Modern World*. New York: The Macmillan Co., 1944.

Shedd, Clarence. *The Church Follows Its Students*. New Haven: Yale University Press, 1938.

―――. *Religion in the State University*. New Haven: Edward W. Hazen Foundation, 1947.

Sweets, Henry. *Source Book on Christian Education as Related to the Colleges and Theological Seminaries of the Church*. Louisville, Ky.: Executive Committee of Christian Education, Presbyterian Church in the U. S. (410 Urban Building), 1942

7. Building for Religious Education

Conover, Elbert. *Building for Worship*. New York: Interdenominational Bureau of Architecture (297 Fourth Avenue), 1945.

*————. *The Church Building Guide*. New York: Interdenominational Bureau of Architecture, 1946.

Conover, Elbert M., ed. *Planning Church Buildings*. New York: Interdenominational Bureau of Architecture, 1945.

Harrell, W. A. *Planning Better Church Buildings*. Nashville: Broadman Press, 1947.

Holisher, Desider. *The House of God*. New York: Crown Publishers, 1946.

Leach, William. *Protestant Church Building*. New York and Nashville: Abingdon-Cokesbury Press, 1948.

Scotford, John. *The Church Beautiful*. Boston: Pilgrim Press, 1945.

V. CURRICULUM FOR RELIGIOUS EDUCATION

Bobbitt, John. *The Curriculum in Modern Education*. New York. McGraw-Hill Book Co., 1941.

Caswell, Hollis, and Campbell, Doak. *Curriculum Development*. New York: American Book Company, 1935.

Hopkins, Levi. *Interaction, the Democratic Process*. Boston: D. C. Heath & Co., 1941.

Jersild, Arthur. *Child Development and the Curriculum*. New York: Bureau of Publications, Teachers College, Columbia University, 1946.

*Stratemeyer, Florence, *et al*. *Developing a Curriculum for Modern Living*. New York: Bureau of Publications, Teachers College, Columbia University, 1947.

VI. METHODS IN RELIGIOUS EDUCATION

1. General Consideration of Methods

Chaplin, Dora. *Children and Religion*. New York: Charles Scribner's Sons, 1948.

Dobbins, Gaines. *The Improvement of Teaching in the Sunday School*. Nashville: Sunday School Board of the Southern Baptist Convention, 1943.

*Eakin, Mildred Moody, and Eakin, Frank. *The Pastor and the Children*. New York: The Macmillan Co., 1947.

DeOvies, Raimundo. *The Church and the Children*. New York: Morehouse-Gorham Company, 1941.

Lindhorst, Frank. *The Minister Teaches Religion*. New York and Nashville: Abingdon-Cokesbury Press, 1945.

Myers, A. J. William. *Teaching Religion Creatively*. New York: Fleming H. Revell Co., 1932.

Slattery, Margaret. *A Primer for Teachers*. New York: Harper & Brothers, 1942.

Weigle, Luther. *Jesus and the Educational Method*. New York: Abingdon Press, 1939.

2. Age Groups

(a) Children

Eakin, Mildred Moody. *Teaching Junior Boys and Girls.* Cincinnati: Methodist Book Concern, 1934.

*Eakin, Mildred Moody, and Eakin, Frank. *Your Child's Religion.* New York: The Macmillan Co., 1942.

Fitch, Florence Mary. *One God—The Ways We Worship Him.* New York: Lothrop, Lee & Shepard Co., 1944.

Jones, Mary Alice. *The Church and the Children.* Nashville: Cokesbury Press, 1935.

——. *The Faith of Our Children.* New York and Nashville: Abingdon-Cokesbury Press, 1943.

——. *Tell Me About Jesus.* Chicago: Rand McNally & Co., 1944.

Munkres, Alberta. *Which Way Our Children?* New York: Charles Scribner's Sons, 1936.

Perry, Ruth Davis. *Children Need Adults.* New York: Harper & Brothers, 1943.

Smither, Ethel. *Primary Children Learn at Church.* New York and Nashville: Abingdon-Cokesbury Press, 1944.

Strang, Ruth. *A Study of Young Children.* New York and Nashville: Abingdon-Cokesbury Press, 1944.

Trent, Robbie. *Your Child and God.* Chicago: Willett, Clark and Co., 1941.

Shields, Elizabeth. *Guiding Kindergarten Children in the Church School.* Richmond: Presbyterian Committee of Publication, 1931.

(b) Youth

Beckes, Isaac. *Young Leaders in Action.* New York and Nashville: Abingdon-Cokesbury Press, 1941.

Bowman, Clarice. *Guiding Intermediates.* New York and Nashville: Abingdon-Cokesbury Press, 1943.

Burkhart, Roy. *Understanding Youth.* New York: Abingdon Press, 1938.

Gray, Henry David. *A Theology for Christian Youth.* New York and Nashville: Abingdon-Cokesbury Press, 1941.

Harris, Erdman. *Introduction to Youth.* New York: The Macmillan Co., 1940.

Moon, Alleen. *The Christian Education of Older Youth.* New York and Nashville: Abingdon-Cokesbury Press, 1943.

Watson, Goodwin. *Youth After Conflict.* New York: Association Press, 1947.

Wickenden, Arthur. *Youth Looks at Religion.* New York: Harper & Brothers, 1948.

(c) Adults

Chamberlain, J. Gordon. *The Church and Its Young Adults.* New York and Nashville: Abingdon-Cokesbury Press, 1943.

Charters, Jessie. *Young Adults and the Church.* New York: Abingdon Press, 1936.

Gorham, Donald. *Understanding Adults.* Philadelphia: Judson Press, 1948.

Maves, Paul, and Cedarleaf, J. Lennart. *Older People and the Church.* New York and Nashville: Abingdon-Cokesbury Press, 1949.

Meland, Bernard. *The Church and Adult Education.* New York: American Association for Adult Education, 1939.

Powell, Wilfred. *Understanding Adults.* St. Louis: Bethany Press, 1941.

Sherrill, Lewis, and Purcell, John. *Adult Education in the Church.* Richmond: Presbyterian Committee of Publication, 1939.

*Westphal, Edward. *The Church's Opportunity in Adult Education.* Philadelphia: Westminster Press, 1941.

Ziegler, Earl. *The Way of Adult Education.* Philadelphia: Westminster Press, 1938.

3. Use of the Bible in Religious Education

Bailey, Albert. *Daily Life in Bible Times.* New York: Charles Scribner's Sons, 1943.

*Bower, William. *The Living Bible.* Rev. ed. New York: Harper & Brothers, 1936.

Bowie, Walter. *The Bible.* New York: Association Press, 1940.

Craig, Clarence. *The Study of the New Testament.* New York: Abingdon Press, 1939 .

Curtis, Muriel. *The Story of Bible People.* New York: The Macmillan Co., 1944.

Chamberlain, Georgia. *Making the Bible Live.* Chicago: University of Chicago Press, 1939.

Fahs, Sophia. *Jesus the Carpenter's Son.* Boston: Beacon Press, 1945.

Finegan, Jack. *Light from the Ancient Past.* Princeton: Princeton University Press, 1946.

Fosdick, Harry Emerson. *A Guide to Understanding the Bible.* New York: Harper & Brothers, 1938.

Goodspeed, Edgar J. *How Came the Bible?* New York and Nashville: Abingdon-Cokesbury Press, 1940.

——. *How to Read the Bible.* Philadelphia: John C. Winston Company, 1946.

Love, Julian. *How to Read the Bible.* New York: The Macmillan Co., 1940.

Miller, Madeleine, and Miller, J. Lane. *Encyclopedia of Bible Life.* New York: Harper & Brothers, 1944.

Smither, Ethel. *The Use of the Bible with Children.* Cincinnati: Methodist Book Concern, 1935.

Soares, Theodore. *The Growing Concept of God in the Bible.* Boston: Pilgrim Press, 1943.

——. *The Origins of the Bible.* New York: Harper & Brothers, 1941.

Wright, G. Ernest, and Filson, Floyd. *The Westminster Historical Atlas to the Bible.* Philadelphia: Westminster Press, 1945.

4. Stories

Eggleston, Margaret. *Forty Stories for the Church School and Home.* New York: Harper & Brothers, 1939.

——. *Thirty Stories I Like to Tell.* New York: Harper & Brothers, 1949.

Fahs, Sophia. *From Long Ago and Many Lands.* Boston: Beacon Press, 1948.

Fox, Frances. *Legends of the Christ-Child.* New York: Sheed and Ward, 1941.

Frost, S. E., ed. *Great Religious Stories.* Garden City, N. Y.: Garden City Publishing Company, 1945.

*Hazeltine, Alice. *Children's Stories to Read or Tell.* New York and Nashville: Abingdon Press, 1949.

Hills, Verna. *Martin and Judy in Their Two Little Houses.* Boston: Beacon Press, 1939.

Hills, Verna, and Fahs, Sophia. *Martin and Judy Playing and Learning.* Boston: Beacon Press, 1943.

———. *Martin and Judy in Sunshine and Rain*. Boston: Beacon Press, 1940.
Lantz, J. Edward, ed. *Best Religious Stories*. New York: Association Press, 1948.
Smith, Elva, and Hazeltine, Alice. *The Christmas Book of Legends and Stories*. New York: Lothrop, Lee & Shepard Co., 1944.
Van Loon, Hendrik. *Van Loon's Lives*. New York: Simon & Schuster, 1942.
Walker, Elmer. *Five-Minute Stories from the Bible*. New York and Nashville: Abingdon-Cokesbury Press, 1948.
Welty, Ivan. *Through All the Seasons, Stories to Tell Young Folks*. New York: Fleming H. Revell Co., 1942.

5. The Arts and Religious Education

*Bailey, Albert. *Art and Character*. New York: Abingdon Press, 1938.
———. *Christ and His Gospel in Recent Art*. New York: Charles Scribner's Sons, 1948.
———. *Jesus and His Teachings; the Approach Through Art*. Philadelphia: Christian Education Press, 1942.
Gheon, Henri. *The Madonna in Art*. Paris: Pierre Tine, 1947.
Maus, Cynthia. *Christ and the Fine Arts*. New York: Harper & Brothers, 1938.
———. *The World's Great Madonnas*. New York: Harper & Brothers, 1947.
Ritter, Richard. *The Arts of the Church*. Boston: Pilgrim Press, 1947.
Smith, Jean Louise. *Great Art and Children's Worship*. New York and Nashville: Abingdon-Cokesbury Press, 1948.
Stafford, Thomas. *Christian Symbolism in the Evangelical Churches, with Definitions of Church Terms and Usages*. New York and Nashville: Abingdon-Cokesbury Press, 1942.

6. Drama and Pageantry

Bates, Esther. *The Church Play and Its Production*. Boston: Walter H. Baker Co., 1938.
Brown, Thelma. *Treasury of Religious Plays*. New York: Association Press, 1947.
Eastman, Fred. *Christ in the Drama*. New York: The Macmillan Co., 1947.
*Ehrensperger, Harold. *Conscience on Stage*. New York and Nashville: Abingdon-Cokesbury Press, 1947.
Emurian, Ernest K. *More Dramatized Stories of Hymns and Hymn Writers*. Boston: W. A. Wilde Company, 1943.
Jurgensen, Kai, and Schenkkan, Robert. *Fourteen Plays for the Church*. New Brunswick, N. J.: Rutgers University Press, 1948.
O'Hara, Frank, and Bro, Margueritte. *A Handbook of Drama*. Chicago: Willett, Clark & Co., 1938.

7. Play and Recreation

Breen, Mary J. *The Children's Party Book*. New York: A. S. Barnes & Co., 1941.
*Harbin, E. O. *The Fun Encyclopedia*. New York and Nashville: Abingdon-Cokesbury Press, 1940.
Millen, Nina. *Children's Games from Many Lands*. New York: Friendship Press, 1943.
Mulac, Margaret. *The Game Book*. New York: Harper & Brothers, 1946.
Powell, Warren, ed. *Recreation in Church and Community*. New York: Abingdon Press, 1938.
Slavson, S. R. *Recreation and the Total Personality*. New York: Association Press, 1946.

8. Discussion

*Auer, J. Jeffery, and Ewbank, Henry Lee. *Handbook for Discussion Leaders.* New York: Harper & Brothers, 1947.

9. Audio-Visual Aids

*Dale, Edgar. *Audio-Visual Methods in Teaching.* New York: Dryden Press, 1946.

Elliott, Godfrey. *Film and Education.* New York: Philosophical Library, 1948.

Haas, Kenneth, and Parker, Harry. *Preparation and Use of Visual Aids.* New York: Prentice-Hall, 1947.

Hockman, William. *Projected Visual Aids.* Boston: Pilgrim Press, 1947.

Rogers, William, and Vieth, Paul. *Visual Aids in the Church.* Philadelphia: Christian Education Press, 1946.

Strauss, L. Harry, and Kidd, J. R. *Look, Listen and Learn.* New York: Association Press, 1948.

Wittich, Walter, and Fowlkes, John Guy. *Audio-Visual Paths to Learning.* New York: Harper & Brothers, 1946.

10. Music

Ashton, Joseph. *Music in Worship. The Use of Music in the Church Service.* Boston: Pilgrim Press, 1943.

*Kettring, Donald. *Steps Toward a Singing Church.* Philadelphia: Westminster Press, 1948.

Shields, Elizabeth. *Music in the Religious Growth of Children.* New York and Nashville: Abingdon-Cokesbury Press, 1943.

Thomas, Edith Lovell. *Martin and Judy Songs.* Boston: Beacon Press, 1948.

Wells, Amos. *A Treasury of Hymns.* Boston: W. A. Wilde Co., 1945.

Wentzel, Fred. *Song of the Earth.* Philadelphia: Christian Education Press, 1946.

Wheeler, Opal. *Sing in Praise.* New York: E. P. Dutton & Co., 1946.

Wiley, Lulu. *Bible Music.* New York: Paebar Company, 1945.

11. Handwork

Almy, Ruth Case. *Simulated Stained Glass for Amateurs.* New York: Harper & Brothers, 1949.

Cox, Doris, and Weisman, Barbara. *Creative Hands.* New York: John Wiley & Sons, 1945.

Ickis, Marguerite. *Arts and Crafts, a Practical Handbook.* New York: A. S. Barnes & Co., 1943.

Parkhill, Martha, and Spaeth, Dorothy. *It's Fun to Make Things.* New York: A. S. Barnes & Co., 1941.

Powers, Margaret. *The Party Table.* Peoria: The Manual Arts Press, 1946.

*Rice, Rebecca. *Creative Activities.* Boston: Pilgrim Press, 1947.

12. Evangelism

Bryan, Dawson, *A Workable Plan of Evangelism.* Nashville: Abingdon-Cokesbury Press, 1945.

*Homrighausen, Elmer. *Choose Ye This Day; A Study of Decision and Commitment in Christian Personality.* Philadelphia: Westminster Press, 1943.

Ownbey, Richard. *Evangelism in Christian Education.* New York and Nashville: Abingdon-Cokesbury Press, 1941.

13. Missionary Education

Casselman, Arthur. *Into All the World*. Philadelphia: Christian Education Press, 1943.

*Harner, Nevin. *Missionary Education in Your Church*. New York: Friendship Press, 1942.

Lobingier, John. *The Missionary Education of Adults*. New York: Missionary Education Movement, 1938.

Soper, Edmund. *The Philosophy of Christian World Mission*. New York and Nashville: Abingdon-Cokesbury Press, 1943.

VII. PRAYER AND WORSHIP

1. Nature of Prayer and Worship

Blackwood, Andrew. *The Fine Art of Public Worship*. Nashville: Cokesbury Press, 1939.

*Buttrick, George. *Prayer*. New York and Nashville: Abingdon-Cokesbury Press, 1942.

Harkness, Georgia. *Prayer and the Common Life*. New York and Nashville: Abingdon-Cokesbury Press, 1948.

Palmer, Albert. *The Art of Conducting Public Worship*. New York: The Macmillan Co., 1939.

Powell, Marie Cole. *Guiding the Experience of Worship*. New York and Nashville: Abingdon Press, 1935.

Smith, Robert S. *The Art of Group Worship*. New York: Abingdon Press, 1938.

Steere, Douglas. *Prayer and Worship*. New York: Association Press, 1938.

2. Prayer and Worship for Age Groups

Barber, Estelle. *Guiding Intermediates in Worship*. New York and Nashville: Abingdon-Cokesbury Press, 1946.

Bartlett, Robert M. *Boys' Prayers*. New York: Association Press, 1947.

Bays, Alice. *Worship Services for Youth*. New York and Nashville: Abingdon-Cokesbury Press, 1946.

Clayton, Ernest. *A Child's Grace*. New York: E. P. Dutton & Co., 1948.

Clemens, Margaret. *My Prayer Book*. Chicago: Rand McNally & Co., 1947.

Hayward, Percy. *Young People's Prayers*. New York: Association Press, 1945.

Jones, Mary Alice. *Tell Me About Prayer*. Chicago: Rand McNally & Co., 1948.

Kelsey, Alice. *More Stories for Junior Worship*. New York and Nashville: Abingdon-Cokesbury Press, 1948.

———. *Stories for Junior Worship*. New York and Nashville: Abingdon-Cokesbury Press, 1941.

Kepler, Thomas, comp. *Fellowship of the Saints*. New York and Nashville: Abingdon Cokesbury Press, 1948.

Lotz, P. Henry. *The Altar Hour*. St. Louis: Christian Board of Publication, 1941.

———. *Worship Services for the Church Year*. With interpretative meditations by Grace Chapin Auten. St. Louis: Bethany Press, 1944.

Paulsen, Irwin. *The Church School and Worship*. New York: The Macmillan Co., 1940.

Perkins, Jeanette. *Children's Worship in the Church School*. New York: Harper & Brothers, 1939.

Shields, Elizabeth. *As the Day Begins*. Richmond: John Knox Press, 1944.

Welker, Edith, and Barber, Aimee, eds. *Thoughts of God for Boys and Girls.* New York: Harper & Brothers, 1948.

VIII. RESEARCH AND MEASUREMENT

Chave, Ernest. *Measure Religion.* Chicago: University of Chicago Book Store, 1939.

Greene, Edward. *Measurement of Human Behavior.* New York: Odyssey Press, 1941.

Ross, Clay. *Measurement in Today's Schools.* New York: Prentice-Hall, Inc., 1941.

IX. BIBLIOGRAPHIES

1. General

Christian Education Bibliography: October, 1934–November, 1944. Selected books and articles in *International Journal of Religious Education,* 13:35-8; 14: 39-40; 15: 34-5; 16: 35-7; 17: 34-7; 18: 34-6; 19: 31-3; 20: 35-7; June, 1937, May, 1938, July, 1939, May, 1940, May, 1941, June, 1942, July, 1943, May, 1944. Also published separately.

2. Religion in Higher Education

Elliott, Harrison. "Religion in Higher Education: Syllabus," in *Religious Education,* XXXVII (1942), 5-22, including bibliography.

3. Religion and the Public Schools

Blakeman, Edward. "A Bibliography: Religious Education and the Public Schools," *Religious Education,* XLIII (1948), 42-50.

Little, Lawrence. "Syllabus on Religion and Public Education" and "Selected Bibliography," *Religious Education,* XLIV (1949), 163-80.

X. SELECTED MAGAZINES FOR TEACHERS AND THE CHURCH-SCHOOL LIBRARY

The Biblical Archaeologist. (Its purpose is to meet the need for a readable, untechnical, yet thoroughly reliable, account of archaeological discoveries as they are related to the Bible.) The American Schools of Oriental Research, 409 Prospect Street, New Haven 11, Connecticut.

Child Study, Child Study Association of America, 221 West 57th Street, New York 19, New York.

Children's Religion, 14 Beacon Street, Boston 8, Massachusetts.

Childhood Education, Association for Childhood Education, 1200 19th Street, N. W., Washington 5, D. C.

The Christian Home, 810 Broadway, Nashville 2, Tenn.

Educational Screen, 64 East Lake Street, Chicago 1, Illinois. (Also publishes "The Blue Book of 16 mm. Films.")

International Journal of Religious Education, 206 South Michigan Ave., Chicago 4, Illinois.

Religious Education, 20 West Jackson Blvd., Chicago 4, Illinois.

Social Action, 289 Fourth Avenue, New York 10, New York.

Also consult denominational journals.

A DIRECTORY

Compiled by LEMUEL PETERSEN

INTERNATIONAL COUNCIL OF RELIGIOUS EDUCATION

206 South Michigan Avenue, Chicago 4, Illinois

International Quadrennial Convention

President, Harold E. Stassen, Philadelphia, Pa.
Vice-President, J. L. Kraft, Chicago, Ill.
Vice-President, Alfred H. Avery, Malden, Mass.
Vice-President, Thomas J. Watson, New York City.
Vice-President, Ralph W. Gwinn, New York City.
Vice-President, Algot F. Johnson, Minneapolis, Minn.
Vice-President, B. A. Whitmore, Nashville, Tenn.
Vice-President, C. H. Dickinson, Toronto, Ont., Can.
Vice-President, Harry Hines, Dallas, Tex.
Vice-President, Edwin B. Lindsay, Davenport, Ia.
Treasurer, J. L. Kraft, Chicago, Ill.
Secretary, Roy G. Ross, Chicago, Ill.

The International Council

Chairman, Paul Calvin Payne, Philadelphia, Pa.
Vice-Chairman, Nevin C. Harner, Lancaster, Pa.
Treasurer, J. L. Kraft, Chicago, Ill.
Recording Secretary, Roy G. Ross, Chicago, Ill.
Chairman, Commission on Educational Program, Harry Thomas Stock, Boston, Mass.
Chairman, Board of Trustees, Luther Wesley Smith, Philadelphia, Pa.

Staff

Roy G. Ross, General Secretary.
Gerald E. Knoff, Associate General Secretary.
Philip C. Landers, Associate General Secretary.
Wilbur C. Parry, Associate General Secretary.
Percy R. Hayward, Editor, *International Journal of Religious Education.*
Lillian Williams, Managing Editor, *International Journal of Religious Education.*
Lee J. Gable, Director of Leadership Education and Church School Administration.
Mildred A. Magnuson, Director of Lesson Studies.
Helen F. Spaulding, Associate Director of Research.
John B. Ketcham, Director of Field Administration.
Mrs. Alice L. Goddard, Director of Children's Work.
Isaac K. Beckes, Director of Young People's Work and Executive Secretary of the United Christian Youth Movement.

Dennis B. Savage, Director of Youth Council Services in the United Christian Youth Movement.

Richard E. Lentz, Director of Adult Work and Family Life Education.

Harry H. Kalas, Director of Educational Evangelism and National Christian Teaching Mission.

Edward W. Gebhard, Associate Director of Educational Evangelism.

Erwin L. Shaver, Director of Weekday Religious Education.

Ruth Elizabeth Murphy, Director of Vacation Religious Education.

Pearl Rosser, Director of Audio-Visual and Radio Education.

John C. Trever, Director, Department of the English Bible.

Richard B. Smith, Director of Financial Cultivation.

Lemuel Petersen, Director of Public Relations.

Clark L. Snyder, Associate Director of Promotion and Finance.

Norman E. Tompkins, Director, Departments of Business and Literature Service.

Helen F. Kindt, Office Manager.

Mrs. Orville M. Smith, Administrative Assistant to the General Secretary.

Luther A. Weigle, Chairman, Standard Bible Committee.

Fleming James, Executive Secretary, Old Testament Section of Standard Bible Committee.

R. H. Gocker, Manager, Conference Point Camp, Williams Bay, Wis.

Norman H. Abbott, Manager, Geneva Point Camp, Winnepesaukee, N. H.

W. Greer Fisher, Director, Eastern Region of United Christian Youth Movement.

RELIGIOUS EDUCATION ASSOCIATION

Executive Office, 20 West Jackson Boulevard, Chicago 4, Illinois

George A. Coe, Claremont, Calif., Honorary President.

Samuel P. Franklin, Pittsburgh, Pa., President.

Ruth M. Shriver, Elgin, Ill., Vice-President.

Emanuel Gamoran, Cincinnati, Ohio, Vice-President.

Thomas J. Quigley, Pittsburgh, Pa., Vice-President.

Weighstill Woods, Chicago, Ill., Treasurer.

O. M. Walton, Pittsburgh, Pa., Recording Secretary.

Board of Directors

Edna L. Acheson, Rochester, N. Y.
Edna M. Baxter, Hartford, Conn.
Israel S. Chipkin, New York, N. Y.
Stewart G. Cole, Los Angeles, Calif.
Alexander M. Duskin, New York, N. Y.
Harrison S. Elliott, New York, N. Y.
Sophia L. Fahs, New York, N. Y.
George Fox, Chicago, Ill.
Solomon B. Freehof, Pittsburgh, Pa.
Frank Grebe, New York, N. Y.
Hugh Hartshorne, New Haven, Conn.
G. Ivar Hellstrom, New York, N. Y.
Charles E. Hendry, Toronto, Ont., Can.
Leo L. Honor, Philadelphia, Pa.

F. Ernest Johnson, New York, N. Y.
Henry M. Johnson, Emory, Ga.
Gerald E. Knoff, Chicago, Ill.
Paul M. Limbert, Springfield, Mass.
E. R. MacLean, Toronto, Ont., Can.
Donald M. Maynard, Boston, Mass.
Ira A. Morton, Denver, Colo.
Ross Snyder, Chicago, Ill.
A. O. Steele, Charlotte, N. C.
J. Edward Sproul, New York, N. Y.
Erwin L. Shaver, Chicago, Ill.
Thomas West, Chicago, Ill.
J. Paul Williams, S. Hadley, Mass.

DENOMINATIONAL BOARDS OF CHRISTIAN EDUCATION AND PUBLISHING HOUSES [1]

Advent Christian Church
Board of Religious Education of the Advent Christian General Conference; Advent Christian Publication Society: 160 Warren St., Boston 19, Mass.

African Methodist Episcopal Church
Department of Christian Education; Sunday School Union Press: 414 Eighth Ave. S., Nashville 4, Tenn.

African Methodist Episcopal Zion Church
Christian Education Department: 128 E. 58th St., Chicago 37, Ill.; Publishing House: Box 1047, Charlotte, N. C.

American Lutheran Church
Board of Parish Education; Lutheran Book Concern (Wartburg Press): 57 E. Main St., Columbus 15, Ohio

American Unitarian Association
Division of Education: 25 Beacon St., Boston 8, Mass.

Associate Reformed Presbyterian Church
Due West, S. C.

Augustana Evangelical Lutheran Church
Board of Parish Education: 2445 Park Ave., Minneapolis 4, Minn.; Augustana Book Concern: 639 38th St., Rock Island, Ill.

Baptist Federation of Canada
Baptist Convention of Ontario and Quebec (Board of Religious Education): 223 Church St., Toronto 2, Ont., Can.
United Baptist Convention of the Maritime Provinces (United Baptist Board of Christian Education): 1 Churchill St., Truro, Nova Scotia, Can.
Baptist Union of Western Canada: 207 Empire Bldg., Edmonton, Alberta, Can.
Baptist Publications Committee of Canada: 299 Queen St. W., Toronto 2B, Ont. Can.

Baptist General Conference of America
Baptist Conference Press: 912 W. Belmont Ave., Chicago 14, Ill.

Church of the Brethren
Christian Education Commission—General Brotherhood Board; Brethren Publishing House (The Elgin Press): 22 S. State St., Elgin, Ill.

Church of Christ (Holiness), United States of America
National Publishing Board (National Publishing House): 44th and St. Lawrence, Chicago, Ill.

Church of England in Canada
General Board of Religious Education: Church House, 604 Jarvis St., Toronto 5, Ont., Can.

Church of God
Board of Christian Education; Gospel Trumpet Co. (Warner Press): E. Fifth and Chestnut Sts., Anderson, Ind.

Church of Jesus Christ of Latter-Day Saints
Department of Education: 47 E. South Temple St., Salt Lake City, Utah

---

[1] Boards of Christian education are listed first, and publishing houses second, for each denomination. If they have the same address, they are run together. The trade names of the publishing houses are in parentheses.

Church of the Nazarene
  Department of Church School: Nazarene Publishing House (Beacon Hill Press): 2923 Troost Ave., Box 527, Kansas City 10, Mo.
Churches of God in North America (General Eldership)
  Board of Education; Central Publishing House: 13th and Walnut Sts., Harrisburg, Pa.
Colored Methodist Episcopal Church
  General Board of Religious Education: 4043 S. Drexel Blvd., Chicago 15, Ill.; Publishing House: 109-11 Shannon St., Jackson, Tenn.
Congregational Christian Churches
  Board of Home Missions, Division of Christian Education; Pilgrim Press Division: 14 Beacon St., Boston 8, Mass.
Cumberland Presbyterian Church
  Board of Christian Education: McKenzie, Tenn.; Board of Publication: 117 Eighth Ave. S., Nashville 3, Tenn.
The Danish Evangelical Lutheran Church in America
  Council of Elementary Religious Education: c/o Rev. A. E. Farstrup, Grand View College, Des Moines 16, Ia.
Disciples of Christ
  United Christian Missionary Society, Division of Christian Education: 222 S. Downey Ave., Indianapolis 7, Ind.; Christian Board of Publication (Bethany Press): 2700 Pine Blvd., St. Louis 3, Mo.
Evangelical and Reformed Church
  Board of Christian Education and Publication (Christian Education Press): 1505 Race St., Philadelphia 2, Pa.
Evangelical Free Church of America
  Evangelical Beacon: 2951 Bloomington Ave., Minneapolis, Minn.
The Evangelical Lutheran Church
  Augsburg Publishing House: 425 S. Fourth St., Minneapolis 15, Minn.
Evangelical Mission Covenant Church of America
  Covenant Book Concern: 1005 W. Belmont Ave., Chicago, Ill.
The Evangelical United Brethren Church
  The Board of Christian Education: 1900 U. B. Building, Dayton 2, Ohio; The Evangelical Press: Third and Reily Sts., Harrisburg, Pa.; The Otterbein Press: 230 W. Fifth St., Dayton 2, Ohio
Finnish Evangelical Lutheran Church of America: Suomi Synod
  Finnish Lutheran Book Concern: Hancock, Mich.
Five Years Meeting of Friends in America
  Board on Christian Education; Friends' Publication Board: 101 S. Eighth St., Richmond, Ind.
Free Methodist Church of North America
  Free Methodist Publishing House (Light and Life Press): Winona Lake, Ind.
The Lutheran Church—Missouri Synod
  Board for Parish Education; Concordia Publishing House: 3558 S. Jefferson Ave., St. Louis 18, Mo.
Lutheran Free Church
  Messenger Press: 2120 Riverside Ave., Minneapolis, Minn.
The Mennonite Church
  Mennonite Publishing House (Herald Press): Scottdale, Pa.
The Methodist Church
  The Board of Education: 1001 Nineteenth Ave. S., Nashville 2, Tenn.; The

Methodist Publishing House (Abingdon Press): 810 Broadway, Nashville 2, Tenn.; 150 Fifth Ave., New York 11, N. Y.

Moravian Church in America
Christian Education Board, Northern Province: 69 W. Church St., Bethlehem, Pa.
Christian Education Board, Southern Province: Box 187, Salem Station, Winston-Salem, N. C.

National Baptist Convention of America
Department of Education, Sunday School Congress; National Baptist Publishing Board: 523 Second Ave. N., Nashville 3, Tenn.

National Baptist Convention, United States of America (Inc.)
Department of Christian Education; Sunday School Publishing Board: Fourth Ave. and Cedar St., Nashville 3, Tenn.

Northern Baptist Convention
The Board of Education and Publication; American Baptist Publication Society (Judson Press): 1701-3 Chestnut St., Philadelphia 3, Pa.

Pilgrim Holiness Church
Pilgrim Publishing House: 226-30 E. Ohio St., Indianapolis 4, Ind.

Presbyterian Church in Canada
Board of Sabbath Schools and Young People's Societies: Rooms 801-9, 100 Adelaide St. W., Toronto 1, Ont., Can.

Presbyterian Church in the United States
Board of Education (John Knox Press): Presbyterian Bldg., 8 N. Sixth St., Richmond 9, Va.

Presbyterian Church in the United States of America
Board of Christian Education (Westminster Press): Witherspoon Bldg., Philadelphia 7, Pa.

Protestant Episcopal Church
Department of Christian Education, National Council: 281 Fourth Ave., New York 10, N. Y.

Reformed Church in America
Board of Education (Half Moon Press): 156 Fifth Ave., New York 10, N. Y.

Reorganized Church of Jesus Christ of Latter-Day Saints
Herald Publishing House: 103 S. Osage St., Independence, Mo.

Seventh Day Baptists
Board of Christian Education: Alfred, N. Y.; American Sabbath Tract Society (Recorder Press): 510 Watchung Ave., Plainfield, N. J.

Southern Baptist Convention
Baptist Sunday School Board (Broadman Press): 127 Ninth Ave. N., Nashville 3, Tenn.

United Brethren in Christ
Department of Christian Education; Publishing Establishment: United Brethren Bldg., Huntington, Ind.

United Church of Canada
Board of Christian Education; Publishing House (Ryerson Press): 299 Queen St. W., Toronto 2B, Ont., Can.

United Evangelical Lutheran Church
Lutheran Publishing House: 200 S. Fifth St., Blair, Neb.

United Lutheran Church in America
The Parish and Church School Board; Publication House (Muhlenberg Press): 1228 Spruce St., Philadelphia 7, Pa.

The United Missionary Church
The Bethel Publishing Co.: 1819 S. Main St., Elkhart, Ind.
United Presbyterian Church of North America
Board of Christian Education: 209 Ninth St., Pittsburgh 22, Pa.
Wesleyan Methodist Church of America
General Sunday School Board; Publishing Association: 330 E. Onondaga St., Syracuse, N. Y.

STATE COUNCILS OF CHURCHES
AND OF RELIGIOUS EDUCATION

Alabama Council of Christian Education: 511 Title Guarantee Bldg., Birmingham 3.
Arizona Council of Churches: P. O. Box 1702, Phoenix.
Northern California–Western Nevada Council of Churches: 220 Golden Gate Ave., San Francisco 2.
Southern California Council of Protestant Churches: 3330 W. Adams Blvd., Los Angeles 16.
Colorado Council of Churches: 302 Trinity Bldg., 1820 Broadway, Denver 2.
The Connecticut Council of Churches: 11 Asylum St., Hartford 3.
Florida Council of Churches: 236 W. Church St., Jacksonville 2.
Territorial Sunday School Association of Hawaii: Box 150, Honolulu 10, T. Hawaii
Illinois Church Council: 100 W. Adams St., Springfield.
Indiana Council of Churches: 622 Board of Trade Bldg., Indianapolis 4.
(Indiana Council of Christian Education functions as a department of the Indiana Council of Churches.)
Iowa Inter-Church Council: 202 Shops Bldg., Des Moines.
Kansas Council of Churches and Christian Education: 633 Kansas Ave., Topeka.
Kentucky Council of Churches: 554 S. Third St., Louisville 2.
Maine Council of Churches: 97A Exchange St., Portland 3.
The Council of Churches and Christian Education of Maryland-Delaware, Inc.: 14 W. Madison, Baltimore 1, Md.
Massachusetts Council of Churches: 14 Beacon St., Boston 8.
Michigan Council of Churches and Christian Education: 42 Michigan Arcade, Lansing 25.
Minnesota Council of Churches: 122 W. Franklin St., Minneapolis 4.
Missouri Council of Churches: 130 E. Jefferson Ave., Kirkwood 22.
Montana Council of Churches: Box 442, Livingston.
Nebraska Council of Churches and Christian Education: Y.M.C.A. Bldg., Lincoln 8.
New Hampshire Council of Churches and Religious Education (Inc.): 18 School St., Concord.
New Jersey Council of Churches: 65 Central Ave., Newark 2.
New Mexico Council of Churches: 420 N. Spruce St., Albuquerque.
New York State Council of Churches, Inc.: 75 State St., Albany 7.
North Carolina Council of Churches: College Station, Durham.
North Dakota Interchurch Council: 13 Roxy Bldg., Fargo.
Ohio Council of Churches: 63 S. High St., Columbus 15.
Oklahoma Council of Churches and Christian Education: 1305 E. 15th St., Tulsa 5.
Oregon Council of Churches: 215 S.E. Ninth Ave., Portland 14.

Pennsylvania State Council of Christian Education (incorporated as Pennsylvania State Sabbath School Association): 2403 N. Front St., Harrisburg.

Rhode Island Council of Churches: 144 Westminster St., Providence 3.

South Carolina Fellowship of Churches: Box 264, Myrtle Beach.

South Dakota Council of Churches and Christian Education: 364 Third St. S.W., Huron.

Vermont Church Council: 189 S. Winooski Ave., Burlington.

Virginia Council of Churches, Inc.: 109 W. Grace St., Richmond 20; Box 307, Bridgewater.

Washington (D.C.) Federation of Churches; 1751 N St. N.W., Washington 6, D. C.

Washington State Council of Churches and Christian Education (including Northern Idaho): 312 Old Times Bldg., Seattle 1.

West Virginia Council of Churches and Christian Education: 1608 McClung St., Box 8, Charleston 21.

Wisconsin Council of Churches, Inc.: 308 Washington Bldg., Madison 3.

OTHER AGENCIES [2]

Interdenominational and Other Religious Organizations

American Association of Schools of Religious Education: c/o Seminary Hill Station, Fort Worth, Tex.

American Association of Theological Schools: c/o College of the Bible, Lexington, Ky.

American Bible Society: 450 Park Ave., New York 22, N. Y.

Association of Schools and Colleges of The Methodist Church: 810 Broadway, Nashville 2, Tenn.

Canadian Council of Churches, Department of Christian Education: Room 417, 299 Queen St. W., Toronto 2 B, Ont., Can.

Commission on Christian Higher Education of the Association of American Colleges: 736 Jackson Place N.W., Washington 6, D. C.

Commission on Jewish Education: 34 W. Sixth St., Cincinnati 2, Ohio.

Cooperative Publishing Association: 2700 Pine Blvd., St. Louis 3, Mo.

Federal Council of the Churches of Christ in America: 297 Fourth Ave., New York 10, N. Y.

Foreign Missions Conferences of North America: 156 Fifth Ave., New York 10, N. Y.

Friends Council on Education: 20 S. Twelfth St., Philadelphia, Pa.

Home Missions Council of North America: 297 Fourth Ave., New York 10, N. Y.

International Association of Daily Vacation Bible Schools: Room 686, 45 Astor Pl., New York, N. Y.

International Society of Christian Endeavor: 1201 E. Broad St., Columbus 5, Ohio (Box 110, Columbus 16).

Jesuit Educational Association: 49 East 84th St., New York 28, N. Y.

John Milton Society for the Blind: 156 Fifth Ave., New York 10, N. Y.

Lutheran Education Association: 7400 Augusta Blvd., River Forest, Ill.

[2] See the *Educational Directory: Part 4—Educational Associations and Directories* for a fifty-three-page listing of many other agencies. Secure from United States Government Printing Office, Washington, D.C.

Missionary Education Movement of the United States and Canada: 156 Fifth Ave., New York 10, N. Y.

National Catholic Welfare Conference, Department of Education: 1312 Massachusetts Ave. N. W., Washington 5, D. C.

National Conference of Christians and Jews, Inc., Commission on Educational Organizations: 381 Fourth Ave., New York 16, N. Y.

National Council of Community Churches: 1320 Cambridge Blvd., Columbus 5, Ohio.

National Council for Jewish Education: 1776 Broadway, New York 19, N. Y.

National Council on Religion in Higher Education: c/o Swarthmore College, Swarthmore, Pa.

National Jewish Welfare Board: 145 East 32nd St., New York 16, N. Y. (Affiliated organizations include Young Men's and Young Women's Hebrew Associations).

National Lutheran Educational Conference: 736 Jackson Pl. N.W., Washington, D. C.

National Protestant Council on Higher Education: 808 Witherspoon Bldg., Philadelphia 7, Pa.

National Woman's Christian Temperance Union: 1730 Chicago Ave., Evanston, Ill.

Protestant Film Commission: 45 Astor Pl., New York 3, N. Y.

Protestant Radio Commission: 297 Fourth Ave., New York 10, N. Y.

Religious Film Association: 45 Astor Pl., Room 686, New York 3, N. Y.

United Christian Adult Movement: 206 S. Michigan Ave., Chicago 4, Ill.

United Christian Youth Movement: 206 S. Michigan Ave., Chicago 4, Ill.

United Council of Church Women. 156 Fifth Ave., Rooms 409-15, New York 10, N. Y.

United Stewardship Council: 153 Hillsdale St., Hillsdale, Mich.

United Synagogue Commission on Jewish Education: 3080 Broadway, New York 27, N. Y.

World Council of Christian Education: 156 Fifth Ave., Room 1107, New York 10, N. Y.

World Council of Churches: 17 Route de Malagnou, Geneva, Switzerland; 297 Fourth Ave., New York 10, N. Y.

World's Student Christian Federation: 13, Rue Calvin, Geneva, Switzerland.

Young Men's Christian Associations, National Council: 291 Broadway, New York 7, N. Y.

Young Women's Christian Associations, National Board: 600 Lexington Ave., New York 22, N. Y.

Other National Educational Associations

Allied Youth, Inc.: The Allied Youth Bldg., 1709 M St., N.W., Washington 6, D. C.

American Academy of Arts and Letters: 633 W. 151st St., New York, N. Y.

American Academy of Arts and Sciences: 28 Newbury St., Boston 16, Mass.

American Academy of Political and Social Science: 3457 Walnut St., Philadelphia 4, Pa.

American Association for Adult Education: 525 West 120th St., New York, N. Y.

American Association for the Advancement of Science: Smithsonian Institution, Washington 25, D. C.

American Association for the Advancement of Science, Section Q (Education): 1515 Massachusetts Ave., N.W., Washington 5, D. C.

American Association of Junior Colleges: 1201 19th St. N.W., Washington 6, D. C.

American Association of University Women: 1634 I St. N.W., Washington 6, D. C.

American Camping Association; Inc.: 343 S. Dearborn St., Chicago 4, Ill.

American Council of Learned Societies Devoted to Humanistic Studies: 1219 Sixteenth St., N.W., Washington 6, D. C.

American Council on Education: 744 Jackson Pl. N.W., Washington 6, D. C.

American Education Fellowship: 11 E. Walton Pl., Chicago 11, Ill.

American Educational Research Association (N.E.A.): 1201 Sixteenth St., N.W., Washington 6, D. C.

American Educational Theatre Association: Speech Department, University of Michigan, Ann Arbor, Mich.

American Institute of Family Relations: 2503 N. Marengo, Altadena, Calif.

American Library Association: 50 E. Huron St., Chicago 11, Ill.

American National Red Cross, National Headquarters: Seventeenth and D Sts. N.W., Washington 13, D. C.

American Occupational Therapy Association: 33 West 42nd St., New York 18, N. Y.

American Philosophical Association: 1219 Sixteenth St. N.W., Washington 6, D. C.

American Psychological Association: 1515 Massachusetts Ave. N.W., Washington 5, D. C.

American School Health Association: 3335 Main St., Buffalo, N. Y.

American Social Hygiene Association, Inc.: 1790 Broadway, New York 19, N. Y.

American Sociological Society: University of Chicago, Chicago, Ill.

American Statistical Association: 1603 K St. N.W., Washington 6, D. C.

Association for Childhood Education: 1201 Sixteenth St. N.W., Washington 6, D. C.

Association for Education by Radio: 228 N. LaSalle St., Chicago, Ill.

Association for Family Living: 209 S. State St., Suite 1426, Chicago 4, Ill.

Association for Supervision and Curriculum Development (N.E.A.): 1201 Sixteenth St. N.W., Washington 6, D. C.

Association of American Colleges: 744 Jackson Pl., Washington 6, D. C.

Association of American Universities: c/o University of North Carolina, Chapel Hill, N. C.

Association of Research Libraries: c/o Director of Libraries, University of Pennsylvania, Philadelphia, Pa.

Boy Scouts of America: 2 Park Ave., New York 16, N. Y.

Boys' Clubs of America, Inc.: 381 Fourth Ave., New York 16, N. Y.

Camp Fire Girls, Inc.: 16 East 48th St., New York 17, N. Y.

Child Study Association of America, Inc., 221 West 57th St., New York 19, N. Y.

Child Welfare League of America, Inc.: 130 East 22nd St., New York, N. Y.

Committee on Friendly Relations Among Foreign Students: 347 Madison Ave., New York 17, N. Y.

Department of Adult Education (N.E.A.): 1201 Sixteenth St. N.W., Washington 6, D. C.

Department of Audio-Visual Instruction (N.E.A.): 1201 Sixteenth St. N.W., Washington, 6, D. C.

Educational Film Library Association, Inc.: Suite 1000, 1600 Broadway, New York 19, N. Y.

Educational Press Association of America: 1201 Sixteenth St. N.W., Washington 6, D. C.

Film Council of America: Room 1228, 431 S. Dearborn, Chicago 5, Ill.

Four-H Clubs: Federal Extension Service, U. S. Department of Agriculture, Washington 25, D. C.

Future Farmers of America: U. S. Office of Education, Washington 25, D. C.

Future Homemakers of America: U. S. Office of Education, Washington 25, D. C.

Future Teachers of America (N.E.A.): 1201 Sixteenth St. N.W., Washington 6, D. C.

General Federation of Women's Clubs: 1734 N St. N.W., Washington 6, D. C.

Girl Scouts: 155 East 44th St., New York 17, N. Y.

International Council for Exceptional Children (N.E.A.): Saranac, Mich.

League of Women Voters of the United States: 726 Jackson Pl. N.W., Washington 6, D. C.

Motion Picture Association of America, Inc.: 28 West 44th St., New York 18, N. Y.

Music Educators National Conference (N.E.A.): 64 E. Jackson Blvd., Chicago 4, Ill.

National Academy of Sciences: 2101 Constitution Ave., Washington, D. C.

National Association of College Women: 2645 Fifteenth St. N.W., Washington D. C.

National Association of Educational Broadcasters: Radio Hall, University of Wisconsin, Madison, Wis.

National Audubon Society: 1000 Fifth Avenue, New York 28, N. Y.

National Committee for Mental Hygiene, Inc.: 1790 Broadway, New York 19, N. Y.

National Committee on Boys and Girls Club Work (Four-H Clubs): 59 E. Van Buren, Chicago 5, Ill.

National Conference of Social Work: 82 N. High St., Columbus 15, Ohio

National Conference on Family Life, Inc.: 10 E. Fortieth St., Room 2803, New York 16, N. Y.

National Congress of Parents and Teachers: 600 S. Michigan Ave., Chicago, Ill.

National Council of Parent Education, Inc.: 221 West 57th St., New York 19, N. Y.

National Council of Family Relations: 1126 East 59th St., Chicago, Ill.

National Council on Work-Study-Play Activities: Seventeenth Ave. and Taney St., Gary, Ind.

National Education Association: 1201 Sixteenth St. N.W., Washington 6, D. C.

National Federation of Business and Professional Women's Clubs, Inc.: 1819 Broadway, New York 23, N. Y.

National Federation of Music Clubs: Room 812, 306 S. Wabash Ave., Chicago 4, Ill.

National Health Council: 1790 Broadway, New York 19, N. Y.

National Home Study Council: 839 Seventeenth St. N.W., Washington 6, D. C.

National Kindergarten Association: 8 West 40th St., New York 18, N. Y.

National Music Council, Inc.: 338 West 89th St., New York 24, N. Y.

National Probation Association: 1790 Broadway, New York 19, N. Y.

National Recreation Association: 315 Fourth Ave., New York 10, N. Y.

National Research Council: 2101 Constitution Ave., Washington 25, D. C.

National Safety Council, Inc.: 20 N. Wacker Dr., Chicago 6, Ill.

National Social Welfare Assembly, Inc. (formerly National Social Work Council): 1790 Broadway, New York 19, N. Y.

National Society for Crippled Children and Adults, Inc.: 11 S. LaSalle St., Chicago 3, Ill.

National Vocational Guidance Association, Inc.: 82 Beaver St., New York 5, N. Y.

Phi Beta Kappa, United Chapters of: 5 East 44th St., New York 17, N. Y.

Social Science Research Council: 230 Park Ave., New York 17, N. Y.

Society for Occupational Research: 608 Kimlin Dr., Glendale, Calif.

Society for Research in Child Development, National Research Council: 2101 Constitution Ave., Washington 25, D. C.

U. S. National Commission on U.N.E.S.C.O.: Milton Eisenhower (chairman), Manhattan, Kan.

Workers Education Bureau of America: 1440 Broadway, New York 18, N. Y.

Educational Boards and Foundations

Carnegie Foundation for the Advancement of Teaching: 522 Fifth Ave., New York 18, N. Y.

Child Education Foundation: 535 East 84th St., New York 28, N. Y.

Commonwealth Fund: 41 East 57th St., New York 22, N. Y.

Edwin Gould Foundation for Children: 422 West 58th St., New York 19, N. Y.

Harmon Foundation, Inc.: 140 Nassau St., New York 7, N. Y.

Henry C. Frick Educational Commission: 422 Frick Bldg., Pittsburgh 19, Pa.

John Simon Guggenheim Memorial Foundation: 551 Fifth Ave., New York, N. Y.

Phelps-Stokes Fund: 101 Park Ave., New York 17, N. Y.

Rockefeller Foundation: 49 West 49th St., New York 20, N. Y.

Russell Sage Foundation: 130 East 22nd St., New York 10, N. Y.

Twentieth Century Fund: 330 West 42nd St., New York 18, N. Y.

International Educational Associations and Foundations

Commission for International Educational Reconstruction: 744 Jackson Pl. N.W., Washington 5, D. C.

Institute of International Education, Inc.: 2 West 45th St., New York 19, N. Y.

International Bureau of Education: Palais Wilson, Geneva, Switzerland.

International Committee for Mental Hygiene, Inc.: 1790 Broadway, New York 19, N. Y.

International Union for Child Welfare: 43 Qui Wilson, Geneva, Switzerland.

United Nations Educational, Scientific, and Cultural Organization: U.N.E.S.C.O. House, 19 Ave. Kleber, Paris 16 M. E., France

World Organization of the Teaching Profession: 1201 Sixteenth St. N.W., Washington 6, D. C.

Biographical Index

ADAMS, JAMES LUTHER: Professor of religious ethics, Meadville Theological School, Federated Theological Faculty, University of Chicago, since 1946. Born Ritzville, Wash., 1901. Educated Univ. of Minnesota (A.B. 1924); Harvard Divinity School (S.T.B. 1927, A.M. 1930); Strasbourg and Marburg (1936, 1938); Univ. of Chicago (Ph.D. 1945). Minister: Second Church in Salem, 1927-32, Wellesley Hills Unitarian Society, 1933-35. Instructor in English, Boston Univ., 1930-32; prof. of psych. and phil. of religion, Meadville Theol. School, Chicago, 1936-40; prof. of theology, 1940-44; prof. of theology, Meadville Theological School, Federated Theol. Faculty, University of Chicago, 1944-46. Editor, *Journal of Liberal Religion*, 1939-44, and member editorial board since 1944; president, Independent Voters of Illinois, 1942-44, vice-president since 1944. Member, Amer. Theol. Soc. and Amer. Sociol. Soc. Author: *The Changing Reputation of Human Nature* (1943). Contributor: *Irving Babbitt, Man and Teacher* (1941), *New Perspectives on Peace* (1944), *Together We Advance* (1946), *Voices of Liberalism II* (1948). Translator (with concluding essay): Paul Tillich's *The Protestant Era* (1948). Editor: "Phoenix Series" on theology, phil. of religion, and social ethics. Home: 5707 Woodlawn Ave., Chicago 37, Ill.

Basic Causes of Progress and Decay 61

BARTLETT, EDWARD RANDOLPH: Pres. Iliff School of Theology since 1947. Born Fort Madison, Iowa, 1889. Educated Iowa Wesleyan (A.B. 1912, D.D. 1926), Boston Univ. (S.T.B. 1917), Northwestern (Ph.D. 1933). Director rel. ed., Topeka, Kansas, 1918; Minneapolis, Minn., 1919; Detroit, Mich., 1920-23. Asst. prof. philos., DePauw 1923-24; prof. rel. ed. and head of dept. 1924-47; prof. Old Testament 1938-47; dean 1941-47. Visiting prof., Northwestern 1930-31. Summers: lecturer Pacific Palisades 1924; I.C.R.E. 1920-22, 1925, 1928; instructor Boston Univ. 1927, Northwestern 1930-31. Visiting prof. Northwestern 1932, Purdue 1938, Southern California 1939. Member I.C.R.E. since 1925, exec. committee Indiana Council Rel. Ed. 1924-39, pres. 1937-47; chairman Amer. Conf. Academic Deans 1946-47; pres. Indiana Council of Churches 1946-47. Member: A.A.U.P.; R.E.A., Society of Biblical Literature and Exeg., Pi Gamma Mu, Phi Delta Kappa. Home: 2100 South Josephine, Denver, Colo.

Religious Education in Church Colleges and Theological Schools 352

BECKES, ISAAC KELLEY: Executive secretary of the United Christian Youth Movement and director of Young People's Work I.C.R.E. Born Vincennes, Indiana, 1909. Educated Vincennes Univ. (1931-33); Indiana State Teacher's College (B.S. 1935); McCormick Theological Seminary (B.D. 1938); Yale University (Ph.D. 1945). Pastor, Presbyterian Church, Monroe City, Ind., 1934-38; Humphrey Street Congregational Church, 1938-43. With the U.C.Y.M. and I.C.R.E. since 1943. Member: Pi Gamma Mu. Author: *Young Leaders in Action* (1941), *Inter-religious Relations on the American College Campus* (1943), *Week-day Religious Education, Help or Hindrance to Inter-religious Understanding* (1946). Home: 6715 Ridgeland Ave., Chicago 49, Ill.

The United Christian Youth Movement 456

BENNETT, JOHN COLEMAN: Prof. of Christian theology and ethics, Union Theol. Sem. since 1943. Born Kingston, Ont., Can., 1902. Educated Phillips Exeter Acad.

(1918-20); Williams College (A.B. 1924), Oxford University (Mansfield College, B.A. 1926; M.A. 1930), Union Theol. Sem. (B.D. 1927, S.T.M. 1929). Hon. D.D.: Church Divinity School of the Pacific (1940), Pacific School of Religion (1943), Williams College (1947). Instructor in theol., Union Theological Sem., 1930-31; asst. prof. of Christian theol., Auburn Theol. Sem., 1931-35, assoc. prof., 1935-38; prof. of Christian theol. and philosophy of religion, Pacific School of Religion, 1938-43. Ordained to ministry Congregational Christ. Church 1939; chairman Council for Social Action (Cong.), 1942-46; member Prudential Committee of American Board for Foreign Missions since 1947; secretary of section on economic order, Oxford Conf. on Life and Work, 1937; secretary of section on Church and the social disorder, Amsterdam Assembly of World Council of Churches, 1948. Member, American Theological Society, Phi Beta Kappa. Author: *Social Salvation* (1935), *Christianity and Our World* (1936), *Christian Realism* (1941), *Christian Ethics and Social Policy* (1946), *Christianity and Communism* (1948). Member: editorial board, *Christianity and Crisis.* Home: 606 West 122nd St., New York, N. Y.

Basic Christian Convictions 26

BLAKEMAN, EDWARD WILLIAM: Research consultant and chairman of rel. ed., Pacific School of Religion, Berkeley, Calif., since 1948. Born Gary, Minn., 1880. Educated Lawrence Coll., Appleton, Wis. (A.B. 1907, D.D. 1918); Boston University, 1907-9; Univ. of Wis. (A.M. 1911); Univ. of Chicago, Univ. of Calif. Ordained minister of the Methodist Church 1908; univ. pastor, Univ. of Wis. 1910-25; dir. Wesley Foundation of Wis. 1915-25, of Calif. 1925-31; lecturer at Pacific School of Rel. 1927-31; counselor in rel. ed. Univ. of Mich. 1933-48. Lecturer Williamstown Institute of Human Relations 1935, 1939. Exec.-board member Mich. Child Guidance Inst. 1938-42. Gen. Conference Meth. Church 1920; chairman Commission to Survey Weekday Rel. Ed. 1920-24; adviser Nat. Council on Rel. in Higher Ed. 1920-27, Universal Rel. Conf. 1927-31. Research Section I.C.R.E. 1940-46; chairman Higher Ed. Section R.E.A. for U.S. and Canada 1942-49. Member: Amer. Acad. of Polit. and Social Science; Conference Church Workers in State Univ.; Nat. Conf. on Science, Philos., Rel.; Nat. Conf. Social Work; Phi Beta Kappa; Beta Theta Pi; Tau Kappa Alpha. Author: *Religion at State Universities, A. Churchmanship for Our Times, Administration of Religion in Universities and Colleges, Personnel* (1942). Home: 296 Arlington Ave., Berkeley, Calif.

Religious Education in Tax-Supported Colleges and Universities 365

BOWEN, CAWTHON ASBURY: Exec. editor church-school publications Meth. Church since 1940. Born Holly Springs, Miss., 1885. Educated Millsaps Coll. 1902-4 (D.D. 1927); Emory Coll. (B.A.); Northwestern 1921. Ordained minister Meth. Episc. Church S. 1908; pastor Stevenson, Birmingham, Dadeville, Ala., 1908-14; pres. N. Ala. Epworth League 1912-13. Prof. rel. ed. Woman's Coll. of Ala. 1914-21, vice-pres. 1921; prof. rel. ed. Millsaps Coll. 1921-25. Chairman Miss. Conf. Sunday School Board 1922-30; asso. Sunday School editor M.E. Ch. S. 1925-30; pres. Gen. Sunday School Council 1926. Member exec. comm. and ed. commission Committee on Basic Philosophy and Policies, I.C.R.E. (chmn. Group Lesson Committee, chmn. comm. on the Graded Series, vice-chmn. comm. on Educational Program), Graded Lesson Syndicate, Leadership Training Publishing Assoc.; sec. editorial dept. Gen. Board of Christian Ed. M. E. Ch. S. 1930-40; chairman Miss. Conf. Bd. of Christian Ed. 1930-36. Mem. R.E.A.; Gen. Conf. M.E. Ch. S. 1934, 1938; Uniting Conf. Meth. Churches 1939; Gen. Conf. and S.E. Jurisdictional Conf. Meth. Ch. 1940; sec. editorial div. Board of Ed. Meth. Ch. 1944; mem. exec. committee Federal Council of Churches. Member: Phi Beta Kappa, Kappa Sigma, Pi Gamma Mu, Theta Phi. Author: *Lesson Materials in the Church School, Literature and the Christian Life; My Child Joins the Church.* Editor:

Cokesbury Worship Hymnal; Boys and Girls and the Bible. Home: Wellington Arms Apartments, Nashville, Tennessee.

Curriculum Patterns for the Church School 101

BROWN, ARLO AYRES: University president emeritus. Born Sunbeam, Mercer County, Ill., 1883. Educated Northwestern U. (A.B. 1903); Drew Theological Seminary (B.D. 1907); Union Theological Seminary, Northwestern U.; Cornell College, Ia. (D.D. 1921); Syracuse U. (LL.D. 1927); University of Chattanooga (Litt.D. 1929); Northwestern U. (LL.D. 1938); Boston U. (L.H.D. 1939). Charges M.E. Ch. 1903-12, deacon 1907, elder 1909; assoc. pastor Madison Ave. Church, New York, 1907; pastor Mount Hope Church, New York, 1909-12, agt. Bd. of Foreign Missions, M.E. Ch., in Jerusalem, 1912-13; exec. sec., Newark Dist. Ch. Soc., 1913-14; supt. teacher training Bd. of Sunday Schools M.E. Ch. 1914-21; pres., U. of Chattanooga 1921-29; pres., Drew University 1929-48. Enlisted in Training School for Army Chaplains, June 1, 1918; commd. 1st Lt., Chaplain, 318th Engrs., 6th Div., A.E.F., Aug. 29, 1918; sr. chaplain same, Dec. 21, 1918; captain, March 26, 1919; hon. discharged June 12, 1919; captain chaplain, O.R.C., 1921-24; major chaplain, 1924-34. Vice-pres., Assn. of Amer. Colls. 1928-29; chairman of I.C.R.E. 1939-48; pres., American Assn. of Theol. Schools 1936-38; pres., Methodist Educational Ass'n 1939-40. Member: Comm. on Conference Courses of Study of Methodist Ch. 1922-48, University Senate, M.E. Ch. 1922-40, Methodist Commission on Chaplains 1943-48, Board of Education of Methodist Ch. 1940-48, Appraisal Comm. of Laymen's Foreign Missions Inquiry 1931-32, International Comm., International Bd., Army and Navy Comm. Member: Phi Beta Kappa, Mason. Author: *Studies in Christian Living* (1914), *Primer of Teacher Training* (1916), *Life in the Making* (co-author) (1917), *A History of Religious Education in Recent Times* (1923), *Youth and Christian Living* (1929). Address: c/o Drew University, Madison, N. J.

Protestantism's Strategy for Religious Education 549

BROWN, MARGARET ELIZABETH: Methodist Board of Ed. Camp Consultant since 1947. Born Rural Retreat, Va., 1901. Educated Radford (Va.) Teacher's Coll. (1919-23); Teacher's Coll. Columbia U., and Union Theo. Sem. (1938); New York Univ. (1945). Teacher Radford High School and asst. instr. Radford T. Coll. 1923-25; Dir. Youth Work, Meth. Holston Conf. 1925-33; member Youth Dept. Staff, Bd. of Ed. Meth. Episc. Ch., South, 1934-39, and The Meth. Ch. 1940-46. Counselor Camp Glenrochie, Va., 1921-24; director of training Camp Cheonda, Lake Junaluska, 1935-39 and Camp Hawthorn (Mo.), Camp Sheldon (Neb.), East Bay (Ill.), Aquabi (Iowa), and on staff of various other Meth. and interagency camps since 1925. Member Am. Assn. of Group Work, Comm. on Camps and Confs., and Comm. on Graded Lessons Series, I.C.R.E. Member Am. Camping Assn. and Pres. Tenn. Valley Section, A.C.A. 1949. Author: *Intermediate Manual, Christian Adventure Camp Manual, Diagrammatic Sketches of Camp Structures.*

Camps and Summer Conferences 338

CHIPKIN, ISRAEL SOLOMON: American Association for Jewish Ed. Born Vilna, Lithuania, 1891. Educated Col. City, N.Y., (B.S. 1908-10), Columbia (1913; A.M. 1915; 1916-20); Jewish Theol. Sem. (1913-16; hon. D.H.L. 1942); Hebrew University, Jerusalem (1928-29); Am. Sch. Oriental Research, Jerusalem (1928-29). Teacher, Principal, rel. school, Prep. School for Girls 1913-16; educational director, League Jewish Youth 1916-20; instru. education and registrar, Israel Friedlander classes, teachers inst., Jewish Theol. Sem., 1920-45; ed. director, Jewish Ed. Ass'n. 1921-40; Ass't. Dir. Jewish Ed. Committee of New York 1940-45; executive director, Am. Ass'n for Jewish Ed. 1945-49; vice-pres. for Research and Experimentation, Jew. Ed. Committee, N.Y., since 1949. Census enumerator,

U.S. Dept. Labor 1910; mem. staff, Bur. Jewish Education, New York, 1910-20. Lecturer, Teachers Coll., Columbia, 1935-41; director, Women's Inst. Jewish Studies 1935-45; founder and educational advisor, Beth Hayeled Bi-cultural Experimental School, Early Childhood Education; Assoc. editor *Reconstructionist;* Research ed., ed., *Jewish Education Magazine.* Director, Jewish Ed. Surv. of Newark, N. J.; Paterson; Worcester, Mass.; Pittsburgh, Pa.; Winnipeg, Can.; Atlanta, Ga.; Miami, Fla.; and Schenectady, N. Y. Chairman, Lena Socolow Palestine Scholarship Fund. Sec. Nat'l Council Jewish Ed. 1926-27, pres. 1927-28. Organizer and sec. Friedlander Conf. Jewish Youth Organizations, 1920-23, vice-pres. Nat. Conf. Jewish Social Service 1937-39, pres. 1941-42. Psychol. examiner U.S.A. 1918. R.E.A. (Vice-pres. 1943-46). Author: *Twenty-Five Years of Jewish Education in the United States.* Contributor: *Encyclopedia of Educational Research, Dictionary of Education, Jews and Judaism.* Member: Soc. for Advancement of Judaism, Jewish Academy Arts and Sciences, Bureau of Intercultural Ed., American Academy Jewish Research, Histadruth Ivrith, Zionist Org. of America, Menorah Association. Address: 1776 Broadway, New York 19, N. Y.

Jewish Education in America 501

CUMMINGS, OLIVER DE WOLF: Dir. of Youth Dept., Board of Ed. and Publication of Northern Baptist Convention since 1946. Born Chester, Pa., 1900. Educated Univ. of Redlands (A.B. 1921, D.D. 1940); Newton Theol. Sch. (B.D. 1924, M.R.E. 1926). Dir. Young People's Work, Ruggles St. Bapt. Ch. (Boston) 1921-22. So. Calif. Bapt. Conv. 1924-26; Dir. Christian Ed., So. Calif. Bapt. Conv. and American Bapt. Pub. Soc. 1926-41. Gen. Sec. Bapt. Youth Fellowship of Nor. Bapt. Conv. since 1941, also of Youth Dept., Council on Christian Ed. of Nor. Bapt. Conv. 1941-46. Served with S.A.T.C. World War I Ch. Com. on Rel. Ed. of Youth and mem. Com. on Ed. Program I.C.R.E. Member: Council on Soc. Progress of Nor. Bapt. Conv., Bd. of Trustees, International Chr. Endeavor Union, National Council Boy Scouts of Amer.; Pi Chi, Phi Chi Phi. Author: *Administering Christian Education in the Local Church* (1936); *Christ in My Life* (1940); *Christian Education in the Local Church* (1942); *Discussion and Program Suggestions for Youth on World Evangelism* (1947). Home: 2312 Kenilworth Road, Ardmore, Pa.

The Youth Fellowship 287

DAVIS, ORVILLE LESTER: Assoc. prof. of rel. ed. and Dir. of the Crusade for Christ program at DePauw Univ., since 1946. Born Bridgeport, Ind., 1900. Educated DePauw Univ. (A.B. 1922), Boston Univ. (S.T.B. 1925), Northwestern Univ. (M.A. 1933). Hon. D.D. DePauw Univ., 1945. Latin and English teacher in Albany Academy, New York, 1923-24; Minister, Congregational Church Clinton, Mass., 1924-25; since 1925 ordained minister Methodist Church serving in Mont.; Manila, P.I.; Md., and Ind.; prof. of New Testament, Union Theological Seminary, Manila, P.I., 1926-31; prof. of Christian Missions and Religious Edn., Gammon Theological Seminary, Atlanta, Ga., 1932-37; principal, Leonard Theological Coll., Jubbulpore, India, 1937-44; prof. of Rel. Ed., Westminster Theological Seminary, 1945-46; Member: Phi Delta Kappa, Member of the Senate of Serampore Univ., India and member of its exec. Committee, Board of Examiners, and Board of Moderators; Bd. of Direction, Hislop Coll., India, 1938-44 (Chmn. 1943-44). Pres. Rotary Club, Jubbulpore, India, 1943-44; Chmn. of Committee on Christian Higher Ed. for the Philippines, 1945. Member: Alpha Tau Omega, Phi Delta Kappa. Editor: *The Philippine Observer* (1928-31), *The Foundation* (1932-37). Youth leader; one-time director of Youth Work in the Methodist Church, Philippine Islands, and vice-pres. of the Philippine Youth Movement. Participant in the program of revision of the theological education curriculum for the bachelor degree in India and the Philippines. Home: 715 East Washington St., Greencastle, Ind.

The Religious Education Association 445

EAKIN, MILDRED MOODY (Mrs. Frank): Assistant professor of rel. ed., Drew Univ. since 1948. Born Wilson, N. Y., 1890. Educated Wilson Acad. (1906); Syracuse Univ. (A.B. 1910); N. Y. U. (A.M. 1934); Syracuse Univ., Univ. of Chicago. Teacher high school, Wilson, 1910-16; dir. children's activities W.C.T.U. 1916-19; assoc. nat. dir., 1919; dir. elementary ed. for seven states, Board of Ed. M.E. Ch. 1919-21, supt. dept. of elementary ed. at central office, Chicago, 1921-32; teaching fellow rel. ed. Drew Univ., 1932-34, instr. 1934-48; dir. demonstration school since 1937; visiting instr. Union Theol. Sem., New York City, summer, 1946. Member: R.E.A., Alpha Chi Omega. Author: *Tales of Golden Deeds* (1923); *Kindergarten Course for Daily Vacation Schools* (1925); *Teaching Junior Boys and Girls* (1934); *Exploring Our Neighborhood* (with pupil's books, *Under The Church Flag* and *In Anybody's Town*) (1936); *Getting Acquainted with Jewish Neighbors* (1944); Co-author (with Frank Eakin): *A Junior Teacher's Guide on Negro Americans* (1936): *Your Child's Religion* (1942); *Let's Think About Our Religion* (1944); *The Pastor and the Children* (1947); *The Church-School Teacher's Job* (1949). Home: 39 Green Village Road, Madison, N. J.; (summer) Bloomsbury, N. J.

Newer Techniques in Teaching 197

EDICK, HELEN MARIE: Assoc. prof. ed., Hartford School of Rel. Ed. since 1943. Born Watertown, N. Y., 1900. Educated Folts Mission Institute (1920-23, 1924-25); New York U. (1933, 1937); Hartford School of Religious Education (B.R.E. 1940-41); Hartford School of Religious Education (M.A. 1942-43); Universitaria de Bellas Artes (Mexico, 1946); Union Theological Seminary and Teachers' College Columbia (1947, 1948). Social Work, Philadelphia 1923, Pittsburgh (Pa.) 1925-27. Head Resident Settlement House Utica (N. Y.) 1927-1940, 1941-42. Member: Professional Rel. Ed. (Hartford), Assoc. for Group Workers (New York). Author: *Thoughts of God for Boys and Girls* (special editions); *Leisure Time Activities in the Church; Children's Day in the Church School* (1945); *Marionettes in Religious Education* (1947). Home: 106 Niles St., Hartford, Conn.

The Community as a Unit of Religious Education 325

ELLIOTT, HARRISON SACKET: Professor, Union Theological Seminary. Born St. Clairsville, Ohio, 1882. Educated Antioch Coll., Yellow Springs, O., 1898-1900, Valparaiso (Ind.) U. (1900-1); Ohio Wesleyan U. (A.B. 1905); Drew Theol. Seminary (B.D. 1911); Teachers College, Columbia (A.M. 1922); Oxford University, England (1931); Yale (Ph.D. 1940); Ohio Wesleyan (Hon. Ed. D. 1949). Secretary to James W. Bashford, bishop of M.E. Ch., China, 1905-8; correspondent Assoc. Press, Shanghai, China, 1906-8; assistant sec. Africa Diamond Jubilee, M.E. Church 1909-10; sec. International Comm., Y.M.C.A., in student publication and relig. work depts. 1910-22, sec. National War Work. Council, Y.M.C.A., 1917-18; teacher National Training School, Y.W.C.A., 1920-25; instr. of religious psychology, Drew Theol. Sem., 1921-23; mem. faculty Teachers Coll., Columbia, summers, 1923-29; asst. prof. rel. ed. and psychology, Union Theol. Sem., 1922-23, assoc. prof., 1923-25, Skinner and McAlpin prof. of practical theology and head dept. rel. ed. and psychology since 1925, dir. summer courses, 1937-43. Ordained to ministry of Meth. Ch., 1944; member, Chairman Boards of Education and Missions, N. Y. Annual Conference. Member Nat. Council of Y.M.C.A.'s; Chairman National Boy's Work Comm. Y.M.C.A.'s, 1927-46; Chairman, Board of Publications, Y.M.C.A. since 1946; Chairman Board of Trustees, New Lincoln School, Inc., N. Y., since 1948. Member R.E.A. (board of directors: vice-pres. 1937-38; pres. 1939-42). Author: *Student Standards of Action* (with Ethel Cutler, 1914); *How Jesus Met Life Questions* (1920); *The Bearing of Psychology upon Religion* (1927); *The Process of Group Thinking* (1928); *Group Discussion in Religious Education* (1930); *Solving*

Personal Problems, A Counseling Manual (with Grace L. Elliott, 1936); *Can Religious Education Be Christian?* (1940). Home: 606 West 122nd St., New York, N. Y.

Individual and Group Counseling 183

FALLAW, WESNER: Howard Prof. of Rel. Ed., Andover Newton Theol. School, since 1947. Born Woodruff, S. C., 1907. Educated Furman Univ. (A.B. 1923-27); Columbia Univ. (M.A. 1936, Ed.D. 1944); Union Theol. Seminary (1934-37). Y.M.C.A. secretary, Charleston, S. C., 1927-33; alumni executive, Furman, 1933-34, assistant prof. and asst. to dean 1937-39; dir. rel. ed., Winnetka, Ill., 1940-46; lecturer, Columbia (Union Seminary), summers 1946, 1948; assoc. prof., Andover Newton, 1946-47. Author: *The Modern Parent and the Teaching Church* (1946). Contributor: *Learning and World Peace: A Symposium* (1948); *Sermons of Good Will* (1948). Home: 111 Institution Ave., Newton Centre 59, Mass.

The Home and Parent Education 236

GIBBONS, RAY: Director Council for Social Action of the Congregational Christian Churches since 1944. Born Cleveland, O., 1903. Educated Oberlin College (A.B. 1924); Oberlin Seminary (1924-25); Union Theological Seminary (B.D. 1928); Teachers College, Columbia (A.M. 1928); Defiance College (hon. D.D. 1948). Ordained Congregational Christian clergyman, 1928. Pastor: Westbrook Congregational Church, Westbrook, Me., 1928-34; First Church of Christ in Northampton, Mass., 1935-43. Dean of Maine Congrl. youth conferences two years. Founder and dean Massachusetts Congrl. youth conferences two years. Chairman Massachusetts Congrl. Comm. on Rel. Ed. two years. Pres. Portland Congrl. Club. Moderator Hampshire Association, Chm. Massachusetts Comm. on Churches and Colleges. Member Division of Christian Education six years. Member: Connecticut Valley Theological Club, Torch, National Religion and Labor Foundation. Instructor Deering School for Pastors two summers. Member National Comm. on Displaced Persons; White Plains, N. Y., Board of Education; Commission on Church, State, and Education. Author: *Action to Match Our Gospel* (1944); *Guidebook for Social Action* (1947); *Protestantism and Public Education* (1949). Home: 19 Midland Ave., White Plains, N. Y.

The Relation of Church and State 479

GODDARD, ALICE LYMBURNER: Director of Children's Work, I.C.R.E. Born Gardendale, Mich. Educated Chaffee Noble School; Wayne University, Detroit; Auburn School of Religious Education (B.R.E.). Director of Rel. Ed., Federation of Churches of Rochester, N. Y., Fort Street Presbyterian Church, Detroit, and other local churches; Detroit Council of Churches. Author: curricular materials, articles, and pamphlets on children's work in the church.

The Total Program for Children 229

HARMS, JOHN W.: Exec. vice-pres., Church Federation of Greater Chicago since 1943. Born Blue Springs, Neb., 1902. Educated Phillips U. (A.B. 1931); Auburn Seminary (1933-34); U. of Chicago (1936-37, 1940). Surveyor, dept. of endowments, board of ed., Disciples of Christ, 1925-26; business manager, Central Christian Ch., Enid, Okla., 1926-29; dir. rel. ed. (Eastern area) United Christian Missionary Society (Disciples of Christ), N. Y., 1931-34; state dir. of rel. ed., Ind., 1934-38; exec. sec. Council of Churches and Christian Ed. of Md.-Del., Inc., 1938-42; pres. Assn. Council Secs. 1941-42. Ordained minister Disciples of Christ (Christian) 1931. Member: Pi Kappa Delta. Contributor to religious journals. Home: 5420 Blackstone Ave., Chicago, Ill.

City and State Councils of Churches and Religious Education 419

HARNER, NEVIN COWGER: Prof. Christian ed. Lancaster Theol. Sem. 1929-45, since 1947. Born near Berlin, Pa., 1901. Educated Franklin and Marshall Coll. (A.B. 1921, D.D. 1940, LL.D. 1946); Lancaster Theol. Sem. (B.D. 1924); Union Theol. Sem. (S.T.M. 1925); Columbia (Ph.D. 1931). Ordained minister Reformed Church in U. S. 1924; dir. rel. ed. Zion Ref. Church, Lehighton, Pa., 1925-28. Pres. Heidelberg Coll. 1945-47. Member: R.E.A., Federal Council of Churches, International Missions of the Evang. and Ref. Ch., Phi Beta Kappa. Vice-chairman I.C.R.E. Author: *The Educational Work of the Church* (1939), *Youth Work in the Church* (1942); *Missionary Education in Your Church* (with David D. Baker, 1942); *Religion's Place in General Education* (1949). Home: 523 West James St., Lancaster, Pa.

The Educational Ministry of the Church 381

HEFFRON, EDWARD JOSEPH: Director of Media Relations, Nat'l Conf. of Christians and Jews since 1947. Born E. Dubuque, Ill., 1905. Educated Loras Coll., Dubuque, Ia. (A.B. 1927, hon. LL.D. 1940); Georgetown U. (LL.B. 1931); Catholic U. (studies in radio law, 1936); admitted to bar, D.C., 1930, to practice before Fed. Communications Comm. 1939. Instr. commercial law Strayer Coll. of Accountancy 1935-42. Dir. Catholic Evidence Bureau, Nat'l Council of Catholic Men, dir. of program for Catholic Hour 1932-35; exec. sec. N.C.C.M. 1935-46; exec. asst. to pres. in charge public relations, Natl. Assn. of Broadcasters 1946-47. Member: Catholic Evidence Guild, Catholic Institute of the Press (N.Y.C.). Home: 676 Riverside Drive, New York City, N. Y.

Roman Catholic Religious Education 519

KALAS, HARRY H.: Director of National Christian Teaching Mission. Born Merrill, Iowa, 1903. Educated Western Union College, LeMars, Iowa (B.A.); Evangelical Theological Seminary, Naperville, Ill. (B.D.); Northwestern University, Evanston, Ill. (M.A.); Hon. D.D., Western Union College. Minister: Union Congregational Church, North Aurora, Ill., 1925-27; Grace Evangelical United Brethren 1928-34; Trinity Evangelical United Brethren, Chicago, 1934-39. Professor practical theology, Evangelical Theological Seminary, 1939-45; Executive Secretary, Iowa Inter-church Council, 1945-48.

Educational Evangelism 75

KNAPP, FORREST LAMAR: General Secretary of World Council of Christian Education since 1940. Born Rio Grande County, Colo., 1899. Educated Colo. State Coll. (B.S. 1921); Yale (B.D. 1924, Ph.D. 1927). Asst. pastor United Church, Bridgeport, Conn., 1924-27; supt. rel. ed. Cleveland Ch. Fed., 1927-28; dir. leadership ed. and mem. board of editors *International Journal of Rel. Ed.*, I.C.R.E., 1929-39, dir. church-school adm. 1931-37, dir. research 1931-32, chmn. Bur. of Research 1933-34, dir. field adm. 1937-39, member educational comm. 1929-45. Exec. sec. program comm. International Convention on Christian Ed. 1930, exec. sec. gen. conv. comm. 1938, mem. exec. comm. and board of trustees since 1940; mem. Council of Ch. Bds. of Ed., 1935-39; mem. Foreign Missions Conf. of N. America; vice-pres. John Milton Soc. for the Blind since 1942; assoc. gen. sec. World Council of Christian Education 1939-40. Lecturer in rel. ed. Northwestern Univ. 1932-33. Member: Pi Kappa Delta, Lambda Chi Alpha. Congregationalist. Author: *Leadership Education in the Church* (1933); *Next Steps in Latin America* (1942). Editor: *The Christian Challenge to the Modern World* (1938); *Christian Education and World Evangelization* (1941). Home: 320 Hayward Ave., Mt. Vernon, N. Y.

The World Council of Christian Education 469

LANKARD, FRANK GLENN: Dean Baldwin-Wallace College, Berea, O., since Feb., 1950. Born Garnett, Kan., 1892. Educated U. of Kan. (1912-13); Baker U. (A.B. 1916);

Boston (S.T.B. 1919); Northwestern U. (M.A. 1921); Garrett Bibl. Inst. (B.D. 1923); Northwestern U. (Ph.D. 1926); Baker U. (LL.D. 1945). Entered ministry M.E. Ch. 1915; ordained deacon 1918; ordained elder 1921; pastor Freemont (N.H.) Community Ch. 1917-19, Leaf River, Ill., 1919-20, Sawyer Ave. Meth. Ch., Chicago, 1920-22. Assoc. prof. bibl. lit. and rel. ed. U. of Chattanooga, 1922-23, prof., 1923-24; instr. Northwestern U. 1924-25, asst. prof. bibl. lit. 1925-29. Prof. bibl. lit. Brothers Coll., Drew Univ., 1929-50; dean 1931-50. Member: Soc. Bibl. Lit. and Exegesis, R.E.A., Amer. Assn. Univ. Profs., Nat. Assn. Bibl. Instrs. (pres. 1937), Eastern Assn. of Coll. Deans and Advisers of Men (Pres. 1938-39), N. J. assn. Colls. and Univs. Board of Dirs., Pi Kappa Delta, Phi Beta Kappa, Phi Delta Kappa (pres. Upsilon Chapter 1921-22), Pi Gamma Mu. Morris County Y.M.C.A. Bd. of Directors (pres. since 1944), Co-ordinating Council of Morris County Y.M.C.A.'s (chairman since 1948), Morris County Council of Social Agencies (vice-pres. and member of Exec. Comm. and of Bd. of Directors). Clubs: Rotary (gov. 182d Dist., 1942-43; offcl. observer for Rotary Internat'l at meetings of Ec. and Soc. Council, U.N., 1946). Author: *A History of the American Sunday School Curriculum* (1927); *Difficulties in Religious Thinking* (1933); *The Bible and the Life and Ideals of the English Speaking People* (1935); *The Wanted Generation* (1937); *The Bible Speaks to Our Generation* (1941). Co-author: *The Altar Hour* (1941); *Founders of Christian Movements* (1941); *Rising Above Color* (1943); *Problems of Faculty Personnel* (1946). Member of Editorial Board, "Know Your Bible Series," by Roy L. Smith, 1943-45. Office: Baldwin-Wallace College, Berea, O.

The Use of Our Religious Heritage 114

LIGON, ERNEST MAYFIELD: Chairman dept. of psychol. Union Coll. Born Iowa Park, Texas, 1897. Educated Texas Christian U. (A.B. 1921, M.A. 1921, LL.D. 1948); Yale (B.D. 1924, Ph. D. 1927). Lab. asst. and asst. instr., Lab. of Psychology, Yale, 1924-27; asst. prof. psychology, Conn. Coll., 1927-29; asso. with Union Coll., Schenectady, New York, since 1929, successively asst. prof., assoc. prof., prof. Founder Union Coll. Character Research Project in association with Westminster Presbyterian Church of Albany, 1935; teacher, summer, U. of Mich. 1945-47; Mead Swing lecturer, Oberlin Coll., 1947; vice chmn. and chmn. Research Sect. of I.C.R.E., 1946-48, council rep. since 1948. Dir. Union Coll. Character Ed. Workshops since 1946. Dir. Schenectady Y.M.C.A. Fellow Amer. Psychol. Assn., A.A.A.S.; mem. Psychometric Soc., R.E.A., Sigma Xi. Author: *A Comparative Study of Certain Incentives in the Learning of the White Rat* (1929); *The Psychology of Christian Personality* (1935); *Their Future Is Now* (1939); *A Greater Generation* (1948). Home: 1079 Parkwood Blvd., Schenectady, N. Y.

Basic Psychological Concepts 37

LIMBERT, PAUL MOYER: President Springfield College since 1946. Born Grove City, Pa., 1897. Educated Franklin-Marshall Coll. (A.B. 1918); Lancaster Theol. Sem. (B.D. 1922); Union Theol. Sem. (1923); Columbia U. (Ph. D. 1929); Franklin-Marshall (LL.D. 1946). Pastor St. John's Reformed Church, Pottstown, Pa., 1922-23. Asst. prof. religion, Franklin-Marshall, 1923-31; assoc. in rel. ed., Teachers College, Columbia U., 1931-32; asst. prof. education and assoc. in New College, 1933-39; prof. education and director field work, Springfield College, 1939-43; lecturer, Union Seminary, 1939-45; program staff, National Board Y.M.C.A.'s, 1943-46. Pres., Springfield Council of Churches, 1947-49. Member: Phi Beta Kappa, R.E.A., Am. Assn. Group Workers. Chmn. Haddam House Editorial Board. Author: *Denominational Policies in Higher Education* (1929); *Educating for Civic Responsibility* (1941); *Christian Emphasis in Y.M.C.A. Program* (1944). Editor: *In War Time and After* (1942); *Professional Competence in Y.M.C.A.* (1946). Home: 36 Dartmouth St., Springfield, Mass.

Agencies of Recreation and Group Services 312

LOOMIS, AMY GOODHUE: Dir. Dept. Relig. Drama, Div. of Education in Home, Church and Community, No. Bap. Convention. Born Grand Rapids, Mich. Educated Univ. of Mich. (1919-22, A.B.); Amer. Acad. Dramatic Art, N. Y. (1922-23); professional theater exper. 1923-33. Dir. dept. drama, North Shore Country Day School, Winnetka, Ill., 1927-28; Goodman School of Theatre, Chi., Ill. 1928-29; Lydia Mendelssohn Theater, Univ. of Mich. 1928-31; Manag. Dir. Summer Theater, Northport, Mich. 1933-35; Dir. Dept. Rel. Drama, Fountain St. Bap. Ch., Grand Rapids, 1935-47; Northwestern Univ., 1937-38; Assoc. Dir. Dallas Little Theater and School, 1938-39; Chairman Speakers' Bureau, Amer. Red Cross, Kent Co., 1941-44; Dir. Dept. Drama, No. Bap. Assembly, Green Lake, Wis., 1944-49; Dir. Relig. Ed. F.S.B.C. 1946-47; Comm. on Relig. Drama, I.C.R.E. 1948; Dir. Rel. Drama Workshop, Green Lake, Wis. under N.B.A. and I.C.R.E., 1949. Chi Omega. Home: 68 Ransom Ave., N. E., Grand Rapids, Mich.

The Creative Arts in Religious Education **137**

LOTZ, PHILIP HENRY: Clergyman, teacher, author, editor. Born Wilton Junction, Ia. Educated Central Wesleyan Coll. (B.A. 1913); Boston Univ. School of Theol. (S.T.B. 1917); Northwestern Univ. (M.A. 1921, Ph.D. 1924); Garrett Biblical Institute (B.D., 1928); graduate work at universities of Iowa, Illinois, and Chicago. Ordained Methodist minister 1913; pastor, Herman, Mo., 1913-14, Detroit, Ill., 1917-18, Palmyra, Ill., 1919. Prof. rel. ed. Kan. Wesleyan Univ. 1923-24, Upper Iowa Univ., 1925-27, Huntingdon Coll., 1929-31. Pastor Oakland, Ill. 1932, Philo, 1933-34, Rock Island, 1935-37, Wenona, 1938-41, Toulon, 1942-45, Forrest, since 1946. Member: Phi Delta Kappa, Sigma Tau Delta, Alpha Kappa Delta. Author and/or editor: *Current Weekday Religious Education* (1925); *Studies in Religious Education* (with L. W. Crawford, 1931); *The Quest for God Through Worship* 1934); *The Quest for God Through Understanding* (1937); "Creative Personalities Series," *I. Vocations and Professions* (1940), *II. Women Leaders* (1940), *III. Founders of Christian Movements* (1941), *IV. Answering Distant Calls* (edited by Mabel H. Erdman, 1942), *V. Rising Above Color* (1943), *VI. Distinguished American Jews* (1945); *The Altar Hour* (1941); *The Legal Aspect of Week-day Religious Education in Illinois* (1943); *Worship Services for the Church Year* (1944); *The Quest for God Through Faith* (1944); *Some Legal Aspects of Weekday Religious Education* (1947); *Honour Thy Mother* (with Grace Chapin Auten, 1949). Contrib. various rel. ed. mags. and lesson series. Address: The Methodist Church, Forrest, Ill.

McKIBBEN, FRANK MELBOURNE: Prof. of Rel. Ed., Garrett Biblical Institute since 1940. Born Conway Springs, Kan., 1889. Educated Southwestern Coll. (A.B. 1914); Boston Univ. School of Theol. (S.T.B. 1918); Northwestern Univ. (A.M. 1924, Ph.D. 1929). Youth Sec. Board of Sunday Schools, Meth., 1919-20; Comm. Dir., Rel. Ed., Evanston, Ill., 1920-23; Oak Park, Ill., 1921-23; South Bend, Ind., 1923-24; Baltimore, Md., 1925-28. Prof. of rel. ed., Univ. of Pittsburgh, 1928-30; prof. of ed., Northwestern Univ., 1930-40. Member: R.E.A.; Phi Delta Kappa. Author: *The Community Training School* (1922); *Intermediate Method in Church Schools* (1926); *Improving Religious Education Through Supervision* (1929); *Improving Your Teaching* (1937); *Christian Education Through the Church* (1947); Ph.D. Dissertation: *A Study of Selected Factors Conditioning Efficiency in Sunday Church Schools.*

Trends in Educational Philosophy **48**

MAYNARD, DONALD MORE: Prof. of rel. ed. Boston Univ. school of Theol. since 1948. Born Emmetsburg, Iowa, 1900. Educated Ohio Wesleyan University (A.B. 1923); Garrett Biblical Institute (B.D. 1926); Yale University (Ph.D. 1936). Minister, Florida Conference, Methodist Church (1927-29). Prof. of Rel. Ed.:

Florida Southern College (1929-31), Scarritt College for Christian Workers 1931-48. Home: 110 Prospect St., West Newton, Mass.

The Total Church as an Agency of Religious Education 221

MUNRO, HARRY CLYDE: Prof. rel. ed. Brite Coll. of the Bible, Texas Christian U., since 1948. Born Cheboygan County, Mich., 1890. Educated Hiram Coll. (A.B. 1916); U. of Wash. (1919); Spokane U. (A.M. 1922); U. of Okla. (1923-24); Transylvania U. (M.R.E. 1925). Ordained ministry Disciples of Christ, 1916; missionary in Alaska for Amer. Christian Missionary Soc., 1916-18; pastor, First Christian Ch., Tacoma, Wash., 1918-19. Prof. philosophy and rel. ed. Spokane U. 1919-23; prof. rel. ed. U. of Okla. 1923-24. Editor of young people's lit., Christian Board of Publ., St. Louis, 1924-29; dir. leadership training, United Christian Missionary Soc., 1926-29. Convention mgr., 1929-30, International Conv. of Rel. Ed., Toronto, June, 1930; dir. adult work and field administration I.C.R.E. 1930-38, dir. adult work and extension 1938-44; dir. National Christian Teaching Mission, 1945-48. Author: *Agencies for the Religious Education of Adolescents* (1925); *How to Increase Your Sunday School* (1928); *The Church As a School* (1929); *The Pastor and Religious Education* (1930); *Christian Education in Your Church* (1933); *The Effective Adult Class* (1934); *Be Glad You're a Protestant* (1948); Founded and edited three years, *Bethany Church School Guide* (monthly). Home: 2721 Forest Park Blvd., Fort Worth, Texas.

The Christian Education of Adults 300

MURPHY, RUTH ELIZABETH: Director vacation religious education I.C.R.E. since 1942. Born Owatonna, Minn., 1898. Educated U. of Redlands (A.B. 1921, 1935-36); Columbia U. (A.M. 1924); New York Baptist City Society, scholar (1922-24). Teacher, Bodfish, Calif. 1921-22; head worker Riverdale Christian Center, Yonkers, N. Y., New York Baptist City Soc., 1924-26. Part-time supervisor in rel. ed. Teachers Coll., Columbia U., 1925; dir. Christian education in charge, Cooperative Weekday Church Schools, First Presbyterian Church, Englewood, N. J., 1926-31; dir. rel. ed. First Baptist Church, Bakersfield, Calif., 1933-35; dir. children's work in mission centers and assoc. dir. Baptist educational center in Harlem, New York Baptist City Soc., 1936-41; service in war emergency areas, 1941-46. Home: 1805 East 72nd St., Chicago, Ill.

The Vacation Church School 260

PARKER, EVERETT C.: Director, Protestant Radio Commission. Born Chicago, 1913. Educated University of Chicago (A.B. 1935); Chicago Theol. Seminary (B.D. 1943), awarded Blatchford Graduate Fellowship. Ordained by Chicago Assoc. Congregational Christian Churches, 1943. Assistant Chief of radio, W.P.A., manager station WJBW, New Orleans; program manager station WHIP, Hammond, Ind., assistant to the manager, Public Service Dept., NBC, 1943-44; director Joint Religious Radio Committee 1944-48. Director, Univ. of Chicago Rel. Radio Workshop; lecturer in radio, Yale Divinity School; lecturer in rel. radio, Columbia Univ.; director of radio, Congregational Christian Churches. Address:297 Fourth Ave., New York 10, N. Y.

Radio and Television in Religious Education 164

PETERSEN, LEMUEL ALVA: Director of public relations, I.C.R.E., since 1947. Born Viborg, S. D., 1919. Educated Univ. of Minnesota (B.A. 1943); Yale (B.D. 1947). Telegraph editor, New Haven (Conn.) *Journal-Courier* 1944-45, state editor 1946. Instructor in journalism, New Haven Jr. Coll. of Commerce. Member: Sigma Delta Chi; author of magazine articles. Home: 12431 S. Princeton, Chicago 28, Ill.

Directory 584

Powell, Marie Cole: Teacher of Bible, Concord Academy; b. Ottawa, Ill., 1882; educated Oberlin Coll., (1900-02); Vassar Coll. (A.B. 1904); Northwestern Univ. and Chicago Theological Seminary; Boston Univ. (A.M. 1935). Teacher public schools Oak Park and Berwyn, Ill., 1905-11, director religious education First Congregational Church, Oak Park, Ill., 1912-16; secretary Congregational Training School for Women 1916-17; director religious education Congregational Church, Hinsdale, Ill., 1917-18, First Cong. Church, Oak Park., Ill., 1918-20. Instructor School of Rel. Ed. Boston Univ., 1928; Associate professor of rel. ed., Boston Univ., 1935-44; instructor, Boston Univ. School of Theology, 1948. Author: *Junior Methods in the Church School* (1923 and 1931); *Guiding the Experience of Worship* (1935); *Boys and Girls at Worship* (1943); *Men and Women Who Knew Jesus* (1949); *New Testament Pioneers* (1949). Member: P.E.O., R.E.A. Home: Independence Road, Concord, Mass.

Worship in Religious Education 126

Ross, Roy George: General Secretary, I.C.R.E. Born Forrest, Ill., 1898. Educated Eureka Coll. (A.B. 1921, hon. LL.D. 1936); Yale U. (B.D. 1924); U. of Chi. (1935). Ordained minister, Disciples of Christ Church, 1923; pastorates (1921-25) —Carrollton, Ill.; West Cornwall, Conn.; Milwaukee, Wis. Director of young people's work, United Christian Missionary Society, Disciples of Christ, 1925-28; executive secretary, Dept. of Rel. Ed., 1929-36; Chm. of Division of Christian Education, 1934-36; trustee and chief executive I.C.R.E. since 1936, Rel. Ed. Foundation since 1938, International Association of Daily Vacation Bible Schools since 1937. International Training School for Sunday School Leaders since 1937. Trustee of Eureka Coll. 1936-42, Disciples Divinity House, U. of Chicago, since 1936. Member: Executive Com., Federal Council of Churches since 1936. Member: Pi Kappa Delta, Theta Kappa Nu, Chi Upsilon, Acacia. Co-author: *The Disciples and Religious Education* (1936), *Faith of the Free* (1940). Home: 5555 South Blackstone Avenue, Chicago 37, Ill.

The International Council of Religious Education 431

Scotford, John R.: Editor of *Advance* since 1943. Born Chicago, Ill., 1888. Educated Dartmouth (A.B. 1911) Union Theological Seminary (1910-12). Pastor of Congregational Churches, 1912-27. Free-lance speaker and writer, 1928-31. Editorial and promotional work, Congr. mission boards, 1931-43. Author: *Spanning a Continent* (1939); *The Church Beautiful* (1946); *Church Union; Why Not?* (1948). Home: 497 No. Fulton Ave., Mt. Vernon, N. Y.

Building for Religious Education 207

Shaver, Erwin Leander: Director of weekday rel. ed. I.C.R.E. since 1942. Born Eau Claire, Wis., 1890. Educated Lawrence Coll., Appleton, Wis. (A.B. 1913, A.M. 1914); Garrett Bibl. Inst. (S.T.B. 1916); Union Theol. Sem. (1917-20); Columbia, (1917-20, A.M. 1918); Northland Coll. (D.D. 1933). Ordained minister Congregational Church, 1917. Pastor Rosendale and Genoa City, Wis., 1912-16; dir. rel. ed., Decatur, Ill., 1916-17; pastor East Rockaway, L. I., N. Y., 1917-20; asst. in rel. ed., Union Theol. Sem., 1919-20; prof. rel. ed., Hendrix Coll. Conway, Ark., 1920-22; dist. sec. Congr. Ed. Soc., Boston, 1922-26; sec. leadership ed. Board of Home Missions, since 1926; instructor summers, U. of Chicago, Boston U., Auburn Sch. Rel. Ed., Reformed Theol. Sem. Made survey of weekday rel. ed. for R.E.A. 1921-22. Member: R.E.A., vice-pres., I.C.R.E., department of supervisors of N.E.A. Author: *Teaching Adolescents in the Church School* (1923); *The Project Principle in Religious Education* (1924); *Young People's Projects* (10 vols., 1925-27); *The Teaching Church* (with B. S. Winchester, 1925); *How to Teach Seniors* (1927); *A Project Curriculum for Young People* (1927); *Programs for Teachers' Meetings* (1928); *Present-Day Trends in Religious Education* (1928); *Training*

Young People in Worship (with H. T. Stock, 1929); *Youth and Worship* (1929); *Shall Laymen Teach Religion?* (1931); *Programs for Workers' Conferences* (Series A. 1932, Series B, 1933); *A Church-School Teacher's Notebook* (1935); *The Worker's Conference Manual* (1938); *The Art of Christian Leadership* (1938); *The Pilgrim Senior Teachers Quarterly* (1939); *100 Ways to Improve Your Sunday School Teaching* (1942); *Directors of Religious Education—A Survey* (1947). Home: 15 Shirley Rd., Waltham, Mass.

The Weekday Church School 274

SHERRILL, LEWIS JOSEPH: Prof. of rel. ed. Louisville Presby. Sem. since 1925, dean since 1930. Born Haskell, Tex., 1892. Educated Austin Coll., Sherman, Tex. (A.B. 1916, D.D. 1925); Presby. Theol. Sem., Louisville (B.D. 1921); Yale (Ph.D. 1929); Northwestern U. (summers 1925-26); Yale (1925, 1927-28); Harvard (1939-40); Davidson Coll., N. C. (Litt.D. 1937). Ordained minister Presby. Church in U. S., 1921. Pastor Covington, Tenn., 1921-25. Exec. sec. Amer. Assn. of Theol. Schools 1935-38, pres. 1938-40, chairman of exec. com. since 1948. Dir. Rel. Ed. Re-study, Presby. Ch., U. S., 1945-48. Served as sec. Y.M.C.A., U. S. Army, 1917-18, pvt., F.A., 1918-19. Author: *Presbyterian Parochial Schools, 1846-1870* (1932); *Religious Education in the Small Church* (1932); *Adult Education in the Church* (with J. E. Purcell, 1936); *Family and Church* (1937); *Understanding Children* (1939); *The Opening Doors of Childhood* (1939-translation into Spanish, 1943); *Becoming a Christian* (with Helen H. Sherrill, 1943); *The Rise of Christian Education* (1944); *Guilt and Redemption* (1945). Home: 1853 Overlook Terrace, Louisville, Ky.

A Historical Study of the Religious Education Movement 13

SNYDER, ROSS: Assoc. prof. rel. ed., Federated Theological Faculties, Chicago Theological Seminary. Born Degraff, Ohio. Educated Ohio State Univ. (1923); Boston Univ. School of Rel. Ed. and Social Service (Ph.D. 1929). Ordained as Congregational minister in 1939. Director of rel. ed. at Prospect Presbyterian Church, Maplewood, N. J.; Winnetka Congregational Church, Winnetka, Ill.; and Chicago Theological Seminary. Member: Quadrangle Club, radio committee of the Church Federation of Greater Chicago, and radio advisory committee, I.C.R.E., Co-author of *Religious Radio* (1948) and author of numerous articles. Dean of the Univ. of Chicago Religious Radio Workshop. Home address: 1364 E. 58th St., Chicago 37, Ill.

Experimentation and Research 404

STIDLEY, LEONARD ALBERT: Dean, Graduate School of Theology, Oberlin Coll., since 1949. Born Fort Madison, Ia., 1898. Educated Carthage Coll., Ill. (A.B. 1921); U. of Ill. (M.S. 1922); Union Theol. Sem. (B.D. 1925); Carthage Coll. (D.D. 1939); Columbia (Ph.D. 1944). Ordained to ministry of Meth. Ch., 1929. Director rel. ed. and assoc. pastor First Meth. Church, Decatur, Ill., 1926-30; assoc. dir. survey Meth. chs., Manhattan, Bronx, Westchester, N. Y., 1930-31; dir. and pastor, Church of All Nations and Neighborhood House, New York City, 1931-37; asst. dir. field work, Union Theol. Sem., 1931-35, 1936-37. Assoc. prof. of rel. ed. and practical theology, Grad. Sch. of Theology, Oberlin Coll., 1937-44, prof. since 1944; visiting lecturer summer session: Union Theol. Sem., 1945; Garrett Biblical Inst., 1946, 1949; Univ. of Michigan, 1947, 1948; Emory University, 1948. Survey for Federation of Protestant Welfare Agencies, New York City, 1936-37; chmn. Ohio Student Y.M.C.A., 1944-46. Served as pvt. 350 inf. A.E.F., France 1918-19. Member: Board R.E.A. (dir. since 1943); I.C.R.E. (chmn. prof. adv. sect. 1944-46; rep. since 1946); Church Conf. of Social Workers, Nat. Assn. Biblical Instrs.; Amer. Assn. Univ. Profs., Gamma Pi Upsilon, Pi Kappa Delta, Theta Chi Delta. Author: *Sectarian Welfare Federation Among Protes-*

tants (1944). Chmn. editorial comm. Religious Education since 1946, editor since 1948. Office: Oberlin Coll., Oberlin, Ohio.

Selected Bibliography of Religious Education 567

STOCK, HARRY THOMAS: General Secretary, Division of Christian Education, Board of Home Missions of the Congregational Christian Churches since 1938. Born Springfield, Ill., 1891. Educated Knox Coll. (A.B. 1914); Chicago Theological Seminary (B.D. 1916); University of Chicago (A.M. 1917); hon. D.D.; Piedmont Coll. (1932); Knox Coll. (1939); Chicago Theological Seminary (1940). Associate Professor of Church History, Chicago Theol. Sem., 1917-22; Secretary of Young People's Work & Student Life, Congregational Education Society, 1922-38; editor, *Pilgrim Home*, 1947. Chmn. Commission on Educational Program, I.C.R.E. since 1948. Member: Tau Kappa Epsilon, Delta Sigma Rho. Author: *Church Work with Young People* (1929); *Training Young People in Worship* (with E. L. Shaver, 1929); *Christian Life Problems* (1927); *Problems of Christian Youth* (1927); *So This Is Missions!* (1933); *Social Issues for Young People* (1933); *A Life and a Living* (1936); *Christian Education in Our Church* (1944); *Ancient Answers to Ageless Questions* (1947). Home: 30 Jackson Road, West Medford 56, Mass.

The Sunday Church School 248

SWEET, HERMAN JAMES: Director of Christian Education, Board of Christian Education, Presbyterian Church, U.S.A., Synod of California, So. Area, since 1946. Born Canova, S. D., 1899. Educated Huron College (A.B. 1918-22); Univ. of Minnesota (1926-29); Yale Divinity School (1938-40); Huron College (D.D. 1944). Instructor English Huron College (1922-26); director Christian education: Westminster Presbyterian Church (Minneapolis) 1926-38, Church of the Redeemer, New Haven, Conn. 1938-40; director of Department of Leadership Education and Church-School Administration, I.C.R.E., 1940-46. U. S. Army 1918; Member: American Legion; ordained by the Presbyterian Church, 1940; Pi Kappa Delta. Author: *Opening the Door for God*. Home: 1218 Park Avenue, Inglewood, Calif.

The Education of Lay and Professional Religious Education Leaders 392

TULLY, ROBERT WARREN: Assistant prof. physical ed. and recreation, Bethel Coll., since 1946. Born Goshen Ind., 1909. Educated Manchester Coll. (A.B. 1931); Claremont Graduate School (A.M. 1943). Secondary-school teacher: Burnettsville, Ind., 1935-37; Beaver Dam, Ind., 1937-38; Gratis, Ohio, 1938-40. Prof. physical ed. LaVerne Coll. 1940-43. Pastor Church of the Brethren, Rocky Ford, Colo., 1943-45; assoc. sec. Colo. Council of Churches, 1945-46. Member: Phi Delta Kappa. Author: *Social Recreation Primer* (1944). Home: Box 87, Bethel College, North Newton, Kan.

Play and Recreation 171

VIETH, PAUL H.: Horace Bushnell Prof. of Christian Nurture, Yale. Born Warrenton, Mo., 1895. Educated Central Wesleyan Coll., Warrenton, Mo. (A.B. 1917); Divinity School of Yale (B.D. 1924); Grad. School of Yale (Ph.D. 1928). Field sec'y and gen. sec'y of Mo. Sunday School Ass'n (now Mo. Church Council) 1917-22; director of rel. ed., Church of the Redeemer, New Haven, 1923-25; director of research, chairman of Board of Editors, *International Journal of Rel. Ed.*, and superintendent of education administration, I.C.R.E., 1925-31. Visiting prof. of rel. ed., Duke Univ., 1931; director of field work and prof. of rel. ed., Yale Divinity School, 1931-39; Horace Bushnell Professor of Christian Nurture, Yale University, from 1939. Adviser on rel. ed., General Headquarters of the Occupation in Japan, 1947-48. Member: Spring Glen Church (Congregational) and chairman of Committee on Christian Ed.; I.C.R.E.; World Council of Christian Ed. Editor: *The Church and Christian Education* (report by commission of I.C.R.E.; chairman). Home: 409 Prospect St., New Haven, Conn.

Audio-Visual Method and Content 150

VOEHRINGER, ERICH FREDERICK: Associate secretary, World Council of Christian Education since 1946. Born Akuse, Gold Coast, British West Africa, 1905. Educated Univ. of Tübingen, Germany, 1923; Mt. Airy Lutheran Theol. Sem. Philadelphia, 1923-26 (B.D. 1927); Univ. of Pa. (1927-30 A.M. 1930); Univ. of Berlin (1931-32, Ph.D. 1933). Assistant pastor, Luth. Deaconess Motherhouse, Philadelphia, 1926-30; missionary and supervisor of schools, Gold Coast, B. W. A. 1933-40; pastor, Grace Luth. Church, New York, 1940-43; Tabor Luth. Church Philadelphia, 1943-46. Home: 211 Hillside Ave., Wortendyke, N. J.

The Development of Religious Education in Other Countries 533

WEIGLE, LUTHER ALLAN: Dean Emeritus Yale Univ. Divinity School. Born Littlestown, Pa., 1880. Educated Gettysburg Coll. (B.A. 1900, M.A. 1903); Lutheran Theol. Seminary, Gettysburg (1900-2); Yale (1902-5, Ph.D. 1905); Carleton (D.D. 1916); Gettysburg (1917); Muhlenberg (Litt.D. 1925); LL.D.: Dickinson (1933), Gettysburg (1934); Ohio University (S.T.D. 1934); Boston Univ. (J.U.D. 1939); D.D.: Queen's University (1941), Princeton University (1946). Ordained Lutheran ministry, 1903; pastor Bridgeport, Conn., 1903-4. Prof. philosophy, Carleton College, Northfield, Minn., 1905-16, dean, 1910-15. Horace Bushnell prof. of Christian Nurture, Yale, 1916-24; Sterling prof. of rel. ed. since 1924; dean of Yale Divinity School, 1928-49. Pres. Minn. Ed. Assn., 1913. Member: International Sunday School Lesson Comm. 1915-29 (chairman, 1922-23); exec. comm. I.C.R.E. since 1920, Educational Comm. 1928-48; chmn. exec. comm., World Council of Christian Education since 1928. Chmn. Comm. on Christian Education Fed. Council of Churches 1924-29, chmn. admn. comm. 1929-32; dir. and vice-pres. Cong'l Home Bd., 1927-36; chmn. Amer. Standard Bible Commission since 1930. Del. to International Missionary Council, Jerusalem, 1928; pres. Amer. Assn. of Theol. Schools 1929-30; chmn. exec. comm. since 1930; pres. Conn. Council of Churches 1931-33. Chmn. Interseminary Commission for Training for the Rural Ministry 1929-42. Visited China to conduct study of ed. of ministers for Chinese churches, Feb.-Aug. 1935. Del. to meeting in Utrecht, Holland, to devise constitution for World Council of Churches, 1938. Pres. Fed. Council of Churches, 1940-42; chmn. Co-ordinating Com. for Wartime Service of the Churches 1942-45; chmn. Planning Comm. for the Nat'l Council of the Churches of Christ in America since 1942. Presided at Birmingham, Eng., meeting of the World Council of Christian Education in 1947. Member Am. Philos. Ass'n; Am. Psychol. Ass'n; R.E.A. (council); N.E.A.; Phi Beta Kappa; Phi Delta Kappa; Alpha Tau Omega; Book and Bond (Yale). Member: Board of Founders, Nanking Theological Seminary since 1939. Holman lecturer on Augsburg Confession, Luth. Theol. Sem., 1921; Sprunt lecturer, Union Theol. Sem., Richmond, 1925-38. Avera lecturer, Duke U., 1926; Duncan lecturer, Presby. Theol. Sem., Louisville, 1926; Norton lecturer, Southern Bapt. Theol. Sem., Louisville, 1928; Pond lecturer, Bangor Theol. Sem., 1937; Goldberg lecturer, Hebrew Union Coll., Cincinnati, 1942; Cole lecturer, Vanderbilt U., 1948. Editor: *Horace Bushnell's Christian Nurture* (1916). Author: *The Pupil and the Teacher* (1911, rev. 1916); *Talks to Sunday School Teachers* (1920); *Training the Devotional Life* (with H. H. Tweedy, 1919); *Training Children in the Christian Family* (1921); *American Idealism* (Vol. X, "The Pageant of America" 1928); *Religious Education* (with J. H. Oldham); Vol. II of *Jerusalem Reports* (1928); *The Religious Education of a Protestant* (autobiography); in

"Contemporary Amer. Theology," Vol. II, 1933; *We Are Able* (1937); *Jesus and the Educational Method* (1939); *The English New Testament* (1949).
The Aim and Scope of Religious Education 87

WILLIAMS, J. PAUL: Prof. Dept. of Religion, Mt. Holyoke Coll., since 1945. Born New York, N. Y., 1900. Educated Baker U., Baldwin, Kan. (A.B. 1922); Garrett Bibl. Inst. (B.D. 1927); Columbia (Ph.D. 1937). Assoc. dir. Wesley Foundation, Urbana, Ill., 1926-27; dir. United Religious Council, Univ. of Mass., 1928-39; assoc. prof. dept. of Religion, Mt. Holyoke Coll., 1940-45, chmn. 1943-46. Summer lecturer: School of Education, Univ. of Ore. 1937-1938, Stout Inst. 1939, U. of Pa. 1940, State Coll. of Wash., 1941, Garrett Biblical Inst. 1947, Union Theological Seminary, 1948. Visiting prof. in School of Rel. Ed. Hartford Sem. Foundation, 1943-46. Pres. Assn. of Church Workers in Colls. and Univs. (Eastern region), 1936, 1937; dir. Survey of Working Conditions Among the Child Laborers of Conn. Valley, 1931; Mem. comm. on rel. organizations, Nat. Conf. of Christians and Jews, 1946-48; mem. div. of Christian Ed. Congregational Christian Churches. Member National Assn. Bibl. Instructors (vice-pres. 1938, pres. 1946), Kappa Sigma, Phi Delta Kappa, Pi Kappa Delta, Congregationalist clergyman. Author: *Some Aspects of Social Adjustment in Methodism* (1938); *The New Education and Religion* (1945). Research editor: *The Journal of Bible and Religion.* Home: South Hadley, Mass.

The Relation of Religion and Public Education 491

Index

Adult program, the
  bibliography, 311
  changed concepts of experience, 303-4
  changing concepts, 302-3
  lag in practice, 307-8
  promising developments, 309-10
  scope of program, 300
  two necessary changes, 301
  United Christian Adult Movement, 305-6
Aim and scope of religious education,
    bibliography, 97-98
Aims of religious education
  democracy at fault, 88-89
  democracy, education, and religion, 87-
    88
  education at fault, 89-90
  religion at fault, 88
American Sunday School Union, origin of,
    21
Aquinas, Thomas, 51
Art
  activity, 142-43
  activity without, 143
  bibliography, 149
  dance, the, 148
  experience as perceptual, 142
Audio-visual aids
  action picture, 153-54
  bibliography, 162-63
  church, 156-57
  distribution of, 157-58
  effectiveness, 150-51
  evaluation schedule, 160-61
  films, 155-56
  illustrated textbooks, 153
  integration with curriculum, 158
  moving pictures, 155
  nonprojected, 153-54
  projected, 154-55
  responsibility in church, 158
  securing a budget, 161
  training of workers, 158-59
  types of, 152-53
  value of, 150
Authors contributing
  Adams, James Luther, 595
  Bartlett, Edward Randolph, 595
  Beckes, Isaac Kelley, 595

Authors contributing—cont'd
  Bennett, John Coleman, 595-96
  Blakeman, Edward William, 596
  Bowen, Cawthon Asbury, 596
  Brown, Arlo Ayres, 597
  Brown, Margaret Elizabeth, 597
  Chipkin, Israel Solomon, 597-98
  Cummings, Oliver deWolf, 598
  Davis, Orville Lester, 598
  Eakin, Mildred Moody, 599
  Edick, Helen Marie, 599
  Elliott, Harrison Sacket, 599
  Fallaw, Wesner, 600
  Gibbons, Ray, 600
  Goddard, Alice Lymburner, 600
  Harms, John W., 600
  Harner, Nevin Cowger, 601
  Heffron, Edward Joseph, 601
  Kalas, Harry H., 601
  Knapp, Forrest Lamar, 601
  Lankard, Frank Glenn, 601-2
  Ligon, Ernest Mayfield, 602
  Limbert, Paul Moyer, 602
  Loomis, Amy Goodhue, 603
  Lotz, Philip Henry, 603
  McKibben, Frank Melbourne, 603
  Maynard, Donald More, 603-4
  Munro, Harry Clyde, 604
  Murphy, Ruth Elizabeth, 604
  Parker, Everett C., 604
  Petersen, Lemuel Alva, 604
  Powell, Marie Cole, 605
  Ross, Roy George, 605
  Scotford, John R., 605
  Shaver, Erwin Leander, 605
  Sherrill, Lewis Joseph, 606
  Snyder, Ross, 606
  Stidley, Leonard Albert, 606
  Stock, Harry Thomas, 607
  Sweet, Herman James, 607
  Tully, Robert Warren, 607
  Vieth, Paul H., 607
  Voehringer, Erich Frederick, 608
  Weigle, Luther Allan, 608
  Williams, J. Paul, 609

Bible, the
  adolescent, 119

611

Bible, the—*cont'd*
architecture, 117
art, 116
authority in faith and morals, 19
bibliography, 125
human living, 179-81
juniors, 118
life philosophy, 119-20
literature, 116
little child, 118
music, 116-17
translation of, 18
ungraded, 118
Bibliography
adult program, 311
adults, 578-79
agencies of recreation and group services, 324
aim and scope of religious education, 97-98
art, 149
arts, 580
audio-visual aids, 162-63, 581
basic Christian convictions, 36
Bible, 125
bibliographies, 583
biography, 122-23
building, 217, 577
camping, 576
camping program, 350-51
Catholic religious education, 532
character education, 572
children, 578
children's work, 235
church college and seminary, 364
church and home, 574
church and state, 489-90
civilization, 74
community, 337
councils of churches, 430
counseling, 195-96, 572-73
curriculum, 112-13, 577
discussion, 581
drama, 149
drama and pageantry, 580
education, 59-60
educational ministry, 390-91
evangelism, 86, 581
experimentation and research, 415
general methods, 577
group work and dynamics, 572
handwork, 581
higher education, 576
historical development of religious education, 25, 570
home and parent education, 246-47

Bibliography—*cont'd*
International Council of Religious Education, 443-44
Jewish education, 518
leadership education, 403, 573
learning process, 571
local church, 575
missionary education, 582
moral and religious growth, 571
music, 149, 581
nature of prayer and worship, 582
nature of religion, 569-70
parents, 573
play and recreation, 182, 580
prayer and worship for age groups, 582
principles and aims of religious education, 570
Protestantism's strategy, 562-63
psychology, 47
public schools, 575
radio and television, 170
religion and public education, 500
religious classics, 188-89
Religious Education Association, 455
religious education in other countries, 548
research and measurement, 583
rural church, 576
selected magazines, 583
sex education, 574
stories, 579-80
Sunday church school, 258-59
tax-supported institutions, 377-78
teaching process, 571-72
techniques in teaching, 206
total church, 228
United Christian Youth Movement, 468
use of Bible, 579
vacation church school, 272-73
weekday church school, 285-86
weekday and vacation schools, 576
worship, 136
youth, 578
youth fellowship, 299
Biography
authors', 595-609
bibliography, 122-23
religious, 121
Boy Scouts of America, religious purpose, 314-15
Boys' Clubs of America, secular agencies, 313
Building for religious education
Akron plan, 216
army barracks and chapels, 211-12
bibliography, 217

Building for religious education—*cont'd*
  church basement, 211
  church parlor, 212
  classrooms, 214
  color and pictures, 215
  command respect, 208
  devotional chapel, 213
  fundamental strategy, 207-8
  gymnasiums, 214-15
  little children, 210
  one-room church, 209-10
  two-room church, 210
  visual education, 215
  worship, 208-9
Bushnell, Horace, 21, 83

Calvin, John, schools proposed, 19
Camp Fire Girls, religious purpose, 314
Camping program
  adolescent, 342
  bibliography, 350-51
  camp versus conference, 342-43
  characteristic elements, 343-44
  interdenominational co-operation, 348
  kinds of summer conferences, 346-48
  relation to larger camping movement, 348-49
  unique values, 344-45
Camps and summer conferences
  beginning of youth summer conferences, 339-40
  glance backward, 338-39
  present development, 340-41
Catholic religious education
  bibliography, 532
  Catholic view of life, 521-22
  inconsistencies, 528-30
  organization of, 530-31
  professional, 530
  rights of parents, 523-24
  "separatism" of separate schools, 523
  and the state, 526-27
  state aid to religious schools, 524-26
  why Catholic schools, 519-21
Character research
  Education Inquiry, 40
  Union College, 39-40, 43-44
Children's work, bibliography, 235
Christian education
  in the family, 94-95
  meaning of, 221
  universal, 18
Christian ethics
  justice, 33
  love for neighbor, 32-33

Christianity
  early, 15-16
  a historical religion, 26
  medieval, 16-17
  modern, 17-18
  nature of, 26-27
Church, the
  bibliography, 228
  congregation teaches, 227
  educational work of, 95-96
  every phase significant, 226-27
  social imperative, 33-34
Church colleges
  administrative problems, 357-58
  bibliography, 364
  courses in religion, 356-57
  objectives of religious education, 355
  religious objectives, 352
  religious orientation, 353-54
  social values, 354
Church and state
  bibliography, 489-90
  in field of education, 486-89
  forms of religious observance, 488-89
  freedom for religion, 482-86
  historical background, 479-80
  recent decisions, 485-86
  religious freedom, 480-81
  sharp focus, 479
Civilization
  authoritarianism, 70-71
  bibliography, 74
  causes of decay, 69-70
  causes of progress, 71-72
  civility, 61-62
  meaning of, 61
  power of co-operation, 70
Closely-graded lessons, origin of, 253
Community, the
  bibliography, 337
  church at head of, 329
  curriculum, 329-37
  curriculum of juniors, 333-34
  curriculum of kindergarten, 330-31
  curriculum of primaries, 331-32
  educational process, 326
  importance of, 325-26
  individual needs, 328-29
  means of religious education, 327-28
  new sense of, 90
  youth groups, 334-35
Convictions, basic
  bibliography, 36
  Christ, 29-30
  Church, 32
  God, 28-29

Convictions, basic—*cont'd*
  Kingdom of God, 34-35
  man, 29
  salvation, 30-31
Council system
  merger into unified, 422-23
  nonecclesiastical co-operation, 420-21
  official interdenominational co-operation, 421-22
Councils of churches
  bibliography, 430
  current situation, 419
  origin of council system, 420-23
  organization and program, 425-26
  philosophy of community relationships, 423-24
  probable future trends, 428-29
  program functions, 426-27
  program organization, 427
  relation to national organizations, 427-28
Counseling
  basic process in, 183-84
  bibliography, 195-96
  conflicts in purpose, 186-87
  counseling relationships, 193-94
  directive and nondirective, 190-91
  emotional attitudes, 184-85
  emotional factors, 185-86
  group, 191-93
  issues of confidence, 187-88
  personality problems, 188
  religion, 194
  transformation of personality, 188-90
Creative arts, revival of, 137-38
Curriculum, the
  agencies, 107-10
  audio-visual, 110
  basically life-centered, 106-7
  Bible in, 114-21
  bibliography, 112-13
  broadly-graded lessons, 103
  church camping, 108
  closely-graded lessons, 103-4
  completely life-centered, 107
  content, 106-7
  content-centered, 106
  cycle-graded lessons, 103
  free, 102, 104
  grading, 103-5
  local-church, 102
  main-line, 101-2
  main-line with variations, 102
  partly content-centered, 106
  patterns, 101-3
  period of confusion, 170-71
  Sunday-morning church school, 108-9

Curriculum, the—*cont'd*
  unified, 104-5
  uniform lessons, 22, 105
  Union College, 44-45
  vacation church school, 108
  weekday church school, 107
  youth and adult fellowship, 109

Democracy, peril of weakening, 92
Director of religious education
  five educational functions, 387-89
  problems of profession, 389-90
  task of the, 386-87
Directory, a
  denominational boards, 586-89
  educational foundations, 594
  international associations and foundations, 594
  International Convention, 584
  International Council of Religious Education, 584
  International Council staff, 584-85
  national educational foundations, 591-94
  other agencies, 590-91
  publishing houses, 586-89
  Religious Education Association, 585
  state councils, 589-90
Drama
  bibliography, 149
  creative, 146-47
  methods of, 145-46
  speaking choirs, 146
Dramatics, formal, 147-48

Education
  bibliography, 59-60
  community-centered, 53
  conflicting metaphysics, 57-58
  dominant philosophies of, 49-50
  individual, 52-53
  is life, 53-54
  objectives in, 52
  a philosophy of, 48
  progressivism, 49
  racial experience, 53
  research, 56
  secularization of, 20, 91-92
  social process, 48-49
  social progress, 55-56
  spiritual values, 56-57
  traditionalism or essentialism, 50-51
  trends in, 51-52
Educational ministry, bibliography, 390-91
Evangelism
  bibliography, 86
  crisis decisions, 78

Evangelism—*cont'd*
  crisis moments, 79
  educator's criticisms, 75-77
  frame of reference, 81
  function of teacher, 82
  gospel songs, 77
  importance of crises, 76
  intellect and emotion, 80
  love, 80
  national teaching mission, 84-85
  orthodox terminology, 77
  pillars of faith, 78
  practical program, 83-86
  psychological laws, 77
  redemption versus growth, 79
  response to God's love, 80-81
  sense of urgency, 79
  synthesis and interaction, 79-80
  ultimate meaning, 79
  verbal appeal, 76
  visitation, 76
Experimentation and research
  basic approaches, 405-9
  bibliography, 415
  Character Education Inquiry, 404
  communications, 412-13
  counseling, 409-10
  developmental approach to religion, 411-12
  family, 409
  frontier areas, 409-10
  group dynamics, 410-11
  measurement movement, 405
  new types of schools, 24

Faith, America's common religious, 93-94
Family, the
  teaches religion, 243
  teaching Christianity, 18
Family education
  way persons grow, 244-45
  working with the church, 245
Family life
  Commission on Marriage and the Home, 238-39
  national conference on, 238
Family religion, incarnating attributes of God, 244-45
Four-H Clubs, secular agencies, 313

Girl Scouts, religious purpose, 317-18
God, grace of, 31

Home and parent education
  current long-time trends, 237-38
  disintegration of home, 236-37

Home and parent education—*cont'd*
  unifying experiences, 237
Humanism, encouraged tolerance, 69

International Council of Religious Education
  associated sections, 437-38
  basic philosophy, 439-40
  bibliography, 443-44
  Commission on Educational Program, 438-39
  Committee on Children's Work, 233-34
  educational committees, 437
  executive leadership, 442
  National Council of Churches, 441-42
  organizational purpose and function, 431-32
  program, 432-33
  quadrennial convention, 438
  services to denominations, 432-34
  structure, 436-37

Jesus, as teacher, 15
Jewish education
  afternoon weekday classes, 505-6
  all-day school, 504-5
  bibliography, 518
  central agencies, 514-15
  content of studies, 507-10
  current trends, 516
  finances, 514
  foundation school, 505
  Hillel Foundations, 374
  problems, 517
  school system, 502-3
  secondary schools, 506-7
  Sunday school, 503-4
  types of schools, 503-7
  youth and adult, 510-13
  teachers, 513-14
  wisdom, 501
Judaism
  academy, 14
  elementary schools, 14
  family education, 13-14
  secondary schools, 14
  synagogue, 14
  teaching adults, 14

Kingdom of God
  eternal, 35
  present reality, 34
Knox, John, proposed schoolmaster, 19

Leaders
  vacation church school, 266

Leaders—*cont'd*
  youth fellowships, 296-97
Leadership training
  bibliography, 403
  concern for, 394
  general church leaders, 399-400
  historical background, 393-94
  laboratory school, 398
  lesson preview, 396
  on the job, 395-96
  other needs, 400-401
  professionally trained, 401-2
  reading, 399
  situation today, 394-95
  Standard Curriculum, 396-97
  workers' conference, 395-96
  workshop, 398-99
Local church, diagram of organization, 225
Love, of neighbor, 32-33
Luther, Martin, schools advocated, 18

Methods in vacation church school, 268-69
Minister
  educational task of, 224-25
  his own director, 381-84
  working with director, 384-85
Ministry, educational approach to, 385-86
Missionary education, for children, 232
Music
  activities in church, 140-41
  bibliography, 149
  children's work, 232-33
  courses in church, 140
  creative experience, 138-39

National Teaching Mission, fourfold program, 85

Parent education
  adult education, 239-40
  bibliography, 246-47
  parent nights, 241
  primacy of home, 239
  readiness of parent, 240-41
  sex practices, 241
Parochial school, Presbyterians organized, 21-22
Personality, discipline, 44
Play and recreation
  activities for character development, 174
  areas, facilities, and finances, 180
  asceticism, 172
  banquets, 178
  bibliography, 182
  church program, 175-76
  committee or director, 175

Play and recreation—*cont'd*
  dramatics, 176-77
  hikes, 177-78
  hobbies, 176
  methods of character development, 173-74
  movies, 177
  music, 177
  philosophy of, 172-73
  program elements, 176-77
  questionable practices, 180
  scholasticism, 172
  specific social activities, 178-79
  team games, 177
  training leadership, 180-81
  worship, 179
Preaching, biblical content, 2
Program for children
  development of children, 229-30
  missionary education, 232
  nursery school, 232
  summer opportunities, 231
  time and length of sessions, 231
Progress
  criticism of, 64-67
  idea of, 63-64
Protestant
  attitude toward progress and decay, 67-68
  priesthood of believers, 68
Protestantism's strategy
  bibliography, 562-63
  camps and institutes, 555-56
  community level, 550
  conclusions, 560-62
  higher education, 557-59
  home, 551
  international level, 559-60
  local church, 551-53
  national scale, 556
  public-school curriculum, 554-55
  weekday religious education 553
Psychology
  bibliography, 47
  experimental findings, 38
  individual differences, 45-46
  methods of measurement, 38-39
  motivation, 41-42
  perceptual situation, 42-43
  schematic diagram of motivation, 42
  schools of, 37
  teaching and learning, 39-40
  trait theory, 40-41
Public school, religious emphasis, 93-94

Radio, workshops, 167-68

Radio and television
  bibliography, 170
  drama and emotion, 165-66
  educational functions, 168-69
  immediacy and personalized, 164-65
  personal follow-up, 166-67
Raikes, Robert, 20
Recreation and group services
  agencies with religious purpose, 313-14
  bibliography, 324
  secular agencies, 313
Reformation, justification by faith, 18
Religion in public education
  bibliography, 500
  core of traditional religion, 498
  divorce between, 491-92
  keep things as they are, 494-95
  nonsectarian spiritual values, 495-96
  support of church school, 498
  teach religion objectively, 496-97
Religious education
  academic development, 24
  aim and scope, 94
  bibliography of historical development,
    25
  co-operation in, 96-97
  creative art in, 141-42
  drama in, 143-44
  educational process, 78
  evangelist's criticism of, 78-79
  local church, 221-22
  ministers and laymen, 222
  movement defined, 13
  over-all planning groups, 222-23
  professionalization of, 23
  trends in college and seminary, 362-63
Religious Education Association
  Association today, 453-54
  bibliography, 455
  contributions of, 450-52
  defined, 445
  editorial service, 452-53
  organization and program, 446-49
  principles and policies, 449-50
  task defined, 445-46
Religious education in other countries
  Asia, 536-39
  bibliography, 548
  China, 537-38
  continental Europe, 545-47
  Great Britain, 541-45
  Japan, 536-37
  Latin America, 533-36
  Moslem countries, 539-40
  Philippines, 538-39

Sermon, in popular Christian education,
  19-20
Summer program, evaluation of conference, 346-47
Sunday church school
  all ages, 250
  associations and conventions, 22
  begun in America, 249-50
  bibliography, 258-59
  catechetical process, 252
  characteristics of early, 248
  current trends, 256-57
  curriculum development, 251-52
  departmentalized system, 250-51
  "homemade" curriculum, 254
  inclusive program, 255-56
  lack of standards, 256
  memorization of Bible, 252
  modified organizational setup, 251
  national conventions, 249
  origin of, 20
  origin of closely-graded lessons, 253
  Robert Raikes, 248
  selected Bible verses, 252
  uniform lessons, 252-53

Tax-supported institutions
  administrative structure, 375-76
  arrival of state-type college, 365
  bibliography, 377-78
  communions alert, 475-76
  curricular religion, 366
  examples in three states, 370
  Hillel Foundations, 374
  Newman Club, 374-75
  patterns of religious education, 366-67
  problem defined, 365-66
  religious agencies, 370-71
  student patronage, 369-70
  United Student Council in the U.S.A.,
    372
Techniques in teaching
  bibliography, 206
  doing, 202-4
  evaluating, 204-5
  graph of relationships, 199
  group planning, 200-201
  observing, 197-98
  planning, 200-201
  questions for observing, 198-99
Theological education
  aims of, 358-59
  curriculum building, 360-61
  new demands on leadership, 362
  present curriculum, 361-62

Uniform lessons, origin of, 252-53
United Christian Youth Movement
    background and organization, 457-60
    bibliography, 468
    comparatively new, 456
    local community, 464-66
    philosophy and objectives, 460-62
    program, 462-66

Vacation church school
    bibliography, 272-73
    course of study, 267-68
      by departments, 262-63
    good administration, 270-71
    joyous spirit, 263
    leaders needed, 266
    methods used, 268-69
    origin of, 264
    summer opportunities, 260
    training leaders, 266-67
    types of co-operation, 265
    values of, 271-72
    what happens in, 261-62
    what it is, 260-61
    who responsible for, 264
Visual education, building for, 215
Visual materials, use of, 233

Weekday church school, the
    achievements of, 279-80
    bibliography, 285-86
    how organized and administered, 275-76
    imposed problems, 282-83
    limitations of, 280-81
    origins and basic principles, 274-75
    problems of, 281-82
    reasons for growth, 278-79
World Council of Christian Education
    beginning of, 469

World Council—*cont'd*
    bibliography, 559-60
    development of, 470-71
    ecumenical bonds, 474-75
    today, 472-74
Worship
    answer to spiritual needs, 129
    bibliography, 136, 582
    at an early age, 128-29
    environment of, 134
    experimentation with, 133-34
    feeling of satisfaction, 129
    for children, 131-32
    for young people, 132
    importance of, 126
    leader of, 128-29
    more meaningful, 132-33
    planning a program of, 134-35
    purpose of, 126-27
    readiness for, 130
    recent trends in, 130-31
    temptation to exploit, 127

Youth Fellowship
    bibliography, 299
    ecumenical potentialities, 297-98
    leadership, 296-97
    nature of, 290-91
    need for unity, 289-90
    points of strength, 292-93
    significant trends, 287
    types of activity, 293-94
    urge to organize, 287-88
Youth movements, young people's societies,
    22
Y.M.C.A.
    boys' work, 320-21
    religious purpose, 318-19
Y.W.C.A., religious purpose, 321-22

Date Due